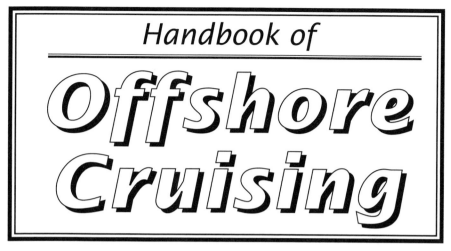

Handbook of Offshore Cruising

The Dream and Reality of Modern Ocean Cruising

Jim Howard

Illustrations by Tadami Takahashi

SHERIDAN HOUSE

First published 1994
by Sheridan House Inc.
145 Palisade Street
Dobbs Ferry, NY 10522

Library of Congress Cataloging-in-Publication Data

Howard, Jim
    Handbook of offshore cruising : the dream and
    reality of modern ocean cruising / Jim Howard;
    illustrations by Tadami Takahashi.
        p. cm.
    Includes bibliographical references (p.) and
    index.
    ISBN 0-924486-35-X
    1. Sailing—Handbooks, manuals, etc.
    2. Sailboats—Handbooks, manuals, etc.
    I. Title.
    GV811.H629   1994   94-4824
    797.1′24—dc20   CIP

Illustrations by Tadami Takahashi

Design and composition by Oxprint Ltd,
Oxford, England

Printed in the United States of America
ISBN 0-924486-35-X

CONTENTS

CONTENTS

CONTENTS

CONTENTS

Dedication

This book is dedicated to my sister Joyce Johnson, who year after year and usually with a smile takes care of my mail and fends off bill collectors and others who try to interrupt my ongoing vacation. Every cruiser should be fortunate to have such a helpful home base.

And to Grey Paulk, who sailed a lot of miles with me and all the while claimed he didn't like sailing – but kept coming back for more.

INTRODUCTION

This book is written for cruising sailors, including those who are now cruising, those who are preparing for long-distance sailing, and for those who dream.

Anyone who has been out cruising for more than a few months will be familiar with the subjects covered here, and will probably have some better or at least different ways of doing things. There is no lack of strong opinion among cruising sailors when it comes to marine gear and materials, systems and techniques, but there is also a curiosity and a willingness to learn and use better ways. Every time I see how someone else does something, I learn – and so I hope this book will provide veteran cruising sailors with at least a few new ideas.

If you are actively preparing to go cruising, and find in this book many new tasks to add to your ever-expanding 'to do' list, I can only say that you probably would have discovered those tasks anyway, and I hope the book will expedite your labors.

If you are still in the dreaming stage, I hope I won't dim the gleam in your eye – although I may take away some of the stars. In any case, keep dreaming. That's the beginning of all sailing adventures.

I have tried to make this book a practical guide to living your own adventure. In reality, the preparation alone is time-consuming, expensive, and frustrating. Some folks have no idea what they are getting into when they begin. Some never complete the job because they run out of time, or money, or interest. If this book discourages some people from trying to become offshore sailors, it will have served its purpose for those readers, because if you become discouraged at the preparation stage you will surely have much greater difficulties farther along.

The word 'cruising' holds different meanings for different people. To me it simply means taking a boat out on the open ocean for more than a day. Where you are going and how long you plan to stay at sea will, of course, have a bearing on the type of boat you need and how you will rig and provision it. Certainly you will plan differently for a trip to Catalina from Los Angeles or to the Bahamas from Miami than you would for a cruise to the South Pacific, an Atlantic crossing, or a circumnavigation. However, all of those trips have one basic thing in common – they involve heading offshore. The ocean is the ocean, and it can be kind or cruel at any time and place, be it two or two thousand miles offshore. When you're 'out there' it doesn't matter if you are rich or poor, man or woman, old or young. The weather and the ocean make no such distinctions. If you and your boat are properly prepared, you will succeed; if not, you can expect difficulties.

INTRODUCTION

I don't consider myself an expert. I am passing along what I have learned, sometimes the hard way, from my own experiences, and summarizing ideas picked up from many books and conversations with fellow cruising sailors. My own biases will be obvious, but I have tried to explain the reasons behind them.

If you spend a few days around a group of long-distance cruising people you will learn very quickly that certain products have distinct reputations. Now and then I mention specific items of equipment – good or bad – by brand name. Be aware that some products are improved upon and some become less reliable through time. Often a small company that manufactures a good product is bought out by a big corporation, and the quality goes down. Brand names are not necessarily good indications. The quality of one manufacturer's winches, for example, can vary from model to model.

If you learn nothing else from this book you will know when you finish reading that there is no perfect cruising boat. The cruising sailor constantly tries to balance costs, speed, weight, size, beauty, comfort, storage space, and numerous other variables. The best you can hope for is a good compromise. But I believe, and I have emphasized throughout the book, that *there is no compromise when it comes to safety and seaworthiness.*

My use of male pronouns throughout the book is simply a matter of convenience, readability, and, perhaps, habit. It should be obvious that sailing is in no way gender-based.

By tradition and by necessity sailors help out other sailors and share ideas and information. I would like very much to hear comments and criticism from you who read this book, so that a future edition can be more useful to other cruisers. Where I am wrong, I should be told about it. If you have a better way to do something, please share your idea. If I've failed to cover an important point, or covered it inadequately, let me know.

If it happens to fit your style, the cruising life is hard to beat. It is not the last frontier, or even a new frontier, and of course it is not what it was ten, fifty, or however many years ago – a fact that has its good and bad points. Every year there are more boats cruising, but the offshore cruising community is still pretty small, and there are still a lot of places where you can find solitude.

Whichever way you choose – to sail alone or in company, to anchor out or raft up alongside friends, I hope we'll have a chance to meet in some pleasant harbor along the way.

Jim Howard
on board *Denali*

Acknowledgements

Very special thanks go to Doug Logan, who edited this book and gave me a lot of valuable advice about rigs and rigging, as well as about writing.

PART I
THE BOAT

BUILDING OR BUYING A BOAT FOR OFFSHORE CRUISING

Building On Your Own

Building your own yacht and sailing off into the sunset is the stuff that great adventure stories are made of. Many people have done it, and a lot more have started to do it. Certainly 'doing it yourself' has many advantages. You can have, within the constraints of cost, a boat that is suited precisely to you and your crew. More importantly, you can be sure of the strength and quality of your vessel. When you make repairs or changes, you will know exactly how to do them. And you can't overlook the pride and joy in sailing something uniquely yours. If you build your own boat, and do so in a careful way, you may save a lot of money that can be used for subsequent travel expenses.

Perhaps you think that boat building is an impossible dream because you lack experience. This should not deter you. There are numerous books explaining techniques. Most of them are highly illustrated, and if you go at it slowly, they will lead you along. Some companies which sell construction materials offer well-illustrated and easily understood how-to books.

Another advantage of building yourself is that the boat's cost is spread out over a long period of time. Instead of making a large initial outlay of money, you build at your own speed and buy materials as you need them.

To build your own boat, you must start with a set of plans. You shouldn't feel uneasy about writing to a designer and telling him the type of boat you hope to build, the kind of sailing you expect to do, and your level of experience in yacht construction. You will be surprised at how helpful and cooperative most designers are.

Now, let's look at some of the difficulties you may face in building your boat. The two most significant are time and space. Both depend on where you live and your occupation. If, for example, you have a job that leaves only one day a week for boat work, it will take many years to finish your project. An inexperienced person building a 36-foot (11 m) fiberglass boat could expect to put in at least 4000 hours of labor, and probably a lot more. If your occupation gives you some free time in the evenings, on weekends, and during vacation time throughout the year, you can project approximately how long it will take to complete the project. If it is a family affair, or if you are building the boat with one or more friends, the completion of the project will be significantly hastened. Some sailors have been so dedicated to building that they have changed jobs to have more time for their project.

Working space can be a big, but not insurmountable, problem. Perhaps there is a nearby boatyard that will rent or lease space in an out-of-the-way place. Although it is preferable to work inside a building, it is not absolutely necessary, and sometimes temporary shelter can be created with scaffolding and plastic sheets. Otherwise look around for some space that is not being used or is under-used. I know one man who is building a boat in a cave. Some people have built yachts in decrepit and abandoned warehouses. The buildings were rather shabby, and of course unheated, but the owner was willing to rent the unused space very cheaply.

You need space mainly for constructing the hull and cabin. If necessary the boat can be moved elsewhere when it comes time to add the keel. Stepping the mast can be done after launching.

When you begin your project be realistic about your commitment. Anyone who has ever built a boat will admit it took far longer than expected. It can be a frustrating endeavor for the inexperienced person, and there will be many discouraging moments as you proceed. But the anticipation and thrill of seeing your creation launched is beyond description.

Partly Finished Boats

One attractive option is to have the hull and deck made by a yacht builder, leaving the interior work and finishing to yourself. Some companies will sell you a boat in almost any stage of completion. Cascade Yachts of Portland, Oregon is a company well-known for this type of construction. There are advantages to this because so much of the finish work is labor intensive and, therefore, expensive. For many people the techniques of working with fiberglass may prove difficult, whereas wood work, and many of the other tasks involved with the finish work of a boat, are better known. Having the hull and deck completed for you means that 20 to 30 percent of the work is completed. Also with a production hull, you can select a proven design, and usually you will have an opportunity to see how the boat is finished on deck and inside.

If this approach appeals to you, find some boats you especially like and write to the builders to ask if they are willing to sell a partially completed boat. If so, you will then want to visit the builder and discuss your ideas. Be straightforward in your discussion and indicate your level of experience and what you want to do on your own. The builder is an experienced craftsman and can guide you in deciding how much you want pre-built and how much to do yourself. He will be able to give advice on the necessary strength and quality of material you need, and perhaps he will sell you materials at a better price than the retail market. Establish a good working relationship with the builder. As your work progresses you will need to consult with him on problems you encounter. He will want to see you succeed because the boat you are building is associated with his company, and if you do a sloppy job it will reflect poorly on his reputation.

Buying a New Boat

There are three ways to go when buying a new boat – a stock production boat, a semi-custom boat, or a boat designed and built for you.

You can select from dozens of 'off-the-shelf' production boats with a wide variety of price and quality available throughout the world. Many are advertised to be cruising boats, but the term 'cruising' has different meanings, and many are not really suitable for long-distance sailing.

The expression 'cruiser-racer' or 'racer-cruiser' is commonly seen in the literature. This description is used to help sell boats to folks who want to take part in races and also go cruising now and then. Some of these boats will, with modifications, serve very well for offshore sailing. We are now seeing more and more light-displacement 'racer-cruisers' with tall and often fragile masts that really are not safe or suitable for offshore cruising. Such boats are to be avoided if you plan to cross oceans.

You will also see many heavy-displacement cruising yachts. There is no question that these are tough, rugged, strongly rigged boats. They are commonly slow and poor performers when going to windward. For some people the security and comfort they offer is a primary consideration, but such boats are not required for offshore sailing. In my opinion, you can make safe passages at better speed in lighter boats that will be a joy to sail on any point, and less expensive too.

It is worthwhile to consider a middle road approach and seek out a well-constructed, proven, sturdily rigged, moderate-displacement boat that avoids design extremes or gimmicky additions. Once out on the cruising trail you will find that most new and used boats follow these principles.

If you are choosing a stock boat, make a point of talking to the designer and builder. A phone call may get you some good advice. Tell them what your plans are, and see if they feel their product is satisfactory for what you want to do. Big companies tend to be less direct in answering your questions, and too often the customer-service representative is more of a salesman than a sailor, but it is worth a try. Talk to other owners of the model you are considering. Ask the dealer or builder for the names of customers who have sailed their boats offshore. Call or write to them for their opinions. There is no better source of realistic information. Each month the sailing magazine *Cruising World* publishes a list of boats whose owners are willing to give you their opinions.

Other Costs

Even after you purchase a standard production boat, you are still a long way from being ready to go to sea, regardless of what the advertisements may lead you to believe. Some dealers offer the boat as it comes from the factory, and others include, at extra cost, a 'sail-away package.' This option may easily cost as much as 20 percent of the base price.

A few years ago the sailing publication *Practical Sailor* described a 34-foot production boat which, at that time, had a base price of $58,000. The owner spent an additional $6,500 to sail the boat away, and within a year had spent another $6,000 for additional equipment. This was not someone who was setting off on a world cruise, but just a typical coastal cruiser. The point here is that you must anticipate many additional costs in preparing a new production boat before it is ready to go offshore.

How much will you spend? It depends on you and what you want to add to the basic boat and how much work you are willing to do yourself. I estimate additional supplies and equipment to be at least 25 percent of the original purchase price.

Semi-Custom Yachts

Having a production boat modified to your specifications while it is being built is worth considering. There are some excellent yards that specialize in semi-custom yachts. They build only a few, basic, hull designs, and almost always to order for a specific customer. A yacht of this type will naturally cost more than a ready-made production boat.

In some ways buying a modified production yacht is like having a boat built just for you – only better. Better, because you have a boat that is a proven design, and its speed, performance, seaworthiness, and overall characteristics are already established. A yacht completely designed and built just for you may be a wonderful status symbol – but a very expensive one. By customizing a production boat, the costs will be substantially less, and yet you will have a boat that is distinctly yours.

To get going on a semi-custom boat, talk with the designer if possible, and start working with the builder right away. Some of your desires may not be realistic or feasible if they adversely affect the boat's strength or stability. The location of bulkheads adds to the strength of the hull, and the size and location of tanks are considered in the yacht's trim and stability. These and other points will be explained to you by the builder, but there are numerous changes you can make to the boat to pattern it to your use. Most production boats have pilot berths and V-berths as standard equipment. If only a husband and wife are going to be cruising, and especially if they anticipate long offshore passages, these beds can be made into storage space. Anyone who plans to cruise extensively will want as many storage compartments as possible and should develop definite ideas about the size and shape of the added cabinets, drawers, and bins. A semi-custom yacht permits you to have cupboards built to fit the storage containers you want to use, or even to hold the specific dishes you want on board.

Production boats come with standard toilets, basins, stoves, lights, engines, and numerous other accessories. These items have been selected by the builder. By standardizing he can buy in quantity, and if his workers routinely put the same items in all boats, production costs are lower. Perhaps you want a different toilet than is standard, or you have a preference in engines, or you want an oven where a two-burner stove is standard. If you want refrigeration or a hot-water heater this is the time to have it done.

Production boats don't come with installed electronics. The new owner has to fit them into the space available. If the electronics are purchased during production, the cabinets to hold them can be customized. The advantage of this is more than cosmetic. It means radios and navigation equipment can be installed where they are most convenient to operate.

On a modified production boat there are also certain changes you may want to make on deck. Some stock boats are set up for racing as well as cruising, and some of the features which the racer wants to have are of little use to the cruising skipper. You may even want to consider heavier rigging if you are going offshore. Other cruising extras such as wind-vane steering and mast steps can be installed at the factory. Certainly you can do these jobs yourself after you buy the boat, but it is nice if they can be done by professionals. Anyone who has decided to add mast steps to a standing mast will tell you it would have been much easier to have had it done at the factory!

One-Off Yachts

The thought of having a cruising boat designed and built specifically for you seems too good to be true. It is a dream that only a few can hope for today, although a few years ago all boats were built that way. Yet, as wonderful as this idea seems, it may have some disadvantages. Unless you have extensive offshore cruising experience, and I emphasize cruising, rather than offshore racing, it is difficult to know what you really want in a cruising boat. Although, so far, there is no perfect cruising boat, most sailors have some definite ideas about what they would like in their next boat based on their present boat. Hence it may be advisable, even if you feel you can afford the luxury of having a boat designed and built for you, to first spend some time sailing in a variety of production boats so you can establish some clear-cut ideas about the boat you want built for you.

The Designer

Those who will have their very own, unique, cruiser need to select a naval architect who specializes in ocean-cruising boats. Don't limit your search to only the 'brand names.' There are numerous independent designers who turn out excellent plans, and with such a person you often have the benefit of more personal attention. Some of the independent architects have a good working relationship with a specific builder, and this cooperation can be important. You want to have a designer with whom you feel comfortable and with whom you can communicate.

Give a lot of thought to what you want in your boat. If you let the designer draw for you what he thinks is best, you might as well stick with a production or semi-custom yacht. Listen to the designer and consider his ideas; perhaps he has some innovative concepts that he is unable to develop in a production design. But before you visit the designer, make a list of specific features you want in your new boat. Most importantly, have your yacht designed with you and your crew in mind.

Countertops should be at the height you like and if you want a certain type of cabinet, ask for it. Beds, settees, and dining tables should be of a size and shape that please you. This is the time to be specific even down to the details of cushion thickness and upholstery. When you eventually go to the builder with your plans, he will make his estimate of construction costs based on the information contained in the design plans. If you fail to stipulate a particular item, he will have to make his estimate based on the materials he normally uses. If it turns out later you don't like his choice, it will be an added expense to change.

If you have a specific way you want your cockpit arranged, then incorporate that into your boat. Some people will argue that too many individual quirks built into a boat may make it difficult to sell. Perhaps that is true but you are not building this boat to sell it, you are building it to sail in comfort and convenience.

The Builder

After your plans are complete the next step is to find a builder. Be sure you can communicate with him in a comfortable way. Talk to the owners of boats he has built. Follow-up service is especially important to those having a one-off yacht constructed. It pays to shop around when trying to select a builder, not only to make price comparisons, but also to see the factory, to get an impression of the quality of workmanship, and to determine if you can establish a good rapport.

From this point on you will be in frequent contact with the builder. If possible, visit the yard several times as your boat is being built, but not so often as to be a nuisance. If the factory is located nearby and you have the time, it is good to visit once a week in the early stages of construction. Your interest in the yacht-building process will be appreciated by the workers and very instructive and informative for you. When you visit take your camera and make a record of the progress. It will be valuable information if you want to change something in the future.

Consider hiring a surveyor or consultant when building a new yacht, especially if the yacht builder is located far away. Having a surveyor inspect your boat as it is being built is not an affront to the builder. The surveyor is your representative and his job is to see that the plans are being followed to the letter.

Establish a schedule with the builder that indicates the expected completion and launch dates. As the building progresses, you should get a feeling for whether or not construction is on schedule. Don't be surprised if the completion date is delayed. Builders seldom make the date they think they will, and with individually built boats this is almost sure to happen because of delays in delivery of special equipment. Be patient with the builder and give him some leeway. On the other hand, excessive delays are seldom necessary. Some builders have a reputation for always being late, you should make inquiries about your builder in this regard before the job begins.

When a one-off is completed, some time should be devoted to sea trials. You and the builder should agree on this before the job begins. Keep the time of year in mind when considering a projected date for sea trials. If the boat is being built in the high latitudes, it may be impossible to hold sea trials in the winter. And while you cannot expect to have the perfect range of varying conditions to test your new boat during sea trials, you should endeavor to put it through its paces as much as possible.

At some point in the sea trials the designer should be present. Production boats seldom yield surprises during sea trials, but an unproven boat may show some minor and sometimes even major problems. It is best to conduct sea trials near the factory, where the builder can make necessary changes and modifications. Once you make final payment and sail away, or the boat is shipped to you, it will be hard to make changes without a great deal of inconvenience to you and the builder. Even after sea trials consider sailing for a few days in the area where the boat was built. This is an opportunity for you and your new boat to become 'friends,' and this may be your one last contact with the builder.

Buying a Used Boat

Second-hand boats have some good attributes, especially if you are on a limited budget or are pressed for time. In buying a used boat you have the opportunity to select a proven yacht design, and to ask owners of similar boats how well they perform. There will probably be an opportunity to sail on a boat of the same design and perhaps even go cruising for a while.

Used boats always bring important extras with them. If the yacht has been sailed for a few years, the previous owners will have made improvements in the boat and added useful equipment. A 10-year-old anchor is just as good as a new one. The sails will seldom be new, but there will often be a good selection on board. This permits upgrading the sail inventory over a long period of time rather than having to buy a whole new suit at once. An extensive inventory may raise the price of the boat, but this will not come close to the replacement cost of the sails.

Sometimes a buyer finds a 'distress' sale – when someone wants to sell his boat quickly. Occasionally it is a boat that has been outfitted for ocean cruising, and the owner or a family member has decided that the cruising dream is really a nightmare for him. He may be so anxious to get away from his boat that he will sell it at an unusually low price. If you happen to be in the right place at the right time, or if you are not in a hurry, you may make a very good deal.

On the other hand, don't expect that an old boat will necessarily be a cheap one. Some boats appreciate over the years. In general, good boats tend to hold their value. An obvious advantage of shopping for a used boat is that there are so many available. At present, it is definitely a 'buyer's market.' One reason for this is that fiberglass boats don't wear out.

Boat prices are affected by various economic and political factors. When the energy crisis first struck in the early 1970s, sailboats became more popular, because they did not use as much fuel as power boats. Also the new popularity of fiberglass in the 1970s helped to accelerate yacht building. Medium-displacement cruiser-racers, around 30 to 36 feet (9 to 11 m) in length were especially popular. Many of those boats are now on the market as their owners upgrade to larger or newer models.

The used-boat buyer can afford to be very choosy, and he should approach the task slowly and thoughtfully. For example, several boats of the same model and nearly the same age may be on the market, and among these you can select the best bargain. Price alone, however, should not be the main consideration. One boat may have a higher price which reflects the equipment on board as much as it does appearance and condition. The extra equipment may more than make up for the difference, *if* it is the type of equipment that you need for your cruising plans. For example, ground tackle, a tender, a good inventory of usable sails, or perhaps some electronic equipment, would be valuable additions. However, be careful and selective when looking at old radios and navigation gear. What you really need for offshore cruising may be somewhat different from what is often found on coastal cruising boats.

After you have narrowed the field down to one or two boats, you enter the negotiating stage. For most of us, this is the least pleasant part, though some people thrive on it. Sellers list their boats at a price that is higher than they expect to get. A buyer should not hesitate to offer a lower price. For every seller who might resent a low offer, there are 10 or 15 who will lower their price. 'Dickering' is a game as old as civilization. A seller may list his boat at a 'firm' price, which supposedly means he will not take less. It is still OK to make a lower offer – perhaps the assurance of a sale will make a difference. Sometimes you can play a waiting game and tell the seller to let you know if he changes his 'firm' offer. If you are not in a hurry time is on your side.

Once you agree on a price, there remains one very important step before buying the boat – having a survey made. At this point the buyer makes a deposit on the boat with the stipulation that it will be returned if the boat fails to pass a satisfactory survey. You will now need to hire a surveyor and have the yacht hauled out for a detailed examination. Appendix 1 describes how a survey works.

Boat Buyer's Budget

How much does it cost to buy a boat and equip it for offshore cruising? The standard answer is, as much money as you have! Unless you are unusually wealthy you will spend more than you hope to, and still have many things on your wish list. For this reason it is important to begin with a budget. Then, based on how much money you have available, you can estimate how much to spend for the boat, how much to spend on conversions if it is a used boat, and how much to spend on new equipment.

No one can tell you exactly how much this will be. There can be some shockers when you start adding up the costs of needed or high-priority gear. A liferaft can cost as much as $4000. I consider a wind-steering vane a necessity for a shorthanded crew, and that will be around $2000. A GPS will be about $1000, as will some radios. The new EPIRBs are in the same price range. How about a couple of new sails at $1500 each? A tender and outboard? A boom gallows is mighty nice on a bluewater boat, and most folks won't want to go to sea without a dodger (sprayhood). Don't forget some extra anchors and the conversion from nylon line to chain for anchoring. Oh, and by the way, with that chain you'll need an anchor windlass.

Many factors are involved in the final expenditure. The only firm figure you can start out with is the cost of the yacht. After that it depends on what condition the yacht is in when you buy it, what modifications you make, how much work you are willing to do yourself, and what new equipment you decide to add. It is very easy to spend an additional 50 percent of the purchase price to prepare a used boat for extensive offshore sailing. In other words, if you buy a used boat for $50,000, it would not be unusual to spend an additional $25,000 before you cast off.

SIZE CONSIDERATIONS

There is a lot more to size than boatlength when considering an off-shore cruising yacht. Boats designed as cruiser-racers under the old CCA rule, for example, might have an overall length of 34 to 38 feet (10 to 11 m) with a relatively narrow beam of around 10 feet (3 m). Many of them are excellent sea boats but not very roomy. A boat of similar length specifically designed for cruising would be more beamy and the interior more spacious. There is a trade-off, of course, because the cruising boat with greater displacement will be slower and less weatherly. Likewise, a yacht with a high flush deck will be roomier than one with a conventional raised cabin. But here is another compromise, because the flush deck yacht will have more freeboard and considerably more windage. The boat will probably be less attractive as well because of the flat sheer.

Costs

Bigger boats cost more money, initially and ultimately. Regardless of their original purchase prices, a 40-foot (12 m) boat will cost more to equip and to maintain than a 30-foot boat, and a 30-foot boat will be more costly than one of 25 feet. A larger boat has more surface area both below and above decks to paint. It requires larger standing and running rigging, bigger winches, and more expensive sails. It usually has a larger engine with a bigger appetite for fuel. Marina charges are based on length, as are haul-out and dry-storage charges. As boat size increases so does the size of the ground tackle and the windlass to handle it.

The next time you are looking at a marine supply catalog, notice the difference in price between a 25-pound CQR anchor that would be adequate for a 25-foot boat, and one weighing 45 pounds, which is recommended for a 38-foot yacht. Notice too the difference in winch prices and the cost of jib-sheet line. A larger boat needs not only larger diameter line, but a lot more of it.

Some costs are fixed regardless of size. Electronics, compasses, and tenders will be the same size for a wide range of boats.

Maintenance Time

In much the same way that boat size dictates the cost of equipment and maintenance, it also determines the amount of time you spend on maintenance. This applies equally to the big jobs like painting and waxing and to more routine matters such as washing down the deck. Most cruisers find it necessary to dive and clean the bottom of their boats fairly often, depending on where they are sailing. Another nuisance job is the removal of seaweed from the waterline. While engaged in these tasks there is time to think, and often your thoughts turn to boat size – especially if the water is cold!

Maintenance time takes away from the time for sightseeing, fishing, reading, or the other things that were the original objectives of cruising. It also seems that bigger boats have more expensive and more complicated equipment. This is not necessary, but it frequently happens. When you have room for more gear, it often comes aboard. Before long there are numerous add-ons such as refrigeration, a hot-water system, pressure water, and a compressor for diving tanks. Big-boat people often collect more and more electronic toys such as TVs, VCRs, microwave ovens, and electric windlasses. Soon more and bigger batteries are needed and eventually an auxiliary generator to supply all these power-hungry shipmates. It is not uncommon in cruising anchorages to see the skippers of larger boats running around trying to find parts for this or that generator or compressor or to find a repairman for the refrigeration, while the folks on the smaller, simpler boats are sitting in the shade or are out snorkeling and taking life easy. Cruising is supposed to be a fun and easygoing lifestyle. Too often, especially with a big boat, you become a slave to all the 'conveniences' that purport to make life easier. The best advice, regardless of boat size, is to 'keep it simple.'

Cruising Plans

Where you plan to go, and how long you plan to take for your cruising adventure, are things worth considering as you shop for a cruising boat. It is easy to underestimate the ratio of days at sea to days in port or at anchor. For most of us a port stay of less than two weeks is unusual. Often it is several weeks, and sometimes the weeks become months.

The log of an average cruising boat shows that passage time represents only 10 to 20 percent of most cruising years. You will be spending long periods at anchor, and size has to do with comfort and being 'at home' on your boat.

If your cruising plans are very limited it may be worth considering a smaller boat than you would take on a more lengthy cruise. But give this careful thought because once you are out cruising you will begin to take life a little easier, your daily pace will slow down, and you will find it more and more difficult to leave your new-found cruising friends and pleasant harbors. What started out as a one- or two-year trip will be modified, plans will be altered, and your cruise will be extended. That is what cruising is all about.

Speed

Many cruising sailors began as racers, and for some of them there is a tendency to cruise as if it were a race. We have to remind ourselves that this is supposed to be enjoyable and not a contest of speed and survival. We can slow down a bit and take it easy. On the other hand, about halfway through a long passage, you may begin to wish you could go just a little faster. Good boatspeed is desirable, and there is nothing wrong with trying to sail your cruising boat at its best speed, as long as it is not uncomfortable or unsafe for the crew.

If all other considerations are equal, bigger boats are faster. Of course, some skippers are better than others or sail their boats more efficiently. But if a boat is overloaded or badly out of trim it will slow down.

The significance of speed to the cruising sailor means less time at sea between ports, and it can also mean more comfort and safety. It may mean getting out of the way of a typhoon or perhaps reaching a harbor in advance of bad weather. But speed is not a substitute for seaworthiness. There are some racing and cruising yachts that are fast but should not be out on the ocean.

The late Eric Hiscock, and his wife Susan, probably chalked up more pleasurable world-wide cruising than anyone else in the history of sailing. Hiscock considered the three most important features in a cruising boat to be seaworthiness, comfort, and speed – in that order.

Suppose that in searching for a cruising boat you find two that you especially like. It may not seem very significant that one will sail at an average speed of a knot or even a half-knot faster than the other. Consider that in terms of a long passage, however, and it is significant. The passage from Panama to Hawaii is about 5000 miles. A yacht that averages six knots will arrive in port a week earlier than one averaging five knots. Does this mean it is impossible or even inadvisable to go to sea in a small or a slow boat? Not at all. There are many impressive circumnavigations that have been made in less-than-ideal cruising yachts. A lot of folks are out sailing in small seaworthy yachts with families in spite of crowded conditions on board. Most of them would prefer to have a larger boat but their budgets do not allow them such a luxury. Ask them if they would rather be sailing or on land trying to save enough money for a more comfortable or faster boat, and they will all say they would rather be sailing.

Displacement

A boat's weight is equal to the weight of the water it *displaces*. In the yachting literature there are frequent references to light, medium, and heavy-displacement boats. These are relative terms that many people use and few understand. When someone refers to a yacht as light, medium, or heavy he usually means the *displacement/length* ratio (D/L ratio) rather than displacement alone. This ratio is determined as follows:

$$\text{D/L ratio} = \frac{\text{displacement in long tons}}{(.01 \text{ DWL})^3}$$

[Long ton: 2240 pounds (1016 kg). DWL: the design waterline length in feet.]

In general, a D/L ratio of less than 200 is light displacement, 200 to 300 is medium displacement, and greater than 300 is heavy displacement. A typical racing boat, for example, would be light displacement and often with a D/L ratio of around 100. A cruiser-racer production boat is commonly medium displacement, and a yacht designed only for cruising would have a D/L ratio in excess of 300. If it is an older cruising boat, or one of the new versions of an old-style cruising yacht, it may well be more than 400.

The preceding information seems straightforward and simple enough, and it would seem logical that the lighter displacement boat will be fast and the heavy displacement boat slow. This may be true, but there can also be some exceptions. For example, cruising boats are almost always overloaded, so no matter what their design displacement and D/L ratio, their 'reality displacement' may be somewhat different. Typical production racers or cruiser-racers are rarely designed to carry the equipment and supplies for an extended cruise. On the other hand heavy displacement cruising boats are designed to be heavily loaded and you can pile gear on them for hours and notice little change in the waterline. Try this on a light displacement boat and the boot-top will soon disappear. The change would be apparent in a medium displacement boat, but not as rapid.

How do you estimate the 'reality weight?' Lin and Larry Pardey, who have written extensively about their cruising experiences, propose that for long distance cruising you should estimate as much as 2000 pounds (900 kg) per person. I would not have believed this suggestion before I began cruising, but it now seems a conservative estimate. You can logically ask, 'What in the world is all that stuff?' It is food, summer and winter clothing, books, extra ground tackle, an offshore liferaft, additional foul-weather gear, cassette tapes, a lot of charts, a typewriter, sewing machine, cameras, trinkets and souvenirs that you pick up along the way, extra fuel and water, repair parts, tools, diving gear, and the good-luck charm your cousin sent to you from Kankakee. With this huge pile of paraphernalia, displacement takes on a new significance, which presents us with a new compromise.

Weight is the enemy of speed, and your heavily loaded yacht will not move as fast as when it was at design displacement. So, the boat you selected for speed may now be so heavy that its speed is markedly decreased, and you might have been better off selecting a heavier boat that was more capable of absorbing the extra weight. This is especially true for light displacement boats. Medium displacement yachts can usually take a few inches of added displacement without too much difficulty.

If you already have a medium displacement yacht and plan to use it for the offshore cruise, you should not get discouraged by the foregoing discussion. Unless your boat is excessively overloaded, the weight probably will not significantly affect seaworthiness or stability, provided you pay attention to trim. It may even increase stability. Most of us 'solve' the problem by painting the waterline higher and higher. I have yet to see a yacht that has been out cruising for a year or more that was not down on its lines. It never fails. *Denali* has had her waterline raised about four inches so far, is still a lively performer and has turned in a few cruising days in excess of 165 miles, even with a lazy skipper.

Size of the Crew

There are a couple of important considerations when it comes to boat size versus number of crew. First is the amount of boat the crew can control, and second is the amount of space they want or need. A few years ago it was generally accepted that about 40 feet was as much as two middle-aged people would want to handle, and 34 feet seemed about enough for a singlehander, depending on the design, crew experience and energy, and cruising area involved. However, there have been many changes in yachts and yacht equipment in recent years that justify revising these figures. Boats are now being constructed of lighter materials, designs have changed, autopilots and wind-steering vanes have been perfected, and the advent of roller-furling/reefing jibs and even mainsails, now permit larger boats and smaller crews. If you have some of this state-of-the-art equipment incorporated into your boat it is not impossible for a crew of two to manage a vessel of 60 feet or more.

But before you run out and purchase a floating condo, keep in mind what was said previously about maintenance and upkeep. In spite of all the high-tech equipment that has come on the yachting scene, no one has invented anything to replace time and hard work to maintain a larger boat. Furthermore, I would not recommend having a boat that cannot be sailed singlehanded if necessary. On most cruising boats watches are stood by only one person, and it is inconvenient and sometimes impossible to call crew on deck every time it is necessary to tack or make a sail change. More important, illness or injury can require singlehanded sailing even though it was not anticipated.

The second aspect of crew size is naturally living space. In his famous book, *Heavy Weather Sailing*, Adlard Coles had this to say about the cabin of one 27-foot boat he sailed in: 'One person can be accommodated in comfort, two in tolerance, three in tenseness, and four in bitter enmity.'

A boat is at best a small space for people to live in, and while most of us can survive in a crowded cabin, we may not enjoy it very much. If someone has to stand up whenever someone else wants to sit down, it gets very tiring. If the saloon table is also someone's bed it is inconvenient. Again, it is a trade-off: if your budget is tight or you are only cruising for a short time, you may have to make do with these inconveniences. If most of us insisted on waiting until we had exactly the boat we wanted, we would never get to sea.

A singlehander or even a couple can probably adapt to whatever they have to work with. With a larger crew, or if you expect to have guests sailing with you, or if you have children on board, then space may become more of a consideration when you go shopping for your boat.

Age and Physical Condition of the Crew

The age of people out sailing the oceans today is truly impressive. Recently a young American sailor, Tania Aebi, completed a singlehanded circumnavigation. When she began her cruise she was 18. There are singlehanders and couples in their 70s who are still out cruising. Age is obviously not a barrier to offshore cruising. There are definite advantages to beginning cruising when you are young, but there are some who began in their 60s. Certainly as you grow older it is necessary to scale down your activities somewhat and to be realistic about what size sails and equipment you can handle.

Like age, the physical condition of cruising people varies. Most cruisers are healthy because it is a healthy way of life. On the other hand there are people out sailing with disabilities. A few years ago, writer/sailor Tristan Jones had to have a leg amputated, but it did not end his cruising. I met one man who built his own yacht and went cruising even though he had only one arm. As an extreme example, a blind man sailed alone from California to Hawaii. And strength is not a prerequisite to sailing. It is not unusual to see women of small stature singlehanding.

When preparing your boat for offshore sailing, you can modify it to suit the strength and ability of your crew. Some people choose to use power equipment for winches and windlasses. These may be electric or hydraulic. I would discourage this practice as it goes against the idea of keeping the cruising boat as simple as possible. If you have trouble cranking in the jib sheet, get bigger winches, or choose a rig with two small headsails rather than one large one, or go to a split rig (ketch or yawl). If a tiller is too hard to handle, use wheel steering.

Another consideration is the choice of cruising area and season. If you select carefully and adhere to the well-known seasonal limitations for specific parts of the ocean, there is little likelihood of getting into serious trouble cruising. A seaworthy yacht and an experienced crew need have no fear of the ocean. Respect, yes, but not fear.

Recommendations

For a couple heading offshore for an extended cruise I suggest a medium displacement boat between 35 and 45 feet (10.6 to 14 m) if it is within your budget. This size, regardless of rig, can be easily managed by two middle-aged people in average physical condition, and can carry enough standard equipment for relatively long offshore passages.

Larger boats, properly rigged, are within the capability of most two-person crews, so I mainly suggest 45 feet as an upper limit because of cost and maintenance. The larger yachts can put a strain on your cruising funds and on your cruising fun if you have to spend too much time on upkeep.

Now what about the range between 35 and 45 feet? Surprisingly, most medium-displacement yachts in this size range don't differ too much in their cabin layout. Yes, they will have differences, but the basics – galley, chart table, main cabin, head, and forward cabin will not be significantly different in most cases. What will differ is the relative size of the foregoing plan. A bigger boat will have a larger and more convenient galley, a more comfortable chart table, a larger dining table, and possibly, more comfortable bunks. The head will be larger and perhaps include a shower, and of course there will be more stowage space throughout the boat.

Be skeptical of the cruiser-racer hulls in the 30- to 40-foot range that attempt to mimic cruising yachts. Sometimes the large production companies will offer a cruiser-racer hull with an option for a 'cruising' interior. They might, for example, offer an 'aft cabin arrangement' or extra 'stateroom' forward or, as was popular in America a few years ago, a center-cockpit version.

'You can't make a silk purse out of a sow's ear.' A boat is only so big, and if you put in an extra anything then something else will have to be smaller. Furthermore, the bulkheads and doors required for 'privacy' take up a lot of useable space. An enclosed aft cabin might seem like a nice option, but if it is too small to be comfortable, it will end up as poor storage space.

Almost any sailor who has been cruising for a while will admit the desire for a bigger boat. Almost in the same breath, or at least a couple of beers later, he will reminisce about a previous (and smaller) boat and comment on how much easier it was to take care of.

CHOOSING THE RIG

The variety of cruising rigs that have been developed through the ages is impressive. If you are a traditionalist, or have an interest in the ancient or exotic, there are many possible rigs to consider. If you are an experimenter or 'dabbler,' you may want to have a go at one of the more unusual rigs. However, my goal is to help you choose a seaworthy, comfortable, and fast-sailing yacht that is within your budget, and to get you out of the gate as quickly as possible. When it comes to selecting the rig, compromises and trade-offs become very obvious. What you want, what is available, and what is within your budget, may be quite different.

Not so many years ago the gaff rig was very common and there are still a number of gaff rigs among the cruising fleet today. The chance that you will build or buy a gaff-headed yacht is slight. However, a brief discussion of the differences between gaff and Bermuda rigs will help explain why we sail the way we do today.

Gaff, Bermuda, and Fractional Rigs

The gaff rig carries a four-sided sail. The head of the sail is attached to a gaff spar, and the gaff is hauled up the mast. For this reason there can be no hardware, shrouds, or fittings on the mast where the 'throat'

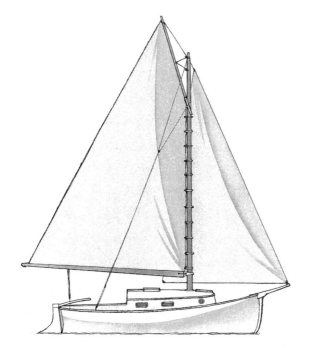

Figure 3.1
Gaff-rigged sloop.

of the gaff has to slide up and down. Sloops, cutters, yawls, ketches, and schooners – the types of rigs we will discuss in this chapter – can all be gaff-or Bermuda-rigged; in the case of yachts with two or more masts, they can be a combination of gaff and Bermuda. Until the second decade of this century the gaff was the primary rig found on sailing yachts, and gaff rigs still held their own until the 1930s.

Gaff-rig masts are short and sturdy but their popularity has waned because they are less efficient than the tall Bermuda. Except for their backstays, gaff-rig masts are easier to hold in place with a forestay and upper shrouds. However, the gaff spar does away with the possibility of lower shrouds and spreaders, and the after stays have to be running backstays in order not to interfere with the gaff. With each tack, the windward running backstay has to be tightened and the leeward backstay slacked. Furthermore, it takes more time, more halyards, and usually more effort, to raise and furl a gaff sail than a Bermuda.

A definite advantage of the gaff sail is that it can be set with the wind coming from any direction. Hoisting a Bermuda main when the wind is anywhere except just about dead ahead is either difficult or impossible. The sail will catch on the shrouds or spreaders and the halyard will try to wrap itself around any projection on the mast – a singlehander's delight.

The terms 'Bermuda,' 'Bermudian,' 'Marconi,' or 'jib-headed,' usually all mean the same thing; they describe what most of us think of as the standard sailboat rig – a tall mast that carries a large, triangular sail hoisted on a mast track or groove.

Although the original Bermuda-type rig had been around for some time in the West Indies, it took a technological advance to make it practical for most yachts. The development of marine-grade glues permitted

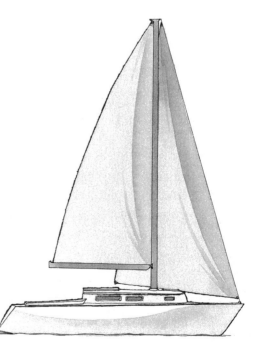

Figure 3.2
Bermuda-rigged sloop.

the building of hollow, and therefore lighter-weight, wood masts. This in turn meant that taller masts could be carried.

Underway the Bermuda rig out-performs the gaff going to windward unless an additional topsail is raised above the gaff main. But the addition of the topsail means more rigging and more work, and the topsail is impossible to carry in increasing winds. There are also problems of sail chafe against the running rigging with gaff sails. That is the reason for all of that salty-looking baggywrinkle in the rigging of a gaffer. Chafe is seldom more than a minor problem on the Bermuda main.

The Bermuda rig permits a taller mast and a mainsail with a long straight luff. It only requires one mainsail halyard, which on most modern yachts is internal. It also presents less weight aloft than the gaff rig. This is an advantage for a small yacht, because it reduces heel and makes for more efficient sailing and less drag. There is no question that a gaff-rigged yacht under sail is a beautiful sight, and if you want to be a bit of a traditionalist it has some appeal. But it is more work to sail and it can be a nuisance for the shorthanded crew.

Fractional rigs are those in which the headstay, instead of running to the top of the mast, as it does in a 'masthead rig,' only goes to a position 75 to 90 percent of the mast height. Some years ago fractional rigs were quite popular, then they nearly disappeared, and now they are back again on race boats. Their reappearance has occurred because they permit lighter weight masts. Fractional rigs, also known as 7/8 or 3/4 rigs, depending on where the headstay joins the mast, are sometimes referred to as 'bendy' rigs. This means that a significant bend can be set into the upper part of the mast to give the main better draft control.

The fractional rig reduces the size of the jib and increases the size of the main. Supposedly, therefore, when the wind pipes up and it is time

Figure 3.3
Fractional-rigged sloop.

to reduce sail area, it is possible, up to a point, to leave the jib flying and reef the main. Certainly it is easier and faster to reef a main than to change a headsail. The trade off is the need for running backstays to give strength and support to the mast abaft the point where the forestay attaches.

For a cruising yacht, fractional rigs seem of questionable benefit and may be a distinct disadvantage. They are often fragile, and require a lot of attention and tuning. They can easily be broken if the running backstays are not attended to promptly on a tack or especially on an unintentional jibe. If you go to the trouble of running backstays why not have a cutter rig, which also offers easy sail reduction?

Sloops

Most of us are best acquainted with the sloop rig; it is by far the most popular boat today because of its convenience and simplicity. With a sloop you can go aboard and be underway in a few minutes. There is only a main and a jib halyard, and the only work in tacking is handling jib sheets. The main is nearly self-tending and only needs adjustment after a tack. The single backstay is much less complicated than runners. But the dependence of the mast on the fore- and backstay means they must be strong and well set up. The mast on a sloop is located far enough aft that working on deck is usually not difficult.

On boats up to about 45 or 50 feet (14 to 15 m), the sloop rig is the simplest way to go. Around 45 feet the sails may begin to be a bit large for a singlehander or small crew. At that size most cruisers start thinking seriously of some alternatives.

Cutters

Cutters are preferred by many cruising sailors, and probably a lot more long distance sailors would own cutters if more of these boats were available. As it is, most production boats are sloops, so that is what a lot of us end up sailing. A cutter has most of the advantages of a sloop plus easier headsail handling. It is possible to convert a sloop to a cutter, but it may not be advisable. Before you try, talk to the designer. In a proper cutter the mast is farther aft than in a sloop rig of the same design.

The main advantage of the cutter is that instead of having one large headsail it has two smaller ones – usually a high-clewed jib and staysail. This permits rapid sail reduction when the wind increases and likewise an easy increase of sail area when the wind drops. A sloop with a good roller-furling jib can be just as easy to manage, but a partially furled headsail almost always loses its proper shape, and thus its ability to drive the boat efficiently – especially to windward.

Without roller furling, sail changes on both sloops and cutters require some foredeck work. However, in heavy weather a cutter can be safer for several reasons: First, it can fly a well-balanced combination of sails – a staysail and a reefed main, whereas a sloop has to carry an inferior balance – a working jib or storm jib along with a reefed main or storm trysail. Second, because the mast on a cutter is farther aft, the

Figure 3.4
Cutter.

staysail-mainsail combination eliminates the need to be out on the bow once the jib is down. Third, cutters with the staysail-mainsail combination generally heave-to better than sloops, whose storm sails are widely separated and harder to balance against each other.

I question the need, though not the convenience, for roller furling on a cutter, even in terms of sail stowage. With properly cut sailcovers the two headsails on a cutter can be left hanked on most of the time at sea and in port – a big advantage over a sloop. The two headsails that 'live' full time on deck on a cutter replace three sails that must be stored below on a sloop.

Rigging is more complicated on a cutter than on a sloop and requires an inner forestay and running backstays in addition to the permanent backstay. However, the backstays do not need to be used in light or moderate conditions on most cutters, and when not in use they can be tied off at the lower shrouds. In light air the cutter becomes a sloop and carries a large genoa. At such times the inner forestay can be detached and brought back and tied off at the mast.

On some cutters a bowsprit is added to increase the sail area and to reduce mast height. This is all right, as long as the main doesn't wind up being too small, in which case the two headsails will have to be changed more often.

Ketches

On a ketch the mizzen is stepped forward of the rudder post, or at least forward of the end of the waterline, and the mainmast is slightly forward of where it is on a sloop or cutter. Some choose a ketch because the rig can carry a lot of sails that are small and relatively easy to handle. Another popular reason for selecting a ketch is that two masts can be a safety factor. In the event of a dismasting, there is still one mast to keep the boat going. This, of course, assumes that the two masts are independently stayed.

Breaking up the sailplan for the sake of smaller sails is a definite advantage on a large boat (over 50 feet), but for smaller boats it is seldom necessary, and with the trend toward lighter, stronger, boats and reliable furling sails, this argument will lose strength in the future. The extra mast means added weight. Weight and windage result in a slower boat. A ketch rig will be slower than a sloop or cutter of equivalent design, and it will not be as closewinded. Rigging, hardware, and sail costs, as well as maintenance time, will be greater on a yacht having two masts instead of one.

There are a number of common complaints about ketches, starting with the position of the mizzen and the problems of wind blanketing on various points of sail. Ketch owners grumble about the problems they have with the main and mizzen interfering with each other. Often they end up sailing with the main reefed or the mizzen furled. When running, the mizzen will blanket the main, and on other points the main may blanket the mizzen. When on a broad reach the ketch may experience excessive weather helm.

On aft-cockpit ketches, the mizzen is always in the way and manages to take up a lot of room in the cockpit. The combination of a mizzen mast and a pedestal steering wheel makes for a crowded cockpit. It is difficult to see around the mizzen mast, and the mizzen boom is known for crew bashing. Standing rigging for the mizzen can make walking on the deck difficult. With a mid-cockpit ketch, some of these problems are eliminated because the mast is behind the helmsman. However, it takes a large ketch to justify the belowdecks layout that benefits from a mid-cockpit. More trade-offs!

The argument that it is easy and quick to reduce sail on a ketch by furling the mizzen is true. But when I hear this I wonder if those who

Figure 3.5
Ketch.

boast about it have reefed a main on a sloop or cutter. It is not a difficult task with a correctly set up slab or jiffy reef system. Reefing the
main on a ketch, by the way, can be a bit more difficult, because the
mast is farther forward and working on deck is more subject to pitching
than on a sloop, or especially a cutter, where the mast is farther aft.

Proponents of the ketch point out that an extra sail (a fisherman
staysail, mizzen staysail, or a mule) set between the main and the
mizzen mast will give the boat additional drive. True, but such sails are
difficult to set, get mixed reviews from their owners, and often add too
much heel. Some ketches have a bowsprit to increase the foretriangle
sail area, and of course it is possible, but not necessarily a good idea, to
have a staysail forward if a bowsprit is installed.

It cannot be denied that a full-rigged ketch, even a small one, can be
a beautiful boat to see sailing, but most of the ketch owners I have spo-
ken to say their next boat will be a cutter or sloop.

Yawls

At first a yawl may seem not that much different from a ketch. However, the mizzen on a yawl is much smaller and is stepped aft of the rudder post or the waterline. This in turn puts the main mast farther aft
and opens up the foretriangle area.

The well-known Caribbean and Atlantic sailor Donald Street owns a
classic 85-year-old yawl, and it is enjoyable to read his comments on
cruising. His enthusiasm about yawls will lead you to believe that there
is no other rig worth considering, and he goes into great detail explaining how a yawl is especially handy when maneuvering in crowded
anchorages. He should know, because his large yawl has no engine. It is
fascinating to realize you can, according to Street, actually back a yawl
under sail alone. But as interesting as it is, it is not an easy task for a
small crew. I have anchored and gotten underway from an anchorage

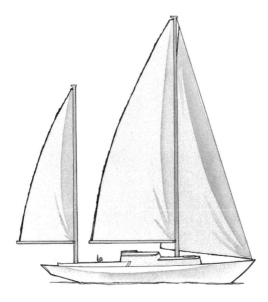

Figure 3.6
Yawl.

on a sloop numerous times without using my engine and have never felt that the addition of a mizzen would have made the job any easier.

For a split rig a yawl is probably better than a ketch. Because the mainmast on a yawl is farther aft than on a ketch it can be stayed better and thus allows a larger foretriangle and less need for a bowsprit. Likewise it is better downwind than a ketch, because the mizzen is smaller and gives less blanket effect to the main. Still, the mizzen of a yawl, though smaller than on a ketch, adds weight as well as time and money in hardware and maintenance; at least it offers less windage.

If a sloop or cutter has a sufficiently wide and strong stern and a short enough boom, it is possible to convert it to a yawl. Some claim this could be an advantage, because it will produce more weather helm in light and moderate air, and it will give some boats good balance in heavy going with the mizzen and jib flying and the main reefed.

Yawl owners are quick to point out that their rig is great for rigging an awning, and they are right. They also point out, as do owners of ketches, that under some anchoring conditions it is convenient to rig the mizzen (it would probably have to be reefed on a ketch) as a riding sail to keep the boat from swinging around.

Schooners

A schooner provides a beautiful sight when under sail, so if you want to give a nice view to others while you are pulling a lot of lines at sea and spending time on maintenance in port, this may be the boat for you. Again, for a big boat, especially an older one with adequate crew, or for the charter business, it has its good points.

Schooners may have two or three masts. If three, the masts are of equal height. If only two, the forward mast is shorter. Schooners carry a variety of configurations. Some are gaff rigged, some have a gaff for-

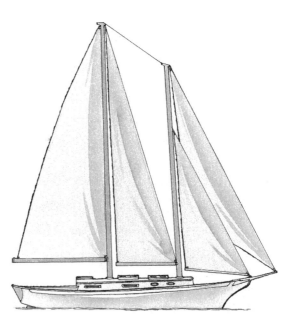

Figure 3.7
Schooner.

ward and a Bermuda mast aft, and some even have two Bermuda masts. Occasionally you still see a staysail schooner.

A schooner's best point of sail is a reach, and at such times you will have a fast and exhilarating sail – but they do not go well to windward, and on a run the main will blanket the foresails. And again, the more spars and rigging, the greater the expense and upkeep.

I admit to a feeling of romance and nostalgia whenever I see a schooner under sail, and I would never turn down the opportunity to go for a sail on one. But owning and maintaining a schooner with a small crew is not my preference.

Cat Ketches and Unstayed Rigs

Most production boats look pretty much the same, and that sameness is patterned after the current style in racers. The few production boats that are supposedly built only for cruising tend to be double-enders which are rugged, heavy, and slow.

A refreshing challenge to both of these principles occurred about 20 years ago when Garry Hoyt introduced a different kind of cruising yacht with a combination of new and old ideas, including cat rig, wishbone booms, and unstayed masts. These were not new ideas. Cat boats and unstayed masts are of ancient origin, and wishbone sails were popular about 60 years ago. However, it was Hoyt's innovative thinking that brought them together with new technology. The cat-ketch turns out to be something between a ketch and a schooner, with two masts of equal, or nearly equal height, one far forward, as it would be on a traditional, single-masted catboat; each carrying a single large sail aft, but no headsails.

The most surprising and controversial aspects of the cat-ketch were the unstayed carbon-fiber masts. When first introduced they met with a

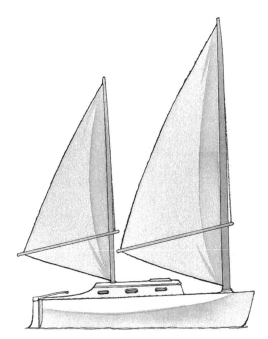

Figure 3.8
Cat ketch.

great deal of skepticism. Indeed, it is a strange feeling to go aboard a boat without any stays or shrouds. Now, after nearly two decades of use, the rig has confirmed its strength and reliability, as carbon-fiber masts have proven to be lighter, stronger, and more practical than aluminum.

The high freeboard and uncluttered deck of the cat-ketch are definite attributes for the cruiser in spite of added windage. Although it is not as fast going to windward as more conventional yachts, the cat-ketch is excellent on a reach, and these are the conditions most cruisers hope to sail under. A major advantage to the shorthanded sailor is that a cat-ketch is self-tacking. The absence of shrouds and stays removes a major worry and maintenance factor.

Included in this general category are the 'hybrid' unstayed rigs, like the current Freedom boats, which carry big, roachy mains and small, self-tacking working jibs. The jibs, which are there mainly to create a slot, are run up on headstays that don't actually contribute to mast support, and have internal wishbone booms (trade-named CamberSpars) to maintain sail shape.

The Best Rig

For many sailors the question of the 'best' rig really means, what is available and affordable. If, on the other hand, you can have whatever boat you want, here is some additional information. A survey of the senior members of the Seven Seas Cruising Association a few years ago showed the types of boats these sailors owned and, presumably, preferred:

Sloops	138
Cutters	138
Ketches	136
Yawls	22
Schooners	13
Multihulls	1

All of the boats in this survey have crews that live aboard full time. Most of them are out cruising, although some probably spend their time exclusively in marinas. Probably the abundance of sloops is related to the fact that most production boats are sloops. The relatively few yawls may be in part because there are few yawls available; the same may be true of schooners. As for multihulls, well, who knows? Maybe their owners don't like to belong to organizations, or maybe they are moving so fast that they don't have time to be included in surveys!

HULL DESIGN

The influence that racing has on cruising hull design is not a new phenomenon. In fact this influence has been present for as long as cruising and racing have been around. This did not present a significant problem for cruising boats until the early 1970s, when the International Offshore Rule (IOR) was introduced and became the guiding light in yacht design. Simultaneously, advances were made in new, high-technology, lightweight construction methods and materials to reduce weight and improve boatspeed. Not all of the new directions were helpful to offshore cruising sailors – and some were harmful.

Under the 'old' Cruising Club of America (CCA) rule, boats were actually weighed in the process of being rated for racing and they were penalized for long waterlines and light displacement. Under the IOR, on the other hand, light displacement became an advantage in the rating formula (and of course in boatspeed) and long waterlines, which improve speed, were rewarded.

As discussed in Chapter 2, all this is fine for racing, but when a light displacement boat is outfitted for cruising, problems arise: If you add a ton of cruising equipment, supplies, and food to a medium or heavy displacement yacht of 35 or so feet you will hardly notice the difference. Try the same thing on a small, light-displacement boat and it is no longer a light displacement yacht – its performance will suffer.

Over the past 20 years, racing boats – what used to be the cruiser-racers – have become specialized machines, lighter and more beamy, with taller masts and larger sailplans. Underwater hull shapes have become flatter, like those on racing dinghies; crew weight is 'moveable ballast,' and internal ballast has been moved higher. In the search for even greater weight reduction and better control of sailshape, masts have decreased in diameter and weight. The number of fractional rigs has increased, along with a reliance on running backstays. At the same time, competition and the desire to win at all costs have pushed this rig farther and farther offshore. This competitiveness has widened the gap between racing and cruising until today few racing boats are good for cruising.

Does this mean that new, lighter-weight building materials cannot or should not be used in offshore cruising boats? No. But it does mean that the prospective boat-buyer needs to balance a number of factors in the search for a strong, seaworthy boat.

Considerations

In the following discussion we will look briefly at some hull factors and consider how they affect performance of the offshore cruising boat.

Figure 4.1
Comparison of racer-cruiser hulls.

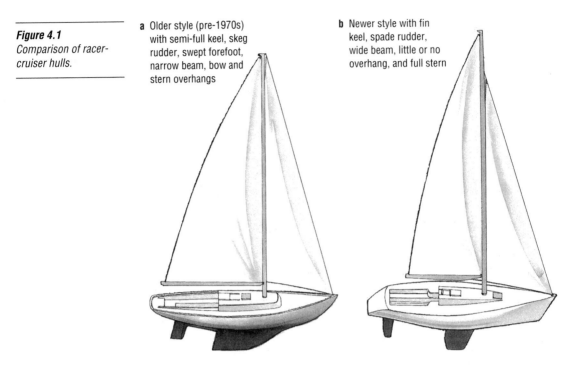

a Older style (pre-1970s)
with semi-full keel, skeg
rudder, swept forefoot,
narrow beam, bow and
stern overhangs

b Newer style with fin
keel, spade rudder,
wide beam, little or no
overhang, and full stern

Since this is not a technical manual please keep in mind that I am making generalizations.

Displacement

There are so many factors to consider when comparing heavier-displacement boats to lighter-displacement boats that it's often difficult even to generalize. However, if we were to compare two such boats, both well-designed and of the same size, the heavier boat would tend to be more comfortable for the crew, able to carry more stores and supplies, and probably have greater ultimate stability. Once again, however, there is a trade-off, at least in terms of comfort: The lighter boat would tend to be faster, which might let it avoid bad weather, or at least sail out of it sooner, thus reducing the amount of time the crew has to spend in discomfort in the first place. The two sides of the displacement question need to be balanced by anyone who decides to head offshore. Usually the right choice is a medium-displacement hull that blends both comfort and speed.

Stability

The subject of stability is much more complex than most of us consider it to be. Here, however, I emphasize the main points of stability for the cruising boat. Stability means the ability of the boat to resist heeling. The greater the stability, the more upright the boat remains as the wind increases, and the more sail area it can carry, which means greater speed. The less the heel, the higher the boat will point and the more effective the keel will be in reducing leeway.

Beam

Production boats today are much more beamy than in the past. Beam increases form stability (the stability derived from the shape of the hull) but at the same time adds to resistance as the boat moves through the water. This is often counteracted by increasing the sail area, which in turn affects stability. Quite obviously a beamier boat has more space below and thus provides more livable space for the crew. However, greater form stability often results in a much less comfortable motion at sea.

Ballast

The days of internal, and sometimes moveable, ballast are gone on ocean-going yachts, and it is just as well. Perhaps an exception in recent years is the development of moveable water ballast which appears to have some advantages.

Nearly all yachts today have external ballast attached to the hull with bolts. This is usually a casting of faired lead that makes up part of the keel. Some fiberglass and metal hulls have the ballast as an internal casting within the keel. This is not to be confused with internal ballast.

Ballast on most ocean cruising boats represents 30 to 50 percent of their displacement. It is important to keep in mind that location is as important as amount of ballast. A complaint about some modern racing boats is that the ballast is placed too high. The deeper the ballast is below the boat's center of gravity, the greater the stability will be.

Draft

For the coastal cruiser, shallow draft may be a major consideration, but when the boat is off soundings and making long passages it becomes a disadvantage. There are some especially nice cruising areas where shallow draft will permit greater choice of places to visit, but a draft of five or six feet is seldom a problem. Deeper draft and lower ballast mean increased stability.

With shallow draft, a boat's ability to go to weather will be adversely affected. Pointing higher of course means the boat makes a better course to windward, as every sailor soon learns. Another point often overlooked is that made by Juan Baader in his book *The Sailing Yacht*, 'If one of two yachts sails close-hauled with an angle of leeway of three degrees and the other with an angle of leeway of six degrees, the first has to overcome an increase in resistance of 23 percent, the latter as much as 56 percent.'

Keel Shape

In an effort to reduce wetted surface and weight, the fin keel has replaced the full keel on most boats in recent years. Full keels, or something between a full and fin keel, are still popular on many boats built only for cruising. In my opinion the semi- or full-keel boat has advantages in the boat's ability to track as well as to make less leeway and to remain more comfortable when hove-to. Furthermore, although perhaps only the owner will appreciate it, the hull form of the 1960s,

Figure 4.2
Underwater hull profiles. These four shapes represent the evolution in yacht design over the past 50 years.

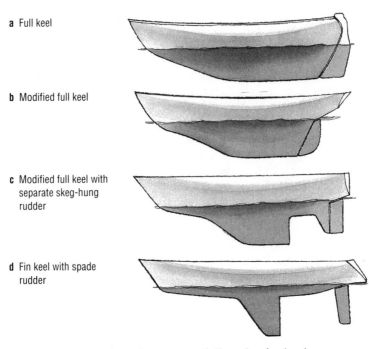

a Full keel

b Modified full keel

c Modified full keel with separate skeg-hung rudder

d Fin keel with spade rudder

which is intermediate between a full and a fin keel, presents a beautiful underwater shape.

Fin keels, however, are here to stay and they are efficient and successful. A well-designed fin keel should give good directional stability, reduced wetted surface, good maneuvering, and windward ability. There is significant variation in fin keels and some types are better adapted to cruising boats than others. Not the least is the restriction they offer to hauling out for repairs and maintenance. The size and shape as well as the way the keel is attached may prohibit the use of some haul-out facilities in remote areas. This is becoming less of a problem as each year more marina and boat repair facilities are built. It can, however, be a financial consideration if you have to rely on a TraveLift or special equipment. There is also the reality of grounding or striking submerged objects. A walk around a yacht repair yard will show examples of underwater hull damage resulting from fin keels hitting submerged objects. The results can be a severe dent in the keel, cracks in the hull at the keel-hull seam, and in the extreme case, sinking.

Rudders

Spade rudders are fine for racing boats and offer many advantages but they have no place on a cruising yacht. A skeg-hung rudder offers greater strength, better directional stability in steering, and better control when heeled, especially in the event of a broach. Keel-hung rudders are part of the package of a full keel. The inboard type with the rudder shaft coming through the hull is believed to be more efficient. However, some traditional-style boats have keels hung on the stern. Proponents of these point out that rudder repairs are much easier in the event of damage. One problem with keel-hung rudders is that they are usually vulnerable to damage if the keel is grounded.

a Outboard transom hung rudder

b Outboard keel hung rudder

c Keel hung spade rudder

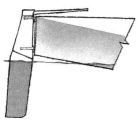

Figure 4.3
Rudder variations.

d Spade rudder with skeg

e Spade rudder

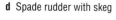

Hull and Capsize

It is unfortunate that so often disasters have to occur before we realize, or are willing to acknowledge, that a danger exists. Sometimes it takes a tragedy to force us to confront a situation that many people recognize but no one seems able to control.

The 1970s competition to beat the IOR racing rule resulted in racing yachts whose speed and performance took precedence over stability and seaworthiness. Ultimately this led to the disastrous results of the 1979 Fastnet Race in which 15 lives were lost.

In response to the Fastnet tragedy, a surge of research and investigation into yacht design and construction and offshore racing rules occurred. Some findings produced information and concepts not previously appreciated as important to offshore sailing. The details of some of these findings are given in a report published by the United States Yacht Racing Union and summarized in the Cruising Club of America's book, *Desirable and Undesirable Characteristics of Offshore Yachts*, edited by John Rousmanière. This important book provides valuable and thoughtful information for anyone who plans to sail offshore for cruising or racing. Especially significant is Chapter 3 by Karl L. Kirkman and Richard C. McCurdy, members of the Technical Committee of the Cruising Club of America. In the following paragraphs I will mention some of the most salient points of their writing.

Many people were surprised to learn that boats which have been dismasted are much more susceptible to capsize, the reason being that the mast offers resistance to roll inertia. This important point suggests the value of a strong rig.

As a result of trying to determine the effect of boat size on capsize due to high (breaking) waves, researchers found that resistance to capsize results from the roll moment of inertia, which is decreased in boats with wide beam. Their studies resulted in a screening factor to estimate a boat's resistance to capsize based on a fairly complicated formula. In addition the researchers came up with a simplified version of the screening formula that anyone can use to estimate a boat's capsize resistance. There is good agreement between the short and long versions. The simplified formula is to divide the gross weight of the boat in pounds by 64. The cube root of that number is divided into the maximum beam in feet. If the result of the calculations is 2 or less the boat passes the screening test.

Obviously these calculations do not mean that any boat that has a screening value of 2 or less is safe to go offshore. But it does give an indication of its relative ability to *resist* capsize. No boat is totally immune from capsize; it can happen to any boat under extreme conditions. If the yacht is dismasted, the screening value is no longer relevant.

The other aspect of the capsize problem is a boat's ability to right itself if capsize occurs. Some yachts cannot right themselves easily or at all; their 'negative stability' is just as good as their 'positive stability.' The length of time a boat is inverted, even if it does have the ability to right itself, has significance for several reasons. It is especially important to remember that while the yacht is inverted it is vulnerable to flooding. The greater a boat's range of positive stability the easier and quicker it will be able to become righted.

Both wind and waves are factors which can lead to capsize. In conditions of breaking waves it will take an unusually large breaking wave to cause capsize. It also takes wave action to help bring the boat back to normal position. If the yacht has a wide range of positive stability, righting will occur quickly. If it has a narrow range, and especially if the positive and negative ranges of stability are nearly the same, it may take a wave with a magnitude nearly equal to the one that caused the capsize to bring it back up.

Capsize can also occur due to strong winds. For some boats a knockdown could occur in non-storm conditions. If a boat takes a full knockdown with the mast in or almost in the water, it is going to take water aboard. Should the boat be near its maximum range of positive stability it will be slow to regain its footing, and during a slow recovery the possibility of flooding will be increased. Furthermore, if, in a knockdown, heavy weights below are shifted, stability may be further reduced. Slow recovery from a knockdown can result in the mast filling with water, and this also will adversely affect recovery and stability.

A boat's righting ability can be determined from its stability curve and results of the capsize study suggest that 120 degrees is a minimum for an offshore yacht. Hull shape and ballast obviously play a significant part in determining a yacht's righting ability.

Beam also plays an important role. It is often mentioned that beam adds to stability. But this is only true of initial stability or stiffness that will occur at normal angles of heel. However, at large angles of heel, such as in knockdowns or those induced by large breaking seas, a wide beam serves to reduce the stability range.

CRUISING MULTIHULLS

I frequently hear monohull sailors criticizing multihulls as too dangerous for offshore passages because they are too fast, too easily capsized,
and too fragile for offshore sailing. Meanwhile, I see plenty of cruisers
on Wharram cats and Jim Brown Searunners in anchorages throughout
the Pacific.

The tenet that multihulls are too fragile for ocean sailing is the legacy
of the days when people believed trimarans and catamarans could provide a cheap and easy way to go to sea. As for speed, multihulls have
established impressive time-distance records in numerous offshore races
and likewise the impression that multihulls frequently capsize is derived
mainly from the same source – offshore racing.

It is remarkable how often cruising books and magazine articles,
written by experienced monohull cruisers, condemn *cruising* multihulls
as unsafe, and cite for their reasons accidents which were incurred by
racing boats. There may be good reasons to reject a multihull as a cruising yacht, but judging them based on the mishaps of racing multis
should not be one of the reasons. It makes about as much sense as
deciding not to drive a car because of accidents that occur on a race
track.

No matter how fast something goes it is human nature to try and
make it go faster. Yacht racing crews are not known for the conservative
approach – often they push their boats to the maximum and beyond.
This happens with monohulls as well as multihulls – the difference is
that monohulls are more forgiving and can take more abuse.

Speed, Low Cost, and Space

It is often said that with a multihull you can have any two, but not all
three, choices of speed, low cost, and space. If a multihull is overloaded
it will not have good performance. To have ample space and load-carry-
ing capacity, it is necessary to build a large boat, and this will increase
the cost.

In spite of their reputation for speed, multihulls are not fast under all
conditions. In rough seas and heavy weather they have to be slowed
down. It is mostly disregard for this factor that has led to multihull
accidents.

This is not to say a well-built multihull doesn't give you warning of
imminent capsize. It does. When the windward hull begins to fly or the
leeward hull begins to bury, it is past time to reduce sail and slow down.
You can disregard this and the boat will keep going for a while and
then, quite suddenly sometimes, the high initial stability will be used up.
Compare this with a monohull that is sailed too hard for the wind or

sea conditions. First the boat will go rail down and be very uncomfortable. Eventually it will round-up out of control and probably broach. Whereas you may blow out your sails or even damage the spar, the boat's high (you hope) reserve stability will usually keep it from capsize.

Space and accommodations are critical factors in multihulls when compared to monohulls. Performance is a major reason for selecting a multihull, but if the boat is overloaded it will quickly lose this primary attribute. With a displacement boat, this is less of a factor. Most medium or heavy displacement monohulls will tolerate a lot of additional loading of gear and still be able to maintain a speed close to design expectations. Likewise, multihulls, and especially trimarans, will not have as much interior space and spaciousness as a monohull of equivalent length. Cruising multihulls tend more toward function than fashion, and their interiors are usually more spartan than monohulls.

As I mentioned, there are a lot of folks doing long-distance offshore cruising in monohull yachts of 30 feet (9 m) and less. No responsible designer or experienced multihull sailor would recommend this for a multihull. Forty feet is a recommended minimum LOA, and 50 feet or more is preferred. This size allows adequate storage for necessary cruising equipment, and can still give you a good turn of speed in comfort and safety. The larger boat, consistent with proper loading, will be more stable and more resistant to capsize. If 50 feet (15 m) sounds enormous, remember that the weight of a multihull of this length is probably not much more than half the weight of a monohull of the same length, and it can be sailed with less crew effort.

Draft

Proponents of multihulls are quick to point out the advantages of shallow draft. Even a 50-foot multihull with the board(s) up will generally draw only three feet or less. This extends potential cruising areas, and is an advantage in a crowded harbor or anchorage where displacement boats frequently have to crowd together in a way that is inconvenient and often unsafe. Multihulls can usually find space and privacy away from the crowd.

Shallow draft offers the owner easy 'haul-out' for bottom cleaning and painting or hull maintenance almost any place there is a tidal fluctuation. This advantage often represents a significant saving of time and money. Another positive aspect of shoal draft is what multihull designer Jim Brown calls 'forgiving draft' where multihulls have survived groundings and strandings that would surely have destroyed a monohull.

There is a trade-off for the advantages of shallow draft. If it does become necessary to haul out in the conventional manner, it may be difficult to find haul-out facilities that can safely handle a large multihull. Usually it requires the services of a crane. Few marina operators are excited when they see a multihull arriving. The extra width of a tri or cat requires the same amount of space as two or three conventional boats, if in fact the harbor even has an adequate slip available. While this is a decided disadvantage now and then, most cruising sailors spend far more time at anchor than they do alongside.

In the same way that some sailors prefer a ketch and others a cutter or sloop, there are different preferences among multihull sailors for a trimaran or a catamaran for offshore cruising. Although overall performance is said to be about the same, trimarans do better upwind and in light air, whereas a catamaran gets high marks on a reach and in heavier winds. The misconception that multihulls tack poorly is a carryover from the past. A cat requires some speed to tack because you are moving two hulls instead of one. A tri will tack more easily than a cat, because it is more like a monohull. Both will jibe with ease and with good control due to the wide sheeting angle. As for accommodations, a catamaran naturally has more space for any given boat length and, depending on the size of the boat and the size of the crew, this may be an important consideration. However, considering that most cruising is done by a husband-wife team, there is ample room for a cruising couple in a 40-foot or larger trimaran. The trade-off in selecting a catamaran over a trimaran is the added expense of two rudders and two engines, or if one engine, two drives. There are attractive, seaworthy designs for either type of multihull and probably a final decision will be based on a combination of factors.

Trimaran Versus Catamaran

Someone accustomed to 'shopping' for a displacement boat may be surprised that there aren't as many good cruising multihulls to choose from. The multihull market has never been one to attract mass production of good cruising boats. Most cruising multihulls are owner-built, and there are relatively few on the market.

Building or Buying a Multihull

The good news is that there are some excellent designs well-suited to a dedicated do-it-yourself builder. Because most cruising multihulls are one-off, home-built boats, designers are accustomed to working with individual builders and offer their customers far more than a set of plans. Better designers are concerned that you build your boat correctly and that you follow their plans precisely. Some require their customers to sign an agreement which prohibits making any modifications to the hull design without the designer's permission. Step-by-step instructions and the opportunity to write for construction advice is part of the service some designers offer.

Building a boat yourself is not the only option. Some professional yards are known for turning out excellent multihulls. If you decide to have a multihull built, choose a builder recommended by the designer. The multihull community is small and the designer will know reputable builders.

Used cruising multihulls are often sold by the owner/builder. A thorough survey is mandatory before buying any used cruising boat. In the case of a used multihull, it may be more difficult to find a surveyor who is experienced in multihull construction and sailing. The best approach is to contact the designer for his opinion and recommendations for a reliable surveyor. Because of the unique designer/builder relationship for most multihulls, the designer may have knowledge of the specific boat.

Multihull Construction

Methods and materials of trimaran and catamaran construction have made significant advances in recent years. These improvements are another reason why much of the stereotyped criticism of multihulls is no longer valid. A primary goal in multihull construction is to achieve a high strength- (and stiffness-) to-weight ratio. Today this can be achieved using modern fiberglass and epoxy materials. Most builders, following the advice of their designers, choose either fiberglass sand-wich construction or the wood epoxy saturation (WEST) system. Either one is suited to the home builder, although the WEST system is perhaps easier and more popular. Epoxy is excellent because of its bonding strength and its ability to eliminate water penetration.

Innovative building techniques for multihulls have likewise brought direct benefits to the individual as well as commercial builders. Best-known is the 'Constant Camber' laminating form patented by Jim Brown. This technique uses wood veneer and epoxy to build hull, deck, and cabin panels.

Capsize

This is the word that comes up immediately in any discussion of multi-hulls. It is not just the thought that capsize occurs, but that once inverted, a multihull stays that way, whereas a well-designed monohull, if its hatches are closed, will recover and right itself. Figure 1, from an article by multihull designer Chris White, in the May 1988 issue of *Cruising World*, compares the stability curves of large multihulls and monohulls. In this graph heeling angle is plotted against righting moment. Righting moment relates to stability and the ability to resist capsize.

Multihulls have high initial stability. The larger the multihull the greater the resistance to capsize because the hulls are farther apart. As can be seen from the graph, it takes a tremendous force to heel a multi-

Figure 5.1

Stability curves of large multihulls and mono-hulls. Courtesy of Chris White.

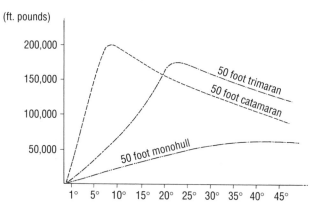

hull (more for a catamaran than a trimaran), which accounts for their well-known ability to give a flat ride and to sit flat at anchor even in strong winds. It should also be clear from this comparison that failure to reduce sail when the boat does heel is an invitation to disaster. Another aspect of capsize is the effect of large waves. Here again boat size is a controlling factor and the larger the multihull the easier it will be to sail.

Probably the major cause of cruising multihull capsize has been improper boathandling; generally as a result of inexperience. Considering that offshore multihull cruising began only about 30 years ago, it is remarkable that there have been so few disasters.

A point stressed by multihull proponents is that even if a capsize does occur, the game isn't over. The major advantage of a multihull is its ability to remain afloat even if upside down. If adequate planning is done before going to sea, the inverted hulls will provide a life-support system indefinitely. In this case a trimaran has a definite advantage over a catamaran because the main survival flotation is provided for in the two outboard hulls (amas) which support the main hull. In several instances where trimarans have capsized the survivors have made a 'hatch' in the inverted main hull and lived, albeit uncomfortably, within the hull. This would be considerably more difficult in a catamaran where cutting an opening into one of the hulls would cause it to submerge further.

Certainly living in an inverted trimaran would not be easy or pleasant, but it would be better than depending on a liferaft. Staying with the boat would provide water, food, shelter, and supplies. An inverted trimaran would be much more likely to be seen by ships or aircraft than a liferaft.

Speed and Responsibility

You cannot sail a multihull with a monohull mentality. The reasons you can't are the same reasons that make multihulls interesting, exciting, and worthwhile cruising boats: their potential for speed, light displacement, shallow draft, and high initial stability.

Anyone who opts for a multihull as an offshore cruising boat is interested in performance and speed. There is nothing wrong with this desire. There isn't a cruising sailor around who would reject better hull speed, especially on a long passage, when most of the days have light and moderate winds. Previously I pointed out that a speed increase of only one knot means a difference of several days on a passage from Panama to Hawaii. Consider what an average speed increase of four or five knots would mean. Faster passages mean less time in which to encounter difficult sailing weather. To avoid unfavorable weather a sailor with a faster boat can change course and put more sea miles between himself and a storm in a shorter period of time.

Along with higher performance comes greater responsibility. There is less margin for sloppy sailing in a multihull, and respecting that margin is the trade-off for faster sailing.

CHAPTER 6

CONSTRUCTION MATERIALS

Before 1960 there was little choice in construction material for pleasure yachts, and essentially all building was done with wood. The introduction of fiberglass changed that, and, in fact, revolutionized the boat-building industry and the world of yachting. Today, probably more than 80 percent of yachts are built in fiberglass, but the use of steel and aluminum is increasing. The surge of interest in ferrocement construction some years ago has now largely dissipated.

Although emphasis is sometimes placed on cost of material when planning a new boat, the hull represents only 20 to 25 percent of the final cost of a boat. The remaining costs will be about the same for fiberglass, steel, aluminum, or wood. A savings of even 20 percent in hull cost will translate to less than 10 percent of the total yacht cost.

Wood

Traditionally, wooden yachts are built of planks laid on a wood frame. Principal types are clinker or lapstrake, carvel, and strip-planking. Clinker construction consists of overlapping strips fastened to closely spaced frames. This method uses no caulking, and the wood swells in the water to make a tight bond. This construction results in an increased wetted surface and added turbulence due to the uneven hull surface. Clinker hulls must be refastened periodically. Carvel planking is accomplished with long strips of wood laid edge-on to give a smooth hull surface. Caulking is forced between the planks which are screwed or nailed to the frames. This building style requires occasional recaulking – a significant job.

Strip-plank yachts are built with nearly square pieces of wood with the edges slightly rounded. The strips are joined by edge fastenings. This method is well-suited to the amateur builder, but it is difficult to repair.

Plywood construction is used successfully on offshore cruising boats and is often selected by amateur builders. A plywood boat must be single-, double-, or multiple-chined, because plywood can only bend in one direction. (Chine is the intersection or angle of the bottom and sides of a flat or V-bottomed boat.) A difficult part of the construction is making proper joins along the chine and adequate scarfs between the plywood panels.

Another type of wood construction is cold-molding, which often incorporates the WEST system. WEST is an acronym for wood epoxy saturation technique. By this method several thin layers or skins of wood veneer are glued together with epoxy. Each layer of the resulting veneer has its grain running in a different direction. Finally the hull is

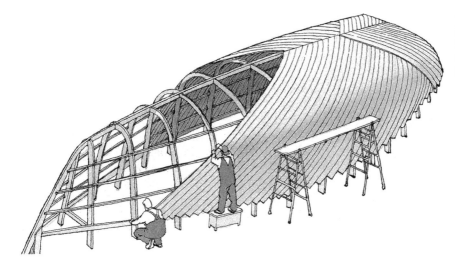

Figure 6.1
*Wood construction
using cold-molding
technique.*

epoxy coated inside and out. The result is a very strong and lightweight hull. The epoxy serves both as a binding agent and as a barrier to water and air. Cold-molding has special appeal to the amateur because the male hull plug is less complicated to build than the plug for a conventional fiberglass hull. The cold-mold method has been especially popular for multihull construction, where lightness and strength are essential.

Steel

Hulls constructed of steel have long been popular in Europe, especially in Holland and Germany. Indeed, when looking at a group of cruising yachts anchored in a harbor, you can usually guess correctly that the hard chined yachts are steel hulls from those countries. However, it is also possible to build a steel yacht with a rounded hull that will be difficult to distinguish from wood or fiberglass.

The major advantages of steel are strength, cost, and its ability to be easily repaired. Probably strength is the most appealing factor because it gives a cruising boat improved resistance to collision and grounding. Both steel and aluminum construction allow the opportunity to have a completely sealed deck. Hardware can be welded to the boat's exterior, thereby eliminating the hundreds of screws and bolts necessary on a wood or fiberglass boat.

Steel is a relatively cheap material, and probably no one-off boat can be made for less. Labor costs are generally lower than on other kinds of construction. An especially important consideration is ease of repair. Welders can be found almost anywhere in the world and repair materials are readily at hand.

Steel is heavy and therefore not popular for racing yachts. For the cruiser, however, this is a less serious problem. Furthermore, weight can add to stability, and yachts of 40 feet or more can be built with a displacement weight ratio of about 300. For smaller yachts, steel is less advantageous, but there are still some excellent steel boats between 30 and 40 feet. Sometimes, to reduce the weight, the deck and house on

Figure 6.2
Yacht construction using steel or aluminum alloy.

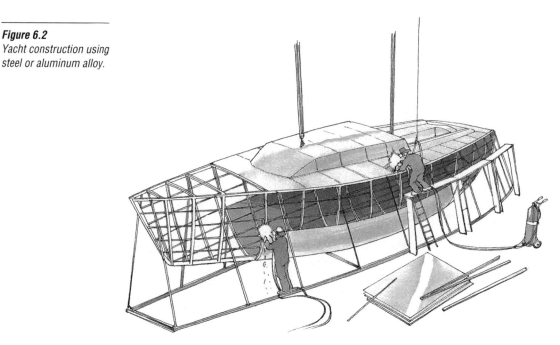

steel boats are made from wood or aluminum. There is some question as to the advantage of this. With a wood deck there is again the potential, and usually the assurance, of leaks at the deck-hull seam and from the fasteners for deck fittings and hardware. The combination of steel and aluminum is possible with certain types of construction, but will be expensive.

It is well known that steel and salt water are not compatible, and a steel yacht immediately brings to mind major maintenance problems. This is much less of a problem than it used to be. Certainly, a steel hull requires responsible attention and frequent inspection but, with hot zinc spraying and epoxy paints, the hull can be maintained in excellent condition by routine preventive maintenance. I would estimate that a steel yacht might require less maintenance than a fiberglass one if you factor in the problems many fiberglass boatowners have with deck leaks and, especially in recent years, with osmosis and hull blisters.

A major concern with steel yachts is electrolysis. Through-hull fittings below the waterline must be made of mild steel, stainless steel, or plastic. Likewise the shaft and propeller must be stainless steel. Even with these precautions, adequate sacrificial zincs need to be installed. It is also advisable to avoid an external lead ballast keel, usually the ballast keel is part of the hull construction, with the ballast isolated from direct contact with sea water.

A steel hull needs insulation to reduce condensation and to cut down on noise. But this is also true of aluminum and some fiberglass yachts.

Although steel yachts are not very common in the U.S., they will probably attract more cruising customers in the future. Each time there is an increase in the price of petroleum and related products, such as fiberglass resin, the balance in favor of steel increases for one-off boats.

Aluminum may become second only to fiberglass for construction of pleasure boats in the future. Even today it is a popular building material in France and it is used elsewhere for racing boats. A principal advantage is its light weight. Aluminum is only one-third the weight of steel, but has two-thirds as much tensile strength. This gives it a great advantage in a displacement/weight ratio.

Aluminum alloy is expensive and requires special welding techniques, but, like steel, it forms a rigid, strong, leak-free boat. Aluminum requires care to avoid electrolysis and galvanic action. Electrical wiring must be a special style that is different from the simple ground system on other yachts. Like steel, the underwater fittings cannot contain bronze or other copper alloyed metals. Sacrificial zinc or pure aluminum bars must be installed and frequently inspected to prevent hull deterioration. On the other hand, an aluminum alloy hull can be left unpainted above the waterline, and this represents a maintenance saving.

In spite of the high initial costs of materials and labor, aluminum is becoming more popular. For shaping a hull, aluminum is easier to work with than steel, and a well-constructed aluminum-alloy hull is assured of good resale value. The fact that there are 'production' aluminum sailboats being built today in France indicates the popularity and success of this material.

Fiberglass

It is interesting to contemplate where yachting would be today without the adaptation of fiberglass to boat construction. This incredible material has permitted the development of production-line methods for yacht construction and opened up the sport of sailing to many people who

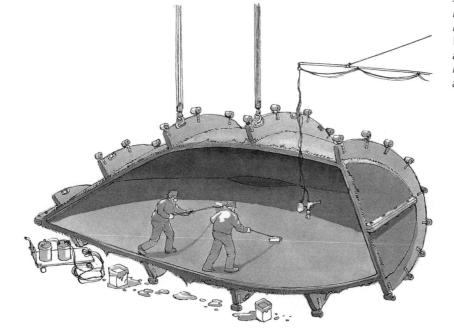

Figure 6.3
Fiberglass construction. Workers are rolling resin and glassfiber cloth in a hull being laid up inside a female mold.

otherwise could not enjoy it. Properly maintained fiberglass boats appear to have an indefinite life span. Even a boat that is poorly maintained will not rot or rust away as happens with wooden or steel boats that are ignored.

Fiberglass construction for production boats requires a female mold which itself is made of fiberglass. The mold is first covered with wax to permit release of the hull when construction is completed. Next it is sprayed with gelcoat which will give the yacht a smooth outer surface. This is followed in some cases by a layer of fiberglass cloth, and then the hull thickness is built up in a series of layers of fiberglass materials called mat and roving. Mat is a thin sheet composed of short glass fibers with random orientation. It serves to build up thickness of the hull, to give good bonding to the alternating layers of roving, and to help eliminate the accumulation of resin pockets in the roving. Woven roving is a coarse glass fabric with the fibers running at right angles. It provides strength and flexibility to the hull. As the mat and roving are laid in the mold, they are continually saturated with resin, which acts as the binding material.

After a desired hull thickness is achieved, longitudinal, and in some instances transverse, strengtheners are added and the hull is removed from the mold. The deck is cast in a similar way, and, after the interior finish work is completed, the hull and deck are bolted together.

In a never-ending quest to improve strength and reduce weight, numerous modifications have been made to the basic fiberglass construction method. Now it is common practice to use some type of core material in the hull and deck. Such sandwich construction results in a stronger and lighter hull. It also adds insulation and reduces noise.

Common core materials are balsa wood and PVC foam. Cores made of PVC include Airex, Termanto, and Divinycell. Airex is elastic and easy to repair whereas Termanto and Divinycell are more rigid, and offer better shear strength for a stiffer and lighter yacht.

For racing boats, where weight is a major consideration, there are other exotic materials used in construction, including Kevlar and carbon fiber, both of which give thinner, stronger hulls. However, the higher material and labor costs limit their application to racing yachts where thin, and hopefully strong, lightweight hulls are desired.

Figure 6.4
Fiberglass hull
laminates.

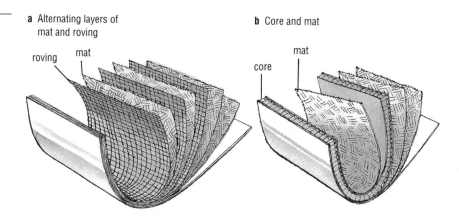

a Alternating layers of mat and roving

roving   mat

b Core and mat

mat
core

Several kinds of resin are used in fiberglass hulls. Traditionally most fiberglass boats have been made with polyester resin. However, epoxy and vinylester, which are more expensive, result in stronger, more flexible, hulls with greater shear strength.

The popularity and success of fiberglass construction have led to ongoing research in new techniques and materials. Each year sees stronger, lighter, and faster production boats being built in a highly competitive industry.

Fiberglass boats have a well-earned reputation for their ease of maintenance, but some yacht owners are surprised to learn that their boat hulls are not completely maintenance free. Unless properly cared for, the gelcoat will lose its beautiful luster. Even boats that are kept in reasonable condition may require painting after ten years or so. Although less of a problem now than a few years ago, the gelcoat surface may craze and pigment may noticeably fade in color and take on a chalky appearance. In boats that are poorly built or raced hard, stress cracks may develop in the hull and especially in the deck.

Any industry as successful and competitive as fiberglass yacht construction is bound to attract some poor builders, and that can include the 'big-name' companies which mass-produce poor quality products. This shoddy workmanship is often not obvious to the overly enthusiastic yacht buyer. But in a short time if the yacht is subjected to heavy or even moderate seas, the discouraged owner finds problems resulting from cheap and slipshod construction methods, including leaky deck-hull seams. Other leaks may occur around through-deck fastenings when the hull flexes. Even bulkheads and internal furniture sometimes come loose, because they were not adequately bonded to the hull. If the owner is lucky these problems will not immediately put the yacht or its crew in mortal danger. However, many otherwise enjoyable cruises have been ruined when clothing, bedding, food, and electronic equipment became saturated due to seawater leaks.

Osmosis Blisters

In spite of the research and technology that have gone into improving fiberglass building materials, these boats continue to be plagued by hull blistering below the waterline. A lot of ideas and theories about the cause and solution to this problem have been suggested, but it persists.

Recent research indicates that blistering is caused by water diffusing into the hull through the gelcoat and reacting with water-soluble material in the fiberglass. When this happens it forms an acidic solution which grows, because of osmotic pressure, to form a blister. Most commonly this occurs at the boundary between the gelcoat and the first layer of the laminate, but it can also occur within the laminate layers.

Attempts to correlate the development of osmotic blisters to any single cause such as water temperature, salinity, age of the boat, or to specific boatbuilders have not met with success. A certain amount of the blistering can be attributed to poor workmanship, but even the best builders have had osmosis problems now and then. Most builders are reluctant to boast that their boats are totally immune. There are instances where hulls have been blister-free for nearly 20 years and then, quite suddenly, the problem occurs. When this happens the owner may be lucky and find only a few blisters, but in other instances it can affect a large portion of the underwater hull and require expensive, time-consuming repairs.

Exactly how to deal with the problem of repairing blisters is still being tested. Commonly the procedure is to puncture and drain the blisters, open them using a high-speed grinder, and let them dry out. Next the blister cavities are filled with epoxy paste, and, after curing, the surface is faired. Finally the hull is painted with an epoxy sealer or barrier coat.

If the blisters are unusually extensive, for example 50 percent or more of the hull, it is often recommended that the gelcoat and perhaps some thickness of the laminate be completely removed by sanding, sandblasting or, more recently, by a cutting or 'peeling' technique. This is followed by a drying out period and then new fiberglass mat and roving may be applied using vinylester resin. This then requires fairing of the new surface and the addition of a compatible barrier coat before bottom paint is applied. When this procedure is done by a professional boatyard, the cost can be 10 percent or more of the boat's value. But even after the hull is completely repaired, there is no guarantee osmosis will not reoccur or continue to exist.

Ferrocement

Perhaps the kindest words about ferrocement hulls would be to say they have not been a great success. Building in ferrocement is an idea that goes back nearly 100 years. In theory it sounds easy and practical. To be able to build a wire frame and then cover it with plaster suggests something that could be easily accomplished by the amateur builder. In the past many believed this to be true, but they found the work complicated and beset with many problems. Numerous attempts at ferrocement boat building sit abandoned in weed-filled lots around the world. On the other hand, some professional boatbuilders and a few amateurs have been able to turn out successful ferrocement yachts. Conventional wisdom now suggests it is unwise to use ferrocement on yachts under 50 feet in length because of weight considerations. It has become obvious that the final cost in time and money for ferrocement is no less than for building with fiberglass, steel, or wood.

In my opinion steel or aluminum are the very best choices for cruising hulls over 35 feet in length because of their strength and their ability to make a boat that will, even after extensive sailing, remain leak free. Although metal lacks the inherent warmth and 'friendliness' of a wooden boat, it is possible to finish off the interior of the yacht in such a way that it is nearly indistinguishable from a more traditional wooden boat.

Many people feel that the added responsibility of maintaining a wooden boat is more than offset by its beauty and the pleasure of sailing it. It cannot be denied that wooden boats have a charm and ambience that cannot be found in fiberglass, steel, or aluminum.

A fiberglass yacht will no doubt continue to be the choice of many cruising sailors in the future. Because of mass production and costs, this type of boat is probably the cheapest and most convenient way for the average person to go cruising.

For the potential offshore sailor, the bottom line is that a boat of any construction material, if well built and properly equipped and maintained, will take you where you want to go – and bring you back.

CHAPTER 7

SPARS AND STANDING RIGGING

There is nothing wrong with having a reliable and powerful auxiliary engine, but when the seas are up and the chips are down, it is your sails that will gain you some sea room and safety, and the sails are only as good as the spars and standing rigging that support them.

Under sail, standing rigging is constantly subjected to the loading and unloading of force. Even at rest in an anchorage, the rig is in nearly constant motion, and all of its parts are continuously stretched and relaxed. Sudden stress loads, such as may come unexpectedly with the passing of a weather front, or due to wind gusts accompanying a rain squall, produce short-term loading far in excess of normal conditions.

Spars

Masts

There is a salty old saying: 'If God had wanted us to have aluminum masts, he would have provided aluminum trees.' My response is that if God had been a sailor at the time of creation, there would be vast forests of aluminum trees today. Aluminum is great for masts and spars, and it has made life a lot easier for the sailor. It is far easier than wood to maintain, and it provides taller and stronger masts than were ever possible with wood. If and when carbon fiber and fiberglass can meet and beat aluminum in price and strength, I will welcome them as well.

The fact that strong, well-built, aluminum masts are readily available and reasonably priced makes it surprising that we see small-diameter, thin-walled, bendy masts being put on so-called cruiser-racers and even cruising boats. They don't belong on cruising boats.

If the racer loses his mast, he is usually within the range of assistance. When the cruiser loses his mast out on the ocean, he is faced with very serious problems, and there is no one around to help him out. Being at sea in a dismasted cruising boat is a frightening and distressing situation. In addition to being rendered nearly helpless and having to put up with a most unpleasant motion, there is now the realization that a dismasted yacht is more easily capsized.

The mast of a cruising boat should be of sufficient diameter and wall thickness, and the rigging of adequate strength, that even if one part of the rigging should give way, the mast will not automatically break or even sustain a permanent bend, if corrective action is taken immediately.

If you are in doubt as to the adequacy of your mast or rigging, get some professional advice. Talk to a rigger who has offshore sailing experience, or write to spar manufacturers and tell them your sailing plans, and everything about your yacht. Consult a reference such as *Skene's Elements of Yacht Design*, for formulas necessary to determine proper specifications.

Aluminum masts are by far the most common type found on boats today, but there are also masts made of fiberglass and carbon fiber. Fiberglass has not been widely adopted, but carbon-fiber masts are now standard on the Freedom yachts, and on many racing boats.

If the mast on your boat is anodized aluminum, you should have no problems maintaining surface appearance, and it is not necessary to paint it. If it is not anodized, it can be painted with a high-quality epoxy paint or whatever coating the spar builder recommends, or it can remain unpainted.

Keel-Stepped and Deck-Stepped Masts

There are several reasons for preferring a deck-stepped to a keel-stepped mast, but few of them apply to offshore cruising. One supposed advantage of a deck-stepped mast is that you have more room below. On a very small yacht this may be valid, but to have a well-supported, deck-stepped mast, it is necessary to have a compression post for support, which also interrupts the open space.

Some people contend that if a deck-stepped mast goes overboard due to a failure of the rigging, it will probably go as one piece, and it may be possible to recover it. Perhaps, but I doubt a shorthanded crew could get a mast back on board in anything but very calm seas – if then.

A deck-stepped mast might be a reasonable choice for those who plan to be cruising rivers or canals where it is not possible to carry a standing mast. If you do decide on a deck-stepped mast, be sure it is heavily supported below, with a pipe or strong athwartships I-beam, and perhaps with both. On deck, the mast base should be set in a heavy-duty tabernacle.

The primary reason for preferring a keel-stepped mast is that it is stronger, and can be better supported. The support, where it passes through the deck, is very important, and can keep the mast from going over or bending if one part of the rigging should suddenly let go. At least it will give you some few extra minutes to tack or jibe the boat, and get the strain off the broken rigging. Also, most keel-stepped masts break somewhere above the partners, which means there's usually a stump to help jury-rig an emergency sail.

Some people object to keel-stepped masts because water often makes its way inside the boat between the mast and mast collar. There are various ways to seal this hole, but the cheapest and easiest is to make a mast boot from a section of a tire innertube. The rubber is cut and trimmed to fit the mast and the mast collar, with about a six-inch overlap. The overlap is well covered with polysulphide or silicon sealant, and then sealed to the mast and to the collar. The boot is held in place with large-diameter hose clamps. To make a neater job, and to protect the rubber from deteriorating, a cover for the boot can be made from canvas or sail-cover cloth.

Mast Collars

Where the mast passes through the deck, a mast collar is needed. It gives lateral support to the mast and, on many boats, it serves to hold wood or rubber wedges that help keep the mast vertical and absorb the lateral force exerted by the mast on the deck. The mast collar also serves as a point of attachment for the mast boot. It is generally believed that the collar should be the same material as the mast to inhibit electrolysis. The collar should be inspected and the whole assembly resealed every year.

Mast Base

The mast heel lies at the base of the mast. It fits in the mast shoe on top of the keel. Examine this arrangement on your boat, and notice if different metals have been used; commonly they are. If the mast is aluminum and the heel or the step is another metal, for example stainless steel, there may be corrosion problems sooner or later.

Even if all metals are the same, complications may arise if the mast base is often wet. Masts with internal halyards invariably allow a certain amount of fresh and salt water inside. The water sometimes pools at the base of the mast. There should be drain holes at the mast base, and they should be kept clear. Even so, some water may collect here and electrolysis will begin to slowly nibble away at the base of the mast column. With a wood mast a similar situation would be an invitation to dry rot.

Figure 7.1
Features of a keel-stepped mast where it passes through the deck and at its base.

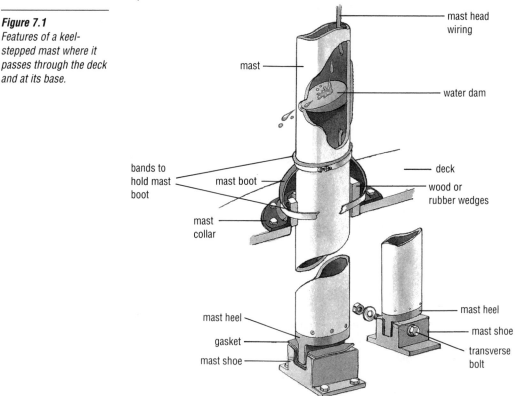

One solution to mast base corrosion on an aluminum spar is to install a dam within the mast, so that water captured inside will exit on deck before it goes below. This can be done by blocking and sealing the mast just below the lowest halyard exit; a job most easily done when the mast is removed from the boat although Richard Henderson in *Understanding Rigs and Rigging*, suggests a clever way to do this with the mast in place. A plate of fiberglass or some kind of inert material needs to be cut to fit snugly inside the mast. The plate is inserted into the mast, slid up to the desired position, and fixed in place by screws. A drain hole should be drilled in the mast, just above the dam, and some sort of sealer poured on top of the dam. It is important to create a sloping surface above the drain hole. This you can do by heeling the boat at dockside and pouring in a quick-setting slurry of fiberglass resin.

If, as is generally the case, there are electrical and radio wires inside the mast that need to be let down through the mast and into the boat, it will be necessary for them to exit above the dam, and then reenter the mast below it.

If you find that the base of your mast has already suffered from electrolysis and is weak, it is possible to carefully trim off the weakened material when the mast is removed from the boat, and replace the mast heel. Unless your rigging is too long to begin with, the mast shortening will probably not require replacing any shrouds or stays.

The mast heel must fit correctly, and bear evenly, on the mast shoe. If there is unequal loading, or the union is not correct and more weight is borne on one side than the other, the problem will affect the whole mast, and it will not be possible to set up the shrouds and stays properly. This can be checked when the mast is put in the boat. If you have problems aligning your mast correctly, check to see if the cause is the mast base.

Most masts are held against the base plate by the downward pressure of the standing rigging. If the shrouds and stays are properly set up there is a substantial amount of pressure to hold the mast down. However, in the event of the mast breaking and only a stump remaining in the boat, it will probably be unsupported. One solution is to secure the mast heel to the step with a transverse bolt, if the heel and plug on your yacht will allow this modification. Before you drill the hole, have a boatbuilder or experienced rigger take a look at it.

Unstepping a mast is a big job on most boats over 25 feet in length, and usually requires a crane. However, if you are upgrading a second-hand boat with the idea of offshore sailing, it is worthwhile to do so to be sure everything is in good condition. With the mast out of the boat, make a very detailed inspection of all fittings on the mast and, if you plan to install steps for climbing the mast, this is a good time to do it.

Mast Tracks and Grooves

Almost all aluminum masts have either a track or groove to help raise and lower the sail and keep the luff close to the spar. Some masts are manufactured with a boltrope groove or slug groove integral with the

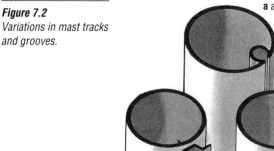

Figure 7.2
Variations in mast tracks and grooves.

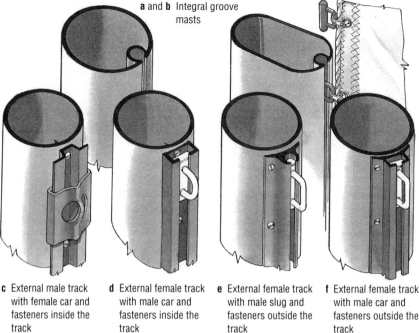

a and **b** Integral groove masts

c External male track with female car and fasteners inside the track

d External female track with male car and fasteners inside the track

e External female track with male slug and fasteners outside the track

f External female track with male car and fasteners outside the track

mast extrusion. This saves having to install and maintain a track, reduces weight, and makes for a stronger mast.

If you have a boltrope groove on your mast, as is common on many recent cruiser-racers, and you plan extensive cruising, the best thing you can do is buy slugs that fit your mast groove, and install them on your mainsail and storm trysail. Raising, lowering, and furling a mainsail with a boltrope alone is very inconvenient for a shorthanded crew, and next to impossible for a singlehander. Chances are, it will take two to hoist it under anything but calm conditions; one on the winch, and one feeding it into the groove. Lowering can be a real mess with the sail dumping itself on the deck and trying to go over the side. These problems are almost completely eliminated if the mainsail is attached to the mast track with cars or slugs.

If the mainsail track on your mast is held in place by screws or rivets, keep a weather eye out for loose fasteners and remove or replace them immediately. A rivet or screw that comes adrift could trap a car or slug and make it impossible to lower the sail. Under the best of conditions this is a big inconvenience, especially if it is above the spreaders. If it happens when you urgently need to put in a reef, it could turn out to be a long day. The best type of mast track is one with metal fasteners that grip a flange outside of the track. These are more rugged than the external tracks that accept flat plastic slugs.

A variety of gear and fittings end up installed on most masts – winches, eyes, cleats, antennas, instruments, and lights. Some require base plates to correct for the mast radius. Best is to have the bases welded to the mast. However, this is often inconvenient unless you are installing a new mast. Even if it can be done, you will not want to do it on an anodized mast. Hence, we usually end up using a wood, stainless steel, or aluminum base plate that must be attached to the mast by tapped fittings and bolts, or screws, or rivets – and this introduces the possibility of electrolysis. In higher latitudes, electrolysis will probably take place very slowly, but if you take your boat to the tropics the corrosion will accelerate. Fasteners on the mast should be carefully chosen, and nothing less than monel or 316 stainless steel should be used. Copper, bronze, or mild steel should never be used on an aluminum mast.

In every case, the base plates and the fasteners should be liberally covered with a good bedding material such as polysulphide when they are installed. Place a rubber or neoprene gasket, with polysulphide applied to both sides, between the fitting and the mast. This is good practice even if the base plates are aluminum.

Mast Steps

Mast steps are highly endorsed, or soundly criticized, by most sailors. In my opinion, steps are a necessity for the shorthanded crew or singlehander. A case is often made for mast steps because they permit you to go aloft more easily at sea. Notice I said more easily; 'easily at sea' is an oxymoron. I have gone aloft at sea in a bosun's chair and with mast steps, and I don't like either one – but if you have to go, and if you are alone, the mast steps are well worth having.

My main reason for endorsing steps is that they make going aloft easy to do in port. I always take a quick trip up the mast for inspection purposes before leaving port. Naturally, if you have crew aboard, they can hoist you up in a chair, but that job is easy to put off and then forgotten. With steps, it is a 10 minute task.

A criticism of mast steps is that they have a tendency to catch and foul halyards. This is true. Soon after I installed them on *Denali* I came to believe that the reason for the steps was so I could go aloft and untangle the halyards that would not have gotten caught if I didn't have the steps in the first place. However, I eventually strung some light line between the steps and the upper shrouds, and the problem was solved. This need only be done above the lower-most spreaders.

Another criticism leveled against mast steps, in comparison with a bosun's chair, is that while aloft, your hands are busy holding on and it is difficult to work. This problem can be avoided by wearing a safety harness and securing yourself to the mast. If you have to work on the mast for an extended period of time, and especially if the job involves a lot of tools and work such as drilling or tapping holes, then a bosun's chair is more convenient. Mast steps add some weight and windage to a mast, but this is one instance where the trade-off is justified.

Before installing mast steps, try to find a boat with steps already installed and ask permission to climb the mast to see how the spacing feels. If you can't find a boat on which to experiment, get some lumber and make a short 'test mast' to determine what is a comfortable spacing for your arms and legs. Remember, you may be wearing foul-weather gear and a safety harness when you climb at sea. If it is the least bit difficult ashore or at the dock, the steps are too far apart.

Once you have determined the step spacing, measure your mast and make a scale drawing of the mast and all the hardware, including winches, spreaders, tangs, and masthead. Plot the proposed location of the steps on the drawing. Some points to keep in mind are: (1) You may be able to use a winch for the first step. (2) Consider the position of the spreaders in relationship to the steps; probably the spreaders will act as a step. (3) Be careful about the placement of steps in the vicinity of tangs; if a tang or shroud lies directly in the front of a step it will not be possible to have safe footing. (4) Near the top of the mast you'll want a pair of steps so that you can stand with one foot on each step when working at the masthead. (5) Those top two steps should be placed so that the masthead is at a convenient working height and you are clear of the forestay or backstay.

Mast steps should have a flat base at least 1 1/4" (32 mm) wide for safe and comfortable footing. Don't ever make mast steps from round stock.

Masthead

Most aluminum masts come from the factory with the sheaves installed for internal halyards, as well as fittings to attach a headstay and backstay. However your masthead is rigged, it should have, at the minimum, main and jib halyard sheaves for internal or external halyards, and fittings to hold blocks for a spinnaker halyard and a topping lift. If either the jib or main halyard breaks, or is lost, the spinnaker halyard and topping lift respectively, can be used as substitutes. They will also come into temporary service if the headstay, backstay, or cap shrouds should be lost. Halyard sheaves should be strong, and frequent inspections should be made to be sure there is no chafe. If your halyards are wire, be sure the sheaves are designed for that purpose.

Whatever you put on top of your mast should be well attached and frequently checked for security. If anything comes adrift and is hanging by a wire, such as a light, some instrument, or an antenna, it will invariably be during rough conditions when you will not be able to go aloft to retrieve it. If left swinging free it may do serious damage to the head of the mainsail.

Booms

The combination of the mainsheet, vang, downhaul, outhaul, and mainsail, all pulling in different directions, puts heavy stresses on the boom. If the boom is of lightweight construction it may bend or break in hard going with everything strapped down tight.

Before going offshore take a good look at your gooseneck fitting. This is a common source of trouble for offshore cruising boats. Some are undersized and not built for hard and continuous use. Often the gooseneck is made of cast aluminum, which is easily broken and difficult to repair. If you have the choice, and you have an aluminum mast and boom, it may be better to have the gooseneck and attachments made of stainless steel. If the boom and mast are wood, then bronze, galvanized steel, or stainless steel may be used.

The boom-end fitting for the topping lift should be especially strong, particularly if you don't have a boom gallows. Likewise, the bails and fittings for downhauls and vangs must be ruggedly built and properly secured with strong rivets or bolts. The same suggestions for mounting hardware on the mast apply to the boom. Most hardware on aluminum booms is made of stainless steel, and held with stainless steel fasteners. If the boom is closed – for example an aluminum pipe with stainless steel caps on the ends – it is a good idea to use a high-quality silicon grease or anhydrous lanolin rather than polysulphide bedding compound on the fasteners, if you ever hope to remove the end caps in the future.

Spinnaker Poles

Some cruising sailors don't want to bother with a spinnaker, but whether you do or not, it can be handy to have a pole onboard to wing out a jib or genoa. Poles that are infrequently used need to have their triggers and snaps frequently lubricated.

Standing Rigging

Maybe it's true that 'Gentlemen don't sail to windward.' But some of the rest of us do now and then. A couple of weeks of steady bashing to windward gives you some time to think about your rigging. Sitting in the cockpit for hours and hours I become very impressed with the tremendous forces of nature. Growing out of that is an appreciation for the strength of my boat's rigging. Then I start to wonder just how strong the rigging really is. I cease to consider the standing rigging as a whole and start to think of it as a collection of individual pieces. All of them are like links in a chain – if there is one weak link, be it toggle, clevis pin, tang, or terminal, it could blow the whole shooting match. On a typical sloop the standing rigging is made up of more than 100 individual pieces.

Wire

Although galvanized wire is sometimes used, stainless wire rope is the most common standing rigging wire on sailboats. The two principal types are 1 × 19 strand and 7 × 7 cable. The designations refer to the type of construction. The 7 × 7 consists of seven bundles of seven strands each. It is more flexible than 1 × 19 and is commonly used on smaller one-design boats where the standing rigging is adjusted to affect sailtrim, and masts are unstepped frequently. The 1 × 19 wire

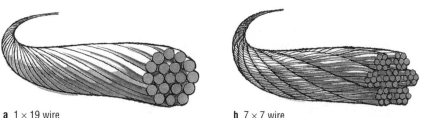

a 1 × 19 wire   b 7 × 7 wire

Figure 7.3
Rigging wire.

is what most of us are accustomed to in yacht rigging wire rope. It is laid up in one bundle comprised of 19 strands. You may find a wide range of prices when you go shopping for wire. It isn't necessary to pay the highest price to get the best wire, but be sure of its origin. Some of the world's developing nations are now manufacturing wire that looks just as good as the best quality available, but it may be unreliable.

Commonly the question is asked, 'What size rigging wire should I have for offshore sailing?' The designer or builder should be able to answer that question, but be sure they understand that you are planning extended offshore sailing. To reduce windage and weight, and because smaller wire is cheaper, some production cruiser-racers are under-rigged.

You may hear the suggestion that for offshore sailing you should always increase your wire to the next larger size. It probably won't hurt to do this, but it may not be necessary. Ross Norgrove in his book, *Cruising Rigs and Rigging*, offers a general rule for determining the wire size for the cap shrouds of a monohull. By his suggestion, multiply the weight in pounds of the ballast keel by two, and this will give an approximation of adequate ultimate tensile strength of the wire. For example *Denali*, with a ballast keel of 6000 pounds (2700 kg), requires stays with a tensile strength of 12,000 pounds, or 5/16" 1 × 19 stainless wire. I could use slightly smaller diameter wire for the shrouds, but I keep everything at 5/16" (8 mm), both as extra insurance, and because I only need to keep track of one size for spare wire and terminals.

Rod rigging is often used on racing boats but it has few cruising proponents. It is expensive, and requires very close attention and precise tuning. Spare lengths are difficult to store, and replacements may be difficult to find along the cruising routes.

Terminals

Rigging wire can break anywhere along its length, but this rarely happens if it is of good quality and is not abused. Shrouds or stays usually fail at or within the terminal. Sometimes the terminal itself cracks or breaks.

There are some choices among terminal fittings. Production boats usually have swage terminals, but other possibilities are Norseman and Sta-Lok, poured sockets, Castlok, and Nicopress.

Swages require expensive machines, so this work is only done by professional riggers. Swage machines are of three types: roller, hammer or hydraulic. By all three methods, high pressure is used so that the metal of the terminal flows into the lay of the wire. Swaging is only as good as the person who does the job, and some rigging failures can be laid to an inexperienced or careless operator. It pays to deal with an established rigger with a good reputation, and to watch the swages being made for your boat. If they don't look right or if they are 'banana-shaped,' don't accept them. Incorrectly made swages put uneven strains on the terminals and they will be more likely to fail.

Swage terminals have a reputation for failure on yachts sailed for a long time in tropical areas. In those latitudes, cracks commonly occur in the swages at deck level. Eventually they enlarge and the terminal splits and breaks. Sometimes examination of the interior of the fractured terminals shows that they contain broken wires.

Does this mean that you should not venture into the tropics with swage terminals? No. But if you plan to spend a long time there, consider an alternative type of terminal.

There is a lot to recommend Sta-Lok and Norseman terminals. They are very strong and are made from machined stainless steel bar stock. Especially important to the cruising sailor, they can be installed quickly and easily with simple tools and no special machines. Initial cost of these fittings is high but you can do your own rigging and thereby save labor costs, and the terminals can be reused by the replacement of the internal split cone. Spare split cones should be carried on board. In the event of a rigging failure, it is possible to install the terminals at sea.

On *Denali* I carry one spare 1 × 19 wire as long as my longest stay, with a Norseman terminal already installed on one end. If I ever have to prepare a stay or shroud quickly, it will only be necessary to cut the wire to the correct length and add one more terminal.

Poured sockets are more complicated to install but are highly regarded, and are probably the best terminal to keep salt water from penetrating the fitting. They are also reusable. Because they are not used extensively, poured socket terminals are more difficult to find. For stainless steel wire, bronze sockets are used. Their strength is attested to by the fact that this type of terminal is used on cables for elevators and huge cranes.

Another terminal reported to be good for resisting salt water penetration is Castlok. Like Norseman and Sta-Lok it is easy to install with only a few tools. The Castlok terminal is filled with epoxy which completely seals out water.

Nicopress sleeves are quick and easy to install on flexible wire if you have the proper tool to do the crimping. I have never tried it on rigid wire such as 1 × 19, and suspect it would be difficult to bend anything larger than 1/4" (6.4 mm) wire around a thimble without special tools. For emergency repairs and for small flexible wire terminals, Nicopress fittings are excellent.

Regardless of the brand or type of terminal fitting you select, it is best to use eye terminals rather than forks. The eye terminal is one solid thick piece, whereas the terminal forks are thinner and more likely to be bent or broken.

Turnbuckles, Toggles, and Split Pins

Turnbuckles, also known as rigging screws, are usually forged bronze or machined stainless steel. Bronze turnbuckles have coarse threads, whereas stainless threads are usually fine. With fine threads, there is a chance of 'galling,' and the possibility of the screws becoming stuck. Either type should be disassembled and lubricated, at least once a year. The best lubricant is anhydrous lanolin or silicon grease. Turnbuckles should be of the open-barrel type so that the amount of thread remain-

Figure 7.4
Turnbuckle, toggle,
clevis pin, split pin, and
chainplate.

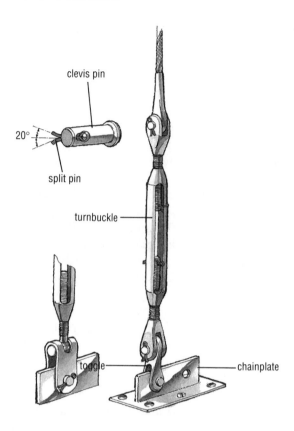

ing on the screw can be seen. The end of the screw should contain a hole to hold a split pin or piece of wire.

Toggles should be installed where turnbuckles attach to chainplates, and where terminals of stays attach to the masthead. Toggles permit the rigging to 'work' without stressing the chainplates or mast fittings. Without them, a twisting force is placed on the fittings and on the wire, which will cause them to fatigue and break. Toggles, like turnbuckles, may be stainless or forged bronze. They, and other parts of the standing rigging, should be fitted with clevis pins of the correct size.

Cotter pins or split pins are used extensively on standing rigging; on the rigging screws, and to hold the clevis pins of toggles, chainplates and tangs. Stainless steel split pins are the best choice. Circular pins are not recommended because they become distorted and are difficult to insert and remove. It is important to obtain the proper size cotter pins and to install them correctly.

Well-equipped yachts carry wire cutters to cut away the rigging in the event of a dismasting. Fine in theory, but often the cutters will be difficult to use in an emergency situation. If cotter pins are correctly installed the quickest way to disengage damaged rigging is to remove the split pins and knock out the clevis pins.

The pin should fit snugly inside the hole of a clevis pin or turnbuckle. That is, it should not wobble around, nor should it require a hammer to insert it. The length of the pin below the head should be 1.5 times the diameter of the piece it fits through. After the pin is inserted, each leg should be bent no more than 10 degrees. If they are bent more than this, they will be difficult to remove. The ends of the cotter pins are often sharp, and should be rounded off with a file before they are inserted. Once they are in place they can be taped to keep them from snagging sails, sheets, or clothing.

Chainplates

Unfortunately, the trend toward lighter and more flimsy rigging in racing yachts and even in racer-cruisers has extended to the chainplates. For offshore work chainplates must be strong and well-anchored. On a fiberglass boat they should be bolted to a structural member and glassed in. Furthermore, they should be easy to inspect. On some boats, they are hidden away in the back of cabinets and often covered over with wood paneling. If your cruising boat was not originally designed for offshore sailing it would be a good idea to be sure the chainplates are adequate, and if not, to install stronger ones. *Skene's Elements of Yacht Design* gives a table showing proper chainplate dimensions for any given wire size.

Tangs

The old-style tangs, which are strongly attached to the mast with a strap or plate, are best for the offshore boat. Most of these were copied from a Herreshoff design, which has stood the test of time. In this type, an end-threaded solid rod extends through the

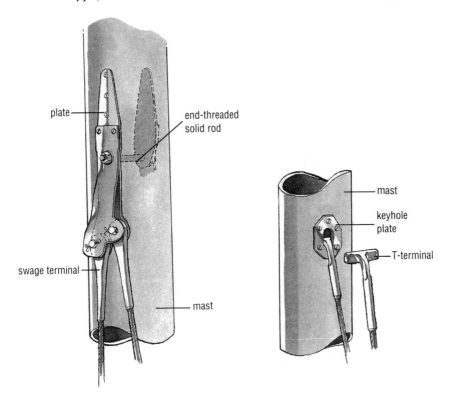

plate

end-threaded solid rod

mast

keyhole plate

T-terminal

swage terminal

mast

Figure 7.5
Tangs.

mast. Where it exits it is supported by a stainless steel strap or plate that is bolted or riveted to the mast. The tangs are hung on the bolt and kept in place by a nut screwed to the rod whose end is peened over. The shroud or stay terminals are held to the tang with clevis pins.

The use of T-shaped terminal fittings that slip into a keyhole plate on the mast is not a good idea for offshore boats, even though they make for easy rigging. Often this fitting does not allow for the wire terminal to 'work' or move as is possible with a tang and toggle or clevis pin arrangement. Due to the rolling and pitching of the boat the wire moves, and if there is no opportunity for a toggle or clevis pin to relieve this motion it will be absorbed by the flexing of the wire and the working of the T-fitting in its socket. Next time you visit a marina with a variety of yachts compare the old style tangs with the new style T- or ball-shaped fittings, and see which one you think will last the longest.

Stays and Shrouds

The purpose of the shrouds and stays is to keep the mast in the boat and to keep it straight. Most cruising sailors don't care to spend time making frequent adjustments as a racer might. For this reason, it is a good idea to spend some time initially to properly adjust your rigging. There are plenty of opinions about how tight or how loose the standing rigging should be. In a standard offshore cruising rig, the main point is that the mast should remain straight on either tack and off the wind as well.

Initial setting of the rigging is done when in port or at anchor. You will probably be pretty close to correct, if you take your time. Be sure your boat is trimmed and loaded as it will be for sailing when you set up your rigging. If you hang a plumb bob from the center of the mast about 10 or 12 feet above the deck it will give you a reference point as you adjust the shrouds. Fore and aft, the mast can be adjusted for a slight rake if that is your preference. When you have the rigging set to your satisfaction, go out and see how it looks on different points of sail. Remember, the main concern is to keep the stick straight. Make only slight changes to the lee shrouds when underway. Otherwise, when you tack it could put large compression strains on the mast.

Running Backstays

Running backstays were standard equipment in the days when most yachts were gaff-rigged. Today, they are most often found on boats with double headsails or fractional rigs. Cutters usually have a strong permanent backstay and set up the runners only under moderate and heavy going. On double-headsail rigs the running backstays lead aft from the mast abaft the fitting for the inner forestay. On deck, they are set up on a track, in a lever arrangement, or with a block and tackle. Some are arranged to be tensioned with a cockpit winch.

When sailing, the windward running backstay is tensioned. On each tack or jibe, the old windward runner is slacked, and the new windward runner tensioned. When not in use, the running backstays are sometimes detached at deck, or sufficiently slacked that they can be tied off at the mast or at the aft lower shrouds.

Some experienced offshore sailors strongly recommend that even a yacht with a single headsail should have running backstays either permanently rigged, or available to be rigged, when an especially difficult passage is expected. It is hard to make a recommendation on this point because it depends on the individual boat, the size of the mast and rigging, and on where you are sailing. I have only a permanent backstay and no runners, and have never felt the need for them – but my boat has a very heavy mast and it is stepped on the keel. If I were to take my boat into the Southern Ocean for sustained sailing I would consider adding running backstays. It would certainly not hurt to add running backstays to almost any offshore cruising yacht. If you decide to do this, get some advice from a designer or experienced rigger.

Spreaders

Spreaders need to be strong, and are usually designed with some flexibility so they can swing slightly fore and aft. They carry large compression forces, and also receive the forward pressure of the mainsail when off the wind. They are tilted slightly upward to equalize the angle they make with the shroud.

Shrouds need to be secured to the spreader tips. If using stainless wire and aluminum spreaders, this can be done by neatly lacing monel, stainless, or even galvanized wire around the shroud and the spreader tip. This, then, should be covered with some soft leather or rubber to prevent sail chafe.

The amount of strain the shrouds put on the mast is influenced by the angle of their leads from the mast. This in turn is determined by the width of the boat and where the chainplates are located, the height of the mast, and the length of the spreaders. Opinions vary on the best shroud angle, but a minimum of 10 to 12 degrees seems acceptable. If the angle needs to be enlarged there are several options, but it would be advisable to talk with the designer and a competent rigger before undertaking any major changes.

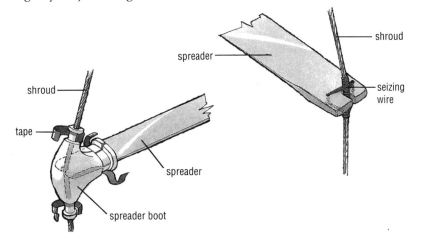

Figure 7.6
Joining of shroud to spreader end.

Bowsprits

Looking at the old sailing ships, with their long, thin bowsprits, makes you wonder how these delicate-appearing spars were strong enough to carry such huge sail area. Looking closer you can see they were always well-supported with stays and shrouds, and the base of the bowsprit was firmly planted on the ship. Most bowsprits on modern yachts are shorter and safer than their forerunners, but they must also be strongly reinforced. On most contemporary boats, an A-frame-type bowsprit is installed, and it often includes one or two anchor rollers, anchor storage, a sturdy bow pulpit, the forestay, and sometimes roller-furling gear for the headsail.

Bobstays support the bowsprit and need to be strong and well anchored. Wire, chain, and sometimes rods are used for the bobstay and associated shrouds. If the angle between the bobstay and the bowsprit is small, a dolphin striker is installed to open the angle and reduce the strain. The bobstay should be frequently inspected because it fulfills an important function and has a lot of different forces applied to it. Underway, it receives constant stress-cycled loads, and it is continually in and out of the water. When the boat is at anchor, the bobstay may be stressed or chafed by the anchor rode.

I end this chapter by once more mentioning that the standing rigging is an interconnected system made up of many simple but important parts. If any one part fails, it puts the whole system in danger. All the parts should be of equal strength. If it is necessary to make a replacement, and a duplicate part is not available, it is better to go up rather than down in strength for the substitute. Frequent inspections of all parts of the standing rigging should be routine procedure. This means going aloft when in port and before leaving on a passage. At sea it is a good idea to look at every deck-level fitting once a day, and to make a habit of frequently looking at the upper rigging with your binoculars.

If your boat is a production cruiser-racer that you are converting to a long-distance cruiser, or if your boat has lived most of its life nearshore, give some thought to the adequacy of your rigging and consider replacing or upgrading the rigging with heavier gear.

Figure 7.7
A-frame bowsprit.

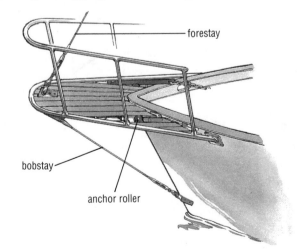

forestay

bobstay

anchor roller

RUNNING RIGGING

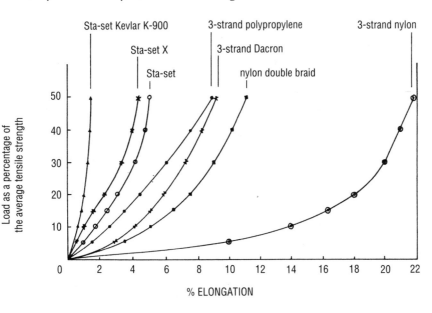

8 CHAPTER

My recommendation for running rigging on a cruising boat is to keep it simple. Forget about expensive and inconvenient go-fast gear. Instead, aim to keep the cockpit and deck as clean and uncluttered as possible. In place of high-tech, the cruiser's running rigging should be appropriate-tech. Some of my opinions on running rigging will probably meet with arguments from the racers.

Line

New materials and improvements in the manufacture of rope have made the sailor's life easier. The first generation of line consisted of plant-fiber ropes which were difficult to handle and stow. The second generation was nylon and Dacron – generally easier on the hands, and far easier to care for. They have produced high strength and low stretch line for running rigging and strong, elastic line for anchoring. Nylon and Dacron can be 'ridden hard and put up wet' without damage if they are protected from chafe. It is difficult to say how long a Dacron sheet will last if you take care of it; certainly many years.

The third, and latest, generation of ropes includes Kevlar, Spectra and other new synthetic fibers. Their main attributes are very low stretch and high strength, but they require even greater care than nylon or Dacron. These latest ropes have taken over the racing scene, but they are too costly for cruising. Some of them are difficult to splice, and they are really unnecessary for routine sailing.

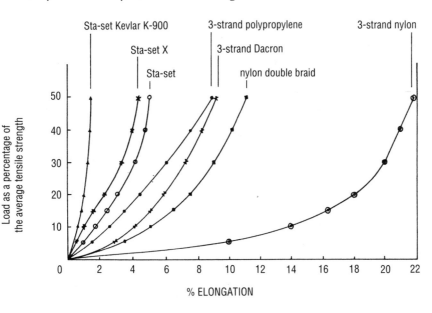

Figure 8.1
Strength of ropes (line) of varied compositions. Courtesy of New England Ropes.

Saving Money

The variety in the type and size of lines available is impressive. To help avoid confusion about which line does what, some sailors outfit their boats with a rainbow of colors. With an inexperienced crew on board it is convenient to say, 'Slack the chartreuse line,' or 'Take in on the yellow line with the blue polka dots,' rather than indicate the specific purpose in mind – although it doesn't work as well at night.

The cruising sailor doesn't need line in a lot of different sizes and colors. And if you keep your rig simple, and your crew knows their boat, you won't need many different lines. Usually, the same size line can be used for various jobs – one size for all halyards and sheets, another for reefing lines, downhauls, and vang, and a third for anchoring and mooring lines.

Compare the cost-per-foot for short lengths of line at the local chandlery, with the price for a 600-foot (185 m) roll from a wholesaler or discount house. Six hundred feet sounds like a lot, but you may be surprised at how fast it can disappear for sheets, halyards, and anchor line. If it still sounds like too much for you, find another boat to split the order with.

The most popular rope materials for the cruising boat, are nylon and Dacron. In looking at each of these, the emphasis is on strength, stretch, cost, and ease of handling.

Nylon

Nylon line is characterized by its great strength and its high stretch. It is the strongest synthetic line suitable for cruising. Under load, it will stretch 15–20 percent. The most common type of nylon is three-strand, but now we are seeing more and more braided nylon. The three-strand is cheaper, and the braided is more comfortable to handle. Both are more chafe-resistant than Dacron. The combined characteristics of nylon line make it the best choice for anchor rode and mooring lines. Most sailors would never consider using nylon for halyards or sheets because of its stretch, and it is true that a nylon sheet or halyard will require retightening after a few minutes of sailing. But if you are cruising on a tight budget, and especially if you have self-tailing winches, nylon can suffice – and it's much cheaper than Dacron.

New, three-strand nylon, right off the roll, is usually stiff and difficult to handle – especially in sizes larger than 1/2" (12 mm). There is some three-strand nylon now being sold that is quite soft to begin with, but I find this flaccid stuff very difficult to splice. The stiffer, older-style nylon is easier to splice, and it will gradually soften up with use. Three-strand line is much easier to splice than braid, either for an eye, or to join two pieces. Also, a braided line splice is stiff and inflexible, and cannot be cleated at the splice.

Dacron

Dacron is the most widely used line for halyards, sheets, vangs, and reefing lines on modern sailboats. Its ease of handling and low stretch, usually less than five percent, make it well-suited for these tasks. Dacron is made from polyester fiber, and is available as double braid, three-strand, or plaited. Braid is most commonly used for halyards and sheets. Perhaps its main disadvantage is that it will chafe very easily if not properly cared for and watched. This, plus its low stretch, are the reasons it is not so widely used for anchoring or mooring. However, it's so pleasant and easy to handle that sometimes its convenience offsets other considerations. I have one 300-foot (90 m) piece of 3/4" (19 mm) braided Dacron that I sometimes use for anchor line. No matter how it is dumped on deck, it will run free when it is paid out. I keep it loosely stored in an old sailbag with the two ends hanging out. In an emergency or at night I can put out an anchor easily and quickly without any tangles. When it comes back on board, it can be fed into the bag without the need to flake it down and tie it up, as is necessary with nylon three-strand.

Wire

If your cruising boat is already rigged with 1 × 19 stainless steel wire halyards that are in good condition, there is nothing wrong with continuing their use. Wire has less stretch than any type of line except Kevlar or Spectra and so it is popular for racing, but it has some disadvantages for the cruising boat. If the wire ever jumps out of the sheave at the masthead and jams, you may have a very difficult and sometimes dangerous time correcting the problem at sea. If you are starting out with a new boat or rerigging an old one for cruising, Dacron will be a better choice.

When strands of wire rope break, as they often do near the eye fittings, or at a rope-to-wire splice, the broken strands become hand-cutting 'meat hooks'. Also, depending on the size of your jibs, it may be necessary to add pendants to them to keep the wire or the rope-to-wire splice off the winch drums or cleats. Some sailors don't mind having pendants on their jibs, but it seems to me just one more complication that can be avoided by using all rope halyards. Also, rope is much quieter than wire if a halyard is slack inside or outside the mast.

I consider all-wire winches to be dangerous equipment. Sometimes the wire on the drum will become buried when the halyard takes a stain and the wire is then difficult to release. Problems with wire winch brakes are notorious. If the brake does not hold, it is difficult to keep the sail up. If the brake accidentally lets go, and the winch handle is still in the winch, it is easy to break an arm, or worse. Wire winches *do* give you the opportunity to crank with one hand and hold on to something for support with the other. This, however, is also possible with self-tailing rope winches.

Halyards

Most yachts today have internal halyards as standard equipment. Some folks still object to them because of the possibility that they will be fouled inside the mast, and because they are so difficult to reeve

Halyards and Sheets

Figure 8.2
Basic running rigging set-up for a sloop. This very simple arrangement allows for easy cockpit work.

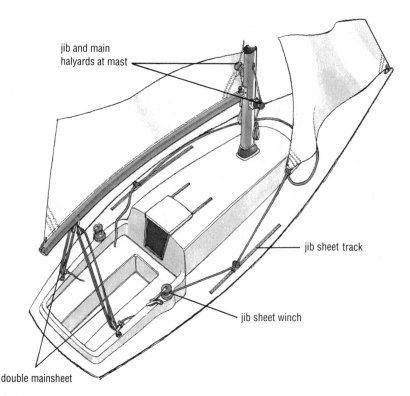

jib and main
halyards at mast

jib sheet track

jib sheet winch

double mainsheet

if a halyard breaks or is somehow lost in the mast. These are valid complaints, but fouling seldom happens with proper care and maintenance. On the plus side, internal halyards cause less windage, less noise, and they reduce by half the chance of a halyard becoming fouled on the mast.

Any hardware installed on the mast should use fasteners no longer than necessary, so they won't foul the halyards inside the mast. Likewise, electric wires run through the mast need to be kept isolated from the halyards. Some masts have a wire tunnel installed at the factory. If not, and you are installing wires, be sure to set the halyards up very tight when the wires are run, and to keep the slack out of the wires once they are installed.

In the past, mast exits for halyards were boxes with one or two sheaves. Today halyards often exit through simple slots in the mast wall. This seems to work fine as long as there is no chafe at the exit. If chafe does occur it can be remedied by fastening a smooth piece of stainless steel inside the mast at the top of the exit hole and outside the mast at the base of the exit hole. Carefully align the mast winches to have a straight run from the exit to the drum.

Again, it is important to have at least two halyards that lead forward and two that lead aft from the masthead, even if your boat is a sloop rig. The spinnaker halyard and topping lift can act as back-up halyards in the event that either the jib, or main halyard should break, become stuck, or let fly. Those spares might also be your emergency standing rigging if a headstay, backstay, or cap shroud should ever part.

Jib Sheets

All the sheets on a cruising boat should be Dacron – or in a pinch – nylon. Leave the wire or combined wire and rope to the racers. Jib sheets will last indefinitely if you keep an eye out for chafe and keep the leads to and from the turning blocks fair and true. The sheets should not touch anything except the sail cringle, the turning blocks, and the winch. Chafe will occur when sheets are caught or snagged on improperly installed cotter pins (split pins), by rubbing against the shrouds when hove-to, or if they lie against spars, stanchions, or lifelines.

Every now and then someone comes up with a new method of securing the sheets to the jib clew, but the safest method is to tie on both sheets with bowlines. Snap shackles or quick connectors of any design are dangerous if you happen to be hit by one on a flogging sail. It is unpleasant enough to be struck by a bowline, but it is much more painful to be beaned by a piece of metal or plastic.

When a bowline is tied, pull it really tight and leave a few inches of tail. A bowline is about as perfect a knot as one could hope to find, but they will come undone if they are not cinched up. Just before tacking, take a look at the bowline on the lazy sheet to be sure it hasn't taken a holiday. At night, you will need to use a flashlight, but the few moments it takes to do this are a lot less than the minutes it will take to straighten out the mess, or the hours necessary to resew a sail that has flogged itself to near destruction. When cruising, you sometimes remain on the same tack for days. It is not a pleasant experience to tack and see a line – the one you were expecting to be the new leeward sheet – trailing in the water. It could be even more unpleasant if you were making the tack to avoid a collision with a freighter.

When making a headsail change, it is often necessary to reposition the jib track car, and it may be necessary, on some boats, to rereeve the sheets to obtain a better lead under the lifelines. At such times, there is a temptation to use snatch blocks on the jib track. Force yourself to overcome the urge. The jib exerts tremendous pressure, and it is possible, under sudden loads, for the snap shackles on the snatch blocks to come undone. Avoid snap shackles on halyards as well. There are too many stories of snap shackles, on mains and headsails, coming undone when the sail is two-blocked. To attach a halyard, use either a bowline or a proper screw-type halyard shackle.

Finally, notice the size and condition of the sheaves on the jib track cars. They should be large diameter, smooth turning, and, if they are some type of plastic, free of any chips or cracks.

Mainsheet

Most mainsheet setups on cruising boats are adopted from racing boat styles, and are often inconvenient or dangerous. Too often they use a track that is either in the way of the companionway hatch, or located in the middle of the cockpit, and the crew is forced to climb over it, or fall over it, a few dozen times a day. It doesn't need to be there –

alternatives exist.

Mainsheet travelers located on the cabintop keep the cockpit clear, but may not be convenient once a dodger is installed. The length, type, and sheeting position of the boom on your boat will have some bearing on how the mainsheet can be run, but it is worthwhile to consider some optional rigs to make it more convenient.

My mainsheet setup is simple and usually keeps the cockpit uncluttered. Instead of a traveler, I rigged two 4:1 vangs, one secured to each side of the cockpit. Except when running downwind, the vangs don't interfere with movement in the cockpit. When tacking, there is excellent control of the boom; as one vang is let off, the other is hauled in, and the boom moves across the cockpit fully under control. Jibing is calm and peaceful. A bit slow for racing perhaps, but I gave up on that stuff years ago. In addition, the vangs permit better sail control and shape.

Other Working Lines

Sail Downhauls

Here is a device that some sailors find useful for cruising; especially on a large sloop or cutter. A sail downhaul is, logically enough, a line to help haul down a headsail or mainsail. On a headsail, a line is attached to the first hank below the head of the jib, and then led to the deck, where it passes through a turning block near the tack fitting, and then back to the mast, or to the cockpit. On the main, it attaches to the first slug or car below the headboard and runs down to the gooseneck – if hoisting and takedown are done at the mast – or to a turning block at the base of the mast, and then to the cockpit. When making a sail change or when reefing, the halyard is slacked off and the downhaul is

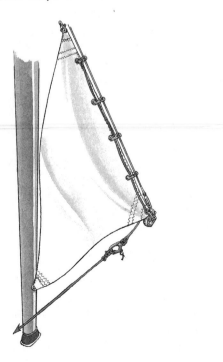

Figure 8.3
Downhaul for headsails.

hauled in. The sail should slide down the forestay or track with little effort. It is one more line to have to keep track of, but it may be useful on some boats. If you have no problems in dropping your sails, don't bother with this rig.

Topping Lifts

A strong, adjustable topping lift should be fitted to the end of the boom to support it when the main is furled or reefed. It is important, even if you have a boom gallows. At times the topping lift is a nuisance and has to be watched to keep it from chafing the leech of the main. But when it is needed it pays for its inconvenience.

The topping lift rides herd on the boom and can keep it from becoming a lethal weapon if the main halyard should ever break or let go. As pointed out earlier, it can also serve as a backup main halyard, and, in an emergency, might have to stand watch as a temporary backstay or cap shroud.

The rigging of a topping lift can vary to fit your boat. It can lead from the end of the boom to the head of the mast, and then down to the base of the mast as an internal or external halyard. If you are leading everything aft it can be one more line to live in the cockpit. Mine is rigged in a way that seems very simple, but I seldom see it so rigged on other boats. It is shackled to an eye on the outboard end of the boom, it then runs to a swivel-mounted turning block at the masthead, and then back down and aft to a cleat on the quarter. In this position it is handy but out of the way, and it can be easily adjusted if necessary.

When the main is hoisted and the strain is taken off the topping lift, it goes slack. Often there is just enough slack to permit it to rub against the leech of the main. Some people prevent this chafe by running stretch cord from the backstay to the middle part of the lift.

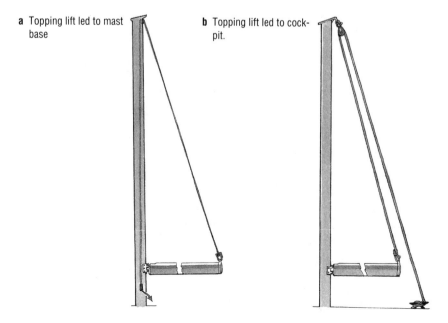

a Topping lift led to mast base

b Topping lift led to cockpit.

Figure 8.4
Topping lifts.

Vangs and Preventers

There are a number of fancy and expensive boom vangs on the market that have been developed for racing boats. The latest 'solid' vangs serve the double function of shaping the mainsail when off the wind, and supporting the boom in place of a topping lift. The more expensive solid vangs are hydraulic, but some combine a spring-loaded tube and a rope tackle. Such vangs should be released immediately if the main begins to flog when eased off. If not, the tremendous jerking forces that are placed on the rigidly held boom may cause the boom to bend. This kind of vang can be dangerous on a cruising boat when a helmsman is not always on duty. Finally, if you store a dinghy abaft the mast, there may not be room for a fixed boom vang. The traditional rope vang is a cheaper and lower-technology alternative.

I keep a combination vang/preventer rigged at all times when I am even slightly off the wind. It is simply a large rope tackle with a 4:1 purchase, similar to the tackles I use for my main sheet. It attaches to the boom, about mid-way along its length, and to a car on the jib track. Mainly it acts as a preventer in the event of an accidental jibe, but it also helps to control sail shape. The line from the cam cleat on the vang's fiddle block is long enough that I can easily release it from the cockpit.

Lines to the Cockpit

It is popular to have all sorts of sheets, halyards, vangs, downhauls, outhauls, and lines led to the cockpit. This technique began with the racers and was aimed at reducing weight and windage forward. Like other trends, it was assimilated by the cruiser-racers and has now become a standard on many cruising boats. It is justified, and even praised, as a safety factor. The theory is that no one needs to leave the safety and security of the cockpit to raise, lower, or reef any sails.

To my way of thinking, there are some flaws in this reasoning and unless the skipper or crew are physically handicapped, I am not convinced a cockpit full of lines is a good idea. Several points:

1. A profusion of lines in the cockpit makes an incredible mess that is confusing and can be dangerous. The tails are often tossed below and clutter up the cabin sole, making it difficult to move around.
2. Turning blocks at the base of the mast increase friction on the halyards and add resistance to winching.
3. Turning blocks, bullseyes, fairleads, and line stoppers all tend to clutter the deck – and it is expensive clutter.
4. If you carry a rigid tender on deck it will probably be stowed aft of the mast. This will be difficult if the deck is covered with running lines and hardware. It is possible if chocks are added to raise the tender off the deck, but then the tender may interfere with the boom.
5. If halyard tending and reefing is done at the mast it means you will be better able to quickly straighten out any problems that

may occur in the process. If you remain in the cockpit for all line handling it is often difficult to see developing problems before they become serious.

6. No matter how hard you try to avoid it, there will be times when it is necessary to go forward on deck because of some complication. You can be fairly sure that it will happen under the worst conditions, such as a sudden squall with an unexpected increase or shift in the wind. At such times your quick response and agility on deck will be important. If you are not 'at home' on the foredeck it will be just that much more difficult and dangerous.

7. When lines are led from the mast to the cockpit they have to somehow pass under or through any dodger (sprayhood). In hard going the spray will make its way under the dodger where the lines are led and in so doing significantly reduce the efficiency of the dodger.

8. Most cruising boats are either shorthanded or singlehanded. Even with all the lines leading aft, it is rare that sails can be efficiently raised or lowered completely from the cockpit. If a cruising boat is rigged with everything going aft, it usually means that someone has to remain in the cockpit while someone else goes forward to tend the sail. This is impossible for a singlehander and it can be inconvenient for a doublehander if it means the off-watch crew must come on deck for every sail change or reef. Doing all the halyard work and reefing at the mast will make for a more efficient operation. If you feel unsafe working at the mast it is possible to build a mast pulpit to give added support.

Two final points. If you do follow the all-lines-to-the-cockpit routine, be sure to have the best quality line stoppers. Some of them severely abrade the line when the brake is engaged. Also, be sure the turning blocks at the mast base are adequately supported from below.

CHAPTER 9

DECK LAYOUT AND EQUIPMENT

A lot of careful thought should go into selecting, arranging, and installing deck equipment. When buying a new or used production boat, some sailors are willing to leave things as they are, assuming the builder and designer have done an adequate job in choice and placement. Those having a one-off or semi-custom yacht made may likewise be willing to leave the decisions to the builder. This is a mistake, because the standard or typical deck equipment is seldom arranged for shorthanded offshore sailing crews.

The Deck

It seems trite to say the deck should be strong, but surprisingly, it isn't on some boats. The deck is a major structural part of the boat that supports and strengthens the hull and mast, and serves as an important anchoring point for safety equipment. The deck is subjected to a variety of bending and twisting forces of tension and compression imposed by the hull, the standing and running rigging, and the sea. While the boat is underway, the deck sometimes takes a tremendous load when waves come aboard. If you can feel your decks flex when you walk on them, they are not strong enough. But even if they 'feel' OK, they should be inspected for strength.

Pay special attention to the deck-hull joint both inside and out, and notice how the structural bulkheads and transverse supports are attached to the deck and hull. On some production boats the poor workmanship is shocking, and a few weeks at sea or even a day of heavy going will reveal how inadequate they are, as bulkheads move or come adrift, and water begins to seep in at the deck-hull joint.

On fiberglass boats the deck-hull seam should be flanged, properly sealed, and through-bolted with fasteners spaced about three inches (75 mm) apart. On *Denali* the deck-hull seam appeared to be well made, but to insure its strength and ability to resist leaks I removed the toerail and glassed over the seam on the outside. This was an expensive, time-consuming job but one I am glad I did. In the past 10 years the hull has had far more bashing to windward than many boats ever encounter.

Deck surfaces should be covered with some type of non-skid to assure safe footing for the crew. Fiberglass boats usually have a non-skid pattern molded into the deck surface, but through time this will lose its grip. If your decks are slippery, they can be painted with a mixture of paint and sand or finely ground walnut hulls, or one of the newer composition materials. Another option is to put down non-skid overlays of rubberized or polymer materials held in place with epoxy cement. Unpainted teak decks are the safest and kindest to the crew.

However, they are a big maintenance responsibility.

Side decks between the cockpit and foredeck are important access routes. They should be at least 18 inches (45 cm) wide if there is a raised cabin. On some yachts the side decks narrow to almost nothing at the cockpit. This is a dangerous arrangement, and in my opinion such boats should not be sailed offshore. Moving between the deck and the cockpit should be easy, and there should be adequate handholds for support.

The decks of most fiberglass boats are cored with end-cut balsa or some type of closed-cell foam. This reduces weight, provides good insulation in both hot and cold weather, and reduces condensation inside the boat during the winter. Because of the core, however, care must be taken when the deck is penetrated with fasteners, or if a hatch is added. Most builders use solid fiberglass or plywood in places where they expect hardware will be installed or in places which need extra strength, such as adjacent to the mast, the bridge deck, cockpit coamings, and parts of the main deck. The builder can show you where the deck is cored and where it is solid, or you can figure it out by lightly tapping the deck with a piece of wood or the plastic handle of a screwdriver. If you cut out a part of the cored deck, it is important to cut back within the sandwich core and then seal it off with epoxy to prevent water from seeping into the sandwich.

In cored sections use care when tightening through-hull fasteners, or cracks will occur in and through the gelcoat. You can avoid this by using oversized backing plates of wood or metal. In some cases it helps to add a sleeve or compression tube around the fastener where it penetrates the core.

This may seem like a lot of work, but getting water in a cored deck can lead to big problems. When I was shopping for a cruising boat I noticed that a popular production boat was often listed with two widely different prices. When I inquired why, I learned that the ones with the high price had had their deck problems repaired, and the ones with the low price had not. In one case the problem was so severe that the cabin overhead and the top of the deckhouse were warped due to water penetration and swelling of the wood core.

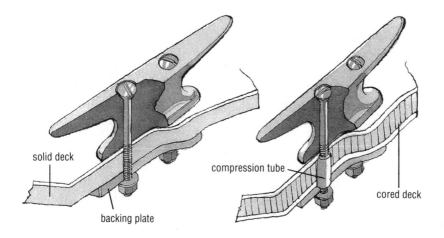

solid deck

backing plate

compression tube

cored deck

Figure 9.1
Backing plate and compression tube for through-hull fasteners.

Bulwarks and Toerails

Most fiberglass boats have the deck-hull seam covered by either a wood or aluminum toerail. The aluminum rail also serves as a place to fasten jib sheet blocks. The low profile toerail so common on nearly all production boats evolved from the convention of having crew sit to weather for ballast on racing boats. On older yachts and on well-designed cruising boats, a raised bulwark lines the edge of the deck. A bulwark makes for safer deck work and often provides needed foot support. After I glassed over the deck-hull seam on *Denali*, I followed Hal Roth's example and installed a raised bulwark rather than replacing the toerail. It was another labor-intensive job, but I am very pleased with it. Since it is raised off the deck, any water that comes aboard rapidly returns overboard. It provides good foot support and is convenient for tying off extra water and fuel containers on a long passage. Now and then it has served to keep a dropped winch handle or screwdriver from going overboard. Its only disadvantage is that I like to keep it bright and each year it is another varnishing project.

Figure 9.2
Raised bulwark as installed on board Denali. *Bulwark supports are made of stainless steel angle iron.*

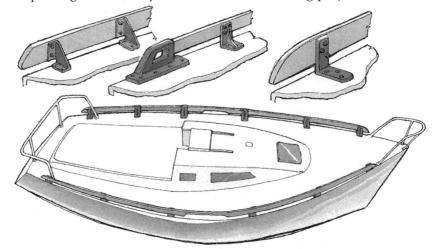

Lifelines and Stanchions

There seems to be a tendency among sailors to take lifelines for granted and assume they are adequate for their primary job of keeping the crew from going overboard. This is a bad assumption.

For most of us who began sailing less than 25 or 30 years ago, lifelines are accepted as standard equipment. However, they are a rather recent addition. Even today, some sailors prefer to sail without lifelines. Their reasoning is that lifelines and pulpits give a false sense of security. They maintain that without them the crew is much more careful. I don't subscribe to this philosophy, but it does serve as a reminder that lifelines are not foolproof. Just because they are on your boat does not mean they will prevent anyone from falling off.

The purpose of lifelines is not to provide handholds and they should not be used as attachment points for safety harnesses. Rather lifelines act as a 'fail-safe' or backup to help keep someone from going over the side if that person should accidentally slip on deck. Don't allow anyone to sit on the lifelines or to use them as handholds to pull themselves aboard from swimming or when boarding the yacht from a tender. Doing so will stretch the lifelines and put an unnecessary strain on the stanchions and the pulpits. Eventually, you'll spend time and money straightening stanchions and stopping deck leaks around through-hull fasteners.

Install strong stanchions in the first place and then regard them with skepticism and suspicion. I have seen boats where lifeline stanchions were ripped from the deck or broken due to only a mild bump against a pier. In another example the stanchion was strong but the deck underneath it broke when the stanchion struck a pier.

Stanchions should be strong and set in deep sockets. Baseplates should be through-bolted and supported by a metal backing plate at least as large as the stanchion base. Stanchions held in the socket baseplate with Allen (hex) screws often come loose due to vibration. If Allen screws are used there should be two screws for each baseplate. If you prefer to have the stanchion and baseplate as one piece, the set screws can be removed and the stanchions welded to the baseplate. The problem with this is that sometimes it is convenient to remove one or two stanchions, for example when launching or recovering a tender. Furthermore, stanchions are occasionally bent. To repair the one-piece type it is necessary to remove the through-hull fasteners – a time consuming task.

Lifeline wire is commonly 7×7 vinyl-coated wire, although it is possible to use 1×19 or 7×19. When installed, the wire should be set up tight because it will stretch. Adjustable pelican hooks are often installed at one or both ends of a lifeline, or at a boarding gate amidships. Not everyone approves of this because of the possibility that a pelican hook will open accidentally. However, those manufactured by Johnson Marine are virtually foolproof. They have a unique locking mechanism and are adjustable so they can be retensioned when the wire stretches. Being able to release the lifeline makes it easier to board, load stores, and launch and recover the tender. Most important, lifelines that can be slacked may make it easier to recover a man overboard. With the standard double lifelines set at about 12 and 24 inches (30 and 60 cm) above the deck, it is extremely difficult to recover a crew over the side, especially if the victim is weak from exhaustion, or is unconscious.

On some yachts I have seen solid railings rather than flexible lifelines. They are constructed of stainless steel pipe or tubing, the same as is used to construct pulpits. This has a lot to recommend it because the railings are very strong and act as solid handholds. They are especially convenient for climbing on board. However, they add weight to the boat and are difficult and expensive to repair.

Pulpits

Pulpits are usually placed at the bow and stern (also called pushpits), and sometimes at the mast. Bow pulpits need to be ruggedly built and firmly fixed to the deck and, like lifeline stanchions, supported by strong backing plates. Pulpits on most boats extend beyond the bow, and no matter how careful you are, they will end up taking some abuse

Figure 9.3
Bow pulpits.

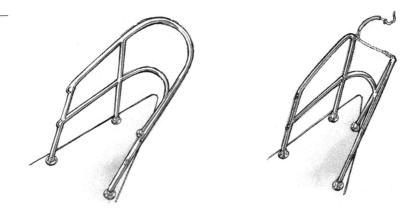

when the boat is moored with its bow to a pier or bulkhead, as is popular in many parts of the world. When moored in this way the boat must be correctly held off the pier, with due consideration for wind, tide range, and boat wakes, before it is left unattended. Even then, with slack lines or falling tide, the pulpit can hang up on the surface of the wall or on some projection sticking out of the wall. These encounters result in damage to the pulpit and the deck, and assure new deck leaks.

Having to leave and board the yacht, or load stores over the bow pulpit, is a difficult maneuver. This is when you will appreciate having a strong pulpit. Some boats have a gate in the upper part of the pulpit to permit easier access across the bow. This is convenient if you are sailing with children.

Pulpits that are well-built and firmly anchored to the deck should have fittings welded on them to attach halyards that are not in use. However, if the halyards are set up too tight they may put excessive strain on the pulpit. Likewise, unless the pulpit is strong and well-attached to the deck, the strain produced by lifeline tension will result in leaks around the pulpit fasteners; another reason not to abuse the lifelines and stanchions.

Most of what has been said for bow pulpits equally applies for stern pulpits. Stern pulpits come into their own as a place to attach a lot of gear. After you have sailed for a while and decided what equipment and fittings are of use to you, it is a good idea to remove the stern pulpit, take it to a shop that does stainless steel welding, and have permanent fittings installed. This will be much neater than having everything secured with hose clamps and line.

Some of the new production boats do not have a stern pulpit but any boat going offshore cruising should have a stern pulpit for safety. I do not trust the current trend on racing boats to have an open transom. Maybe it is OK for racing, but good crew is hard to replace on a cruising boat.

You will see boats with antennas, taffrail logs, water generators, horseshoe life rings and other man-overboard gear, fuel and water containers, bicycles, sailboards, solar panels, water generators, stern anchors, fenders, outboard engines, barbecue grills, and fishing reels, mounted on the stern pulpit. There is no denying the convenience, but too much weight on the stern won't do you any favors and may effect steering and windward performance. If your boat has a wind-vane steering, the aft end of the pulpit needs to be kept clear to permit access to the vane. Too much gear back aft may also disturb the wind flow around the vane and wreak havoc with your steering. Some boats incorporate fold-up ladders into the pulpit; this is fine as long as it doesn't interfere with the steering vane.

More and more boats have stainless steel 'radar arches' above the stern pulpit and some production boats now come with fiberglass arches. I don't care for them for several reasons. They tend to accumulate more and more 'things', which add windage and weight. I am also concerned that in hurricane conditions at sea or in port these arches will be left up and thereby increase windage. I also think they detract from the beauty of a boat's lines.

Large yachts sometimes have pulpits installed on each side of the mast to give support to the crew hauling on a halyard or pulling down a reef. Occasionally they are also seen on smaller boats. Mast pulpits can be a good idea – provided they are substantial and correctly located. They should be sufficiently high (at least 36 inches, 90 cm) to give support to someone leaning back and strong enough to act as a secure brace in a heavy seaway. They should be far enough from the mast to allow free movement of a winch handle and the crewmember using it.

Figure 9.4
Mast pulpit.

Deck Cleats and Chocks

There are few production boats that have enough deck cleats and chocks of the proper size for cruising. There should be a minimum of two, and preferably three or four, large, heavy cleats on the bow and at least one on each quarter. There should also be midships chocks and cleats for breast lines. All of these on a 30- to 40-foot boat should be able to hold two or three half-inch (12 mm) lines. Cleats should be the type held in place by four bolts and have strong backing plates.

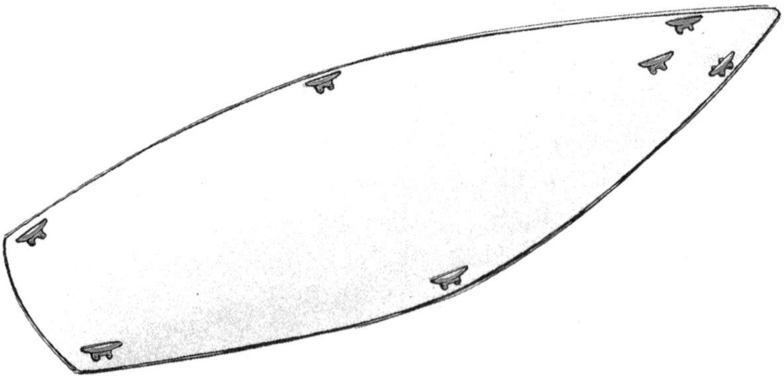

Figure 9.5
Deck cleats.

It is easy, after lying to a protected dock at your home port, to assume your mooring gear is adequate. However, when cruising it will sometimes be convenient or required for your boat to go alongside a wide variety of piers or docks for customs or immigration inspection, to obtain fuel or water, or because there is no place to anchor. Under the best conditions when going alongside a pier or dock, you will have a minimum of four, and more often six lines ashore, and each must be attached securely to the boat. Someday you will find yourself moored to a pier and dealing with strong tidal surges or current, or perhaps a storm will keep you in port. At such times you will want a lot of lines to the shore and maybe to anchors as well.

Along with cleats there must be chocks to lead the lines off the boat. Chocks, too, should be able to hold two or three lines at once, and must be through-bolted and secured with backing plates.

Fairleads from midships cleats can be a problem. Sometimes eyes are built into the bulwark or toerail to lead mooring lines. Under quiet conditions this is OK, but if there is a sudden surge on the lines, it is possible that the strain could damage or rip out a toerail or bulwark. Likewise some people lead lines from the cars on the jib track. This works sometimes but it may also result in a warped or broken track and leaks. It is better if the lines from the midships cleats lead directly off the boat without passing through a fairlead. However, every mooring and docking situation is different and will tax your ingenuity to make the boat secure. The more chocks and cleats you have, the easier the job will be.

Strong cleats and chocks will be needed if you ever need to be towed or pulled off of a grounding or if it becomes necessary to stream a drogue or lie to a sea anchor. Under such circumstances the safety of yacht and crew may depend on having proper cleats. Cleats can be made from wood, aluminum, bronze, galvanized steel, stainless steel, and monel. Any one of those materials is fine if the cleat is large and strong.

On wooden boats bollards or samson posts are often installed on the bow and sometimes the stern. These are excellent for securing a variety of lines. They are also used on some fiberglass boats. Like cleats they require a heavy backing plate. Even with a samson post, you should also have cleats on the bow.

Position cleats in such a way that the line leads to it at an angle of 15 to 25 degrees to the horn of the cleat. When locating the cleat think about the various ways in which it may be used. For example, bow cleats may need to receive lines from both bow chocks.

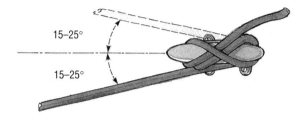

15–25°

15–25°

Figure 9.6
Proper lead for line to deck cleat.

Rollers are used to help launch and retrieve an anchor. The best ones are frames built of stainless steel, bronze, or galvanized steel with a roller of rubber, nylon, or some similar material that can tolerate chain or rope. When buying choose with care. There are some rollers that look good but are cheaply made and will not last.

Bow and Stern Rollers

Unless you really enjoy difficult tasks, a bow roller is worth having on any boat over 30 feet. Perhaps you are young, full of energy, and enjoy hauling the anchor line hand over hand when gunkholing. But that is different from getting underway in a blow that is likely to set you on a rocky lee shore.

If you are using all chain for anchoring, a bow roller is absolutely necessary. If space and weight considerations permit, it is better to have two bow rollers – one on either side of the forestay and extending slightly beyond the bow. Sometimes it is necessary to use two anchors, and deploying and recovering your gear will be much easier and safer with two bow rollers. The best rollers have a long, U-shaped trough that holds the anchor shank while the flukes or plow rest on the roller. The edges of the roller where the rode exits should be rounded. Often these are sharp edges which can cut through line in short order during a blow.

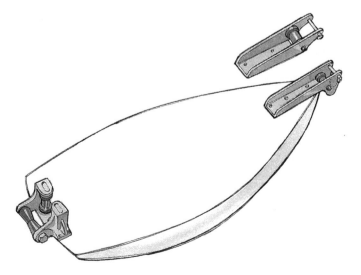

Figure 9.7
Bow and stern rollers.

As I mentioned, some boats with bowsprits have the anchor rollers built into them. This makes for easy deployment and storage. Bow rollers are subjected to heavy vertical and lateral strains and sudden shock and cyclical loading. They must be heavily through-bolted and backed by a strong backing plate inside the hull. It is advisable to mount a piece of solid or laminated teak or similar wood between the bow roller channel and the deck to help absorb the heavy loading.

An anchor roller on the stern is a convenience but not a necessity. It is, however, worthwhile to install a roller chock on the stern. This device is helpful in making frequent adjustments to a stern anchor and putting out extra dock lines. Such a fitting on *Denali* permits me to lead stern mooring or anchor lines to the jib sheet winches.

Anchor Windlass

It is rare to see a long-distance cruising boat without some type of windlass to retrieve its anchors. Very often the windlass is placed far forward on the foredeck. This seems logical, because it puts the winch near the bow roller, but it is not a good idea. All weight on the boat should be as low and as far from the ends of the boat as possible. Chances are pretty good that you will end up using chain for your main anchor; and since the chain locker needs to be directly or almost directly below the windlass, both windlass and chain locker should be moved as far aft as possible in order to maintain trim and buoyancy forward. Except for boats designed specifically for cruising, most designers never anticipated 200 to 300 feet (60 to 90m) of chain on their boats.

On *Denali* I placed the windlass as far back on the foredeck as possible and built a new chain locker into the forward cabin. A thick-walled, heavy PVC pipe between the windlass and the chain locker

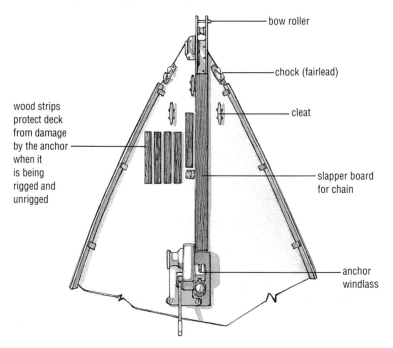

bow roller

chock (fairlead)

cleat

wood strips protect deck from damage by the anchor when it is being rigged and unrigged

slapper board for chain

anchor windlass

Figure 9.8
Foredeck layout on Denali.

brings the chain below. By this modification I was able to relocate the windlass more than six feet back from the bow, and to move the mass of chain which weighs 300 pounds (135 kg), aft by four feet and lower it by about two and a half feet – a significant contribution to trim and probably to sailing ability.

Having the windlass farther aft makes it easier and safer to work on the foredeck. A windlass near the bow also interferes with the lead of dock lines. With the windlass aft, it is necessary to install a 'slapper board' to keep the chain from damaging the deck.

Many production boats these days have a self-draining locker near the bow to hold an anchor, line, and sometimes even a windlass. While this is fine for the daysailor or gunkholer it has no place on the oceangoing yacht other than for storing fenders. Even then, be sure the drain is free or the space will surely fill up with water. Perhaps the best solution would be to seal the drain, fill the compartment with closed-cell foam and glass over the deck, and consider it added positive flotation for your yacht.

The windlass should be through-bolted and have a hefty backing plate below it. This cannot be overemphasized. When anchored, the strain of the anchor line should not be left on the windlass, but should be transferred to the cleats. However, you will forget to do this some time, and when you do the windlass serves as an expensive cleat. Furthermore, occasional heavy loads on the windlass cannot be avoided when hauling in the anchor. Without a strong backing plate it is possible to damage the deck.

Boom Gallows

The boom gallows supports the main boom when it is not in use in port, sometimes when reefing, and especially to strap down the boom in storm conditions. A wildly swinging boom is one of the most dangerous accident-producers on board. The gallows also functions as a fail-safe if the main halyard or the topping lift should let go. I have heard of one person knocked overboard and lost, as well as of numerous head injuries, on boats that did not have gallows installed. Recently I read a book in which the author said boom gallows were old-fashioned and no longer needed on cruising boats. Maybe on his boat, but not on mine. Having cruised with and without a gallows, I would not put to sea without such a convenient item.

A gallows has some other uses as well, depending on how and where it is rigged on the boat. If it is located forward of the cockpit it provides a convenient handhold when going forward on deck, and it acts as a support when taking sextant readings. It can be used to support a cockpit awning. My gallows is strong enough to serve as a tie point for spring lines when alongside a dock. It is also used as a clothesline and to hang a stalk of bananas in the tropics.

Where you locate a gallows will depend on how your boat is rigged. Commonly it is located near the front or in front of the cockpit. If you have a long boom that extends over the cockpit it may be placed aft. Take your time and think about how it can be located to give the best

Figure 9.9
Boom gallows.

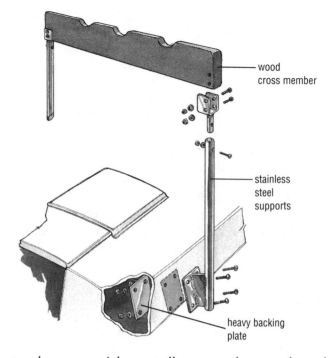

wood
cross member

stainless
steel
supports

heavy backing
plate

support and most use. A boom gallows must be securely anchored to be useful but it should be removable. Stainless or galvanized pipe, one and a half inch (38 mm) or larger can be used for the vertical supports. The cross member, which supports the boom, should be wood. Usually the wood piece has three shallow depressions in which the boom can lie. It is a good idea to cover these troughs with leather or rubber to reduce chafe. Some gallows are made entirely of pipe. My first attempt at building a gallows was of this type but I subsequently changed to wood because it was kinder to the boom.

Dodgers

I can't think of any item more important to crew comfort in the cockpit than a full-sized dodger or spray hood. In cold weather, when it is raining, or when there is a heavy sea running with continuous spray and an occasional wave coming aboard, a good dodger will help maintain a happy crew.

It is one thing to be wet and cold for a few hours when daysailing, with the certain knowledge that a hot shower and dry clothes are only a few hours away. It is something else to be wet and cold for days. Even those who have taken part in ocean races may fail to grasp the importance of a dodger. Larger racing boats usually have enough crew that, in heavy going, they can take turns on deck and in the off times go below, dry off, and rest. On a small boat with a crew of one or two it may be necessary to remain in the cockpit for hours, or at least to frequently visit the cockpit to maintain a watch; this can go on for days.

On one passage I experienced a period of bad weather that lasted nearly five days. Much of that time I remained in the cockpit. My generous dodger more than paid for itself at that time. By snuggling up

Figure 9.10
Cockpit dodgers.

a Dodger base attached with snap fasteners on a spray shield

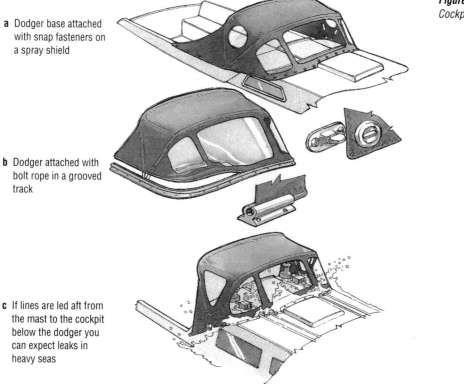

b Dodger attached with bolt rope in a grooved track

c If lines are led aft from the mast to the cockpit below the dodger you can expect leaks in heavy seas

in the forward part of the cockpit on the lee side, I could fend off most of the rain and spray and still maintain a watch by occasionally peeking around the edge of the dodger. Without a dodger or with a poorly built one I could not have remained on deck for very long.

When making a landfall or approaching a harbor in cold or otherwise unpleasant weather, a dodger will help you stay alert and allow you to go on deck whenever you need to. Without a good dodger many people put off leaving the warmth and security of the cabin knowing they are bound to get cold and wet when they do. In some situations this procrastination can be dangerous.

A good dodger must be constructed of heavy, water-resistant material and should be sewn with triple stitches using heavy UV-resistant thread. The metal bows that support it need to be made of one inch (25 mm) gage tubing. The dodger will invariably be used as a handhold, so it must be strong.

The skirt of the dodger should be securely attached to the deck or spray shield. This can be done with snap fasteners, or a bolt rope can be sewn into the skirt of the dodger and a grooved track installed on the deck; otherwise water will surely pass under the dodger. If your boat is not equipped with a spray shield, consider adding one.

Plastic windows to improve visibility and to allow more light below are installed in most dodgers. Windows are nice, but they will lose their transparency after a few months at sea. When I recently replaced my dodger I made the new one without windows. It is just as effective as the old one and looks better without the dingy windows.

Rigid dodgers, just one step away from a pilothouse, are now becoming more common on cruising boats. The advantages are obvious, but keep in mind that they will add windage and could be a distinct liability in a hurricane at sea or in port.

Hatches

The strength, security, and watertight integrity of the oceangoing boat's hatches warrant detailed attention before heading offshore. On too many production boats the hatches are inadequate. Hatches used for crew access and sailhandling should be capable of being opened from the outside as well as the inside. Only a few hatches provide this safety and convenience feature. Try to find hatches designed so that the handles and dogs will not catch sheets and feet.

The main companionway is a huge opening. If your cockpit is pooped and the hatch boards are not in place the cabin can be flooded in a matter of seconds. Main companionway hatches should have two or preferably three hatch boards, and each board should have some type of slip bolt or latch to keep it in place in the event of a knockdown or capsize. You occasionally see main hatches with hinged doors that open in the middle. If you have this type it should be replaced with boards in a groove. There are times at sea when it isn't safe to expose the whole hatch opening to the elements. As difficult as it may be to climb in and out at such times, it will be better to leave in the lower one or two boards. In heavy going it may be necessary to keep all boards in place. Some sailors refuse to have a companionway, and only enter the cabin through a deck hatch.

Usually one of the companionway hatch boards has some sort of louver or ventilation opening. About 99.9 percent of the time this helps to provide some airflow through the boat when it is closed up. However if you are lying to a dock or sailing downwind and a hard rain comes from astern, a lot of water can make its way below. It is possible to install a sliding cover to prevent this, but it is just as easy, less expensive, and probably more effective to have a large plastic bag to slip over the hatch boards.

A sliding hatch over the companionway is standard equipment on most yachts. On better-built yachts the sliding hatch escapes into a 'garage' when the hatch is opened. Without this shield you are sure to get a lot of water below, even with a dodger. It is possible to build such a cover or have one built.

Hinged deck hatches should be of top quality. A leaky hatch is a nuisance and can result in damage to supplies and equipment stored below. Often the problem is simply an aging gasket, worn lip, misalignment of the hatch, or inadequate dogs. Any of these should be corrected before heading out. Test hatch repairs by playing a stream of pressure water all over and around the hatch. Even then, you may be surprised to see the ocean making its way into your boat drop by drop. Hatches on some boats are so poor that it may be necessary to rebuild

Figure 9.11
Deck hatch. Low profile hatches made with strong hardware which can be opened both from inside and outside are the best option for a cruising boat.

or replace them completely. Goïot, Bomar, and Lewmar hatches have a good reputation, and most of them are constructed of clear or tinted polycarbonate that is almost bulletproof.

Before leaving on an extended cruise, purchase enough gasket material to repair all hatches on your yacht. Nearly every hatch manufacturer uses a different size and type gasket, and finding spare parts out on the cruising trail will usually prove impossible.

Hatches are expensive. The best ones are built with aluminum or stainless steel frames. Three important features are the ability to seal properly, the way the hatch is supported when open, and the way it dogs down when closed. Consider what the hatch will be used for. If it is only for ventilation you may not need a large hatch. However, if you plan to use it for crew access, and especially for handling bulky sailbags, it needs to be large and free of obstructions. Some hatches are conveniently large but have fastener fittings that make it nearly impossible for one person to pull out a sailbag without catching it on the fittings. Think about how the hatch will work if you are singlehanding and have to make a sail change in rough seas. Check the way in which the hatch dogs down. Are the dog handles convenient to handle with gloves on and large enough to permit you to get a good grip? Notice the way in which the hatch is supported when open. Are the supports strong and easy to adjust? Will they get in the way of hauling out a sail bag or when handing a sail below? One of the best supports is produced by Moonlight Marine. This is a stiff spring that holds the hatch half-way open and then folds down when the hatch is closed. Because it is a spring, the hatch can be fully opened to drag out a sailbag by stretching the spring.

Every deck-opening hatch should have two safety features which you will probably have to add yourself. There should be an eye attached to the inside of the hatch that is large enough to accept two turns of half-inch (12 mm) line, and there should be a similar eye or cleat somewhere nearby inside the boat. This will permit you to secure the hatch with line in the event that one or more of the dogs should break or become defective. Another important fail-safe is a spare cover for every hatch. These should also have an eye on the inside. Emergency hatch pieces

Figure 9.12
Hatch safety features.

a If possible, add an eye bolt to the inside of deck hatches. This will permit the hatch to be secured if a hinge or dog should break

b A temporary deck hatch can be made of wood and kept stowed below for emergency use

c Spare companionway hatch board as carried on *Denali*. In addition to being an emergency replacement for lost wash boards, it is commonly used in heavy weather

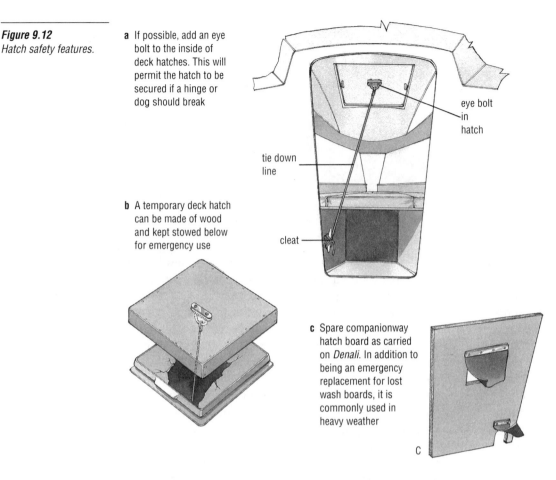

can be made from ³/₈" (9 mm) or heavier marine grade plywood. The possibility of loosing a hatch is remote, but if it happens it will no doubt be under bad conditions, and the last thing you need at that time is a huge gaping hole in the deck. A monohull taking on water through a hatch would have a survival time of only a few minutes. If you think it is impossible to lose a hatch, consider a jib sheet catching on an open hatch during a tack or unplanned jibe. In addition to a spare forward hatch, I also have a spare hatch board to replace the boards of the companionway patterned after that described by Richard Henderson in his book *East to the Azores*. I have used this board several times in heavy going. It has no louvers but it does have a heavy rubber flap for peeking outside and for passing food from the galley to the cockpit. It also has a smaller rubber flap at the base which will permit the exit of an emergency bilge pump hose.

Windows

In my opinion the window 'styling' on some cruiser-racers today is deplorable, not only because I don't think a boat should look like a pair of designer sunglasses, but more importantly, because in most cases the windows are too thin, too big, inadequately secured, and easily cracked or broken. Windows, whether they are opening ports or fixed plates of

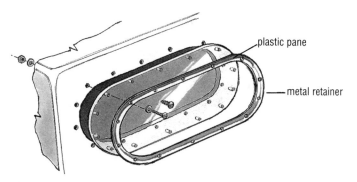

plastic pane

metal retainer

Figure 9.13
*Window. Small windows
with round corners are
best for the offshore
cruising boat. They
should be securely
fastened with screws
or with through-hull
fasteners.*

acrylic or polycarbonate, are part of the boat. They are located where holes have been cut into the hull. Holes weaken the structure and hence whatever covers those holes needs to be strong. Large windows, as nice as they may be while in port, are a definite liability at sea. They should be no larger than 9 by 15 inches (22 cm × 38 cm). Windows with round or oval shape are stronger than square ones. The window material must be very strong and scratch resistant with a minimum thickness of 3/8" (9 mm). Windows should be attached by screws or through-bolted and bedded with marine grade adhesive/sealant to prevent leaks.

Opening ports are a convenience you will appreciate in tropical areas when it is impossible to have too much ventilation. However, some opening ports are flimsy. As nice as the airflow is, water flow or drips are intolerable and can result in expensive damage. There is nothing produced today that is superior to the old-style round brass portholes with thick glass, but few sailors today are willing to put up with their cost and weight. Furthermore, the cabinsides on most modern yachts are not high enough to accept such ports. If you can install opening ports, select those that are well made and not cheap copies. As with hatches, be sure and have a large supply of gasket material.

Every cruising yacht should have storm windows or window covers for every fixed or opening port onboard. I am unaware of any yacht builder that offers storm windows as standard or even optional equipment, so you will have to design and install them yourself. The most obvious need for storm windows is to protect your yacht against damage from the weight of large breaking waves which could board your boat in a storm. However, experienced offshore sailors tell us that there is probably greater risk for window breakage on the lee side when a yacht is suddenly thrown on its beam ends and damage is caused by pressure.

Storm windows must be designed for quick and easy installation under difficult conditions. On one occasion when I felt it prudent to put on my storm windows it took me nearly an hour to do so. I had to work by crawling along a rolling deck while wearing foul-weather gear and a safety harness.

Storm windows or covers can be made of wood or heavy acrylic or polycarbonate. A clear material is preferable because it permits more light below. The interior of a boat is gloomy enough in a storm, and windows will probably be your main method of maintaining a watch under storm conditions.

Figure 9.14
Storm window covers.

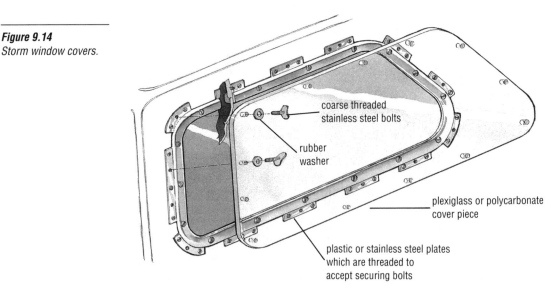

coarse threaded
stainless steel bolts

rubber
washer

plexiglass or polycarbonate
cover piece

plastic or stainless steel plates
which are threaded to
accept securing bolts

On-Deck Storage

A tender stowed on deck must be tied down securely and may require chocks to hold it in place. Most yachts have wooden handholds on the cabintop, but they were not designed to be used as tiedowns. A better option is to install through-bolted padeyes with backing plates. On a long passage the security of the tender should be checked and lines tightened as necessary.

Liferaft storage should be on deck, not somewhere down below in a locker. The chances of having to use a liferaft are extremely unlikely, but if one is needed, the need will be immediate. Nearly every account of a yacht sinking due to striking or being struck by some object tells of the boat going down in an extremely short time. In *The Sailor's Handbook*, edited by Halsey C. Herreshoff, a graph shows that a 30-foot (9 m) yacht with a two-square-inch (13 cm²) hole in its hull could sink in three minutes, and one with a 14-square-inch (90 cm²) hole could go down in five seconds. Such facts of life suggest the value of having the raft readily available and easy to launch. Some yachts carry the liferaft on the cabin top and some have it in the cockpit. Either way it must be tied down securely – and in such a way that it can be quickly deployed. On *Denali* the raft is stowed in front of the mast and held in place by half-inch line and quick release knots.

Most cruising sailors would prefer to keep the decks as clear and uncluttered as possible. However, after cruising for a while, more and more gear ends up on deck. This includes water and fuel containers, bicycles, sailboards, boathooks, mops, outboard engines, and an incredible variety of gear. The best advice is to tie everything down securely and be ever-watchful for the possibility of chafe on sails or sheets. Try to keep the weight as low as possible.

My fuel tank only holds about 20 gallons (75 l). To supplement this I often carry six five-gallon jerry cans on a long passage; three on each side at the base of the shrouds. They are carefully tied down at the beginning of a cruise, but invariably they work loose under hard going and need to be checked frequently.

Some gear, such as winch handles at the mast or an emergency knife for cutting the lashings on the liferaft will need to be stored where they are needed. It is possible to buy rubber or plastic holders that can be secured to the mast or wherever needed, or you can make your own from PVC pipe.

As you arrange and improve your deck, think about safety, convenience, trim, strength, and water-tight integrity. When buying new fittings and equipment, select the best and strongest you can afford. Take the time to install everything in such a way as to prevent leaks. Storms are the exception rather than the rule, but when they do occur you will want to be able to securely 'button up' your boat for maximum safety and comfort.

10 COCKPIT ARRANGEMENT

Of all the 'people space' on a yacht the cockpit is the most important. No other part of the boat is more frequently occupied at sea and in port. Underway the watchstander or person on the helm will spend countless hours here in every imaginable kind of weather and sea condition. In port the cockpit is the gathering place; from time to time it functions as work area, living room, dining room, and sometimes bedroom and shower.

Cockpit arrangement deserves careful thought and planning for the comfort and safety of the crew. When building your own yacht or having one built for you, take the opportunity to design a well-thought-out cockpit. When shopping for a new or used boat, consider the size and arrangement of the cockpit before making a final decision. If you already have a boat you will surely want to make some changes to the existing layout before going offshore.

Size

Because the cockpit is so important and has so many functions the first assumption might be that it should be large and spacious. However, for an ocean-going yacht a small cockpit is preferable. The reason is simple: a small cockpit holds less water than a large one. If and when the boat is pooped by a wave, the water in the cockpit adversely affects stability by adding tremendous weight to the after part of the yacht. The smaller the cockpit, the less water and weight will be added to the boat when pooped and the faster the boat will be able to recover.

Suddenly finding yourself in a completely flooded cockpit is an awe-inspiring ordeal you will not soon forget. Terrifying as this experience is, it should not be as dangerous as it seems if ... There are many 'ifs' here. *If* your yacht is solidly built, well-designed and not already overloaded. *If* the companionway hatchboards are in place. *If* it is a one-time occurrence. *If* you have adequate cockpit drains.

When a wave fills the cockpit most of the water is rolled out very quickly, but much still remains in the footwell. This water can only escape through the cockpit drains. If they are undersized or clogged it will take too long when minutes are important. Companionway hatchboards locked in place will keep most of the water out of the cabin. But if the companionway is open a lot of water will get below, and until it is pumped out (which under the circumstances may take some time) it continues to lower your freeboard. The combination of water in the cabin and a large, poorly draining cockpit can put the yacht in jeopardy and make it vulnerable to additional boarding by waves. Subsequent waves may subject the deckhouse and superstructure

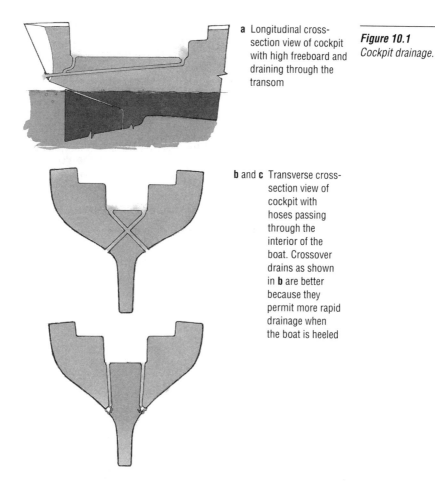

a Longitudinal cross-section view of cockpit with high freeboard and draining through the transom

Figure 10.1
Cockpit drainage.

b and **c** Transverse cross-section view of cockpit with hoses passing through the interior of the boat. Crossover drains as shown in **b** are better because they permit more rapid drainage when the boat is heeled

to damage and bring injury to the crew.

It is worthwhile to determine how much water your cockpit can hold and how fast it will drain. At some convenient time when dockside, plug the cockpit drains and fill a convenient fraction of the footwell with fresh water. Then pull the plugs and see how long it takes to drain. (If you make this test take into consideration engine controls and other fittings that may be located in the footwell. Be sure they are watertight.) From this information you can calculate the approximate amount of time for the whole cockpit to empty. If it is more than five minutes it is too long. Chances are you will not be happy with the results. William Van Dorn in his book *Oceanography and Seamanship* says that cockpit volume should not be more than four cubic feet for each ton of displacement. Note also that the drain test is made under ideal conditions. When sailing you cannot expect the water to exit as quickly. Some cockpits have straight rather than crossover drain lines. Consequently when the boat is heeled the more deeply submerged drainhole will cause the cockpit to drain more slowly than in the dockside experiment.

On some yachts the cockpit drains should definitely be increased in size for offshore sailing. More recently built yachts have sufficiently high freeboard so that cockpit drains lead aft through the transom and can be enlarged to permit rapid draining. On older boats the drains commonly run inside of the hull to through-hull valves below the waterline. *Denali* is in this category and her cockpit is also too large. To improve the drainage of the cockpit I added two drains to the existing two. A lot of people would object to this, as it adds two more holes in the hull. But the few times I have been pooped I was glad to have the extra drains.

If your cockpit is too large the drains can be increased in size and in number. It may also be possible to reduce the volume of the cockpit by glassing in closed-cell foam blocks, adding water-tight lockers, or raising the level of the footwell.

Cockpits can also be too small. A few yacht designers, notably those who create bulletproof double-enders, have sometimes carried the small-cockpit ethos to its ridiculous conclusion and made cockpits so tiny that even a small dog would have trouble trying to turn around. As a result the cockpit is uncomfortable at sea and too small for any purpose in port. I believe that on a boat between 30 and 40 feet (9 to 12 m) long four adults should be able to sit comfortably in a cockpit, and the benches should be long enough for an adult to lie down.

Layout and Equipment

Tillers and Wheels

The most serious business of the cockpit is steering and line tending. Whether you have a wheel or tiller and where it is located will dictate how the other equipment is arranged. The decision as to wheel or tiller is one of personal choice. On boats up to 40 or sometimes even 45 feet a tiller is manageable. On larger yachts a wheel is more convenient. I prefer a tiller if possible because it is the simplest method of steering. The tiller attaches directly to the rudder stock and there is little that can go wrong. A wheel adds one more item of equipment to be maintained, adjusted, and repaired, and it is an expensive piece of equipment to begin with. Some object to a tiller because it takes up too much space. That of course depends on the size of the cockpit and where the rudder shaft is located. The same objection can be made about a wheel and pedestal on some yachts. Most tillers are hinged so that in port they can be lifted up out of the way, thereby increasing room in the cockpit. Wheels however are usually fixed in place and pedestals certainly are.

The placement of a tiller or wheel affects cockpit safety. I have seen yachts on which the wheel is so large and poorly located that it is difficult for anyone to move around it from the steering position to the forward part of the cockpit under calm conditions, and it cannot possibly be done in a safe manner under heavy going. These are the so-called T-shaped cockpits that seem to be so popular lately, with the cross bar of the 'T' filled by the oversized wheel. I assume these huge wheels help the owner imagine his mini is a maxi. My objection to them is that when singlehanding it is difficult or impossible for the helmsman to steer and tend the sheets at the same time. It seems obvious to me that the 'T' cockpit is for sailing with a crew only.

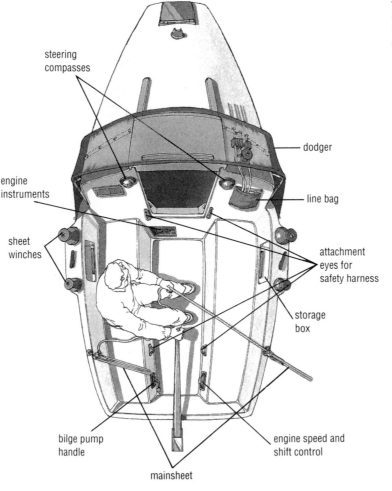

steering compasses

engine instruments

sheet winches

dodger

line bag

attachment eyes for safety harness

storage box

bilge pump handle

engine speed and shift control

mainsheet

Figure 10.2
Cockpit layout for an offshore boat.

Offshore, one person should be able to tack or jibe the boat without assistance. This is important even if you are sailing with a crew of three or more. It is inconvenient to have to call for assistance for every tack, and sometimes there isn't time to have someone help you. To make the cockpit more convenient it may be necessary to relocate sheet leads and winches or to change the sheeting method and position of the mainsheet. Large self-tailing winches add a lot of convenience.

You can be very innovative in how you arrange a cockpit. There is no right or wrong way; only the way that is best for you and your crew. If you have a tiller and want a wheel or vice versa it is possible to make the change. Also there are other kinds of wheels than the pedestal-mounted type. The Edson Company, the major manufacturer of wheel steering equipment, offers several options. One that is especially good is a wheel connected to a rack and pinion. It takes up little space by using direct gearing to the rudder-head and thereby eliminates pulleys, cables, and chains. For the singlehander a tiller is usually easier to use because the helmsman can stand in one place with the tiller between his legs and have his hands free to work the jib sheet winches and the mainsheet.

Figure 10.3
Rack and pinion wheel steering.

Before making major modifications to the cockpit, mount the gear you will be using for wind vane and autopilot and see how it affects the arrangement. Lines leading from the wind vane use up a lot of cockpit space on some boats.

Radar

A radar screen should be mounted in such a way that it can be seen by the person steering. On most sailboats the radar screen is mounted inside the main cabin in order to keep it away from spray and rain – a good idea. If thoughtfully located it can be seen from the helm and still remain out of the weather. Except in pea soup fog the radar is used only as a reference, and the ability to look at the screen should not be sacrificed at the expense of the person on watch being able to maintain a 360-degree view of the horizon. In that sense a radar screen is like a compass and only needs to be glanced at from time to time.

Bilge Pump

A high-capacity hand-operated diaphragm bilge pump connected to the main bilge of the yacht should be operable from the cockpit in such a way that the helmsman can pump the bilge while steering and without needing to open any cockpit lockers. (A discussion of bilge pumps appears in Chapter 13.)

Cockpit Lockers

Cockpit lockers are probably one of the most poorly designed features on production yachts. Often they will leak under heavy going and permit a significant amount of water to enter the boat. For this reason some offshore sailors refuse to have cockpit lockers. If possible the best arrangement is to have only one, and have it bulkheaded and sealed off from the rest of the yacht. We are victims of designers and builders who assume that only a small percentage of their customers will take their boats into rough offshore conditions. They save the production cost of installing locker bulkheads and seals, and at the same time advertise vast 'stowage volume'.

Unless you have sailed your boat in some really heavy going, assume your cockpit lockers will leak to start with and try to improve on their design. This is especially important on modern fiberglass cruiser-racers which, in addition to leaking lockers, often have very small bilges – a bad combination. In a likely scenario you're sailing offshore and unexpectedly get into some heavy weather. Soon spray is flying everywhere and occasionally several gallons of water drop in the cockpit. Eventually you get everything shipshape and even though it is heavy going you have a good feeling that your boat is properly trimmed and set up for the prevailing conditions. At this point you go below to change into some dry clothing or make a cup of coffee. Entering the cabin you find several inches (or centimeters if you happen to be sailing in metric conditions) of water sloshing around inside the boat. The first reaction is, 'My God, we're sinking'!

A few minutes of frantic pumping relieves your anxiety as the water in the cabin recedes and you can relax. Still a bit wild-eyed you wonder where all that water came from and start looking around. The stern tube packing gland is OK, all the through-hull hose connections are secure, the forward hatch is tight, the mast collar is dry, and none of the windows are leaking. The bilge water tastes salty, so it can't be a leaky freshwater tank. The deck-hull seam appears to be in good condition. What is the source of all that water? Eventually you realize it is a combination of leaking cockpit lockers and a bilge that is too small; both of which are 'standard equipment' on many fiberglass boats.

You can't do much about the size of a boat's bilge but you can improve the lockers. Perhaps they can be sealed off in the cockpit and access gained to the stowage space from inside the boat. If this is difficult or impossible to achieve due to the design of the boat, it may be possible to isolate the lockers from the rest of the boat with bulkheads and to build in one-way drains. The easiest and most common approach is to improve the seat drains by making them larger, put better gaskets around the edges of the lockers, install strong lid hinges, and add heavy-duty closures that hold the lids down with a pressure fit.

No one likes to think about worst-case scenarios, but it is the best way to approach the cockpit locker problem. This is exactly what happened recently when a new boat being sailed to a New England boat show got into some heavy weather. During a knockdown a cockpit locker that lacked a hasp or gasket flew open and water poured into the bilge and cabin. The boat was lost but the lucky crew was saved by a U.S. Coast Guard search and rescue team.

Visibility from the Cockpit

Visibility from the cockpit when steering and when on watch is both a comfort and a safety consideration. When hand-steering you must have visibility in all directions, even if this means standing up. When motoring it should also be possible to reach the engine controls, keep an eye on the engine instruments, and be able to glance at the compass.

A dodger (or spray hood) across the front of the cockpit or a tender stowed on deck aft of the mast will restrict visibility. Sitting well aft in the cockpit permits the best view, but this is often difficult or uncomfortable because of rain and spray. The ability to look forward also depends on the type of rig and what sails are flying. If the cockpit seat backrests have a reasonable outboard slant to them it is usually possible to see comfortably around the dodger.

There is bound to be a trade-off somewhere in trying to achieve a balance between comfort, safety, and good visibility in a cockpit. It is unlikely that you will always be able to stay warm and dry and still have a good view of the whole horizon from the cockpit of a small cruising boat. I prefer to sit under the dodger and get up and look around once in a while than to be wet or cold. In shipping lanes or when near land there may be no other choice than to stand up most of the time or sit far enough aft to have a good view. At such times you will be happy if you are not a singlehander and there is someone to share the watchkeeping.

Comfort

Comfort should be a major aim. Most shorthanded offshore crews use some sort of automatic steering device. As wonderful as these self-steerers are, they are not foolproof and the time could come when you will be forced to hand-steer for many days. Under the best of conditions this is tiresome, but if the seating is uncomfortable the person at the helm will be easily fatigued and do a poor job.

Cockpit seating should provide good back support and the ability to brace your legs when the yacht is heeled. Bear in mind that what is comfortable for someone six feet (1.82 m) tall may not be comfortable for someone shorter. When you are sitting to windward the leeward seat is commonly used for foot support. The usual distance between the seats is about 26 inches (65 cm). If the distance is too little or too much it will be tiring. The inside cockpit coamings should be high enough to support the lower and middle back, and should slope outboard about 15 degrees. The 'comfort number' for the width of cockpit seating is 16 to 18 inches (40 to 45 cm). On boats designed for racing the backrest is often low or even nonexistent. It would be sheer torture to make a passage in a cockpit designed this way. If you go long-distance cruising

Figure 10.4
Cockpit comfort and safety. In choosing a cockpit be sure it offers comfortable support for your back and adequate distance to brace your legs when the boat is heeled.

you will be 'wearing' the cockpit for long periods of time under a wide variety of conditions. It is possible to make comfort modifications to a cockpit, but expensive. Take the time to 'try on' the cockpit before you buy a boat.

Being dry is an important part of cockpit comfort. In addition to a dodger, weather cloths can help protect the cockpit crew from rain, spray and waves. These cloth panels are secured to the lifelines along the cockpit sides; they not only reduce the amount of spray that enters the cockpit at sea, but add privacy at anchor. Before installing weather cloths consider the location of sheet leads and the amount of room needed for winch operation. Also consider how they will affect boarding the boat from a dinghy.

It is important that the cockpit benches remain as dry as possible. This can be achieved with adequate seat drains and by having wood slats on the benches. Sitting for very long on wood slats will soon give 'bottom fatigue' that can be alleviated with individual cushions. Some people claim that cushions are dangerous because they can slip out from under foot when someone is leaving or entering the cockpit. That is true, but the need for comfort justifies their careful use. On *Denali* I have large closed-cell cushions about one and a half inch (4 cm) thick. Under really heavy going they are a nuisance because they tend to slip down into the footwell. But the rest of the time they are quite comfortable and it is convenient to stretch out and lie down on them when not on watch, and to sleep on them at night in the tropics. Teak grating in the footwell will help to keep feet dry when sailing. The grating should not interfere with drainage, and should never be varnished or it will be too slippery to walk on.

Another aspect of comfort is neatness. Sheets and halyards trailing all over the cockpit are uncomfortable and dangerous. If you have a lot of lines to contend with, make up canvas pockets for holding the tails and attach them in the cockpit and footwell.

It is convenient to have some sort of easily accessible storage area in the cockpit which can be used without opening a locker. A variety of things are nice to have readily at hand – winch handles, short pieces of line, mainsail ties or gaskets, sponges, a scrub brush, or some fishing tackle, to name a few. On yachts with wide coamings open boxes can be built in, but be sure they have some sort of drain.

It is not a good idea to keep binoculars, hand-bearing compasses, and flashlights in the cockpit at sea, but they should be handy to the crew on watch. It is usually possible to locate some small boxes for this gear just inside the companionway.

Safety

The least comfortable thing of all is falling or being swept out of the cockpit. Any offshore cockpit should have strong padeyes for attaching safety harnesses. Like stanchions and cleats, these fittings need through-bolts and strong backing plates. To decide where safety harness attachment points are needed, put on your bulkiest of foul-weather clothing and safety harness and simulate steering, working the winches, pumping bilges, and so forth. Make sure you can move aft in the cockpit in the event you need to work on the wind steering vane, release the man-overboard equipment, or stream a drogue. One clip-on point should be installed just outside the companionway so that someone coming on deck can hook on before entering the cockpit. When locating this fitting keep in mind that at some time one or all of the hatchboards may be installed in the companionway hatch when the crew enters the cockpit.

In summary, arrange the cockpit to make it seaworthy, safe, and comfortable for you and your crew. So much time is spent here under all types of conditions that safety and comfort are prime considerations. Once you have it the way it seems best, take a test cruise for a few days and make additional changes as necessary.

CABIN ARRANGEMENT

Safety, convenience, and comfort are the principal considerations for organizing and arranging the main cabin. It is difficult to relax and be comfortable in an unsafe or inconvenient position when sleeping, cooking, navigating, or just sitting. Likewise, if getting in and out of a bunk or working in the galley is inconvenient it will most likely be unsafe and uncomfortable.

We usually seek the impossible when trying to improve the layout of a cruising home. There are so few options. The desire is to have a place where one, two, or more people can live in reasonable comfort and have a kitchen, living room, bedroom, toilet, shower (sometimes), and a place to store clothing, food, books, tools, and plenty of specialized gear. It's a lot to ask.

General Considerations

First a few words of reassurance. No matter how small or big your boat is, be assured that after a few months of cruising you will wish you had more room. The larger the boat, the more convenient and comfortable it will or should be. But many people have made successful and enjoyable sustained cruises and circumnavigations in yachts less than 30 feet in length. Lin and Larry Pardey have written several excellent books on their worldwide cruising. Their first 11-year circumnavigation was made in a 24-foot cutter without an engine. Remember, also, that even though the smaller yacht is less spacious, it will also cost less and be easier to maintain.

It is one thing to put up with an inconvenient layout for an overnight trip, a weekend, or even for a few weeks of cruising. But if this will be your home every day for months or years it is quite another thing. Bunks that are too short or narrow will not be comfortable. If the height of the countertop or stove or chart table is too low, food preparation and navigation duties will be drudgery. It should be possible to sit comfortably in the cabin when off watch, or in port, relaxing, reading, or listening to music.

Singlehanders can be as eccentric or unconventional as they wish, but once there are two or more people on board it is necessary to consider the need for individual space. One person should be able to move about without constantly bumping into another. It is difficult to appreciate the significance of this while comfortably sitting in your home, but it will become apparent when you must remain on board for two or three days waiting for a rainy tropical depression to pass.

Figure 11.1
Typical main cabin layout.

Safety

After sailing aboard *Denali* for several months and beginning to feel as if I was living in a short tunnel, I visited a beamy, heavy-displacement cruising yacht the same length as my boat. When I went below there was so much room it felt like a stadium. 'Ah', I thought, 'how nice to have so much space.' But, once over the initial surprise, I had a vague feeling that something wasn't quite right. Then I realized there was too much space. Moving around in that large cabin required several steps without the possibility of a handhold.

On any boat there will be times when the motion is violent and unpredictable. Underway, you quickly learn to always hold on to or be braced against something. Being suddenly hurled across the cabin is an invitation to injury; the wider the space, the greater the chance of being injured. Even on my boat. with a width between cabinets in the main cabin of only 6½ feet (195 cm), I was once momentarily knocked unconscious when the boat took a sudden roll and I went flying into a bulkhead.

Convenient handholds should be any place where someone might be standing up. This is usually achieved by having overhead handrails running the length of the cabin, port and starboard. There should also be handholds on each side of the companionway for entering and exiting the cabin, and they should be large enough to be grasped while wearing heavy gloves. Extra handholds may be needed in the galley and at the chart table; even if the chart table has a seat you will often work there standing up. Underway the cook is always braced to maintain balance, and also needs something to hold on to. Commonly there is a vertical pole incorporated into the half bulkhead that separates the galley from the rest of the cabin. A lot of cooking is done with one hand holding a handrail. There should also be handholds in the head compartment to be used when sitting or standing.

It should be possible to sit comfortably in the main cabin under any sailing condition, with the body supported and braced if there is much motion. All table, desk, and projecting cabinet corners should be rounded. The height of counters needs to be sufficient to give support at the hip. A surface just below knee height is especially dangerous.

When installing clocks, barometers, lights or decorations, have safety in mind. Locate them away from places where someone might be standing, sitting, or leaning. Consider what it would be like to fall against them. On yachts with opening ports, the dogging latches are especially dangerous because they are often at head or eye level. Underway they should be covered with foam rubber.

Large mirrors and pictures with glass frames are better left ashore. Small mirrors with plastic frames are a better choice and even these should be hung on the inside of cabinet doors. For pictures use clear acrylic instead of glass.

Burning or scalding from cooking accidents is a constant concern on the offshore yacht. In addition to being extremely painful, a burn may be slow to heal on a boat where it is difficult to keep dry. It is often recommended that the cook wear a safety belt or some sort of harness while working in the galley. This is a matter of preference. A harness gives protection from falling against or away from the stove, but it also limits your ability to move quickly out of the way. If you decide to use a galley belt (which is not really a belt but a thick strap to lean against), it should be made of strong nylon webbing and well-padded in the middle. All material should be triple-stitched, and the belt should be attached to strong padeyes in the galley area.

In bouncy conditions I recommend that the cook should wear heavy, bib-type foul-weather gear trousers. The full-length PVC aprons worn by workers in fish markets would also be excellent. Further, in rough seas the cook should be wearing shoes.

Slippery cabin soles are a menace. In rough seas, or on rainy days, there is usually some water that gets below. The cabin sole needs to be finished to protect the wood, but choose a varnish that does not produce a high-gloss slippery surface. Most people don't want non-skid decks below because they are uncomfortable for bare feet. Having a carpet sounds nice, but once it gets wet it will be difficult to dry and to keep dry. Salt crystals are hygroscopic and salt in the fabric will keep it damp and make the cabin smell like a wet sheepdog.

It is essential that the steps on the companionway ladder have a non-skid surface. After years of replacing non-skid strips on my companionway ladder, I finally got some heavy-duty exterior deck tread, as is used on steel decks, and installed it with epoxy glue. It looks better, gives much better footing, and appears as if it will last forever.

Fire extinguishers need to be located in at least three places on a boat with a standard layout – one in the galley, another in the forward part of the boat, and one in a cockpit locker. The greatest risk of fire is in the galley, and so it should be possible to grab an extinguisher and fight the fire from forward or aft.

Drawers, and the doors of lockers and cabinets, always appear safe when you are sitting peacefully in a marina. Offshore, with a bit of a sea running, it may be different, and you may think there is a poltergeist on your boat as cabinet doors mysteriously swing open and their contents are dumped out, or drawers slide open at unexpected and usually inconvenient times. Instead of, or maybe in addition to ghosts, there are some other forces at work. If a yacht is beating to windward and happens to fall off a wave crest and heel at the same time it is not so difficult for a drawer, even with a proper notch, to jump open. Invariably it is a drawer that holds about 87 small items – great fun to pick up and re-stow with the boat heeled.

Cabinets and lockers with finger locks are designed to be opened by poking your finger through a hole and depressing a spring-loaded trigger (elbow door catches). The trigger can also be released if some item in the cabinet comes adrift. Similarly, it is possible for loose gear to jam the lock so it is impossible to open the cabinet. I recommend replacing internal spring latches with external latches where possible, and adding a second external latching mechanism so that if one is broken or damaged the locker can still be used. I use slide-lock closures and also a simple key lock.

Most of the foregoing suggestions have to do with avoiding personal injury. On a long passage you will be a long way from medical help. A serious injury that disables a crewmember adds anxiety and increases the work load for the rest of the crew.

Figure 11.2
Drawers and cabinet doors.

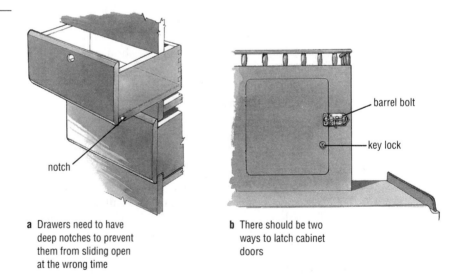

notch

barrel bolt

key lock

a Drawers need to have deep notches to prevent them from sliding open at the wrong time

b There should be two ways to latch cabinet doors

Interior Layout

The interior arrangement of most yachts between 30 and 40 feet or so is depressingly similar. But there are some practical reasons for this. The midships section of a boat is the most comfortable area on board. Spend one or two nights trying to sleep in the forward cabin while beating to windward and you will probably choose American Airlines for your next vacation and golf as a new hobby. Galleys located anywhere but aft on medium-displacement yachts are miserable to try and cook in. Engines do a better job of propelling the boat when they are located aft.

On yachts over 40 feet, and maybe on smaller ones if you are building or buying a custom boat, the opportunity exists for more creative and personalized arrangements. Some designs offer two or more interior layout options. But if you already have a boat, or if you buy a used one, it will be easier to learn to live with things pretty much the way they are than to undertake a major rearrangement. This is especially true of a production boat in which the interior 'pan' and accommodations play a large role in the structural integrity of the boat. Still, there are a variety of small changes that can be made in the main cabin to make it more comfortable, convenient, and personalized.

Galley

On some older boats the galley was forward, even on relatively small boats. This layout usually harks back to the days of the paid cook. The poor soul had to prepare meals under difficult and cramped conditions so that the owners could have a larger main cabin. Perhaps it wasn't too bad because many of those kindly old cruising yachts had a gentle sea motion most of the time. On modern, medium-displacement boats, cooking forward would be a feat of endurance and survival. Most crews would end up living on instant soups and crackers, if they were lucky.

These days the cook is usually part of the family crew and prefers to be near the cockpit, where the boat's motion is easier, communication is better, and there is more fresh air. Often the cook has a few other jobs as well, such as captain, navigator, deck hand and engineer. Cooking is sometimes combined with watchstanding, meals are often eaten in the

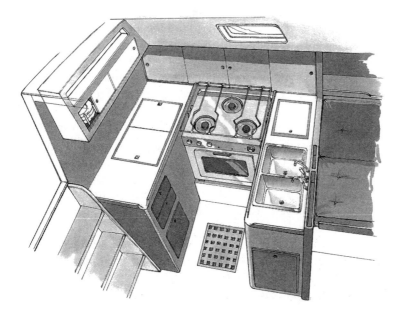

Figure 11.3
A convenient galley arrangement.

cockpit, and a galley adjacent to the companionway ladder makes it all easier.

A typical layout has the galley immediately to port or starboard upon entering the main cabin. Traditionally it is located to port, for an interesting reason: A sailing yacht on starboard tack has right-of-way over most other vessels, and in theory should not have to worry about tacking. Therefore, if the boat is sailing or hove-to on the starboard tack, the galley is on the low side, where it is supposedly easier to cook. Few people today take that into consideration, but it still remains valid – in theory. If you want to try testing your right-of-way sometime, choose your traffic carefully. I would not advise selecting a supertanker or a Panamanian freighter.

Compared to a home kitchen, the boat's galley represents a major sacrifice in space. However, the galley can be made into a highly efficient area, where the cook can stand in one place and do everything. After living on a boat for a few months you may wonder why you needed so much kitchen space when living on land.

Sinks

If space permits, it is convenient to have a double sink, and the deeper the better. How deep will depend on your waterline when sailing. If the sink stays half full of seawater on one tack or the other, it will be of use only half of the time. The closer the sink is to the centerline, the easier it will drain on either tack.

There should be a pump for fresh water from the boat's tanks and one for salt water from the ocean. Few yachts come with a salt-water line installed, so it will be necessary to add a through-hull fitting or a T-connection at the engine cooling-water intake valve. Seawater, of course, can be obtained by putting a bucket over the side, but as a routine procedure this is inconvenient, and if done in a careless way, dangerous. With salt water easily available at the sink the crew will get into the habit of using it for washing dishes.

Some yachts have pressure-water systems installed in the galley. You may find this a convenience, but it is not a necessity. In addition to being an added expense and another maintenance item, pressure-water systems make it easy to waste water. A foot or hand pump at the sink is easy to use, and the fact that it must be pumped encourages people to only use what they need.

Choose galley pumps carefully. Most of those put on production boats will die an early death when used constantly. Finspray made by White Star of New Zealand are excellent hand pumps. They are double-acting, so that water comes on both the up and downstroke. The fresh- and salt-water pumps in my galley are Finsprays, and they have been in almost daily use for ten years with only routine maintenance.

Stoves

An adequate and reliable stove is a high-priority item for cruising. Appetizing, nutritious hot food is a health and morale factor. It is also a safety factor. Under the most difficult conditions a hot meal will

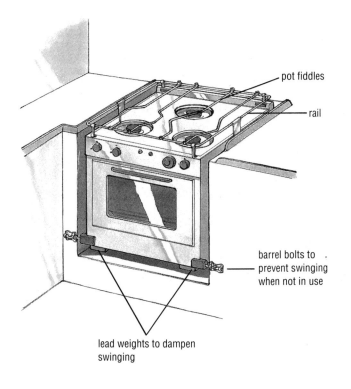

pot fiddles

rail

barrel bolts to
prevent swinging
when not in use

lead weights to dampen
swinging

Figure 11.4
*Galley cooking stove.
Stove should be
gimballed for use when
cooking but it should
also have locks to
prevent it from swinging
in heavy going. A rail
and pot fiddles should
be installed on the
burner plate. Gimballing
on some stoves is
improved by installing
lead weights under the
oven.*

improve your physical and mental ability. Some sailors are satisfied with a two-burner stove, but an oven is an added benefit. Baking bread and pastries is easy, and an oven permits a more varied menu.

Stoves on offshore yachts should be gimballed to operate safely. An un-gimballed stove will be difficult and dangerous to use at sea. Most gimballed stoves are installed on a fore-and-aft axis to allow for heel. This is a tradition but not a necessity. An athwartship stove is also possible but it will require a special gimballing device such as that manufactured by Paul Luke, so the stove can swing to accommodate pitching as well as heel.

A gimballed stove needs to swing freely, but not wildly. Sometimes ballast must be added. Diving weights attached underneath the oven work well. When the stove is not in use, hooks or a barrel bolt can be added to hold it in place. A rail should be installed all the way around the burner plate to keep pots from sliding off the stove. Pot-holder clamps which attach to the rail make cooking safer in rough seas.

It is surprising that something so basic as a stove should be so expensive, but yacht stoves are always high-priced. Enamel-finish stoves look nice when they are new, but soon show signs of rust. If possible choose a stainless steel stove.

Get some opinions from experienced cruisers before buying a new stove. This is especially important with LP gas stoves because they are fairly complex mechanically if they have automatic lighters and burners that shut off if the flame goes out accidentally. Of all the day-to-day equipment on a yacht, the stove is one of the highest-use items. A poor stove will add a lot of frustration to sailing. Some of the brands highly regarded by cruising sailors are Dickenson, Mariner, and Force 10.

Fuels used for boat cooking include alcohol, kerosene, diesel fuel, LP gas, and compressed natural gas. Alcohol is considered safe by some people because an alcohol fire can be put out with water. While this is true, alcohol has a low flame point, and if it somehow escapes from the stove and ignites it can flow easily and make an accidental fire very difficult to extinguish. Cooking with alcohol is slow. Whereas alcohol used to be low in price it is now expensive and often difficult to find. If you have an alcohol stove it can be converted to kerosene or gas by purchasing new burners. Having had experience with two onboard alcohol fires, I strongly recommend this conversion.

Kerosene has its share of advantages and disadvantages. It is the traditional cooking and heating fuel of cruising boats. The advantages of kerosene are safety, cost, and availability. Any type of fuel must be treated with care both in storage and use, but the high flame point of kerosene makes it difficult to ignite accidentally unless it is pressurized, preheated, or has a wick. Accidental fires seldom occur with kerosene and explosions are nearly impossible. Leaking burners, however, can lead to boat fires, so any leaks in the system should be repaired immediately. A lighted stove should not be left unattended.

Compared to other cooking fuels kerosene is usually cheaper. It is available everywhere in the world and is sometimes easier to find in remote and undeveloped countries than in industrialized countries. It is often cheaper to buy from a bulk dealer if you take your own containers.

Unfortunately, kerosene is a dirty fuel. Its use will require more frequent cleaning and painting of the cabin interior. This is true even with high-quality, clean fuel, and much worse if it is of poor quality and contaminated. Burners become clogged and operate poorly with contaminated fuel. Kerosene is supposed to be the hottest burning, most efficient, and economical fuel, but in fact it seldom performs as well on a boat as it does in a testing laboratory.

Most kerosene stoves use a pressure tank and burners must be preheated before lighting. The typical burner has a small cup built into the base to hold alcohol for preheating. This can be a messy and difficult job on a bouncing boat. An alternative is a small wick cup which is filled with alcohol and clamps around the burner base. A more efficient technique, and one recommended by Taylor, a boat stove builder in England, is to preheat the burner with a small gas blowtorch that uses a disposable propane or butane canister.

For years I had a kerosene stove and oven because I believed the traditional brouhaha about the dangers of LP gas and the economy and availability of kerosene; none of which are necessarily true today. I suspect this creed was initiated by Noah or Columbus, or some other big name, and has since been handed down from father to son as part of the oral tradition of sailing. But the happiest day of my sailing life was when I changed from kerosene to LP gas. No longer was it necessary to preheat the burners, pump up the pressure tank, inhale kerosene fumes, or repair pesky burners. With LP gas, cooking is a lot easier, the overhead in the main cabin is white again instead of smog brown, and the boat no longer smells like a fuel barge.

Propane, and sometimes butane, are the two types of LPG used on yachts. They are dangerous to use because they are heavier than air and, if accidentally ignited in a closed space like the bilge, can cause a violent explosion. On the other hand, LPG is wonderfully convenient and these days is available in all but the most remote parts of the world. Probably most cruising yachts now use LPG for cooking.

Compressed natural gas is now used on some boats in North America. It is safer than LPG because it is lighter than air. However, it is expensive and often difficult to find, even in the U.S.A. It is not practical for boats going abroad.

Stoves using diesel oil are sometimes found on boats sailing in the high latitudes. They are excellent for heating as well as cooking, but are too hot for use in the tropics. They are also heavy and require a flue and sometimes a blower. Electric cooking is possible, but requires a power supply that cannot be satisfied without an auxiliary generator. Microwave ovens are beginning to appear on some boats and will probably become more popular in the future. Coal and wood are no longer used for cooking on small boats, but are still in use for fueling small cabin heaters.

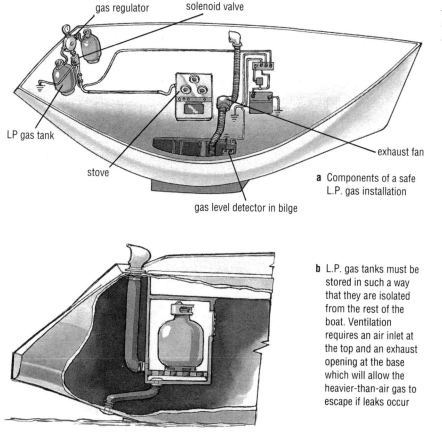

gas regulator   solenoid valve

LP gas tank

stove

gas level detector in bilge

exhaust fan

Figure 11.5
L.P. gas system.

a Components of a safe L.P. gas installation

b L.P. gas tanks must be stored in such a way that they are isolated from the rest of the boat. Ventilation requires an air inlet at the top and an exhaust opening at the base which will allow the heavier-than-air gas to escape if leaks occur

Refrigeration

The thought of trying to 'survive' without refrigeration, or at least an icebox, probably sounds impossible, but life on board really can be maintained without it. Less than 50 percent of cruising boats have refrigeration, and far more people in the world live their lives without refrigeration than with it. Many kinds of food can be kept aboard for long periods of time without refrigeration if properly stored.

Before spending money on refrigeration, try to determine if the existing icebox on your boat is adequately insulated. A lot of them are not, and trying to improve on a box already installed is a major project. Adding refrigeration to a poorly insulated ice box will have you and your batteries in a nervous state of exhaustion. Invariably, the engine will have to be operated one or more hours each day, and few cruising boats can afford to carry enough fuel to justify so much engine time. At an anchorage you will become unpopular in a hurry if yours is the noisy boat that is always running its engine.

If you can satisfy your refrigerator with solar power it is a viable option. A couple of years ago in a fit of uncontrolled affluence, spawned by a newly acquired credit card, I surrendered to a desire for an occasional equatorial cold beer and bought a 12-volt DC portable refrigerator. I have been quite pleased with it. In the low latitudes the solar panels can more than keep up with the power demands.

Ice is readily available in some places, especially fishing harbors, but it is a nuisance to haul around, and it has a finite life at sea. Elsewhere, it may be difficult to find, except in the form of expensive small bags of ice cubes that don't last long.

If you do decide to have permanent refrigeration, buy the best quality equipment, have it installed by a boat refrigeration expert, and then learn how to maintain and repair the system. If you plan to sail to remote places there will be no one to help you and no spare parts available. The claim that carrying a large supply of frozen foods will save money, if true, also means that the loss of a freezer full of food due to faulty equipment will be a costly loss.

An LPG refrigerator system warrants consideration. There are no moving parts and it does not require electricity. It has been designed and developed in America for recreational vehicles and is readily available, relatively cheap, compact, and self-contained; it comes with its own insulation, which saves having to build in an insulated box on your boat.

The dangers of LPG for stoves also apply to refrigeration. Some people object to having an LPG flame burning constantly on their boat at sea but are willing to risk it in port. Considering the ratio of sea time to anchor time for most sailors, it is reasonable to consider a gas refrigerator for use only in port.

Chart Desk

It is probably heresy to suggest it, but I doubt that 'navigation stations' are even needed on most boats. Convenient, yes, but necessary, no. The maxim that 'form ever follows function' should apply. On a large yacht with ample space, a chart desk and all of its associated amenities are fine. However if having a navigation station means giving up or reducing space for sitting and relaxing, sleeping, or storage, it is worth considering alternatives.

In my experience most chart work is done standing up. Electronic navigation equipment should be situated so it is easy to see, but these days it is all direct readout and it isn't necessary to sit down to use it. Likewise radios, which are used infrequently, hardly require an office for their use. It is convenient to sit down to work out a celestial fix but it isn't necessary to sit at a chart desk.

On a small yacht space is at a premium. It is realistic and indeed necessary for areas to have shared functions. A chart can be laid out on the main cabin table instead of on a chart desk that remains unused most of the time. The top of a storage area such as an icebox or refrigerator can also serve as a chart desk.

On some boats the chart is kept on a hinged board. It folds down when in use and can be folded up and out of the way when not needed.

The Main Cabin

The main cabin on most yachts is devoted to settees, a table, and storage space. A typical arrangement on yachts with beams of 12 feet (3.65 m) or less, is to have a settee along each side of the cabin and a permanently installed or fold-down table in the center or slightly off-center.

Tables

One option is to have a table with a U-shaped bench partially surrounding it. If well-designed and properly located, this arrangement will open up the passageway forward. Underway it is much easier to use the table on one tack than the other. On some boats the tables can be lowered and the U-shaped bench converted into a double bunk. This is OK for occasional times when guests are aboard, but on a routine basis underway or in port it is not convenient.

Tables with fold-down leaves are usually a nuisance. With the leaves down your legs are cramped, and with the leaves up the passageway forward is blocked. Tables built with internal storage boxes are fine as long as the box does not interfere with legroom.

On large boats, and especially older ones, the table may be gimballed. Modern yachts have gotten away from this practice as gimballed tables require relatively heavy ballast to keep them steady, as well as secure locking devices and extra reinforcement where they are attached to the boat. Any table should have a raised edge and a non-skid surface mat to keep dishes from sliding around, and should be firmly anchored to the boat as it will be used as a support or brace.

Cabins

It is convenient to have separate cabins if space is available, and the concept of the 'owner's cabin' or 'stateroom' sounds nice and looks good on the design drawings. Sometimes, however, the concept gets ahead of reality, and the so-called stateroom ends up being cramped and uncomfortable. Be especially leery of boats under 40 feet with aft cabins. Some clever layouts are able to achieve this, but on others it is a joke. If the split arrangement has a passageway leading aft, be sure it is really a passageway and not a crawl space. On some center-cockpit yachts the aft cabin is completely separate from the rest of the boat. This has the attraction of privacy, but also some disadvantages. Underway it may be difficult or impossible to enter or leave the aft compartment without spray or rain entering, and it requires a lot of climbing up and down to go back and forth.

Bulkheads and doors built only to make more rooms take up a lot of space. Often boats that seem very spacious have achieved this appearance at the expense of storage space. If a boat has few cabinets and lockers it will only have a lot of room until you go to sea.

Settees

On yachts less than 40 feet in length, the most comfortable place to sleep underway is in the central part of the boat; forward and aft there is likely to be a lot of motion. For this reason the settees are often used as bunks while underway and often, by necessity, in port as well. A settee used for both sleeping and sitting should be the sliding kind – about 15 inches wide for sitting and 24 to 30 inches when slid out for sleeping. Such bed-seat combinations should be designed to lock when in either position.

A quarterberth is an excellent place to sleep, provided it is not too difficult to enter, and it doesn't give the sleeper claustrophobia. Pilot berths are often comfortable, although they may be difficult to climb in and out of if the yacht is heeled. On most any small boat the pilot berths will be converted to storage cabinets.

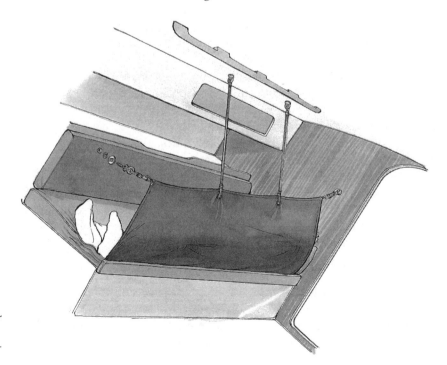

Figure 11.6
Lee cloths. All berths, except quarterberths, should have lee cloths or lee boards available.

All berths except the quarterberth need lee boards or lee cloths to make them safe for sleeping underway. Lee cloths are more convenient because they can be easily stored when not in use. A lee cloth should be made of some type of heavy, water-resistant material and have large, reinforced grommets. It should fasten securely at the base of the bunk and tie to strong fittings in the overhead. The cloth should be about 18 inches high.

Forward Cabin

If you are lucky you will have a spacious forecabin that can serve multiple purposes. Often it is used as a bedroom in port, and as a storage area on a passage, with sailbags, bicycles, food supplies, and a myriad of gear. On some boats the forward cabin is a large open space; on others there are sail bins or permanent bunks installed. If it is an open space consider building in a partial bulkhead to add strength to the hull. In the process of installing this it may be convenient to build a chain locker or some convenient storage compartments. If this is done the area can still be used for sleeping by installing fold-down pipe berths.

Head

Standard routine puts the head forward, separated from the rest of the main cabin by a bulkhead. The head does not need to be in a completely enclosed compartment unless you prefer it that way. It will be much better ventilated and comfortable if it isn't. A door, or more realistically a curtain, can separate it from the main cabin and from the forward cabin. There may be a few times when this is not a convenient arrangement in port. However, that minor inconvenience is far outweighed by the advantages it offers and the increase in space you will have.

If the head compartment contains a shower it will need a drain pan and separate plumbing. On most small boats, however, the shower is more likely to be taken in the cockpit. If you can afford the luxury of hot water and a pressure-water system it will make for more enjoyable cruising, but such things are not a requirement and most yachts do no not have them. Abundant fresh water (big tanks or a watermaker), hot water (water-heating system), and pressure water (special pumps and plumbing) mean additional expense and maintenance.

Even a permanently installed toilet is not an absolute necessity. Some sailors object to them because of the cost, the necessary maintenance, and the through-hull valves involved. They get by quite well by building a seat with a bucket beneath. If you install a toilet, get one that has a reputation for reliability and low maintenance. Two of the best marine toilets on the market are the Lavac and the Blake, which are both made by the same company in England.

Whatever toilet you have on board, make sure you have spare parts for one complete overhaul. To reduce repairs, carefully and completely explain to any guests how the toilet is operated and post detailed instructions next to the toilet. Most people unaccustomed to the head on a boat are totally confused about its correct use.

Toilet repairs are rather low on the list of enjoyable maintenance projects.

An anti-siphon relief valve or vented loop must be installed in the pump-out hose of the head if the bowl is below the waterline. Without it, water may siphon back into the boat. I have seen two boats sink because of this. Anti-siphon valves should be examined periodically for correct operation. It is possible for them to become clogged with salt crystals. On my boat I keep the toilet through-hull valves closed except when the head is in use. That saves a lot of worries.

The closer the head is installed to the centerline, the easier it will be to use and to pump out when underway. On some boats it can only be pumped out on one tack if there is much heel. A 'toilet tack' is usually inconvenient.

There is no reason for the head to be located forward if there is space elsewhere. It would be quite reasonable to install it aft near the main companionway and combine it with a hanging locker for wet foul-weather gear.

Cabin Lighting

Lights inside the boat need to be enough, but not too much. I deplore the painfully bright dome lights so commonly located smack in the middle of the main cabin overhead. They flood the cabin with a harsh, unforgiving light, and if turned on at night while underway will immediately destroy the helmsman's watchkeeping vision. Small individual lights, such as those made by Aqua-signal, are preferable. They are adjustable to any angle and produce a small, soft spotlight for reading. For use in port I have three small fluorescent lights that consume little power and produce a soft light. In the past, yachts relied on kerosene lamps, and even today some sailors use them to conserve electricity. Unfortunately, their smoke will produce the same discoloration and smell as a kerosene stove. Lamp chimneys are easily broken, and in the tropics kerosene lamps add heat to the cabin. Still, the charm and friendliness of lamplight justify their use, and it is sad to see them disappearing.

The overall ambience or 'feeling' of the main cabin depends on the color scheme and the amount and type of wood paneling and trim. Many people like the richness and warmth (and perhaps nautical look) of a teak or mahogany interior, but after a few weeks or months such cabins begin to feel like caves. Lighter-colored wood, white-painted surfaces, and bright formica counters and cabinet doors, will add some cheer and light. Likewise, the choice of fabric on the cushions will change the cabin appearance. Patterned upholstery is generally preferred over solid colors, as it does not show dirt and stains.

Cabin Ventilation

Ventilation plays an important role in comfort, health, and maintenance. The primary goal of ventilation is to move air through the boat without letting water in. It sounds like a simple goal to achieve, and most of the time it is, as long as the boat is underway in calm conditions

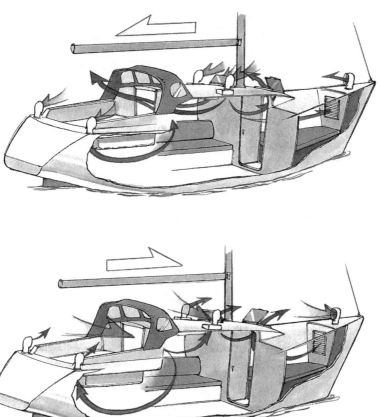

Figure 11.7
Ventilation. Proper ventilation is achieved by experimenting with various combinations of open and closed vents and hatches.

or if there is any breeze at anchor. Maintaining proper ventilation becomes more difficult when sailing in heavy weather conditions or in port when there is no wind.

Hatches and ventilators are the main ways by which air is carried in and out of the yacht. There is a tendency to open all the hatches on a warm day, with the thought that this will cool off the boat and provide a comfortable movement of air. However, the correct use of hatches and vents will provide more efficient airflow. This is especially important when sailing, because it allows the maximum circulation of air and the minimum amount of spray to enter the boat. It is also important in port when the yacht must be left unattended or when it is raining.

Each hatch and vent allow a certain amount of air flow depending on their size and the strength of wind. Likewise, the direction in which the hatch or vent is opened relative to the wind will determine how much air can enter and leave the boat. A concise and logical discussion of yacht ventilation appears in the book *Desirable and Undesirable Characteristics of Offshore Yachts*, in the chapter titled 'Ventilation' by Thomas R. Young. This discussion emphasizes that ventilation is a system and that the elements of the system – the vents and hatches – need to be in balance. Proper balance can be achieved by adjusting the orientation of the hatches and vents to keep air moving in and out of the boat, consistent with eliminating sea spray or waves and rain, relative to the airflow direction.

We mainly think of ventilation in terms of health and comfort for the crew; a continuous circulation of fresh air is needed for normal respiration, to eliminate unpleasant odors from the boat and, in hot weather, to provide a cooling flow of air. But ventilation also performs other functions. On a wooden boat, the presence of water standing inside the hull and the lack of proper ventilation are a constant worry due to the possibility of rot. With fiberglass boats this concern is largely eliminated, but it is still important to air out lockers and closed storage areas. Failing to do so allows the growth of mildew, which adds to cleaning chores. A buildup of humidity in lockers and cabinets will accelerate rust on tools and spare parts, allow mold to develop on clothing, and destroy electrical and electronic equipment.

In the discussion of galleys I mentioned the dangers of LPG gas accumulating in the bilges. Proper airflow through the boat will help to reduce this possibility.

In addition to the ability of a vent to allow air in and out, it also must be built to keep water out. Yacht supply catalogs offer a wide selection of vents, and many of them are a waste of money for the offshore yacht. Most useful are the genuine Dorade vents, which are water-resistant but not waterproof, and some of the low-profile mushroom vents. Often vents are referred to as Dorade vents but in fact they are not, and underway in even light or moderate conditions, seawater easily enters the yacht through these openings. The accompanying illustration shows the correct dimensions and construction for a Dorade vent as originally designed for the yacht *Dorade* in the 1930s. Compare this with the Dorade-type vents on your boat and you may be surprised at what you find.

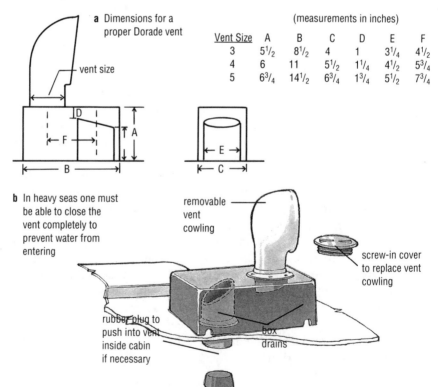

a Dimensions for a proper Dorade vent

vent size

(measurements in inches)

Vent Size	A	B	C	D	E	F
3	$5^1/_2$	$8^1/_2$	4	1	$3^1/_4$	$4^1/_2$
4	6	11	$5^1/_2$	$1^1/_4$	$4^1/_2$	$5^3/_4$
5	$6^3/_4$	$14^1/_2$	$6^3/_4$	$1^3/_4$	$5^1/_2$	$7^3/_4$

b In heavy seas one must be able to close the vent completely to prevent water from entering

removable vent cowling

screw-in cover to replace vent cowling

rubber plug to push into vent inside cabin if necessary

box drains

Figure 11.8
Dorade vent.

Even Dorade vents must often be completely sealed when underway to keep them from bringing water into the cabin. A properly made Dorade will have a deck plate that can be used to replace the cowling when the vent must be secured. On *Denali* I also have large rubber plugs that can be pushed into the vent openings from inside the cabin, which is quick and easy.

Mushroom or low-profile vents come in a variety of sizes and styles. These are not high-volume ventilators, but they are sufficient to improve airflow through lockers and small compartments. In the past this type of vent was used for exhausting air and required airflow over their surfaces. Now the Nicro Corporation has developed low-profile vents with solar-powered fans, made for intake or exhaust.

In tropical areas the need for adequate airflow in port or at anchor is obvious. Wind scoops rigged over open hatches will greatly increase cabin comfort. They are simple do-it-yourself projects, or they can be purchased from marine supply outlets, catalogs, or canvas shops.

On hot days when there is no wind blowing, a fan may be the only alternative. Small 12-volt DC fans use relatively little power and will move a lot of air in a stuffy cabin. They are also handy to have in cold weather with a cabin heater to keep the warm air from accumulating on the overhead.

Cabin Heaters

Those planning to sail and live aboard outside of the tropics will find a cabin heater a worthwhile addition. Even in the summertime throughout the temperate zone there are times when a heater is a welcome companion. At sea or in port a heater will help dry out clothing, as well as the cabin interior in rainy weather. Even slightly cool weather is miserable if you are wet. For high latitude sailing a heater becomes a necessity.

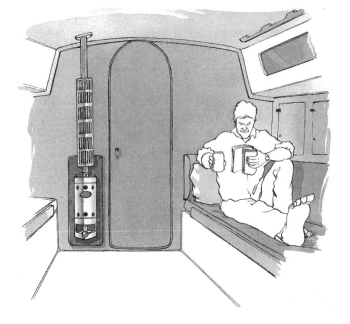

Figure 11.9
Cabin heater. A cabin heater will greatly improve cabin comfort in middle and high latitudes.

Heaters, like cooking stoves, use a variety of fuels and have the same inherent safety problems. Any permanent cabin heater should be vented to the outside through an insulated chimney. This exhaust must have a vent designed to maintain draft for the fire and to keep out rain and spray. Poorly designed or incorrectly installed chimneys and vents are the reason some heaters create problems. In some instances it is necessary to install a force-draft fan in the chimney to start and sometimes to maintain the heater properly.

The boat's own ventilation system, as just discussed, plays a role in the success and safety of a cabin heater. If the intake and exhaust of air are not in balance with the heater and its chimney, the fire will not burn properly, and may cause carbon monoxide poisoning or suffocation. The possibility for this is especially serious at night in cold weather when the cabin is closed up and the stove and heater are on for warmth. Under all circumstances, more than one hatch should be kept open and the cabin should be under a slight pressure rather than a vacuum when a heater is in use.

Determining the proper method of heating a boat involves more than the heater itself. How well the boat is insulated will have a lot to do with how easy it is to heat, and it will also affect condensation. Live-aboard boats with hulls built of fiberglass, steel, or aluminum often have condensation problems in cool climates. This can vary from being a nuisance, with water dripping off the cabin sides and overhead, and the attendant problem of mildew and mold, to costly damage to books, clothing and equipment. One of the advantages of a fiberglass boat with a cored or sandwich hull is that it suffers few condensation problems. If your boat does have condensation problems, they can be reduced by adding ceiling boards or some sort of insulation material such as cork.

Even correctly insulated boats can have condensation problems if they use heaters that are not vented to the outside. All liquid fuels, and some gas fuels, produce water in the process of burning, and that water will end up as condensation. Cabin heaters that are vented carry the water vapor to the outside.

Unvented heaters, usually kerosene or gas, are not generally recommended for boats, but sometimes they are convenient and easy to use if you only need heat now and then. If they are used, pay close attention to ventilation and provide adequate fresh air to the cabin. Under no circumstances should such heaters be left unattended or kept burning at night when the crew is asleep.

A low-technology, short-term alternative for cabin heat is to use ceramic (clay) flower pots inverted over lighted stove burners. I have used this method, and although of minimal benefit it is better than nothing for an occasional cool evening.

In a recent survey of cruising people made by the Seven Seas Cruising Association, some of the heaters highly praised by one crew were roundly condemned by another. Force 10, Espar, and Dickinson cabin heaters seemed to receive the fewest complaints from users. Eberspacher is a popular European brand.

PART 2

THE SYSTEMS AND THE EQUIPMENT

ENGINE AND PROPULSION

We sailors love to brag about how we use the power of the wind to cross oceans. We make a big deal out of how we conserve natural resources. But when our engines go on vacation without us, it's a different story. When I think about how many hours and how much money I have spent on my engine compared to the amount of time and money spent on sails, it makes me wonder if I really am a sailor. When I consider how many miles I have traveled under sail, and how few motoring, I wonder why I even have an engine.

Whether we like it or not, engines have become part of sailing. There are some folks out there getting by just fine, or so they say, without engines. But most of us, albeit begrudgingly at times, bear the burden of expense and maintenance for the convenience and expedience an engine provides.

For the offshore sailor, an engine fulfills a much different function than it does for the weekend gunkholer. This difference should be considered when preparing for cruising. Most blue-water sailors use their engines for three purposes: charging batteries, entering and leaving ports, and sometimes for motoring when there is absolutely no wind. There are a few who use their engines almost continuously, either because their boats are poorly designed (or built) and won't go to windward, or they are carrying so much auxiliary electrical equipment on board that they have to run the engine for hours each day to keep up with the power demands.

Once, after sailing from Japan to Guam, a trip of 11 days, I was complaining that I had used nearly five gallons of fuel during the trip. Another cruiser buying fuel at the same time looked at me in surprise and said he needed more than 100 gallons for his trip of 5 days from the Palau to Guam. He had a heavy, beamy ketch that couldn't get out of its own way, and his fuel tanks held more than 160 gallons. His boat was equipped with a pressure-water system, a hot-water heater, refrigerator and freezer, and probably numerous other convenience items.

If you don't have an engine you will be a better sailor – or at least you had better be – and you can take a lot of pride in getting around that way. Certainly, these days, solar panels and wind and water generators make it possible to get rid of the engine and still have sufficient electricity on board for cabin and navigation lights, radios, and other essentials in most latitudes. Lack of an engine, however, will definitely restrict you from visiting some ports and anchorages; most harbors are designed with the assumption that all boats and ships have engines. Entering under sail alone may be illegal or cause inconvenience to other marine traffic.

We need to strike a balance between use and need. Consider the engine a tool and an aid. Traditionally, the engine on a sailboat is called an *auxiliary engine*, and it should fulfill that role. Let it be your slave and not your master.

Engine Type and Size

It really isn't worthwhile considering anything other than a diesel engine on a cruising yacht. Years ago, production boats in America mainly used gasoline engines. Fortunately, this has changed. Gasoline engines are cheaper and lighter, but they are far more hazardous than diesel. Gasoline has a low flame point and is highly explosive. Ignition systems and carburetors often cause problems, and the fuel consumption rate of a gasoline engine is higher than that of a diesel engine. If you have a gasoline engine on your boat, it will be to your advantage to replace it with a diesel before you set off on a long cruise.

Determining the best size (horsepower) engine depends on the size of the boat. There is no reason to have an engine that is larger than necessary. The general rule is to select an engine that will move the boat upwind in a moderate breeze at design hull speed (1.25 times the square root of waterline length in feet). Too much weight in the boat, the wrong size propeller, or fouling on the bottom will reduce speed. There are also factors that can increase the speed, including a feathering or variable pitch propeller and lightweight construction materials. In terms of efficiency, hull speed is a realistic criterion; putting in a larger or more powerful engine will be inefficient and more expensive to operate.

Considerations When Selecting an Engine

Most small marine diesel engines offer the option of a hand-crank for starting if the electric starter should fail. This is an ideal backup, and much cheaper than purchasing a spare starter motor. It isn't always easy to hand crank an engine, but it can be done. Before going to sea the crew should learn how to start the engine with the crank. When installing a new engine be sure there is sufficient room to swing the crank. It may require some modification to the engine compartment. It is possible to start some diesel engines when sailing if the boat is moving fast enough. This is done by releasing the decompression levers, putting the engine in gear and then closing the compression levers when the engine fires. Don't plan on this working, however, if you have a folding or feathering prop.

Considering the importance we attach to engines it seems strange that the space provided for them is often badly located, poorly designed, and undersized. Probably the reason for this is that on the showroom floor it is human space, not engine space, that sells boats. How often do you see a picture of an engine compartment in a boat advertisement?

If I am ever fortunate enough to design or build my own boat it will have an engine compartment that is easily accessible on at least three and preferably four sides. There are yachts in which the engine box is located in the middle of the cabin. A bit short on aesthetics perhaps, but there's easy access to the engine, which makes it more likely that it will be well-maintained and reliable. If an engine is stuck back in a tiny, cramped compartment it will almost always suffer from poor maintenance. With a little bit of thought in planning and building, an engine room can be designed with removable panels to permit easy access to any part of the engine.

A noisy engine is a nuisance to everyone in and around the boat. A muffler system will reduce outside noise. Cutting down on noise inside takes some work, but is worth the trouble. It requires adding multi-layer insulation to the sides and top of the engine box. The best sound-proofing insulation is the type with a foil cover over alternating layers of spun fiberglass, plywood and thin lead sheeting. When improving on the engine compartment for noise remember that a diesel engine must have a large supply of clean air to operate, so don't cover up or eliminate any ventilation.

Even with a quiet engine, give your neighbors in the anchorage a break. When you run your engine to charge batteries, pick a time that is least likely to interfere with others who may be sleeping, eating, or relaxing in the cockpit. Usually, the best time is between 1000 and 1200 or 1400 and 1600.

Diesel engines have come a long way in the past 20 years. Formerly they were expensive and heavy. Fortunately, both of these factors have been reduced. Due to an expanding market for small diesel engines, design improvements have made them easier to install, maintain, and repair.

But engine costs extend beyond the initial investment. In spite of their reliability they will eventually require repairs as well as routine replacements of filters, injectors, and pump parts. When selecting an engine, inquire about which company has the best reputation for service, repairs, and repair-part costs. Some have a dismal record. Likewise, find out the experiences others have had with various engines in terms of performance and reliability. A well-known engine that is marketed worldwide is better because of the possibility of finding repair facilities and parts. Yanmar, Isuzu, and Perkins have good reputations. Saab is known for its sturdy and reliable engines. Volvo-Penta made for years one of the most reliable and tough engines, but lost many of its customers because of the high cost of repair parts.

Fuel System

One of the nice things about diesel engines is their simplicity. If they have an uninterrupted supply of clean air and fuel, and are adequately cooled, they will run almost indefinitely. For this reason the fuel system should be high on your list of routine maintenance.

Clean fuel is the top priority. In some ports it is possible to buy diesel at a discount from sources that supply fishing boats and commercial craft. This can be a risky business and not worth the savings. Usually it is better to buy from an automobile service station even though the price may be slightly higher. When adding fuel to the boat's tank, use a filter. Pantyhose make excellent filters.

Figure 12.1
Fuel system.

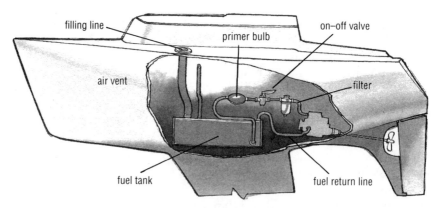

filling line

primer bulb

on–off valve

air vent

filter

fuel tank

fuel return line

Fuel tanks must be kept clean. Tank cleaning is a messy job, but may be necessary at least once a year. Even though you have scrupulously maintained a clean fuel policy, it is surprising how much water and other impurities can collect at the bottom of a fuel tank. Some water will gradually accumulate as it separates from the fuel. It also collects due to condensation in the tank. Keeping the tank full will reduce condensation. Often the bottom of the tank will contain a flocculated material caused by bacteria, especially in the tropics. If the engine is not used for an extended period of time a bacteria inhibitor should be added to the fuel.

It may be possible to run a diesel engine for a long time without cleaning out the tanks and have no problems. Then, one day you will operate the engine when the seas are rough and the tank is only partly full. Foreign matter and water from the bottom of the tank will get stirred up with the fuel and be picked up by the fuel line, and the engine will run rough or stop completely from a clogged filter or injector.

All diesel engines that I know of come with fuel filters installed. These are usually closed containers that have a replaceable fiber filter of some type. They should be inspected at least as frequently as recommended in the owner's handbook. An additional fuel filter should also be installed in the fuel supply line. One with a large transparent sediment bowl is best. It permits you to see the color and clarity of the fuel as it comes from the tank, and it will also show if there is any air in the fuel line. The filter should have a water separator and a drain plug at the bottom of the bowl. This type of filter will also have a replaceable filter element. Filters made by Racor are highly recommended. Be sure and have spare filter elements for all of your fuel filters.

On *Denali* I installed a squeeze bulb, of the type used for priming an outboard engine, in the fuel line between the tank and the first filter. This permits me to pump fuel through the system by hand if necessary, and to purge air from the lines when performing maintenance. On several occasions it has come in handy when the fuel pump was not operating correctly or there was an air leak in the fuel line.

Put some effort into making fuel line connections secure to keep air out of the system. Usually connections on the engine are made with thin copper washers. Be sure to have some spares in your repair kit when setting off on a cruise.

A cut-off valve should be located in the fuel line between the tank and the first filter. Unlike a gasoline engine, which has an electric ignition switch, a diesel engine cannot be turned off by turning a key switch. The only way to stop it is to cut off the fuel or air supply. (Yes, you could also cut off the cooling water supply but that would be a rather expensive way to stop the engine!)

There should be a method for sounding all fuel tanks instead of relying on a gauge. A sounding rod can be made from a wood, plastic, or brass rod, with the marks on it to indicate the amount of fuel remaining in the tank. Tanks should be removable if it becomes necessary to repair them or have them steam-cleaned. Stainless steel tanks are the most convenient.

The last part of the fuel system that causes problems is the fuel pump. Most engines are equipped with a reliable diaphragm pump, but they all need repair eventually. Manufacturers sell fuel pump repair kits and it is a good idea to have one or two on board. I recommend also having a complete spare pump. It may be that when the old one 'packs up' you don't have time to overhaul it. It will be quicker to simply replace it with the spare and do the repair later.

Cooling Water

Engine cooling for small marine diesels is usually either direct seawater (raw water) cooling or indirect with a heat exchanger. With direct cooling, seawater is pumped through the cooling system of the engine and returned overboard through the engine exhaust system. The main elements of the cooling water supply system are the through-hull valve, a water strainer or filter, water pump, thermostat, and zincs.

The through-hull water-intake valve should be a marine-quality ball valve with an easily accessible handle to close it quickly in the event of a

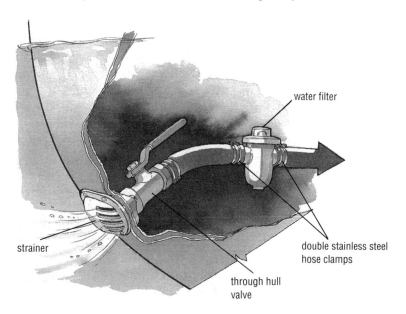

water filter

strainer

double stainless steel hose clamps

through hull valve

Figure 12.2
Engine cooling water intake system.

break somewhere in the line. The intake opening should have a guard to keep large objects from obstructing it. This is especially important in harbors and near shore where various kinds of trash, especially plastic bags, are often floating at or just below the surface. A grill-type guard is best. Screens with a fine mesh are not as good because even small pieces of seaweed can clog them. Racing sailors don't like to use the grill-type guard because it produces a small amount of turbulence. Remember, this is cruising, not racing.

Between the through-hull valve and the engine a water strainer should be installed. These are standard on some production boats, but not all. They are a good investment and will probably pay for themselves in avoiding water pump repairs. Water strainers have a basket inside which is periodically removed for inspection and cleaning. Commonly you may find a small crab or even tiny fish that have made the strainer their involuntary home. If you are using your engine in an area in which the water obviously contains a lot of foreign debris or sediment, the strainer should be checked frequently.

From the strainer, the water goes to the water pump directly or, on some engines, by way of the reverse gearbox. The water pump is usually an impeller-type that is mounted on the engine. It is about as simple a pump as you could hope for, but it requires at least annual inspection. Like the fuel pump, it is not difficult to repair. Repair kits should be carried, as well as a complete spare pump to permit quick replacement if necessary.

A thermostat is installed in the heat exchanger. It should be looked at about once a year for correct operation. Spares should be on board. On some engines there are one or more sacrificial zincs installed in the cooling system. Be sure and inspect, and probably replace, them at least annually.

Exhaust System

Nearly all small sailboats use a 'wet-type' exhaust system. With a wet exhaust, the cooling water, after leaving the engine, is mixed with the exhaust gases and exits through the exhaust pipe. How this system is arranged on your boat will depend on the type of engine and on where, and how, the engine is located relative to the waterline. If it sits below or partly below the waterline, as is commonly the case, the important elements of the system are (1) a loop and anti-siphon valve in the cooling water line, (2) a waterlift, and (3) a high loop and through-hull valve in the exhaust overboard discharge line.

If the point where the cooling water enters the exhaust gas line is below or less than six inches (15 cm) above the waterline, an anti-siphon valve must be installed in a loop in the cooling water line. This loop must rise at least six inches above the yacht's waterline. If this is not done, a siphon can form in the cooling water line when the engine is not running. When that happens, water from the cooling water intake valve can fill the cooling water lines at least as far as the waterlift, and then back up into the exhaust manifold and enter the exhaust ports of

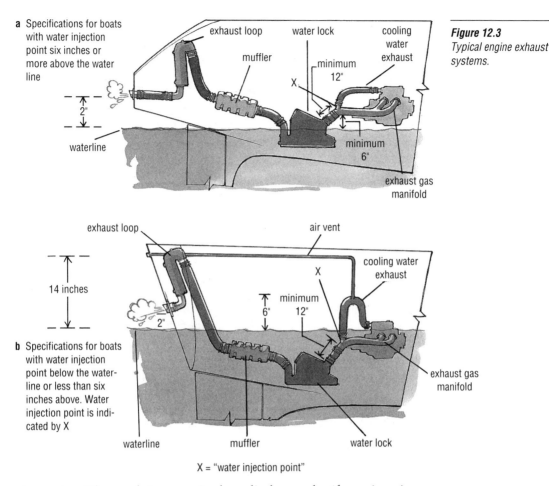

a Specifications for boats with water injection point six inches or more above the water line

exhaust loop   water lock   cooling water exhaust

muffler   minimum 12"

X

2"

waterline

minimum 6"

exhaust gas manifold

Figure 12.3
Typical engine exhaust systems.

exhaust loop   air vent

14 inches   cooling water exhaust

X

minimum 6"   minimum 12"

2"

b Specifications for boats with water injection point below the water-line or less than six inches above. Water injection point is indicated by X

exhaust gas manifold

waterline   muffler   water lock

X = "water injection point"

the engine. The result is water in the cylinders and a 'frozen' engine, as well as water in the lubricating oil.

The waterlift functions as a combination muffler and temporary holding tank to reduce the temperature of the exhaust gases and engine cooling water. It eliminates the need for a high-temperature exhaust line leading to the overboard discharge and results in a safer, cooler, and more easily maintained exhaust system. A waterlift is a box with inlet and outlet pipes. The outlet pipe reaches nearly to the bottom of the waterlift. Cooling water and exhaust gases from the engine enter the waterlift and accumulate there until sufficient exhaust gas pressure builds up to force the water and gases out of the box. If you watch the exhaust on most boats you will notice that it comes in pulses or surges. Each pulse of water is in response to the pressure buildup in the water-lift.

A waterlift must be located on the centerline of the yacht and lower than the engine; specifically at least six inches (15 cm) lower than the point at which the cooling water enters the exhaust gas line from the engine. The waterlift must always be lower than this point, even when the yacht is heeled or when it pitches. Otherwise the cooling water will be able to flow from the waterlift into the exhaust manifold and flood the engine cylinders. If it is impossible to place the waterlift far enough below the exhaust manifold, the alternative is to construct a 'dry riser stack'. This is a steel pipe (better make it from stainless steel), that puts a loop in the exhaust gas line that rises above the yacht's waterline. Such a riser will be very hot and it must be insulated. The preceding illustrations, prepared by the W.H. Den Ouden Company of Holland, indicate the minimum distances for the various components of the exhaust system. Some engine manufacturers recommend slightly different configurations. By all means check your engine's handbook.

There are various waterlifts on the market. They include those made from mild steel, stainless steel, fiberglass, and plastic. Those of mild steel will rust out in a short time, and the stainless steel ones are heavy and expensive. Fiberglass and plastic waterlifts are the best choice. The Vetus Waterlock is a reliable and inexpensive plastic waterlift. I installed one 10 years ago to replace a huge rusty monster, and am quite satisfied with it.

There are three ways that water can accidentally enter the engine cylinders. The first way is by the accidental siphoning of intake water when the engine is not running, as previously described. The second way is via the exhaust pipe. A boat at anchor or on a mooring may violently pitch in strong wave or surge conditions. At such times it is possible for water to make its way into the exhaust and eventually to the engine exhaust manifold. This can also happen when sailing if the boat is heeled over or pitching, and it can happen in large following seas. A high loop should be installed in the exhaust line between the waterlift and the point of overboard discharge. It should rise about 16 inches (40 cm) above the waterline.

Generally, the loop alone is enough to restrict water entry. However, if the yacht is heeled far over or sustains a knockdown, the vertical loop may become horizontal. For this reason it may be advisable to also install a through-hull valve where the exhaust exits the boat. If the overboard exhaust opening is located in a convenient position, for example through the transom, it is equally reasonable to shove a wood or rubber plug into the opening instead of using a valve.

Finally, flooding of the engine can occur under certain starting conditions. Whenever the engine is turned over with the electric starter the water pump sends water into the cooling system. If for some reason the engine is difficult to start and the starter is turned over for a long time, water will accumulate in the waterlift because there is no exhaust gas pressure to force it out. It is possible to introduce so much cooling water into the waterlift that it backs up into the exhaust manifold and floods the cylinders. The only way to eliminate this possibility is to drain the waterlift box if you have had a slow time starting the engine.

Perhaps the foregoing discussion sounds like overkill, with so many fail-safe devices. However, it takes very little water to freeze an engine cylinder. The inconvenience and expense of repairing a flooded engine is a complication worth avoiding. The first time it happened to me I had no idea what the problem was. I ended up sailing from St. Lucia to St. Croix without using my engine. It was an excellent, although enforced, learning experience as I managed to sail into and exit six anchorages on Guadeloupe, Dominica and St. Croix. The cylinders also got flooded on a trip from Japan to the Marshall Islands. There were some rough seas and water came in through the innovative exhaust system I had recently designed and installed. I began to suspect trouble when I saw seawater flowing out through the air intake on my new Yanmar engine. As horrible as that sounds – and it is an especially horrifying sight when you are at sea – it is not quite the end of the world. If you suck out all the salt water and spray some WD-40 or oil in the cylinders, and then slowly turn the engine over by hand without compression, you should be back in business. Don't forget to also change the engine oil after one of these experiences.

Another type of cooling system is indirect, and uses a heat exchanger. Most marine diesel engine manufacturers offer this as an option. By this method, the engine, as on an automobile, has its own self-contained fresh-water cooling system. Salt water is still brought to the engine, but instead of passing through a water jacket it passes through the heat exchanger and cools the fresh water. This is an expensive modification that adds an additional water pump and equipment to the engine. However, it is considered by many to be a worthwhile investment because it keeps salt water out of the engine and permits the engine to operate more efficiently. It does not eliminate the wet exhaust problem, and a waterlift is still required.

Engine Mounts and Shaft Couplings

A diesel engine must be 'shock' mounted to eliminate transmitting vibration to the shaft. There are five points that have to be considered – the four attachment points where the engine is secured to an engine bed, and the shaft connection. If an engine is only operated when the boat is level and in relatively calm seas almost any mounts will work. However, in rough conditions engines have been known to break loose of their mounts, and a loose engine rolling around can put a hole in the hull.

There are a number of different mounts to choose from, and often the manufacturer will sell and recommend a specific type. It may be difficult to get good advice on engine mounts. Perhaps it is best to seek the advice of a company that only makes engine mounts, or talk to a yacht builder.

Once the mounts are installed they need to be examined now and then to be sure they have not vibrated loose and that the rubber has not deteriorated or cracked. In heavy going check the mounts more frequently. After you have gotten to know your engine you will recognize its vibration characteristics by sight and by sound. If the vibrations seem abnormal, take immediate action. The first act is to reduce engine speed and examine the suspension system. If necessary, stop the engine until you can take corrective action. An unusual vibration pattern is not always due to engine mounts. It can also be due to some type of engine malfunction or problems with the shaft or propeller. Regardless of the cause, quick action is required.

The connection between the engine and the propeller shaft must also be flexible. If the engine is in straight alignment with the shaft a nylon-type spacer or 'donut' may be sufficient. More elaborate and flexible couplings such as the CVA Aquadrive will assure smoother, vibration-free operation.

Production boats are built to accommodate a specific engine. If you change engines, the size and shape of the engine bed, and the engine compartment, may require modifications. This can be a complicated and costly operation. Figure it into the cost if you are installing a new engine.

Drive Shaft and Associated Hardware

From the engine coupling to the propeller there remain some important parts of the propulsion system. These include the stuffing box, stern tube or shaft tunnel, strut, and cutlass bearing.

Stuffing Box and Packing Gland

In a typical installation the stuffing box, which holds the shaft packing, is connected to the stern tube by a piece of flexible rubber hose. This set-up is reliable but should be checked frequently to be sure the hose clamps and hose are in good condition. If the hose clamps should let go, or if the hose should break, it would be possible for the boat to sink in a very short time at sea or in port.

The stuffing box is made of bronze and consists of a packing gland and two nuts. One nut permits tightening of the packing gland, and the other one is a lock nut. These nuts are of large size and usually the easiest way to slack or tighten them is with a special wrench or a large pair of slip-joint pliers. Learn how to do this before going to sea. Usually the space in which you have to work is narrow and uncomfortable. The discomfort of working here will be aggravated if you are in a

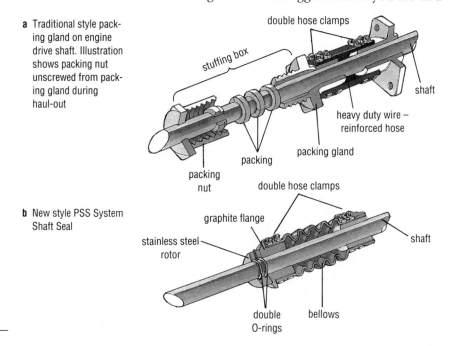

a Traditional style packing gland on engine drive shaft. Illustration shows packing nut unscrewed from packing gland during haul-out

double hose clamps
stuffing box
shaft
heavy duty wire – reinforced hose
packing gland
packing
packing nut

b New style PSS System Shaft Seal

double hose clamps
graphite flange
shaft
stainless steel rotor
double O-rings
bellows

Figure 12.4
Packing glands.

rolling sea. If you know in advance how to tighten the nuts, it will only take a few seconds to do so.

On your next haul-out, check the condition of the shaft packing and renew it if necessary. At the same time inspect the shaft where it is in contact with the packing to check for wear. The packing is either braided flax impregnated with a lubricant or a more modern version of this made with Teflon. Pieces of packing should be cut to fit the diameter of the shaft. When the individual pieces are laid around the shaft their end joints should be staggered. The packing nut should be lightly tightened to bear down slightly on the packing, and then the lock nut brought securely in place. Don't use force. A light touch will do. Conventional wisdom used to be that when the shaft is turning the stuffing box should have a very slight drip. The practice now is that the packing nut is tightened just enough to stop a leak. Recently, a new type of stuffing box, supposedly maintenance free, has become popular. A rubber bellows is attached to the end of the shaft tunnel, and has a carbon flange on the other end that rides against a stainless steel rotor secured to the shaft with set screws and O-rings. Reportedly they work fine when new, but when the bellows age or any foreign object gets between the carbon flange and the stainless steel rotor, they can fail. Of the two or three brands on the market, the PSS Shaft Seal has the best reputation.

Stern Tube and Cutlass Bearing

The stern tube and shaft tunnel on a fiberglass boat should be strong and well built into the hull. Examine it now and then for any possible cracks or wear. At the point where the shaft exits the hull or at the strut, if one is in place, there will be a replaceable cutlass bearing. This is a brass or plastic tube lined with rubber ribs. Try to gently wiggle the shaft to determine the condition of the cutlass bearing. If there is play in the shaft the bearing should be replaced during a haul-out.

The cutlass bearing is probably held in place by two or more set screws which will have to be removed. If the strut has been painted over

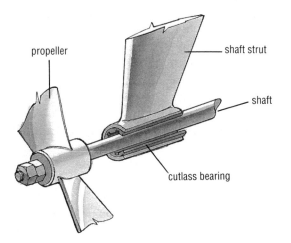

Figure 12.5
Cutlass bearing.

it may take some looking to find the set screws. Sometimes the shaft bearings are difficult to remove. If the bearing is in a strut it can be eased out by carefully tapping a pipe of about the same diameter and thickness against it. Otherwise some careful surgery with a hacksaw blade and long-nose pliers will eventually free the bearing. Carry a couple of spare cutlass bearings on board; they are often difficult to find in out-of-the-way places.

Propellers

The most common propellers on cruising yachts are fixed, folding, or feathering. Fixed-blade propellers are the cheapest, but they produce the most drag when sailing. If you have a two blade prop, drag can be slightly reduced under sail by locking the shaft with the blades in a vertical position. Drag can be completely eliminated by removing the prop before embarking on a long cruise; something few sailors are willing to do. In an attempt to reduce drag some folks let the shaft freewheel. This is effective at high speeds. However, it is not recommended, because it wears out gears, bearings, and seals. It is also noisy.

Figure 12.6
Propellers.

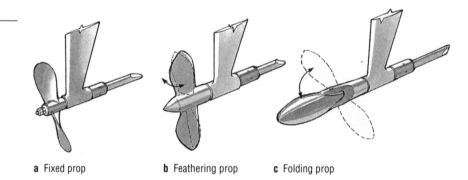

a Fixed prop   **b** Feathering prop   **c** Folding prop

If you have any doubts about the correct size propeller for your boat you can usually get advice from the designer or a propeller manufacturer. A propeller of the wrong size will significantly reduce the efficiency of your engine.

Folding props are popular on racing boats, but often they fail to fold properly when not in use. A more serious problem with folding props is that sometimes, when engaging the engine in forward, and often when going into reverse, the blades do not open symmetrically. When this happens it puts a damaging torque on the shaft. Of the various folding propellers, the Gori receives high marks for performance. The blades on the Gori prop are geared and always open symmetrically.

In recent years the feathering propeller has become very popular for racing boats and now for cruising yachts as well. Most highly regarded is the Italian-made Max Prop. Users claim significant improvement in boatspeed with the Max Prop, and praise its reliable operation. Furthermore it works better in reverse than most propellers.

There are also variable-pitch propellers, but probably few sailors on small boats would want to go to the trouble to install them. For a large motor-sailing yacht they would probably be worth the effort and cost.

Engines are usually operated from the cockpit by remote-control cables. Remote cables should be securely fastened and occasionally checked for rust and loose fasteners. You must get acquainted with where and how the cables connect to the engine, and be able to get to them in an emergency if they stick or jam. It is not a wonderful feeling to have the throttle or the gearshift freeze when coming into an anchorage or alongside a dock.

The prudent skipper will check out the operation of the throttle and determine that the engine will shift into forward, reverse, and neutral every time the engine is started. Make this a routine procedure and an absolute must if you haven't used your engine for several days.

On a passage from Savannah to St. Croix I did not use my engine for 13 days except to charge batteries. In the process of anchoring among a fleet of very expensive-looking yachts at St. Croix I used the engine to back down to set the anchor, and experienced a combination of misfortunes: the anchor did not hold and the engine stuck in reverse. By the time I was able to get to the engine and put it in neutral by hand, I had barely missed hitting two other yachts and had managed to foul my dragging anchor on another boat's mooring. Fortunately no damage was done except to my pride. For the balance of my stay in that harbor I was well-known to the locals as the guy with the unique anchoring technique.

When motoring or motorsailing, watch that a sheet or line doesn't get wound around the engine throttle handle and suddenly put the engine in or out of gear, or cause the engine to accelerate unexpectedly. It happens.

Engine Controls and Instruments

Figure 12.7
Engine instrument control panel.

The type and positioning of engine instruments are important. Most engines come with a convenient wiring harness that makes for easy installation. Unfortunately, standard instrument panels these days tend to use indicator lights instead of gauges or instruments for water temperature, oil pressure, and battery charge indicators. Such indicators are aptly referred to as 'idiot lights' because they don't require any thought or comprehension: One moment everything is fine, the next moment you've got a crisis on your hands. Engine problems, however, are progressive. A gauge will often tell you when something is not quite right, and you can observe a trend developing and take action before it is too late. This is especially important in terms of engine temperature.

I replaced my idiot lights with gauges. It turned out to be a complicated job that spanned three continents before it was finished. There are different types of senders with different thread sizes and different monitoring ranges. There is a significant amount of rewiring necessary as well. It is a job that some mechanics won't touch simply because it is not routine. One company that will give you good advice and recommendations is Frank W. Murphy Manufacturers of Tulsa, Oklahoma, makers of monitoring equipment for marine engines. They will give recommendations on senders, gauges and wiring to replace idiot lights on any engine. The most important instruments are oil pressure, cooling water temperature, ammeter, and an engine hour meter to help you remember when maintenance is due.

Engine instruments should be located so that they can be conveniently read while conning the boat. They must be protected from rain and spray. Usually this means putting them in a box with a permanently sealed acrylic cover. The on-off key and starter switch should likewise be protected.

Figure 12.8
Protected compartment for engine ignition key and starter switch in the cockpit.

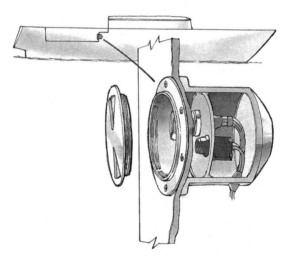

Engine Alternatives

The most obvious alternative to an engine is no engine. In the introduction to this chapter I mentioned some of the advantages and disadvantages of a sailboat without an engine. To go to sea without an engine is not impossible, unsafe, or irresponsible, but it will be inconvenient at times. Some do so to be purists, others don't want the hassle of an engine, or the weight, occupied space, and expense – and some folks are a bit macho. Most of them end up asking for a tow now and then.

Those without engines sometimes carry one or two large oars that can be used to row or scull their boats in light air in port. Having a sculling oar on board is a good idea even if you have an engine. On the occasions when my engine has let me down I've wished that I had an oar on board, but I always forget about it after the problem is solved.

Small racing boats often use an outboard engine. There is no reason why an outboard can't be used on a cruising yacht as well, at least for maneuvering in harbors. Those who disdain having an inboard or an outboard engine on their boat may be willing to use an outboard on their tender and tie the tender alongside for moving in restricted waters.

If you are setting out on a long cruise that will take you to remote places, here is some advice to help keep engine problems to the minimum.

Dealing With Engine Problems

Set up and follow a preventive maintenance program. Usually such a plan is included in your engine owner's manual. Keep a record of engine hours so you know when various maintenance tasks should be performed. Use a page in the back of the log book for this. Sometimes the owner's manual will indicate that certain checks should be made annually. If you are using your engine every day it may be necessary to do these jobs more often.

Have on board a complete parts list and shop manual for your engine. They can be purchased from the manufacturer.

Find a parts supplier who is willing to send repair parts to you by airmail wherever you happen to be in the world. Ask him how you can pay, and if it is possible to place orders by telephone or fax. Doing that before you leave can save you a lot of difficulty later on. I order engine parts from a company in Seattle, Washington, which accepts credit cards for payment, and is easy to call or fax from anywhere. Most cruisers who have been out sailing for a few years have one or more horror stories to tell of how they had to wait for weeks or months to obtain repair parts for their engines.

Write to the manufacturers of your engine and find out what spare parts and special tools they recommend to carry on board. Talk to other cruisers with engines similar to yours and ask what their experiences have been and what spares they recommend. Finally, talk to a marine diesel mechanic for an opinion. It seems to be difficult for local repair men and even company representatives to understand the way cruising works. They cannot envision a world in which it is impossible to simply make a telephone call and have the parts on hand in a day or two.

Learn about your engine. Study it with the parts and repair books in hand. Take advantage of any opportunity to work on a diesel engine or to attend a course on diesel engine repair. All diesel engines are similar in principle, and learning about one is a good introduction to any other. If you have an engine on your boat now, but do not plan to go cruising for some time in the future, start doing all the maintenance and repairs yourself instead of automatically turning them over to a mechanic. When out cruising, you will be the only mechanic around.

Break away from engine dependency. Far too many sailors think that an engine will always get them out of trouble. This is not true. There are many stories of wrecked boats whose fate was the result of someone who relied on an engine instead of on sailing ability. Whenever using your engine be a skeptic and expect it to fail. For example, when entering and leaving port under power, have sails (and anchors) attached on deck and ready to use. Anticipate how you will deal with the situation if your engine fails to perform. Even if you have religiously maintained your power plant, it may quit unexpectedly due to contaminated fuel, a blockage of cooling water due to trash in the water, or a part that fails unexpectedly.

Even a perfectly maintained engine will suddenly cease to function if a rope becomes wrapped around the shaft and propeller or if you hit some underwater obstruction.

Whenever possible, anchor and get underway without using your engine. When you select a spot for anchoring, do so with the thought that your engine may fail to operate when it is time to leave, or that it may become necessary to get underway should a storm develop. When it is possible to do so, enter harbors and ports under sail. It is OK to have your engine running but not in gear when you sail in and out of harbors or anchorages. Find the balance between being too timid to use your sails and too macho to use your engine.

PLUMBING

A plumber once told me that all he really needed to know to do his job was that sewage runs downhill and payday is on Friday – or words to that effect. On a cruising sailboat things are even easier than that and you don't have to worry about Friday.

Plumbing on a sailboat includes the internal fresh-water system and the external salt-water system. These systems are remarkably simple and easy to install and to maintain, if quality fittings are used. Before heading offshore for an extended cruise, all valves, hoses, and hose clamps should be carefully inspected. The crew should know the location of all through-hull fittings and how to open and close them.

Salt-Water System

Most of the valves, hoses, pumps, and fittings on a sailboat have to do with salt water. They deserve close scrutiny because they let the ocean in – only temporarily, we hope – and then out again. Every opening through the hull represents the potential for trouble. Some of the traditional books on cruising emphasize the need to minimize or even eliminate through-hull fittings. I think that philosophy is overstated in these days of fiberglass hulls, reliable hardware, and dependable sealants. Still, it is important to keep an eye on all parts of the system, and not take anything for granted.

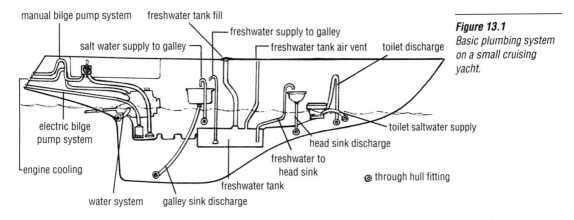

Figure 13.1
Basic plumbing system on a small cruising yacht.

Bilges

No matter how careful you are or how tight your boat is, there are times when water will invade the hull. On rainy days or in heavy going when the companionway hatch is left open, even for a short time, water will make its way inside the boat and into the bilge. Traditionally, yachts had huge bilges. These provided excellent storage space right where it should be, low and in the central part of the boat. It also made pumping out the bilge an easy, and usually infrequent, task.

Modern fiberglass boats seldom have adequate bilge sumps. Many of them will not hold much more than a few gallons of water. For this reason it is necessary to be able to pump bilges quickly before they overflow and water starts sloshing all over the boat. It is bad enough if clothes, food, books, and charts are damaged. The problem is greatly aggravated if any oil happens to be in the bilge from spills in the engine compartment. If oily water overflows the bilge it can make for a difficult clean-up job and be a significant safety hazard when moving around in the cabin.

Whether they leak or not, all boats manage to collect water at times. When this happens, and water collects in pockets, it will often result in bad odors and can cause warping and discoloration of floorboards. If the water happens to accumulate around the foot of the mast it can cause corrosion and damage to the mast base. It should be possible for water that happens to enter the boat at any place to flow directly to the bilge. To permit this, especially in modern, shallow-bilged boats, it may be necessary to add limber holes or fill in low places with fiberglass resin or epoxy.

Bilge Pumps

A cruising boat should have a minimum of three bilge pumps – a small electric pump for routine and occasional pumping, a reliable, permanently mounted manual bilge pump, operable from the cockpit, and a high-capacity emergency, manual bilge pump that can move large quantities of water. It should be portable, so that it can be used anywhere on the boat or transferred to another boat that may be in trouble.

There are a number of reliable small electric bilge pumps, such as the Rule brand, on the market. Production boats usually come equipped with a small, submersible, electric pump with a float-activated switch. These have good and bad points. The favorable aspect is that if the boat is taking on water when no one is on board, it will solve the problem until either the battery runs down or the pump burns out. Even when the crew is on board, this type of pump has the advantage that the sound of its frequent operation will alert them that a problem exists. The bad news is that it is possible for the float switch to become stuck in the on or off position.

A manual bilge pump should be located so it can be operated in the cockpit by the helmsman without having to open any lockers. A diaphragm pump with a pumping rate of at least 15 gallons per minute is recommended. Two bilge pumps that really meet these recommendations are the Edson 18 and the Whale Titan. These pumps are similar except that the Edson 18 is available with an aluminum or a bronze body and the Whale Titan is constructed of plastic. Of the two, the Edson 18 is superior but it also costs about twice as much. Either pump can be mounted inside a locker with a through-handle into the cockpit. The Edson 18 requires more mounting space. If you decide to purchase the Whale Titan, be sure that is what you are getting. There are other bilge pumps made by Whale that are not of equal quality.

Diaphragm pumps are the best type of manual pump to use because they are less likely to become clogged when foreign material gets in the line. All pumps, however, should have an adequate screen or strum box on the intake end of the hose. This screen should be easy to reach for cleaning. A wide variety of debris has a way of getting into the bilge, and it is easy for the screen to become clogged just at the time it is most needed.

The portable, emergency-use, high-capacity manual pump should have reasonably long (15- to 20-foot), flexible intake and exhaust hoses. The only pump that I can recommend for this job is the Edson 30. This pump can move 30 gallons per minute – if you are strong enough to pump that fast.

Figure 13.2
A portable emergency-use bilge pump should be standard equipment on any offshore boat.

It is unlikely you will ever need to use the emergency pump, but it is excellent insurance and reassuring to know it is ready. It should be tested at least once a year, and each crewmember should take a turn at operating it.

Installing Bilge Pumps

When installing a permanently mounted electric or manual bilge pump, pay attention to the hose runs and the location of the overboard discharge in the topsides. It might very well be that the pump will be most needed someday when the boat is heeled, and pumping against the pressure of the seawater just makes the job that much more difficult. Furthermore, seawater can siphon into the boat through the bilge discharge line if it is below the waterline *when the boat is heeled*. On some boats it will be necessary to install a vented loop with an anti-siphon valve to prevent ingress of water. If possible, route the discharge through the transom. When installing hoses, avoid right-angle bends in the lines. They can reduce the pump efficiency by as much as 50 percent.

There should be two complete sets of repair parts for each manual bilge pump on board. Such items are seldom stocked in out-of-the-way places, and there are so many models of bilge pumps that marine supply stores don't try to keep up with spares for all of them. In an emergency it is possible to repair a diaphragm using a piece of rubber, heavy plastic, or the PVC fabric from foul-weather gear.

Through-Hull Fittings

There is nothing mysterious about through-hull fittings and valves. There are three items to be aware of: the through-hull fitting, which is a flanged pipe and flanged nut, the valve itself, and a tailpiece. The through-hull fitting is first installed using a below-the-waterline grade bedding compound-sealant. On the inside of the through-hull pipe there should be two ridges, located 180 degrees apart. These provide places where a flat bar or the end of a pipe wrench handle can be inserted to hold the pipe in place while the backing nut is tightened. The valve is screwed onto the through-hull fitting with some Teflon tape on the threads. Finally the tailpiece is screwed into the body of the valve, also with Teflon tape on the threads. Depending on the type and thickness of the hull, it may be necessary to install a wood backing plate or even to glass in the wood piece.

Determine the type and quality of through-hull fittings and valves or seacocks now installed on your boat. This is especially important on older boats. Through-hull fittings are typically bronze, although in recent years there has been a swing to plastic.

Gate valves have no place on a boat, and it is amazing they are still

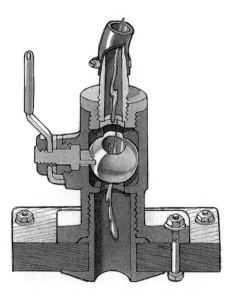

Figure 13.3
Through-hull valve.

around. Gate valves can be easily jammed open if any debris gets caught on the seat of the valve, and the valve stems have a nasty habit of corroding and breaking. It is a strange and memorable feeling to open or close a gate valve when you are 3000 miles from anywhere and have the stem and handle twist off. You stand there for a few moment staring at the alien object in your hand, trying to understand how it got there. If your boat happens to have any gate valves, replace them no matter how good they look.

For many years the bronze, tapered-plug, seacock was the standard valve for yachts. Even these can become worn and fail to stop water flow when they are closed. The best seacock these days is a quality ball valve. It has a bronze body, stainless steel ball valve, and Teflon seat. It requires almost no maintenance and has a long life under normal use. Do some comparative shopping for ball valves. I have seen the exact same valve for sale by a chandlery and by a plumbing supply house for widely different prices. Be sure the handle you buy is stainless steel.

It is now possible to buy high-quality non-metallic through-hull fittings and valves, and they are gaining in popularity. They have definite advantages because they are light in weight and will not be subject to electrolysis. Of particular importance is that they are not likely to be destroyed if the boat is struck by lightning – something that has led to sinking in the past. I am not sure if the jury is in yet on plastic through-hulls and valves. They are pretty much standard these days for knot-meter transducers, so why not for valves? If you do choose non-metallic through-hulls and valves, be absolutely sure of the quality of material. Those made of Xytel and Marelon by DuPont are reported to be extremely strong but the arm connecting the lever to the ball has a nasty habit of breaking after a few years of use. I recommend waiting a few years for the plastic valves to prove themselves.

Make an inspection of all of your through-hull valves a few days prior to hauling out for maintenance and bottom painting. A simple test is to close the valve and carefully remove the hose connection. Be prepared for some water in the hose to drain out. Then watch the valve and see if it is seeping or letting any water through. If the valve is not doing its job there will be some leakage and the valve can be overhauled or replaced during haul-out.

Hoses used on salt-water valves or seacocks should be made of clear vinyl with nylon braid reinforcement. At every connection there should be two stainless steel hose clamps. When you are shopping for hose clamps take along a magnet and be sure that all parts of the clamp are stainless steel. Don't take anyone's word for this. Test each clamp yourself. Some plastic hose clamps are now appearing on the market. They should be avoided.

If all of the foregoing recommendations are followed, there should be no problems of broken or leaking valves. But for one more fail-safe, attach a tapered, softwood plug of appropriate size to each through-hull fitting. Most yachts carry such plugs on board, but if they are stowed in some inaccessible place they will be of little use in an emergency.

Fresh-Water System

The potable water system on a yacht includes the deck filling connection, storage tank(s), hoses, and pumps. Be sure the deck fill has a good closure and think about a spare screw cap, or at least a rubber bung in case the permanent one goes swimming. Water tanks need an air escape line that rises higher than the deck filling valve. One way to make this is to run a hose from the tank(s) up through the deck and inside a stanchion. The air line is necessary to keep a vacuum from forming when pumping out of the tank, and to permit more rapid filling of the tank.

Water tanks are usually stainless steel or fiberglass. They need to be looked at once or twice a year, or more frequently if the water begins to taste strange. I clean my tanks with a cloth and baking soda and then rinse them out before filling. It may also be necessary to clean out the hoses if the boat has been sitting idle for a while.

ELECTRICAL SYSTEM

The 12-volt direct current (12 VDC) electrical systems used on sailboats are simple and reasonably safe. Any electrical work requires caution for the amateur or professional, but 12 VDC is far safer than the 110- or 220-volt AC that is widely used on land. Almost any job such as running wires, connecting up a control panel, taking care of the batteries, monitoring use of electricity, or installing lights and electronics can be done by you and your crew.

Electrical problems on sailboats usually result from loose connections, salt-water contamination, or overloading the system by adding more electrical and electronic equipment than it can support. Overloading is especially a problem on cruiser/racers that are converted to long-distance cruisers. The original equipment on a cruiser/racer is designed for daysailing or short sailing trips where the engine is frequently used and power is only needed for starting the engine and occasional use of cabin and running lights. The same boat on an extended cruise will use the engine infrequently, but power consumption will increase with long periods of using running lights and cabin lights as well as an increased collection of electric and electronic equipment. If power-hungry items such as an anchor windlass, radar, or refrigeration are added, the crew will need to run the engine more and more to charge batteries, and will eventually need better sources of power.

Energy Requirements

In preparing for offshore cruising, calculate your expected power consumption to see if the electrical system is adequate. This can be done by listing all the electrical equipment on board, its expected energy requirements, and the number of hours it will typically be operated each day. Figure 1 is an example of a power-use 'budget' that you can modify to suit your boat. This will give you an approximate idea of your electrical needs in amperage hours, or amp hours. From this you can make some ballpark estimates of how your supply and demand may balance out.

If, for example, you estimate you need 90 amp hours and you have an alternator that is rated at 40 amps, you would theoretically need to run the engine (which runs the alternator) for two and one-quarter hours each day (40 amps/hr $\times$ 2.25 hours = 90 amp hours). In reality it is not so simple, because the system is not perfect. Furthermore, the alternator rating of 40 amps is based on its output at high engine RPMs, and you will probably be running your engine at a much lower setting.

Figure 14.1
Electrical budget sheet.

EXPECTED POWER CONSUMPTION

Equipment	Amperage	Daily Hours	Amp-hours
Cabin lights	_____	_____	_____
Running lights	_____	_____	_____
Bilge pump	_____	_____	_____
VHF radio	_____	_____	_____
SSB radio	_____	_____	_____
Weatherfax	_____	_____	_____
Loran	_____	_____	_____
GPS	_____	_____	_____
SatNav	_____	_____	_____
Radar	_____	_____	_____
Refrigeration	_____	_____	_____
Autopilot	_____	_____	_____
Depthsounder	_____	_____	_____
Stereo	_____	_____	_____
_____	_____	_____	_____
_____	_____	_____	_____
_____	_____	_____	_____
Totals	_____	_____	_____

Wiring Diagram

Boats commonly start their lives with a very simple and easy-to-trace electrical system, but through time equipment is added and you lose track of what wire goes to which piece of equipment. If you have bought a used boat it is important to trace out the electrical system early on, not only to understand its organization, but also to check for faulty or improper wiring. Sometimes older boats have such terrible wiring that it may be necessary to rip most of it out and start over – not as difficult a task as it sounds.

A wiring diagram can be basic or elaborate. It can simply show where the wires run from the batteries to the control panel, and to the lights or pieces of equipment they supply, or it might show greater detail and include all fuses, circuit breakers and switches.

Once you have diagramed your electrical system, keep it updated. As new wiring and equipment are added, change the diagram accordingly. When I bought my present boat, the wiring system included running lights, engine instruments, four cabin lights, a bilge pump, and one VHF radio. Now there is an autopilot, a new set of running lights, eight new cabin lights, SatNav, GPS, a radar warning indicator, RDF, a stereo cassette player, SSB radio, a refrigerator, computer and printer, radar, weatherfax, depthsounder, knotmeter, and electrically controlled safety features for the propane stove. Obviously, this is a system that went from light and simple to rather heavy and fairly complicated. As I added each piece of equipment, I was sure that I would remember how each new item had been wired, and which wire was which. Now, I find that my memory was not as good as I thought, and I wish I had put more detail into my wiring diagram. For a new owner coming on board it could be confusing.

Wiring and Connections

When rewiring, or adding equipment, it is important to calculate the correct wire size as determined from the amperage required and the round trip distance between the power source and the equipment. The tables in Appendix 2 show the recommended AWG and metric wire sizes. Notice that they list current drops of three and ten percent. For electronic equipment a drop of three percent is tolerable, and for other equipment, ten percent.

Don't try to get by with a wire twisted or wound onto the screw or clip fitting. Such connections will not last long, and they offer the possibility of electrical short circuits. You should have some kind of soldering tool that you can use on board. The choices are 12 VDC, a butane soldering tool, or an old-style iron that can be heated on the stove. Terminals and splices should be soldered (with rosin-core solder), to prevent breaking of the wire by vibration or corrosion by salt water. Soldering takes more time, but it is worth the trouble.

Typically, 12 VDC terminals are installed with an electrician's crimping tool, or a pair of pliers. It is OK to make the initial connection in this way, but the wire-to-terminal join should still be soldered before it is put in use. There is always a lot of moisture and salt on a boat that can enter between the strands of the wire and eventually corrode the wire and weaken the connection. If the plastic covering comes off in the process of soldering that is no problem.

Select wire with care and be prepared to pay for quality. There are various grades of electrical wire. That used for most wiring in houses and on simple appliances is not adequate for boat use. Marine-grade wire is sealed in a plastic covering, has more strands to insure greater flexibility, and is tin-plated for proper soldering. Most terminal connectors are also tin-coated copper. Hence, soldering tinned wire to these terminals will reduce galvanic action and keep the connections corrosion-free for a long time.

Wire that is not designed for use under high humidity and moisture will quickly corrode and break down. One way to see this is to strip

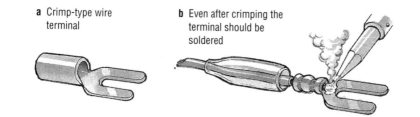

a Crimp-type wire terminal

b Even after crimping the terminal should be soldered

Figure 14.2
Electrical wire terminals.

143

back the covering from a piece of wire on your boat that has been in use for a while. If the wire still has a bright copper color, it is all right, but if it is dark green or black, it means that moisture has penetrated inside the plastic cover and begun to corrode the wire.

Ancor brand is widely recognized in North America as the leader in marine wire. It is expensive, but it will be more resistant to corrosion. It is an excellent idea to code the wiring system with numbered or lettered plastic labels, which can be purchased from an electronic or electrical supply company. Each wire should have a number designation repeated at five- or six-foot intervals. Color coding is a nice idea, but you can spend a lot of time and money trying to find all of the colors you need.

The System

This section is an overview of a typical sailboat electrical system. It is only a starting point, a sketch map of the campus. To improve your electrical skills read Beyn or Brotherton, which are devoted specifically to 12 VDC. Other valuable references that cover the engine and electrical system are books by Calder, Goring, Spurr and Pike.

Figure 14.3
Basic electrical system.

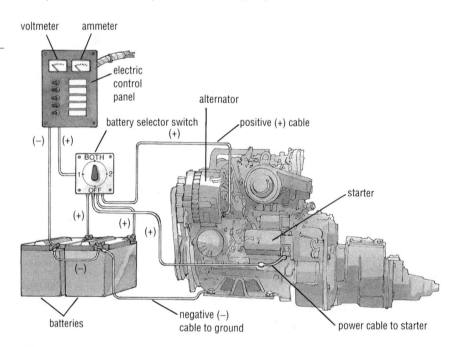

Alternator

This is where the electrical power is generated. The alternator is driven by a belt from the engine's flywheel. In most cases small diesel engines are sold with an alternator installed on the engine. Such alternators are only adequate for keeping batteries charged for daysailing or weekend trips. It is possible to install larger-capacity, deep-cycle batteries, but this does not completely solve the problem because the batteries still need to be charged and the small alternator is not up to the job. To improve this situation, it is necessary to install an alternator controller or to add a higher-output alternator.

An alternator controller serves to bypass the original voltage regulator installed on the alternator. Alternators were developed for use on automobiles, not boats, and the car's demands for electrical power are much different. Almost the only time you need electrical power for a car is when it is in operation. On a sailboat, electrical power may be needed whether the engine is in operation or not. The car alternator produces maximum charging as soon as the engine is started, and then the charging rate is reduced. On a boat in which electrical power is used constantly, it requires a lot of engine time to bring a battery up to full charge. An alternator controller permits a continuous high rate of charge so that the batteries will charge more quickly. Alternator controllers can be automatic or manual. The automatic type is more expensive, but the manual type requires more careful operation by the crew. Most offshore sailors use their engines so little, and then mostly to charge batteries, that the manual alternator controller is sufficient.

Before I left Georgia to sail to the Pacific I went from a 40-amp to an 80-amp alternator. A year later I installed an alternator controller. Two years after that I put in a 140 amp alternator and tossed out the alternator controller. Now, with that setup, plus four solar panels, I have all the power I need. In the tropics I rarely even need to use my engine to charge batteries. But if I do, the charging goes quickly with the engine running at idle speed, while the alternator supplies 90 amps and charges both of my 120-amp-hour batteries.

A number of companies produce these high-output alternators and advertise in the sailing magazines. One of the major suppliers is Balmar of Seattle.

Battery Selector Switch

If you have more than one battery on your boat – and you should have at least two – it is necessary to have a battery selector switch. The selector switch has four positions: Battery 1, Battery 2, Both, and Off. This allows you to delegate one battery for starting the engine and the other for electrical needs, and gives you the option to charge one or both batteries when the engine is running.

In the past, standard procedure on yachts has been to use one battery for engine starting only, and one (or more) to supply power for electrical equipment. Before the engine was started the 'engine battery' was selected and after the engine was in operation the selector switch was changed to one or the other, or both batteries for charging. When the alternator is not charging, one or the other is selected for use and the other is reserved for starting.

Another method is to alternate between batteries each day for 'household' electrical needs and, depending on your power usage, to charge batteries every two to four days. This method requires more responsibility on the part of the crew to frequently monitor battery charge condition, but it provides a more efficient operation and longer battery life.

It is important to know the type of battery selector switch you have and how it operates. Some battery selector switches are such that if they are turned to the 'off' position while the engine is running they can burn out the alternator and other equipment.

Batteries

In deciding how many and what size batteries you will need, refer to the 'power consumption table' mentioned earlier in this chapter. This will tell you how many amp-hours you expect to use each day. Your batteries' storage capacity should be at least twice this amount. For example, if you anticipate a normal amp-hour use of 100 your batteries should be 200 minimum, and more would be better.

Recommendations for deep-cycle marine battery use suggests not letting batteries discharge more than 50 percent for most efficient use. A fully charged battery will have a voltage of 12.6 volts, and a half discharged battery will read 12.2 volts. To determine this requires an accurate voltage meter; preferably a digital meter. A battery that is down to 12.2 volts is still capable of starting your engine if necessary.

There are so many different kinds of batteries, and so many assurances of perfection by battery manufacturers, that it is difficult to decide what is best for your boat. Typical automobile batteries are not suited for constant use as on a cruising yacht. 'Deep-cycle' batteries are built to be able to withstand repeated charge and discharge. They are designed to put out a small amount of amperage for a long time, compared to a typical automotive battery, which will deliver a large amount of amps for a short time. Some batteries, supposedly designed specifically for boats, are nothing more than batteries produced for other purposes – except that they cost more. Deep-cycle batteries manufactured for heavy equipment operation will work fine on a boat.

The place and method of battery storage is an important consideration. When a battery is charging, it heats up and emits explosive gases, so there must be adequate ventilation. To be properly maintained, a battery should be inspected frequently, and this requires accessible storage. Maintenance includes making sure that the electrolyte level is correct and of the proper strength. The battery must remain clean and the cable connections kept tight.

Hard starting and poor charging are often due to loose battery connections or corroded battery terminals. In fact when trying to trace any electrical problem on a boat the best place to start your search is at the battery terminals. Make sure the connections are tight and that there is no buildup of corrosive material at the terminals.

Batteries must be held securely in place with non-metallic brackets or straps. The electrolyte in a battery is acid, and if the battery moves or tumbles in heavy seas the acid will spill and be a hazard to crew and equipment. Batteries are heavy and can become lethal weapons if they break loose in a knockdown or capsize.

There is no need to consider batteries as expendable items that must be replaced every year or so. A properly selected and maintained bank of marine batteries can last more than 10 years. The major reason for short battery life is incorrect charging and discharging procedures.

Voltmeter and Ammeter

Between the battery selector switch and the electrical control panel, a voltmeter and ammeter should be installed. The voltmeter indicates the amount of charge going to the battery while it is charging. Both dial and digital type of meters are available; the digital is preferred because it is more precise.

An ammeter gives an indication of the amount of current being used. It is located in line between the battery selector switch and the positive bus bar of the electric control panel. Monitoring this meter will help you control power usage and indicate when too much equipment is in use.

Electric Control Panel

Most production boats are built with an electric control panel already installed. Older boats used a fused board, but in recent years all boats come with circuit breakers, which are more convenient.

Boats that have been used primarily for daysailing and local cruising will probably need to have a second panel added to accommodate additional electrical and electronic equipment. This is much better than overloading the existing panel, and it is best to have a separate switch for each piece of gear.

An electric control panel consists of a positive bus bar which is wired to the battery control switch, a negative bus bar which is connected to the negative terminal of the batteries, and a series of fused or breaker-type on/off switches. Each switch should be labeled with the equipment it controls. The positive wire for each piece of equipment or system (as in the case of cabin lights) is connected at its respective switch on the positive bus bar. The negative wires can be connected anywhere on the negative bus bar.

Usually the control panel switches are in one or more vertical rows. It is a good idea to arrange the order of the switches in some sort of logical sequence to permit easy operation in the dark. For example, on my boat, which has two vertical columns of switches, the top left switch is for the cabin lights and the remaining five below it are all for the running lights and deck lights. I arranged them that way so that in an emergency situation where the possibility of a collision exists, all of the outside lights (running lights, anchor light, bow and stern light, strobe, and spreader lights), can be quickly turned on without having to figure out which is which.

Some control panels have indicator lights to show when equipment is on or off, and to make the switch labels easy to read. As an added safety precaution the electric bilge pump should be on a separate circuit with its switch located next to the main control panel.

In setting up or adding equipment to the control panel, take care to not overload it. Notice that each switch has a fuse or circuit breaker with a designated maximum amperage. Overloading circuits can reduce the performance of the equipment it serves, and is also dangerous: if you exceed the maximum, the circuit breaker should trip or the fuse should blow, but if it doesn't, a fire may result. If you have to connect more than one piece of equipment or system to a switch, the combined load of the two should not exceed the fuse or circuit breaker maximum.

Instructions for wiring electronic equipment often indicate that the gear should be wired directly to the battery. The reason electronic manufacturers suggest this is to assure maximum efficiency for their equipment, and to avoid fluctuations in voltage and possible damage due to power surges. While this was a problem with old-style generators, it is not a problem with modern alternators, and it is much more convenient to wire to a control panel. If in doubt check with the manufacturer.

In locating or relocating an electrical panel, mount it in a place where it will be kept dry at all times, and where it will be easy to service. Most panels are made to be set into a hull liner or bulkhead with four or more screws. This means that to change wiring or to inspect it, all of the screws must be taken out. A more convenient way to mount the panel is on a hinged door that can be swung out for inspection of the wiring in back.

Alternating Current (AC)

Shore-power

Some marinas offer shore-power connections to yachts alongside docks and pontoons. Voltage of these systems will vary depending on the country, but are usually 100- to 120-volts AC. *This power cannot be routed to the boat's 12 VDC system.* For a yacht to use alternating current from shore-power it must have an additional wiring system designed for AC use only. If you expect to use shore-power frequently and want to install receptacles on board for its use, they should be completely different and separate from the boat's DC system to avoid electrical shock and destruction of equipment.

AC power and voltage are inherently more dangerous to handle than 12-volt DC. In some marinas the AC electrical systems are not well maintained and often have been modified by inexperienced users. Use them with caution and be sure they are properly grounded when used on your boat. If you add AC power capability, also install a 'ground-fault circuit interrupter', which stops current flow if the electric ground is lost. In addition, there should be a circuit breaker installed on your boat's AC shore-power system.

A typical use of shore-power is to charge batteries, in which case an AC-powered battery charger will be needed. As an offshore cruiser you will soon realize that in many parts of the world there are no marinas, and even when they do exist, shore-power is not usually provided. Life will be easier if you learn to live without it.

Inverters

Formerly, converting from DC to AC on a small boat required bulky equipment that produced AC power only suitable for certain equipment. Now, a new generation of inverters has appeared which will give smooth AC power even to such delicate electronic equipment as computers, TVs, VCRs, as well as microwave ovens and normal household appliances. This is an attractive option because most 12 VDC appliances made for 'marine use' have a high price. At present the new generation of small, lightweight inverters are expensive conveniences. In the future they will probably become lower priced as the market expands.

Lightning Protection

Protecting the boat and crew from lightning is a subject few of us understand. There are a lot of stories and legends about sailboats and lightning, and remarkably little factual or reliable information. One of the best analyses of the subject appeared in the June 15, 1988 issue of *Practical Sailor*. This no-nonsense discussion includes comments by people whose boats were struck by lightning, and a list of equipment to provide protection.

Most of us have heard about the so-called 'cone of protection' that characterizes sailboats. With a grounded mast, any lightning striking within the area of the cone of protection will be diverted to the mast which offers some assurance of safety to the crew.

Whereas the possibility of a boat being struck by lightning is remote, it does happen. There are certain areas of the world in which lightning strikes are more prevalent, but it can happen anywhere. The boat can receive a direct hit at sea or in port, or a side hit from a boat nearby that is struck first. It is not possible to prevent lightning from striking your boat, but there are some things you can do to provide protection from damage if the boat is hit.

It is well known that lightning 'seeks' the shortest path from the sky to the ground, and the mast of a yacht offers a shortcut. If your mast is the chosen shortcut, it should at least provide a direct exit path for the lightning. You don't want it wandering around looking for a place to go!

One kind of path is made by assuring that the mast is in direct contact with the keel, if the keel is of the external ballast type. This is not the case for deck-stepped masts, and it may not necessarily be the case even for a keel-stepped mast. Some masts are insulated from the keel to prevent electrolysis, and some boats have keels encased in fiberglass.

The most reliable system is to have a lightning rod installed at the masthead, extending higher than any antennas or instruments. It should be connected to the keel (via a keelbolt, for example) by #8 AWG wire. (See Appendix 2.) Otherwise, the wire from the masthead should be connected to a through-bolted ground plate on the outside of the hull below the waterline. The ground plate should be as close to the base of the mast as possible. A lightning protection system applies equally to boats with wood, metal, or any other type of mast, although for non-metallic masts it is especially important.

Another suggestion for grounding, occasionally espoused, is to link the mast and rigging with heavy electrical cable, such as welding cable, and attach it to a length of chain, which then can be trailed in the water during an electrical storm. Some sailors even rely on this as their only lightning protection. Although this may seem like an easy or 'quick-fix' solution to the problem, it has its drawbacks. This is just some more

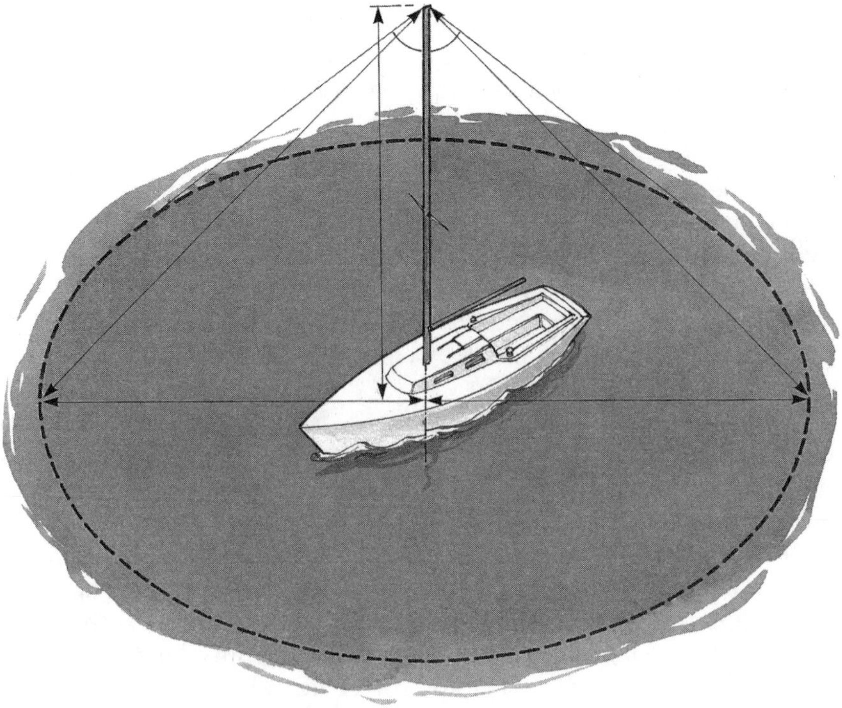

Figure 14.4
Lightning cone of protection.

gear to keep track of, and in a sudden, unexpected storm you may have many other tasks that will prevent you from rigging a temporary grounding device. Once a lightning storm is in progress, I for one, would not want to tempt fate by connecting metal wires to the mast and rigging.

Accounts by people whose boats have been struck by lightning indicate that sometimes the equipment is unaffected, sometimes only fuses are blown, and sometimes the various radios, navigation equipment, depthsounders, engine alternators, and starters are completely destroyed. Regardless of what preparatory steps you take, the crew must exercise good judgment in an electrical storm. Most important is to stay out of contact with the mast, rigging, lifelines, engine controls, or anything else that is metallic and a possible conductor of electricity either from the direct lightning strike or from induced voltages. The safest place to be is inside the boat, and so anyone not needed on deck should stay below.

Of course, you should avoid lightning storms if possible. Sometimes this cannot be done, but often, especially in the tropics, thunderheads can be seen far in advance and it is possible to change course until you are in the clear.

Bonding

Although separate from the lightning protection system on a boat, bonding is related to it. On non-metal boats with a 12-volt DC electrical system, a bonding system is often recommended to provide a low-resistance electrical path inside the hull between isolated metallic objects which are subject to electrolysis. This is especially important for metals in contact with salt water. A bonding system also provides a low-resistance electrical path to ground in the event of excessive voltages that can occur if the boat is struck by lightning. In addition, a bonding system will reduce radio interference.

That's the good news. The bad news is that there is a wide range of opinion on whether bonding is necessary or even desirable. Whereas some knowledgeable people, such as the American Boat and Yacht Council, consider bonding mandatory, there are some engineers and electrical experts who consider it a waste of time and money.

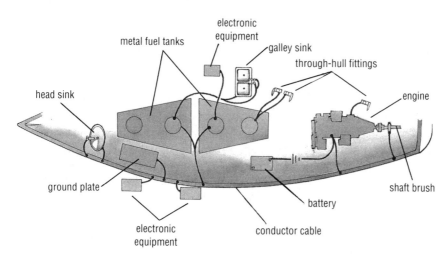

Figure 14.5
Bonding recommendations by the American Boat and Yacht Council.

For those who consider bonding a good idea, the accepted method of installation is to run a fore-and-aft conductor cable the length of the boat, but not in the bilge. This should be an uninsulated copper or bronze strip with minimum thickness of 0.8 mm and width of at least 13 mm; if wire is used, it should be uninsulated copper wire with a diameter of at least #8 AWG. (See Appendix 2 on electric cable sizes.) All permanently installed metallic objects are attached to it with #9 AWG or larger wire – metal tanks, metal plumbing fixtures, through-hull fittings, the chassis of radios and other electronic equipment, and the engine (also the shaft if it is separated from the engine by a non-metallic coupling).

Alternative Energy Sources

It always takes me a long time to believe that something new is going to work for my boat. I still haven't gotten around to roller furling, and I remain skeptical of electronic charts. It doesn't really bother me that my cutting edge is rather dull, because by the time I get around to accepting what everyone else already knows is wonderful, I can buy the lower-priced version that has all of the bugs worked out of it.

Solar panels are an exception to this, however. I finally discovered them about two years ago after nearly everyone else had them aboard. But my conversion was instantaneous and I am a true believer. They really have improved my way of cruising.

I have four three-amp solar panels. They are mounted in two pairs on the stern pulpit and can be adjusted through nearly 270 degrees of arc to catch the sun from dawn to dusk. Between 30 degrees north and 30 degrees south latitude they have sustained all of my electrical needs on every clear day. Now I only run my engine once a week, and that is only done for the good of the engine. With this power source I run an ice box, my computer, cabin lights, stereo and electronic toys, as well as running lights when underway. Solar panels are passive and maintenance-free. It is important, however, to have a charge controller to avoid damaging the batteries by overcharging. Keep a close watch on battery electrolyte as well, because the batteries are being charged continuously each day.

In most cruising anchorages you will see *and hear* a number of wind generators whirring away. Some boats have them permanently mounted for use underway and in port. Others just hoist them up in the rigging when swinging on the hook. The performance is excellent on some days, but a drawback is the noise they make. Interestingly, I never notice the noise mine makes, but those on other boats often keep me awake. I rarely use my wind generator any more – it's one more piece of gear to keep track of. Whereas I can ignore solar panels completely, the windmill has to be taken up and down whenever I switch anchorages. Furthermore, whenever I leave the boat to go ashore, I don't like to leave it unattended, so I turn it off and let a lot of potential power blow on by. I also think of those whirling blades as a bit dangerous.

Water generators are another item I have experimented with. I have used mine very few times because it is a hassle and the output does not seem to me to justify the trouble. It surely does affect boatspeed. I have never heard any cruiser mention using a water generator on a routine basis.

A lot of boats carry small, portable gasoline generators capable of producing AC or DC current. They are very handy to have for running power tools, and to charge batteries in a pinch. Most are small enough that nearly any sailboat can find a place for one. If you do decide to have one aboard, ask around for opinions on the best models. Before you buy, listen to the generator in operation. Some are much quieter than others. Honda generators have a good reputation for maintenance-free operation.

ELECTRONICS

Electronics for offshore cruising can be as lavish as you can afford or as simple as you need. With the plethora of beeping gadgets offered for sale, it is often difficult to distinguish between tools and toys. Advertisements strive to convince us that without this gear, the safety of our boat and crew is in jeopardy, and that with it, the ocean will look as serene as a Botticelli painting.

Regardless of the electronics you decide to have on board, keep two facts in mind:

- *You can get along without any of it.* There are hundreds of boats out cruising that use only the most basic equipment, not significantly different from what was used 100 years ago. Ironically, some of these boats have electronics on board, but the owners have become weary of the cost and inconvenience required to maintain them.
- *You will be forced to get along without it.* The time will come, if you sail long enough, when the electronics will let you down, either due to a power problem or equipment (receiver or transmitter) malfunction. When it does, the situation will be either inconvenient or dangerous, depending on how much you depend on the equipment.

Having said that, I must add that I am just as guilty as anyone of having my share of toys – and I love them. I think GPS is wonderful. Yes, it has indeed made me very lazy, and although I do still use my sextant, I don't use it as religiously as I used to. I consider the new 406 MHz EPIRB one of the most significant safety breakthroughs in modern sailing history. I give very high marks to the weatherfax; it gives me greater freedom and less dependence on other sources of weather information. However, it is important to distinguish between convenience, usefulness, and need when trying to balance the electronic budget.

General Considerations

It is true that many of the electronic devices available to the small-boat sailor offer convenience, simplify cruising, and serve to relieve anxiety in difficult situations – sometimes it is false relief, but relief nonetheless. On the other hand, none of this equipment is cheap, and some of it will eventually require expensive repair. In short, most of it is in the category of luxury or convenience – the things you buy with 'disposable income.'

The life of most electronics is rather short. If you manage to get five years of uninterrupted service out of most of it, consider yourself fortunate. The only piece of electronic gear that has survived the five-year limit on my boat is a VHF radio. Usually, a piece of broken equipment, when sent to a repair facility, often at significant expense, is found to be reparable, but the price of the repair is about half the cost of a new unit. When selecting possible electronic gear for your boat, make your choice based on your cruising plans. If you already have Loran C and it covers the area you will be sailing in, why bother with GPS at this time? On the other hand, if you are choosing between Loran, SatNav, or GPS, the only choice is GPS.

A radar is very useful if you are sure to be sailing in areas of fog, but otherwise it is hardly necessary on a cruising boat. A commonly cited use for radar is making landfalls and entering harbors at night. GPS is usually as good as radar for making a conservative landfall. Even so, a prudent yachtsman will heave-to and wait for daylight before entering an unknown or poorly lighted harbor, even with a radar on board. I have had a radar for the past seven years. In that time I have entered about 150 harbors and ports, and have only considered using it once or twice.

If you are spending a year or more preparing your boat for a long-distance cruise, put off buying any electronic gear as long as possible. Without exception, electronics become cheaper with time. GPS is an excellent example. In five years it went from $8,000 to less than $1000. In another five years you will probably be able order a GPS receiver with a proof of purchase certificate from a box of Wheaties, and get a decoder ring as part of the deal. The only time there is a price increase for electronics is when a new model appears. And when that happens it usually means you can pick up the older model at an even lower price.

For those on a limited budget, electronics should be the very last thing to purchase, after everything has been done to make the yacht seaworthy.

No matter what type of electronic navigation equipment you select, don't become complacent and fail to also use your sextant whenever you can. It is still the simplest and most practical navigation tool on board. There will be days when the weather is such that the sextant is impossible to use, and you will rejoice at having the electronics to help. But there will also come a day when the electronics will let you down and the sextant will see you through.

If there are two or more crew aboard, keep your celestial navigation skills sharp with a little competition. Have one crewmember maintain a plot using the sextant and another maintain a separate plot using the electronics. Alternate responsibilities every few days.

Nearly all on-board electronics these days can be installed by the crew – but pick locations carefully. Most of the modern equipment is fairly rugged but will not survive very long if it becomes doused with sea spray or rain. The more barriers you can put between the electronics and the marine environment, the better. Few of the readouts need to be in view. The only exceptions are the radar screen and depthsounder, both of which should be visible to the helmsman.

VHF

A VHF radio is the most useful transceiver radio on board. VHF is line-of-sight communication, so the range is seldom much more than 30 miles, depending on the heights of the transmitting and receiving equipment. It will be considerably less in some areas and with some radios.

VHF has several important uses on board. It is the primary method for communicating with other vessels at sea. Almost all commercial shipping continuously monitors VHF Channel 16. Merchant ships at sea are usually willing to give you current weather reports, a navigation position, or even just chat for a few minutes. When approaching land, VHF is useful for obtaining weather or navigation information from shore stations, or to get advice on entering harbors. In some areas of heavy ship traffic there are continuous or periodic broadcasts giving important updates on navigation aids and weather. In most areas of the world local coast guard and military facilities monitor VHF Channel 16 for those in need of assistance. When entering an unfamiliar harbor, VHF can be used to obtain information on where to proceed for anchoring, quarantine, and customs and immigration procedures.

Throughout the United States and its possessions the National Oceanographic and Atmospheric Administration (NOAA) broadcasts continuous weather summaries that can be received on VHF radios equipped with weather channels.

When sailing in heavy fog, before I had a radar, I would broadcast my position, course, and speed on VHF Channel 16 as a SECURITY-category message if I suspected there were any ships around. A sailboat is easily overlooked on a ship's radar. My assumption was that by frequently announcing my location it might alert the ships in my area and cause the watch to be more vigilant.

There is an excellent variety of marine VHF radios available, both fixed models and handhelds. Since signals are sent and received line-of-sight, the fixed models with masthead antennas have much greater range than handhelds. They operate on the boat's 12 VDC power supply, and can typically transmit at as much as 25 watts. Handheld units have neither the range nor the transmitting power (three to six watts), but they do a good job in most situations, and they have the advantage of an independent power supply and portability. On singlehanded or shorthanded boats it's often inconvenient or dangerous to leave the helm and go below to talk on the radio; the handheld solves that problem. More importantly, if you ever have to abandon ship and take to your liferaft, a handheld radio could be your most valuable aid to being rescued. Almost without exception, those who have survived long periods of time in a liferaft describe seeing several ships before they were eventually rescued. They tried to contact the ship with flares, smoke signals, flashed lights, or a heliograph, without getting any response. Yet almost all ships on the high seas have a radio continuously tuned to VHF Channel 16.

The ideal solution might be to have a fixed-mount VHF as the primary radio and carry a handheld as a backup. However, if your budget permits only one radio, I'd recommend a handheld. It can do most of what a fixed radio can do; it's smaller, does not require a masthead antenna or wiring, and can be an important link to safety if you have to abandon ship.

Multiband Radio Receiver (150 KHz to 29.999 MHz)

This might be considered the most basic and singularly important piece of electronic equipment to have on board. Its ability to receive time signals for proper celestial navigation is reason enough to have a multiband receiver. In addition it receives regional marine weather broadcasts and hurricane tracking reports. Some multiband receivers can be used with a printer to collect weatherfax maps. If you buy a multiband receiver, be sure it has this ability. Even if you don't want a weatherfax now, you may in the future. An important secondary function of the multiband receiver is as a source of entertainment, news, and information at sea and in port. Not so long ago the huge, heavy, Zenith Transoceanic was used on many boats. Today's models are compact, not much larger than a hardback book.

SSB

Single sideband (SSB) radiotelephones provide long-distance, two-way communication. They can be used for emergency calls or routine traffic to shore stations or to other vessels; for placing calls to a high-seas telephone operator, or for receiving weather broadcasts. SSB can be used to transmit and receive voice messages on Federal Communications Commission (FCC) authorized frequencies between 2 MHz and 28 MHz.

For U.S. boats a station license is required for SSB, but it is a simple matter to obtain one and there is no test or examination to use the radio. A license is required for the ham operator and if you have the proper ham radio license you can use an SSB to talk to other ham operators. Otherwise you can only listen. Thus, for those who only want to transmit over long distances SSB offers the least complicated method. However, the equipment is generally more expensive than that used by a ham operator.

Ham

For some sailors ham radio is a major part of cruising. Day and night they keep several maritime ham nets humming throughout the world. In addition to camaraderie, a lot of sailing hams appreciate the security of staying in touch with a maritime mobile net, especially for regional weather forecasts. For a lot of cruisers the opportunity to use a phone patch and talk to friends and family back home is reason enough to be a ham operator.

To be a ham operator it is necessary to pass a test and obtain license and call sign. Information can be obtained from the American Radio Relay League, Newington, Connecticut 06111. Of course, you do not need to be a ham operator to listen to the broadcasts and weather summaries.

A ham radio transceiver is virtually the same as a SSB radiotelephone, except that it is restricted to transmitting on ham radio frequencies. In fact a ham radio can easily be modified to allow you to transmit on all frequencies – in other words to use it as an SSB. While this is not legal, it is permissible to use the modified radio in an emergency, and should be limited strictly to that. Unlike SSB, it is not permitted to conduct any form of business via ham radio.

Appendix 3 is a worldwide listing of ham nets used by cruising sailors.

If you decide to have a SSB radiotelephone or a ham rig aboard, a proper antenna, antenna tuner, and adequate grounding are essential. For some sailors this is more than a do-it-yourself project. At least get some professional advice to avoid disappointment.

SatCom

Satellite communication is the easiest, most convenient, and clearest form of long-distance marine communication. One of its most significant potential uses is a service named SafetyNET which broadcasts marine safety information and weather broadcasts. Although SatCom is already in operation it is still in the 'big ticket' price category and well beyond what most cruisers are able to pay for its convenience, but probably in a few years it will be standard equipment for cruising.

Navigation Electronics

Impressive advances in technology have been made in electronic navigation in the past few decades, and all of it has brought convenience to the cruising sailor in the form of Decca, Omega, Loran C, SatNav, and GPS. None of this gear was developed solely for yachting – we represent too small a market to encourage research and development. However, the interest in pleasure boating has grown sufficiently to encourage manufacturers to add small-boat equipment as a sideline, and for some of them it has become a big sideline.

With all of this equipment, the convenience of rapidly and effortlessly obtaining a precise position by merely turning on a receiver is enticing. For the cruising sailor, however, cost, power requirements, size, weight, simplicity of operation, and ease of installation also play a role. Imagine installing a radar without the assistance of a technician! That would have been unheard of just a few years ago.

Assets of the various electronic navigation systems include multiple waypoints, course and speed over the ground; range, bearing, and even time to a destination; signals for waypoint arrival; off-course steering, and anchor alarms, to name a few. Many systems can interface with various other instruments and electronic compasses – even radar – and tie all the information into an electronic map – and feed it to the autopilot. Zounds!

It really is a bit mind-boggling, and the application to yacht racing is obvious. But, at the risk of being a spoilsport, I have to really strain to see the value of most of this stuff for the offshore cruising boat. Yes, the basic positioning and performance functions are valuable, but the ability to watch an electronic display of the boat's track through the water is, in my opinion, unnecessary. Just grab the basic GPS receiver and run.

GPS

GPS (Global Positioning System) is now replacing Loran, Decca, Omega, SatNav, RDF, and, for some sailors, no doubt, the sextant. It is the most efficient navigation system ever developed, and there are several handheld receivers available that weigh less than two pounds. I remember lusting after Loran C as little as 15 years ago, but the price was far too high for me. Since then it has come down to less than $300. In the meantime SatNav has gone through a similar evolution and is now almost *passé* with the advent of GPS.

GPS is now giving 24-hour coverage throughout the world. It is certainly the best option for ocean-sailing yachts. On the other hand Loran and even SatNav will continue in operation for several more years in certain parts of the world. Depending on your sailing plans, they may be quite adequate.

GPS provides continuous fixes obtained from several satellites and gives accurate positioning anywhere in the world. It also offers all the functions familiar to Loran users – programmable waypoints, course and speed over the ground, range and bearing to waypoints, and so on. It is almost too wonderful.

The Global Positioning System satellites are operated by the U.S. Department of Defense, which can and does degrade the time signals from the satellites to provide a maximum position error of 100 meters. Without this 'Selective Availability' turned on, GPS receivers offer much more precise accuracy. Still, on an offshore cruising boat, a constant position fix within 100 meters is enough accuracy for most of us.

Radio Direction Finder

Yes, there still is such a thing as a radio direction finder (RDF) and it can still come in handy, even in the world of GPS. In spite of its imprecision RDF is an excellent and relatively inexpensive backup. When all else fails it can help you find your way home.

I am seldom successful at obtaining very precise fixes using an RDF, even with three or more stations. However, it provides an approximate position and it is especially valuable as a homing device. Some of the old RDF receivers were difficult and inconvenient to use and store on board. The new handheld models, such as the Lokata 7 made in England, are easy to use and remarkably accurate.

A small transistor radio can be used as a type of RDF to indicate the direction of a commercial radio station – if you are roughly aware of your position and the location of the transmitting station. But be careful, a transistor radio can indicate both the bearing to the radio station and its reciprocal.

Radar and Radar Detectors

Like other electronic equipment, the adaptation of radar units for use on pleasure craft has captured the attention of numerous manufacturers. It is now possible to buy small, compact raster-scan radars at budget prices. For some sailing situations radar is a valuable navigation tool. In rough seas, and sometimes in rain, it may present a very disappointing picture. If the yacht is heeled 20 degrees or more the radar's range is greatly diminished. Small fishing boats and other sailboats constructed of wood or fiberglass may be invisible on radar. Some radar units are power hungry and cannot be run continuously without frequent battery charging.

Radars have warning systems that can be used to monitor selected sections of the screen with alarms set to sound if a target appears in the selected sector. This warning system can be used at sea or at anchor if your boat drifts. Both are practical uses for radar. However, frequently at sea if the boat is heeled or rolling the alarm system is unreliable. The anchor alarm is a much more attractive option, although a depth-sounder alarm is usually more suited to this task.

There is a strong argument that radar is more reliable than GPS for making landfalls or sailing in poorly charted areas. The problem is that GPS is absolutely correct, whereas, in some parts of the world, the data on which charts are drawn is as much as 200 years old. The early cartographers were enviably accurate in the shoreline details, but sometimes their location of islands or landmasses themselves were out of position by miles, though usually much less. Therefore, when sailing in close proximity to incorrectly charted land, the radar will be more beneficial than GPS. They are both telling you the truth, of course, it's just that there is more than one kind of truth as you have probably suspected all your life.

Is this situation alone sufficient justification to have a radar? I don't think so. Up-to-date charts all warn you about features that are out of correct position. Furthermore, by the time you are close enough to get in trouble with GPS you should be exercising your piloting skills.

In summary, radar is really not necessary on a cruising boat unless you are planning to sail in areas of heavy fog.

A related piece of electronic equipment is the radar detector. The one I have is the Watchman, manufactured by Lokata in England. It is a passive listening device similar to detectors used in cars to warn the driver of police radar. The units used on automobiles, however, will not pick up a ship's radar signal. The Lokata Watchman has a small antenna which can be located inside your boat. If you are within the sweep range of a ship's radar the Watchman will emit a 'beep' with each pass of the sweep. This serves to alert you that a ship is in your vicinity – usually less than five miles away – and permits you to track the ship in fog. It also detects some land-based military radar and military surveillance patrol aircraft radar.

Although all ships have radar they may not be using it in clear weather. I was surprised on a recent passage from Hawaii to San Francisco where I met five large ships during the three weeks passage and not one of them was using its radar during the day or night.

Depthsounder

Most of us restrict our use of the depthsounder to keep from running aground and to assist in anchoring. Don't overlook the value of a depthsounder as a navigation tool. Often it can be used with one, or preferably two, visual fixes to give a very accurate position if a reliable chart is at hand. On some coastlines, sailing by depthsounder in restricted visibility or at night is a primary method of navigation.

Although some boats still use the flasher-type depthsounder, digital readouts are more convenient and the liquid crystal display (LCD) type are easier to read in bright sunlight than the light-emitting diodes (LED). If you have the space and can afford to purchase a paper print-out type depthsounder, it will not only show depth, but record the trend in the change of depth, the configuration of the bottom, and indicate the type of bottom. Valuable information when anchoring.

When selecting a depthsounder, consider the power consumption and beam width. Most sounders use little electric power, but there is considerable variation between models, and now and then it may be desirable to operate the unit for extended periods of time.

The depthsounder's beam width is an important consideration for sailboats. With the boat heeled, a narrow beam transducer will tend to

Figure 15.1
Variable beam widths of depthsounders. Depthsounder readings will vary depending on the type of beam used. In shallow and shoaling water a narrow beam may indicate that the water is deeper than it really is.

give deeper readings than a wide beam. It is important also that the transducer be correctly mounted. For a cruising boat this usually means a transducer which extends through the hull with proper fairing. A fairing block can be purchased from the manufacturer or you can create your own with epoxy or fiberglass resin. Usually the manufacturer will give specific where-to and how-to information for locating the transducer. The readout should be placed where it can be easily read by the helmsman in bright sunlight.

All depthsounders have some sort of alarm system with either pre-set or 'dial in' depths. I rarely use a depth alarm and prefer to monitor the depth by looking at the readout frequently. Too many times in a tight situation when I use the alarm, it is triggered by a fish, or a turtle swimming below the boat, and I nearly jump out of my skin each time it happens. Depth alarms are perhaps useful at anchor to give an indication if you are drifting.

As with any electronic equipment, 'don't put all your eggs in one basket.' Every boat should have a sounding line with a lead weight on board for backup.

Weatherfax

Until just a few years ago weather facsimile receivers were restricted to big ships. The equipment was bulky, expensive, and inconvenient to use because of the 'wet paper' printers. All of this has changed in a short time. Compact, lightweight weatherfax units are now easy to install on any cruising boat. As boat electronics go, a self-contained weatherfax is still relatively expensive ($2000 and up). However, it is possible to buy just a signal processor (and printer) and hook it up to a shortwave radio, which will reduce the price almost in half. If you have a personal computer (PC), and printer, and a shortwave radio, you can buy software that will have you receiving weatherfax maps for a bit over a hundred dollars.

The international system of fax map transmissions puts the small-boat sailor in touch with graphic weather displays nearly anywhere in the world. Up to four times a day you can collect regional weather maps and one-, two-, and five-day forecasts. There are also other products available, depending on the originating station – satellite photos, cloud cover maps, wave and current maps, maps showing the location of the Gulf Stream and other currents, and hurricane or typhoon tracking bulletins. The U.S. Government publication, *Selected Worldwide Marine Weather Broadcasts*, Appendix 14, gives the schedules of weatherfax broadcasts throughout the world.

Weatherfax may seem to be a luxury item, but if so, it is certainly a practical one for some sailing situations. When on an ocean passage, and when anchored in remote places, it is often impossible to obtain weather forecasts that are useful to a small sailboat. Regional voice radio broadcasts are transmitted by a variety of governmental agencies throughout the world, but they are designed to give brief summaries for large commercial ships and they emphasize heavy

Weather Data Electronics

weather. Usually they mention only winds greater than 30 knots, seas greater than 12 feet, and the position of significant low-pressure centers. A weather map, on the other hand, gives you the whole picture and the opportunity to consider developing weather patterns. Regardless of the station from which the weather map originates, the meteorologic symbols follow a universal scheme. Anyone can learn to read a weather map and collecting and studying the daily maps in sequence will improve your understanding of weather systems and your forecast skills.

When I left America in 1985, I thought about installing a weather-fax but decided it was too expensive. A few months of sailing in the Far East changed my mind. There, weather changes very rapidly as frontal systems continually move off the Asian continent. These fast-moving, relatively small systems are not of sufficient significance to warrant mention on regional weather broadcasts from Guam, but they are discernable on a regional weather summary map. Now I consider weatherfax to be one of the most important 'luxuries' I have on board.

Navtex

Another convenient source of weather and navigational information in coastal areas is Navtex. This is an international radiotelex system which eventually will offer worldwide coverage within 200 miles of major continental coastlines. Messages concerning weather and important notices to mariners are continuously broadcast, and special alerts are signaled as necessary. All messages are printed in English on a paper roll, and the receiver can be set to record only certain category messages. For ocean passages, Navtex would be of little use. For extended cruising in coastal areas, for example Northern Europe or the Mediterranean, it is handy.

Electronic Performance Instruments

Numerous tempting electronic instruments are displayed in the marine supply catalogs. All of them have been developed for racing and the cruising sailor can easily live without any of them, save perhaps, a knotmeter/log. A knotmeter will add precision to your dead reckoning and, if you are willing to spend the time playing with sheeting angles and sail combinations, a knotmeter can help make you a better sailor.

Having sailed for years without an electronic windspeed and direction indicator I cannot imagine needing one, and I would definitely put it in the category of luxury items for the cruiser. You quickly learn to estimate windspeed based on the appearance of the sea surface and seat-of-the-pants inspiration. It isn't necessary to have an instrument read-out to tell you when to reef or make a headsail change – at least not more than once or twice. Furthermore, these instruments will all occasionally need to be repaired or replaced. A good masthead fly, such as the Windex, is an excellent indicator of apparent wind direction, as is a piece of yarn tied to a shroud.

Electronic compasses are certainly nifty gadgets and their precision is unquestioned. However, they are expensive and simply not needed for cruising. If you happen to own a boat with an electronic compass, be sure to also have a magnetic compass mounted in the cockpit.

High-tech racing yachts now employ integrated instrument systems that combine all of the various readouts of position, true and apparent windspeed and angle, boatspeed, and when to put the cat out. All of this is fed to a computer and processed to produce an impressive array of information which, if interpreted and used correctly, can help the boats win races. As impressive as all of this appears, and as expensive as it all really is, it requires accurate calibration and frequent adjustment to be of much use. Bottom line: you don't need it.

EPIRBs

EPIRB is the acronym for *Emergency Position-Indicating Radio Beacon*. An EPIRB is the marine equivalent of the ELTs (emergency locator transmitters) originally developed for aircraft. The purpose of an EPIRB is to transmit a radio signal indicating that an emergency exists. It is a transmitter only, and sends an emergency signal on specific VHF channels designated by international agreement and preset by the manufacturer. It does not require any tuning or adjustment; it has only one switch, which the user turns on in the event of an emergency in which assistance is urgently required. Some models are designed to float free and be activated automatically if the vessel should sink. Most sailboats use a less expensive EPIRB which must be manually activated.

EPIRBs are required equipment on commercial ships. For private boats they are optional, and may be installed at the yacht owner's discretion, although most offshore yacht races require participants to have them.

EPIRBs have been responsible for saving many lives over the years, but their misuse has resulted in an incredible number of false alarms at a tremendous cost in money and time. A few years ago the U.S. Coast Guard reported that 97 percent of the emergency signals received are erroneous.

As originally developed, civilian EPIRB signals were broadcast on 121.5/243-MHz with the intention that aircraft or other ships could pick up the signal. The development of satellites greatly improved the opportunity for intercepting an EPIRB signal, but it turned out that the frequencies are too busy for precise satellite use. Furthermore, the 121.5/243-MHz signals are not picked up by satellites in most of the southern hemisphere which is one of the most popular cruising venues.

A new EPIRB system, known as COSPAS/SARSAT, has recently been inaugurated. It is designed for satellite technology, and transmits on 406-MHz. There is an almost 100-percent assurance that the signal will be picked up by a satellite anywhere in the world. It offers a position accuracy of within 1.5 miles, and within two and a half hours of the distress signal being transmitted, the position is known by a SAR (search and rescue) agency. The 406-MHz EPIRBs, if properly registered by the boat owner, will send an encoded signal that refers to the

Figure 15.2
The new 406 EPIRBs offer rapid alert and response to vessels in distress.

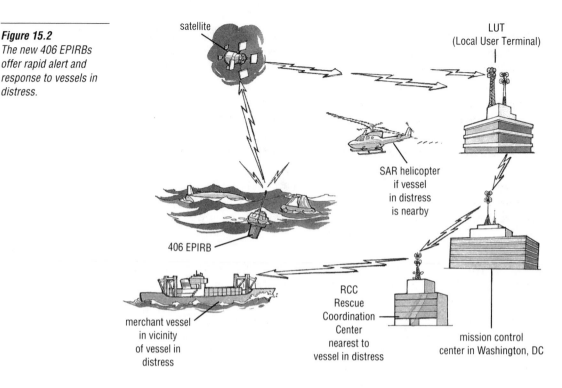

satellite

LUT
(Local User Terminal)

SAR helicopter
if vessel
in distress
is nearby

406 EPIRB

merchant vessel
in vicinity
of vessel in
distress

RCC
Rescue
Coordination
Center
nearest to
vessel in distress

mission control
center in Washington, DC

name, size and registry of the vessel in distress and the approximate number of crew.

These new-generation EPIRBs are expensive – three or four times more costly than the old style. But in just the past two years the price has begun to come down as more companies begin production. I have had an opportunity to observe how rapidly the signals can be received and how immediately the U.S. Coast Guard can activate a SAR mission, and I consider the new 406-MHz EPIRBs very important onboard safety equipment.

There is nothing complicated about installing an EPIRB. It comes with a long-life, self-contained battery. There are no electrical or electronic connections to make. It only requires fastening the EPIRB holder in some convenient place on the boat.

Miscellaneous Electronics

Some cruising sailors install cassette or CD players, VCRs and TVs, for use in port, as well as various other entertainment electronics. In selecting these items there is usually no great advantage in buying equipment supposedly designed for marine use. Almost anything made for automobiles will work for your boat and will be cheaper. I suspect that the advertised statement that something has been 'marinized' for boat use, really means it has been sprayed with CRC and the price raised. Exceptions are some stereo speakers which are more water-resistant than others.

Small, handheld navigation computers are available from various companies. These are a real benefit to celestial navigation. They will probably improve your computations and will certainly encourage you to use your sextant more frequently. Different brands feature different functions; some important and some only flashy gimmicks. Shop around for the one that does what you want it to do.

If you already have a high-performance calculator which can be programmed or which accepts a navigation 'chip,' you may be able to use that for your sailing navigation. In addition to solving celestial navigation computations most of the nav computers are convenient in trip

---

Priority List of Electronics

The following recommendations are for a cruising boat that is going to make an extended cruise of several months or longer.

Radios

Minimum: A multiband radio receiver and an inexpensive VHF handheld transceiver.
Additional: A SSB or ham radio transceiver for long-distance communication.

Navigation equipment

Minimum: A hand-held RDF and depthsounder.
Additional: GPS, unless you already have SatNav or Loran. Be aware that Loran coverage is spotty or non-existent in some areas, especially far offshore. Furthermore, some Loran chains are now being shut down. In late 1992 the Hawaii Loran system was discontinued.

Weather electronics

Weatherfax if you can possibly afford it.

Instruments

Minimum: None
Additional: Knotmeter/log

EPIRBs

Minimum: 406-MHz EPIRB
Note: Although the old 121.5/243-MHz EPIRBS are still for
sale and much cheaper than the 406-MHz, I would not
recommend buying one for most cruising. They have been
shown to be less reliable than the 406-MHz and their area of
satellite reception is more restricted.

Miscellaneous

A radar detector is a great shipmate for singlehanded and short-handed sailing. A navigation calculator will make celestial computations easier.

planning, when determining rhumbline and great-circle routes. I have used a Hewlett-Packard calculator with a navigation chip, as well as the Merlin. The HP is functional and speeds up calculations. The Merlin is absolutely fun to use and turns celestial navigation into an enjoyable daily game. It has definitely made me want to use my sextant more frequently.

Radio Dependence

A final word has to do with the assumption that a ham or SSB radio is a necessity in the event of serious calamity at sea. It cannot be argued that these radios have been used to aid in assisting sailboats in distress and in saving lives. However, having this equipment on board is no assurance or insurance against disaster, nor will it solve your problems if disaster occurs.

Boat disasters are very rare, but when they do happen they are seldom simple. They are often the result of a series or combination of complications, and the resulting damage is often multiple. Flooding may be accompanied by the loss of electrical power or the loss of the mast, and with it the backstay antenna or the whip antennas. A yacht that is sinking after being holed will usually go down so fast that the crew's primary concern will be to launch and board the liferaft and not to send radio messages. These points are not made to frighten or discourage potential mariners; only to point out that sending off a radio message in an emergency is seldom an easy procedure.

It is a big ocean and even if you do get some sort of message out, and if it is received, there may be a significant delay before anyone comes looking for you. Unless the position you give is absolutely precise, your liferaft or disabled boat will make a very difficult target to find. There are two devices I am willing to stake my life on in such circumstances: they are the 406-MHz EPIRB and the handheld VHF.

CRUISING SAILS

Consider first the minimum requirements. After the basic needs are met, additional sails can be added to the inventory depending on your budget and the amount of storage space you are willing to give up to sail-bags. My suggestion for basics is definitely skewed toward the heavy-weather end of the scale even though this will probably involve a relatively small percentage of your sailing time. But if you encounter heavy weather without proper sails you put your boat and crew in jeopardy. If you encounter light air without the proper sails your only penalty will be slow speed – frustrating perhaps, but not dangerous.

For a sloop there are five basic sails – mainsail, storm trysail, storm jib, working jib and a lapper (genoa) of about 120 percent. A cutter or double headsail rig would also carry a staysail. For a ketch or yawl a mizzen is added to the list. These sails can be considered a basic wardrobe and should all be made for cruising. If not new, they should still be in very good condition when you begin your cruise. Sails inherited from racing will probably need to be strengthened with reinforcement patches at the tack and clew, and you may even want to add some stitching to the seams.

After basic sail needs are met, and if your budget can stand it, the next sail on the list should be a larger genoa, perhaps 150 percent or larger, depending on your boat and where you plan to sail. And after that would be a light air drifter/reacher or a spinnaker. There are various other staysails and special-cut sails you may want to purchase, but keep in mind that sails use up a lot of valuable storage space, and that most cruising sailors settle into a rather lazy routine that involves as few sail changes as possible. Keep your sail inventory simple and basic until you have cruised for a while. Then add the particular sails you find you need, rather than starting off with a large inventory and finding there are some you never use.

On an extended cruise you will have an opportunity to use all of your sails at some time, but you will find that most of your sailing is done with a certain combination. For example on my sloop the combination of lapper and double-reefed main probably accounts for 50 percent of the sailing; a full main and large genoa perhaps 30 percent; double- or triple-reefed main and working jib 10 percent; and the cruising or regular spinnaker about 10 percent. The storm jib and trysail are flown less than one percent of the time – but it's usually a memorable one percent.

Decisions on sail selection will be dictated by the type of sailhandling equipment on your boat. If you use roller-furling gear, sails will have to

Sailhandling

be made to fit that equipment. This is largely a matter of personal preference, but consider your decision carefully. There are obvious advantages in the ease and convenience of furling sails, but there are some disadvantages, as well.

Furling Headsails

Roller-furling headsails have come a long way in recent years, and today there are a number of systems to choose from. The advantages of furling gear are well-known by many daysailors and coastal cruisers. We have also seen numerous examples of singlehanded yachts on long races, such as the BOC race, using roller-furling gear, and this speaks well for this equipment. Keep in mind, however, that these racing boats are state-of-the-art and have had experts, often factory representatives, install their equipment. Some of them have support teams on hand at each port of call to repair or replace any problem gear. This is a far cry from the cruiser who might end up with problems in some out-of-the-way place with no prospect of assistance. Warranties are of little value if you are 5000 miles away from a dealer or manufacturer.

More and more we see advertisements for boats in which all the sails are furling, and sometimes these include ketches and staysail schooners. To go one step farther, some of these boats have furling gear and winches that are operated by electric power. This may be an important consideration for some, but it is seldom necessary, and the supposed added convenience may be more than offset by the added maintenance it requires. Such systems do permit small crews to sail larger yachts, but how long will you keep sailing in the event of power loss or mechanical problems?

It is important to recognize the difference between furling and reefing. Don't assume that roller-furling completely alleviates the need for headsail changes, or that, as the wind increases, it is only necessary to roll up the sail to deal with changing conditions. A reefed roller-furling sail will not set as well as a smaller sail, and some are not good at all – although the situation has improved significantly through the use of foam luffs. You cannot expect one sail to satisfactorily reef from 150 percent down to a working jib. Some sailmakers say a 150-percent can be reefed to perhaps 110 percent and that a 110-percent can be reefed to about that of a storm jib. But you should also have a dedicated storm jib.

Even with roller-reefing headsails for cruising boats, continuous incremental reefing is not recommended. Rather, as the headsail is reduced in size, there are specific size positions at which to stop. This way, foot and clew patches can be added to the sail to help achieve better sailshape and reduce chafe. It also makes it easier for the crew because they can have predetermined settings for the sheet leads that need to be changed with each change in sail size.

Regardless of the type roller-furling you have, there will still be times when it is necessary to carry a smaller headsail. When that time comes, you need to be able to remove the roller-furled sail or to have another stay on which to set a smaller sail such as a working jib or storm jib.

This can be a forestay set slightly aft of the headstay or, more realistically, a removable intermediate stay. The latter may require the additional installation of temporary running backstays. There will also be times when it is necessary to completely remove the furled sail, for example to reduce windage when preparing for a typhoon at sea or in port.

Any time it is necessary to remove a furling headsail at sea, be sure it is done quickly and efficiently. Trying to control a large headsail in strong winds with a shorthanded crew is not just difficult, it is dangerous. It is reason enough that a lot of people stay with hanked-on sails in spite of their apparent inconvenience.

In selecting a furling system give careful consideration to what is involved in removing the furling sail. Think about the worst-case scenario and ask yourself how it would be done on your boat with your crew in heavy weather. Also consider how you will remove the sail in the event that the furling equipment malfunctions and the sail will not roll up. It *does* happen.

Jibs with boltropes or tapes which feed into an extrusion or foil are extremely difficult to control as they come down on deck and are often equally difficult to feed into the extrusion. As they come out of the extrusion they must be controlled or they will immediately spread out all over the foredeck or go over the side. Under heavy going this can be dangerous as well as inconvenient. The aerodynamic advantage of a foil, as used on a racing boat with a large crew, may prove an inconvenience and disadvantage on the typical shorthanded cruising boat. Hanked-on sails are much easier to handle and can be easily controlled by one person with the sail lowered and partially bagged before it is removed from the stay.

If you decide on roller-furling, seek advice from experienced offshore sailors who have used a particular brand for a long time under a wide variety of sailing conditions. Find out what type of additional rigging they use for heavy-weather conditions.

Comparative discussions of furling headsail equipment have appeared in *The Practical Sailor* (November 1, 1983; March 15, 1987; May 15, 1988; and November 1, 1990). The specific models discussed have all been upgraded by now, but much of the discussion centers on the pros and cons of different styles of furling equipment. Remember, too, that the remarks are not specifically oriented to the offshore boat.

Each year there are new models of jib furlers. Regardless of how attractive a new jib furler may seem, it is better to stick with an established brand with a proven reputation. Let the near-shore sailors experiment with the new types for a few years.

Mainsail Furlers

In recent years a number of new mainsail furling systems have been developed. Some of these furl the mainsail inside the mast, and others furl the sail on a luff wire just behind the mast. Although I regard these systems with the same caution mentioned for roller-furling jibs, such rigs might well appeal to those who feel they are getting too old to wrestle the main for reefing and furling.

There are also systems whereby the main is stowed inside the boom. This is reminiscent of the roller-reefing boom popular years ago, with two major advantages: the battens can remain in the reefed sail, and sailshape is undistorted.

This equipment is expensive. Costs include hardware, sail modification or replacement, a new mast or boom if 'in-spar' furling is chosen, and professional labor for the installation.

Furling mainsail systems may, depending on the boat, require additional standing rigging or a change in the rigging. Performance will be sacrificed somewhat because of added weight and windage, the necessity for a smaller sail, and less perfect sailshape. But these are all factors that some cruising sailors can gladly live with for the sake of convenience.

Mainsail Reefing

A few years ago roller-reefing booms were the rage. They used a geared crank to wind the boom as it reeled in the sail. Now they have all but disappeared, and it is just as well. The supposed advantage was ease of reefing but it never seemed possible to roller-reef and get a decent set to the sail. Some of the newer booms come equipped with internal lines for reefing. Most of them are adequate for the cruiser although the way some of them are rigged adds a lot of unnecessary hardware and puts a lot of lines in the cockpit.

Putting in and shaking out mainsail reefs is a frequent exercise offshore, and it pays to have a reefing system you're comfortable with. If you choose one of the mainsail furling systems mentioned in the section above, your reefing problems will be covered in most situations, although, depending on the system, perhaps not with ideal sailshape. Otherwise the best answer is the now-traditional slab-reefing (jiffy-reefing) system.

There are several variations on this theme – reefing lines inside the boom or external; single-line reefing systems in which the tack and clew can be pulled down simultaneously as the halyard is lowered; reef points or no reef points in the main; gooseneck tack hooks for mainsail luff rings versus multi-part tackle downhauls, and so forth. It will pay to study all these options carefully aboard other boats, and to consult experienced cruising sailors and professional riggers, before settling on any particular set-up. As always, it's better to start simple and keep complexity as an option for later. Following that philosophy, the simple slab-reef method will probably serve you well.

Lazyjacks

It is interesting how sailors constantly discover for the first time ideas that have been around forever. Lazyjacks are back again after pretty much going into retirement with the passing of the gaff rig. It is easy to see why they are popular again. For sails with boltrope luffs, lazyjacks are about the only way to conveniently furl the main. What is difficult

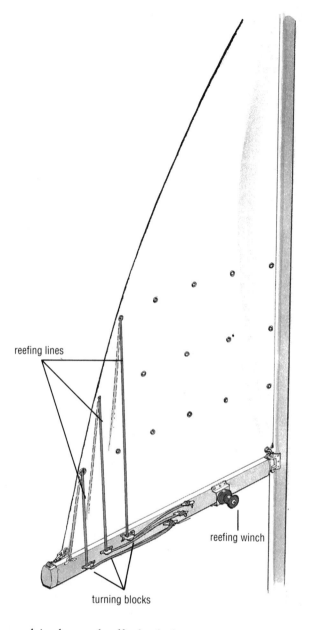

reefing lines

reefing winch

turning blocks

Figure 16.1
*Slab or jiffy reefing
setup. This is the
simplest mainsail reefing
system.*

to understand is the tradeoff: the bolt rope is used to make the main more streamlined and to reduce windage, but the lazyjacks create windage. It is true that a mainsail with track cars will be a bit difficult to fake down when it is brand new, but after a few weeks of use it will soften up and be more manageable. I don't believe lazyjacks are necessary on yachts under 40 feet if they use mainsails with slides or cars – as should be the case on a shorthanded boat.

Conventional Sailhandling

In spite of the popularity of roller-furling for headsails, and now mainsails, many cruising boats continue to use traditional hanked-on jibs and put up with the necessity of occasional headsail changes. Often this decision is a matter of economy and in some cases it reflects a conservative attitude. To a large extent it is an attempt at simplicity and reliability.

There is a lot to be said for keeping sailhandling simple, easy, and as maintenance-free as possible. But this probably means different things to different sailors. Perhaps for you this will include furling sails, and all lines, sheets, and controls leading to the cockpit.

If in doubt, start out with the simplest and most traditional methods and then add specialized sailhandling equipment as you go along, as you learn new ideas from others, and as you find out what equipment is proven and reliable. Furling sails are not a requirement for offshore sailing, and on a yacht of 40 feet or less it is not difficult for a husband-wife team or a singlehander to work with hanked-on sails. If that is what you have, and you are comfortable with your sailhandling, don't be in a hurry to change.

Sailmakers and Materials

The Sailmaker

If you are starting out with a new boat you have an opportunity to obtain sails made and designed for offshore work. Otherwise it is a matter of adapting what is available and perhaps improving or adding to your inventory through time. When I bought my present boat it had a rather tired set of sails, but they were good enough for a couple of years. During that time I sailed the boat extensively and made some decisions about what sails to buy. Taking my time allowed me to spread the cost of new sails as I gradually built up my sail inventory. It also gave me time to seek out a sailmaker who was experienced in building cruising sails. I was lucky in this respect, because the person I found had spent several years cruising the South Pacific and he knew a lot more about what I needed than I did.

Almost all sailmakers will assure you that they know exactly what is best for you, but in fact few of them really do. The main business for most sail lofts comes from racing sails, and few have personnel who have the cruising experience or who appreciate the realities of cruising. It is to your advantage if the sailmaker you select is willing to visit your boat to make the proper measurements and, when the sails are completed, to spend a few hours sailing with you. This adds to your cost, but you will benefit in the long run. Even if it is necessary for you to take your boat some distance to a sailmaker, it is worth doing it to have the right sails.

It is rare indeed that you can get the best sails by mail order. Sometimes the quality and workmanship is adequate, but major or even minor corrections to the sail can be costly and time-consuming if they have to be returned to the maker.

Price is certainly a consideration, and good cruising sails will not be cheap. Buying a sail, even a well-made sail, at a discount price will not do you much good if it isn't right for your boat. Having a sail re-cut is often unsuccessful and can be expensive.

The more you can learn about cruising sails, the greater will be your chances of ending up with the proper sails. This includes knowing what to request when you order a sail, discussing price and quality with the sailmaker, evaluating what you pay for, and knowing how to take proper care of your sails.

The rapport you establish with your sailmaker is important. If he is good, he will want much more information from you than the yacht's designed sailplan. Other considerations include the type of sailing you expect to do, the size of the crew, and a lot of specific information on sheeting angles, height of the pulpit and lifelines, position of the turn-buckles and other rigging hardware, the type of reefing, the position of reefing hardware, and so forth. If you have a production boat, check the sailplan measurements. The builder or previous owner may have made modifications that do not appear on the plan.

Some sailors claim that a small loft is better to deal with in terms of cruising sails. Often this is true if you are dealing directly with a sail-maker who has cruising experience. I have found that small lofts charge less for their sails, and there is no guarantee that lofts with famous names will produce better sails than smaller independent lofts. Famous names are achieved mainly through building racing, not cruising, sails, and by advertising. Some names are franchised, and even if the loft is well-respected elsewhere, it is not an assurance that the local franchise loft will produce quality cruising sails.

Sailcloth Type, Weight, and Quality

A major spinoff of yacht racing has been the improvement in sailcloth. Not so many years ago all sails were of cotton and flax. The develop-ment of Dacron represented one of the greatest benefits to sailing because of its long life, ease of handling, and low maintenance. Today, even the classic or character boats rely on Dacron sails. In recent times, low-weight and low-stretch Kevlar and Mylar sails have become stan-dard equipment on racing boats. For the cruiser, however, they offer no advantage. Kevlar and Mylar are slippery and difficult to handle and furl. They require special care in storage, and when flying are easily damaged by chafe. Of particular importance to most cruising sailors is that these high-tech fabrics are expensive. Probably the day will come when new methods of laminating high-strength fabrics will make them suitable for the cruiser, but in the meantime, Dacron is the only way to go for mainsails and headsails. Nylon is used for spinnakers and some light-air sails.

There is a wide variety of sailcloth weight and quality. Going by weight alone is not a simple matter, for a number of reasons. Different manufacturers of sailcloth use different criteria for determining weight. Weights are usually given in ounces or grams per square yard or meter, but in addition the finishing process and specific type of finish will determine the sail's actual weight, and this may vary somewhat even for a single manufacturer. Major manufacturers make sailcloth of different quality in order to be competitive in the world market, and the prices vary accordingly. Therefore, just because your sails are made of a brand-name cloth, quality is not guaranteed.

It is the complexity of weight, cost, finish, and quality that makes the buyer greatly dependent on the knowledge and expertise of the sailmaker. This is one more reason to select a loft that has some previous experience with offshore cruising boats.

Finally, price alone cannot be used as a criterion. Sailmakers can always reduce the cost of a sail by using lower-quality materials, and this may be to your disadvantage in the long run. On the other hand, some sails, depending on their use, can be built of cheaper sailcloth without adversely affecting the sail.

Choosing Your Cruising Sails

Mainsail

The main is your most important cruising sail. Except for heavy weather use of a trysail, the main is in nearly constant use underway. It should be heavier than your other sails, but not so heavy that it slows down the boat. It should probably be made of cloth that is one ounce heavier than a sail normally used for daysailing and weekend cruising.

Have the main ruggedly built, with adequate chafe protection. To decide where sacrificial chafe patches are needed, use the sail for a few days under a variety of conditions. Then take the sail down and have reinforcements added where chafe is indicated.

Experienced cruisers recommend triple stitching of all seams. This

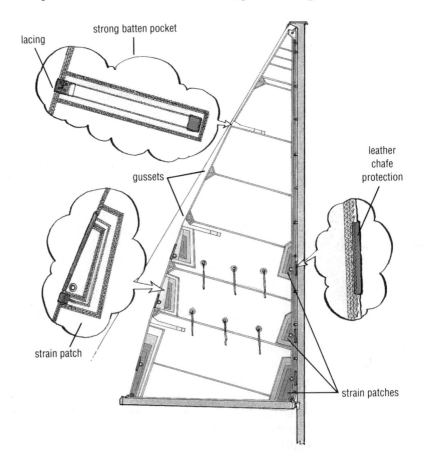

Figure 16.2
A cruising mainsail.

adds to the cost of the sail, but will be a benefit in the long run. A mainsail is difficult to repair on board, even if you have a sewing machine. The stronger the main is to begin with, the longer it will last.

Large strain patches should be installed at the tack, head, and clew to carry the load. Likewise, strong strain patches should back up each of the reef cringles. Often the heaviest loads imposed on the main are when it is reefed. Go one step further and have gussets added where panel seams join the luff and leech.

Commonly, cruiser-racer mainsails have two or three sets of reef points. For the cruiser two sets may be enough. The first set should reduce the sail by about 20 percent and the second reef by 50 percent or more.

Batten pockets need to be sewn or laced shut at the leech. Various arrangements can be used to make the battens easy to remove if the sail is frequently taken off the boom and stored below. For the cruising sailor, however, the main will probably stay on for months or years. Unless the batten pockets are sewn or laced shut, the battens will soon find their way overboard. For even better protection against chafe on the leech, and to keep battens in place, add gussets at the batten pockets.

When you have a new mainsail made, be sure the battens lie flat when the sail is reefed. Some sailmakers who are experienced cruisers recommend that batten pockets be made separate from the sail and then sewn on. With this type of arrangement a torn batten pocket is easier to repair, and you can carry a spare pocket to substitute for a torn one.

At least one complete set of battens, or better yet several feet of batten stock, should be carried as on-board spares. Being careful of how you treat your mainsail will add to the life of the battens.

The type of main you choose is a matter of personal preference. A few year ago battenless mainsails were popular. They were supposed to alleviate the problems of lost and broken battens and the frustration of battens getting caught on the shrouds. Now the other extreme is in vogue – fully battened mainsails. You can read the arguments for and against full batten mains in the sailing magazines. In the meantime, note that most cruising boats have traditional mainsails with partial battens. Make your own decision and don't let someone sell you on an idea just because it is the latest trend.

Other than chafe, exposure to sunlight is the biggest threat to mainsail damage and deterioration. When sailing there is nothing you can do to protect your main from sunlight, but in port it should always be kept completely covered by a proper-fitting, UV-resistant sailcover. It is easy to think that a day or two of leaving off the sailcover is not significant, but every day the sail is left exposed is one day closer to having to replace it.

Headsails

If you use hanked-on headsails, add a set of reef points to all of them except perhaps to a large genoa. It is true that headsails are not convenient to reef, nor will they set as well as smaller sails. However,

Figure 16.3
Reefable headsails.

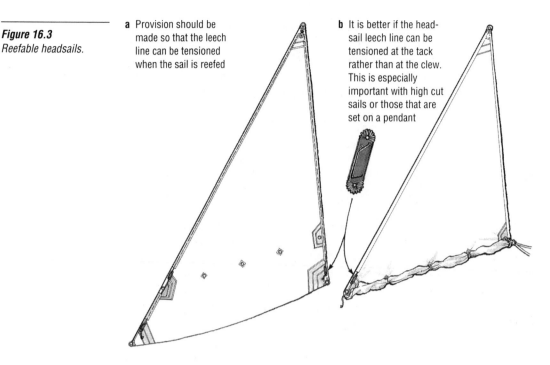

a Provision should be made so that the leech line can be tensioned when the sail is reefed

b It is better if the head-sail leech line can be tensioned at the tack rather than at the clew. This is especially important with high cut sails or those that are set on a pendant

being able to reef a headsail doubles the potential use of the sail for a relatively small additional cost. Consider, for example, a sail inventory consisting of a lapper, working jib, and storm jib. If sailing conditions require the working jib, but it is torn or damaged, you will probably be forced to use the storm jib, which will not give adequate drive. A reefable lapper could save the day.

Club-footed headsails – those attached to a small boom – are seldom seen on recently built boats, but they have been popular in the past. Their purpose is to make the boat self-tacking. This may be an advantage for coastal cruisers who are forced to make frequent tacks to work their way up a river or estuary, but for the offshore sailor club-footed jibs are unnecessary and seldom work well in the sail plan. My biggest criticism is that they are dangerous. A club-footed sail will eventually injure someone on your boat, no matter how careful you are. Best advice if you have one of the monsters onboard is to get rid of it.

When buying new headsails for cruising, order high-cut sails. They will not chafe on the bow pulpit or the lifelines, they will give the helmsman better visibility, and they are less likely to scoop up water that might either damage them or put excess loads on the standing rigging. If some of your smaller headsails set low on the deck it may be possible to raise them higher with a pendant permanently installed on deck. If you already have deck-sweepers, add sacrificial chafe patches before you head offshore.

High-cut sails can, however, present a problem for adjusting leech lines. If the adjustment must be made at the clew, as on a conventional sail, it is often impossible to reach when sailing. Your sailmaker can modify the leech line by running it up to a small turning block at the head and down the luff, where it can be adjusted near the tack of the sail. All leech line fittings should be sewn, not riveted.

If your headsails have reef points, be sure the leech line exits at each reef. This is also true of the luff on the mainsail. Otherwise it will be impossible to remove 'flutter' when the sails are reefed.

Storm Sails

With the onset of heavy weather, you are beset with several tasks, such as putting on a storm jib, installing storm shutters, and perhaps extra navigational duties if you need to clear a headland or lee shore. Moving about while wearing heavy foul-weather gear and a safety harness on a wave-washed deck is fatiguing. So the better prepared you are, the less difficult it will be.

Storm sails should be dedicated strictly to their original purpose. The trysail should have pendants and sheets permanently attached, and should be practiced with, to be sure the lines are of correct length. The trysail luff is commonly set on the main track, and is secured at the tack by a pendant cleated to the mast. This pendant should allow the sail to be hoisted several feet above the boom. The foot is set free. Sheets are attached to winches or to cleats in the cockpit. It may be convenient to use the mooring cleats on the quarters. The sheets and pendant should be clearly marked to indicate where they should be cleated. Only when the tack pendant and sheets have been cleated in place should the trysail be hoisted. Unless you have rigged a storm trysail under difficult conditions, don't assume it will be a simple operation. In really heavy going it can sometimes take more than an hour just to get the main down and secured and the trysail properly set and flying.

It is often recommended that the trysail be permanently rigged and stored in a bag at the base of the mast. For this purpose some boats

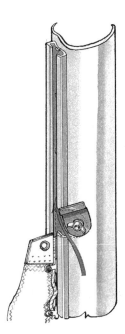

Figure 16.4
Gate in mainsail track to facilitate installing storm trysail.

have an additional short track to which the trysail luff cars are attached. The short track can be switched to the main track to bypass the cars of the lowered main. On *Denali* I do not have a separate track. However the luff track has a gate that can be opened to feed in the trysail cars. This is somewhat less convenient than a separate track, but the few times I have used the storm trysail it has worked OK.

Opinions vary on trysail size and weight. It should be as heavy or preferably slightly heavier than the main, and not more than 30 percent of the area of the main. It should be heavily reinforced with patches at the head, tack, and clew. The storm trysail is a simple but important sail. Be sure it is well made and don't fail to inspect it at least once a year.

Much of the foregoing applies equally to a storm jib. It, too, should be heavy and well-made, with an area about half that of the working jib, a permanently installed tack pendant and, depending on your particular boat, a pendant at the head.

It is best to hoist a storm jib on an inner forestay. This puts the storm trysail and storm jib closer together, gives a better slot effect and balances the sailplan, and prevents the bow from falling off to leeward. It will improve storm sailing and greatly improve heaving-to. It is also easier and safer to hank the jib on an intermediate stay than on the headstay.

For boats with roller-furling gear it is especially important to have the storm jib rigged on an inner forestay. In real storm conditions the furling sail is best removed. But, if for some reason that is not possible, the inner forestay is the only way the storm jib can be rigged.

If your boat is cutter-rigged and both headsails are roller-furling, consider how you will rig a storm jib or storm staysail. Some people maintain that a roller-furling staysail can serve as a storm staysail. Perhaps this is true under ideal conditions, but storms are rarely accompanied by faultless operation of equipment. For a shorthanded crew caught in a sudden gale at night, there is scant possibility that they will have the time or the energy to remove the furled sail. At such times you need an alternative for rigging a storm staysail.

Light-air Sails

You won't be cruising for long before you will want to add one or more light-air sails when your budget can bear the added cost. Some people recommend a medium- to lightweight 140- or 150-percent headsail, and others go for a drifter/reacher.

Light-air days are frustrating, and the boat may not move with anything less than an ultralight sail. Therefore the idea of a drifter/reacher makes sense. Another option is the so-called cruising spinnaker. It is usually tacked at the bow, but can also be used with a spinnaker pole. It will not take you too close to the wind, but it is easier to handle than a conventional spinnaker.

Some cruising sailors never consider flying a spinnaker because they think of it only as a racing sail. While it is true that a spinnaker can be more than a handful under many conditions, especially in heavy air, it should not be rejected out of hand. In light air a spinnaker can be a real

a Launching and recover-
   ing a spinnaker is much
   easier with a sleeve

Figure 16.5
Spinnaker sock or
sleeve.

b Details of a spinnaker
   sock

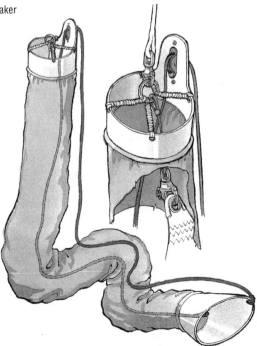

friend to the cruiser, and make a big difference in performance. Take your time rigging the spinnaker. A spinnaker sock, sleeve, or snuffer will do wonders to make it behave. I have spinnaker sleeves on both a cruising spinnaker and a regular spinnaker, and they make raising and lowering these sails quite easy.

Downwind Sails

For many years two large headsails set on twin spinnaker poles was standard procedure for downwind sailing in tradewinds. The original purpose of this rig, which was developed in the 1930s, was to permit the yacht to self-steer, with the sheets rigged to the tiller or wheel. Wind steering vanes and autopilots for small yachts have eliminated the need for this set-up, and these days few boats still sail with two poled-out jibs.

Sail Care and Maintenance

As mentioned, preventing chafe and protecting sails from sunlight when not in use are the two best ways to assure long life for your sails. As inconvenient as it may seem, a sail that has been taken down should immediately be stowed below. Leaving sails on deck, even if they are tied down, is not a good idea. It gives them continuous exposure to sunlight and presents the possibility for damage or loss. If you make it a practice of leaving unused sails on deck you can be assured that eventually one will get washed overboard. Trying to recover a sail that has gone partly or completely overboard is a difficult exercise.

The other cardinal principle of sail care is to make repairs as soon as possible. Even a minor tear or abrasion can quickly enlarge to a major rip that may completely destroy the sail. Repairs while underway are never easy, but at least temporary repairs must be made. Some of the most desirable sailing areas are far from any sail loft, so you should be ready to make your own repairs.

To increase the life of stitching, seams should be coated with Duraseam or a similar product. This is best applied to new sails, but can also be put on used sails if the seams are thoroughly cleaned of salt crystals.

A variety of sail needles stored in oil or vaseline, a sailmaker's palm, sail thread, waxed twine, and two or three yards of spare sail cloth are minimum sail-repair materials. In addition you can add more sophisticated equipment as recommended in the books on sail repair. Bainbridge rip-stop sail tape works well if the sail is clean and dry. It can also be stitched on as a patch. Even the old reliable duct tape sometimes works. For emergency repairs, a patch can be applied with rubber cement, but if possible the sail should be correctly patched by sewing.

Some cruising boats carry a sewing machine for sail repairs. This also permits you to make your own sailcovers, awnings, and various other canvas projects. Machines sold specifically for use on yachts are expensive. You may be able to find an old homestyle sewing machine that will work almost as well for far less money. Some of them will work with a hand-crank or foot treadle. Before you buy any machine, test it to see if it is capable of sewing double or triple thicknesses of the type and weight cloth used for your sails. The needles commonly used for home sewing are too weak for sail repairs, but heavy-duty needles can be purchased.

17 SELF-STEERING SYSTEMS

Try to imagine all of the improvements in small-boat sailing since the days of Joshua Slocum – stronger and lighter construction materials, advanced design techniques, satellite navigation, radar, weatherfax, better understanding of heavy-weather sailing, small diesel engines, improved man-overboard procedures, watermakers, better fabrics for comfortable clothing, the replacement of cotton and flax sails with Dacron and Kevlar, dependable anchors, aluminum masts, DC/AC power inverters, stainless steel fittings, and synthetic rope for every purpose.

Now, suppose Neptune came tromping aboard your boat in a particularly bad mood one day and said, 'OK, Captain Oak, I'm tired of pandering to all you fiberglassed, electronic, polyester polliwogs. Starting right now we're going back to the good old days of wooden ships and iron men. Say goodbye to all of your high-tech goodies. From now on it's hand, reef, and steer for every man-jack among ya' . . . Well, OK, you can keep one of your toys – but only one.'

I don't know about you, but without hesitation I would choose to keep my wind-steering vane gear, and forget about all the rest.

The first offshore passage I ever made was a 1300-mile trip from Savannah, Georgia to St. Croix in the Caribbean. There were two of us onboard and we made the trip in about 13 days without the benefit of any type of self-steering. As I recall our passage consisted of steering, sleeping, steering, navigating, steering, eating, and steering. I would never do that again if I could avoid it.

The fact that Joshua Slocum made the first singlehanded circumnavigation impresses me not only because he did it, but because he did it without a wind-steering vane. It is quite correct to say that a well-balanced and properly trimmed boat will self-steer to windward, and that double headsails will steer the boat downwind. However, it isn't as wonderful as it sounds. Furthermore, there is a lot of sailing that falls between those two extremes.

Mechanical wind-activated self-steering vanes have been around in some form for almost 50 years, but it is only in the past 20 years that they have really become popular and widely available. Electric autopilots for large ships are not new either, but those built for small sailing craft have not been long on the scene. Their popularity and development parallels that of mechanical units.

The choice between an autopilot and a wind-steering vane is based mainly on where you are going and what you will be doing. If you are looking at bluewater passages under sail in a boat of 50 feet or less LOA, the first choice should be a wind vane. For larger boats and for motorsailers, an electrical self-steerer will be more practical. It is a convenience to have both, but the wind vane will do most of the day to day steering.

Mechanical Self-Steering

A few years ago there were few mechanical steering vanes to choose from. Today there are quite a few on the market. Stick with those with a well-established reputation. It is sometimes advantageous to have the latest and most up-to-date equipment on your boat, but for something as important as a steering vane it is probably better to let others do the testing on the new models. A well-researched, detailed summary of wind steering vanes by Deborah Bennett appeared in the January 1 and February 15, 1989 issues of *Practical Sailor*.

There are three principal types of mechanical wind-steering vanes: trim tabs, auxiliary rudders, and servo-pendulum. Deciding which is best for you depends to some extent on personal preference, but mainly on the type of boat you have and its intended use.

All wind vanes follow the wind and have no relationship to compass direction. Ideally, you set your sails for the course you want and then engage and adjust the steering vane to that point of sail. If the breeze veers or backs, the vane will maintain its relative position to the wind and the yacht's course will change accordingly. Offshore, the wind often remains nearly constant for long periods of time and most shifts are gradual. Close to land there is a greater chance of frequent windshifts and it may be easier to hand steer or use an autopilot.

Trim Tabs and Auxiliary Rudders

On traditional boats with outboard rudders, a wind-steering vane connected to a trim tab on the main rudder is commonly employed. Some of these are remarkably simple, and can be home-built. Trim tabs are also used with auxiliary wind-vane rudders. In this case the auxiliary rudder is connected to the tiller or wheel by steering lines. This works well for boats with hydraulic steering, or if the ship's rudder is turned by a worm gear. It is also recommended for center-cockpit boats and those with very high freeboard. Auxiliary vanes tend to be heavy and less convenient than the servo-pendulum type. Some of them can serve as emergency rudders if the main rudder is damaged, although it seems likely that damage to the main rudder would damage the auxiliary as well.

Servo-Pendulum Steering

For most displacement yachts up to about 45 feet in length, the servo-pendulum is the best choice for long-distance sailing. The most popular models now available are rugged, dependable, easily maintained, and – of special importance to the cruising sailor – they have a proven record of performance. They work with the boat's main rudder which was designed to steer the boat in the first place.

How it Works

What appears to be a rudder on the servo-pendulum mechanism does not function like a rudder at all. More than anything else it acts somewhat like a sculling oar, so oar it is called. The oar does rotate slightly on a vertical axis, but it mainly swings (hence pendulum), from side to side on a horizontal axis. It is connected by gears and linkages to a wind-vane that sticks up into the wind.

Consider the servo-pendulum vane at rest, in a situation where there is no wind. The *vane*, usually a piece of thin plywood, and the *pendulum* or *oar*, usually made of fiberglass or stainless steel, will both come to rest in a vertical position if there is no wind and the boat is not moving. The vane seeks a vertical orientation because it has a counterweight. The oar, in this calm condition, is vertical because it is controlled by the vane. Once the wind starts blowing and the boat begins to move, the vane is tilted to leeward from its vertical position. This through a linkage and beveled gears causes the oar to rotate slightly on a vertical axis. When this happens the oar is forced by the slip stream of the water flowing by to swing to one side. It is this force which is translated to the tiller or wheel by lines and blocks and changes the boat's heading, bringing it back to a balanced position relative to the apparent wind. As the boat is sailing a balance is never achieved because the wind is tending to push the bow away from the wind and the sails are trying to make the bow come up into the wind. Hence the vane, the pendulum, and the rudder are constantly making small steering adjustments.

For the wind's effect on the vane to be rapidly translated to the oar, and the oar's force to the wheel or tiller, all of the gears, linkages, and their bearings must be very responsive and as friction-free as possible. If they are not, the wind will get ahead of the steering. At the same time, some damping, for example a counterweight on the vane, is required, or the unit will oversteer.

Getting Acquainted with the Gear

Those who approach the use of yacht equipment with the attitude of 'plug-it-in-and-away-we-go' may have some problems with mechanical steering vanes. The boat must be balanced and the sails correctly trimmed for a vane to do its job properly. Sailing close-hauled is usually no problem, and a balanced boat will just about sail by itself when hard on the wind. From close reaching to running, however, requires more attention to boat balance, sailtrim, and sail size.

I recall my first experience with a wind-steering vane. In the rush to leave for the Caribbean from Georgia before the winter storms set in, I did not find time to test my new Aries vane, and I departed thinking I could learn about it underway. I did. It was a beat all the way from Savannah to the Virgin Islands and the steering vane worked like a charm – I came rolling into St. Croix feeling I had personally discovered the greatest thing since the sextant.

The next leg took me across the Caribbean to Bonaire off the coast of Venezuela. Within a few hours of leaving St. Croix's Teague Bay, I was quite disillusioned and distressed about my new toy. Try as I might, I could no longer make the vane work properly. The boat rounded up continually and sailing was miserable even with the wonderful tradewinds broad on the beam. I ended up with a lot of hand steering and a log book full of ruminations. I am embarrassed to admit that it took me nearly three days of frustration and a lot of tinkering, before I realized that I had too much sail up and everything strapped in too tight. I was overpowering the steering vane. That was the cause of the round-ups. Once I tucked a couple of reefs in the main, made a headsail change, and let things slack off a bit, the Aries worked like a Swiss watch.

Selecting a Servo-Pendulum Vane

In choosing a wind-steering vane, look for durability, ease of operation, simple maintenance, and low weight. These factors are often interrelated. Stainless steel is perhaps the best choice of construction material. It is strong, stands up well to salt water, and can be repaired almost anywhere there is a welding shop. But stainless steel is heavy and it puts weight on the stern of the boat where it is least desired. Aluminum is a logical second choice, but it is less rugged, less resistant to the marine environment, and repair facilities are not so abundant.

It is difficult to build an aluminum vane without using some other metals, and this invites frozen fittings and difficult repairs. The use of new types of plastics has helped somewhat to alleviate this problem.

In looking at the better-known servo-pendulum styles, there are five models that stand out. Three are 'traditional' in design and follow closely the original design concepts of H.G. (Blondie) Hasler. These are the Aries, the Monitor, and the Fleming. Departures from this are the Sailomat and the Windpilot.

Aries

The Aries is the 'old standby' and has logged more hours and miles at sea on cruising and racing boats than all of the other brands together. While its basic concept has remained the same for many years, its designer and builder, Nick Franklin in England, frequently modified it and constantly tried to improve it. A lot of ancient Aries are still out there doing their job after many years. Some of them look their age, but they continue to be highly reliable with relatively little maintenance.

Cast aluminum makes up most of the unit but parts of it, depending on the age and model, are bronze, stainless steel, and plastic. It weighs about 64 pounds (29 kg).

Denali has an Aries wind-steering vane and it is the best-made and most reliable piece of equipment on my boat. Anytime I have needed parts, Mr. Franklin's service has been excellent.

It is indeed unfortunate that the Aries is no longer in production. However, there are still a lot of them around and occasionally it is possible to find a used one for sale. A good supply of repair parts are still available from England.

Figure 17.1
Aries vane.

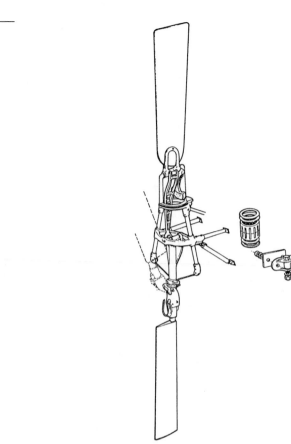

Fleming

This is an all-stainless steel wind-steering vane made in New Zealand. The main components are cast stainless. The Fleming became very well-known from the praise it received in the 1983 BOC around-the-world singlehanded race. There are three models.

The Fleming requires more frequent lubrication than other vanes, but this is not a serious drawback. The quality of workmanship and stainless steel construction result in an incredibly tough unit that can stand up to hard going in strong winds. In light air it is reportedly less responsive than might be desired. The primary complaint about the Fleming is its weight of 70 to 80 pounds (32 to 36 kg), depending on the model. It is the heaviest of all the steering vanes.

Monitor

The U.S.-made Monitor is now the best steering vane in production. It is constructed of stainless steel tubing and is therefore lighter than the Fleming or the Aries. It weighs about 52 pounds (24 kg), which adds to its popularity. Welded tubing is not as strong as cast stainless steel but of course it is not as heavy either and that is one of the trade-offs that is so much a part of cruising gear. The Monitor has been around long enough to have proved itself as a solid citizen and it is bound to develop the same mystique that the Aries has enjoyed for years.

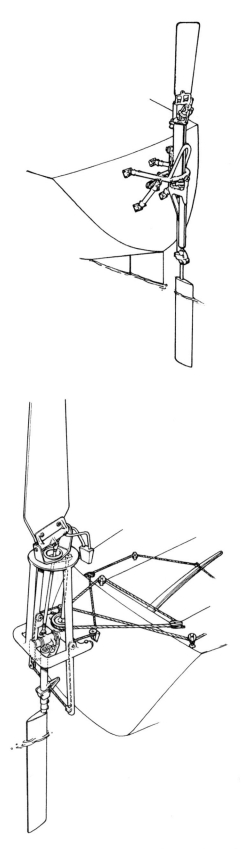

Figure 17.2
Fleming vane.

Figure 17.3
Monitor vane.

Sailomat

This Swedish-designed and -built servo-pendulum is aluminum. It has a streamlined, uncluttered profile which is a significant design departure from all other pendulum vanes. The Sailomat weighs between 55 and 60 pounds (25 and 27 kg), depending on boat size. It is still a fairly 'new kid on the block' and is rarely seen out on the cruising circuit.

Figure 17.4
Sailomat vane.

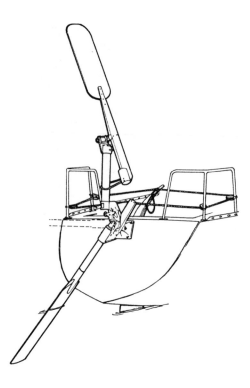

Windpilot

The German-made Windpilot Pacific is similar in appearance to the Sailomat. It is mainly of aluminum construction and weighs just over 46 pounds (21 kg). Like the Sailomat it is a relative newcomer to the cruising-boat market. Windpilot also makes other vane models that use auxiliary rudders and a combined auxiliary rudder and pendulum.

Additional Considerations

Most damage to steering vanes occurs when maneuvering in harbors and around docks, not at sea. In selecting a wind-steering vane, find out how complicated it is to take the unit on and off the boat. If you frequently use a stern anchor, some vanes can be a nuisance and give you a lot of worries about damage. A decided advantage of one of the older Aries models is that the whole unit can be taken off or installed quickly and easily. No other vanes are so convenient. If you only expect to be anchoring or lying to a mooring, the need to take the unit off and on is less important.

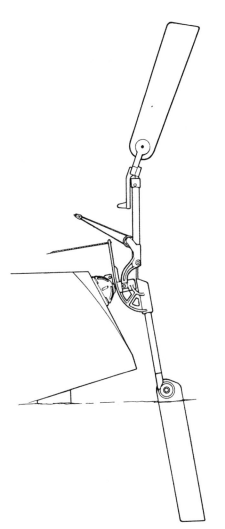

Figure 17.5
Windpilot vane.

Determine also how the pendulum will react if struck by some object in the water. This doesn't occur very often, but it does happen. It is important that the rudder or pendulum be designed to kick up out of the way, or to 'break' in a controlled manner. If it fails to do so it can destroy the whole steering mechanism.

Autopilots

Autopilots have become very popular among coastal cruising boats over about 30 feet. Offshore cruising boats, even those with a proven and satisfactory mechanical wind-steering vane, often carry an autopilot to use when motoring and for very light air.

Sailors who limit their sailing to weekends are usually satisfied with their autopilots. However, in any gathering of full-time cruising sailors the subject of autopilots will usually evoke a heated discussion. Some brands have a reputation for failure and a less-than-wonderful service record.

Part of the problem is that the portable-type autopilots that live in the cockpit are subject to water damage, no matter how well they are made. The sea eventually finds its way inside, and that is the end of the electrics and the electronics. Further evidence of the importance of keeping autopilots out of the weather is the relative lack of problems with units that have drive motors located belowdecks.

There are also complaints that some autopilots are underpowered or easily broken. Often the problem is not that the pilot is underpowered, but that it is driven too hard by the boat. An autopilot is not Superman, and if there is too much sail up, or if the boat is not trimmed correctly, neither an autopilot – nor a helmsman can keep it under control.

Autopilots are now key elements in long-distance singlehanded races throughout the world. Whereas these races formerly featured mechanical vanes, the boats have all turned to the electrical units for reasons of weight and precision. Wind-steering vanes are too heavy and not responsive enough for multihulls and light-displacement monohulls. Because a round-the-world or across-the-ocean singlehanded race is such an event of endurance, it is logical to ask what autopilots the racers use and to take their advice. It turns out that racers commonly rely less on a particular brand name and more on multiple back-up units. A cruising sailor may feel lucky to be able to afford to have one autopilot on board, but a racer, if he is well-sponsored or can otherwise afford it, will probably have a locker full of autopilots and just keep replacing broken units as he goes along.

On my boat I have both a wind vane and one of the cheaper autopilots. That combination works well for me. Probably 95 percent of my steering is done by the wind vane. The autopilot is reserved for motoring or sailing in very light air. The rest of the time it is stowed below.

MAGNETIC STEERING COMPASSES

With the advent of so many convenient electronic sailing aids, we tend to forget the importance of the magnetic compass. Yet even with Loran-C, SatNav, and GPS the simple magnetic steering compass remains the basic instrument for navigation. When everything else fails it will be the main device used to find a safe harbor.

Fluxgate compasses have become popular in the last few years and are needed on boats with integrated electronic navigation systems. However, they are expensive and are not required for safety nor will they make offshore cruising easier. Even with a fluxgate compass on the boat there should still be a large, easily-read, well-lit, and properly compensated magnetic compass mounted in the cockpit.

Anatomy of a Magnetic Compass

The standard yacht compass today is internally gimballed. It has an aluminum compass card surrounded by fluid inside a clear plastic or glass hemisphere dome attached to a plastic or metal case. The dome is part of the compass housing but it also acts to magnify the compass card. The larger the dome the better, because it will have more fluid and thus greater dampening, as well as being easier to read. A five inch (13 cm) dome compass contains almost twice as much compass fluid as a four inch (10 cm) dome and the smaller the boat the larger the compass should be. The reason for this is that the larger boat will be more stable. The smaller boat will have a more lively movement and therefore will benefit from a more stable compass.

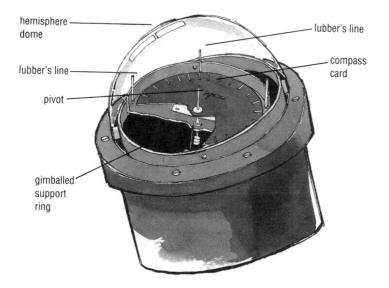

Figure 18.1
Steering compass.

Steering compasses should always have one or more lubber's lines for easier steering. On modern yacht compasses the lubber's lines are small wires or posts attached to the gimballed supports. They lie next to but do not touch the compass card. The lubber's line in the forward part of the compass (and on some bulkhead compasses on the after side as well) is aligned parallel with the boat's centerline and indicates the course being steered. On a binnacle-mounted compass, lubber's lines may also be located at 90 degrees relative to the heading. These are used for determining when a point is exactly on the beam. Additional lubber's lines are often installed at 45 degrees off the centerline. They provide a reference for steering when the helmsman is sitting or standing to one side of the compass, and assist in estimating courses on opposite tacks.

Legibility

Some compasses are easier to read than others. This is subjective in part, but it also has to do with compass size, the interval of the numbers, the spacing of the degree marks (ticks), and the orientation of the compass card itself – forward-reading, aft-reading, or a combination of both.

With a forward-reading compass you are looking at or 'reading' the forward side of the compass card. This is the most convenient, because the card display is the same as on the compass rose of a sailing chart: If the boat is pointed north the directions on the card lie in their correct relative position; east is on the right, and west is on the left. On an aft-reading (also called edge-reading or direct-reading) compass you are looking at a beveled compass card and reading the side of the card closest to you. This is less convenient when steering because numbers on the left and right of the course being steered are the reverse of their true orientation. This can cause a good bit of consternation to someone accustomed to a forward-reading compass, and frequently he will tend to steer in the wrong direction until becoming accustomed to the new orientation.

Some compass cards can be read both on top (forward-reading) and on the side (aft-reading) and this type should be satisfactory to everyone.

Compass Lighting

Using a subdued red light to illuminate the compass is important, so that watchstanders can maintain proper night vision. Light intensity should be correct for comfortable and easy reading by the helmsman. All yacht compasses should come with some type of illumination, but it may be necessary to modify the light for safe and efficient use. It is possible to paint compass light bulbs with red fingernail polish to achieve or improve night lighting. Some compasses use a red card with a white light, which is quite effective. Be sure to have spare light bulbs for your compass. Bulbs used to be standard; now they are different for each brand.

When trying to decide what is the best compass for you, make price the last – instead of the first – consideration. If you are setting out for an extensive cruise you will spend many hours looking at your compass, and the one you select should be easy to read and comfortable for your eyes.

For offshore cruising, as opposed to racing or short-distance cruising, I strongly recommend a bulkhead-mounted compass; if possible, two, one on each side of the companionway hatch. Even if you use wheel steering and have a pedestal there should still be a bulkhead-mounted compass. Pedestal compasses are convenient to read only when you are standing at the wheel. Even then it is difficult during a long watch because the helmsman has to continually look down at the card and then up to watch where the boat is going. Also, when you are heeled it is seldom possible to use the lubber's line on a pedestal compass without a significant parallax error.

In contrast it is usually easy to read a large, properly mounted bulkhead compass from anywhere in the cockpit. More often than not on an offshore cruising boat, there is no one standing behind the wheel or holding the tiller anyway, because the boat will be sailing with autopilot or wind-steering vane. In times of heavy seas or even a rain shower the person on watch may be hiding under the dodger with only a look around the horizon every five or ten minutes. It should be possible to read the compass conveniently from this location as well.

If you do decide on a pedestal-mounted compass, avoid loading down the pedestal with all sort of electronic gadgets and instruments, as if your boat were Captain Kirk's starship *Enterprise*. Such instrument clusters are difficult to read while steering or sitting anywhere but directly behind the wheel. Continuous exposure to rain and salt air will give the instruments a shortened life, and all of the wires and gauges operating in close proximity to the magnetic compass may add to deviation.

Purchasing Your Compass

When you go shopping for a compass take along a tape measure and look at the compass from the same distance as you will be using it in your cockpit. Squint your eyes and look at it again to simulate the difficulty of reading it in a rain squall. Some compasses that look good in bright daylight are not at all easy to read in the rain. Ask to look at the compass in a dark room with a night light. Inadequate lighting will add to steering fatigue. Be sure the compass has a built-in compensator for correcting deviation. Most compasses have compensator magnets installed, but on some they are an option, and others have no compensators. Without them compass corrections may be difficult.

When you have found one or more compasses you think you like, give each one a simple test for steadiness. Rock the compass forward and back to simulate pitching, and then from side to side to see how it responds to rolling. Take it slowly and rapidly through wide angles of tilt in both directions and check its steadiness and ability to regain steady state after movement. Next put it on a flat surface and slide it back and forth and sideways. The compass card and the lubber's lines should remain steady throughout these simple tests. Compare several compasses to gain an appreciation of one being better than another.

Before buying a bulkhead compass take into consideration the slant of the bulkhead in your cockpit. Unless the compass is properly mounted it will give spurious readings when the boat is heeled. R.E. White in the October 1, 1984, issue of *Practical Sailor*, pointed out that a boat with a bulkhead slanting five degrees when sailing at a 30-degree heel will have a compass error of $2^{1}/_{2}$ degrees – equal to a half-mile error over a distance run of only 12 miles. To determine this multiply the sine of the angle of heel times the degrees of slope of the bulkhead. In the example given this is the sine of 30 degrees (0.5) times five (degrees), equals $2^{1}/_{2}$ degrees.

You can overcome the bulkhead problem by shimming the compass to a true vertical position using a tapered wood collar (leveling block). A few compasses are designed to be mounted on a slanted bulkhead, or they can be special-ordered from the manufacturer. However shimming is not a difficult task.

Before making a final decision consider the warranty and repair service. Unfortunately compasses tend to be like electronics, and within about five years you will probably need some sort of repair. For example, if you are cruising extensively in tropical regions, the sun's UV rays may result in yellowing of the plastic dome or even the development of an air bubble in the compass. How can the compass be serviced? Are there repair stations throughout the world, or does the compass have to be returned to the manufacturer? Read the remarks about repair in the owner's pamphlet that should come with the compass. This booklet should also give installation advice.

If you plan on cruising over a wide range of latitude find out if your compass has been compensated for dip, and if so for what geographic area. Dip is the vertical component of the earth's magnetic field (not to be confused with variation). Usually a manufacturer will adjust compasses for the country in which they are being sold, and as such they will work OK in adjacent zones. Figure 2 shows the dip zones for

Figure 18.2
Compass dip zones.

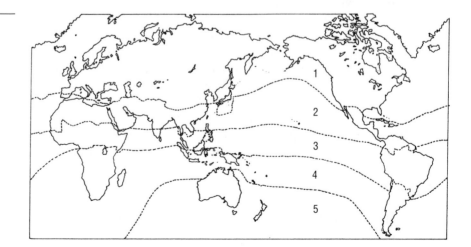

which the Suunto Marine compasses are calibrated. For example, a compass with dip adjustment for North America (zone 1) should work fine in zones 2 and 3 but may show dip effects in zone 4 and especially in zone 5.

If a compass is not adjusted properly for dip in the local area, the card tilt will cause the compass to give incorrect readings or it will be difficult to read. If you encounter this problem or if you expect to be sailing in a zone far from where your compass was dip compensated, have it recalibrated at a compass repair facility. Two of the compasses on *Denali* experienced dip problems when I sailed from Japan to the South Pacific. About two days before my landfall in New Zealand I realized my steering compasses both read several degrees off the course I was actually steering.

Few people in the northern hemisphere seem to be aware of dip so don't be surprised if the compass salesman can't answer your questions about it for the compass you want to buy. He can however send a fax message to the manufacturer for you to find out how your compass is dip-corrected.

Mounting a Bulkhead Compass

There are several factors to consider in locating the compass, and you may have to rearrange existing equipment to achieve all of them. You will probably have to cut a hole in the cabin bulkhead. You'll want to get it right the first time, so 'measure twice and cut once.'

Locate the compass where it can be easily read from a variety of positions in the cockpit. Sometimes while steering you will be sitting down and other times standing. Remember too that the proper height of the compass will depend on whether the card is aft-reading or forward-reading. The compass needs to be away from electrical equipment and wiring. Most modern electronic readouts such as a depth sounder, windspeed, or speed indicator will have little if any noticeable effect on a magnetic compass, but any 12-volt DC wiring near the compass should have the wires twisted to eliminate influence by the current.

Taking Care of the Compass

The most important point in caring for a compass is to keep it covered when it is not in use. Most yacht compasses have plastic domes and with time the sun's UV rays will cause the dome to become yellow, and it may be nearly impossible to read the compass card. Yellowing can be reduced by cleaning the dome with a non-abrasive polish such as automobile wax. With long exposure to the sun, however, the dome will crack or craze and eventually leak. If the compass manufacturer does not supply or sell a compass cover, have one made from canvas. The importance of covers cannot be overstated. If you have two steering compasses in the cockpit, it is worthwhile to leave the unused one covered.

19 TENDERS FOR CRUISING

The importance of a proper tender comes as a great surprise to some sailors when they begin cruising. For years they have been used to staying in a marina or harbor where they could tie up to a pontoon or pier. But once out on the cruising circuit they discover that in-port time is usually anchor time. Marinas are few and far between in many of the best cruising areas, and those that do exist may be costly.

Tying to a commercial pier is sometimes possible but it is seldom desirable. Harbors that cater to fishing and cargo vessels are usually dirty and too often you have little privacy. Docks are not built with sailboats in mind, so it is often difficult to give your boat adequate fendering. The frequent wakes from passing ships and harbor craft make life aboard uncomfortable. After staying in such harbors it is usually necessary to spend several hours cleaning oil and scum from the boat and fenders.

At anchor it is cleaner and quieter. In tropical areas, there will be a pleasant breeze most of the time. Problems with mosquitos, gnats, and cockroaches are greatly reduced, and the possibility of rodents coming aboard is eliminated. You have much more privacy because anyone coming to visit must have a boat or make arrangements with you beforehand. If adverse weather develops a boat alongside a pier may find itself trapped and unable to cast off. It is always easier to get underway from a mooring or when anchored. But anchoring does necessitate a reliable dinghy to shuttle the crew back and forth and to carry groceries, fuel, and water to the boat. In some places it is your responsibility to transport customs and immigration officials to and from your boat for inspections and paperwork.

There are two principal choices for a dinghy – an inflatable or a rigid boat. At first inflatables may seem the most desirable. They are stable, easy to stow, and can carry a lot of people and equipment. They make good dive boats because they are easy to enter from the water. Rigid boats, however, are more practical for extended cruising because of their ease of maintenance, ability to be rowed, and for their strength. A particularly important point in favor of a rigid dinghy is that it can be put in the water much faster than an inflatable. We will look at the characteristics of both, and then return to a summary comparison of the two.

Inflatables

Inflatables vary greatly in quality. Usually, but not always, the quality is reflected in the price. Well-known brand names are not always an indication of what is best. As with most yacht equipment, advice from

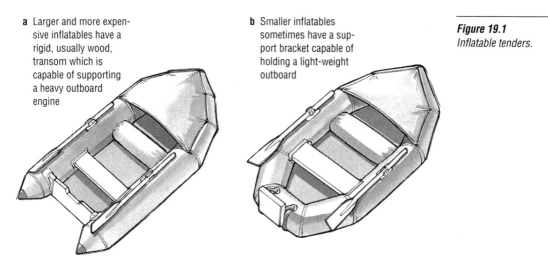

a Larger and more expen-
sive inflatables have a
rigid, usually wood,
transom which is
capable of supporting
a heavy outboard
engine

b Smaller inflatables
sometimes have a sup-
port bracket capable of
holding a light-weight
outboard

Figure 19.1
Inflatable tenders.

experienced cruising sailors who use their inflatable constantly is worth considering.

Construction, Materials, and Design

The simplest inflatable is a single chamber of unreinforced PVC (polyvinyl chloride) fabric. This type never stays properly inflated and tends to be soft, as the fabric stretches like a balloon in hot weather – although some are better than others, depending on the quality and thickness of the PVC. Usually the seams of the inflatable are formed by heat sealing in the same way that seams are formed on PVC foul-weather gear. Unless these seams are thick and well-constructed the boat will have a very short life. All of that aside, having only a single inflation chamber is not a good idea – a puncture and the boat will deflate and quickly become simply a piece of flaccid, floating plastic.

Inflatables made with reinforced fabrics will be more expensive but are stronger, safer, and have a longer life. In this type of construction a fabric is impregnated to give it added strength. Fabrics include nylon, polyester, Kevlar, neoprene, Hypalon, and PVC. The coating or impreg-nating material is commonly Hypalon or neoprene, both of which are types of synthetic rubber. Hypalon is presently considered to be the best by most manufacturers. Sometimes a fabric such as nylon is given an outer coating of Hypalon to provide protection from the sun and weather, and an interior coating of neoprene, because of its ability to hold air. Others use Hypalon or a combination of Hypalon and neo-prene on both sides of the fabric. Hypalon, when combined with neo-prene, stands up well against oil, acids, and mildew. It is abrasion resistant, and maintains its color. PVC is also used as a coating or impregnating material, and has similar attributes to Hypalon and Hypalon-neoprene combinations.

There are two processes for fabric impregnation. One is knife coat-ing in which the impregnating material is built up in layers. Fabrics made up in this way may, through time, delaminate or separate. The preferred impregnation method is calendering, in which the fabric passes between rollers and the coating material is deeply pressed into the cloth. Calendering is a more expensive process, but the fabrics are rigidly bonded and not subject to separation.

In shopping for an inflatable try to determine the type and quality of the seams where the fabric is joined to form the air cylinder. The strongest type is a lapped seam in which the two edges of the fabric are overlapped and covered with seam tape. Otherwise the seams may be butt-joined or flanged.

Multiple chambers are necessary for safety. Chambers are formed by building cone-shaped or hemispherical walls into the tube. In addition to the main air chamber, the better models have an inflatable keel. This gives the boat better directional stability – especially important when using an outboard.

Figure 19.2
Inflatable construction features.

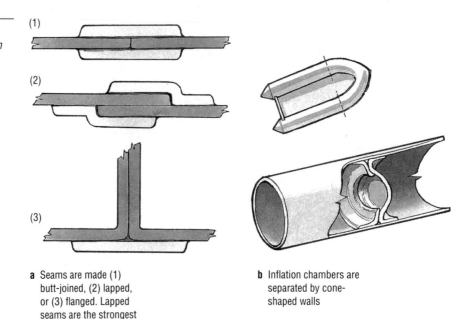

(1)

(2)

(3)

a Seams are made (1) butt-joined, (2) lapped, or (3) flanged. Lapped seams are the strongest

b Inflation chambers are separated by cone-shaped walls

Floorboards

Floorboards are a nuisance to install and remove in an inflatable, but they are worth the trouble. They give strength to the boat, but equally important they make it easier and more convenient to use. Stepping into a rubber tender without floorboards is guaranteed to get your shoes wet, along with any packages you might want to stow. Furthermore, floorboards make it much easier to stand up in the boat and they give the boat better performance when motoring.

Air Filling

Take a good look at the air-filling valves and the air pump when selecting an inflatable. The valves should be able to accept a large-volume hose and be designed to partially unscrew for rapid deflation. Foot-pumps vary in quality – some are quite flimsy. Usually the better-made boats have the best pumps. The pump should deliver a high volume to permit rapid inflation. You can also buy a small electric air pump or use a scuba tank or compressor. This is much quicker, but must be done with caution to prevent overinflation. Recommended procedure is to do only the initial inflation with the high-pressure source and to finish the job with a conventional foot pump.

Maintenance

Inflatables that are in constant use require a good bit of maintenance. Unless your inflatable is of good quality and you are able to make minor repairs yourself, it will provide you with many headaches when cruising. In remote places it may be difficult to find repair facilities, and air-shipping the boat back to the manufacturer or dealer, or having a new inflatable sent to you, will be costly. It is possible to have an inflatable repaired at a facility that services aircraft and ship liferafts.

It is important to protect the fabric from deterioration. The introduction of Hypalon has improved fabric life, but it still needs additional attention. A coating of Armor-All will help keep the surface in good condition. Some owners paint their boats with Hypalon paint, or use a canvas cover.

Chafe and abrasion are constant problems for rubber boats. They occur on both inside and outside surfaces. Sacrificial rubber strips cut from an old tire innertube can be glued over potential trouble spots. Wear occurs chiefly inside the inflatable along the edges of floorboards and at the seam where the pontoon is attached to the floor. Dragging the boat across a beach or any rough surface will abrade the bottom. Here also, the addition of rubber chafe guards will help.

When you go ashore in your dinghy and leave it in the water tied to a dock, consider possible abrasion against pilings or the bottom if there is a tide range. Coral, barnacles, oysters, sharp rocks, and metal projections on docks will all result in punctures to the pontoon. Coming back to your tender after a day ashore and finding it partially deflated is not pleasant; especially if the inflation pump is on your boat half a mile from shore and you have a load of groceries to transport.

Ocean cruisers who remain at an anchorage for several weeks and leave their inflatables continuously in the water may end up with a difficult bottom-cleaning task. Fouling organisms attach just as quickly to your tender as they will to your boat. Scraping marine growth off the bottom of an inflatable is difficult to do without damaging the fabric. One way is to take the boat ashore and clean the bottom with diluted chlorine bleach and a plastic scrubbing tool. First apply the bleach to the organic material and let it stand for about 10 minutes, or until the marine growth turns nearly white. Then use the plastic scrubber to remove the growth.

Prevention of fouling may be easier than the cure. If you plan to keep the tender in the water continuously, the bottom can be painted with a cheap grade of boat antifouling paint.

Towing

When gunkholing, it is sometimes convenient to tow the inflatable between anchorages over short distances in protected waters, or to pull it up on the stern pulpit so that only the aft portions of the pontoons are touching the water. It should never be towed when going offshore, with an outboard installed, or with other equipment inside. A sudden increase in the wind or a large wave, even the wake from a passing boat, can capsize an inflatable.

If you expect to tow an inflatable often, add towing rings and use a bridle. The standard bow eye installed on an inflatable will not last long if routinely used for towing. Furthermore, when being pulled by only the bow eye, the inflatable will yaw back and forth, putting added cyclical loading on the fitting. Port and starboard towing rings can be purchased from an inflatable dealer and you can install them yourself.

Selection

An inflatable represents a significant investment, and considering the variety and number offered for sale it is necessary to make your selection with care. In the 1988 and 1992 SSCA (Seven Seas Cruising Association) Equipment Surveys the Zodiac and Metzler inflatables were soundly criticized. Owners mentioned leaking air chambers, fabric deterioration, poorly made seams, deterioration of the fabric in sunlight, poor handling ability with engine and with oars, and the fact that Zodiac service was poor. Avon, Achilles, and the relative newcomer, Tinker, earn high marks from their owners. Likewise a November 1991 evaluation of inflatables by *Practical Sailor* showed Avon to be the favored choice.

Rigid Tenders (Dinghies)

Rigid tenders come in a tremendous array of sizes, shapes, and construction materials, and quality is likewise variable. For the cruiser the most important consideration is the dinghy's strength and ease of rowing. Even if you anticipate using an outboard engine or a sail, the first consideration is how well it can be handled with oars. Other important points are the amount of freeboard to keep you, your crew, and your supplies from getting soaked when maneuvering in choppy water or waves; the amount of flotation, the weight, and the length, which will control storage.

Hull Design

Tender design is an important consideration. The two main hull shapes are prams with a transom at each end, or dinghies with conventional pointed bow and flat transom. A pram provides maximum volume for length. A flat-bottomed pram is perhaps the easiest type of tender to build of wood. It is fun to sail in protected waters, but not good for rowing in anything other than calm conditions. Prams with rounded or V-bottoms are more maneuverable and versatile than those with flat bottoms.

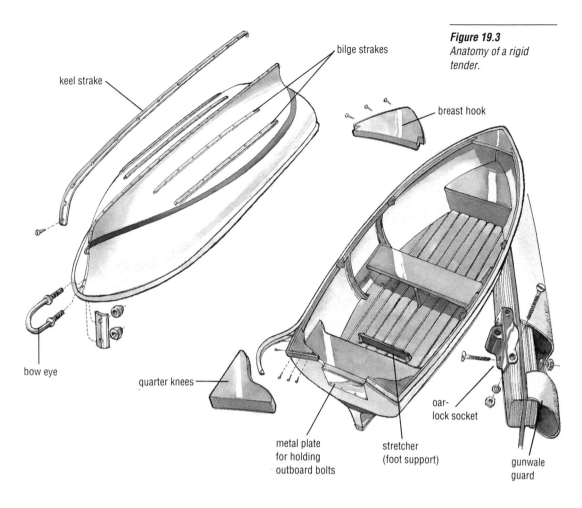

Figure 19.3
*Anatomy of a rigid
tender.*

keel strake

bilge strakes

breast hook

bow eye

quarter knees

metal plate
for holding
outboard bolts

stretcher
(foot support)

oar-
lock socket

gunwale
guard

A sleek, narrow-beam dinghy that sails well presents a pretty picture but is seldom the best choice for a yacht tender. A dinghy with a pointed bow and fine entry will move nicely through the water, but if the bow is too narrow, especially in a short dinghy, valuable space will be lost. More important, perhaps, is the underwater configuration. A conventionally shaped, flat-bottom tender has the same drawbacks as a flat-bottomed pram and will be hard to row. It does offer good initial stability, but in any kind of a sea it will be difficult to handle.

A more desirable design is a shallow V-shaped or rounded bottom with at least a hint of a keel and a skeg that runs all the way aft. These features give better directional stability under sail or when rowing. A round bottom is the strongest and most seaworthy dinghy, but the equally popular and generally cheaper V-bottom, though less strong, makes an adequate tender.

There are several two-piece rigid dinghies on the market, and some of them are well-made and relatively easy to put together. This can be a very important consideration where space is a limitation because the two halves can be nested.

Improving a Tender

In former times tenders were always made of wood, and many of them were extremely beautiful boats that rowed and sailed well. Today, fiberglass is the most common material used and there are a few aluminum dinghies as well. On fiberglass tenders flotation is usually blocks of foam that are glassed in, often to form the seats. The cost of a tender is a reflection of the amount of labor that has gone into its construction as well as the quality of the hardware and fittings. Some of the less expensive fiberglass tenders are sufficiently strong and have adequate flotation because they must meet U.S. Coast Guard standards, but the hardware and trim are often rather shoddy. For example, only the better and more expensive tenders have adequate strakes on the keel and bilges. In fact most fiberglass tenders have none. Only a few drags across a gravel or sand beach, or especially up a cement ramp or even a wood dock, and the bottom will be damaged. Usually the skeg is wood with a thin fiberglass covering, and if the wood is exposed it will quickly splinter or delaminate.

Strakes of wood, brass, or stainless steel strip will eliminate time-consuming reglassing of the bottom. Adding strakes is something you can do yourself. At a minimum a strake should be installed on the keel, and if practical they can also be installed on the bilges.

If the dinghy has been constructed without a breast hook and quarter knees, these should be added to improve hull strength. These additional supports are especially important if an outboard motor is going to be used.

Some tenders come with an inadequate fender or gunwale guard, or the gunwale is flimsy and easily broken. A guard or fender strip is important to protect the dinghy itself, and to prevent damage to other boats. Marine supply catalogs offer various styles of fender guards, but it is also possible to make your own from discarded fabric-covered firehose, heavy nylon line, or plastic hose.

It may also be necessary to improve and strengthen the transom. If an outboard is to be used you can install a wood, brass, or stainless steel plate on the inside and outside of the transom to keep the outboard engine clamps from damaging the hull. A metal strip added to the top edge of the transom will add strength and valuable chafe protection when using the dinghy to lay out an anchor.

Finally, the bow eye may need to be reinforced. This eye is mainly used for mooring, anchoring, and sometimes for towing. Unless it is stoutly made and ruggedly through-bolted with an adequate backing plate, it may pull out and bring about the loss of the tender. Similarly, U-bolts installed on the transom will facilitate lifting and provide a good place to secure a stern anchor, as is sometimes needed when the dinghy is tied-off ashore.

Oars, Oarlocks, and Oarlock Sockets

Rowing oars need to be strong and long. On inflatables they are notoriously short, but even those that come with rigid dinghies are seldom long enough. Adequate length is needed for maximum rowing power, especially through surf or to windward. According to Donald Street, the proper length of oars is twice the beam of the tender plus six inches. Unfortunately, for a dinghy less than about 10 feet (3 m) in length, it is impossible to have oars of the proper length that can be stored inside the dinghy when not in use. The best oars are made of spruce or ash, and are of one-piece construction, not laminated. Whatever you do, don't try to get by with the cheap oars made of plastic or aluminum and plastic. They will not stand up to hard use.

Another weakness of many inexpensive tenders are the oarlock (rowlock) sockets. Often they are poorly made and require replacement. This cannot be emphasized too strongly, because one of the tender's most significant functions is to row out extra anchors in the event of heavy weather. Invariably this will have to be done under difficult conditions. If an oarlock or socket should give way in a tight situation, your sailboat's safety may be in jeopardy. Likewise, going back and forth between the boat and a beach sometimes requires maneuvering through the surf zone. This type of rowing and control can put a tremendous strain on the oars, oarlocks, and sockets.

In some cases the oarlock socket is nothing more than a metal insert in a thin piece of wood trim. Much better is a heavy bronze or stainless steel socket which is bolted rather than screwed through the gunwale. Stainless steel is preferred because bronze sockets will wear into ovals and make for poor rowing.

A proper dinghy will have two rowing positions to permit the oarsman to sit amidships or forward, depending on the distribution of the load. Both positions should be provided with proper sockets. An additional socket installed on the transom permits you to scull the dinghy if one oar is lost or broken.

The best oarlocks are the solid ring type. These stay on the oar when it is removed from the socket and are hard to lose overboard. They should be strong and well made. Aluminum and plastic are not adequate. Even galvanized steel may deteriorate in just a few months of steady use. Once the galvanized coating is worn away they will rust and bleed, and the metal will eventually give way and break. Bronze or, if you can find them or have them made, stainless steel, will last a lifetime. Oar sleeves are needed to help keep the oar in position and to protect the wood.

The Problem of Stowage

If you think an inflatable can be a nuisance, a rigid dinghy sometimes creates even more problems. The main one is stowage. Whereas an inflatable can be deflated and stored away in a locker, a rigid dinghy demands a place to live when underway, and on a small boat there are few choices for storage. Those who have really big yachts may find davits a logical way to hang up the tender out of the way, but on most cruising boats this is not practical. The only place for davits is at the stern, and this is impossible if you have a wind steering vane. I doubt that stern davits are advisable on most boats under 50 feet because of the added windage and weight.

All that is left is stowage on the bow or between the mast and the cockpit. The bow is a poor choice because the tender will forever be in the way when making sail changes and when handling anchoring gear. It is quite dangerous to try and work on a rolling, pitching foredeck if you have to share it with a selfish, fat tender.

A more practical location on most aft-cockpit boats is the cabintop between the mast and the dodger. Most medium-sized cruising boats end up with the tender tied down in this position. The distance between the mast and the dodger will thus determine the size dinghy your boat can carry and hence, length often ends up being the deciding factor on what tender you select.

The conventional stowage position is upside-down. If the cabintop has a ventilation hatch, the overturned tender may permit you to keep the hatch open much of the time when sailing and thereby improve ventilation. A sailing dinghy with a daggerboard or centerboard trunk may make it difficult or impossible to open the hatch underneath. Keep that in mind when shopping for your rigid tender.

Figure 19.4
On-deck dinghy storage. To properly secure a dinghy on deck it is usually necessary to add chocks and through-deck tie-down eyes. Often it is possible to use the area below the dinghy to stow light-weight items including fresh provisions.

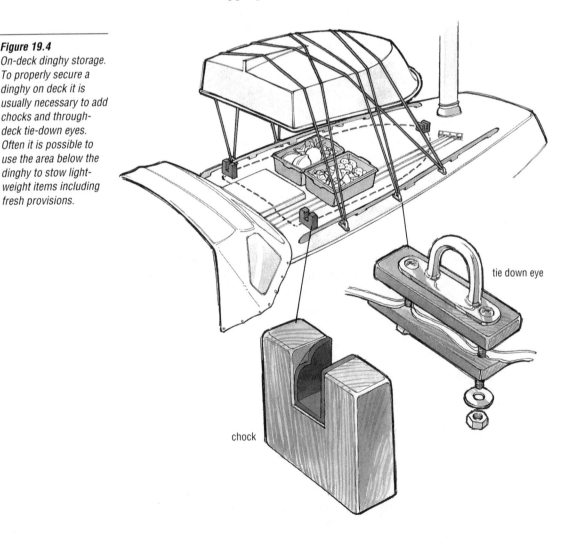

tie down eye

chock

Once you find a tender to fit the cabintop the next consideration is how to secure it. If you have halyards and other lines running from the mast to the cockpit, it will probably be necessary to use chocks to raise the dinghy off the deck.

The tender must be well secured. In heavy seas any waves coming aboard will put severe strains on the lashings. Handrails, which usually run port and starboard on the cabintop look like the logical solution, but they are seldom strong enough to do the job. If you really bowse the lines down snug, the result will either be broken rails or leaks into the cabin liner. A better idea is separate eyes with strong backing plates on the inside of the cabin.

Launching and recovering the dinghy will take a bit of ingenuity, but it is not as difficult as it might seem. If there are two crew on board and the tender is not too heavy, it can be lifted by hand and set over the side into the water. Leave the dinghy painter tied to the boat. It is most embarrassing to smoothly ease your dink in the water and then watch it float away.

If the launch and recovery have to be done by one person, or if they are too heavy for two crew to handle, let the main halyard help out. The halyard is attached to the tender's bow eye and it is lifted bow-first. Slowly crank the main halyard winch until the stern of the tender is just ready to clear the deck. It can then be swung aft and over the lifelines. Next, a bridle is attached to the tender's quarters and led to a turning block aft, and a couple of fenders are rigged between the tender and the side of your boat. Then, alternately slacking the halyard and the stern bridle, the tender can be launched without shipping any water. Yes, it takes a bit of practice to get it right.

When bringing the tender back aboard all you need to use is the main halyard. I usually let the dinghy hang on the main halyard while I rinse any sand or mud out with a few buckets of water. Otherwise the dinghy is hauled up with the main halyard secured to the bow eye. When the dinghy transom is slightly lower than the lifelines it can be swung aft and over the life lines. The dinghy's transom is then set on the cabintop in its storage position location, with the bottom of the dinghy facing aft. The bow of the dinghy is then slowly lowered by slacking the halyard. If you have positioned it correctly it will just about slip back where it belongs.

Summary

For the weekender, gunkholer, coastal sailor, and even for the long-distance racer, an inflatable tender is often quite adequate. For the cruiser who will be venturing forth to a variety of anchorages and must be self-sufficient, a well-made, rigid dinghy that rows well and has a large carrying capacity with adequate freeboard is needed. Ninety-five percent of the time the dinghy's main purpose will be to ferry the crew back and forth to land and to carry supplies to the boat. Often these are big loads, especially when it is necessary to transport water and fuel from shore to ship. For these tasks an inflatable will do fine if it has an outboard. But when the outboard packs up you will find inflatables very difficult to row for any distance, and if there is a headwind or chop they are pure misery. This is not just an inconvenience: more than one sailor has been lost by being swept offshore when he could not overcome the effects of wind or tide when trying to row an inflatable.

A major consideration for the cruiser, however, is that time when the tender is urgently needed to row out a second, or kedge, anchor. In this case speed and reliability are the important considerations. Again, this job can be done quite well with a good inflatable boat if it is ready to go and if the outboard does not fail. But total reliance on an inflatable is not prudent. If the urgency of the situation does not allow enough time to inflate and rig an inflatable, the time lost could mean the difference between success and failure. Under the stress and urgency of these conditions there is also the opportunity to accidentally damage or puncture an inflatable. But most important is the absolute fact that you cannot row out a heavy kedge or second anchor, or even a light one for that matter, with an inflatable if there is a headwind, a choppy sea surface, or any significant sea running. I recommend a rigid tender first. Then, if you have room on board and in your budget for an inflatable and outboard engine it will be an added convenience. Even with a crew of only two it is often advantageous to have two tenders available. Invariably, whoever is left on the boat will suddenly find some compelling reason for wanting to go ashore and have no way to get there. Certainly an inflatable makes a better dive boat.

Either type of tender can be taken along, in addition to your liferaft, if it is ever necessary to abandon ship.

Dinghy Techniques

Rowing Fundamentals

In calm waters and with little load in the tender, almost any kind of rowing stroke will get you around. But when going against a headwind, or in chop or waves, and with a load aboard, you want to get the maximum efficiency from your efforts.

Rowing is not just effort by the arms. You need to use your whole body for greater power. Your feet need to be well braced. This may be achieved with a stretcher (foot support) or, in a small tender, by placing the soles of your feet, or heels, firmly against the transom. As much as possible, your body and shoulders should lean forward in preparation for a rowing stroke. Then, as you dig in and pull on the oars, the power comes from your whole upper body, not just your arms. As you move the oars through the air to prepare for the next stroke, the wrists are dropped (rotated) to feather. This is all done in an uninterrupted, smooth, and rhythmic way. To achieve a coordinated motion requires practice.

As you pull the oars through the stroke, get the maximum distance from your sweep. As the blade goes through the water, it should travel along a nearly horizontal line, just below the water surface. Digging deeply into the water is a waste of effort.

With proper rowing, the tender does not yaw back and forth, but rather tracks in a straight line. On a trip of some distance, like back and forth between your mooring and shore, steering is improved by lining up some distant reference point, or preferably two points in line to make a range. If you are sighting on land, this is usually easy to do. When your only reference is the sea and sky, try sighting on a cloud. Rowing alone, it is necessary to now and then look over your shoulder to be sure you are on course. If you have a passenger, he can give directions.

Once you have mastered the basic skill of rowing, learn to 'back water', or row in reverse. This is useful when coming alongside a boat or at a landing. By backing on one oar and rowing on the other, you can turn a dinghy around in its own length.

Difficult Rowing

In rough seas, for example when there is a significant chop or large swells, it is often easier to row by pulling when in the trough of the waves or swell, and pausing on the crest. In difficult conditions remember the most efficient course is usually not a straight line to your destination. If there are large waves, it will be safer and easier to 'tack' back and forth to your destination. Sometimes, with a large following sea, it will be more convenient to turn the tender around and let the seas carry you to your destination, while using the oars to keep the bow into the waves.

When confronted with a strong current it is necessary to use good judgement, plan your trip carefully, and then be prepared to make changes as necessary. In the most common situation, you need to aim for a point far up-current from your desired destination and to 'crab' your course. Anyone who has sailed against a current will understand this immediately, but it should be explained carefully to inexperienced crewmembers who are using the tender. In most instances, problems in misjudging current will only lead to inconvenience and extra work for the rower. However, there have been cases where the dinghy and its hapless crew have been carried offshore by strong current flow.

Beach Landings and Departures

Landings made on beaches will vary widely depending on the nature of the shore and conditions of wind and sea. Sometimes, the prudent decision will be to remain aboard your boat until conditions improve, rather than attempt a dangerous landing. In a bay that is unfamiliar it will pay to climb to the spreaders on your boat and study the surrounding shoreline to seek out the safest place to put ashore.

Even after a choice has been made, be prepared to abort the attempt if it looks dangerous or even questionable as you approach the shoreline in the tender. If there are even small breaking waves at the beach, you are usually safe if you stay outside of the breaking zone while you row or motor the dinghy along the beach looking for a good landing spot. Take your time. Notice the wave pattern. Usually waves travel in sets and you will notice that sets of higher waves are interspersed with waves of lesser height. Let several sets go by until you have a feeling for the pattern before you begin your run in.

Figure 19.5
Rowing techniques.

a When rowing in large swells it is often easiest to pull hard in the troughs and to rest on the crests

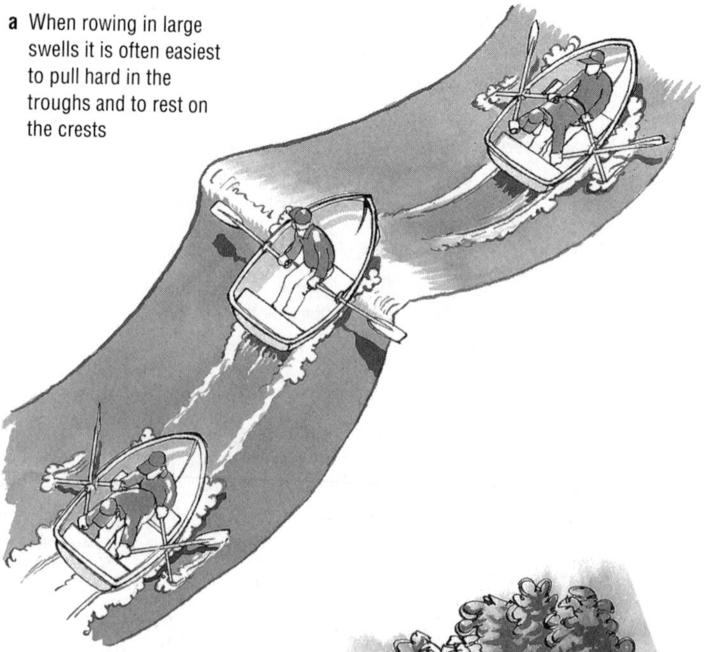

b When rowing across a current it is necessary to aim for a point up current from your destination and to 'crab' across the current

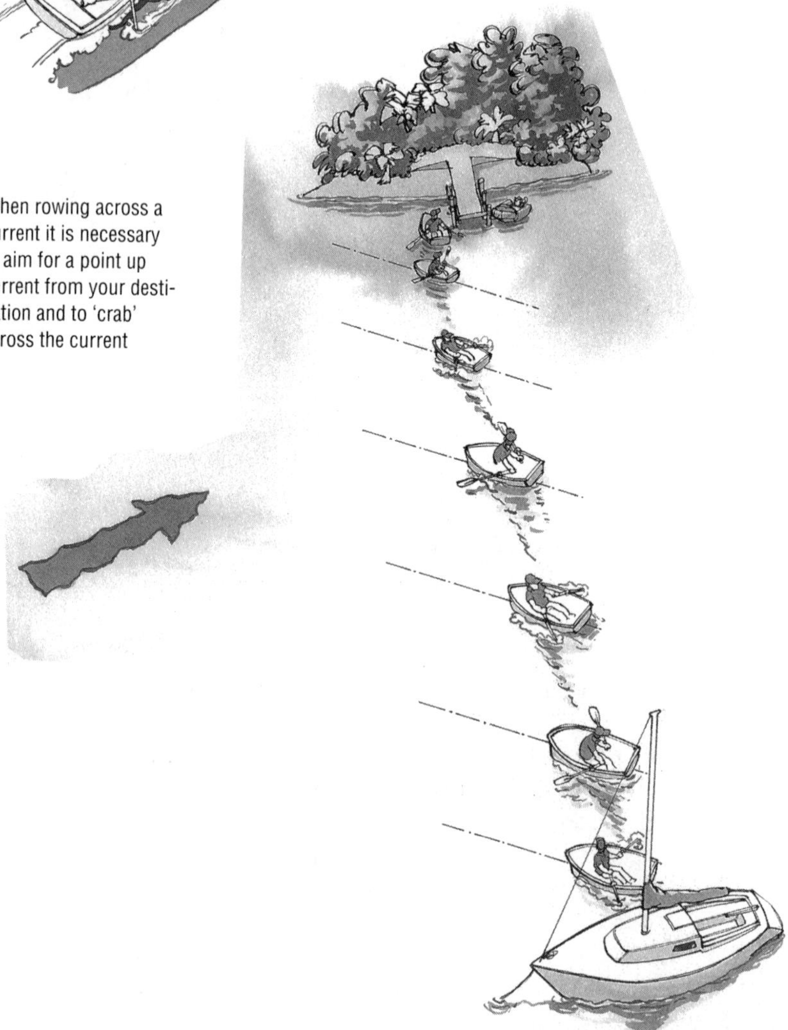

If there are others with you in the tender, brief them on what to expect and how to react as the boat moves on to the beach. It is also important to tell them what to do in the event of a capsize. Naturally, in such situations, everyone should be wearing a lifejacket.

On a gently sloping beach it is easier to keep control of the tender. As soon as it grounds, the crew needs to jump out and drag or carry the tender on up the beach to avoid being pooped or broached. Often with the crew out of the boat it will be possible to keep it floating as you bring it up the beach. At some point however, it will be necessary to carry or drag it above the surf line. If it is an inflatable, it is best to carry it, as dragging may abrade or even rip out the bottom.

Beach landings are sometimes complicated if you use an outboard, because at some point the engine needs to be put in neutral, turned off and then tilted up and locked in the raised position. If this maneuver is combined with jumping out of the boat and running it up on the beach it can be difficult and dangerous. Often it is safer and easier to bring the tender through the surf zone using only the oars.

Launching from the beach may be more difficult than landing. The crew needs to get the boat floating, pushed off, and then quickly board all in one rapid maneuver. If you are using an outboard the initial maneuvering must still be done with oars. It is not safe to have anyone alongside in the water with the engine in operation. The rower needs to really 'lean into it', put some water below the boat, and get through two or more wave crests before trying to start the engine. At the same time it is necessary to keep the bow pointed into the waves. The effort, although intense, is usually brief, and once outside of the surf zone the dinghy will bob about like a happy duck riding up and down on the swells. All loose gear should be tied to the boat in any beach landing or launching with much surf.

Beaches with steep underwater slopes can be especially difficult to negotiate because the waves or swells break suddenly rather than gently. With a steep beach profile it is possible for the dinghy to trip at the edge of the beach and broach or suddenly roll over. Added to these dangers is the fact that such beaches often have a strong flow of water returning seaward, or undertow, which can carry those in the water offshore and lead to drowning. If you suspect a beach has these characteristics, it will be better to search for a different landing place.

Some of the unpleasant surprises in beach landings occur if the shore is soft mud and the crew may sink up to their knees or even waist in sediment when jumping out at the shore line. At the other extreme is a beach of coarse pebbles where the footing is poor.

Trim

Load the tender carefully to obtain proper trim fore and aft, as well as athwartship. A dinghy that lists to port or starboard will be difficult to row, and it will tend to take on water if there is any wave action. Similarly, you will experience difficult handling when the bow or stern is too high or too low. The tender should be nearly level or slightly down by the stern when rowing. You can arrange seating of the crew to achieve this. When boarding the dinghy from the yacht or from a pontoon or dock, the person rowing should enter first and then steady the boat and direct others. Keep in mind that people boarding for the first time are probably a bit frightened and apprehensive, and have no idea what to do or what to expect. Give them clear and simple directions and have them move slowly and carefully. Likewise, when leaving the tender, the rower should stay aboard, keep control of the boat, and supervise others.

Tenders with outboards require a somewhat different approach. All tenders with engines are heavy in the stern, so be especially careful when there is too much weight aft. Boarding is much easier in an inflatable because the boat is more stable than a rigid dinghy. However, if the engine operator enters first, as is recommended, he or she will need to shift position as the passengers board. Then, it may be necessary to move about to start the engine and again once underway to maintain proper trim. Inflatables, even when lying alongside a boat or a dock, have been known to flip over if there is too much weight in the stern, and the bow is caught by a strong gust of wind.

Dinghy Equipment

Certain minimum equipment should be onboard your tender whenever it is used. In addition to the obvious need for a long, strong painter you should carry a bailer of some sort, a sponge, a small anchor, and about 100 feet of about 1/4- or 3/4-inch anchor line. The anchor and line may be needed when you tie off at a dock or landing, but more importantly it is your fail-safe if you should get carried away by the current, if you lose your oars, or if the outboard engine quits in a difficult situation.

It is recommended, and in some cases required, that everyone wear a lifejacket when in a dinghy. Of course, lifejackets are often a nuisance and it is rare that you see them being used in yacht anchorages. For children and non-swimmers, however, they should be mandatory. Any time you think you should be wearing a PFD, wear one. If you expect your children to wear a lifejacket, you should set the example. (See Chapter 28.)

If you expect you will be using the dinghy at night, bring along a flashlight. When you are in an unfamiliar anchorage either at night, or when fog or haze are possible, consider leaving the yacht's anchor light on to help find your way home.

For outboard operations a few basic tools and a spare sparkplug are recommended as part of the dinghy's standard equipment.

PART 3
THE VOYAGE

TRIP PLANNING

Designing a voyage is one of the highlights of sailing for me. It is a vicarious trip as I think about the new places to visit. Where do I want to go, how much time do I have, and what is the best and safest season to expect favorable weather, winds, and currents? Those are the first questions.

In the past the principal guide for selecting a route was *Ocean Passages for the World*, published by the British Government and available from chart dealers throughout the world. Although it is written to serve commercial ships, it retains some of the original information from the days of sailing vessels and is of interest to the small-boat sailor. Presently, Jimmy Cornell's book, *World Cruising Routes*, is a good source of voyage-planning information. It is a helpful reference for anyone getting ready for a circumnavigation or any long-distance sailing trip.

Heavy Weather

Weather

Cruising sailors are frequently asked by landlubbers how many hurricanes or typhoons they have encountered at sea. Luckily, most of us can say none. Any cruising sailor you meet who has a seabag full of hurricane stories is either poor at route planning, foolhardy, or more likely, a good spinner of yarns.

It is true that severe unexpected heavy weather can happen on any ocean at any time. But most storms are seasonal, and if you are conservative in planning, it is unlikely you will face significant danger. Many cruising people have spent years sailing throughout the world and never encountered any 'survival conditions' at sea or in port.

Rain, Fog, and Cold

Avoiding heavy weather is a primary concern but there are other seasonal considerations as well. The possibilities of rain, fog, and cold, are also important. Rain can be a positive or negative factor in choosing a route. It is downright miserable to spend days sailing in rainy conditions. Small boats get pretty grungy after a few days of continuous rain. But rain also means an opportunity to resupply fresh water.

Fog is seasonal and sailors prefer to avoid it. Near land, fog is dangerous and makes for very tense sailing because of the danger of collision and grounding. On the open ocean, fog is less of a concern unless you are in or crossing shipping lanes. However, long periods of fog will give the sextant a rest and put the navigator on edge. On some passages it is nearly impossible to avoid a few foggy days.

It is difficult to avoid cold weather in reaching some sailing destinations. But given a choice, I'd select a route and season of warm weather.

Wind and Currents

Most ocean currents are persistent throughout the year but vary seasonally. The major unidirectional currents, such as the Gulf Stream and the Kuroshio, must be reckoned with in order to take advantage of their help or to minimize their ill effects. Winds in many parts of the world change dramatically in strength or direction depending on the season. Every passage is planned by the winds. Average wind and current conditions on your route can be determined by studying the Pilot Charts.

Shipping Lanes

An important consideration in route selection for shorthanded and singlehanded yachts is the position of shipping lanes. Most sailors prefer to stay away from the main shipping routes because of the danger of collision. There are others who feel there is greater safety in being near the shipping lanes in the event they need assistance. In my opinion the risk of collision seems much greater than the possibility of needing assistance. When laying out a rhumbline course for any passage, it is a good idea to mark your charts to show the position of the shipping lanes as a reminder of areas in which to be especially alert. The location of the main shipping routes is given on the Pilot Charts.

Sailing Aids

Pilot Charts

These regional summaries display the ocean subdivided into five degree squares. For each square there is a wind rose showing average strength and direction. Pilot Charts also illustrate the typical direction and strength of surface currents. Other important information on the Pilot Charts includes the main shipping lanes, number of days in which fog can be expected, typical hurricane paths, mean water temperature, and a variety of other pertinent data depending on the area covered. Appendix 14 lists the various Pilot Charts for the world oceans.

Pilot Charts are compiled from data collected by ships over a long period of time. The data represent averages and must be used with that in mind. It is unlikely that you will make a passage and find that things exist exactly as summarized on the chart. However, Pilot Charts present reasonable trends and are a valuable guide to route planning.

Charts

Sailing charts can eat up a big chunk of a yacht's budget. In recent years the price of charts has increased significantly. This is unfortunate, because it encourages some sailors to put to sea without sufficient up-to-date charts on board. How many charts you take with you is a matter of personal preference and budget. Some folks are content to use only regional charts, whereas others insist on having detailed entrance charts for every port they may want or need to enter.

Charts of the same area published by different countries may look remarkably different because of cartographic technique and style. However, countries all share their hydrographic data, hence the charts are all based on the same soundings and surveys. For example, if you examine an American or British chart of waters controlled by Japan, you will see a notation to indicate that it is based on Japanese hydrographic data, or it may even refer to a specific Japanese chart. The fact that a chart is printed in a foreign language has little significance, because chart symbols share an international language and anyone who can read one chart can read another. It makes sense to buy charts based on price or on a preferred cartographic style. Depending on currency exchange rates, it may be much cheaper to buy from one country than another.

The cruising sailor's primary concern is to know what is deep and what is shallow, and often he wants to know this quickly without having to read each depth reading. On a chart with too much data and no color system, it is difficult to pick out shallow areas quickly. British Admiralty (BA) charts are by far the easiest to use. They are not cluttered with too many soundings, and often shallow areas are colored for quick identification.

Obtaining Charts

New charts can be purchased directly from the government or through a map distributor. Most chandleries only sell charts for their local area, so it may be necessary to find a major agent if you are looking for adequate coverage for an ocean passage. Among bookstores, The Armchair Sailor in Newport, Rhode Island, is unique in maintaining a huge worldwide chart inventory. In addition they offer a free regional checklist and order form that includes every chart, sailing aid, and reference book that you could possibly need. Their comprehensive coverage also includes cruising guides, books on weather, nature guides, and even books on birds, shells, and fish.

British Admiralty charts are available through major chart supply agencies. All of the major ports throughout the world have chart dealers that supply merchant ships, and they should be able to get any chart you need.

Among cruising sailors, there is a lot of swapping of charts. Trades can also be made through some sailing associations. For example the Seven Seas Cruising Association (SSCA) frequently lists people looking for charts of various regions and those who are willing to trade charts they no longer need.

It is also a common practice to borrow charts from fellow cruisers and have them photocopied. In some places copy services are able to duplicate half- or full-sheet maps on one sheet of paper. Copies represent a tremendous savings over having to buy a new chart, but take time to inspect and compare each copy with the original to be sure nothing has been accidentally left off, or that parts of the map are not out of focus. Sometimes borrowed charts have numerous pencil lines and various other notations that may obscure important information. Consider also that original charts are usually printed on high-quality, distortion-free paper, whereas copy paper is cheap and of poor quality. Making copies of copies is not recommended as it introduces too many possibilities for loss of detail.

It is worthwhile having some tracing paper stashed away in the chart desk to permit hand-copying charts when necessary. If you make a tracing of a map, take the time to do a thorough job. Information that may seem insignificant at the time you make the copy may subsequently be very important when you are using the tracing to negotiate a reef passage or to approach a harbor entrance.

Chart Scales

For open ocean passages it is not necessary to have detailed charts. Those printed at a scale of 1:10,000,000 are suitable unless there are numerous reefs or shoals along your route. For navigating in the vicinity of shallow areas, a scale of 1:500,000 is usually adequate, and for coastal navigation and harbor entrances a scale of 1:50,000 is sufficient. If you can afford to buy detailed charts, they will make your sailing easier, but they are not required to get you where you want to go.

The most important point is to not put to sea without the necessary charts. I would rather delay a cruise than head offshore without the proper charts. The few times I have lacked the needed charts have caused me a lot of disquiet. Sometimes I have sailed a gap of a few miles with no coverage between charts. I always knew full well that there were no hazards within this void, but it still made me anxious. It can be argued that none of the early ocean explorers had charts. But they had large crews and lookouts up in the rigging. Furthermore, we only hear about the successful adventurers. The ones who never came back didn't write books. Don't be too conservative when buying charts. Even though you plan to go to a specific place, you may find it necessary to deviate somewhat from your schedule. It is advisable to have charts for alternative islands or harbors along your route and near your expected destination.

Sailing Directions (Pilots)

The British and United States governments each publish a series of books called *Sailing Directions* or *Pilots*. The British version, which some consider more useful, are hardbound, and the U.S. publications are loose-leaf for keeping in a three-ring binder. Both the British and the U.S. versions give thorough descriptions of foreign coastal areas throughout the world, including information on commercial harbor facilities.

Sailing Directions are published to assist large ships and contain far more information than most of us will ever need. However, they are handy to have on board. For example if you are lacking a detailed chart for a coastal area or a major harbor entrance, you can almost draw a chart based on the information in the pilot. The possibility of spurious currents is discussed, and where pertinent the pilots describe features that announce the approach of unusual weather. For example, in parts of the Western Pacific, tradewinds are now and then replaced by westerlies which spell danger for many atoll anchorages. The pilot indicates the unique weather patterns that give as much as 36 hours warning.

Included in the U.S. Sailing Directions are regional volumes on the open ocean areas such as the North Pacific. These volumes are useful when preparing for long ocean passages.

The U.S. government also publishes eight volumes of the *Coast Pilot* which is like *Sailing Directions* and covers the coastlines of the United States and its possessions.

See Appendix 14.

Light Lists

There is a series of seven publications by the U.S. government called Light Lists for various regions of the world. They indicate all the navigational lights for each country in the regions covered. Lights are also shown on your charts, so these lists are a supplement to the chart. The lists give each light's characteristics, its exact latitude and longitude, its height and elevation, and a brief description of the light structure itself.

There are times when light lists can be handy to have on board but in fact cruisers rarely use them because they are never up to date. The issuing agencies publish addenda to keep them current, but few people have the time or energy to try and keep up with the changes.

For the coasts of the U.S. and its possessions, there is a seven-volume set of Light Lists prepared by the United States Coast Guard.

See Appendix 14.

Radio Publications

The U.S. and British government both sell two radio publications that are useful to yachtsmen. One lists the location, range, and signal characteristics of radio direction finder (RDF) stations and radio beacons and time signals throughout the world. The other, which is of more value to the cruising yachtsman, gives the time and type of maritime weather broadcasts for all countries of the world. It includes voice, code, weatherfax, and radiotelephone transmissions.

How necessary these are to you depends on where you are sailing and how much space you have on board for little-used publications. Often station and frequency information for weatherfax and radiotelephone transmissions are included in booklets that come with the equipment. Prior to setting off on a voyage, you want to have a list of necessary frequencies, but it isn't necessary to have them for the whole world. I finally gave away these books after hauling them around for about 10 years.

See Appendix 14.

Tide and Current Tables

Depending on where you are sailing, knowing the time, strength, and direction of tidal currents may be critical to cruising safety and convenience. This is difficult to appreciate unless you have sailed in areas of strong tides. Yet in some parts of the world, failure to take tidal currents into consideration can lead to groundings and yacht damage.

The U.S. Government publishes tidal current tables for the U.S.

coasts and tide tables for areas outside America (Appendix 14). Other countries publish tide and current tables for their waters. If you plan to sail extensively in one area, purchase the local tables.

Cruising Guidebooks

Some sailors like to play Columbus and go off adventuring as if they were the first people to ever cross an ocean. They claim they want to avoid structure and regimentation, and they shun the use of cruising guides. Others are eager to learn anything and everything they can about the areas they plan to visit. I am in the latter group and derive a lot of pleasure reading guidebooks on the way to a new destination.

There are numerous cruising guides available for those who care to use them. Most are valuable additions to a yacht's library and will pay for themselves several times over in terms of the money and time you will save by knowing in advance the best places to anchor, recommended shopping areas, and the location of fuel, water, and repair facilities. Some are very general in their descriptions, others give fine-scale detail. For example, Earl Hinz's excellent book *Landfalls of Paradise* covers practically the whole Pacific Ocean area. It discusses sailing routes, provides information about individual islands, and gives sketch maps of major harbors and anchorages.

The authors of cruising guidebooks are often fair game for yachties who love to point out the errors they have found in the books. But like any other sailing information, the advice and directions given in cruising guides must be used with discretion. The better cruising guides are written by sailors, and for them to visit all of the places they write about takes time. They are traveling like the rest of us, and their boats, like ours, have two speeds – slow and stop. Thus, it may be several years from the time the author gathers the information until the book is published. During that time, both natural and man-made features may change – harbor entrances may have a new set of breakwaters, marinas may have improved or become bad, immigration and customs regulations will have been revised. But in spite of these inconveniences, any information is better than none at all, and most cruisers find the guides helpful.

Cruising guides are specialized publications and are sold only by booksellers who deal in maritime publications, by the publishers, or chandlers. The time to buy the cruising guidebooks is before you leave home. Don't expect to find them in the area they describe.

There are also a number of excellent tourist guidebooks these days that are written for people who, like most sailors, are traveling on a limited budget. They will tell you where to find the post office, inexpensive restaurants, and laundromats; they will also offer a realistic appraisal of a country's history, the significant tourist attractions, and a no-nonsense guide to local customs. Foremost among these are books published by Lonely Planet and Moon Publications.

The best and most up-to-date sources for cruising information are the newsletters published by cruising associations. Of these, the Seven Seas Cruising Association (SSCA) is perhaps the best known. Each month it publishes a newsletter called the *Commodores' Bulletin*. It is made up of letters from some of the organization's more than 3000 members.

These letters provide a valuable source for cruising information. They are first-person accounts from around the world. Writing style and opinions vary with each writer, but they contain information on good and bad anchorages, accounts of ocean passages, experiences with various types of yacht equipment, and the latest word relating to customs, immigration, harbor and canal fees, and a wide variety of other information. SSCA is one of the best bargains among my cruising expenses. I carry several years of back issues on board, and frequently refer to them in planning a passage.

Anyone can be a member of the SSCA and receive the Bulletin by paying the yearly dues. Even if your cruising plans are several years away, it is worthwhile to become a member now in order to begin to gather a backlog of information. The SSCA address is given in Appendix 13.

The Ocean Cruising Club is an international association administered from the United Kingdom. It was founded in 1954 for long distance cruising sailors. OCC members receive a regular newsletter that reports news of voyaging members and other Club activities. Around the world nearly 100 OCC Port Officers in more than 35 countries can assist visiting members with local information. Another important British organization is the Cruising Association. They publish several useful cruising guides for the British Isles, Europe and North Africa. The address for the OCC and the Cruising Association are given in Appendix 13.

Cruising Associations

Experienced cruising sailors will tell you to be very liberal with your time estimates when planning a cruise. That Boeing 747 that just passed overhead will go as far in two hours as your boat will go in two weeks. The average run for boats between 30 and 40 feet in length is about 100 nautical miles per day. Sure, we all like to talk about the days when we logged 160 or even 200 miles. But we seldom mention the days when there was no wind or when we were hove-to because of too much wind.

It is impossible for anyone to tell you how long to plan for a trip. The best advice you can get is from someone who has already done it, but it may not apply to you and your style. A circumnavigation of three years is possible, and some have done it in less time, but five or six years is much more realistic. For others it can extend into decades. My own circumnavigation began nearly 10 years ago and I still haven't gotten out of the Pacific Ocean.

Putting it Together

CHAPTER **21** PROVISIONING

Food

Planning food for a long ocean passage may seem awesome. Although it is an important task, it isn't so complicated. If any errors in judgement are made, they should be on the side of too much rather than too little. For a first cruise it may be worthwhile to make out an estimated day-by-day menu. It isn't important that you actually follow your plan, but it will help in making adequate food purchases. After provisioning for a few voyages you will become an expert on food estimates.

Selection of specific food items will depend on the crew's likes and dislikes, so the proposed menu should be agreed upon by all hands. Contrary to some people's concept of sailing, it *is* possible to eat well and have a variety of foods even on a small boat. The size of your boat and whether you have a freezer will affect what you buy. Even if you have a freezer, adequate backup foods must be carried in the event that conveniences should fail.

Stocking Up

Food purchases can begin weeks or even months in advance of leaving. Dry stores such as grains, pasta, flour, dried or freeze-dried foods, and canned foods and drinks can be purchased early. As the departure day comes closer you will have more than enough other tasks at hand.

Shopping early also allows time for testing what you are buying. For example, if you normally only buy fresh foods you may find that canned and dried items are less palatable, and it may be necessary to look around for foods you like.

Timely planning permits buying at reduced or discount prices, especially if you are buying in bulk. Fresh produce such as eggs, long-life milk, fruit, and vegetables can be put off until the last week, but where and how they will be stored on the boat should be considered in advance and the space for them reserved.

In addition to the quantity of food you consider adequate for a cruise, there needs to be a supplement for emergency use. An overage of about 50 per cent is a reasonable amount to plan for – more if you have space. This reserve is to get you by in the event of unexpected problems or delays, not all of which are emergencies. A recent letter to the SSCA Bulletin described the experiences of the crew on a 47-foot gaff-rigged yawl that took 97 days to go from Tarawa to Honolulu – a distance of little over 2000 nautical miles. The passage was originally planned to go directly from Kiribati to California but the boat encountered unexpected calms, gales, engine problems, and some minor rigging difficulties. All problems, none a real emergency. Fortunately they were well supplied with food and water. That kind of a trip is unusual, but it can happen and every cruiser has heard one or more stories of folks who have had extremely long passages. In the 1989 race from Auckland, New Zealand to Fukuoka, Japan, one crew misjudged food requirements and ended up eating emergency rations out of the liferaft supplies. A rather humorous story in retrospect, but it could have developed into a serious situation.

An adequate water supply is critical. Whereas it is possible to go without food for long periods of time, survival will be only a few days without water. Give careful thought to planning an adequate water budget. This includes estimating average use for the expected passage, plus a reserve of at least 50 percent. It is not prudent to rely on being able to replenish your supplies from rainwater. Often this can be done, but rain does not show up on cue. On my passage from Panama to Hawaii of 47 days it rained only once, and that was during a gale when it was too rough to catch rainwater easily.

Water Replenishment

Conservation

Dedicated conservation of fresh water is important. Some sailors shut off the fresh-water supply to the sink in the head when offshore to avoid the possibility of accidental loss of water. Boats with pressure-water systems often use only a manual pump when off soundings. I have found that a hand pump rather than a foot pump also encourages water savings. Especially important is to have a salt-water hand pump at the galley sink. All dish washing can be done with salt water once away from land. Salt water is also fine for bathing, provided a very small amount of fresh water is used for a rinse. Clothes can be washed in seawater if they are rinsed in fresh water before drying. Finally, some cooking can be done with a combination of salt and fresh water. It is easy to get by on two liters of fresh water per person per day for drinking and cooking. Until the crew has become accustomed to conserving water, it is advisable to sound the water tanks frequently to be sure of your reserves.

Rainwater

Top off the tanks with rainwater when possible. A procedure for this should be considered before you leave port. One way is to put a reef in the mainsail, which will catch the water flowing down the sail. The outboard end of the boom can be raised a bit with the topping lift so the fresh water can run down the reef toward the mast and be caught in a bucket or funnel and hose near the gooseneck. Usually the sails and spar have a coating of salt crystals, so the water should be allowed to wash out the salt for a few minutes before collecting water for the tank. In port a rain catcher can be combined with a cockpit or deck awning.

Storage Tanks

Recommended practice is to have at least two water tanks for the sake of safety: If one tank becomes contaminated or develops a leak the boat's whole supply will not be lost. Unfortunately, most racer-cruiser type production boats are fitted with only one, usually small, water tank. An additional water tank may need to be added, or a collapsible tank carried on long passages. Many boats carry additional water supplies on deck in plastic containers. The water in on-deck bottles should be treated with chlorine to prevent the growth of algae.

Water Treatment

Any water brought on board from a land source may be contaminated. In most countries of the world the water is reliable, but in some places it is not. Treat the water if you have any suspicion. More than one cruising yacht has found itself several days from land with its entire water supply contaminated.

Watermakers

Small watermakers now being manufactured are useful for supplementing a yacht's water supplies. Though still a bit pricey they are becoming more popular due to their convenience. Recovery Engineering manufactures a small reverse-osmosis unit that operates on 12-volt DC current. The Power Survivor 35 is reported to produce about a gallon per hour with a four-amp power requirement. A gallon a day is adequate for a crew of two. This is a worthwhile option to consider for long-distance cruising. Another attractive unit is that produced by Balmar Products of Seattle. This is the Aqua-Pac, which is a combined reverse-osmosis watermaker and battery charger. It is powered by Yanmar 4.2-HP air-cooled diesel engine. Balmar claims it will produce up to 75 liters of fresh water per hour, as well as 100 amps for charging batteries. This would solve two of the biggest problems faced by cruising sailors. The Aqua-Pac is a high-priced item and though compact it requires more space than is available on most cruising boats of less than 40 feet.

Provisioning Ports

Some ports are well known by cruisers as especially good places to stock up on particular items. For example, Guam and Hawaii are good provisioning points because of a wide variety of U.S. food products at reasonable prices. New Zealand is well-known for meat and dairy products.

If you stay for an extended period in any country you can usually learn about the most economical places to stock up on supplies. In some places it is possible to join a food co-op. These organizations are privately run and each member contributes a few hours of work each week. In return you can buy quality foods in bulk at discount prices.

If you are stocking up for a long period at sea it is sometimes possible to buy food in bulk from a ship's chandlery. These are the suppliers for large merchant ships and often they will sell to sailboats as well. This is not like shopping at a supermarket. Rather, the supplier may show you a printed list of what they have available, and you can buy only in case lots. If a case of something (usually 24 or 48 items) is too much for you, it may be possible to have two or three boats make purchases together and then split up the case lots.

Duty-free markets are by and large a thing of the past. A few still offer some bargains, but usually they only apply to luxury items, and often prices are no better than in discount stores. You will have the option to buy duty-free liquor and tobacco in some ports and there is no limit on what you can have on board until you come back to your own country. The best source of information on this is other cruising boats you meet along the way, or the local customs officers. Usually duty-free items must be taken aboard just prior to departure. If you arrive in a new country and you have an unusually large supply of tobacco or liquor on board, customs can require that it all be kept in one locker and the locker sealed by customs agents for the duration of your stay in that port.

In remote areas, shopping for fresh foods is done at outdoor markets where local people bring their excess produce. Usually this takes place once or twice a week and the prices are generally low and the sellers honest. No matter what you buy, market days are an exciting and inter-esting experience. It is a good way to meet the local people and to get an introduction to new foods. If you plan to buy fresh produce at these markets you need to go early and take your own shopping bag. Usually, anything you buy is simply handed to you, and it is your problem to have something to put it in. It is a good idea to take along several small plastic bags as well as a canvas or net sack for the ride back to the boat in the dinghy.

In some anchorages local people will come out to your boat in canoes to sell fruit and vegetables, and sometimes they are more inter-ested in trading than in cash transactions. Used clothing, pencils, candy, tobacco, shoes, old tools, used rope, and fish hooks are just a few of the things they will be interested in.

Bargaining is a way of life in many places. Even if you don't like to bargain it will be necessary to do so. The usual practice is to offer half the asking price and then you work your way from there. Don't be too distressed if you think you are not paying enough. It has been a few years since Magellan or Columbus came this way, and local people seldom come out short on a trade.

The Other Side of Provisioning

The amount of trash and garbage that a sailboat creates is relatively minor and it is easy enough on the vast surface of the ocean to overlook a few bits of garbage here and there. But unfortunately a lot of that stuff doesn't sink and the decay rate on some materials is measured in years or decades.

A lot of potential trash can be eliminated by how you provision your boat. For example you can make the effort not to buy things that are over-packaged. Even where you cannot avoid items such as the infa-mous bubble-packs which marine supply stores are especially guilty of using, the packaging should be left ashore. Obviously plastic, using that noun in its broadest sense, is the worst offender. But what about tin, aluminum, glass and paper? It is pretty well accepted that there isn't any

Figure 21.1
Provisioning at anchor.

great harm in jettisoning glass bottles and aluminum and tin cans in the deep sea. They will make their way to the sea floor, sometimes miles below us, and simply become a home for some denizen.

I confess that I have given the heave-ho to my share of cans and bottle over the years but on recent passages I have been experimenting with garbage and have found out that it is just as easy to bring it back to land and dispose of it where at least there is some sort of responsible recycling activity underway. Bottles and cans can be washed out with salt water to remove any food particles. Metal cans are easily flattened. Bottles present a slightly more bulky problem but even on a passage of three or four weeks you won't have all that many bottles.

Unlike the products made directly from plant materials which become nature's compost in a matter of days, the products of industrial societies do not rot, dissolve, or disappear and the long range impact is potentially more serious than mere aesthetics.

STORAGE

Lack of storage space ranks pretty high on my list of frustrations, and it seems to be a problem I share with all cruising sailors. Over the past several years I have packed, repacked, and rearranged my boat four or five times, and nothing seems to create more storage space short of getting rid of my accumulated junk. Even buying a larger boat, I'm told, only brings temporary relief from the eternal quest for more storage. As soon as we have more bins, cabinets, drawers, and lockers, they become full of things we consider essential even if we managed to get along without them before.

Weight

In stowing a boat for offshore cruising, a primary consideration is stability and trim. One aim is to keep the weight out of the ends of the boat for better balance, and to maintain buoyancy. If possible, anchors should be stowed low, in the middle of the boat. On a long offshore passage, some or all of the anchors can perhaps be kept under settees in the main cabin. Likewise, canned food, diving equipment, and similar heavy objects should all be kept low. You have little choice about the location of anchor chain, although it may be possible to move the chain locker back from the bow as discussed in Chapter 9.

Sails and line, which are light for their volume, can be placed forward and aft depending on convenience and handiness.

Accessibility

Having things you need where you can reach them conveniently is an important goal. Supposedly, you need everything on your boat or it would not be there – but there is a hierarchy of use and need. The first consideration is equipment to maintain a safe boat. Second, you can arrange things according to how frequently they are used. Third, you can change stowage depending on whether you are at sea or in port.

Emergency Equipment

Easy access to emergency equipment comes first. This includes items for very infrequent but potentially instant use, such as man overboard equipment, fire extinguishers, emergency bilge pumps, flares, the liferaft, abandon-ship bag, EPIRB, and specific tools needed for damage control. Because most of this equipment is seldom used it tends to get in the way and eventually ends up out of the way, buried beneath other equipment in a obscure locker. This is a bad policy for two reasons.

True emergencies on a boat are rare events, and the majority of cruising people spend years without ever having to resort to any heroic measures to save their lives or their boat. On the other hand, accounts of crews that were forced to abandon ship or confront some other crisis almost always emphasize the suddenness of the event. There may be little that can be done to save a rapidly sinking boat other than to save yourself. Likewise a dismasting or major damage to the rigging requires fast action. Damage-control and survival equipment must be readily at hand. Flares to alert a ship of your whereabouts must be immediately available. These are not times to have to stop and wonder where they are, or to dig down in a locker to find them.

Keeping emergency equipment accessible also encourages you to be conscious of its condition and readiness. A liferaft, abandon-ship bag, or signaling flares may be damaged by water or other causes and go unnoticed when stowed out of sight. A pair of heavy-duty rigging cutters will freeze up in no time if they accumulate a little moisture in the bottom of the hanging locker.

Frequently Used Items

Storage of non-emergency equipment and supplies should be based on their frequency of use. Engine spares, paint, varnish, and special tools will only be needed during repair periods in port. Certain charts and pilot books are necessary for the current leg of a voyage, but others can be put away. Only clothes for the local climate are needed; the rest can be stashed away.

Most cruising boats carry a large supply of dried and canned foods. It is not necessary to have all of it available all of the time. When setting out on a passage, one or more lockers that are easy to use should be stocked with what you expect to consume on that leg.

It is unnecessary to have all of the boat's tools at hand underway. Locate basic tools where they are easy to get to, and put the rest away. On *Denali* I keep a basic set of tools in the pockets of a cloth tool holder that hangs next to the chart table. Everything is within easy reach, and I don't have to root around through a locker for the needed screwdriver. Damage-control tools (heavy wirecutters, sledgehammer, wrecking bar, axe, and saw) are in a locker at the base of the companionway ladder. Other tools, including a power drill, grinder, sander, and an assortment of wrenches, live peacefully out of the way below a settee.

Even items devoted to entertainment and relaxation can be categorized into frequent and infrequent use. Most of us carry a trove of books and cassette tapes. Before leaving port, I usually load up the bookshelf with a variety of titles for that particular voyage, and put the rest of the library out of the way.

In-Port or At-Sea Use

Things limited to in-port use can be put out of the way at sea. For example, bicycles can be placed in the forepeak when sailing. They are light and will not significantly affect trim. Anywhere else, they will be in the way. Many sailboats carry the tender's outboard motor on the stern pulpit. This is convenient when gunkholing or making short passages, but on an offshore passage it is better stowed below.

In port, seagoing equipment goes into hiding. The sextant can be put farther back in a locker, and sails can be relocated to make the boat more convenient for extended port visits.

Safety and Security

The rules here are 'no loose gear' and 'a place for everything.' This does not mean that the boat needs to be in a continuous state of emergency readiness. It does mean that every piece of gear should have a storage place that will keep it from being broken or from becoming a hazard in rough seas. It also encourages the crew to put things away. If there is a handy box just inside the companionway hatch for binoculars and hand-bearing compass, there is less chance that they will be left on a cockpit bench or under the dodger. Likewise, storage for the sextant should be secure and easily accessible when sailing. A sextant should either be in someone's hand or in its storage box at all times.

As unpleasant as it may be, think about your boat in a knockdown or capsize, and then decide if you have safe and secure storage. Begin with the forepeak and chain locker and then work your way aft. Think about each cabinet, locker, and drawer. How about the chart table and icebox? The stove? Consider items stored beneath the settees, in the quarter berth, the cockpit lockers, and in any deck storage boxes. If your boat will survive a knockdown without loose gear and equipment becoming lethal weapons, or your cabin turning into a quagmire, it is safe and secure for offshore passages. Conditions on boats that have rolled or pitchpoled are sobering. In his book *Once Is Enough*, Miles Smeeton recounts conditions aboard *Tzu Hang* after pitchpoling:

'There was paper pulp everywhere from labels and books and charts. It looked like the output of a pulp mill. Mixed in with it was broken glass, marmalade, bottled meat no longer in bottles, seventy broken eggs, soggy loaves of twice-baked bread, ashes and coke. The whole was tied together with glutinous tendons from skeins and skeins of colored wool – marlin, fishing line, caulking cotton, and fishhooks all helped bind it together. This was topped off by odd clothing, soaking Dunlopillo cushions, and seats, and out-of-place floorboards.'

Record Keeping

Loading and stowing a cruising boat requires considerable time and ingenuity to make everything fit. Sometimes a locker will be repacked several times before the best use of space is found. Foods have to be repackaged and labeled. Bottles need special padding to prevent breakage. Stowage may take several days.

With such time and thought spent on the task, you might expect that the location of every item would be indelibly printed on your mind. Yet, a few weeks into a cruise, you may have to spend hours searching for a jar of anchovies (small problem) or a fuse for the bilge pump (big problem). A storage record will help. It can be simple or elaborate, depending on your love of detail. It can be a map of the boat, a list of the lockers and their contents, a list of items and their location, or some

Figure 22.1

Storage diagram. Each shelf, locker, bin, or cabinet should be given a location designation to help in making a storage log book.
The following abbreviated designations can be used: p, port; s, starboard.
s, shelf; b, bin; l, locker; c, cabinet.
For example in this diagram some of the designations are: pl1, port locker 1; pc4, port cabinet 4; sb2, starboard bin 2; ss5, starboard shelf 5.

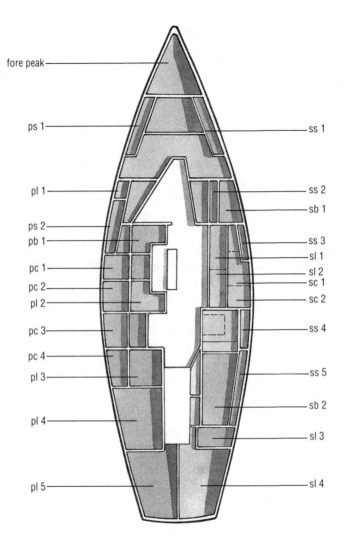

sort of combination and cross-reference. You will eventually find your own system. I have a diagram of my boat showing each of the more than 50 individual cabinets, lockers, bins, drawers, boxes, and shelves. Each storage area has a designation and the contents of each space is listed in the stores notebook.

The notebook is also a way to keep track of expendable items such as food, fuses, oil filters, camera film, and similar items. Use a pencil for the record of the contents because the list will frequently change. Some very orderly cruisers keep daily records of food supplies by indicating in their record book each time something is used or transferred to the galley. This has obvious benefits when it is necessary to restock the boat. Some sailors even have a cross-reference by alphabetical listing. A lot of work? Yes. But then, cruising should be enjoyable and if you enjoy this kind of precision, go for it.

The record book has other uses as well, such as keeping track of charts, pilot charts and pilot books. I record the more than 60 different fuses, light bulbs, and batteries needed for various pieces of equipment, as well as how many are on board. I am forced into keeping some kind of order of this mess, not because I am organized, but because I am too lazy to have to figure it out more than once. My notebook also contains a list of all of the first-aid and medical supplies.

Some boats are wetter than others, but all boats risk the possibility of water damage to supplies, clothing, and equipment from time to time through deck leaks, condensation, or water coming aboard unexpectedly as rain or spray. Lockers that are seldom emptied or inspected may accumulate water over a long period before it is noticed. Regardless of how dry you think your boat is, you may change your mind after beating to windward for several days. **Waterproofing**

Put everything you can in waterproof or at least water-resistant containers whenever possible. Zip-lock bags and Tupperware-type containers with snap tops come in handy. Small machines for vacuum bagging and heat sealing are now on the market and can definitely apply to the cruiser.

Finding new storage space is an exercise in creative thinking, followed by some creative modifications. Look around for unused or under-used areas. Bunks are most obvious. Production boats of 30 feet or more are advertised as able to 'sleep seven.' Usually this means two berths in a forward cabin, two settees, two pilot berths outboard of the settees or a convertible dinette, and a quarter berth. If you are a crew of two, some of that space can be converted to storage. The pilot berths can be closed in to make convenient cabinets. The bunks in the forward cabin will most likely be needed for storage at least at sea. The quarter berth often ends up as a storage area. On most boats access to the quarter berth is not very convenient at sea, but it can serve as a place for seldom-used items. **Creating Space**

Snoop around, and you will probably find small voids that were built into your boat. I converted more than a cubic foot of unused space under the stove enclosure into a storage bin by installing an access plate. The area is low, and near the center of the boat. It now contains diving weights and spare hose. Even in an otherwise crowded engine compartment there may be space to add a couple of shelves to hold replacement parts for the engine. Look inside existing cabinets to be sure the space is being completely utilized. Sometimes, by adding, removing, raising, or lowering a shelf you can create better storage.

Square or rectangular-shaped containers, all the same size (such as snap-top plastic boxes) utilize shelf space very effectively. In building new cabinets and shelves, consider what will be stored there. If you find storage containers that you like, build the shelves to fit the containers. Nalgene makes a variety of square, wide-mouth, screw-top plastic bottles in various sizes. Their square shape permits maximum use of available shelf space. I use the large ones for storing rice, flour, dried beans, and pasta.

Figure 22.2
*Maximizing storage.
Making the most of the
least amount of space is
important on a small
boat.*

a Hand tools hung in a
cloth apron allow easy
access and maximum
storage in minimum
space

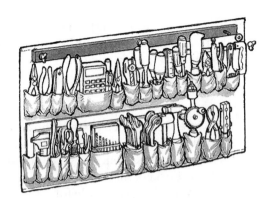

b Food stored in con-
tainers of uniform size
and shape saves space.
Square or rectangular
containers take up less
space than round ones

It is often possible to build a bookcase on the forward bulkhead of the main cabin. In designing a bookcase, consider the sizes of books you plan to take with you, and build the shelves accordingly. Don't forget some shelves for cassette tapes. Stretch-cord across the front of the shelves will hold everything in place.

There are a number of books offering suggestions on ways to add and improve storage space on small yachts. Look in the bibliography for titles by Bingham, Burke, Collins, Maté, and Spurr.

Food Storage

When you change from a life ashore to a life on board, it is necessary to adopt a new style and approach to food purchase, stowage and, to some extent, cooking. It is still possible to eat most of the foods you are accustomed to, and it is not necessary to resort to prepared, instant foods.

Perishables

Some vegetables keep for a long time on board if they have dry, well-ventilated storage. Newspaper often serves as excellent material in which to wrap fruit and vegetables. Just be sure it stays clear of the bilges. Frequently inspect the condition of all vegetables and fruit and throw away any spoiled food. Potatoes and onions may last up to two months if properly stored. Beets and carrots can last for a couple of weeks. Pumpkin and squash are good for several weeks. Cabbage has a long life if individual heads are wrapped in newsprint and kept dry. Usually the outer leaves will become rotten in a week or so, but they can be removed and discarded, and the rest of the head can be used. Tomatoes, if purchased before they are ripe and before they have been refrigerated, can be stored for one or two weeks. More fragile fresh vegetables such as lettuce, eggplant, green beans, and peas will seldom last more than a few days.

Dry, well-ventilated storage and frequent inspection also apply to fruit. Grapefruit, oranges, lemons, and especially limes will keep for several weeks. Some people recommend wrapping citrus fruit in aluminum foil, but it didn't work when I tried it. In the tropics you can often purchase a stalk of bananas at a very low cost. Bananas picked green and kept in a dark, cool place on the boat will last for two or three weeks. They should be inspected daily and as each banana begins to turn yellow it should be cut from the stalk and used.

Net bags hung out of the sun, and open-weave plastic baskets and crates, provide adequate storage with good air-circulation for perishable vegetables and fruit. I have kept fruit and vegetables for weeks in open crates under the dinghy on deck with good results.

With vegetables and fruit it is important to be selective when purchasing for a long passage. Try to buy directly from the farmer, or at least from a farmer's market, to be sure of freshness. Produce that has spent any time under refrigeration will not last long without it.

Eggs keep on board for as much as two months. One method of preservation is to lightly coat the eggs with cooking oil or vaseline, and to store them in cartons to prevent breakage. With this method, the cartons need to be turned over once a week. Some people use water glass (silicate of sodium) as a coating. The best method I have found is to dip each egg in boiling water for five seconds and then into cold water for another few seconds. In each of these methods the purpose is to seal the egg to reduce spoilage. Whichever method you choose, use only very fresh eggs that have not been refrigerated. After a few weeks at sea, test each egg before using, by giving it a float test. If it floats, feed it to the fish.

Hard cheese will keep for an extended time if sealed in wax. But just like perishable fruit and vegetables, cheese needs dry, ventilated storage out of direct sunlight. It is sometimes possible to buy a large wheel of cheese, cut it into smaller portions, and seal individual pieces with hot wax.

Dry Foods

Included in this category are grains, flours, beans, pastas, nuts, powdered milk, coffee, tea, freeze-dried foods, and dehydrated foods. All of these will keep indefinitely on a boat if properly stored. Most important is to keep them in strong, waterproof containers. Paper and cardboard containers have a very short life in the humid environment of a boat. Plastic bags, although often strong, are easily punctured. Even a pinhole will be sufficient to let moisture enter the food and render it worthless. The aim of proper storage is to prevent the development of mold, and to also keep out insects.

Plastic bottles with screw caps and plastic snap lid boxes that can be tightly sealed are the best. If they are kept tightly shut when not in use their contents will often last years. How well dried food lasts often depends on how it has been cared for before it comes on board. For example, weevils, or at least their eggs, may already be in flour when you buy it, so try to buy the freshest staples. For some reason weevils seem to be inhibited from developing in flour if a few bay leaves are put in the storage container.

There are a lot of dehydrated vegetables and fruit that are really excellent. The problem is finding them in the stores. I have been especially impressed with green peas, green beans, and corn, and of course potato flakes. I have had the best success in finding these products in co-op stores and health food stores.

Canned Goods

Canned foods are not as tasty or nutritional as fresh foods, but you may sometimes find them convenient for boat use because they contain fluids. When canned goods are brought aboard, standard practice is to remove paper labels and relabel with a permanent marker. This eliminates the possibility of paper ending up in the bilge, and having to play 'fruit cocktail roulette' at mealtime. It certainly doesn't hurt to remove labels and mark the tins, but the real need for this depends on where and how you store the cans. Probably this ritual dates back to the days of wooden boats with huge bilges that held hundreds of pounds of canned goods. I don't bother with label-plucking anymore, and I have yet to have a label come adrift. But then, I don't keep any cans below the boat's waterline.

Another complaint against tinned foods is that the cans rust. The remedy for this is to keep the cans as dry as possible, and rotate the stock.

Foods in glass jars are less of a problem, although the lids may still rust. Glass containers, however, should be carefully packed. Splinters of broken glass on the cabin sole are unpleasant. I used to have a rule of no glass jars aboard, but I have mellowed now that I have learned to load cabinets and lockers carefully.

For beer and soft drinks, glass is often preferable to aluminum cans. These days aluminum cans are so thin that they easily abrade and leak. If they get the slightest bit of salt water on them they can quickly corrode.

Stories of food poisoning are enough to make anyone wary. If there is the least suspicion that the food is spoiled, the can or bottle should be discarded. Food poisoning at sea is totally debilitating and has led to death on sailboats.

Convenience Foods

Sailors accustomed to making short cruising trips often buy instant foods, like meals sealed in plastic bags that can be dumped into boiling water to cook. Obviously, this is a matter of personal choice, but usually prepared foods are expensive – you pay as much or more for the package as for the food. On a long passage, I reckon such meals would soon become boring and unappetizing. Quick-fix meals, however, do have their place on board for occasional use, especially for snacks during a night watch or in heavy weather when there is little desire to spend much time in the galley.

Water Storage

Depending on your cruising plans, it may be necessary to add additional water tanks to the boat. It is not difficult to install a collapsible plastic tank in some convenient place for a long passage. It comes equipped with vents and plumbing fittings already installed. If either permanent or temporary tanks are added, consider their effect on trim. Fifty additional gallons of water weighs 417 pounds (188 kg).

It is possible to carry extra plastic water jugs on deck – if they are carefully tied down. This is an alternative for boats short of space below. You see few small cruising boats without their tank farm of fuel or water bottles on deck. On any passage you should carry one or two water bottles on deck as emergency rations for the liferaft. Make sure these bottles are only partially filled, so they will float high enough to be visible.

In rough going, jugs stored along the rail are subjected to waves coming on board and may break loose. Before leaving port, tie them down as if preparing for a rounding of Cape Horn. It is unpleasant to get up in the middle of the night to retie bottles at sea with the lee rail awash.

Whenever there is any reason to suspect the quality of water you take aboard, it should be treated with chlorine bleach. One teaspoon (5 ml or 80 drops) of Clorox or Milton bleach, which contains 5.25 percent available chlorine, per five gallons of water is sufficient. Let it stand for 30 minutes before adding it to your water tanks. Be very careful in adding Clorox, as too much will give the water an incredibly strong and disagreeable flavor. Tea and coffee will taste like it was made in a YMCA swimming pool.

Clothing Storage

The sailor's wardrobe normally includes clothes for sailing, for going ashore, and, most important, foul-weather gear. Storage of clothing uses up a lot of space.

Well-sealed plastic bags, and especially snap-top plastic boxes, are good for short- and long-term clothing storage. Mildew is a constant problem on a boat, so any clothing that is put in a sealed container should be absolutely dry. Likewise, any locker containing clothing should have adequate ventilation. Other than foul-weather clothing, it is not advisable to store clothes on hangers. The constant motion of the boat will cause the fabrics to abrade.

Foul-weather clothing should be kept where it is easily accessible. After use, it should be turned inside out to be sure the lining is dry before it is stored. Most rain-gear these days has a quick-drying lining. After a long passage during which the foul-weather gear has been used, it should be washed inside and out in fresh water (a rain shower works fine), and then dried. Be sure to give all zippers and fasteners a liberal coating of silicon spray or silicon grease.

Books and Charts

Books are easily damaged if not kept dry and well ventilated. An open bookcase away from spray or dripping water is best. Books kept in closed lockers will live longer if placed in sealed plastic bags.

Most cruising boats carry a large supply of sailing charts, and some may not be needed for a year or more in the future. A number of ingenious ideas have been developed for storing charts, but one of the best I have seen is lightweight PVC tubing, made completely watertight with PVC caps. These can be stored nearly anywhere on the boat.

Cameras

Camera and film storage present a special problem. A camera needs to be secure and dry, yet available to capture an unusually beautiful sunset or sunrise, nearby dolphins, whales, or birds, or to record some activity on the boat. Consider using a 'sports bag.' These are soft, PVC bags with both zip-lock and Velcro closures. They contain inflatable air chambers which give added protection when the camera is stored and allow the bag to float if it is dropped in the water.

Store film in the driest place you can find. Leave it in its plastic container and put that into a plastic, snap-top box. As soon as possible after the film is exposed, send it off for processing. Exposed film will readily absorb moisture and be worthless.

Electronic Equipment

As far as possible, electronics should be kept in ventilated cabinets, although most of them don't put out much heat these days. Other electronic equipment, such as TVs and computers will live longer in sealed waterproof containers. If practical, desiccant, such as silica gel, should also be placed inside the container. Upon arrival in port, storage containers should be opened and allowed to air out. Pelican Products make excellent large and small storage cases. I use them for my computer, my cameras, and my emergency gear. They are absolutely waterproof and will float.

Spare Parts and Tools

Spares not needed on a routine basis can be stored out of the way. If the spares are susceptible to water damage they should be sealed in plastic bags. Most hand tools will rust very quickly, no matter where they are kept on a boat. To prevent this, they can be cleaned and painted or given a light coat of oil or grease before they are put away. I keep all of my spare fasteners, split pins, and similar small stuff in plastic bottles.

Fuel and Flammables

All flammable fuels require careful storage. Diesel and kerosene are relatively safe because of their high flame point, but fuel oil spills make decks and cabin soles extremely dangerous.

Any fuel spill sufficient to produce a sheen on the water surface is subject to a fine in the U.S. and some other countries. Be careful – even the slightest amount of oil from the bilges will show up around the boat if the bilge pump is used. In addition to the legal aspects of even minor fuel spills is the work it will create for you and any other boats in your vicinity, as the oil tends to adhere to a boat's waterline, especially if there are any algae growing there. Whenever you pump bilges or transfer diesel fuel, in port or near shore, watch the water around your boat. If any sheen appears, it should be immediately dispersed by spraying it with a few drops of dish-washing detergent.

Gasoline is an especially dangerous fuel. Most cruising sailors would prefer to keep it off their boats, but it is used in outboard engines and portable electric generators. Watch out for hot days when a plastic fuel jug with gasoline will heat up, expand, and force vapor or liquid to escape. Gasoline storage should be kept to a minimum and containers should be placed in a separate cockpit locker or deck box isolated from the rest of the boat. There should be an overboard discharge at the base of the locker, as well as an air vent at the top.

LP gas cylinders also need to be kept isolated from the rest of the boat, or else stored on deck. An LPG locker must be vented at the top and also have an overboard gas escape route at its base. All fuel lines, fittings, and connections have to be correctly installed, maintained and routinely inspected to avoid possible leaks. On a yacht that is constantly in motion with a gimballed stove there is always the potential for leaks.

CHAPTER 23

PSYCHOLOGICAL ASPECTS OF CRUISING

There is a big difference between living with others on land and living together in the confines of a small boat. Seemingly insignificant personality traits that escape notice elsewhere quickly come to the surface. At sea you share a small space, and there is nowhere to go to get away from your shipmate(s) until you reach port. Crewmembers who can remain friends after several weeks at sea and still want to continue sailing together can get along anywhere. Other than a trip into outer space or duty at an Antarctic research station, nothing puts more demands on personal relationships than cruising on a shorthanded yacht.

It is important to know your crew before you head off soundings. Just because someone is a good friend or acquaintance of long standing does not mean your friendship will survive an extended time at sea. To avoid problems take some short trips first. If that works your chances of being able to sail together on a longer trip are better. To set off across an ocean with someone you haven't sailed with extensively is a dicey undertaking.

Leadership

The old saw that a ship cannot have two captains is fact. There are many things in life that benefit from a consensus approach, but sailing is not one of them. Someone has to be the captain, and whoever isn't captain is crew. This is not to say that plans should be made without the crew's input and ideas. They can and should be. But when critical decisions must be made, they seldom benefit from committee meetings, and usually there isn't time. A few boats operate with a rotating captain. If that idea appeals to you, fine. But at any one time only one person can be the captain.

Potential Problems

Perhaps the two biggest concerns on an offshore boat are fatigue and boredom. Fatigue will be dealt with elsewhere with regard to heavy-weather sailing and when approaching harbors. Boredom is not so common but on a very long voyage it can happen to some people. Many of us are able to avoid boredom by reading, doing maintenance chores, navigating, or pursuing some hobby. I don't recall ever being bored when sailing. For me there is too much to do. Most people should be able to handle three weeks at sea without getting cabin fever. Of course if someone is unhappy, seasick, or depressed, the chances of becoming bored will increase.

I have heard it said that there is less chance for psychological problems for a crew of two or more than for a singlehander. I think it depends on the specific individuals, how they interact, the duration of the cruise, and the type of sailing they are involved in. Stress plays a role here, and an apparently harmonious and cooperative crew under halcyon conditions may become quite otherwise after a few days of heavy weather. Fear and apprehension are potential problems for all cruising sailors, and personally I have a hard time distinguishing between the two. Apprehension is something that all of us feel some of the time, but especially when we first begin cruising. It is to be expected, because we really don't know what will happen, and we wonder if we will be able to cope with the rigors of life at sea. Apprehension before and in the early stages of a trip is not unusual, but after a few hours at sea the feeling should disappear. There isn't a sailor alive who isn't apprehensive from time to time when he encounters some difficult or potentially dangerous situation for the first time. Likewise it is impossible to avoid feeling apprehensive at the approach of a storm no matter how many storms you have weathered. This type of apprehension is OK as long as it is channeled into efforts to prepare the boat for heavy weather, and it is far better than overconfidence.

There is another kind of apprehension that accompanies a challenge – entering an unknown harbor, maneuvering through a tricky atoll channel, or threading your way among a group of islands at night. It's a rush in its own way and part of the fun of sailing. I don't think most people go sailing in search of difficult situations, but we know they will happen now and then. They are usually met and conquered with a feeling of accomplishment and a smile.

Cruising sailors usually have little to say about absolute fear. In facing difficult or potentially dangerous situations, you become so involved in solving the problem that there is little time to entertain fear. Then, quite suddenly, the crisis is over. In retrospect most experiences seem less awesome – and end up as good sea stories. I think fear comes from having to face a situation I don't understand. In that sense it is akin to apprehension. Maybe Franklin D. Roosevelt's saying, 'The only thing we have to fear is fear itself,' applies to this situation.

The captain should avert fear in the crew. When a difficult situation is developing, it is the captain's obligation to explain what may happen, what action is planned to cope with it, and what will be expected of the crew. Everyone on board should have some responsibility in dealing with a potential crisis or difficult task. This way the crew will become so involved with solving the problem that they will put fear on the back burner.

It is not unusual for someone preparing for his first long passage to develop a feeling of panic a short time before the cruise is to begin. I have experienced this and have heard others refer to it as well. A few days prior to my first long offshore trip (1300 miles), I woke up in the middle of the night with a sudden thought that I was making a big mistake. Another time when I was about to sail from Panama to Hawaii, a trip I knew could take as long as two months, I felt some apprehension about my ability to be alone for so long. But the apprehension was overshadowed by a curiosity to see if I could cope with the experience.

Some first-time sailors fear that they will experience claustrophobia at sea in a small boat. The question that bothered me before my first offshore passage was quite the opposite – I wondered if I would be able to cope with all of the space of the open ocean. As it turned out neither situation has ever bothered me at sea. I seem to achieve a comfortable balance when sailing and feel my boat is a world and the sea a universe, and that we are pleasantly interrelated.

Voices in the Night

Almost every time I leave on an ocean passage after being in port for several weeks, some unusual visitors come aboard the first few nights. Most of the visitors are animals. Dogs, chickens, the occasional cat, and the odd pig. OK, I don't actually see them, but I hear them clearly. Then, after a day or so, the animals go away. Perhaps they don't enjoy sailing or maybe they get tired of my sea stories and jokes.

As the voyage continues, and the boat and I settle into a routine, human visitors sign aboard. Again, they don't make a visual appearance, but I know they are there because of their voices. Usually they arrive at night, but sometimes I hear them during the day.

I may be reading, daydreaming, or snoozing, and someone will call my name. Often it is the voice of a friend from many years ago, some-

Figure 23.1
Under heavy going or if the crew is tired, un-expected visitors may join the passage.

one I haven't seen or even thought about in years, but I recognize it immediately. Less often it will be a stranger's voice. On more than one occasion when lying down in the cabin, I have gotten up to see if someone has come into the cockpit, or if perhaps there is someone nearby on another boat or in a liferaft.

Actually seeing the people who come aboard my boat in the middle of the ocean is more unusual. This only happens in hard going, such as after fighting a gale for a day or so. We seldom talk much. Mostly we just sit around and eye one another suspiciously. I reckon they are as skeptical of me as I am of them. We maintain a sort of peaceful co-existence, and eventually they depart.

One night on a passage to the Marshall Islands, however, an unusual event took place. There had been a few days of increasing heavy weather, and *Denali* was hove-to waiting for the winds and seas to subside. I got bored lying down below and went up on deck for a while. In the cockpit I scrunched up under the dodger to avoid the occasional rain squalls. Now and then I would doze off for a few minutes. Quite suddenly I noticed that I was no longer in the cockpit. Instead, I was pleasantly gliding around about 100 feet up in the air. My safety line was still attached to the boat but it was much longer than before. It was an enjoyable experience. Eventually, though, I grew a little anxious and wondered if I would be able to safely land in the cockpit when I came down. It turned out to be quite easy.

Who's There?

A few years ago I would have been reluctant to discuss some of these phenomena. As it is, singlehanders are sometimes considered to be sort of close to the edge, and I did not feel like supplying data to someone's research project. However, I have learned that my experiences are not so very different from those of others. In fact the stories mentioned by some are far more arcane than anything I have experienced so far.

Joshua Slocum told of someone coming aboard his boat at sea and taking the helm for several hours. At the time Slocum was violently ill and unable to stay in the cockpit and steer. His visitor claimed to be a member of the crew of Christopher Columbus.

Some solo sailors have recounted seeing people standing at the top of the mast, and others have been absolutely sure that there were people hiding from them on the boat – people they never saw, but whom they heard talking to each other.

So who are these strange people and animals that go cruising with us now and then? Where do they come from and where do they go? How do we explain other strange phenomena?

Investigations of these strange happenings indicate they can be classified as visual or auditory. Some are illusions and others may be hallucinations. Illusions are real objects which appear to be something else. An example would be a slack jib sheet that appears to be a snake. An hallucination is when we imagine someone or something is there when in fact it cannot be.

A study of singlehanded sailors in the 1972 OSTAR produced some interesting results. Half the people interviewed had experienced some type of illusion or hallucination during the crossing. Few singlehanders who have written of their adventures fail to mention one or more imaginary happenings.

In the book *Dr. Cohen's Healthy Sailor Book*, the author suggests that these various phenomena can be attributed to being alone, to loss of sleep, or to stress. This sounds like a reasonable explanation, and looking back at my own experiences I can relate those causes to the events I have encountered. I am sure my flying escapade was caused by stress and exhaustion. When I hear human voices, it is partly the result of being alone, because it has never happened when someone is sailing with me.

I have my own theory to explain some of these 'alone' phenomena. When I go to sea after being on land for several weeks or months and hear animals I believe it is caused by my mind adjusting to boat noise. A boat has its own unique set of sounds, but if the mind is not acquainted with a sound, it may attribute it to a similar sound. Hence, in my case, the sound of animals.

The dogs, cats, and other animals all relate to the normal squeaks and groans of the boat. After a few days the animals go away because my mind has learned to associate the new sounds with their actual source, such as wind in the rigging, the hull working, or lines straining against the blocks.

With regard to voices of old friends, or even strangers, I believe these come when my mind is in a very relaxed state. In our daily lives on land we are constantly assaulted by a variety of 'noise', and our time is taken up by a lot of routine activities. When sailing, for me at least, my mind becomes free, relaxed, and unencumbered by trivia. Then memories can float freely to the surface.

It is reasonable to ask if these various illusions and hallucinations are bad, dangerous, or something to be avoided. In my opinion they are nothing to avoid as long as I understand them for what they are. Those that come about due to lack of sleep, fatigue, or stress can be viewed as a benefit, because they serve as warnings that I need to get some rest or to somehow relax, and that my level of performance is not quite up to par. As for the auditory sensations that happen when I am rested and relaxed, I think they are great. It is an opportunity to recall old friends and past experiences. Now and then I don't even mind cleaning up after a few pigs and chickens.

CRUISING WITH CHILDREN

It is not possible to say how many families cruise with children but I would estimate it to be nearly 10 percent. A visit to one of the more popular cruising areas, and especially ports where cruisers winter over, will quickly convince you that children are part of the cruising scene. Gwenda Cornell's book, *Cruising With Children*, is a useful source of information on family sailing. Ms. Cornell's writing is based on a circumnavigation she, her husband, and two children made during a six year period. When their travels began, their daughter and son were seven and five years old respectively. In addition to documenting her own experiences, Cornell interviewed cruising families with children during the voyage.

Having children on board will not make cruising any easier. Numerous special considerations are necessary, including safety factors at sea and in port, the children's education, and health care. But for those families that have successfully made the transition to life on board the rewards far outweigh the problems. The opportunity permits you to be a full-time family, in which the children can learn first-hand that the world is full of many different kinds of people, ideas, and lifestyles. They acquire an appreciation and understanding of the environment that can be gained in no other way. Cruising children acquire a unique sense of responsibility and self-sufficiency and, at the same time, an appreciation of the importance of teamwork.

Safety

Safety is the first concern of all parents. Babies and very young children are the easiest to care for as they can be made safe and secure in a relatively small space. Toddlers and youngsters who are anxious to climb around are more of a problem. Beyond age three, children need a lot of supervision and protection from injury, but after five or six years of age, they quickly acquire the ability to move about the boat on their own.

Parents need to give a lot of thought to the possibility of injury inside the boat. Extra handholds need to be installed at the child's level, and additional supports may be needed on the companionway ladder. Likewise, children must be taught to stay away from hot stoves or heaters. Children's berths may require high leeboards and extra cushions.

On deck, the usual procedure is to install safety netting from deck level to the top of the lifelines, and to have weather cloths around the cockpit. *Any time a small child is on deck he or she must be watched by an adult – in port as well as at sea.* Rules concerning when and where to wear a lifejacket or safety harness or both should be made and adhered to. Most children quickly learn to adapt to the movement and motion

Figure 24.1
Families with small children are seen in every yacht harbor.

of the boat and only require a safety harness in stormy conditions.

Often we think mostly about dangers at sea, but accidents are just as likely to happen when at anchor. Cruising children need to learn to swim and be confident in the water from a very early age. It is well established that babies have no inherent fear of the water, and can be taught to float and swim. This does not preclude the need to wear a life-jacket when in the tender or at other times when there is a possibility of falling overboard. But if babies and small children are acquainted with swimming and how it feels to wear a lifejacket in the water, they will not panic if they should fall overboard.

As children grow older they can share in many onboard tasks, such as standing watch with their parents and eventually standing watch on their own, at least during daylight hours. In port, boat kids become proficient at rowing and sailing the tender, even when they are only six or seven. By the time they are teenagers most of them are competent watchstanders and can do any of the sailing chores under normal sailing conditions.

Medical Problems

Children on boats have far fewer medical problems than their land-bound contemporaries. Being physically active and spending most of their time outside is a healthy way to live. With nutritious food and lots of fresh air and sunlight, they suffer much less from the illnesses that typify conventional lifestyles. Parents need to acquaint themselves with basic medical techniques but they should do this anyway if they are sailing. There are various books of medical advice for parents that can be kept on board. Boats with ham radio or single-sideband can receive medical advice if necessary when at sea. In port, medical assistance is available nearly everywhere in the world, and routine physical and dental checkups can be scheduled when in major ports.

Education

A primary concern of parents is their children's education, and this is often given as the main reason to not attempt family cruising. Surprising as it may seem, this is an unnecessary worry if the parents are willing to be part-time teachers. Modern society has built up a mystique about education that is unrealistic and ungrounded. There is ample proof that children educated on boats using correspondence courses supervised by their parents, are able to re-enter school at the high school or university level without difficulty. Often, boat-educated children are not only equal but superior to their classmates.

There are excellent English-language correspondence courses for all grade levels. However, because of their personal preferences or financial considerations, some parents do most or all of the teaching themselves. Textbooks are available in all languages, and any educated adult should be able to stay slightly ahead of their children. Furthermore, there are numerous books on education theory and practical aspects of teaching. Often the teaching duties are shared by the parents, and between them they can teach what best suits their talents.

A myth of education is the time that it requires. Whereas children even in the primary grades may spend many hours each day in school, much of that time is devoted to things not really essential to education. Children up to the age of 11 or 12 do quite well on about two hours of 'onboard school' each day. Teenagers are adequately taught with three hours daily.

A significant advantage of teaching your children is that they can learn at their own pace and get as much additional help as you are willing to give. Every child learns at a different rate for different subjects whereas in a classroom they must proceed at the tempo of the established teaching schedule.

In addition to providing onboard education, some cruisers enroll their children in local schools whenever they spend extended times in port. The benefits of this reach out beyond the purpose of formal education. This opportunity is a cultural experience and permits them to become proficient in other languages as well.

A lot of the real learning by cruising children is unconsciously and indirectly tied to the nature of their lives. Certainly no school could hope to teach them so much about nature, the environment, or other cultures that they experience as they travel.

Problems

It is fair to ask about the drawbacks and limitations of the cruising life for children. One obvious consideration is that they will usually have less contact with other children. For this reason it is often considered better if there are at least two children on board. On the other hand, most children without siblings are able to cope satisfactorily with the situation. In port, they will always find other children to meet and play with from other boats, or from the local community. But lasting friendships are seldom possible, and this is a definite disadvantage.

Sailing children spend far more of their lives in the presence of adults than they would living in a normal community. I am always impressed with the maturity and self-confidence of children in cruising families. Usually their knowledge, ability, and conversation are far above what would be expected for their age.

You can anticipate some complications when children who have been sailing for an extended period of time return to school on land. Usually difficulties are not due to their educational level, but to the fact that they have led lives of more freedom and independence. Sometimes they find that their peers are rather naive and childish. Often they may, initially at least, feel left out because they are ignorant of various TV programs, sports heroes, popular singers, and movie stars. Such difficulties may be temporarily inconvenient, but are soon overcome.

Even experienced cruising families are divided in their opinions as to the best age for children to go sailing. Gwenda Cornell recommends the ages between five and thirteen years as best. Children younger than five require more care and supervision, whereas older children that have been involved in a typical school and social life for a few years may have trouble with the transition to life on board.

If a child is expected to begin cruising as a teenager it may be very difficult unless he or she is truly excited and interested in the prospect. Teenagers are certainly old enough to be included in the planning and discussion of the cruise, and should not have to be forced to take part.

For all children, their reaction to abandoning a routine way of life for a cruising adventure will depend greatly on how they are introduced to sailing. Most of them, if they are old enough to understand what is happening, will be excited and look forward to the adventure if they first learn to enjoy the pleasures of sailing. On the other hand, if they are apprehensive or frightened by a poor introduction, they may never fully enjoy themselves or have a happy life on board. Take a soft approach in acquainting your family with sailing. Start gradually, beginning perhaps one or two years in advance of setting off on an extended cruise.

FINAL PREPARATIONS

Shakedown Cruise

I made two preparation cruises before I finally began cruising full time. I first sailed to the Caribbean from Georgia. I had only owned the boat for about a year at that time, but I had made a lot of changes and additions including a wind-steering vane, dodger, boom gallows, a new sheeting arrangement for the main, an anchor windlass and chain, extra storage space in the cabin. Throughout this voyage I kept a notebook of likes and dislikes and returned home with more modifications in mind.

A year later I took off again for a quick 1600-mile round trip to Bermuda for a final shakedown. After that I felt ready to begin a circumnavigation and five months later I left for the Far East via Panama and Hawaii.

A shakedown cruise is not only for the boat. It is also an opportunity for the crew to improve cooperation and to see what personality difficulties may need addressing. The fact that people too often fail to do this is witnessed by the number of boats offered for sale at major sailing crossroads like Panama, Hawaii, St. Thomas, and Gibraltar. There are too many sad stories of crews and even marriages breaking up at the end of the first leg of the long-dreamed-of voyage. Often practice cruises could have prevented this.

It is extremely unfair for anyone to expect his spouse or family to take to cruising without gradually working up to it. Yet I frequently meet people who do just that. There is a big difference between an afternoon sail followed by drinks at the yacht club and a 30-day passage with a few days of foul weather thrown in. It is hard for anyone to make that transition abruptly.

The skipper who has spent most of his time on a racing boat can come totally unhinged when the new crew consists of his wife and children or the next-door neighbors. It may well be that they don't enjoy being yelled at nor do they enjoy sitting on the weather rail. Families are sometimes introduced to a whole new personality when the head-of-the-house puts on his yachting cap. Most people are apprehensive the first time they do almost anything. An initial ocean passage is crammed full of 'first time' happenings.

A series of short preliminary cruises will not only identify personality and communication problems, but they will also help an inexperienced crew get used to extended cruising. A shakedown cruise should be scheduled at least six months or a year before the anticipated departure date of a circumnavigation or even the first extended offshore passage.

Realities of Departure

Watching the preparations for a space launch at Cape Canaveral gives a good impression of what it can be like to get ready for an extended offshore passage. Final preparations are always more difficult when they follow an extended time of repair or renovation work. The big jobs have all gotten done, but frequently the little ones still remain. It is frustrating to find equipment that was working OK before the repair period is now on the blink. For example this is often when electronics will take a vacation. There can be other unexpected glitches as well; one time just before departure after an extended period in port, I found that mice were having a field day in a couple of my sail bags. They had nibbled a number of holes in the working jib and lapper.

It seems the tasks will never end. But a day will finally come when there is no choice but to say, 'That's it! I'm out of here!' There will still be some things left undone, and a few supplies that did not arrive as scheduled. But still you go.

The remarkable thing is that the minute you do leave all of the pressure is off. There is a big sigh of relief, and all those things that seemed absolutely essential to do but could not get done are suddenly irrelevant.

Saying Good-Bye

Never underestimate the interest your departure will arouse. Perhaps it is a throw-back to the supposedly romantic days of ocean passages on large ships; something that few of us have ever experienced except by

Figure 25.1
Bon voyage!

watching old black-and-white movies. When I left Japan after staying several months in one port for a haul-out, more than 50 people got up very early on a cold winter day to see *Denali* off for the South Pacific.

Don't expect your non-sailing friends to understand the problems you will have trying to leave on time. The first rule in the departure game is to be vague and never set a precise date for your getaway.

'Oh, sometime in the fall,' is much better than, 'October first.' Even as the time comes closer, suggest a date two or three weeks beyond when you really expect to leave. It will probably come close to being correct. I have never left on time, and once overshot my first estimate by nearly three months.

Even after you make the final sailing date announcement, I recommend yet another ploy. Have a full-scale bon voyage departure when everyone can come, say good-bye, and wave as you sail off into the sunset. Once you are out of sight, find a quiet protected bay or harbor where no one knows you, and sit quietly for two or three days to get your ducks in a row. Do the final stowing away of equipment and food and, most important, get some rest. It is amazing what it will do to calm the crew and get the trip off to a good start. If you have to clear out with customs and immigration, do it from your hideaway harbor and only when you feel really ready to go.

If it has been some months since you have been sailing or if you are leaving on a long cruise, a detailed departure checklist can save a lot of grief. An example is given in Appendix 11.

26 ROUTINE AT SEA

On a sailboat the immediate world is a few square feet of living space surrounded by a few square miles of ocean. Society is usually only one or two other people or only yourself, or maybe a dog or cat. To some this may sound terrifying and to others it is heaven. But even in the limited confines of a small yacht, a certain daily routine develops. Meal preparation, navigation duties, and maintenance all take time. Depending on where you are sailing and the philosophy of the crew, you may spend a lot of time on watch. Some days you are very busy with frequent sail changes, and other times you don't touch anything. Some days go by when there so little to do that the crew is free to do whatever he or she feels like.

Not all 'free time' is enjoyable. No one feels wonderful when hove-to in heavy weather, and there is nothing to do but wait it out. Time passes really slowly. Often the boat's motion and your stomach's motion are not in sync. On such days, there are no 'happy campers.'

Wet foul-weather gear, a closed up cabin, poor ventilation, and probably a few leaks, make for an uncomfortable, humid cabin. A grey cheerless sky only adds to the gloom. When it gets like this, I often spend my time in the cockpit scrunched up under the dodger enviously eyeing the gliding sea birds that seem to love these conditions. You and your crew should talk about these days before sailing and acknowledge that there will be some along the way.

In the next few pages we'll look at the typical activities that take up time during an ocean passage. Don't expect a schedule for life at sea unless you are in the navy. On the cruising boat there are too many variables, and each person and each vessel will develop its own rhythm in response to conditions.

Navigation

The amount of time you spend on navigation will be determined by where you are sailing and your equipment. It will also depend on whether you view navigation as an art, a science, or a hobby. Some sailors see navigation as a necessary task, others derive a great deal of pleasure from it.

In recent years electronic aids have made this job less time-consuming. But regardless of their convenience, offshore cruisers should use the sextant whenever possible to maintain the skills and practice the routine of celestial navigation. It isn't easy to shoot morning and evening stars from the deck of a small sailboat, and personally I don't enjoy it much, but anyone can maintain a reasonable plot by advancing sun lines most days.

There are a few small-boat sailors who have bemoaned the introduction of Loran, then SatNav, and more recently GPS. Apparently they think these electronics make life too easy and encourage anyone to go sailing. I feel differently. I have made several passages when the sun did not show itself for four or five days at a time; and I have been delighted to have an electronic assist. I did not take up cruising to increase tension in my life, and I'm for anything that makes sailing safer and more enjoyable. Maybe there were people who shunned the sextant when it first appeared in the second half of the 18th century; although I doubt it.

On a long ocean passage, navigation can be fairly relaxed. It may be worthwhile to aim for precision, but it is not crucial in the middle of the ocean. Approaching land is a different story, however, and an otherwise easy-going navigator suddenly becomes busy. Near land, the navigator must maintain a continuous plot and update it with any hard data that becomes available. Never pass up a fix or bearing, because it may soon disappear in rain, haze, fog or darkness.

Weather Observations

The better you become at forecasting the weather the more self-assured you will be. Significant weather changes give warnings as much as two or three days in advance. If you know what to look for and recognize these changes, you have an opportunity to prepare and sometimes to alter course to avoid the worst. You should get used to recording barometer readings every few hours. Anyone who has waited out a typhoon or a significant low pressure system can tell you the importance of doing this.

Limited weather forecasts are available throughout the world by voice broadcasts in English, by code, and by fax. Numerous yachts now carry a weatherfax receiver on board. This is a valuable source of information, and the weather maps can help you improve your skills as a forecaster. A good book on maritime meteorology is a valuable addition to any yacht's library.

Repairs and Other Jobs

It is unusual to be at sea for more than a few days without something needing to be repaired, and on a long passage there will inevitably be a few maintenance and repair chores to do. A two- or three-week ocean passage may well represent more wear and tear on a boat than a year of weekend gunkholing or daysailing. Basic hand tools, sail repair materials, and miscellaneous fasteners, tapes, lubricants, and glue or bedding compound should be readily available at all times.

Anything that affects or threatens to affect the sailing ability or safety of the boat should be repaired or jury rigged as well as possible right away. Waiting a few days just because you are almost to your destination is not a good idea. If heavy weather comes before reaching port, it may be impossible to correct a problem that could threaten the seaworthiness of the boat. So far I have been lucky and have had few problems that I could not fix or get by with. However, I have on occasion had to sail into port without the use or backup of an engine, because the problem was beyond my ability to repair at sea. One time, I had to repair a badly weakened gooseneck at sea by drilling and tapping a new set of holes and then cementing the fasteners in place with epoxy glue.

Comfortable sailing days are excellent times to do splicing and other rope work. If you are a writer, some of your sea time can be devoted to making notes and outlining various projects.

Meals

Part of the sea routine includes preparing and eating meals. Proper meals are important to the health and well-being of the crew. Responsibility for food preparation is different on each boat. It begins before you go to sea when you plan food purchases according to quantity and variety of foods needed for your passage.

Meals at sea are less elaborate than on land, but they still require attention to make them appetizing and nutritious. It isn't necessary to have a precise menu plan for the whole trip unless you enjoy that kind of detail. Most crews find it is a good idea to bring along a cookbook or two, not just for cooking directions but to also offer ideas for a varied menu. Eating the same thing day after day becomes boring, and it has been emphasized again and again by experienced sailors that substantial hot meals are important to safety and morale in heavy weather.

Most people find that on a voyage they eat less because they are expending less energy than in port. On long passages I usually eat two meals a day, one about mid-morning and one just before sunset so I can have the galley cleaned up and the dishes washed and put away before dark. I also make bread about once a week at sea and often in port as well.

Relaxation and Leisure

The most popular activity for cruising sailors is reading, and it is common to see dozens or even hundreds of books on board yachts. Cruising sailors swap books enthusiastically when ashore. On an easy passage it is not unusual for me to read about one book a day.

It is worthwhile to collect a large and varied selection of books before leaving your home port. In foreign countries books may be very expensive or unavailable. If you have children on board give special attention to books. There may be few opportunities to swap, and children's books are not easy to find in many places.

For some, ocean passages offer an opportunity to study technical and professional subjects. It is also possible to enroll in a correspondence course on something in which you are interested. I envy such well disciplined sailors. Cassette tapes, compact discs, Walkmans, even videos are popular on cruising boats. Some sailors bring their hobbies aboard. Knitting and other needle crafts are well suited to yacht life, as are carving and scrimshaw. Musical sailors often bring their instruments aboard.

Fishing seems a reasonable hobby to pursue for the offshore sailor, but for most cruisers it is largely a passive activity where a lure is trailed behind the boat.

Finally, there is the simple art of doing nothing and enjoying it; some call this daydreaming. It can consume many hours. Simply gazing off into space, absorbing the beauty of the ocean or the night sky. Letting your mind wander or concentrating your thoughts on some subject of interest. The world that most of us live in on land is so full of distractions and obligations that we rarely have the opportunity and freedom to let this happen. When sailing offshore, we have many opportunities to do this with impunity.

Figure 26.1
Underway activities.

Sleeping

It may seem strange to mention the importance of getting adequate sleep and rest when sailing. Many people have the impression that there is little else to do. However, for some, especially in the initial stages of a voyage or during heavy weather, sleep is difficult and they become apprehensive and stay awake for long periods of time. This can cause problems when difficulties arise and you aren't able to do your best because you're tired. Even if you don't think you can sleep it is smart to lie down and rest.

Those who try to do everything themselves when there is a crew of two or more are doing themselves and their shipmates a disservice. When you become physically or mentally fatigued you will make mistakes in judgment and put your crew and your yacht in jeopardy – especially when approaching land, when crossing shipping lanes, and in heavy weather.

Getting proper rest is not always easy. First you should make yourself as comfortable as possible. This means having proper ventilation and may mean rigging lee cloths or lee boards. Next, never make the mistake of lying down in your foul-weather gear or wet clothing. Take the time to rest in a comfortable, warm, dry bunk. Even short rest periods will improve your performance and well being.

Exercise

On most small sailboats the crew gets an inadequate amount of exercise. There just isn't enough space. On a long passage this can be a real problem. I discovered this after a passage of several weeks. On my first night in port I went walking for a couple of hours just to stretch my legs. When I returned to the boat my legs were in such great pain that I couldn't sleep.

In spite of the lethargy that often sets in on a cruise it's advisable to set aside a few minutes each day to do some sort of in-place exercise – sit-ups, leg lifts, etc. It you have diving weights on board you can use these to do various exercises. Some sailors have found that yoga helps them maintain better health. Basic yoga postures and stretching exercises are simple to do and require little space. In calm weather it is possible to occasionally stop and have swim call. One crewmember should obviously remain on board to see that the boat doesn't go off on its own and to watch for sharks.

Standing Watch

According to international maritime law, maintaining a proper watch is a duty, a responsibility, and a necessity. It is a well-known rule that 'vessels will maintain a proper watch at all time.' In view of that it is absurd to think that any nation would allow any vessel to put to sea without adequate crew to keep watch. But every year there are well-publicized singlehanded yacht races including overnight, trans-oceanic, and around-the-world events. None of these races are held in secret and in fact governments usually encourage them as a way to stimulate the yachting industry in their country. Government agencies often take part in the organization and administration of the events.

There are also many singlehanded sailors out cruising and no one ever attempts to stop them from sailing. But there is no way that a singlehander can 'maintain a proper watch at all times.' It is questionable if in fact a crew of two people can do so. I have heard doublehanders condemn singlehanders as unsafe and have them tell me how they always have someone on watch. In my opinion that is bunk. I have sailed singlehanded and doublehanded and with larger crews on ocean passages, and I have had as many close calls when there was crew as when sailing alone.

When I began singlehanding I was confused about how to provide a proper watch and still get enough rest to avoid fatigue. At that time I was sailing in the Caribbean where passages seldom lasted more than 12 hours. Under those circumstances it was easy to catch up on sleep after anchoring. When passages became longer I learned to sleep and wake up at one- or two-hour intervals to look around for ships. This practice had merit but still did not represent adequate watchstanding. A collision can easily occur within less than 30 minutes from the time a ship is first sighted, even under clear conditions, day or night.

Some sailors claim they have a 'sixth sense' when sleeping that causes them to wake up if some danger is at hand. I am skeptical of such powers. On a few occasions I have woken unexpectedly and seen a ship in the distance, but many, many more times when something unexplained disturbed my sleep there has been nothing unusual happening. Furthermore there are more examples of yachts going on the rocks or being hit by ships than there are of clairvoyant escapes.

After a few long passages I developed my present philosophy for offshore watchstanding. It has grown out of my experience of seeing extremely few ships while I am on long passages away from the shipping lanes, and my certain knowledge that I cannot possibly maintain a proper watch without becoming exhausted. So my main concern now is to avoid fatigue and get as much rest as possible. I think this approach keeps me fit so that should some situation arise – a storm or potential collision – where my best performance is needed, I will be at my best to deal with it. By remaining alert and rested, I do a better job of sailing and navigation, and that makes passages faster and safer. Regardless of day or night I sleep whenever I feel the need, and in my waking hours I tend to necessary jobs on the boat, and spend time reading and relaxing. Most of my time at sea is spent in the cockpit, and I am frequently looking about without thinking about it; I probably maintain a better watch than I realize.

The two important exceptions to this procedure are when crossing shipping lanes and when making a landfall. From studying the Pilot Charts I know when I can expect to encounter the shipping lanes. In those areas I reestablish a routine and stay awake sometimes for more than 24 hours.

In the past, power and sailing ships followed predictable routes between major ports and these routes are marked on the Pilot Charts. It is worthwhile when planning a passage to annotate your charts to show where the shipping routes will cross your rhumbline.

In recent years the development of routing services has changed the picture somewhat. To take advantage of weather and currents many ships now receive daily advisories on course and speed from land-based routing services. Consequently their paths are less predictable than previously. Slower, smaller ships however still ply the traditional routes.

Usually it is not too difficult to stay awake and reasonably alert up to 48 hours, but after that my efficiency and alertness are rapidly affected by fatigue. The most difficult passages are the ones lasting only two to five days like those among the island groups of the South Pacific. Here there are often unexpected and spurious currents, as well as the danger of islands and reefs that are incorrectly charted.

Duties of the Watchstander

Watchstanders should have a clear view of the horizon from the cockpit and a comfortable, reasonably dry place to sit. In inclement weather it is sometimes more convenient to sit in the companionway and periodically enter the cockpit to look around. During daylight hours the person on watch can usually also read or do various maintenance chores. Even cooking is possible if you are careful not to become too engrossed in it and forget your prime responsibility as a lookout.

A dedicated watch is necessary near land or if there are any ships in the vicinity. There are too many accounts of people who 'just stepped below for a moment to make a cup of coffee' and ended up colliding with a ship, going aground, or becoming stranded on a reef.

When a ship, landfall, lighthouse, or other aid to navigation is first sighted, the watch should immediately take compass bearings. For ships, repeated bearings are needed to determine the possibility of a collision course. If there is even a remote possibility of a steady bearing or of passing close aboard you should change course.

If the watchstander needs help from other crewmembers to tack or jibe to avoid collision, they should be alerted well in advance of the maneuver. Someone who is called on deck at the last minute, especially if he has been sleeping, will be confused and disoriented when he enters the cockpit and may add to the tension and confusion of a critical maneuver.

It is the responsibility of the watchstander to maintain sail trim and keep an eye out for changing weather conditions. At least once each watch it is a good idea, if practical and safe, to inspect the deck for any existing or developing problems such as loose gear, chafe, missing cotter pins from standing rigging, etc.

Watch Schedule

Setting up a watch schedule will vary depending on the size and ability of the crew. On boats with a crew of two, such as a husband and wife, it is usually an informal arrangement. Even a crew of two, however, should discuss a proposed watch system before leaving port. A crew of three or more should set definite watches to be fair to all. In most cases a watch should not exceed four hours. In difficult conditions, two hours is a maximum.

If there is a designated navigator, his or her watches can coincide with sight-taking. Most small-boat crews share duties, and a compatible and informal watch-standing routine can be easily established.

Even with a shorthanded crew, a cooperative attitude between the on- and off-watch crew should prevail. Consideration prevents minor irritations from turning into ill feelings. For example, because proper night vision is so important to the on-watch, the off-watch should keep cabin lights subdued. If it becomes necessary to turn on a bright light below, the watch should be informed in advance so they can shield their eyes or close a hatch.

Likewise the on-watch should be considerate of the resting crew. Even the slightest noises in the cockpit can be heard throughout a fiberglass boat and may awaken or disturb someone trying to sleep. Dropping winch handles, tapping your feet, or even singing are the little things that can drive your shipmates bonkers on a long passage.

If definite watch periods are set up, it is the responsibility of the oncoming watch to relieve on time. Usually the on-watch will wake the relief crew 15 or 20 minutes before their turn. To be fair, the person called should get up promptly and relieve on schedule.

It is your responsibility to the rest of the crew to stand a proper watch. If you cannot stay awake, or become seasick, or for some other reason you cannot fulfill your responsibilities, it is better to get someone to relieve you. Your fellow crewmembers are depending on your good judgment.

CHAPTER 27 HEAVY WEATHER AT SEA

Storms occupy a lot of a sailor's time but fortunately most of that time is spent talking about storms rather than experiencing them. Sailing magazines are full of frightening stories, and many fine cruising adventure books tell of storms and rough seas. Let's face it, a cruising yarn without a decent storm is as flat as a leftover glass of beer. The thought of storms, however, raises a specter much greater than their reality.

Almost everything we hear about heavy weather sailing comes from personal narratives. Therefore, it helps to know something about the personality and level of experience of the person describing a storm, if you want to learn much from the story. With repeated telling the wind often becomes stronger and the seas higher. Once, someone was telling me about his friend who had sailed through a terrible storm with huge seas. I was impressed, and would not have wanted to have been on that cruise. Later I learned that the story originated with one of my crew when I brought *Denali* from St. Thomas to Savannah the previous year. Although it had not been an easy trip, I could not remember 20-foot seas or several other reported events.

The best known and best written book on the subject is *Heavy Weather Sailing* by K. Adlard Coles. This is a book that should be read and reread by anyone who goes offshore. It has taught me many things. However, it is important to remember that Coles' book primarily cites examples of heavy weather encountered by ocean-racing boats. Any boat going to sea must be prepared for heavy weather, but the cruising sailor has a lot more options than the racer, not the least of which is to stay in port rather than get underway if there is concern about the weather.

In trying to learn as much as you can to prepare for heavy weather, you will find that reading the words of experienced cruisers is worthwhile. The opinions of Hal and Margaret Roth, Eric and Susan Hiscock, Bob and Nancy Griffith, Lin and Larry Pardey, and Steve and Linda Dashew are good examples. They have been there, and they know what they are talking about. From their writings we learn three fundamental truths, as well as many specific technical points.

First, all of these sailor-writers emphasize the importance of prudence. This begins with careful trip planning to take advantage of the best season and the best routes. Discretion extends to waiting to begin a voyage until there is favorable weather, rather than trying to meet a schedule and setting out in marginal conditions. Don't be too proud to turn back, heave-to, or seek shelter when conditions deteriorate.

Second, experienced sailors all make the point that there is no set procedure for dealing with heavy weather. Every situation is unique, and each boat reacts differently and must be sailed differently under storm conditions. This is most vexing to inexperienced cruising sailors. We would prefer to have a concise trouble-shooting checklist to follow, but there are no specific procedures other than the ones you develop from your own experience. For example, it would be folly for the Pardeys in their traditional wooden yacht *Taleisin*, with a length of 30 feet and a beam of almost 11 feet, displacing 9 tons, to expect to employ the same storm tactics as the Dashews in their 67-foot, high-performance aluminum cutter, *Sundeer*.

Finally, even though the art and science of sailing is as old or older than civilization, it is not static. The best sailors know that there are always new lessons to be learned and new techniques to employ.

Preparation

It is axiomatic that any boat venturing offshore should be ready at all times for the possibility of heavy weather. Yet we know this is seldom true. Structurally, our boat may be ready – but we are probably not. After sailing for weeks in salubrious conditions, anyone becomes a bit slack. Therefore, with the suspicion or first indication that a storm may be in the offing, it makes senses to start preparing for rough seas. Begin preparing as far in advance as possible to prevent a panic atmosphere. This will give you time to think about and discuss your storm tactics, and, most important, you will feel prepared. Gradual changes in atmospheric conditions, or weather broadcasts, usually provide 12 to 36 hours advance warning of a storm.

I recommend following a checklist. Most of my suggestions are common sense, but under the stress of expecting a storm, especially a major one, it is easy to forget the minor points. The following suggestions serve as a guide, but each boat and each crew should have its own list of specific tasks.

1. On Deck

Topside preparation should begin early while it is still easy to move around on deck. Anything that can be, should be stored below, especially items which cause windage. Gear that must stay on deck should be checked for security and perhaps double lashed – spinnaker poles, for example. I hope you are not towing a tender, but if so, get it on board and properly lashed down. Inspect the liferaft canister to see that it is properly secured but ready to be launched. Are the jacklines properly secured? All standing rigging should be inspected at deck level for security and chafe protection. Standing rigging above deck level can be looked at through binoculars. Now is the time to take down the roller furling jib. If you use an inner forestay or running backstays for heavy weather, they should be installed early before complicated deck work becomes difficult. Hoist the radar reflector.

Any unneeded sails should be put below. Replace the lines on the wind-steering vane if they are showing any wear. Inspect man-overboard equipment, and be sure it is ready for deployment.

Depending on your boat, special covers may be needed for vents and hatches. If the vent openings are easily removed or closed, it is advisable to leave them in place as long as possible to give maximum comfort to the yacht's interior. Storm window covers should be installed, or made ready to install. It is better to put them on early because it is a difficult task once rough seas are encountered. If you have a storm hatch for the companionway, it should be installed now.

Look to see that cockpit drains are clear. If there is any doubt, pour a bucket of water down each drain to assure it drains freely. Open and inspect cockpit lockers for loose gear. Check all closures and locking devices on cockpit lockers.

Have some shock cord ready in the cockpit to attach to the helm or wheel in the event it becomes necessary to heave-to. Try it out to be sure it fits and is in good condition.

2. Below Decks

All loose gear should be stored. Anything that cannot be put away should be securely tied down. If you have double closures for your lockers, use them now. Check the contents of lockers, drawers, bins, and cabinets for loose gear. If necessary use cushions, pillows, or rags to keep loose gear from rolling around in storage spaces. In addition to the annoyance of listening to something banging about, loose gear can be damaged, or cause damage, or even force open a locker door. If you have storage space below the settees, be sure the covers are secured so that in a knockdown or worse the contents will not be thrown into the cabin. Rig lee cloths or lee boards on all bunks that will be used.

Check the condition of safety harnesses and foul-weather gear, and have them ready to wear. Especially check zippers and fasteners on foul-weather clothing to be sure they are functional; they will probably need to be lubricated. Determine if flashlights are in working condition, and have spares at hand. If possible check the operation of running lights.

Look at your engine and electrical system. If there is more than one fuel tank, switch to the tank with the most fuel. Determine the condition of batteries, and if necessary run the engine to have them fully charged. On some boats it is necessary to close or plug the engine exhaust system to prevent sea water from backing up into the engine in following seas. If that is necessary, remove the ignition key and attach a note to it to remind yourself that the exhaust system is closed.

Empty bilges of any water, remove any debris in the bilges, and check bilge pump strainers for obstructions. Operate electric and hand bilge pumps to be sure they work. Inspect the emergency bilge pump to see that it is accessible and that hoses and pumping handle are ready to use.

Have storm sails ready. If they have not been used or examined recently, check to see that sheets and pendants are attached.

Inspect flares, flare guns, and emergency signaling equipment. Be sure that different types of flares (white, red, smoke flares, and parachute flares) are clearly labeled. Inspect condition of firefighting equipment and first-aid supplies. Check the security and location of your emergency bag and EPIRB.

3. General Considerations

Record the barometer reading and continue to monitor it at hourly intervals. Most people keep a log book, but if you don't, set aside a piece of paper to keep a continuous update on barometer readings. Determine your position by celestial or electronic navigation and maintain a careful DR. Deteriorating weather almost always includes overcast skies, and it may be impossible to get a reliable fix for several days. Even if the skies are intermittently clear, it is often difficult or impossible to take precise sextant readings in rough conditions.

Review storm techniques for your boat. Consider your position relative to the approaching weather system, and determine the probable windshifts and your choices for avoiding a lee shore.

Proper nutrition and rest are important. Once the storm arrives you may need to spend long hours in the cockpit. Rough seas always mean uncomfortable conditions below, and sleeping may be difficult. Probably more mistakes result from physical and mental fatigue than from inexperience. If you are physically and mentally alert, your safety margin under any condition is greatly improved. This is not the time to be consuming alcoholic beverages.

'Galley strategy' is part of storm preparation. Some meals, snacks, and hot beverages can be prepared in advance. The stove fuel tank can be checked to be sure there are adequate reserves. Any loose gear in the galley should be put away.

If you or your crew are subject to seasickness, preventive medicine should be taken hours in advance of the storm. Most people can avoid being severely sick if they take precautions early on.

As preparations progress, and once you have things shipshape, take time to discuss storm procedures with your crew. This includes sail changes, tacking and jibing, and deploying drogues, warps, and sea anchors. Don't overwhelm them with too much detail. If possible, sit down with a pencil and paper and make sketches to illustrate your comments. Likewise show them the probable storm position relative to your position, and its expected direction of movement. Avoid creating fear. Staying calm, injecting a little humor, and making realistic explanations, will help keep everyone relaxed. Don't be glib or macho: if things get really difficult your crew will be depending on you, and you will be depending on them.

Heavy Weather Techniques

It would be great if there was as much information offered on light-air sailing as there is on heavy-weather tactics. Nearly every issue of your favorite sailing magazine offers still another bit of advice on what to do when the 'Big One' hits. It doesn't hurt to read the stories, but heavy weather sailing is like falling in love; you need to experience it to appreciate it.

In this section I will discuss basic heavy weather techniques. I gladly acknowledge up front that I have not had to use some of these methods myself. That admission is an important message in itself. *Denali*, in three trips from the East Coast of the U.S. to the Caribbean and Bermuda, and after eight years sailing over much of the North and South Pacific and Far East, has never been pressed hard enough to require anything more extreme than heaving-to and twice going under bare poles. Her storm jib and trysail have seen very little action. No doubt this is in part due to luck, but it is luck superimposed on a strong sense of self-preservation and conservative trip planning.

My suggestions are given with the caveat that, (1) each boat, depending on its size, shape, and displacement, will have to be handled in a different way in storm conditions, (2) each storm is different, and (3) even the same storm will affect you differently depending or where you are and what sailing methods you employ. There are no formulas or specific rules, but there are general techniques that work for most boats.

Some storm techniques are passive and some are active. The nature of the seas and the wind will largely dictate what methods you employ and in what order. The first consideration is having sea room, and plenty of it. Taken in its broadest sense, sea room can even mean choosing to leave the apparent security of a harbor and going to sea, rather than being caught in an anchorage that could become a trap.

Most sailors are aware of the dangers of being too near land in a storm. But ocean areas with broad, shallow continental shelves are also to be avoided, as are any banks or shallows, even if far offshore. In such places tremendous seas can develop when large waves feel bottom. Likewise, strong tidal flows and major ocean currents are extremely dangerous when their flow is in opposition to the direction of storm winds. As we shall see, heaving-to is usually the first technique to be employed. But, if there is any possibility that you will be set down on a lee shore, you must press on until clear or until there is a safe margin. The longer you wait to do this, the more difficult it will become. Sea room to me is measured in days, not in hours. A typical storm lasts about 36 hours, but that is an observation, not a law. Some storms become compound events and go on for several days. Continuing to sail the boat actively as long as you can is sometimes necessary to put as much distance as possible between you and the expected storm path.

Heaving-to

As windspeed and sea state increase, the boat will let you know the need to reduce sail. Actually, you should make sail reductions in advance of the boat starting to protest. As you continue to shorten sail there will come a time, depending on the point of sail, when it is no longer comfortable or very enjoyable to keep going. This will usually be before you have reached the point of putting up storm sails. If you are beating into large seas, you may decide to bear off to a more comfortable course. Often this is not practical or realistic due to a lee shore, or because the decision to bear off will take you too far from your rhumbline.

Heaving-to is generally the first line of defense in rough going; you should practice this maneuver before beginning a long cruise. Every

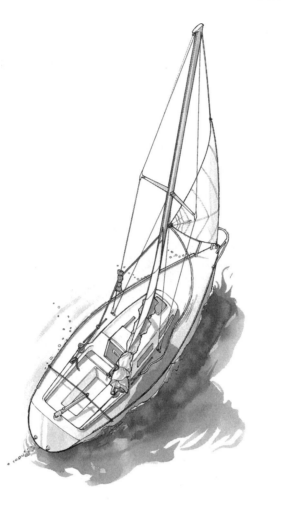

Figure 27.1
Heaving-to.

boat heaves-to in its own way. Sometimes sailors think they are hove-to because they have followed the recommended procedures, but in fact they are still making headway or forereaching. Practice heaving-to some place free of current, but where you are able to monitor your position by taking bearings. Pick a day with moderate winds.

If you are heaving-to for more than a few minutes, the headsail should be reduced to avoid chafe against the shrouds. Even with a small sail the windward jib sheet must be provided with chafe protection. An expensive Dacron sheet will be abraded in minutes.

You want a balanced rig, so if you are using a small headsail, the mainsail should be reefed accordingly. For example, with *Denali's* sloop rig I generally heave-to with the working jib and a triple reef in the main. If you have a double-headsail rig, the boat will balance better if the headsail is set on the inner forestay.

To heave-to, tack the boat but do not release the jib sheet. This way the boat falls off on the new tack but the jib is backwinded. The tiller is brought slightly to leeward and tied off with shock cord (it is the opposite with a wheel). You will have to experiment to see what works best for your steering system. The objective is to balance the boat with the backwinded jib and opposed rudder. The wind against the jib is trying to push the bow to leeward; the rudder down to leeward is trying to make the boat come up into the wind. If properly balanced the yacht will cease its forward motion and only be affected by downwind drift.

If the sail and rudder combination are not in balance, the boat will continue to move ahead slowly, or forereach. There are times when this is allowable or even desirable, but it is important to learn to balance the boat so that it will not forereach. If you cannot avoid forereaching, try a different sail combination. Some boats do well under reefed main alone or even with just a storm trysail. A ketch may need a small headsail and mizzen or mizzen alone. Some sloops reportedly heave-to successfully by setting a riding sail, such as a storm jib, on the backstay. Often in the Far East you see long, narrow fishing boats with nearly flat bottoms and minimal keel, hove-to for fishing in this manner.

The bow will usually be off the wind by 40 to 50 degrees and the motion comfortable. Improved comfort will be especially obvious if you have been beating to windward for some time. When you have achieved the desired balance, the boat will be drifting downwind with a slick formed to windward.

Once hove-to, the crew can usually relax, sleep, cook, and overcome some of the tension that always accompanies storm conditions. The motion should not be uncomfortable and the decks will no longer be swept by waves. Often they dry off. This is the time to get rest and sleep. Probably the storm will soon abate, but if it doesn't, rest will be important for the coming hours. Even though heaving-to relieves a lot of work, it is important for someone in the crew to make periodic checks on deck for chafe and to see that the boat has not begun to forereach.

There may be other times as well when you will want to heave-to. Often good judgement tells you to heave-to at night when approaching a harbor or area of difficult navigation to wait for better light. Sometimes cruisers stop and heave-to simply to rest, to cook, or to make repairs.

Lying Ahull

Yachts that follow the usual cruising routes seldom, if ever, find a need to employ techniques beyond heaving-to. However, if seas continue to build, an alternative to heaving-to must be pursued.

How do you know when it is time to consider doing something other than heaving-to? The increased motion of the boat and the obvious strain on the sails and rigging will give you the message.

The usual next step is to 'lie ahull' or stand under bare poles. In this case all sails are struck and the helm is put to leeward. Again, don't lash down the helm – use shock cord to give it some play. If you fail to do this it is possible to break the tiller, or your steering cables, or even the rudder.

As long as you are not experiencing large breaking seas, 'hulling' is a safe maneuver. On some boats the motion will be uncomfortable, and often on deck the noise of the wind whistling through the rigging can be unnerving. Below, however, it is fairly quiet and you can at least lie down and rest.

Lying ahull, the boat will align itself at right angles to the wind. The hull and rigging now act as a reduced 'sail.' The boat will try to round up, but the helm lashed to leeward will counteract this tendency. The amount of freeboard will affect how much 'sail area' exists and thus, how much lee helm is needed. Likewise, the size and shape of the boat's keel and submerged profile will determine the amount of drift to leeward. Fin-keel boats can expect to make a lot of leeway. A slick will form to windward similar to that described under heaving-to. It will likewise serve to dampen the approaching waves and help give a smoother ride. However, rolling can be very uncomfortable on some boats. A few sailors mention streaming warps to windward when lying ahull, and claim it further calms the seas.

I have only chosen to lie ahull twice in *Denali*. I do not relish heavy weather, but I can truly say that once the boat was set up to lie under bare poles it was an exhilarating experience. The seas were sufficiently large that there was no possibility of making progress under sail, but the waves were not breaking, and she lay nicely at right angles to the wind and seas. For hours we went gently up and down as if on some clever amusement park ride. At one moment we would be on a wave crest, and could scan a vast, rolling sea. Next we would be down in a broad trough with only walls of water in sight.

When taking a passive position in heavy weather, protect your wind steering vane equipment. While hove-to or lying ahull, the boat may now and then be violently pushed backwards. I have already emphasized the importance of securing the tiller or wheel with shock cord to protect the rudder. Steering vane equipment should also be protected and this may require removing part or all of it.

From Passive to Active Response

When waves begin to break, or if seas become confused due to secondary wave train or a wind shift, it is time to change strategies. Trying to carry on under bare poles for too long can put your boat in serious trouble. A large breaking wave can pick up a boat and drop it violently into a trough. We commonly think that breaking waves mainly cause damage when tons of water are suddenly dumped on the weather side of the boat. While this can happen, there are numerous substantiated reports of yachts being picked up by a breaking wave and hurled down to leeward on her beam ends. The tremendous pressure that results can break windows, destroy pulpits and lifelines, and fracture or break the cabin or hull.

Running off

When breaking seas take form, you have little choice, save perhaps the use of a sea anchor, than to run off downwind. This means putting the seas on the quarter, rather than dead aft, and exercising timely action on the helm to bear off when necessary from especially large following seas to prevent being pooped. This may be done under bare poles or with one or more stormsails to aid in directional stability. A decision will have to be made whether to stream some type of drogue or warps.

Whereas heaving-to and lying ahull are passive maneuvers, running off is an active response to storm conditions, and usually requires someone on the helm. If it is necessary to hand steer, there must be frequent changes at the helm. Few people can perform this task efficiently for more than an hour at a time. On a shorthanded yacht this is an important consideration. Downhill steering in heavy seas can be a frightening experience at first, because of the frequent need to bear off to avoid large seas that can lead to a broach. However, after a few minutes to get the feel of it, it proves less difficult. This type of steering affords few moments to relax, but you soon develop a reflex response to the seas. Some crews report remarkable success in running off in storm conditions using their wind-steering vanes. If that works you can consider yourself fortunate, but few sailors will want to leave the cockpit unattended.

The most controversial aspect of running off is boatspeed. In the initial period of running off, it may be necessary to make adjustments and to try to achieve proper speed consistent with directional control. The question of whether to stream a drogue or warps and, if so, what type and how long, must be considered. Sometimes this decision is tempered by the yacht's relationship to a lee shore. If the option exists, it is dictated by how far off your desired course you are willing to travel, and, certainly, by your ability to control the boat.

A wide variety of objects have been trailed from boats when running off, and different yachts have used different techniques. The simplest method is to trail long lines. Some boat carry hawsers just for this purpose. Others include a combination of rope and chain, and sometimes anchors and tires are added. In just the past few years some really quality drogues have become commercially available. Foremost among these in popularity seems to be the Galerider, sold by Hathaway, Reiser & Raymond.

Whenever any weight is added to a warp, it is necessary to place a swivel in the line to keep the warp from becoming twisted and fouled.

Figure 27.2
Comparison of sea anchor and drogue.

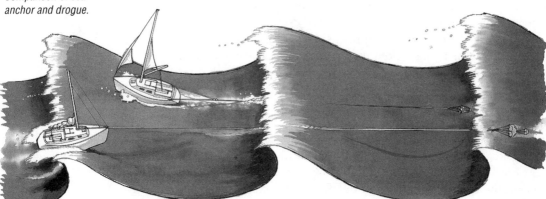

Nylon is the best line to use because of its elasticity. It acts as a shock absorber, prevents a jerking motion, and reduces excessive strains on cleats and other attachment points on the boat.

Different opinions exist about whether to rig a single line or a loop, but if it is a single line there needs to be a bridle to attach it to the boat. And, with either a bridle or a loop, the attachment needs to be made forward of the rudder. The farther forward the better – up to about 60 percent of the boat's waterline length. On a sailboat, the best you can usually do is to attach the bridle or loop to the cockpit winches.

Experienced sailors warn that anything used as a drogue be streamed well aft of the boat. Otherwise it is possible for the device to catch up and even be hurled at the boat by an overtaking and breaking wave. Also, there must be sufficient line so that both drogue and boat can be on the crests and in the troughs at the same time, to prevent jerking strains. Six hundred feet (about 180 meters) of half-inch (10 or 12 mm) three-strand nylon line should be adequate for yachts in the range of 30 to 40 feet. It may not be necessary to use all of this line.

A major advantage of using a single line is that it will be easier to adjust. For example if you are streaming an anchor, tires and chain, etc., in a bight, the heavy drogue gear will need to be centered in the loop with a swivel. This means the length has to be considered initially and may be difficult to adjust. With a single line it can be let out or hauled in as needed.

Regardless of what equipment or technique you employ it is important to remember that the purpose is to control boatspeed and directional stability. Don't let form get ahead of the function, and don't follow the procedures of someone else just because he happens to be a famous sailor, or expect that what worked for someone else's boat will work for yours. A lot of the traditional methods are for traditional boats.

When trying to assess the question of streaming warps, it is easy to become confused. One experienced sailor will report how his life and his yacht were spared disaster by streaming warps. You will read of another equally qualified voyager who found that his boat nearly pitch-poled until he cut the warps adrift and increased boatspeed.

Logic tells us that there is something wrong here. Is it the boat, the captain, the sea conditions, the type of storm, luck, or a combination of factors?

In his recent book, *Seaworthiness: The Forgotten Factor*, C. A. Marchaj has shed some light on this question. He points out that in the early stages of a storm, the wave heights are often steep in comparison to wave length. At such times, streaming warps may be your best option if running off, because they give greater directional stability to the yacht. In a sense the warp is doing the steering and boatspeed is being reduced. Later in the storm the wave height-to-length ratio is reduced, but wave velocity increases. Now, the main concern is to reduce the relative difference in speed between the boat and the wave form. If you continue to run off, you need to sail faster, which means reducing, taking in, or casting off, the warps or drogue. The seeming simplicity and logic of this assessment by Marchaj have the results of tank tests and modeling to back them up.

Use of Oil

The practice of slowly dripping oil to form a slick and thereby dampen the effect of waves is perhaps the oldest storm technique there is. It goes back thousands of years, yet few sailors think to employ this method today. It can be done by hanging a bag of oil-soaked rags over the side or by just puncturing a can of oil with a small opening and letting it gradually drip into the sea. This is not a technique to be used by itself but it can be used in conjunction with other methods described in this chapter. I have never used oil but it seems to me it would be effective, especially when making a transition from one type of storm technique to another. For example, when preparing to run off and stream a drogue there will be a lot of work to do on deck. Anything that will help to create a more stable work platform is worthwhile.

Lying to a Sea Anchor

Misunderstanding exists among sailors about sea anchors and drogues. Most obvious is the frequent misuse and confusion of the two names, and second is a lack of understanding of their proper application, deployment, and use. To add to the confusion some marine supply catalogs fail to properly distinguish between drogues and sea anchors. A few sell small, poorly designed, cheaply made, cone-shaped devices that are worthless in either role.

A drogue is deployed from the stern to slow down the yacht when running off. In contrast, a sea anchor or para-anchor is deployed from the bow. In theory a sea anchor is just what the name implies: it acts like an anchor, but instead of being buried in the sea floor it is buried in the sea. Proponents of para-anchors maintain that 'bow-to-the-sea' is the safest and most defensive position in a storm. The bow tends to part the waves, and seas that do come aboard lose a lot of their destructive capabilities and load before they reach the cockpit.

Compare this to seas coming from astern; for example if you mistakenly deployed a sea anchor off the stern or were carrying too large a drogue. In that case, the cockpit could be easily pooped. Furthermore, many modern boats present a broad, flat stern which will take the full brunt of the approaching seas. This can damage the stern section of the boat, subject the after part of the hull and cabin to wave damage, fill and swamp the cockpit, and affect stability, as well as make life miserable for the cockpit crew.

Deploying a sea anchor from the bow in heavy seas is not new. It has been employed by fishing boats for many years. Some kinds of surplus parachutes, particularly those used for dropping cargo, were first employed by fishing boats and subsequently adopted for yachts. Now several companies manufacture them under the name of para-anchors.

For several years Victor Shane of Para-Anchors International has been waging a publicity campaign to point out the benefits of using properly rigged para-anchors for cruising yachts. Although he has a vested interest in selling para-anchors, his efforts and research into their use has gone far beyond pure profit motives. He has urged anyone who has used a para-anchor at sea to describe the experience. In accumulating these data Shane is not concerned with whose product was used, and he has not filtered the data to eliminate failures of para-anchors. Rather, in cases where they have not been successful he has analyzed the results to see how the techniques can be improved.

Shane's recent publication, *Drag Device Data Base*, published by Para-Anchors International, gives case histories of a variety of monohull and multihull yachts and commercial fishing boats that have used para-anchors under a wide variety of conditions. This interesting assemblage of information, and the personal remarks by individual captains, serve to strengthen the case for sea anchors.

With the proper size sea anchor deployed from the bow, most boats will lie nearly straight into the sea, usually about 10 degrees off the wind. It is necessary to let out sufficient scope so the boat and the sea anchor are cresting on their respective waves at the same time. If this is not done, it will cause a jerking motion that puts severe strains and loads on the boat. It will also cause a very unpleasant ride. A rule of thumb is to use an amount of line equal to 12 times boat length. Individual sea anchor manufacturers will advise what size line to use for your boat. Follow their recommendations. Lighter line may not be strong enough and heavier line may be too stiff to give the needed shock-absorbing stretch. A strong swivel is needed between the line and the sea anchor, or the rode will tangle and eventually render the sea anchor useless.

It can be a dangerous operation to release the sea anchor and pay out several hundred feet of line from the rolling deck of a small boat. Procedures should be thoroughly reviewed beforehand.

It is difficult to say where the use of a sea anchor belongs in the hierarchy of storm tactics. Some sailors claim that deploying a sea anchor is the only procedure necessary, and with sufficient sea room, a sea anchor is deployed early in the game. They don't bother with heaving-to, lying ahull, or running off. Rather they start off with a sea anchor and use it as their only line of defense. Certainly a sea-anchor is adequate for the low end of the scale of storm build-up. What its upper limit is has not been established. Other crews hold a sea-anchor to be the last resort. Perhaps that is just as well, because deciding to recover a sea anchor and then running off in really heavy going does not sound like something most people would want to try. More likely the sea anchor would have to be cast adrift and lost for good. Then, if running off is unsuccessful, you may be in an especially uncomfortable situation.

Post-Storm Conditions

At some point you suddenly realize that the worst is over and things are beginning to abate. There is a great feeling of relief, perhaps a realization of fatigue, but always a sense of guarded happiness and even pride that you and your boat have made it OK. The clouds dissipate, the sun shines brightly, and there is a sparkling cleanliness and beauty to the ocean and sky where just a few hours before there was gloom and discomfort. Now you become anxious to resume your voyage and make up for lost time.

In spite of your eagerness this may not be possible quite yet. If you have been hove-to, lying ahull, or attached to a sea anchor, the clearing skies and reduced windspeed certainly herald a return to favorable conditions. But the seas continue to be treacherous and remain high for several hours. Progress, on any point of sail, may be difficult or impossible. In fact, the greater the reduction of wind with sloppy seas, the more difficult it becomes, because there is nothing to drive or even steady the boat, and you may thrash about for hours. In these unpleasant conditions even seasoned sailors may become seasick and it is often difficult and dangerous to move about on the boat because of its unpredictable movements. Such situations become more dangerous if a second storm system begins to generate a new wave train with a different orientation or period. Then a highly confused sea may result and occasionally exceptionally large waves will develop.

Under these conditions, often after a very large and powerful low pressure system has passed, you repeatedly try to get your boat going but finally accept the frustration and heave-to for a few more hours until the large waves die down.

Personal Observations

Every instance of heavy weather sailing that we go through broadens our sailing education and permits us to meet the next one with more confidence. We gain a better understanding of techniques and have an opportunity to think about new ideas to apply next time. Equally important, we have learned some things about ourselves and our abilities. Our self-confidence has improved, our respect for the dangers of over-confidence have been further developed. Perhaps we have learned to recognize fatigue and exhaustion; a difficult but important lesson.

As inconvenient as it may be at the time, it is worthwhile to maintain some sort of record in the logbook about the nature of the storm and a description and estimate of windspeed and direction, wave height, length, and period. Note the techniques you used, how they worked, and what things you did wrong. Don't be reluctant to record your personal feelings regardless of what they were.

We are still a long way from having pat answers to some questions about storm techniques. This situation will probably always prevail. However, there is a trend in recent years to pay more attention to the need for better survival techniques. Studies such as those by Marchaj, the introduction and testing of new survival equipment and techniques, and the accelerated research by private and public organizations, all point to a new concern and suggest that cruising will continue to become safer in the future.

SAFETY AT SEA AND EMERGENCY PROCEDURES

Someone once told me, a good captain is not someone who performs heroic deeds in a crisis situation. Rather, it is someone who avoids the crisis in the first place.

Sailboat safety is characteristically considered in terms of what equipment we carry on board and the latest techniques we have learned from some seminar or short course. While those things are important, there is, I believe, a more intrinsic factor that precedes ways and means. Simply stated it is a 'safety attitude', and it will go a long way toward assuring a successful cruise.

Proper attitude does not necessarily mean always wearing a safety harness at night, nor does it mean having complied with all of the Coast Guard rules, even though it is advisable to do so. It does mean figuring out how to avoid trouble rather than having to worry about getting out of trouble. It means taking timely action to avoid dangerous situations. It means using good judgement, or at least the best you can conjure up considering your ability and experience. It includes knowing yourself well enough to recognize physical and mental fatigue. A safety attitude may mean heaving-to or lying ahull, rather than trying to enter a port at night. It could also mean leaving the apparent security of a harbor, even though other boats remain, when you suspect it may become a lee shore. In some cases it may be the inconvenience and even embarrassment of returning to port a few hours or days after leaving, because of some problems with the boat – or even because things are just 'too much' for you to handle.

Maintaining a safety attitude can mean being passive when others are active, or active when other are passive. Even watching what the experts do is not necessarily the proper way. Enough experts lose their boats from time to time. Decision-making improves as experience grows, and acquiring experience never ends. Anyone who assumes he has it all figured out will soon find out he doesn't.

Some of what makes up a safety attitude is intuitive. If something doesn't seem quite right to you, then something is wrong. You avoid intuitive feelings at your peril. The best example of this is delaying a sail change when the wind is increasing. It is all too easy, with the relaxed style that cruising encourages, to tell yourself that you can probably press on for a while, or that perhaps the increase in wind strength is only a short-term event. It never is. If you take action before it becomes a necessity, a sail change is usually easy and uncomplicated. When you wait too long it becomes dangerous in terms of working on deck and in risking damage to the sails and rigging. The same applies when setting out in marginal weather or deciding to make an ocean passage in the hurricane season with the reasoning that it probably won't happen.

Crew Safety

Safety Harness

How frequently you wear a safety harness is a personal decision. The best rule of thumb is that if you think you need it, you probably do. On one boat the standard procedure is to wear a harness at all times. On another it may be worn only at night. If the boat's motion is such that it is impossible to move around without constantly grasping something for support, it is certainly best to wear a harness. But there is more to a safety harness than simply putting it on.

Choose your harness carefully. Some are poorly or minimally designed. Most harnesses are strong and the various manufacturers proudly tell you how many pounds of pull they can withstand. However, some harnesses are uncomfortable and cannot be made to fit properly when used with bulky foul-weather gear and a lifejacket. Often they consist simply of a belt and two over-the-shoulder straps that need constant adjusting. The better, new-style harnesses, such as those made by Switlik, fit like a vest and give good support to the whole upper part of your body.

Some foul-weather gear jackets have built-in safety harnesses, but even this style may be dangerous. A few jackets simply have the harness belt sewn into the coat without proper back support. If you fell overboard from a moving boat the pull would all be concentrated on your back and could result in severe injury.

Even if you do select foul-weather gear with a built-in harness, an additional safety harness should be on board for each crewmember. In warm climates it is too hot to wear the foul-weather jacket, but the harness is still needed.

A harness is only as strong as what it is connected to. There should be a hook-on fitting in the cockpit close enough to the companionway hatch to allow you to clip on while still below, before coming on deck. There should also be one or more hook-on points in the cockpit to permit you to move as far aft as the stern pulpit if you have to deploy a drogue or make repairs or adjustments to the wind steering vane. Through-bolted padeyes make the best attachment points; jib track cars and stanchion bases are second-best, and lifelines themselves should never be used.

It is probably not necessary to install special attachment points for a safety harness at the mast, as there are usually enough cleats and other strong fittings to clip on to.

Jacklines

All offshore boats should install jacklines (safety lines or jack stays) to add to crew safety when moving on side and foredecks. Jacklines should run from the cockpit to the foredeck on each side of the boat. By hooking your safety harness tether line to the jackline you are always attached to the boat. On most boats the jacklines lie on deck; on others they are raised and run on the inboard side of the deck, often along the cabintop.

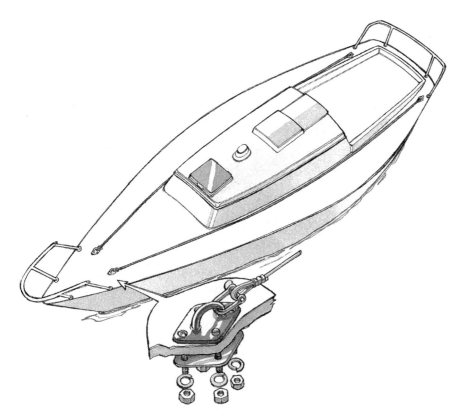

Figure 28.1
*Jacklines rigged on an
offshore cruising boat.*

Jacklines must be securely attached on both ends. If your bow cleats have open centers they make a good attachment point forward, and likewise stern cleats may be used. Otherwise, through-deck fittings with strong backing plates, not just washers, should be installed to anchor the jacklines. Vinyl-coated lifeline wire is a standard material to use for a jackline because the plastic covering protects the deck from scratches. The problem is that the vinyl coating allows the line to roll when stepped on, and can easily throw you off your feet in rough seas. A better alternative is nylon webbing.

If the jackline lies on deck it should be either inboard or outboard – not in the middle. Usually if it lies right alongside the cabin it will be safely out of the way.

Personal Flotation Devices (PFDs)

The PFD is one of the most troublesome, inconvenient, and necessary safety items on your boat. No one likes to wear them. However, there are times when they are necessary regardless of comfort or appearance.

In the past several years, largely due to the lessons learned from the 1979 Fastnet Race disaster, there has been a lot of research into what the proper lifejackets should provide for maximum crew safety, and what is required to make them convenient to use. The fact is, regardless of how well they are made, or how important they are to wear, most sailors avoid using them if they are bulky and uncomfortable.

The traditional U.S. Coast Guard-approved Type I PFDs, or Offshore Life Jackets are required on offshore boats in America. They are still the best non-inflatable jacket you can use because they provide sufficient flotation (about 24 pounds, 11 kg) to keep an unconscious person floating with support for the head. Furthermore, they are strongly made, and even if the flotation is punctured, the jacket will continue to give complete support. The problem is that they are inconvenient to wear.

The logical alternative is a CO_2 inflatable PFD which is much more comfortable and easy to wear, and which permits freedom of movement. The better-quality inflatable PFDs also have more flotation than the non-inflatable type – they often provide up to 35 pounds. Their use, however, requires more responsibility. Unless they are frequently examined and properly maintained, the CO_2 cartridge or the firing mechanism may become corroded by salt water. Furthermore, they must be stored carefully when not in use to prevent them from becoming punctured. Unless they are worn at all times when on deck, inflatable PFDs do not satisfy U.S. Coast Guard regulations for pleasure boats. Consequently, many sailors have the Type I non-inflatable PFDs on board to satisfy the law, but actually use the inflatable vests.

Recently some combined-use equipment has appeared on the market: foul-weather jackets are now being sold with optional zip-out inflatable liners. There are some obvious advantages to this design. However, like the foul-weather jackets with the built-in safety harnesses, they should not be the only PFDs on your boat. There will be times when you need the PFD but it is too uncomfortable to wear the jacket.

Some safety harnesses also have flotation collars attached. One of the Switlik safety harnesses mentioned above can be purchased with an attached flotation collar which provides 35 pounds buoyancy. There is a lot of merit in this combination. When offshore, many conditions that warrant wearing a harness also warrant wearing the PFD.

Keep in mind as well that there are other times when a PFD of some type is strongly recommended – for example, when rowing or motoring your tender. In some anchorages going ashore may require taking the tender through a surf zone where there is risk of capsize.

Foul-Weather Gear

Some consider foul-weather gear a comfort item; to others it is apparently a fashion item. In fact, it is safety equipment. While on watch or working on deck you will be able to perform your tasks more efficiently and for a longer time if you are as warm and dry as possible. When people become cold and wet (the onset of hypothermia) their stamina lessens, and their efficiency and judgement are impaired.

There is such an incredible variety of foul-weather gear offered for sale that it may be confusing trying to reach a decision on what to buy. The stuff designed for fashion may get you by for a daysail or for going ashore in the tender on a rainy day, but it is a different story when you have to spend several hard days beating to windward or riding out a gale.

Figure 28.2
Foul-weather gear for offshore sailing.

Good foul-weather gear is expensive, but not all expensive foul-weather gear is good. The only way to find out what works is to try it out yourself, or to talk to someone who has sailed extensively with a particular brand, in a wide variety of conditions, on a shorthanded boat. On boats with large crews there is usually an opportunity to go below occasionally and change into dry clothing and relax. When cruising shorthanded, an extended period of rough weather may require many hours or even days during which there is little opportunity to shed the oilskins.

When trying on foul-weather gear, put yourself through a wide range of motions. Take your time and try to imagine how it will feel under difficult sailing conditions. Sit down, stand up, bend over, and try reaching and stretching. Imagine yourself at the mast, reaching up and pulling down on a halyard – or sitting on the foredeck gathering in a heavy wet sail. Think about pulling in an anchor line under wild and wet conditions. How will the foul-weather gear feel when you step up or climb down ladders or topsides? Consider how well it will fit when you are wearing a bulky sweater or only a T-shirt. Put it on with a safety harness and with a PFD and try moving around. If it has a self-contained safety harness, see how difficult it is to use. If all of this seems like a lot of trouble just to buy a suit of foul-weather gear, notice the price tag and you will quickly realize you are making an investment!

Most jackets have hoods. Check to see if it can be drawn closely around your face and still provide good visibility. Can you look around without having to adjust the hood? There should be a high collar flap, usually Velcro-sealed, which closes over the base of the hood but doesn't bury your face or make it difficult to talk, eat, or breathe. Some hoods have a small amount of padding added, and this will make it more comfortable when you are sitting in the cockpit and leaning back.

The jacket should close with a zipper covered by a wide flap with

Velcro fasteners. The zipper is a primary consideration. It should be a coarse track with a large car. The zipper and the car should both be plastic. On many jackets the track is plastic and the car is aluminum. It will invariably corrode and become jammed.

The jacket should extend well below the waist. Some models extend well below the hips. There is an advantage in this if you sometimes wear the jacket alone. The jacket should have big patch pockets with large flaps and Velcro closures. Pockets rarely stay completely dry for very long, but the longer the better, and the flaps will help with this. Some pockets have drain holes, but these usually serve to let water in as well as out. It is better to have pockets that keep water out. Fleece-lined, hand-warmer pockets with flaps should be installed in the mid-chest position. It is remarkable how comfortable these are, even if your hands are wet.

Sleeves should have elastic bands on the inner lining at the cuffs and the outside should be fitted with Velcro straps which permit you to tightly close the outer sleeve. Even at that, many people add rubber straps. Water will come in mainly at the neck and wrists, so make every effort to keep those points well sealed.

Pants should be of the bib type, with the bib coming high enough to cover your chest. This provides added warmth and dryness. There should also be hand-warmer pockets with good flaps and Velcro closures on the bib. Pay special attention to the shoulder straps and fasteners. The best straps are broad and flat, and cross high on the back rather than near the waist. This will keep them from twisting. The fasteners which attach the straps to the bib need to be large, strong, and easy to fasten and unfasten by feel. The zipper opening on the pants should be of the same type and quality as described for the jacket, and the track should run to the crotch with a flap on the inside. The outside flap covering the zipper should be the same design as that described for the jacket, and likewise have a Velcro closure.

The knees and seat should have reinforcing patches, as these areas receive the greatest abrasion on a non-skid deck. The pants legs should be large at the base so that they can extend over boots if necessary. Like the jacket sleeves, the inner lining should have elastic closures at the ankles, with Velcro closures on the outside to assure a snug fit around the legs or around a pair of boots.

All seams should be welded or taped, depending on the construction material. Sewn seams that are exposed will leak eventually. The lining on jackets and pants should be made of nylon or some material that dries quickly. The importance of this cannot be overemphasized. All foul-weather gear will become damp inside from sweat and leaks, no matter how good it is. Those with proper liners will dry within minutes when taken off and turned inside out.

Select a bright color of yellow, orange, or red. In my opinion white and blue foul-weather gear should be illegal. The next time you are at sea in rough conditions notice what colors you see in the ocean. Imagine how difficult it would be to recognize a person wearing blue or white in the water under those conditions. Some people claim that white reflects the sun and is therefore cooler on a hot day. This is probably true, but it does not alter the importance of overboard safety. There should be patches of light-reflecting tape sewn to the foul-weather jacket for use at night.

Although good foul-weather gear is expensive, the right stuff does its job and it will last a long time if properly cared for. Whatever brand you decide on, be aware of the various models. Major manufacturers offer several types of suits, and often it is only their 'offshore' quality that is worth buying for cruising. Jacket and pants are sold separately. If you find that a jacket from one brand and pants from another work best for you, buy a mixed suit.

If you still have some money left after buying the best foul-weather gear you can find, there are some other items of clothing you might want to consider. These include float coats, float suits, dry suits, and lightweight foul-weather gear. Float jackets and float suits, or coveralls, have inner linings of Airex or some other type of closed-cell flotation material. Their primary use is to keep you afloat if you fall overboard, but I have found them great to wear just to keep warm, especially at night. In heavy going in cold conditions, I sometimes wear a float suit under my regular foul-weather gear. The best float suit I have found is that made by Mustang. Float jackets alone do not substitute for a PFD, but will help to keep you warm when sailing and are better than nothing if you should go over the side.

Dry suits, such as those worn by dinghy sailors, are nearly the ultimate for keeping warm and dry, but most of them are so inconvenient to get in and out of that few sailors use them offshore. The contortions you have to go through on a rolling boat to use the head when wearing a dry suit will convince anyone very quickly that they are too much trouble. Even more cumbersome are the cold-water survival suits; however, these are highly recommended if you are sailing in high latitudes because they give the ultimate in hypothermia protection. They are completely waterproof and made from neoprene.

Most foul-weather gear that is adequate for offshore work is too hot and bulky for the tropics. It is wise to have a set of cheap, lightweight gear for those conditions. Some of the smock-type jackets that extend down to the knees are comfortable in the tropics.

Because high-quality foul-weather gear is so expensive, it makes sense to take good care of it. Whenever you take it off it should be turned in-side-out and hung up to dry. After an ocean passage it should be rinsed in fresh water – a rain shower is fine – and the zippers should be lubricated with silicon grease. Then it should be thoroughly dried and hung up in a dry place.

The choice of boots and shoes varies with personal preference. Boots should be high enough to keep your feet dry under normal conditions. The best models have some sort of closure at the top to help keep the water out. The combination of this closure and foul-weather pants with Velcro closures at the base will go a long way toward keeping your feet dry. All boots and deck shoes should have soles that give a positive grip on deck. There is a lot of competition in the deck shoe business because they have become fashion items. Each year there are more and more new styles and designs. Just pick a sturdy pair of shoes that fit your feet and your budget.

Some sailors prefer to go barefoot, and that is often the most comfortable way. However, in stormy conditions deck shoes should always be worn to improve your footing and to protect your feet.

Going Aloft

In Chapter 7 I recommended the use of mast steps for the shorthanded crew. Mast steps can be very dangerous, however, and require careful use. There are some terrible stories of people who have fallen when climbing and caught their feet or legs in the steps. Whenever going aloft wear a safety harness so you can hook on to the mast when working, or to hold yourself in position if a boat wake or swell should come along when you are up the stick.

Always wear shoes when going up the mast. Under any circumstances going aloft at sea is a tricky business and should only be done when there is no other alternative. Even if you have mast steps, it may be safer to use a bosun's chair at sea. Often even a slight rolling sea will make it so difficult to climb the steps and hold on that it will be nearly impossible to accomplish any work.

When a bosun's chair is used it is still necessary to wear a safety harness and, if possible, to have a safety line hanging down to the deck that a crewmember can hold to help steady you. If you are working with any tools that could drop, have your crew move out from under the chair while you are aloft. If it becomes necessary to go aloft with any sea running, consider heaving-to to improve stability. In attaching the bosun's chair to a halyard, don't trust a snap shackle. Tie a bowline in the halyard if it is rope. If it is wire, put a safety rope through the eye that holds the snap shackle to the halyard, and tie it with a bowline to the chair eyes or D-rings. If you have never gone aloft at sea, it will only take one trip to convince you that it is not an easy job.

Working Over the Side at Sea

Sooner or later nearly everyone has to go over the side at sea, usually because a line or piece of net has become fouled on the propeller or rudder. If the seas are not rough it need not be a dangerous operation – although certain precautions and some common sense are important.

Before going in the water, think through the whole operation. Decide what tools you will probably need, think about how you will reboard the boat, set up your safety equipment, and, if there is another crewmember, have him be the shark watch. Work out a means of signaling.

When I have to go over the side at sea, I trail a 200-foot (60 m) line with a float behind the boat. I also tie a rope around myself and attach it to the boat, and I wear mask, snorkel, and fins. For reboarding the boat I use a boarding ladder. This job requires a lot of care even under calm conditions because the hull is rising and falling with swells and can easily cause injury.

Man overboard is probably the most dreaded emergency event that can happen on an offshore boat. Everything should be done to prevent someone from falling overboard, but if it does occur, you need good recovery procedures and a crew that knows how to use them rapidly.

Man Overboard

In the past, various man-overboard recovery techniques were proposed, but all of them were based on having a large crew. Today, most cruising boat crews include two people – commonly a husband and wife. Throughout the 1980s, offshore racing and cruising sailors examined man-overboard gear and the procedures involved in recovering a crewmember who has fallen off the boat. Results of this research produced significant improvements.

Recovering someone from the water is a two-part maneuver. First, stay as close as possible to the man overboard, and second, get him back on the boat. It is shocking to consider that even after a lost crewmember is located it may be impossible to get him back on board. However, exactly that has happened too many times.

Anyone who falls overboard can quickly become fatigued from hypothermia, from the exertion of trying to swim or stay afloat, or from the shock and trauma of the experience. Often victims are too exhausted even to help the crew help them reboard the boat. This problem is increased on boats with high freeboard and in rough seas.

Some people assume that stern-mounted boarding ladders will make rescue operations easier. Boarding ladders are fine for swimming in calm water, but they are ineffective for recovering an exhausted person from the water. In the open ocean, even under moderate sea conditions, the hull will continually rise and fall with waves and sea swell and can cause injury to anyone in the water.

Development of the Lifesling by the Seattle Sailing Foundation, in the early 1980s, changed the method of rescuing and bringing a crewmember back on board. Subsequent research by the Safety-at-Sea Committee of US Sailing (formerly the United States Yacht Racing Union), and the United States Naval Academy Sailing Squadron, brought about new methods to keep the victim and the boat in close contact and to permit rapid recovery – the so-called 'quick-stop' method.

The Lifesling is a horseshoe-shaped flotation device attached with large D-rings to a floating line, 150 feet (45 m) in length. The flotation collar and line are kept in a bag near the helmsman with the end of the line secured to a strong point on deck such as a stern cleat or padeye. Commonly the Lifesling is hung on the stern pulpit.

As soon as someone goes over the side, the helmsman rounds up into the wind and tacks the boat *without releasing the jib*. That is, the boat is tacked but the jib is left aback. While this is happening the helmsman also releases the Lifesling into the water. If this sounds like a lot for the helmsman to do, it isn't: as soon as the boat begins to tack it will bring itself around and the helmsman has time to release the Lifesling. The tug of the Lifesling flotation collar will pull the rope out of the bag as the boat falls off the wind.

The boat is sailed in a circle around the victim until contact with the line is made. Usually this can be done within two or three passes. As soon as contact is made, the helmsman brings the boat head-to-wind and drops the sails. It is important to drop the sails immediately to prevent pulling the flotation device away from the victim. The person in the water must be able to get into the flotation collar, but otherwise it is not a difficult maneuver.

The helmsman then pulls the overboard person to the boat either by hand or with a winch. It is best if the victim is brought alongside between midships and the stern on the windward side to keep the boat from drifting down on top of him. Once alongside, the victim should be hauled as far out of the water as possible, with a winch if necessary, and the Lifesling tether belayed. The victim is now safe. The next maneuver is to get him back on board.

This final stage of recovery may be the most difficult without some mechanical assistance. The recommended procedure is to use a three-to-one block and tackle. The upper block is attached to a halyard and hoisted far enough off the deck to give the victim room to clear the rail or, preferably, the lifelines when he is hoisted on deck. This means that the block and tackle must have a long fall – at least 40 feet (12 m) – and be rigged and available in advance. Do not expect to substitute a rope boom vang at the last moment.

The lower block is attached to the D-rings on the Lifesling flotation collar. The working part of the tackle is then led through a block on deck, such as a sheet block, and then back to a winch. The Lifesling collar and victim can now be lifted aboard.

On many boats it will be possible for a strong crewmember to lift the victim directly with a halyard winch. However, the maneuver should be practiced with the block and tackle because it requires less physical effort. In an emergency, it may be necessary for the weakest crewmember to rescue the heaviest.

Notice that this whole maneuver is done without the use of the engine. There is always the possibility of lines becoming entangled in the propeller. Not running the engine relieves the helmsman of one more task and it eliminates the possibility of injury to the victim by a turning prop.

The remarkable aspect of the combined quick-stop method and the Lifesling technique is its relative simplicity. In hundreds of practice runs using human 'test victims' the system has proven successful. This includes small women lifting large men back on board. Like any maneuver employed in a stressful situation, it requires an efficient, set procedure with no time lost trying to find necessary equipment or remembering how to perform the task. Recovery seldom takes more than 20 minutes.

If you recall any of the traditional methods for man-overboard recovery, it can be easily seen that this new method is far superior. The only way to assure it will work for you is to practice the procedure with the crew so that everyone understands the technique and can quickly locate and deploy the necessary equipment.

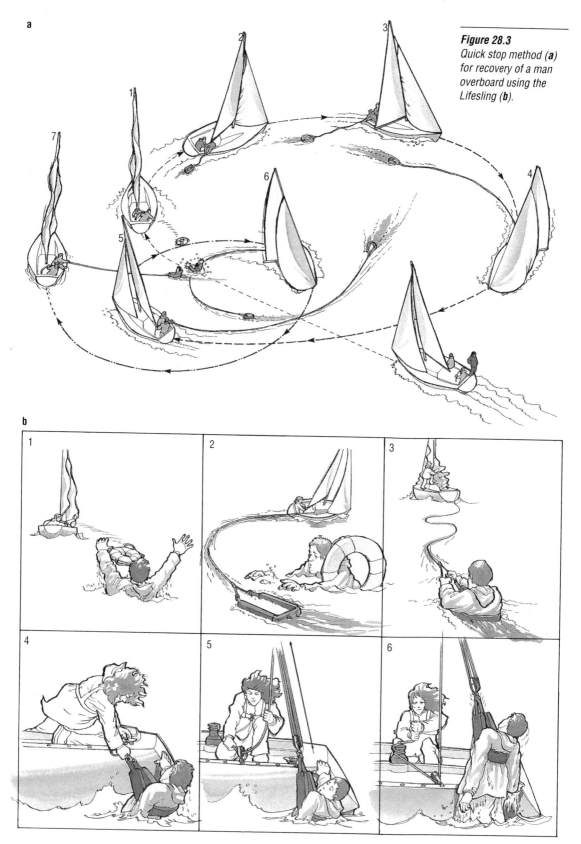

Figure 28.3
Quick stop method (**a**) for recovery of a man overboard using the Lifesling (**b**).

Boat Safety

In this section we will consider various emergencies that can put the boat in jeopardy. The actions that must be taken to save the yacht and crew frequently need to be done instantaneously and instinctively. There is seldom time to sit and think about what action is required. Fortunately, few of us have ever experienced these emergencies. Unfortunately, there is seldom a way to practice them through simulation. You can, however, think through a plan of action for each potential emergency for your boat. Each procedure should be written down and reviewed before a passage. The emergency procedures will be revised and updated as you learn more from other sailors, from reading, and from thinking about procedures as your experience grows.

Preventing Collisions at Sea

It is difficult to think of any collision between a sailboat and a ship that could not have been prevented by timely action on the part of either party. Yet every offshore cruising sailor can recount one or more close calls with a ship. And there are stories enough of collisions that have ended in loss of life.

I am a conservative sailor, but still I have had four close calls – one in broad daylight and three at night. One nighttime experience was with a fishing boat in the North Atlantic, another with a coastal tanker on the Venezuelan coast, and the third with a freighter in the heavy shipping lanes north of the entrance to Tokyo Bay. In looking back, I can now understand how I could have avoided those adrenalin-producing experiences by being more alert, more timely, and more evasive in my maneuvers.

Those who cruise in small boats can just as well forget about who has the right-of-way. As far as I'm concerned the other vessel, regardless of how big or small, always has the right of way! First I make it a practice of assuming the other ships are totally unaware of my existence – and probably more than 95 percent of the time they are. Second, I am a 'pleasure boat' and with few exceptions the other vessels are working boats. I don't feel I should in any way impede their progress or cause them any inconvenience. Third, especially in the case of other pleasure craft or small fishing boats, I make the egotistical assumption that the other fellow is not as good a skipper as I am and that, in a tight situation, he may panic. If there is the slightest possibility of collision, being macho is an invitation to disaster. It is well known that collision avoidance requires the greatest attention near land and when crossing shipping lanes. Coastal areas are obvious, and primary ship routes are indicated on the Pilot Charts. How you approach these areas makes a difference. Sea lanes should be crossed at right angles to reduce the amount of time in the danger area. Coastal approaches are safer if planned to avoid the main shipping and fishing activities. In either case it may be necessary to go some miles out of your way, but it is usually worth the extra time to do so. It may even be advisable, especially when sailing shorthanded or singlehanded, to heave-to a day or so in advance of encountering heavy shipping and get some rest. The density of fishing boats and freighters in coastal zones requires a continuous watch.

Added to this are the increased navigational and piloting chores to assure a safe landfall and harbor approach.

Collision between a yacht and a ship gives rise to several possible scenarios, none of which is encouraging to the yachtsman. Survival may depend on whether the ship is even aware that it has been involved in a collision and stops to render assistance. It further depends on whether your boat remains intact after the collision, and if not, whether you have time and opportunity to launch a liferaft.

There are also collisions with objects other than ships. Logs and various other floating objects have been frequently cited as the cause of sailboats being damaged or sunk. Container ships occasionally lose containers over the side at sea and these hazards to navigation float out of sight just below the surface. It may be impossible to avoid them by day or by night.

There are also numerous documented accounts of whales attacking and sometimes sinking sailboats.

Take Early Action

Collision avoidance is more than just maneuvering out of the way. When there is the least suspicion of being on a converging course your actions must be obvious, precise, and even exaggerated. For example, when meeting another vessel or being overtaken don't just bear off or harden up. Tack or jibe. Your actions must be very clear to the other ship if, in fact, it even sees you. Likewise in a crossing situation you should fall off sufficiently to pass well astern of the other boat and never try to cross ahead or push your luck.

The importance of early and timely action cannot be overstated. One of the most terrifying situations to find yourself in is a 'luffing match' with a freighter. This is especially likely to happen in crowded shipping lanes near land. Under those conditions the bridge watch on the ship is probably very alert and anxious to avoid you. But if you wait too long to change course, then he may decide to do so. You will be busy tacking your boat, and as you harden up on the new course you might suddenly discover that he has also altered course to avoid you, and now you are again closing your range at a relative speed that may be in excess of 20 knots. Now there is no time to take a series of bearings to determine converging courses. You must quickly tack again, only now you are under a great deal of stress. This is when mistakes are made, such as an override on the winch, backwinding a sail, or going into irons. At this point you look up and realize the ship is incredibly close and has once more altered course to compensate for your first tack! If you get out of this one unscathed you can consider yourself indeed fortunate.

I often read about sailors in such tight situations who rush below to call on the radio, get a flare gun to fire off a warning signal, or break out their signaling lamp. These are impressive stories, and when well-told put me on the edge of my chair. However, in my experience the tension and pressure of the moment have kept me 'welded' to the tiller with my only thought being to try and get out of the way. Furthermore, if things have proceeded to the point where both vessels are maneuvering, you are already aware of each other.

A VHF radio is great for communicating with another ship if it is done far enough in advance. However, in an emergency situation there is seldom time to do so. How many times have you called on a radio and immediately begun a conversation? Invariably, the radio volume and squelch control have to be adjusted, and more often than not, you and the ship's watch officer will not be speaking the same language. Radio communications may divert both parties from the need to properly conn their vessels.

Flares are dangerous tools that must be used carefully. In a tense situation it is possible to fire a rocket flare right into your rigging or sail. A hand-held flare can easily injure you or a crewmember and at best it will totally destroy your night vision.

I have, now and then, turned on my strobe, spreader lights, and anchor light, and shined a flashlight on my sails when it appeared another vessel did not see me, or when talking to a ship by VHF and trying to help it locate my position.

Limitations on Lights

Most sailors are rather naive about the range and visibility of their navigation lights. For a sailboat under 40 feet in length, all that is required are port and starboard running lights with a range of one nautical mile and a stern light visible for two miles. If under power you should also display a masthead light visible for two nautical miles. This isn't very much when you consider that you may be converging with a ship at a combined speed of 25 knots. That is two and a half minutes between the time your running lights might be sighted and the time of a collision. This is a shorter period of time than needed by most large ships to maneuver out of the way. Even if you have stronger lights than the minimum requirements, and they are located at the masthead as they should be, about the best you can hope for is that they will be noticed within six or seven minutes (three miles) of a possible collision. Furthermore, remember that big ships are not looking for sailboats. Their concern is with other large ships. Above all else, keep in mind that the fact that you see them is absolutely no assurance that they see you – they probably do not. Stay away from other vessels, and do everything you can to see and be seen, especially in the shipping lanes and when approaching land where shipping and fishing boat activity is more dense.

Among a group of cruising sailors in a rap session, various suggestions will be heard on how to make your boat more visible. Some suggest using a strobe continuously at night, or always using an all-around white masthead light. Neither of these are legal but it can be argued that the primary objective is to be seen and to take whatever action is necessary to make sure you are.

Without question, a strobe will help to make your boat visible, but there are three good reasons why using a strobe is not recommended. First, a strobe is supposed to be an emergency signal or request for assistance. If sailboats continually use it only for identification it will soon lose its significance and other ships will come to ignore all vessels showing strobes. In the meantime, a strobe may attract a ship to come and investigate, which will increase, rather than reduce, the possibility of collision. Finally, it is difficult to judge distance correctly when looking at a distant strobe. The high intensity and intermittent flash from such a small source make it hard for the observer to estimate how far away it is. This also adds to the danger of being run down by a ship. Strobes should be restricted to emergencies, or for illumination for only a few moments to help identify your position, for example when a ship is trying to locate you after you have made radio contact.

Displaying an all-around white masthead light, actually your anchor light, seems to me a good idea, and one that I routinely employ. It is illegal because you are not at anchor, and a ship approaching from ahead or on either bow could read it as an indication that you are under power. But on the high seas either of those considerations is of little consequence. The anchor light will make your boat easier to see, and if it is noticed, the watch on the other vessel is more likely to use his binoculars and then see your running lights.

Other than the negative effect on your night vision, it can be quite effective to turn on spreader lights or use a flashlight to help illuminate your sails. I do this routinely when in the vicinity of small fishing boats. At the same time I attempt to maneuver out of their way. The speed and course of small fishing vessels are often highly erratic and it is my belief that if they realize I am a sailing boat, they will give me a bit more sea room. In some areas where sailboats are seldom seen this can have the opposite effect. On the west coast of Korea, lighting my sails served to attract fishing boats, some of which nearly collided with me as they came in close, often at high speeds, to investigate the alien.

Radar Reflectors

A radar reflector is far from infallible, but it provides one more layer of safety. Most models are so inexpensive and easy to rig that there is no reason to sail without one. The radar return echo from a fiberglass boat is minimal and though a radar reflector only improves that slightly, it is better than nothing. In rough seas a small boat's reflector return will probably be lost in the sea clutter. In fog, however, when the bridge watch of a large ship should be paying close attention to the radar screen, it may be of significant value.

There are several radar reflectors on the market and the price varies greatly from cheap to expensive. A few years ago *Practical Sailor* made a comparative study of reflectors and found that the simple octahedral aluminum reflector, made by Davis Instruments, worked as well as models costing three or four times as much. Subsequent tests have continued to support this. All of the reflectors tested produced variable returns from different directions, because they all have 'dead spots' from which the echo return is weakest. However, on a sailboat underway, there is so much variation in the reflector's movement, that the dead spots will not be consistent, especially if the reflector is rigged with a line rather than in a rigid position.

Figure 28.4
Radar reflector at spreader oriented in the catch-rain position.

Orientation of the common octahedral reflector is important – a lot of sailboats have them rigged incorrectly. The correct position, as recommended by the manufacturer, is in the so-called 'catch-rain' position. That means it should be suspended in such a way that water falling on the reflector would theoretically be trapped in the hollows. In this position the reflector gives the best radar return.

Holing and Flooding

A minor collision with a ship, fishing boat, or some item of flotsam or jetsam can result in a hole in your boat, followed by rapid flooding. At the risk of sounding too pessimistic, a lot of collision damage may just be too significant to overcome on a small fiberglass boat. It is fine to say you should attempt to do everything possible to save your boat. Sailing books and magazines describe various damage-control procedures. But conventional wisdom suggests that in many instances your main concern and effort might be better directed to preparing to abandon ship if sailing shorthanded. As previously pointed out, a four-square-inch hole could cause a 30-foot boat to sink in about one minute, and even a two-square-inch hole could bring about the sinking in about 3 minutes.

Accounts by survivors of boats that have been holed and sunk are frightening when you realize how quickly their boats went down. Often things happened so fast, they considered themselves fortunate to be able to deploy and board their liferafts. The advice that you should not abandon your boat as long as there is a chance it will stay afloat is true. But it is also true that if you must abandon ship, the more water, food, clothing, and equipment you can take with you in the raft, the better your chances for survival. Trying to organize all of this activity is no small undertaking.

There are other causes of flooding that may be well within your capacity to control. These include a broken through-hull valve or, more likely, failure of a hose or hose clamp connected to a through-hull valve. Overcoming and correcting these difficulties may not be easy. If anything other than massive sudden flooding occurs, the first action is to try and determine the source and take corrective action. You should be well enough acquainted with your boat to be able to check every through-hull fitting within moments. If you have prepared your boat properly there will be an emergency soft-wood plug located adjacent to every through-hull fitting, and the valves will be easily closed. In addition to checking hose fittings and through-hull fittings, the engine shaft packing should be checked, as well as the possibility of back siphoning through a bilge pump discharge. Don't overlook the most simple possibility that someone may have failed to close an intake or exhaust hose to the head. Likewise, check to be sure the newly found leak is salt water. The problem could be in a leak in the fresh water lines.

Often, finding the source of the problem when sailing shorthanded is complicated by the need to remove the continually accumulating water, and at the same time maintain an adequate watch. Determining the source of unknown flooding, even if you can stay ahead of it by pumping the bilge, will put even the most competent sailor into a tense state. You may tell yourself that it is probably a minor problem but having to pump the bilge every ten or fifteen minutes, and at the same time search for the leak, can cause you to conjure up wild ideas about the source of the problem.

Flooding is sometimes a result of damage due to grounding. When this type of damage occurs it may be possible to make temporary hull repairs from the outside by nailing or screwing a patch over the hole. Small holes may be temporarily stopped with rags or cushions. A big problem faced by the owners of some fiberglass boats is that of ceilings or liners that restrict easy access to the hull. In an emergency, your only alternative is to remove the material that is in the way. An axe and small wrecking bar, both of which should be carried on the boat, will help in clearing an opening. Flooding of the hull interior can sometimes occur if the cockpit is pooped and the companionway hatch is not secure.

Grounding

Going aground can be anything from being temporarily stranded and quickly getting underway again by use of the engine or a kedge anchor, to running up on a reef or being carried or thrown high and dry on hard or soft ground. The message that comes through in every case is the need for fast action: you must free yourself as quickly as possible. This is no time for committee meetings. Grounding can occur under such a wide variety of conditions that there is no set procedure or specific technique to follow for recovery. The paramount task is to get off the ground if there is the least possibility that the boat can stay afloat once it is free.

The initial problem of going aground may quickly worsen due to the pounding of the hull by surf and waves. Frequently, the boat is eventually carried further aground, or higher on the shore or reef. In tidal areas your course of action will be determined by the stage of the tide when you go aground. If the boat cannot be quickly moved, you may need to get out several anchors to prevent getting into a more perilous situation. With a falling tide and a rocky or coral substrate, a primary concern will be to support and protect the hull or to prevent it from falling over.

Abundant ropes and anchors, which every cruising boat should already have on board, may be your most important tools. The action you take will be patterned to the particular situation. Read the accounts of those who have suffered grounding to get an idea of possible recovery techniques. Some of these stories are incredibly inspiring and encouraging when you see how, under seemingly impossible circumstances, sailors have been able to recover their boats – sometimes after weeks or months of work.

There seems to be no particular type of boat or construction material that will guarantee survival from grounding. Fiberglass is considered by many to be vulnerable to rapid damage in a grounding situation. Others propose that a steel yacht will survive under many situations where boats of other construction materials are lost. Reports by those who have survived various types of groundings cast doubt on the assumption that any one hull material is superior in all cases. It seems that boats of various hull shapes and materials have been saved or lost under a variety of situations.

Sometimes the disaster of a grounding is soon overshadowed by the need to survive if the event has taken place on an uninhabited island or atoll, or in some remote part of the world. Acquaint yourself in advance with survival techniques, and think about how you will salvage everything possible from the boat.

Rudder Damage and Emergency Steering

Loss of a rudder, or serious damage to it will quickly disable a boat. This is a contingency that should be considered in advance. A single-hander friend of mine once lost the rudder on his heavy, 27-foot boat on a passage from the Caribbean to Maine. He ended up at sea for three months before he was taken in tow and brought to port. Others who have suffered this kind of damage have rigged a number of ingenious devices to help their disabled craft.

Like most of the other emergency situations mentioned in this chapter, prevention of damage is the first line of defense. In that regard it may be worthwhile to consider strengthening or even replacing the rudder on your boat. Some of the rudders on recent production boats are too light and flimsy. It is understandable that a rudder shaft might be bent when a yacht is grounded, but it is inexcusable for one to be bent as a result of sailing in gale conditions, as sometimes happens.

There are a number of emergency steering systems proposed in various sailing books and magazines. Many of them seem totally unrealistic to me, and I doubt that the creators of these ideas have actually tried out the techniques they propose. Nevertheless, you should experiment with different systems and have one ready to use if you lose your rudder or rudder control.

Every passage-making boat should have an emergency or spare tiller on board. If your rudder is intact and you have a boat with pedestal steering, it is highly unlikely that the emergency tiller provided by the builder will work efficiently offshore. Usually these tillers are designed to fit behind the pedestal; they are too short for adequate leverage, and are exhausting to use for more than a few minutes at a time, even when fitted with control lines to the cockpit winches. Take the time to modify the emergency tiller or replace it with one that clears the pedestal before heading offshore.

Preparing for loss of a rudder is more challenging. It is a mistake to glibly think you can toss together some sort of wick-wire, jury-rig when the emergency arises. Rather a suitable emergency rudder should be fabricated and tested in advance of a possible emergency. What you come up with will depend on the hull configuration of your boat and what resources you have at hand.

On my boat I prepared an emergency rudder by using the large, 1/2"-thick plywood board that serves as an engine compartment access plate. I had some stainless steel hardware made to attach it to the transom using the fittings that hold my wind-steering vane. It is not a work of art but it will steer the boat.

Rigging Failures and Dismasting

A proper mast and adequate standing rigging that are continually inspected and maintained should stay in a boat under any condition short of the ultimate storm. Still, we are all human and guilty of over-sights, and sometimes fail to recognize developing problems. I pride myself on frequently going aloft to inspect my mast and rigging. Yet once, when I removed my mast during a haul-out, I was shocked to find a significant crack in one of the shroud tangs. It would soon have failed under sail, and I wondered if it was a recent happening or something I might not have seen in spite of numerous trips aloft. Looking and seeing are not necessarily the same!

When a shroud or stay goes, immediate emergency support can be achieved by rigging a halyard in its place. This is not sufficient support for sailing unless sails are reduced significantly, and even then it should only be done in an emergency, such as gaining ground on a lee shore. As soon as possible a new stay should be rigged or the broken one mended.

Installing an upper shroud or stay at sea will prove to be a difficult task under anything but the most calm conditions. It may therefore be safer and easier to make a temporary repair until you can make it to port, heave-to, or anchor in the lee of some protection.

Strong, temporary repairs to stays can be made with cable clamps, also known as bulldog clamps, and wire rope clips. At least six of these, for each size wire on your boat, should be carried on board. How they are installed is important. If you are making an eye, three clamps should

Figure 28.5

Emergency rigging with cable clamps (bulldog clamps).

a Clamps are installed with the U on the short end of the wire rope

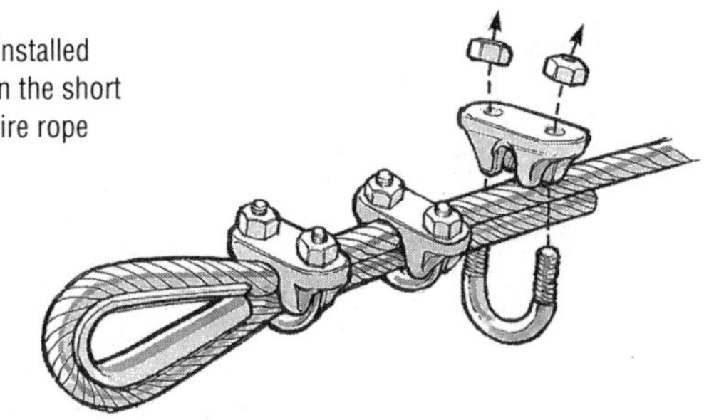

b Table of cable clamp rigging specifications. (*Courtesy of Broderick and Buscom Rope Company*)

Rope Diameter Inches	Minimum Number of Clips	Amount of Rope to Turn Back (Inches)
1/8	2	3 1/4
3/16	2	3 3/4
1/4	2	4 3/4
5/16	2	5 1/4
3/8	2	6 1/2
7/16	2	7
1/2	3	11 1/2
9/16	3	12
5/8	3	12
3/4	4	18
7/8	4	19
1	5	26
1 1/8	6	34
1 1/4	6	37

be used, with the 'U' sides of each clamp against the short end of the loop. If you are adding a support piece there should be three clamps on each end, similarly rigged. Once the temporary repair has been made the nuts on the clamps should be checked and retightened as necessary every day or so, as the wire settles into the clamps.

One or two extra turnbuckles (bottle screws) and toggles should be on board. Such fittings, or even reasonable substitutes, are seldom available in remote places. A temporary turnbuckle repair can be made by using shackles and many turns of light line. Likewise, two shackles can take the place of a toggle for an emergency repair.

If the mast does go over the side, you are faced with at least two major problems. The most obvious one is the need to set up a jury-rig so you can keep the boat moving. However, before you get around to that, there is the immediate problem of what to do about the part of the mast in the water. Under any conditions, a mast in the water still attached to the boat by shrouds, stays, and halyards, presents an immediate danger as serious as the dismasting itself. Unless the mast is disconnected quickly there is the possibility that it will hole the boat and thereby present another set of damage-control problems.

All boats should carry a set of heavy-duty wire cutters of sufficient size to cut the boat's largest rigging wire. Few yachtsmen, however, have ever used their wirecutters *in extremis*. To do so is not a simple matter;

especially on a rolling deck under emergency conditions. Most wire cutters have to be braced against a stable surface to perform their job. Trying to use them over the side of a pitching, rolling deck is dangerous. It is much easier to remove the split pins from the toggles or turnbuckles and knock out the clevis pins with a hammer and drift to disengage the tensioned and tangled rigging wire – if the split pins are correctly installed in the first place. The proper method of inserting split pins in standing rigging fittings is described and illustrated in Chapter 7.

Once the mast is disconnected from the boat it will probably need to be abandoned if the yacht is far from land. More than likely it will quickly sink if it is aluminum. There is seldom much chance of recovering and bringing it aboard.

Various ingenious jury-rig sails have been set up after dismastings. Usually they call for the use of a well-stayed spinnaker pole or even oars from the tender. A broken or bent boom can often be put back into service by lashing or clamping it to a spinnaker pole. Obviously, the mainsail area will have to be reduced and the boat sailed carefully. It may be just as easy to remove the boom and let the sail fly loose-footed with sheets led to cockpit cleats or winches as with a storm trysail. Each situation will present its own set of challenges.

Fire and Explosion

A fiberglass boat with a lot of woodwork, fabric-covered foam cushions, a tank full of engine fuel, and LP cooking gas cylinders, is a fire and explosion waiting to happen. On most boats the only things that will not burn, melt, or explode will sink! That includes the liferaft. The potential for fire is ever-present, and if one occurs while sailing, you are on your own. The message therefore is clear: Every effort should be made to prevent fire, adequate firefighting equipment should be aboard, and the crew should know how to use it.

The most common place for an accidental fire is in the galley. This can occur if there is a fault in the fuel supply line or burners, if cooking oil catches fire, if a burner is accidentally left on and something flammable contacts it, and in many other ways.

A stove should never be left unattended. If a crewmember who is cooking is suddenly needed to help out on deck, even for a short time, all burners should be turned off. Sometimes a task on deck becomes more involved than expected, and your attention to the problem topsides will cause you to forget about the stove or prevent you from going below for an extended period of time.

In another situation it is possible for a burner flame on an unattended stove to go out due to a gust of air that funnels below. With alcohol, kerosene, and some poorly designed LP gas stoves, the fuel may continue to flow through the burner and then be ignited by another source, such as another burner, that is on.

Shut-off valves for LPG must be installed and used for safe operation. A recommended procedure when you finish cooking with LPG is to leave the burner on, turn off the fuel at the tank, let what is in the line burn out at the burner, and then turn the burner off. An alternative and more convenient way to control LPG is to install an electric fuel line cut-off. Marinetics and others make systems with electric on-off switches and indicator lights that can be located near the stove. To use the stove, the control system switch is turned on, a red light appears, and a solenoid switch opens a valve at the tank. After cooking the switch is turned off, the valve closes, and the light goes off. Burners that automatically turn off if the flame goes out are a standard feature on better stoves. It is further recommended that a spark-free exhaust blower be installed to clear possible gas from the bilges. Gas leak detectors are part of the on-off switching for some control units. With this option, it is not possible to turn on the gas until the bilge has been checked for gas fumes. Likewise, any time a gas leak is detected, the gas supply to the stove will be cut off.

There are various portable fire extinguishers available in a range of sizes. The three principal types are dry chemical, CO_2 and vapor (Halon). Their use is classified according to the type of fire they should be used on.

Class A fires involve burning wood, paper, cloth, etc., which can be extinguished by quenching and cooling the flames. For this type of fire, fresh or salt water is sufficient. On deck it would be OK to use water, but inside the boat throwing a bucket of water on a Class A fire might cause damage to electrical or electronic equipment.

Class B includes flammable petroleum products, grease, and burning liquids. In this case the fire must be smothered and oxygen eliminated. Dry chemical, CO_2, or Halon will control these fires.

Class C fires are those involving electrical and electronic gear. CO_2, Halon, or dry chemical extinguishers are all adequate. It may, however, be impossible to clean electronic equipment once it has been sprayed with dry chemicals.

Halon is the first choice and CO_2 the second choice for yacht fire extinguishers because of their ability to fight the fire and their ease of clean-up. In a confined space CO_2 can be hazardous to the crew if its fumes are inhaled whereas Halon is safer. Halon is also more effective than CO_2 for on-deck fires because it extinguishes the fire by chemical action, whereas CO_2 is most effective in a closed or confined space. The long-distance cruiser should also consider the need to have extinguishers periodically inspected. Away from major commercial areas it may be impossible to find a testing and filling service for CO_2 and especially for Halon.

Think carefully about where to locate fire extinguishers. A sailboat of less than 40 feet ought to carry at least three fire extinguishers capable of fighting class B and C fires. One extinguisher can be located where it can be easily reached by the helmsman or cockpit crew. A cockpit locker is a logical location. Another should be in or adjacent to the galley, and a third in the forward part of the boat. For example, it might only be possible to fight a galley fire by approaching it from the cockpit or by entering the boat through the forward hatch. An engine room blaze might have to be attacked from within the main cabin or from the cockpit, depending on the boat's configuration.

The crew should know where the extinguishers are located, where fire is most likely to occur, and anticipate firefighting procedures. Very few people have ever had to fight a fire. For that reason each crewmember should have an opportunity to fight a practice fire ashore with a fire extinguisher. There are specific techniques for using a fire extinguisher. Small fire extinguishers of the type carried on a boat are exhausted in less than 30 seconds, so they must be used efficiently.

Survival

The remainder of this chapter deals with survival. Up to now we have considered general matters of safety, prevention of accidents, avoidance of dangers, and the action to be taken to save the yacht. The emphasis now changes. From this point on our concern is with saving the lives of the crew. We will address this subject with the assumption that it is necessary to abandon ship. However, the situation could also exist in which a badly disabled sailboat itself is the liferaft.

Small-boat survival equipment and techniques have changed dramatically in recent years. Improved liferaft construction, the development of handheld reverse-osmosis watermakers, and the recent deployment of the COSPAS/SARSAT EPIRB system collectively have made offshore cruising safer than ever before. Indeed, some argue it has become so safe and secure as to take away the adventure. They bemoan the fact that too many marginally qualified sailors have joined the fraternity of offshore cruising and 'iron men in wooden ships' have been replaced by plastic people in polyester boats.

Perhaps there is some truth in this lament, but the fact remains that once you struggle aboard a liferaft in the middle of the ocean, your fate rests largely on how well you have prepared yourself to deal with emergencies. Preparation includes equipment and supplies, knowledge of survival techniques, and the will to survive.

The accounts of survivors who have recorded their experiences of days, weeks, and even months in various shipwreck situations serve as a guide to our preparations. Aside from inspiring us with their will to survive, they pass along an incredible amount of precise, detailed practical information that, in addition to a lot of luck, we will need to succeed.

Learning Techniques

Survival is by definition and necessity an acquired skill, but there is still a lot we can do to prepare ourselves for difficult situations. One of the best ways is to read about the experiences of others. That information is much more important than the checklists made up by those who have never experienced a real survival situation. There are several books describing liferaft survival. Perhaps the three most significant books are *Sea Survival – A Manual* by Dougal Robertson, *117 Days Adrift* by the Baileys, and *Adrift* by Steven Callahan. Another handy summary is Michael Cargal's, *The Captain's Guide to Liferaft Survival*. As you read these books, have pencil and paper at hand and make notes as you go along. Decide what equipment you feel should be added to your emergency supplies.

There are numerous other books on the general subject of survival that are worth reading, especially if you have never spent much time in wilderness areas. The cruising sailor needs to consider survival on land as well as at sea. There are instances where sailboats or liferafts have ended up stranded on abandoned islands or on the shores of remote continental areas.

After you have read the books you will have a better idea of what to expect and what to include in your list of emergency equipment. The liferaft with its supply of emergency equipment is your first concern; an EPIRB is second; third is the emergency pack, and finally anything else you can gather up, including a handheld VHF radio, can be added to your survival supplies.

Liferaft

When you select a liferaft with standard survival equipment, be aware that (1) all liferafts are not the same; (2) the water, emergency food, and survival equipment that come in any standard liferaft are adequate to sustain life for only a few days; and (3) reliable liferafts are expensive; their cost may be as much as 10 percent of the cost of your sailboat.

In America, there has been a lot of discussion in recent years as to what is the best type of liferaft. The arguments include shape, size, color, support for the awning or canopy, and the type of ballasting system. Some of this discussion comes from manufacturers who are defending their specific design. The most important points are that the liferaft have a double layer of buoyancy tubes, a self-erecting canopy with an overhead inflatable arch tube, an inflatable floor, and large ballast pockets.

Don't even bother to consider the aircraft-type liferafts, which consist of a single buoyancy tube without a canopy. They are not adequate. Perhaps they will suffice for the weekend or coastal sailor who is seldom out of sight of land or beyond short-range radio communication. However, I even question the validity of that reasoning. The ocean is the ocean, and even if you are only a few miles offshore and have to abandon ship, the only liferaft you want is the best one you can have. Keep in mind that the need to abandon your sailboat may be because of damage sustained in heavy seas. When that happens you are leaving one boat for another, and the new one had better be able to survive where the old one did not!

The size of a liferaft is a point that often generates discussion. It is a fact that putting six people in a six-person raft is a joke – but not a funny one! It is beyond belief to think that six people could survive for any length of time in such cramped conditions. Some, however, argue that only one or two people in a six-person raft will not provide enough weight, and the emergency craft will easily capsize. In my opinion, there are enough examples of success with only one or two people in a six-person raft to discredit this suggestion. For a boat with a crew of three or four I would suggest an eight-person raft.

Any crew heading offshore should spend some time examining an inflated liferaft of the same model and size as the one on their boat. In addition to giving them an appreciation of how small a liferaft is, it will acquaint them with what it looks like inside and out, what the arrangements are for boarding, procedures to keep it inflated, and what features and equipment there are in that model raft. Looking at photographs and videos, or briefly seeing an inflated liferaft at a boat show is not enough. You and your crew should sit inside the craft at the least.

Some people propose going through the whole maneuver of inflating the raft with its CO_2 supply, seeing it released from its canister, floating it in water, and boarding it to simulate a real emergency. It is a good idea to do so, but inflating a raft frequently with CO_2 is not advisable and can cause deterioration of the pontoon fabric. However, prior to an annual inspection, it is possible to inflate the raft with a hand pump to acquaint the crew with its characteristics.

Ocean-use liferafts come with a certain amount of standard emergency equipment installed. Often the manufacturer or the inspection station offers some options in addition to the standard or minimal requirements. Sometimes this is to bring the raft into conformity with offshore racing requirements. Study these equipment lists to understand exactly what is in your raft. In most rafts there is sufficient room to add additional equipment when the raft is initially packed or when it is inspected and repacked.

How and where a liferaft is stored aboard your boat is important. Most can be purchased in a soft valise or a rigid plastic canister. The valise is designed to be kept in a locker and the rigid container is for deck storage. Except when there is some unusual problem in storage, an on-deck location is best. Once more, the accounts of many of those who have had to abandon ship emphasize how unexpectedly and how fast their boats sank. Trying to wrestle a bulky, heavy liferaft valise out of a locker will only add to the confusion and stress of the moment.

The canister and raft make up a heavy package that must be securely attached on deck. At the same time, the raft should be able to be quickly inflated and deployed. Some rafts come with hydrostatic releases to assure the raft will float to the surface and inflate if the boat should sink. I suppose the hydrostatic release is a positive feature. However, there is so much rigging on a sailboat that could catch the raft that it is better for the crew to deploy it by hand.

My six-person raft canister is tied down directly in front of the mast to through-bolted eye bolts with 3/4" line tied with quick-release knots. When at sea I also keep a large, sharp, sheathed diving knife tied to the canister to cut the tie-down rope if necessary. The pull line to the CO_2 inflating cylinder inside the raft extends through an opening in the canister and is tied to an additional line stored in a bag at the mast partners with the bitter end tied around the mast.

Abandon-Ship Supplies

Even a brief knowledge of the experiences of those who have successfully spent extended periods of time in a liferaft points out the importance of having various equipment and tools to help sustain life in excess of the minimum gear included in a standard offshore liferaft. 'The more the better' would seem to be the best advice. Obviously, there is a limit to what can be fitted into a liferaft pack, so it is necessary to make up an additional emergency pack or abandon-ship bag. Even that must be assembled with discretion, lest it become so unwieldy it is difficult to move on deck and into the raft.

How much extra equipment you can add to your liferaft will largely depend on the size of the canister or valise. Some manufacturers pride themselves on how small their canisters are. This is fine in terms of deck space. However, the tiny, compact package will reduce or completely eliminate the possibility of adding needed supplementary gear.

Likewise, notice that most liferaft manufacturers use the same size canister for 4, 6, and 8 person rafts. Obviously, the larger the raft, the less extra equipment you will be able to add to your liferaft for any given canister.

My recommendation is to make up a complete list of all the things you consider necessary or desirable to take with you, and give each item a priority number. Then, when you have your liferaft packed, take the highest priority items to the person who is doing the job and have as many as possible packed in with the raft, beginning with number one and going down the list. What is left can be put in an emergency bag or bags.

There are three items I absolutely recommend putting in the liferaft. First is a small, reverse-osmosis desalinator which will produce a cup of fresh water from sea water in about 15 minutes of pumping. One such small desalinator, the 'Survivor 06' is made by Recovery Engineering. Also consider packing a solar still as a back-up to R-O desalinator, but not as a substitute. Solar stills are difficult to operate and take care of in rough seas and, of course, in cloudy weather they have a very low output. Fresh water is without question the single most basic commodity needed for survival, and its importance when abandoning ship is second only to the liferaft itself.

A small, emergency EPIRB is the second emergency item of major importance. If you have a full-sized EPIRB mounted somewhere in the boat you may or may not have time to take it with you. If there is another one packed in your liferaft you will be sure to have at least one available.

The third essential item is a VHF radio. Almost without exception, people in liferafts see ships but are unable to attract their attention. A VHF radio will solve this problem.

The two difficulties of having a VHF in a liferaft are battery life and waterproofing. West Marine now sells a waterproof, emergency VHF radio with a lithium battery, good for five years. An alternative would be a regular handheld VHF stored in a waterproof container with a solar panel.

Beyond those three essentials there are numerous other items such as additional flares, fishing equipment, storage containers, and patching materials for the raft that are highly recommended. Appendix 9 lists the contents of my liferaft and emergency bag as an example.

Signaling Flares

A boat in distress or wishing to call attention to its position for safety purposes has several options. Most common is the use of a radio transmitter, but in some circumstances flares may be more reliable.

Flares and smoke signals are required on all boats, but you will want more than the minimum requirements. There are several types of pyrotechnic devices and each has a different use. Orange smoke is primarily for signaling an aircraft during daylight. Once ignited, some orange smoke canisters are handheld and others are thrown into the water. Their duration is 90 seconds to five minutes, depending on brand.

Red handheld flares, rocket flares, and parachute flares are for day or night use, but their primary use is at night. White handheld flares are used to warn of an emergency and to indicate your position, for example in avoiding a collision. They should be used judiciously, and only when there is a clear indication that an emergency exists that you cannot avoid by maneuvering.

Rocket flares produce a red color to indicate distress. Some are handheld and others are fired from a pistol or flare gun. Parachute flares have the best chance of being seen. The range of rocket flares is variable depending on the type. When you buy them be sure you understand what you are getting. The most powerful are the SOLAS-(Safety of Life at Sea)type which are now required for major offshore races. They are the best you can buy, but they are expensive. They do not require the use of a flare gun. The firing of any type of flare requires careful handling. For maximum effectiveness they should be fired with consideration of wind and cloud conditions.

Most handheld locator flares and smoke signals produce hot slag. Hold them in such a way that the wind will blow the hot residue away from you and away from the boat.

When firing rocket-propelled distress signals, your arm should be pointed about 85 degrees above the horizon. Once in the air, a rocket will turn into the wind, so it should be launched in the downwind direction. If there are very low clouds, less than 1000 feet, the firing angle should be about 45 degrees above the horizon to prevent them from going above the cloud cover.

Flares have a recommended shelf life of three to three and a half years. Be sure the ones you buy are new. On board, they should be stored in a clearly marked canister that is watertight but easy to open. Every crewmember should understand the purpose of the various kinds of flares on your boat and know how to fire them. Flares have become so expensive that is difficult to justify practicing with new ones. However, when you replace outdated flares, some of the old ones can be used for practice, with Coast Guard approval.

29 APPROACHING HARBORS AND ANCHORAGES

Since dawn the island has been in sight, and with each hour it rises higher on the horizon. Birds have become more numerous and the unmistakable fresh smell of earth and vegetation is in the air. The crew is in good spirits, but it has been a long and sometimes arduous passage, and they are a bit weary of being at sea. Everyone is looking forward to visiting a new place and getting a chance to stretch their legs on terra firma.

The captain talks about the first cold beer in several weeks, and with great anticipation someone else describes a huge dish of ice cream. Because the trip has taken several days longer than expected, another crewmember is eager to call home and allay the anxiety of friends and family.

But distances are deceiving and at noon the destination is still a long way off. Then as the shadows lengthen in the late afternoon it is obvious the harbor is still four or five hours away. Evening comes and lights begin to appear in houses along the shore, and thoughts of a quiet evening at anchor permeate the boat.

At nightfall a decision has to be made about whether to continue on and find the way in the dark or to heave-to and complete the voyage in the morning. The captain looks at the Pilot Book and consults the chart. It shows very little detail and the harbor is too insignificant to be listed in the Pilot. Someone at the last anchorage mentioned the unreliability of the unlighted channel entrance markers. Even though the crew is sure they can find their way in by going slow, the captain decides to heave-to for the night.

It is a wise decision.

It isn't always necessary to delay an entrance until daylight. If the weather is good, the harbor is well marked with lighted beacons, and you have detailed charts, it is usually safe to make a night entrance. Sometimes it is even easier to enter at night when the flashing lights make the channel buoys, range markers, and breakwaters more obvious than by day. Fiji's Suva Harbor entrance is a good example. Often in daylight the leading marks are obscured in haze and industrial smoke. At night the steady red approach beacons are easily lined up for a safe passage through the reef. Likewise, when entering large commercial ports of major industrial nations, the aids to navigation are so profuse and precise that you have to work pretty hard to make a mistake. In Japan I never once hesitated about making port at night. Indeed I felt it was often safer at night. Japanese vessels are fanatic about conforming to rules, navigation lights are abundant and reliable, and in areas of heavy shipping there are well-established traffic separation zones.

Tired crews make mistakes. That is a fact. If you have been sailing under hard-going for several days the crew may not be at their best. Often it is difficult to recognize physical and mental fatigue in yourself, and most of us won't admit we are not at our best. And it's hard not to be eager when the first hot shower and cold beer in several weeks lie a couple of miles away.

Once, approaching Bermuda after a singlehanded passage of seven days from Georgia, I nearly put my boat on the reef. It was daylight, and there was no reason for mistakes. But somehow I incorrectly plotted my hand-bearing compass readings. Based on my assumed position I changed course to round the south end of the island. A short time later I happened to look down and could see numerous coral heads just below my keel. In a panic I jibed the boat and headed back to sea and was extremely lucky to escape unscathed. Had it been nighttime it would have been a different story. I am sure that was the result of unrecognized fatigue.

On my checklist for departing and entering port (Appendix 11), you'll note that the first item is to ask yourself if you are tired. If the answer is 'Yes' the decision to wait until the crew has some rest should always be made. If you decide to wait for morning light, it is sometimes easier to tack out for two or three hours and then tack back in to arrive

Condition of the Crew

Figure 29.1
When nearing a destination late in the day it is often prudent to heave to or anchor, rather than attempting to enter an unknown harbor in the dark.

near the entrance with proper light conditions. I make this a practice when I am tired or if, in heaving-to, there is the possibility that the boat will forereach or drift into dangerous waters.

Usually it is easier to recognize physical than mental lassitude. If you have trouble concentrating or if you set out to do a task and then forget your objective, and especially if you have even mild hallucinations, you can be sure you are tired. It would be nice if someone could come up with a self-administered test for mental fatigue, but if you are the captain, it is up to you to keep an eye out not only for your own but also your crew's fatigue.

I have had otherwise reliable crewmembers on the bow when entering a harbor at night who completely missed seeing buoys and fishing floats because they were tired but would not admit it.

Approach Strategy

When approaching land, navigation shifts into high gear, as does watch-standing. A day or so before an expected landfall the prudent skipper will review the chart and pilot book for the destination. The effects of tide and currents need to be considered. The possibility of off-lying reefs, shoals, and banks may pose special hazards, especially if they are several miles offshore.

As soon as possible take advantage of land areas and navigational aids to establish and maintain a current pilotage plot. Binoculars, hand-bearing compass, and stopwatch will now replace the sextant. Even if you have Loran, SatNav, or GPS on board, visual navigation should be maintained. At night be careful to precisely identify lights. Flashing lights should be timed with a stopwatch and checked against the chart or Light List.

Near large ports it is worthwhile to tune VHF Channel 16 and listen for weather information and harbor conditions. In some countries the Coast Guard or similar agency will put out messages announcing any non-functioning navigation lights, hazards to navigation, or special weather alerts.

Yacht Preparation

When making a landfall or entering a harbor for the first time, I feel the same excitement as a child opening a package at a birthday party. No matter how much I may have heard or read about a new place and regardless of how carefully I have studied the charts in advance, a new destination is never quite what I expect it to be. This is one of the most pleasant aspects of cruising, and subconsciously it may be one of the most compelling reasons for sailing. Each destination is a challenge and most of us thrive on the confrontation and test that it offers. There is a personal pride and good feeling in bringing the boat safely to its destination after an extended passage. What the Kiwis call 'getting the warm fuzzies.'

It is great to be a hotshot and come into an anchorage under sail, and to round up, lower the sails, and drop the hook in one smooth and flawless operation. But before you attempt this in a new anchorage be sure of what you are doing. Numerous glitches can make you appear to be a complete idiot as well as affording an opportunity to damage your boat or someone else's. The impression you make when you arrive at a new anchorage is the one you will have to live with for the duration of your stay.

Some experienced sailors seem to know instinctively what to do by way of preparing their boat for anchoring or mooring; others prefer to follow a checklist.

An unknown harbor may hold surprises. Perhaps you expect to go alongside a pontoon or pier and then find out at the last minute it is necessary to anchor. Even if you are absolutely sure you will not anchor, you should have anchors rigged and ready to release when entering port as a fail-safe against engine problems, or, if you are sailing, the loss of wind in the presence of a strong current or tidal set. On the other hand, if you are planning to anchor, you should still have fenders and mooring lines ready in case you are forced to go alongside another boat or pier.

Give yourself some options and backups. If you are sailing in, it doesn't hurt to have your engine on and in neutral, in case you run into difficulty. Even when motoring in don't be in a great rush to unhank your sails or put on the sail covers. Leave the sails ready to hoist quickly in anticipation that the engine might pack up at the wrong time. It happens.

Best Times for Harbor Entry

Certain hours may be more favorable than others for entering an anchorage or port. The most important example of this is when navigating in areas of reefs and shoal water. In that case the cardinal rule is to never approach these areas when the sun is ahead or too low.

Tidal currents, tidal surges, or longshore currents can also be important considerations. In places where there is significant tide range it may be impossible to sail or motor against the current at maximum ebb. A strong flood tide can also be dangerous if it results in too much boat-speed and loss of steering control. The effects of tide-produced currents and longshore currents must also be considered with prevailing wind conditions. For example, a harbor entrance where tide and wind are in opposition can create huge waves.

Whenever planning a passage in a channel or across an area of shallow water, give due consideration to the state of the tide both in terms of whether it is rising or falling and the phase of the lunar cycle. Tide range will sometimes determine if you have sufficient depth, but it will also provide a margin of safety if you go aground. A boat that goes aground at high tide, and especially on a spring high tide, may not be able to get underway without some expensive assistance – if in fact you are in a place where help is available. Information on unique entrance conditions is given in the Pilot Books and in various cruising guides.

Those who develop their sailing skills in areas where there is relatively little tidal effect may come to grief elsewhere because they fail to appreciate just how difficult tide-induced currents can be. My first years of sailing were on the Georgia coast where the seven-foot (2 m) semi-diurnal tides and extensive shallow estuaries result in strong currents at the change of tide. That background taught me to respect tidal currents, but I still managed to get into a serious grounding on a sandbar in Kun-san Harbor on the west coast of Korea where the tide range approaches 33 feet (10 m). Even though I was 'hard aground,' the current was so strong the flow continued to push me along. Eventually I gained enough depth to get steerage again and could find my way back to the main channel.

In some places, having a set of published tide tables is necessary, and sailing times should take advantage of the most favorable conditions. I recommend negotiating narrow channels at slack tide just before it begins to flow in the direction you are going. Sometimes it may even be advisable to begin before slack while there is still a waning opposing current. If there is too much current with you it will be difficult to maintain proper steerage way. Finding yourself without adequate maneuverability among large ships or a fishing fleet in a narrow chan-nel is a terrifying experience. I had such a 'white knuckle' trip through the notorious Kanmon Straits between Honshu and Kyushu on my first day sailing in Japan. It was a good introduction to the country because after that everything else seemed easy.

The best time to enter a commercial harbor may depend on other traffic. If an entrance used by large ships is complicated, don't hesitate to use your VHF to check with the harbor control for clearance. Usually it is not difficult to share an entrance with big ships. A far more rigor-ous exercise is to fight your way among the local fishing fleet as it departs or returns to port. Working through dozens of fishing craft headed in the opposite direction is not easy under power and can be ter-rifying under sail. The difficulties are exacerbated in places where fish-ermen are not on good terms with yachties.

When entering some commercial harbors you are supposed to call on VHF 16 and request permission from the harbor control, harbor mas-ter, or port authority to enter. Many yachts ignore this and they are sel-dom reprimanded for their neglect. On the other hand it can be to your advantage to do so, because part of the purpose for the call is to aid the harbor authorities with traffic control. If it happens that a large ship or tug with a string of barges is on its way out, the authorities will usually ask you to wait or at least warn you of this or any other hazards.

Where to Anchor

The more up-to-date information you have when entering a new harbor or anchorage the easier it will be. Usually the best and most current source of knowledge will be what you learn from other yachts along the way. Pilot Books can be of some use but they mainly apply to ships, and recommended anchorages are in deep water. Cruising guidebooks pro-vide good information and offer detailed sketch maps. Often, however, you will be on your own, and it may be necessary to sail or motor around for a while until you find a likely spot. Regardless of how much advanced information you have, study whatever charts or sketch maps are available and give yourself some options. For some reason most of us are seized with some unexplained sense of urgency when entering a harbor to rush to find a place to anchor or tie up. Taking your time and looking around a bit may save you having to relocate. I usually look for other yachts and anchor or tie up with them. Even if you don't want to anchor right near them, other yachts can offer you valuable information, such as the bottom type and what the best anchor and scope is. It is convenient to have a VHF hand-held radio in the cockpit in the event someone wants to call and give advice.

Whatever input you get from other people, from the guidebooks, or even the information on the chart, it should not be accepted as fact until you have decided for yourself that it is correct. Conditions can change through time so the chart could be incorrect or someone's impressions could be wrong or confused.

Before Going Ashore

Once you have the boat anchored or tied up and the deck gear squared away you may be anxious to go ashore. Don't be in too big a rush. Make absolutely sure your boat is safe and secure. Many sailors prefer to wait a few hours before leaving their boat to see how it will lie to the new place. There may be currents that you have not anticipated or a change in wind or sea conditions that make your anchorage hazardous. A seemingly secure position alongside a pier may become untenable when the fishing fleet returns in the evening. You may have chosen a spot that is illegal or belongs to someone else or it may be the ferry boat landing. Usually if you are tied up in a space that belongs to a commercial vessel someone will tell you, but sometimes they don't.

One time in Japan I came into a small harbor at night and tied up in what seemed to be an out-of-the-way place. A night watchman who spoke some English came by and I asked him, 'Is this a good place to tie up my boat?' He replied, 'Oh yes, a very good place.' And it was indeed until about three o'clock in the morning when the horn blast of an angry ferry boat captain sent me frantically stumbling about to get *Denali* untied and underway to a less 'very good place.'

If you voyage to places that are seldom visited by yachts be prepared for complications, misunderstandings, and the possibility of bad advice on where and how to anchor or moor. Further complications can arise if you do not share a common language. At Inchon, Korea, another place with 30-foot tides, the harbor authorities wanted me to tie up with the fishing boats which simply sit on the mud when the tide goes out. *Denali* was only the second cruising yacht that had been there and my attempted explanations about how sail boats are different from the flat-bottomed fishing boats was finally understood. However, they still did not see why my boat lying on its side half the time was any problem. Eventually they did let me tie up to a floating dock when I said I was afraid my mast might damage a fishing boat at low tide.

Conventional wisdom says to ask for advice. But in a new port or strange anchorage you are advised to stay with your ship for a while until you feel it is safe and secure before leaving it unattended.

**Post-Passage
Letdown**

One of the danger times for the cruiser is shortly after anchoring. Often at the end of a long passage you are running on second or third wind and the diminishing dregs of adrenaline without realizing it. With the anchor down or the boat alongside with fenders in place and mooring lines secured, all of that mysterious energy that has kept you sharp and psyched up while coming into port suddenly drains away. You may become completely exhausted in a matter of minutes.

Arrival exhaustion is one more excellent reason for using a checklist. It will help to assure you have taken care of the most pressing chores. No matter how tired you are the boat should be made shipshape before taking a rest.

In the process of entering a harbor the hand-bearing compass, binoculars, and VHF hand-held radio often end up in the cockpit. Forgetting to put them away at the end of the passage is an invitation to theft. Leaving sails on deck could lead to their damage or loss if a strong wind comes up after you have turned in. Taking several rounds of compass bearings after anchoring is as important as any other navigation duty.

As tired as you may be it is better to force yourself to stay awake for at least an hour after anchoring. Occasionally it is necessary to continue standing watch after arrival. One way to stay alert after anchoring is to stay busy by completing the checklist, catching up on the log, or making a list of needed repair tasks. Before you go to sleep consider setting an alarm clock to wake you in an hour or so. Sometimes depthsounders or radar alarms can be used but nothing beats a crewmember getting up and looking around every hour or so until the boat is safely settled in its new home.

ANCHORS AND ANCHORING

You can make fast passages and set new records; you can write books about sailing and tell incredible sea stories – but if you can't anchor your boat properly you will be remembered as an incompetent sailor.

How do you learn anchoring? What books do you read or what course do you take? Where is Anchor University? In my opinion, you don't *learn* anchoring – you experience it. It is worthwhile to read a few books on the subject, but to become proficient you have to get out there and do it over and over under a wide variety of conditions. Even at that you will not become perfect, only better.

If you do an adequate job of anchoring no one will notice. But if you make a mess of it you can be certain that not only will everyone see you, they will remember it, and help you remember it for years.

It is important to make the distinction between anchoring and being at anchor. 'Anchoring' means finding a proper place to drop the hook and successfully securing the boat in that place. 'Being at anchor' means remaining safely in that place without putting your boat or the boats around you in danger. It may also mean protecting yourself from other boats that are poorly anchored.

Forces Acting on an Anchored Boat

Winds and waves are interrelated, but whereas windspeed and direction are easily quantified, wave and sea conditions are more chaotic. The effect of waves on an anchored boat depends on a host of factors including boat size, freeboard, rig, underwater hull shape; topographic features of the surrounding land mass and the sea floor below; the density of boats in an anchorage, and the experience and preparedness of the crew, the quality and quantity of ground tackle, and currents, which can be generated by wind, by waves, by tides, or by river outflow. In certain situations current may be the primary force to be reckoned with, but generally in heavy-weather conditions it is much less of a factor than wind and especially waves. Furthermore, currents tend to be cyclic and predictable, whereas wind and waves are not.

ABYC Table of Horizontal Loads

A good scheme to summarize and quantify the forces acting on a boat at anchor is the Table of Horizontal Loads prepared by the American Boat and Yacht Council (ABYC). The values in the table assume that the boat is anchored by the bow with room to oscillate, and that it has moderate shelter from the sea. In other words it is in a protected harbor, bay, or lagoon. Notice that as the wind doubles in strength, the load increases by a factor of four.

In determining the amount of a yacht's surface area affected by wind and waves, the ABYC's calculated surface area is not the direct bow-on view, but rather the surface presented with the boat 30 degrees off the wind. This is to take into account the yawing that occurs when a boat is anchored in a strong wind.

A look around any marina will clearly show that there is considerable variation in surface area even between boats of the same length. For example my boat has low freeboard, long overhangs, streamlined stern, and narrow beam. Her windage is much less than that of modern production boats of the same length with more beam, higher freeboard, flat transoms, and bluff bows – all of which add surface area.

Compared to sailboats, most powerboats appear to have far more surface area and offer greater wind resistance. However, there is more surface area to sailboats than is commonly recognized. Masts, booms, stays, shrouds, halyards, lifelines, pulpits, boom gallows, and dodgers all together add significantly to total surface area. You may be surprised if you calculate the amount of windage on your boat that is represented by the standing rigging. You can roughly determine this by multiplying the thickness of the wire by the total length of all of your shrouds and stays. Add to this the surface area of the mast and spreaders and it may be nearly equal to the surface area of that part of the hull which faces the wind when the boat is yawing.

Permanent structures which create windage on a boat cannot be avoided. But when preparing to ride out a typhoon or hurricane at anchor, it is possible to significantly reduce windage. You can remove dodgers, un-needed halyards and furling headsails. The mainsail can be removed from the boom and even the boom itself can be stored belowdecks.

To enter the ABYC table, locate your boat's LOA and see how it compares with the number for beam. If the beam of your boat is greater

Table 30.1
American Boat and Yacht Council (ABYC) table of horizontal loads.

Table 1

LOA (feet/meters)	Dimensions (in feet/meters) Beam sail	power	15 knots Beaufort 4 Moderate breeze (lunch hook)	30 knots Beaufort 7 Moderate gale (working anchor)	42 knots Beaufort 9 Strong gale (storm anchor)	60 knots Beaufort 11 Storm
			Horizontal load on boat as measured in pounds/kilograms			
20/6	7/2.1	8/2.4	90/40.5	360/162	720/324	1440/648
25/7.5	8/2.4	9/2.7	125/56.25	490/220.5	980/441	1960/882
30/9	9/2.7	11/3.3	175/78.75	700/315	1400/630	2800/1260
35/10.5	10/3	13/3.9	225/101.25	900/405	1800/810	3600/1620
40/12	11/3.3	14/4.2	300/135	1200/540	2400/1080	4800/2160
50/15	13/3.9	16/4.8	400/180	1600/720	3200/1440	6400/2880
60/18	15/4.5	18/5.4	500/225	2000/900	4000/1800	8000/3600

than that given for your LOA, go to the next line down (higher value). For example if you have a sailboat with an overall length of 30 feet (9 m) and a beam of 10 feet (3 m) you would drop down to the next line.

Four principal levels of windspeed have been selected to show horizontal loads to be expected for different size boats. For example, the working anchor and associated gear for a 25-foot (7.5 m) boat should be able to handle a 490-pound (220.5 kg) load. For a 40-foot (12 m) boat under the same conditions the working anchor should be able to cope with 1200 pounds (540 kg). Knowing these data will serve to guide you not only in choosing the proper anchor, but in selecting rope, chain, shackles, swivels, and windlass. It may even give you something to think about in terms of the strength of cleats, bow rollers, and chocks on your boat.

15 Knots of Wind

Fifteen knots typically represents the upper end of easy sailing conditions. It is the point at which we normally begin to reef the main and make a headsail reduction. According to ABYC calculations a 'lunch hook' could be used under these conditions. This is a lightweight anchor of the type you might use while gunkholing in protected waters. However, it is not the kind of anchor you would want to use overnight.

30 Knots of Wind

All power and sailing boats, no matter where they sail, should carry an anchor and ground tackle capable of withstanding 30 knots of wind. Even boats that spend their whole life in protected bodies of water will find times when winds of this magnitude occur unexpectedly. This calls for a 'working anchor', or what you would normally use for anchoring.

42 Knots of Wind

This category can definitely be considered storm conditions for a small boat, and the anchor to do the job for this magnitude of loading can be considered a storm anchor. However, don't be too alarmed by the horizontal load values given for this category. As we will see, anchors for loads even at this level are not excessively large.

Likewise don't assume that you must have a lunch hook, a working anchor, and a storm anchor. On most boats, one anchor does all of these jobs. This is not to say you should only have one anchor on board. Any experienced sailor recommends a minimum of at least two, one of which should be adequate as a storm anchor.

60 Knots of Wind

Anyone who has anchored or sailed in 60-knot winds will remember the event, and will not speak of it in a casual way. The next time you are tossing back a few at the yacht club bar and someone starts talking about the time he was sailing in 60 knots of wind and decided it was about time to tie in the third reef, you can suggest that he buy a new wind indicator or find a new audience for his story. Sixty knots is 'big guns' and most cruising boats will be hove-to, under bare poles, or flying storm sails long before they experience Beaufort 11.

At anchor it is an equally memorable event. If you have to be anchored in such conditions, you will want to have as much protection from waves and seas as possible. You will have out your strongest and best anchor and maybe anything you can borrow, and you will have removed unnecessary windage from the deck and mast.

Surge Loading

It is important to notice that the ABYC table only mentions loads produced by wind. Yet, as pointed out by Earl Hinz in *The Complete Book of Anchoring and Mooring*, the effect of wave surge can result in intermittent loading twice as great as that caused by the wind. The amount of surge loading for any particular boat will depend on its displacement and length. However, for an average cruiser-racer there is enough leeway built into the table to accommodate surge loading. For example, Hinz calculated the total ground tackle load for his Morgan Out Island 41, a beamy, medium-displacement boat. He included horizontal load estimates and a surge factor of about twice the horizontal load. The result was still within the recommendations given in the ABYC table for a 40-foot boat. If you want to determine loads for a multihull or a boat of unusual shape or displacement, more specific calculations will be necessary.

How Anchors Work

When you consider that humans have been anchoring boats for a few thousand years it seems surprising that we continue to have problems. But a view of yacht harbors anywhere in the world suggests that anchoring is still an imperfect art. Why? In part it has to do with the nature of the game. When the anchor leaves the deck we seldom know exactly where it is going, or if it is taking hold properly. However, it helps to understand how an anchor achieves good holding under different conditions.

Anchors are designed to either penetrate (bury) into the sea floor or hook the bottom. In practice a penetrating anchor may act as a hook anchor and a hook anchor may be effective by burying, but they are most efficient when used for their designed purpose.

Penetrating Anchors

Penetrating anchors achieve holding power by virtue of their large flukes. As the anchor enters the substrate, the broad fluke surfaces develop resistance-to-drag from internal friction (sheer resistance) with the sediment. Obviously then, initial penetration is a primary concern in the development of burying anchors.

Penetration should occur quickly after the anchor finds the bottom, and to do this the anchor must be correctly oriented. This is asking a lot, because when you dump the hook over the side, it is difficult to control how it will land on the sea floor. Attempts to improve orientation have led to a variety of innovative anchors. Consider the evolution

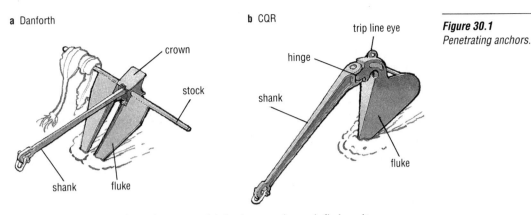

a Danforth

b CQR

Figure 30.1
Penetrating anchors.

from the traditional anchor, in which the stock and flukes lie at opposite ends of the shank, to those in which the stock is adjacent to and parallel with the flukes, and, more recently, to the stockless anchor.

Once the anchor is on the bottom, it should begin to bury as soon as tension is exerted by the anchor line. If it fails to penetrate quickly, it may slide over the substrate surface, and once this happens, it may continue to slide or bounce and fail to take hold.

Anchors with stocks are thrown off balance and thus, no matter how the anchor lands, a fluke will penetrate the substrate when the anchor line comes under tension. In the case of a stockless anchor, penetration is accomplished because of the hook shape and plow-like flukes.

Hooking Anchors

These anchors do not depend on penetrating the substrate to perform their function. Rather, their purpose is to catch on an irregular sea floor surface – broken rock, rounded boulders, living coral, or coral rubble. In situations where an uneven bottom is covered with a thin veneer or pockets of sand of variable thickness, a hooking anchor will often save the day. Likewise it may be the only type of anchor that will hold in hard mud or clay.

Hooking anchors are often successful in areas where the bottom is covered by sea grass, because the flukes can take hold through the plant cover. In contrast, a burying anchor that fails to penetrate the root mat will slide across the surface.

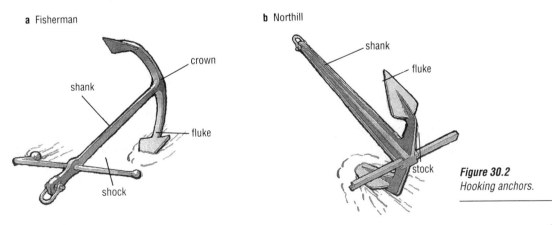

a Fisherman

b Northill

Figure 30.2
Hooking anchors.

Type of Substrate

Sediment type is often the key to success or failure in anchoring. Once initial penetration is achieved the quality and quantity of the substrate becomes important. Sometimes the type of sediment – for example sand and mud – is excellent for anchoring, but it occurs in a patchy distribution of variable thickness over a hard rock substrate. Perhaps a small burying anchor can hold, but a larger anchor will not. In places with such inconsistent bottoms it is important, if possible, to dive to inspect the anchor and probe the substrate around the anchor to be sure it is thick enough. In some estuarine settings I have encountered situations where sand and mud provided excellent anchoring, but it was only a thin veneer overlying a dense compact clay.

A mud substrate can be difficult depending on its consistency. Hard-packed mud or clay may not be penetrable by a burying anchor. At the other extreme, water-saturated mud, especially of consistent grain size, will not offer any resistance to the anchor and, although the anchor may sink deeply, it will not take hold.

I once offered some first-class entertainment to the dozens of people lounging around the wharfs in the picturesque harbor of St. George's, Grenada in the Caribbean. The town basin there is a huge, muddy cul-de-sac. Even though the depthsounder indicated a bottom, the anchor had nothing to hold on to. It simply hung suspended in a mud bath and could not take hold when I backed down to make it set. My repeated attempts were greeted with applause and shouts of encouragement until I gave up after a couple of exhausting hours and sought out the local marina. I later learned that such shows of skill by visiting boats are a common occurrence.

Freshly deposited volcanic ash can likewise cause difficulties. I anchored for three days in the shadow of the active volcano on Pagan Island in the Northern Marianas. I let out a lot of chain and a heavy anchor but the bottom seemed to have the consistency of a bowl of yogurt. Apparently I was 'anchored' by virtue of a heavy weight hanging down in a thick ash slurry. Throughout my stay I kept my sails hanked on, because a windshift would have required a rapid departure from a lee shore.

A reasonably detailed navigation chart will tell you the general nature of the sea floor material to be expected.

Scope and Anchor Line Approach Angle

If there is any point about anchoring that consistently gets the novice in trouble, it is the failure to lay out adequate scope. Scope is the amount of anchor line relative to water depth. Scope largely determines the approach angle of the anchor line to the anchor, which in turn controls the orientation of the shank and fluke angle.

If the approach angle is more than eight degrees, the shank can lift, the fluke angle will be reduced, and the anchor will either trip over itself or begin to slide. Once this happens the anchor may not be able to re-penetrate and will skid, bounce, or plane across the sea floor as the boat drifts.

Figure 30.3
Anchor line angle and scope.

a Approach angle of anchor rode to substrate should be less than eight degrees

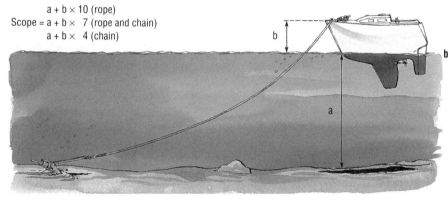

$$a + b \times 10 \text{ (rope)}$$
$$\text{Scope} = a + b \times 7 \text{ (rope and chain)}$$
$$a + b \times 4 \text{ (chain)}$$

b In determining scope don't rely only on the depthsounder reading. Measure from the bow and also take tide range into consideration

Proper scope is achieved by laying an anchor line with an adequate catenary or sag between the boat and the anchor to act as a shock absorber. This depends on water depth, the type and length of anchor line, and the wind and sea conditions.

The conventional amount of scope for a working anchor is 10:1 for an all-rope rode, 7:1 for combined rope and chain, and 4:1 for all-chain. In determining scope it is important to measure from the bow roller (or wherever the anchor line joins the boat) to the sea floor. The careless sailor may think of depth only in terms of what is shown on the depthsounder, but on most boats the depthsounder is at least two or three feet below the waterline and the deck may be four or more feet above the waterline. In shallow water seven feet is a significant percentage of the scope.

Always consider tide range when anchoring and determine scope based on the high-tide depth. A tide range of five or ten feet makes a big difference in determining scope in shallow water.

Testing Anchors

Numerous testing projects have been undertaken in recent years to evaluate small-boat anchors. They include tests in rivers, lagoons, on beaches, and in laboratories with a variety of measuring apparatus. Although certain trends appear from these tests, they still leave much to

be desired. Often tests are made under the auspices of an anchor manufacturer and, not surprisingly, the sponsor's product always comes out
the best. In other instances the test results are equivocal due to variations in substrate, or wind, or testing methods – which makes it difficult
to draw comparisons between different brands and sizes of anchors.
Sometimes testing methods are so unrealistic in terms of anchoring a
small boat that the significance of the test results is suspect.

Read the tests and make your own conclusions. But in the final
analysis ask what ground tackle people who are cruising full-time use.
They represent the real test results.

Choosing Your Anchor

Those new to sailing are often amazed to see the number and size of
anchors carried by experienced cruisers. It is not unusual for a cruising
boat to carry anchoring equipment (windlass, chain, line, and anchors)
that equals three or four percent of the boat's displacement.

Plow

The best anchor for the widest variety of conditions is a plow, and the
best known plow is the CQR. This is the anchor you see most often on
cruising boats. Next in popularity is the Bruce. There are other plow
anchors now on the market and others will surely appear in the future.
At the present time none of them has proven to be better than the CQR
or the Bruce.

When a plow comes to rest on a sand or mud bottom it will lie on its
side. As a pull is exerted, the point of the plow will begin to penetrate
the bottom and continue to do so until it is fully buried. The only
exception to this would be if there were not sufficient scope or weight
on the anchor line: the shank of the anchor must be nearly horizontal
for the anchor to bury properly. This is achieved by giving adequate
scope and weight to hold the shank down. An all-chain rode accom-
plishes this best. If using nylon line there should be a length of chain
between the anchor and the line which, in addition to adding weight to
the shank, will resist chafe.

A primary attribute of a plow is its ability to rotate and remain
buried if the boat shifts due to changes in wind direction. No other
anchor will do this as well the plow.

Although a plow performs best in sand and mud substrates, it will
sometimes work in grass and even in rocks. It is not the best anchor for
these conditions, but it may be the most convenient, or all you have.
The CQR can be carried easily on a bow roller.

In recent years the Bruce has received a lot of publicity. It is a simple
one-piece plow with large flukes. When it lands on a sandy or muddy
bottom it has to rest on one fluke. As a strain is taken it rolls so that
both flukes penetrate the substrate and dig in. Like the CQR, it will
continue to dig in and reposition itself as the boat changes directions
with a shifting wind. Its rigid, broad-hook shape means that it can
sometimes work well in boulders, broken rock, and coral. It stows well
on a bow roller, but it is difficult to stow in a locker when not in use.

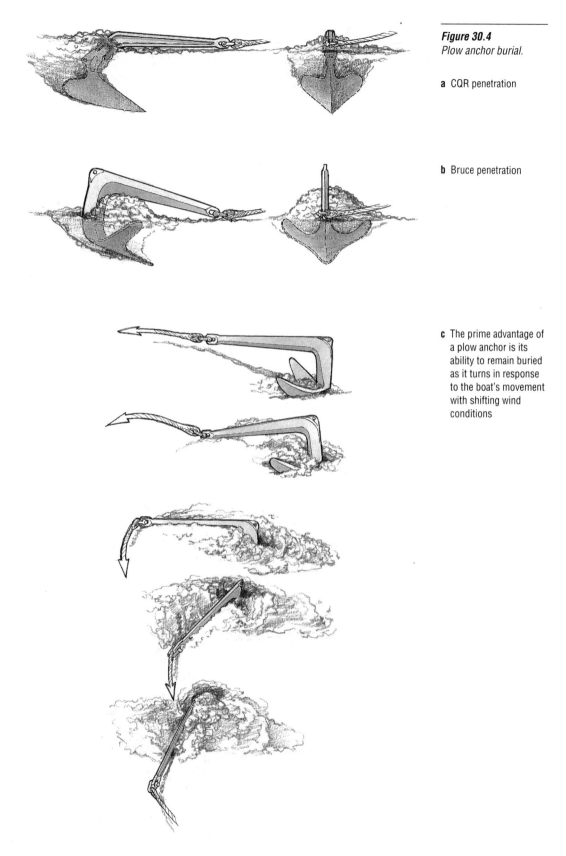

Figure 30.4
Plow anchor burial.

a CQR penetration

b Bruce penetration

c The prime advantage of a plow anchor is its ability to remain buried as it turns in response to the boat's movement with shifting wind conditions

Danforth

This anchor is as well-known as the CQR and of equal popularity, but there is confusion about what a Danforth anchor really is. The name originally came from the inventor R.S. Danforth who developed this anchor in 1939. Subsequently it became famous in World War II when it was used by large landing craft to pull themselves off the beach after discharging cargo. In some ways it resembles the older 'stockless' or Navy anchor. But the Danforth is much lighter and has greater fluke area.

The Danforth is referred to as the 'stock-stabilized, pivoting fluke' anchor. It is also called the 'lightweight' or the 'LWT.' There are numerous 'lightweight' anchors, but often when that term is used it implies a Danforth. Although many anchors are referred to as 'Danforth,' the original Danforth is a specific design that has proven its ability for certain anchoring conditions.

The true Danforth is characterized by large, flat, pointed flukes attached to the stock. The flukes are able to rotate about 30 degrees either side of the shank. When fully dug in, the Danforth offers the greatest holding power for its weight of any anchor, as long as the pull is straight. If the boat shifts on its mooring, however, for example in response to changing wind direction, the Danforth may fail to rebury. Furthermore, once a Danforth begins to drag it resists digging in again.

When a Danforth is lowered to the bottom it comes to rest in a flat position or quickly achieves that orientation if it happens to land on its stock. As pull is exerted on the shank, the flukes rotate down and begin to penetrate the bottom. A gradual initial strain will help assure successful penetration. But if a strain is taken too fast it is possible for the anchor to skid along the bottom and refuse to take hold – especially if the boat is rapidly drifting back. Again, the shank must be near to horizontal or the anchor cannot take hold.

A Danforth will not usually penetrate or hold in gravel or weeds. In boulders and coral it may hold by acting as a hook. The Danforth is less convenient to carry on a bow roller than a plow. It stores flatter than a plow, but its long stock often makes it difficult to manipulate in and out of a locker. Watch out not to pinch your fingers between the flukes and the shank.

The Danforth company is now owned by Rule Industries and they have come out with several new anchors that carry the Danforth name which may cause confusion as to what is a true Danforth anchor. What they refer to as the Hi-Tensile and Standard Traditional Danforth Anchors are the latest versions of the original Danforth lightweight.

Figure 30.5
Danforth anchor burial. The Danforth has the best holding power when a straight pull is exerted.

Both of these clones follow the original Danforth design, but the Hi-Tensile is stronger and more expensive than the Standard. There is also a Danforth Deepset anchor, which is advertised as having increased holding power.

Further complicating the saga of Danforth anchors is the fact that many people incorrectly use the term Danforth as a generic term for any anchor that looks somewhat like the original Danforth design. In my opinion it is foolish to buy a Danforth copy unless the anchor has been tested and proven beyond doubt to be adequate.

Fisherman

The fisherman anchor is known as a kedge, old fashioned, Herreshoff, yachtsman, Nicholson, Luke, and a few other names, depending on design differences or the manufacturer. It wasn't so many years ago that this was the one and only anchor for boats, but it has been replaced by the CQR, Bruce, and Danforth.

The fisherman is not 'user friendly.' It is difficult to launch and recover, and cumbersome to carry and stow on deck. On modern boats it is hard to get a fisherman anchor into the water without putting a few dings in the gelcoat. Most fisherman anchors today come in three pieces (stock, shank, and arm), and are thus relatively easy to store in a locker. When a fisherman falls to the bottom and tension is applied in sand or mud, one fluke will dig in, but it can easily drag. It thus relies more on its weight than do the other types of anchors. Furthermore, the fisherman is much more likely to foul. Because so much of the anchor remains exposed the anchor line can easily become caught if the boat swings. If that happens, the fisherman can be rendered useless. The Herreshoff design improved on the traditional yachtsman anchor by making the flukes diamond-shaped rather than triangular. An even more streamlined fluke is sometimes used in which the fluke is straight or pick-like. But this type has virtually no holding power in sand because the small flukes offer little surface area resistance.

In spite of its disadvantages there is a definite place on board the offshore cruising boat for a fisherman anchor because it is a hooking, not a burying anchor, and it works well in rocky areas where the fluke can usually find something to catch on. Sometimes a plow or Bruce will also work in this situation but the fisherman is more reliable. The other instance where the fisherman may give you holding is when there is a surface crust that it can penetrate. Other anchors in this situation commonly fail to penetrate and may only slide along the surface.

The fisherman is also the most reliable when anchoring in loose gravel or pebbles. This is always one of the most difficult substrates to anchor in. To be effective, however, a fisherman must be heavy, and usually this means twice the weight of whatever CQR or Danforth is recommended for your boat.

Others

In addition to the anchors mentioned above, there are some that have special attributes. The stockless or Navy anchor relies mainly on its weight and the weight of attached chain. Its sheer mass and bulk do not make it a good small boat anchor. The Northill often offers good holding in sand and excellent holding in rocks. However it is very difficult to handle and to store on the boat. A rock pick, which is like a large fishhook, is effective in rocky substrates but it has no other use. A grappling hook with three or more prongs can serve as a lunch hook in a rocky bottom and is handy for recovering lost chain.

How Much Weight?

Although it seems reasonable to think of weight as an important factor in selecting the proper anchor, it is not as important as anchor design. In fact it is a combination of bottom type, anchor type, scope, catenary, and weight for any given boat that must be considered in relationship to the drag forces of wind, wave, and current.

Weight *is* indirectly important in some anchors because of the need for greater fluke area to achieve greater holding power; i.e. a larger surface area of the flukes means a larger and usually heavier anchor. All anchor manufacturers give their recommendations on the proper anchor for your boat in terms of the anchor's weight, but of course it is really the size of the flukes that makes the difference with a burying anchor.

With regard to manufacturers' recommendations, keep in mind that they may not have an offshore cruising boat in mind. We make up a very small part of their business. Sometimes they will indicate the drag force that their anchor will resist, but they usually base their recommendations on coastal cruising boats. Most offshore sailors will increase a manufacturer's recommendation to the next larger size.

Lacking any other information, a general rule of thumb for the Danforth or CQR is one pound (0.45 kg) of anchor weight for each foot (0.3 m) of boat length. In the case of the fisherman anchor it would be about two pounds of anchor weight for each foot of boat length.

Whatever anchors you buy, make a point of personally selecting your anchor from the distributor. Anchors may vary considerably in actual weight, so take the trouble to weigh them when you buy. You might as well get the most anchor for your money.

Anchor Rodes

Too often, inexperienced sailors buy cheap, poorly made, or non-certified chain, shackles, swivels, and rope to put on their newly purchased expensive boats. Sometimes this is done out of ignorance or to save money, but it also results from poor advice and confusion over terminology. We are confronted with a plethora of vague and similar-sounding terms such as minimum tensile strength, maximum tensile strength, average tensile strength, maximum working load, average working load, working load limit, breaking load, and breaking strength. It isn't enough to guess at what these terms mean or to assume what they mean.

Chain Load Terminology

Breaking load, proof load, and working load are the important buzz-words for chain.

Minimum breaking load This is sometimes referred to as 'minimum ultimate load.' It is the same as 'breaking load' or 'breaking strength' and is the load at which the chain breaks when repeated samples are tested on a standard test machine. Usually breaking load is two to five times the working load. It is important to know the specifics for your chain.

Proof load This is referred to sometimes as 'proof test.' It is a test load that is applied to chain during or after manufacture to find possible defects. It is half of the breaking load and twice the working load. It should be possible to obtain a certification of proof load from the manufacturer. In a proof test, the chain is stressed to twice its recommended working load (a quarter of supposed breaking load), and then each link is inspected for fracture or distortion.

Working load Also referred to as 'working load limit.' This is the most important term. It is 20 to 25 percent of the breaking load. This is the number that you should be sure you know for your chain. Don't confuse it with any other 'load' data.

For example, a working load of 750 pounds (337.5 kg) would typically have a proof load of 1500 pounds (2 × 750) and a breaking load of 3000 pounds (4 × 750).

Types of Chain

The two broad categories of chain are open and stud link. The latter, however, is only for heavy chain of the type used on large commercial and military ships. Open link is what is used on sailboats, and there are four types to be considered: proof coil, BBB, high-test, and alloy. All of these look about the same, but they are different in several ways.

Table 30.2
Proof coil chain charac-teristics. Grade 30 proof coil chain's minimum breaking load is 4 times working load limit. Proof load is 2 times working load limit. Table from Crosby Group, Inc.

Table 2

Trade size (in.)	Size material (in.)	Working load limit (lbs.)	Maximum inside length (in.)	Minimum inside width (in.)	Maximum length 100 links (in.)	Weight per 100 feet (lbs.)
$3/16$	.217	800	.98	.30	98	39
$1/4$	.276	1300	1.24	.38	124	65
$5/16$	.315	1900	1.29	.44	129	100
$3/8$	.394	2650	1.38	.55	138	144
$1/2$	.512	4500	1.79	.72	179	250
$5/8$	.630	6900	2.20	.79	220	421
$3/4$	.787	10600	2.75	.98	275	649

Proof coil Proof coil chain (Table 2) is manufactured from low-grade carbon steel and is widely used throughout the industry. Different manufacturers will have slightly different types of chain within this category. For each type, the manufacturer's product description will indicate strength.

BBB For a given size of chain, BBB is made up of shorter links and is stronger, more flexible, and heavier. Every link is inspected as part of the manufacturing process. BBB is being phased out and is now difficult to find.

High-test High-test, or high-strength chain (Table 3) is considered by some to be advantageous for small boats because of its high strength-to-weight ratio. This chain is manufactured from higher tensile carbon steel (hardened and tempered) and is much stronger than the lower grade carbon steel used for proof coil chain.

Alloy chain One step up from high-test. It is made of steel alloy (Table 4).

The supposed advantage of high-test and alloy chain is that you can carry a smaller size and therefore lighter chain, or carry additional chain for the same weight as proof coil. This advantage, however, is not as attractive as it first appears, for two reasons. Whereas proof coil chain is easy and inexpensive to regalvanize the same process for high tensile chain is more complicated and not widely available. Furthermore, high-test and alloy chain lose strength due to embrittlement when they are hot-dip galvanized. Thus the working loads given need to be reduced by at least 10 percent for high-test and 30 percent for alloy to allow for galvanizing. Each time the chain is subsequently galvanized its strength will be further reduced. For some chain it is recommended that it only be regalvanized once.

Another disadvantage of high-test chain for the cruising boat is that using smaller size high-test chain means you will need greater scope (hence longer chain) to have adequate weight to produce the proper

Table 30.3
High test chain. Grade 40 high test chain's minimum breaking load is 3 times working load limit. Proof load is 2 times working load limit. Table from Crosby Group, Inc.

Table 3

Trade size (in.)	Size material (in.)	Working load limit (lbs.)	Maximum inside length (in.)	Minimum inside width (in.)	Maximum length 100 links (in.)	Weight per 100 feet (lbs.)
$1/4$	.276	2600	1.24	.38	124	70
$5/16$	.315	3900	1.29	.44	129	106
$3/8$	.394	5400	1.38	.55	138	154
$7/16$	.468	7200	1.40	.65	129	205
$1/2$	.512	9200	1.79	.72	179	267
$5/8$	.630	11500	2.20	.79	220	402
$3/4$	.787	16200	2.76	.98	276	567

catenary for shock absorption. Finally there is a financial consideration. The initial cost of high-test chain is nearly twice that of proof coil.

Hence, the final decision on whether it is to your advantage to buy standard proof coil chain or opt for the more expensive high-strength chain will depend on what and where you expect to sail, and how critical weight is to your boat.

Galvanizing

No matter which chain you decide on, you want the chain to be hot-dip galvanized to protect it from seawater. Sometimes chain is listed as 'self-color.' This is the term given for chain as originally manufactured and before galvanizing. When buying chain, be sure the strength and price are based on hot-dip galvanized chain.

Windlass Compatibility

If you are buying a windlass to fit existing chain or chain to live with an existing windlass be sure they are compatible. Some windlasses have interchangeable wildcats (the sprockets on the anchor windlasses that grasp the chain as the chain is hauled in and out). Take the wildcat head with you when shopping for chain, or try a short test piece of chain on your windlass. This compatibility cannot be overstressed. If the chain and wildcat do not fit together properly it is possible to lose control of the chain as it is being hauled in or let out. The result could cause injury to you and damage to your boat.

Rope

It is less complicated to select anchor line than it is to select chain. Nylon line has become the standard for anchoring, and few experienced sailors will use anything else. Nylon line is characterized by its great strength and its high stretch. Under load it will stretch 15 to 30 percent. The most common type of nylon for anchoring is three-strand. Nylon

Table 30.4
Alloy chain. Grade 80 alloy chain's minimum breaking load is 4 times working load limit. Proof load is 2.5 times working load limit. Table from Crosby Group, Inc.

Table 4

Trade size (in.)	Size material (in.)	Working load limit (lbs.)	Maximum inside length (in.)	Minimum inside width (in.)	Maximum length 100 links (in.)	Weight per 100 feet (lbs.)
$9/32$ $(1/4)$	.276	3500	.90	.34	90	72
$5/16$	.343	4500	1.00	.48	100	108
$3/8$	.394	7100	1.25	.49	125	148
$1/2$	.512	12000	1.64	.64	164	243
$5/8$	.630	18100	2.02	.79	202	351
$3/4$	.787	28300	2.52	.98	252	584
$7/8$	.866	34200	2.77	1.08	277	705

braid is also available, and although it is easier to handle than three-strand, it is usually only half as elastic, and quite a bit more expensive.

As with chain, we are faced with the need to understand the varied descriptions used by different manufacturers and the meaning and limits of relative strength of anchor line when selecting what we need.

In deciding on the proper size three-strand nylon rope for anchor line, it is important to determine breaking strength (Table 5). This may be called 'average breaking strength,' 'breaking load,' 'tensile strength,' or some other term, depending on the manufacturer. By knowing the breaking load you can determine a proper working load strength for your boat.

For nylon three-strand line the recommended working load is only 11 percent of the breaking strength of the line. Furthermore, this recommendation is based on nylon line that has been well cared for and is in good condition. It also assumes that the eye splices are properly made and protected from chafe.

Thus, reading the ABYC table (Table 1) you would choose a nylon line in which 11 percent of its breaking strength would be compatible with loading equivalent to winds of 30 knots. For example, a 35-foot boat could expect loading of about 900 pounds in 30 knots of wind. A half-inch nylon line would provide more than enough strength and stretch, i.e. 11 percent of the 9000-pound breaking load.

For ground tackle there is a natural tendency to be tempted by the bigger-is-better philosophy and to assume that added protection is gained by buying anchor line of a size larger than recommended. However, the advantage of nylon as anchor line is its ability to stretch – its shock-absorbing characteristic. You can think of the anchor line as a huge rubber band. In heavy weather conditions the line is constantly

Table 30.5

Strength of 3-strand nylon line. Table from New England Ropes.

Table 5

Diameter		Weight	Tensile
(in.)	(mm)	(lbs./100')	strength
3/16	5	1.0	1,200
1/4	6	1.5	2,000
5/16	8	2.5	3,000
3/8	9	3.5	4,400
7/16	11	5.0	5,900
1/2	12	6.5	7,500
9/16	14	8.2	9,400
5/8	16	10.5	12,200
3/4	18	14.5	16,700
7/8	22	20.0	23,500
1	25	26.4	29,400

stretching and retracting. Without this attribute there would be tremendous strain put on the boat's deck fittings and a constant cyclical tugging at the anchor that could jerk it out of the bottom. If you use three-strand nylon that is too big for your boat it will not stretch.

Because the average working load of nylon line is taken at 11 percent of breaking strength, it means there is a significant safety margin for occasional heavy loads. However, a boat should carry one anchor line in new condition that is kept only for emergency or storm conditions. Furthermore, whenever you have endured a sustained period of time anchored under storm conditions, the anchor line should be carefully examined. If there is any doubt as to its strength it should be replaced.

There are a few sailors who choose to use polypropylene line for anchoring because it floats and it is cheaper than nylon. In my opinion this is a mistake. Polypropylene has only half the stretch of nylon, it is much harder to handle, and it deteriorates when exposed to sunlight for a long period of time. The fact that it floats may help keep it from being fouled or caught in the propeller, but this can also be prevented with a bit of care, and the slight advantage of a floating line does not offset the strength, stretch, and durability of three-strand nylon.

The Cruiser's Choice

Most cruising sailors prefer an all-chain rode for routine anchoring. Although this means a bit more work in anchoring and added weight and expense, chain is good insurance and gives peace of mind. When I think back to my earlier cruising when I only had rope, I recall repeated problems with the anchor not holding, of swinging in a wide arc with the danger of hitting other boats, and especially the frequent need to use two anchors. Since I began using all-chain rode I cannot recall a single time I have needed two anchors, other than when sitting out a typhoon. All-chain rode also makes it easier in a crowded anchorage because less scope is needed.

Some people claim that rope is easier to use than chain, but that is only true if you do not have a proper anchor windlass. In my experience, chain is easier to use than rope because it pays out easier and is more convenient to stow.

Shackles and Swivels

How many times have you seen (or used) an undersized and understrength shackle to connect an anchor to the anchor chain because the pin on the proper strength shackle would not fit through the chain link or because you did not have a proper shackle onboard? This is a common practice. Take a look around any marina – some of the Rube Goldberg lash-ups between the anchor and the chain are truly amazing.

Some sailors buy the cheapest shackles they can find. Obviously, however, ground tackle is no stronger than its weakest part, and even if you have proper chain and line, you need other fittings of the same or greater strength.

You will notice a variety of shackles in your chandlery. The two principal shapes are chain shackles and anchor shackles. The anchor shackle (Table 6) is bowed and designed so that when used with an eye or thimble there is no friction or binding. There are also several types of pin styles available, but the common screw pin is quite adequate. Be sure the pin is wired or well moused each time it is used so it will not back out. If the pin or shackle becomes worn it should be retired from active duty.

A proper shackle or swivel is galvanized and will have its size and breaking strength embossed on the body. If your chandlery does not carry this type of shackle keep looking until you find the proper kind. It would be ridiculous to lose your boat because of a cheap shackle.

Oversized 'end links' on your anchor chain will make it easier to connect the chain to anchors or line. If you are buying new chain, some manufacturers will sell you specific lengths provided with oversized end

Table 30.6
Screw pin anchor shackle. Breaking load is 5 times working load limit. Proof load is 2.2 times working load limit. Table from Crosby Group, Inc.

Table 6

Nominal size (in.)	Working load limit (tons)	Dimensions (in.)										
		A	B	C	D	E	F	G	H	L	M	P
$3/8$	2	.66	.44	1.44	.38	1.03	.91	1.78	2.49	.25	2.03	.38
$7/16$	2.6	.75	.50	1.69	.44	1.16	1.06	2.03	2.91	.31	2.38	.44
$1/2$	3.3	.81	.63	1.88	.50	1.31	1.19	2.31	3.28	.38	2.69	.50
$5/8$	5	1.06	.75	2.38	.63	1.69	1.50	2.94	4.19	.44	3.34	.69
$3/4$	7	1.25	.88	2.81	.75	2.00	1.81	3.50	4.97	.50	3.97	.81
$7/8$	9.5	1.44	1.00	3.31	.88	2.28	2.09	4.03	5.83	.50	4.50	.97
1	12.5	1.69	1.13	3.75	1.00	2.69	2.38	4.69	6.56	.56	5.07	1.06
$1 1/8$	15	1.81	1.25	4.25	1.16	2.91	2.69	5.16	7.47	.63	5.59	1.25
$1 1/4$	18	2.03	1.38	4.69	1.29	3.25	3.00	5.75	8.25	.69	6.16	1.38
$1 3/8$	21	2.25	1.50	5.25	1.42	3.63	3.31	6.38	9.16	.75	6.84	1.50

links. Otherwise you can take the chain to a welder and have special links added. This may be a rather major task, and will also mean that the chain or at least the new links will need to be galvanized. A good time to add oversized end links would be just before the chain is regalvinized. In either situation *be sure* that the end links will fit through your chain pipe.

Without end links you can still make proper connections of adequate strength with the correct shackles. The problem comes with being sure that the pin of the proper size shackle will fit through the chain link. Chain manufacturers sell shackles to fit their chain, and recommend using the next larger size shackle for any give chain size. On my boat I have 3/8" proof coil chain and can use 1/2" anchor shackles.

Opinions vary on the use of swivels. I use a swivel because it prevents twisting of the chain if the boat swings when anchored. I feel that the less stress and twisting put on the chain, the longer it will last. However, like shackles, the swivel must be certified for its strength by the manufacturer. If you use a swivel of the type that has a fork fitting on one end, the fork should not be secured to the anchor because it can be subjected to bending forces and break. A better choice are swivels with eyes on both ends (Table 7). If you only have a swivel with a fork connector, there should be a shackle between it and the anchor.

Table 30.7
Chain swivels. Breaking load is 5 times working load limit. Table from Crosby Group, Inc.

Table 7

Size (in).	G-401 Stock no. Galv	Working load limit (lbs.)	Weight each (lbs.)	Dimensions (in.)											
				A	B	C	D	E	G	J	M	R	T	U	V
1/4	1016233	850	.13	1.25	.69	.75	.62	1.12	.25	.69	.31	2.25	2.75	1.69	1.25
5/16	1016251	1250	.25	1.63	.81	1.00	.75	1.38	.31	.81	.38	2.72	3.34	2.06	1.47
3/8	1016279	2500	.61	2.00	.94	1.25	1.00	1.75	.38	1.00	.50	3.44	4.19	2.50	1.88
1/2	1016297	3600	1.12	2.50	1.31	1.50	1.25	2.25	.50	1.31	.63	4.25	5.25	3.19	2.44
5/8	1016313	5200	1.75	3.00	1.56	1.75	1.50	2.75	.62	1.50	.75	5.13	6.31	3.88	2.94
3/4	1016331	7200	3.09	3.50	1.75	2.00	1.75	3.25	.75	1.88	.88	5.78	7.22	4.94	3.46

Selecting an Anchoring System

In this section we will consider the selection of ground tackle following the ABYC table of horizontal loads.

Conventional wisdom suggests equipping your boat with adequate ground tackle to deal comfortably with 42 knots of wind. This is taken to be your storm anchor and storm rode. Within this category there is sufficient safety margin to cover the unusual or unexpected Beaufort 11 or more violent conditions. Remember, this assumes that your gear has been well maintained and frequently inspected. It does not cover the situation where you buy a set of ground tackle, let it sit forgotten in the bilge or lazarette for 10 years, and then expect it to protect you the first time it is used.

Recall that the working load of three-strand nylon line is taken at 11 percent of breaking load, and that for chain the breaking load is generally three to five times the working load. Likewise certified shackles are rated higher than the chain with which they are used. Hence, our objective is to put together a 'system' of anchoring equipment that is geared to working-load conditions of a steady moderate gale – Beaufort 9 or 42 knots of wind. In my opinion every boat that goes offshore should have this as a minimum, plus some redundancy.

The equipment to be surveyed includes the CQR, the traditional Danforth Hi-Tensile, the Bruce, and the Fisherman-type anchors. I select these because they are the typical anchors found on full-time cruising boats, and they have proven themselves with many years of success.

For convenience let us consider a 32-foot sailboat with a beam of 10 feet. Referring to the ABYC table (Table 1) we move up to the LOA category of 35 feet. From this we find that our target number for working anchor conditions is 1800 pounds. Subsequent selection of chain, rope, and shackles is based on this. (Note that manufacturers use different methods to make anchor size recommendations. Contact them directly for details.)

CQR

Table 8 shows the recommendations made by Simpson-Lawrence, the manufacturers of the genuine CQR. As can be seen, they give some leeway in making a decision for our sample 32-foot boat, and recommend anchors from 25 to 35 pounds. I would consider 25 pounds as a minimum, and prefer the 35 pound, especially for serious cruising.

Bruce

Suggestions made by Bruce are shown in Table 9. They use a different approach but we can go by their suggestions for working anchors, which they recommend up to Beaufort 7 (30 knots) and storm anchors for force 9 conditions. Their recommendations are for a 22-pound Bruce as a storm anchor and an 11-pounder as a working anchor. They also recommend a minimum chain lead of 20 feet of 5/16" chain on 1/2" three-strand nylon anchor line.

I consider this advice a bit optimistic, and would feel more comfortable with the next size larger anchor. Most cruising boats I have seen have had Bruce anchors larger than those recommended in Table 9.

Table 8

Boat length feet/meters	CQR WEIGHTS IN POUNDS						
	15	20	25	35	45	60	75
8 m/26 ft	▓	▓					
10 m/32.5 ft		▓	▓	▓			
12 m/39 ft				▓	▓		
14 m/45.5ft				▓	▓		
16 m/52 ft					▓		
18 m/58.5 ft					▓	▓	
20 m/65 ft						▓	▓
22 m/71.5 ft						▓	▓
24 m/78 ft						▓	▓
26 m/84.5 ft							▓
Recommended chain size	$1/4$"/6 mm	$5/16$"/8 mm	$5/16$"/8 mm	$5/16$"/8 mm	$3/8$"/10 mm	$7/16$"/8 mm	$9/16$"/14 mm

Table 30.8
CQR anchor recommendations. Data supplied by Simpson Lawrence, Ltd.

Danforth Traditional Hi-Tensile

Two tables (10a and 10b) are used to determine the recommended Danforth. Table 10a offers suggested minimum holding for winds of 20 knots and 60 knots, and Table 10b refers specifically to the Hi-Tensile traditional Danforth. Following their recommendations for our 32-footer we would consider minimum holding of 1200 pounds for 20 knots of wind and 2300 pounds for 60-knot winds. These numbers are confusing and difficult to correlate with the ABYC calculations; however, the Danforth numbers suggest to me a 20-pound working anchor and either a 35-pound or 60-pound for maximum protection – although it would appear the 35-pound Danforth Hi-Tensile should be quite adequate in the latter case.

Fisherman

In this case the general rule is two pounds of anchor weight for each foot of boat length. That rule of thumb seems to be simply a matter of convention and experience without much scientific basis. However, unless there is something for it to hook on to, you are relying mainly on weight and scope.

Chain

In selecting chain for our 32-foot cruising boat we again consider the horizontal load for Beaufort 9 conditions and want a chain which has a working load or maximum working load of 1800 pounds. For proof coil (Table 2) this would be $5/16$". It will have a working load value of

Table 30.9
Bruce anchor recommendations. Data supplied by Bruce International, Ltd.

Table 9

Anchor weight				Maximum boat dimensions						Rode				Minimum		Anchor shackle			
Storm		Working		Length O.A.		Beam Sail		Beam Power		Nylon Rope Dia.		Chain dia.		chain length		Pin dia.		Body dia.	
kg	lb	kg	lb	m	ft	m	ft	mm	ft	mm	ins	mm	ins	m	ft	mm	ins	mm	ins
2	4.4	–	–	5	16	2.1	6.9	2.3	7.5	10	3/8	6	1/4	1.8	6	8	5/16	6	1/4
5	11	2	4.4	7	23	2.7	8.9	2.9	9.5	10	3/8	6	1/4	4.3	14	8	5/16	6	1/4
7.5	16.5	5	11	8.5	28	3.0	9.8	3.3	10.8	10	3/8	6	1/4	6.1	20	8	5/16	6	1/4
10	22	5	11	9.8	32	3.3	10.8	3.6	11.8	14	1/2	8	5/16	6.1	20	10	3/8	8	5/16
15	33	7.5	16.5	12	39	3.8	12.5	4.2	13.8	16	5/8	10	3/8	6.7	22	11	7/16	10	3/8
20	44	10	22	14	46	4.2	13.8	4.6	15.1	16	5/8	10	3/8	7.0	23	11	7/16	10	3/8
30	66	15	33	17.4	57	4.8	15.7	5.4	17.7	22	7/8	13	1/2	7.9	26	16	5/8	13	1/2
50	110	20	44	22	72	5.6	18.4	6.3	20.7	25	1	16	5/8	8.5	28	19	3/4	16	5/8
80	176	30	66	27.5	90	6.3	20.7	7.0	23.0	32	1 1/4	19	3/4	9.4	31	22	7/8	19	3/4
110	242	50	110	32.3	106	7.3	23.9	8.1	26.6	38	1 1/2	22	7/8	10.4	34	25	1	22	7/8
150	330	80	176	38	125	8.6	28.2	9.2	30.2	44	1 3/4	25	1	11.0	36	29	1 1/8	25	1

Table 10a

Minimum suggested holding power for anchoring in winds to 20 knots	Boat length	Minimum suggested holding power for anchoring in winds to 60 knots
150 lbs.	0-10 ft.	270 lbs.
275	10–16	500
580	16–25	1050
900	25–30	1600
1285	30–34	2300
1575	34–38	2850
1960	38–44	3550
2940	44–54	5300
3420	54–60	6150
4070	60–66	7400
4760	66–72	8150

Table 10b

Holding power (lbs.)	Weight (lbs.)
500	5
960	12
1500	20
1800	35
3100	60
3600	90
4000	150
4400	190

Table 30.10
Danforth anchor recommendations. Data supplied by The Rule Group.

a Holding power in winds of 20 and 60 knots

b Holding power and anchor weight

nearly 1900 pounds and a breaking load of four times this much, and should provide an adequate margin of safety for an unexpected storm. For cruising I recommend a minimum of 200 feet of chain.

Rope

Recalling that the working load for three-strand nylon anchor line should be 11 percent of the breaking load, our 32-footer should have $1/2$" or $9/16$" line (Table 5). That is 11 percent of a tensile strength of 9400 pounds, which gives a working load of 1034 pounds. This is what we want for 30-knot (Beaufort 7) working anchor conditions, but what about Beaufort 9 and 11?

The problem is that if we go to a heavy nylon three-strand line to match the force 9 and 11 conditions, we will lose its most important property – elasticity. Instead, we should rely on the ability of the 1/2" or 9/16" line to bear an occasional 50-percent load. Following such storm loading, the line should be thoroughly examined and probably replaced – at least as a storm rode.

When using a nylon line and chain lead you must decide how much chain to use, and there are varied opinions on this. Some say the length should be equal to the sum of the boat's draft plus the height of freeboard at the bow. This assures that the anchor will be clear of the bottom when the chain/rope connection comes aboard and the boat can be gotten underway. The manufacturer of CQR recommends a minimum of one foot of chain per each foot of boat length.

Certainly the minimum should be an amount of chain that is equal in weight to the anchor. Beyond that, the more chain the better, and if the manufacturer gives a minimum figure, it should be adhered to. Furthermore, when anchoring in coral there should be sufficient chain to assure that none of the rope will come in contact with a coral head, even if it means adding buoys to the anchor line.

Shackles and Swivels

Shackles and swivels should be one size larger than the chain in use, provided the shackles are compatible in quality with the chain. Thus, from Table 6 we would choose 3/8" shackles. If the decision is made to also add a swivel it should likewise be of the same quality and size as the shackle (Table 7).

Is it Enough?

By following the above recommendations have we guaranteed that we can meet any anchoring challenge? Provided there is enough scope, the foregoing recommendations should be adequate for almost any situation. The ABYC estimates are conservative, and we have chosen the maximum in the various categories. Naturally it would be possible to call for larger anchors and heavier chain, but it would probably be a waste of money and add unneeded weight to the boat.

In the case of ground tackle it is better to buy more, rather than larger, gear. This is to see you through if you should lose or be forced to abandon your anchor and rode some day, and it also means you can lay out additional anchors if necessary.

Anchor Windlass

There is a lot of convenience in an electric or hydraulic windlass, but there is a greater amount of inconvenience if it doesn't work properly. And there is ample opportunity for a windlass that sits up on the bow of a sailboat constantly subjected to waves and spray, to go on the blink. For a boat up to 40 or even 45 feet I recommend a manual anchor windlass. Furthermore, I recommend that it have a horizontal axis that permits the operator to stand up and use a back-and-forth cranking motion. This is far superior to the vertical shaft type which requires you to hunker down on deck to crank in the anchor. The Simpson-Lawrence manual windlasses have been around for a while, and seem to have stood the test of time.

If you do decide to install an electric or hydraulic windlass, be sure it can be conveniently operated manually as well. This means actually trying it out in the manual mode and thinking about how it will be to bring in 200 feet of chain and a heavy anchor.

The windlass should be located as far aft on the foredeck as is possible and convenient. The chain locker should also be as far aft as possible. This keeps a great deal of weight out of the bow and helps maintain fore and aft trim. It also makes working on deck easy and safer.

With any kind of windlass it is necessary to have a hefty backing plate belowdecks. Otherwise, the windlass can be torn loose if a sudden or unavoidable storm load is imposed on it. For fiberglass boats the windlass should be mounted on a wood base to prevent the deck from being crushed.

Snubbers

A windlass has only one purpose. It is to lift and control the chain as it goes out and as it comes in. It is not a cleat or a samson post, and it should not be used to hold the boat at anchor. As soon as anchoring is completed the load on the chain should be transferred to one or more snubber lines. These are lines of three-strand nylon that transfer the load from the windlass to one or more deck cleats. The chain between the windlass and the point where the snubber is attached should be slack.

In addition to the favor it does the windlass, the snubber adds to the elasticity of the anchor rode. In fair weather conditions most of the spring in the chain will be taken up by catenary but if it really begins to blow, the nylon snubbers fulfill a critical role in preventing the anchor from pulling out of the bottom, or a cleat or the windlass from being ripped off the deck.

Snubbers can be attached to the chain by a chain hook, by tying a rolling hitch in the line, or by a chain stopper. The chain stopper is the best choice. It gives the best protection because it shares the load with two lines to deck cleats. The chain hook is to be avoided because it puts a kink in the chain and reduces its effectiveness.

No one seems to offer advice on how long the snubber lines should be. Mine are each 40 feet long and I normally deploy them about 20 to 25 feet from the deck. Be sure to give the snubber lines adequate chafe protection where they pass through chocks or fairleads on deck.

Chain Locker

As mentioned earlier, if your boat is a typical racer-cruiser it will be necessary to build a chain locker. It needs to be nearly directly below the windlass and again, as far aft as convenient and possible. Make the locker spacious. If it is too narrow the chain will pile up as it is delivered from the windlass, and will eventually need to be knocked down or it will refuse to feed into the locker. This can be extremely inconvenient for a shorthanded or singlehanded crew.

The bitter end of the chain should be tied securely with line near the base of the chain locker to a strong bulkhead or other solid part of the boat. The purpose of this is too keep from losing the chain if, for example, the brake on the windlass fails when you are cranking the chain in or out. On the other hand, the line from the chain to the boat should be accessible so that it can be cut in an emergency.

Fair Weather Anchoring

Anchoring problems are usually blamed on the wind, the waves, the anchor, or poor holding. But human error accounts for most of the problems.

There is seldom any great rush to get the hook down quickly in a new anchorage. A 'do it quick' attitude sometimes comes about from the feeling that everyone is watching us to see what mistakes we will make. Careful preparation, no matter how long it takes, is better.

Overconfidence is also an invitation to mistakes, and too many experienced sailors have lost their boats because of it.

Reading the Chart

A sailing chart offers far more information than we normally use. Details of harbors include reefs, rocks, shoals and other hazards, but there is more.

When studying a chart to select an anchorage, notice the curvature of the shoreline and estimate how winds from different directions will develop swell. Look at the bottom characteristics; if most of the bottom is sand or mud but one portion is rocky, you can be sure the rocky area exists in response to wave action, and you will want to avoid that area for anchoring.

Study the topography of the land. Notice where you hope to anchor with regard to hills and valleys. An anchorage in front of a valley may result in windy conditions. Likewise, anchoring at the mouth of a river can mean strong currents – especially in tidal areas. Determine what kind of wind conditions could put you on a lee shore and consider what your options will be for getting underway if that happens. Determine from the chart the kind of bottom conditions to be expected. The more detailed your chart is, the better this information will be.

If the area is new to you, try to find out as much as possible about the place where you plan to anchor. Be aware of the location of underwater powerlines or pipelines which restrict anchoring, and especially, overhead power lines that limit access. Stay well clear of ferryboat routes. They have legal obligations to maintain specific passageways, but if you are anchored too close to their route you will be constantly disturbed by their wake.

When planning an anchorage in advance, select some alternatives. The desired bay may be full of aquaculture operations. What appears on your chart as a remote cove with a tiny village may turn out to be a busy, crowded harbor not at all favorable to anchoring.

The sailing chart is the main source of information, but it is not the only one. For all popular sailing areas of the world there are cruising guide books, and many of them have detailed maps and suggestions on specific anchorages.

Preparing to Anchor

When nearing land an anchor should be made ready. If you have been on a long passage, you will need to move an anchor from a locker to the bow – often a difficult and dangerous job while still at sea. It may be easier to first rig an anchor ready for deployment at the stern. I normally do this while still at sea, and then attach the bow anchor after I am within the protected water of the anchorage.

Final Decisions

Once you are in the harbor or anchorage, slow down and evaluate the situation. One of the most important things you can do in a new place is sail or motor around to check depths. I sometimes spend 30 minutes or more doing this in a new place. Even after I have decided where I intend to anchor, I go back and forth across the area to be sure there are no unexpected obstructions and to assess how the wind will affect my drift during the process of anchoring.

Notice if the other boats are using rope or chain, and if they are using one or two anchors. It is advisable, and absolutely proper procedure, to ask anyone who is anchored what type of bottom exists and the kind of anchor they are using. Don't be shy. Other cruisers are always willing to share this information. Their advice may save you time and trouble.

When ready to anchor, check that everything is ready. Specific preparations will depend on how your ground tackle is rigged, but the foredeck should be cleared of any unnecessary gear. Check to see that the anchor line or chain is ready to run free, the windlass has been tested, all shackles have been wired, and that the foredeck and cockpit crew both understand the anchoring plan and have worked out some simple hand signals for communication.

Let the anchor hang free from the bow roller so it can be lowered quickly when you reach the desired spot. Slowly make an upwind approach with enough speed to maintain steerage. Let the boat ease to a stop by dropping the jib or putting the engine in neutral, so that the boat is almost dead in the water. If you have made some practice runs before, this should be easy. Then, using the wind and with some help from the engine as necessary, the boat should begin to move aft. If you are using the engine, back down at low RPMs – about idle speed. At this time the anchor is let go smoothly but not too fast. Whoever is controlling the anchor line should know the water depth and be able to watch the depth marks on the anchor line or chain as it is paid out. If too much line is let go too fast, it can pile up on top of the anchor and become tangled or prevent it from setting. If too little line is let go the anchor will not take proper hold and drag, and the boat will drift.

When a scope of about three times depth has been achieved the anchor line should be snubbed by taking a turn on a cleat or setting the brake on the anchor windlass. If there is any wind let it control this initial set and put your engine in neutral. Achieving a proper set requires a gentle touch – applying too much engine power at this time can easily destroy all of your previous work, because the anchor can be jerked free of the bottom and refuse to set. This is true with almost any kind of anchor in some substrates.

Keep the boat at a three-to-one scope until you feel it is no longer moving aft. Take your time. Then continue to back down in response to the wind or by using the engine at low power until you have the proper scope.

When desired scope is achieved, the final set is made using the engine if possible. It is important to continue a slow and smooth technique at this point. Gradually increase reverse power in small increments. Bring up the engine speed by 200 RPMs and let it remain for a minute or two. Then increase another 200 RPMs. As this is going on the rudder must be tended to keep the boat from swinging. At the same time the crew should keep their hand or foot lightly touching the anchor line to feel for bumping or vibration that indicates the anchor is moving across the bottom. The anchor should be well set by the time you have proper scope and engine RPMs equivalent to about half power.

If you are unable to get a proper set the only alternative is to bring the anchor back aboard and start over. When the anchor comes up, notice if any of the bottom sediment has stuck to it. This may offer a clue to the problem. Otherwise try again – and maybe again and again. Sometimes a second, third or fourth attempt will finally be successful. Other times it will be necessary to kick the windlass (if you are wearing shoes), cuss a bit under your breath, and then try to find a new place with a more favorable substrate. Try not to snarl at your crew. At this point they are just as frustrated as you are.

After Anchoring

Once a proper set is made, the work is not over. Give the boat some time to settle down. This is a good time to clean and tidy up the foredeck and add chafing gear to the anchor rope or the snubber line to the anchor chain. When those tasks are done take a round of bearings with the hand-bearing compass. Sight on at least three and if possible four prominent objects. If you are doing this in daylight, consider what objects you may be able to see at night. If you are in an anchorage with no lights it is sometimes possible to see the outline of a cliff or a prominent rock even at night if conditions remain clear. Occasionally check your position until you are comfortable that your anchor is doing its job. Any time there is a significant windshift or any time you 'feel' things may not be quite right, recheck your bearings.

Plan an escape route. If an unexpected wind should come up that might cause you to drift into danger at night or in restricted visibility, you may need to move the boat under difficult conditions and in limited visibility. Write down the heading(s) that you will need to exit your anchorage.

When the situation permits, take the opportunity to dive on your anchor to see exactly how it lies. You may be surprised. If it is not convenient to dive, but the water is clear, use the dinghy and take a look at the anchor with a dive mask or underwater viewer. Actually seeing the anchor well buried gives a lot or reassurance. Seeing that it is poorly positioned should give you the stimulus to improve the situation.

If there is any indication of increasing wind, or the likelihood of the approach of heavy weather, consider laying out a second anchor. If you need to do so, the earlier it is done the easier it will be. Trying to row out an anchor in windy, choppy waves is difficult and dangerous.

It is just as well to accept the fact that anchoring is a spectator sport as much as baseball and bullfighting. Almost any time you anchor, the arena will be packed with eager spectators watching your performance. You are the star attraction on stage. The only difference is that you never know until the final curtain if the production has been a comedy, a tragedy, or an heroic adventure. It is seldom a love story.

PART 4
IN PORT

HEAVY WEATHER PROCEDURES IN PORT

There are plenty of books and sailing magazine articles about heavy weather at sea, but they seldom address what to do when the wind pipes up while at anchor, on a mooring, or tied to a dock. Yet cruising boats spend far more time in port than at sea. Although storms in port rarely involve the loss of life, they do account for far more severe yacht damage than storms at sea – damage that could be prevented by better preparation and more timely action.

In port we tend to let our guard down. The crew is having a good time sightseeing, snorkeling, completing boat chores, or enjoying the company of new friends. Little notice is taken of the barometer; we may forget to listen to the daily weather reports, and the weatherfax gathers dust. But heavy weather is as much an in-port as an offshore phenomenon.

This chapter emphasizes hurricane conditions because they are surely the most deadly and most specifically destructive storms. However, don't underestimate the fronts that each year manage to do their share of damage to anchored boats.

Safe Harbors

Some parts of the world are still sufficiently remote that there may be little warning of a storm approaching. Weather satellites are making this less common, but in their early stages, during the transition from tropical disturbance to tropical depression, damaging winds may be overlooked, under-estimated, even unreported.

Those who are used to home ports with storm-proof or nearly storm-proof harbors will seldom find such facilities in remote areas, and cruising sailors are often on their own to find a safe harbor in which to sit out a gale, storm, or hurricane. This fact alone is a good reason to bear in mind the statistics and stay out of the high-risk areas during storm seasons. Too often we push our luck because several years have gone by without a major storm in a particular area. French Polynesia had not had a hurricane in 23 years but in the austral summer of 1982-1983 there were five within five months.

It pays to maintain a 'storm mentality' even when cruising in the safe season. This means keeping in mind an escape route and option of where you can go if a windshift turns your anchorage into a lee shore. Take advantage of any available weather forecasts at least once a day.

To Stay or to Go

Before I began cruising I read a lot of books about how to deal with storms. More than one writer advised sometimes going to sea rather than remaining in port when a hurricane or significant period of heavy weather was on its way. When I read these suggestions I found it difficult to believe I would want to head out to sea with a hurricane on the way, and I hoped that I would never have to make that choice.

Now, after having experienced some hurricanes in port, I still feel it would be difficult to leave the safety of almost any anchorage with a large circular storm on the way. But there certainly could be times when such a decision would have to be made. I still hope I never have to.

The decision to try and put a lot of distance between yourself and the storm center must be made when the hurricane is still a long distance away, bearing in mind the storm center's position relative to your course, its anticipated track, and the type of winds to be expected. Otherwise, trying to outrun a storm in a sailboat is a fantasy. In advance of the depression there will be rough seas, strong winds, and difficult sailing. Just because your boat is capable of making seven knots, don't use that figure in planning your escape – you may be forced to go much slower in rough seas. Don't plan on using your engine to escape either, because the seas will probably be too rough to make this an option.

The truth is, by the time most people are willing to recognize the danger for what it is, the storm is too near to permit a safe escape. Furthermore, hurricanes often start out moving slowly and then rapidly accelerate as they build. Thus, if you elect to try and outrun a storm that is moving at five knots, don't expect it to continue at that speed.

Picking a Hurricane Anchorage

Staying in a marina is not necessarily a guarantee of safety in a hurricane. In many instances the best thing you can do is leave the marina and seek out a more protected place. Often marina pilings and docks are not storm-resistant, and there are always some boatowners who really don't care what happens to their boats. They fail to add extra lines and don't take the time to remove high-windage items. As a result, their boats put additional strain on the pilings and docks, and then may break loose and crash into boats that are properly prepared. The fact that they are insured will not do you any good if they hole your boat.

In seeking a safe anchorage there are several factors to keep in mind:
– wind
– waves and fetch
– tidal surge
– bottom composition
– depth
– type of shoreline
– other boats
– potential flying debris

The Way of the Wind

In most cases wind is not the main concern for the boat sitting out a hurricane. Rather it is the combination of wind and waves. If the fetch can be eliminated or reduced, a properly anchored boat will survive the wind.

Where wind *can* be a singular factor is in the case of a super typhoon or hurricane with sustained winds in excess of 130 knots. Under those conditions luck may play as big a role as anything else. But you can stack the deck in your favor by stripping the boat of all excess topside gear that creates windage. This will reduce the work required by your anchors and mooring lines to hold the vessel in place.

Two factors that may end up being a combination of good planning and good luck, or good planning and bad luck, is how the boat lies relative to the wind during the approach and the retreat of the hurricane, and where you happen to be relative to the eye of the storm. If the wind stays mainly on the bow or stern throughout the storm and the boat is securely anchored, chances for survival are greatly improved. But if the boat ends up beam-on to the strongest winds you will be lucky to get away without serious damage or loss.

Avoiding Fetch

Try to avoid areas where waves can build up over a long fetch of water, or at least endeavor to find a spot with the least amount of fetch. Preferably the potential fetch direction will not be the same as the direction from which the maximum winds are expected.

Under hurricane conditions large waves can build even with a short fetch. Your boat will withstand far more wind if there are no accompanying big waves. A wildly plunging bow will either work the anchors loose or put tremendous loads on the bow roller, chocks, and cleats. This situation also creates very dangerous conditions for the crew working on deck to adjust lines and improve chafing gear.

Escaping Tidal Surge

In places where there is a significant tide range the added effect of storm winds can create tremendous tidal increase or surge. It may exceed 20 feet above normal tide level. Take that into consideration when anchoring and tying off the boat. Nylon can stretch up to 50 percent, but under a huge tidal surge mooring lines have been known to snap and deck fittings to be ripped out of the hull.

Tidal surge was a major cause of damage when Hurricane Hugo moved away from the Caribbean and hit the southeast coast of the United States near Charleston, South Carolina, in 1989. In that broad coastal plain area, normal tides are about six feet. Storm tidal surge raised it to nearly 20 feet. Whole marinas, including floating docks and boats, were ripped from their moorings and carried away.

As a boat is lifted on the rising water it will lose more and more of its protection from the wind, and at the same time become more affected by fetch. In a tidal creek, for example, you may have good protection at low tide, but with a rising tide there will be more effect from the wind, and, if the tidal rise is accompanied by a tidal surge, the boat may be raised up until it has no wind protection at all. At the same time the surge may turn a tidal flat or marsh into a broad, flat expanse over which a significant fetch can build damaging waves.

The particularly devastating aspect of tidal surge is that it precedes the storm center and may put your boat in a much more vulnerable position when the main storm hits.

If you are in a tidal area, go as far inland as possible to distance yourself from the effects of tidal surge, which gradually decreases away from the coast.

Helping the Anchor

If you find an anchorage before the rest of the crowd, you have the privilege of deciding where you will settle in, and can take time to find good holding. Sandy mud, sand, and semi-compact mud are usually the best holding. Watch out for very soft mud, which can give a false feeling of security – the anchor may just sink and sink, but never find anything to take hold on. Long, narrow bays may appear to offer ideal storm protection, but provide lousy holding – especially if there is a river or stream that empties into the bay where the bottom is commonly composed of soft sediment and plant debris.

Sometimes the substrate will not be your main concern: If you are hiding out in a narrow tidal channel among the mangroves, tying off to the trees is your first line of defense, and the bottom is less important.

Staying Shallow

As a general rule it is a good idea to work your way into as shallow a depth as can be safely negotiated. This is especially true when tying off to mangroves or other trees. An added advantage of shallow depth is that it will put you farther away from larger boats and thus reduce the chance of being damaged by them. Even when anchoring in an open harbor, the shallower the depth, the greater the scope you can achieve with your anchor lines.

Selecting a Shoreline

An important factor in choosing the anchoring site is the surrounding shoreline. If the boat should break away from its anchor it is much better to drift onto a sandy beach than onto rocks or a coral reef.

Consider also the position of the storm anchorage in relation to the harbor entrance or reef passage. There is always the possibility of a boat being blown offshore if the anchors should fail. In Hurricane Hugo some boats in St. Thomas Harbor were reportedly blown out through the channel entrance and never seen again.

Choosing your Neighbors

As you make your final decision on where and how to lay out your anchors, take a look around you. The potential damage from other boats has to be one of the most frustrating and maddening problems to face when selecting a storm anchorage. It seems that neglectful owners are invariably well insured, so that if their boats are destroyed in the storm it may prove an inconvenience, but not much else. In some instances the owner may even hope the boat will be destroyed so he can buy a new one with the insurance money.

It is the uncared for, unattended, and improperly anchored boats that come adrift in a storm and wreak havoc with the other boats in the anchorage. This can be a problem of major proportions in areas where there is a large charter fleet. Boats used for bareboat chartering are often leased, not owned, by the charter company. When a major storm is coming, some charter operators put insufficient effort into properly anchoring the leased boats. This does not apply to all charter companies, and in fairness it must be said that they are usually understaffed to do the job properly. But the consequence is that these boats may end up destroying the uninsured boats of cruising live-aboard sailors.

There are also absentee owners who leave their boats at anchor for many months and only fly in now and then to go sailing. Chances are good that these yachts will go adrift in a major storm.

Likewise, watch out for huge, shallow-draft powerboats. Too often they will work their way into the shallow anchorages and then be improperly anchored. These monsters have so much windage that unless they are extremely well anchored they will go charging off on their own at the height of the tempest. Multihulls can also be a hazard to those nearby. Usually trimarans and catamarans can take advantage of the shallowest, and often the safest part of an anchorage, and offer no competition to displacement boats. However, in strong winds, multihulls can be picked up and moved by the wind and end up crashing into other boats.

Large and small commercial fishing boats are another class of vessel to be wary of. These boats are characterized by flat bottoms, heavy displacement, high windage, and poor maintenance, and in a major storm they frequently break loose from their moorings. They are roughly built of steel or wood and designed to take a lot of abuse. If one gets loose in a storm anchorage it can bounce around and destroy a lot of fiberglass boats in short order.

In addition to trying to select where you anchor, notice how boats that come after you arrange their anchoring. If you feel they are anchoring too close, you have every right to tell them so, and to politely but firmly request that they give you enough room to swing on your anchor, and to maneuver if you decide to get underway by sail. If someone anchoring near you is doing a poor job, you are well-advised to offer to help him. This may be that this is a first-time experience for the other boat, and they can use all of the help they can get. Either way you have to look out for your boat.

Airborne Hazards

Hurricane winds in the range of 70 to 100 knots pack a tremendous amount of power, and can easily propel tree branches, tarps, and sheets of plywood through the air. Winds over 100 knots can break loose gear that is supposedly well-secured. Sand and dirt carried by such winds is painful and can be blinding without eye protection. Winds in a severe hurricane or typhoon are often greater than 100 knots.

There is not very much that will escape the force of wind when it exceeds 180 miles per hour. At windspeeds approaching that magnitude it isn't just a matter of loose debris that poses a threat. Buildings will be ripped apart and become airborne. Coconuts torn from trees become deadly missiles.

In choosing a storm anchorage, try to avoid areas in which there is the potential for loose material that could bombard your boat, such as old or abandoned buildings or houses that appear to be poorly constructed. Be especially on the lookout for sheet-metal roofs. Sand and gravel piles are also dangerous. When going on deck be especially alert to the dangers of flying debris. If you happen to have a hard hat such as those used for construction or a bicycle or motorcycle helmet, wear it.

Setting Anchors

The decision on how to set your storm anchors is sometimes a gamble. If you are fortunate enough to be snuggled into a small, protected spot, many of the decisions will be made for you by virtue of the limited space available. Anchoring in a bay or lagoon is tricky because your anchor strategy depends largely on where you think you will be relative to the passage of the storm center and the width of the eye. If the storm center passes overhead you will experience the maximum winds from two different directions, whereas if you are on the periphery of the circulation the winds will vary over a smaller part of the compass.

In the second instance it is easier to prepare, because you can put out an array of two or three anchors from the bow. As the storm moves by you will shift position gradually but always be lying to the cluster. With two anchors the spread would be about 45 degrees, and with three anchors about 60 degrees. With two or three separate systems you have the option of hanging off one or balancing between two or three as necessary. You will also have immediate backups if an anchor line should break or become fouled, and the array reduces swinging.

If you expect the eye to pass near or over your location, it may be better to lie to one anchor, or better yet two anchors in tandem. The single anchor set is a typical anchoring system and needs no additional comments. The tandem is one of the strongest anchoring systems you can achieve, since the holding power of the combined anchors is greater than the sum of their individual capacities. The tandem can be made very effectively with CQR or Bruce anchors, because both have eyes welded to the plow (the only anchors I know of that have this feature). Earl Hinz, in *The Complete Book of Anchoring and Mooring*, recommends that the distance between the two anchors be equal to five to eight fluke-lengths of the smaller anchor.

The strength of this rig is mainly due to the fact that the anchor at the end of the rode maintains almost zero chain lead angle, and thus exerts its maximum holding power. The inner anchor makes this possible. The outer anchor should be the larger of the two.

It is not easy to get both anchors to dig in properly with a tandem set. I would recommend diving to check how they are lying and to set them by hand if necessary. There is also some question about how the tandem rig will work if the boat is swinging. For example, if the anchor closest to the boat is rolled out of the substrate, it may not reset itself properly. On the other hand, the extra weight of the two anchors and

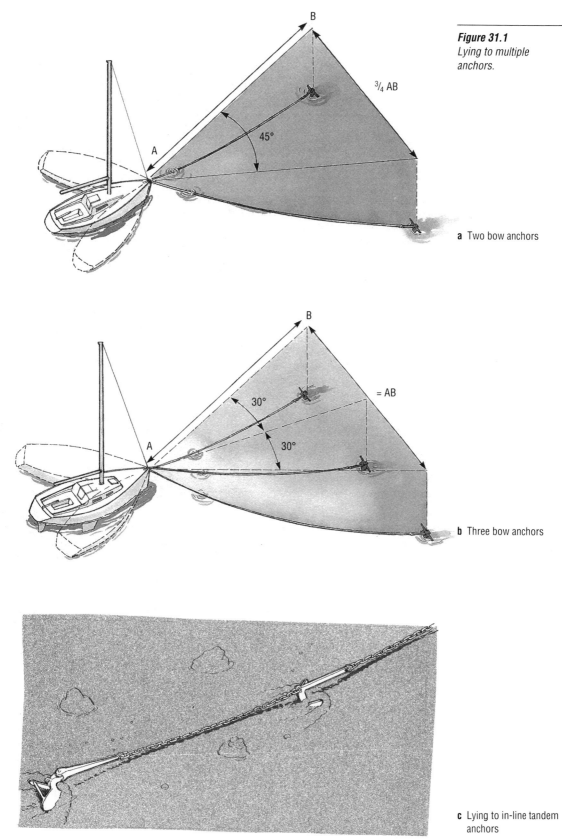

Figure 31.1
Lying to multiple anchors.

Figure 31.1
Lying to multiple anchors.

B

³/₄ AB

45°

A

a Two bow anchors

B

30°

= AB

30°

A

b Three bow anchors

c Lying to in-line tandem anchors

the improved possibility of at least one of them digging in makes this method attractive.

Any other anchors and rodes that you have on board should be made up ready to launch but kept tied down on deck. These will be used in the event that the primary anchoring system should fail.

Anchor Rodes

All rodes prepared for a hurricane must be at least partly made up of nylon line. You do not want to use a rode that is made up completely of chain. Under normal anchoring conditions the sag (catenary) in the chain between the boat and the anchor serves as a shock absorber. But with increasing winds the chain will pull straight, or nearly so, and once that happens the catenary is gone and there is no more 'give' in the chain. Now, if there are any large waves or sudden gusts and surges on the boat, there is nothing to absorb the shock loading. Either the chain will break, the anchor will pull out of the bottom, or deck fittings may be ripped off. Nylon line, especially three-strand nylon, has a lot of stretch and can provide the shock absorber needed, but the size of nylon line must be correct for the weight of your boat. Using a nylon line that is too large will have the same effect as chain.

Tying Off to the Land

Sometimes it is possible to work your way into a small tidal creek or river, or a well-protected lagoon or indentation in the shore, where you can tie off to trees on one or both sides of the boat. Mangrove trees are the finest anchors you could hope for, but any kind of tree will serve as a good tie point. Even strong bushes may help if there are no trees. Rock formations, coral heads, pilings, and the hulls of wrecked ships may all provide the tie points. Overlook nothing and use everything available to secure your boat.

When relying mainly on tie-offs to the land, start out with a basic pattern of port and starboard lines from the bow, from amidships, and from the stern. From that you can continue to build a veritable spider web of lines to the land. Use lots of chafe protection on the boat and on the 'anchors' ashore.

If it is only possible to tie off to land on one side, anchors should be laid out from the bow and stern, and if possible from amidships. It is possible to use a bridle if you do not have enough anchors. With either the side tie, or when tying off to land on both sides of the boat, there should still be strong anchors set fore and aft.

In preparing for a hurricane you will wish you had more chocks and cleats on board. As the lines and backup lines and their chafing gear begin to pile up one on another there will soon be a shortage of attachment points on the boat.

After a line has been cleated off, the remaining tail can be led to the mast and secured with a bowline at the partners. This is a final fail-safe. The mast, *if it is stepped on the keel*, is the strongest tie-off point on deck, and if all else fails it will hold the line.

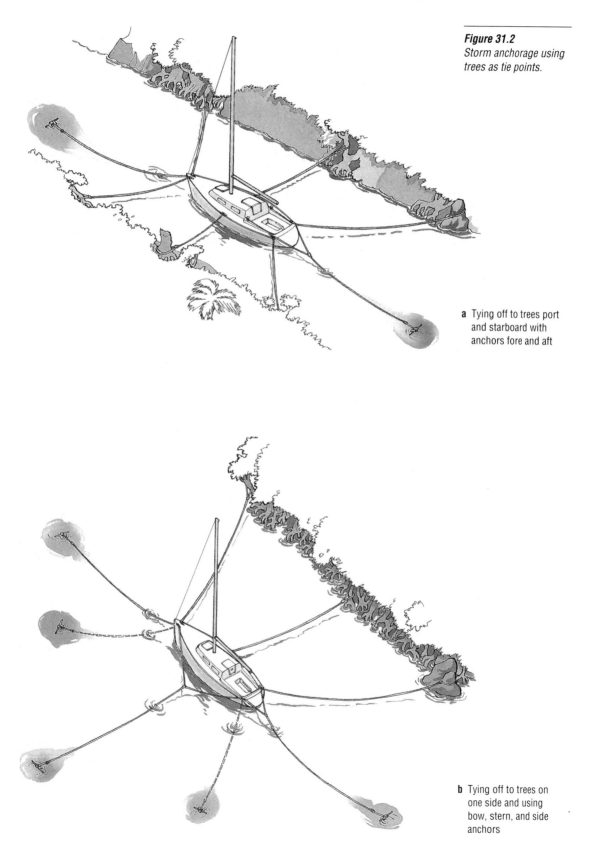

Figure 31.2
Storm anchorage using trees as tie points.

a Tying off to trees port and starboard with anchors fore and aft

b Tying off to trees on one side and using bow, stern, and side anchors

343

Chafe

In hurricane conditions, chafe probably leads directly or indirectly to the loss and damage of more boats than any other cause. In recovering the ground tackle of boats that broke away from their anchors during storms, divers often find the anchor well dug in, the chain lead still secure, and the nylon line still properly attached to the chain. But the 'boat' end of the nylon line invariably is a frayed and ragged remnant that was cut by chafe.

During any heavy weather, but especially in a hurricane, all lines must be continually monitored for chafe. Action should be taken immediately if any evidence of chafe is found. In the hurricanes I have gone through, I have always found chafe that needed to be attended to and lines that needed to be adjusted during the storm. Because of those experiences, I am reluctant to anchor near a boat that will sit out a storm without any crew on board.

A great variety of materials can be used for chafing gear. Reinforced nylon hose (the type used for fuel, water, and bilge hoses on most boats) is especially useful for this purpose. Leather, especially elk hide, is superb. If necessary, cloth, towels, or almost any fabric will work.

Short hose pieces are convenient because they can be slipped over the line, but this must be done before there is a strain on the rode. Sometimes when the line is adjusted it may be difficult to get the hose piece back in its proper place to prevent chafe. Once it is in place it needs to be tied to the line it is protecting. This can be done by building up a series of overhand knots on each end of the piece of hose with small line or shock cord. Chafing gear should be placed everywhere that anchor or mooring lines are in contact with the boat, such as the bow roller and chocks.

If you are tying to trees on shore, chafing materials must also be used there. Although there will be less movement on the lines ashore, there will be some, and probably no one will be there to watch for chafe. For lines tied to trees it is often convenient to use a loop of shackled chain and to cover the chain with old pieces of fire hose.

Boat Preparation

On deck, the objective is to reduce windage in every way possible. This requires a lot of work, but if you have been timely in getting to your hurricane anchorage, there should be plenty of time to prepare the boat in an orderly manner. Begin by removing all awnings and weather cloths, the dodger, and any other equipment that is stowed on deck. The mainsail should be removed and, if you can find a way to do it, the boom can go below as well. If for some reason the mainsail has to stay, it should be tightly lashed to the boom.

Roller-furling sails should be taken down and stowed. If a furled sail should come loose and unroll in the heavy winds, it will surely be destroyed. But before it finally blows out, it will increase windage so much that the boat may be carried off its anchor. Taking down a furling jib is not an easy task if there is much wind, so do this job early.

The wind-steering vane equipment and wind generator need to be disassembled and put below. If you have a radar arch or tower, any gear that is mounted on it should be removed, and the frame itself should be disassembled if possible. Solar panels may need to be removed depending on how they are mounted. I even take down my Windex and masthead navigation light in preparation for a hurricane.

Halyards should either be removed or replaced with very light line (messengers). With internal halyards, and if you have mast steps, put a stopper knot in the end of the line and pull the knot up to the top of the mast. After the storm climb the mast steps and pull the halyard back down.

An inflatable tender should be deflated and put below. If there is a rigid dinghy it should be taken ashore and tied down in some safe place, if practical. You will be able to catch a ride back with some other boat if it is too far or too difficult to swim back to your boat.

It should be clear from the foregoing that the deck and rigging should be as free of any equipment as possible. Liferings and man-overboard equipment should be placed in the cockpit well.

Depending on your boat, it may be necessary to put storm covers over hatches to prevent water from coming in. Vent covers should be made up and ready to install. If there is any possibility of flying debris, put on your (storm) window covers.

Belowdecks, the tasks are about the same as when preparing for heavy weather offshore. Any loose gear should be put away and all cabinets and lockers should be securely closed. In storm-force wind and waves, the boat will be in constant motion. Waves may at times cause violent pitching, and strong gusts may lay the boat over on its beam ends.

Run the engine if necessary to top off the batteries. Check out all bilge pumps to be sure they are in operating condition. This means actually pouring a few buckets of water into the bilge and pumping it out. Examine the bilges and suction hose strainers to be sure they are free of debris. If it is necessary to transfer fuel or water, do it now. Lay out flashlights and be sure they are in working condition with fresh batteries.

Watching Out for the Other Guy

Once your boat is secured and you have determined that you have done everything you can to prepare, have a look at nearby boats that have not been attended to. Try to find another skipper to go with you and check the ground tackle on any unattended boats. It is a good idea to have another person along in the event that the owner or the Coast Guard should show up and accuse you of looting.

On the unattended boat, add chafing gear to the mooring lines, and if possible add lines to trees ashore, or even put down additional anchors if they are available. If conditions permit, dive on the anchors of nearby boats to see how well they are buried and perhaps improve their position.

It could very well turn out that the work you do to hold someone else's boat in place is as important as what you do with your own boat.

If the other boat goes adrift, rams into your boat, and causes it to sink, then all the work you have done to prepare will have been in vain.

Yachts on Land

If a hurricane or other large storm should come when you are hauled out, there are still things you need to do. Most tasks are the same as described for the boat that is afloat. Windage is just as dangerous here as for the boat that is floating. In some ways it may be more dangerous. For example, if the skipper fails to take down the roller-furling sail and it should come loose it could result in the boat being blown off its hard-stand supports. Whereas a boat in the water may heel severely and then recover, a boat that is hauled out has no water cushion.

In preparation for high winds, extra support stands should be added, and lines should be run from the boat to tie points on the ground. Just as when at anchor, check out the boats around you to be sure they are properly secured. There is always the danger in a yard that one boat will topple over and set up a chain reaction in which a whole series of boats will be damaged as they fall against one another. I have heard of two instances where boats that were hanging in Travelifts went through severe hurricanes unscathed, while other boats in the yard were blown off their supports.

When hauled out, be especially wary of flying debris that could damage your boat. Around most yards there is a lot of loose gear lying about that could become missiles in a strong wind.

Crew Preparation

If there is a safe place to go on land, children may be better off there than on the boat. If it should become necessary to abandon the boat during the storm, the fewer people the better.

For the crew that remains aboard, lifejackets and safety harnesses should be kept at hand until the storm hits, and after that they should be worn. For working on deck in the storm, a dive mask will protect your eyes from the driving rain and spray.

While all of the other preparations are going on, prepare some food for the coming day or so. A pressure cooker will come in handy to make up some hearty soup or stew that can be reheated later. When the storm is a few hours away you may want to also prepare coffee or other hot beverages in advance, to be kept in a thermos.

Consider setting up a radio schedule if there are other boats nearby. Use one of the available VHF channels and arrange to call at a specific time each hour to exchange information or reassurance during the storm. Determine the schedule of weatherfax and voice weather reports so you can monitor the progress and position of the hurricane.

Finally, get as much rest as possible. This may sound impossible with all of the tasks that you need to perform, but it is important. As the storm approaches and during its passage you will be busy and will need a lot of energy to take care of your boat. Lie down and rest at every opportunity. Even if you cannot sleep, the rest will be good for you.

Staying Aboard

The question of staying aboard your boat or staying ashore during a hurricane comes up for discussion after every major storm, with proponents for both choices. Each situation has to be looked at on its own merit, but I don't consider it something to vote on. A lot of the people who speak out on the issue, and especially those who recommend not staying aboard, are those with plenty of insurance on their boats. Very few cruising sailors have boat insurance. Either it is not available or it is too expensive. Your anchors, your good sense, and your willingness to stay aboard and tend to the boat during the storm *are* your insurance. In some situations, the boat can be saved by running the engine in forward or reverse as necessary to take a strain off the anchors.

If you do stay on the boat, make some provisions for abandoning ship if necessary. This is a really tough one to call, because by the time you decide it is necessary to abandon, conditions will have become so critical that it may be nearly impossible to do so.

Those who decide to abandon their anchored boats during a storm report the dangers of getting into waters that are filled with floating debris and diesel oil. High waves, wind, and strong currents can be anticipated. Even if there is a tender available, it may be impossible to row it through the heavy seas. Some who have had to abandon recommend wearing a wet suit, which provides flotation, protection from debris, and helps avoid hypothermia.

Preparing a packet of emergency gear is part of storm preparations. This is true whether you go ashore before the storm arrives, or plan to ride it out with the thought in mind that you might need to escape, or for when you go ashore after the storm. Items to take with you include money, passport, ship's papers, and the log book. Depending on where you are and where you plan or hope to stay on land, take extra clothes, a sleeping bag or blankets, and a good pair of shoes. In tropical regions sailors commonly go barefoot or in sandals, but if you have to negotiate coral or beach rock, you must have foot protection. Include a first-aid kit along with the rest of the gear.

If possible, take along food and water. Following severe storms it is often days before facilities are restored or stores are opened. Water supplies are often disrupted or contaminated. In remote places you may end up sharing the home of a local family, and your contribution of food will be welcomed.

In preparing an emergency bag keep a 'worst-case scenario' perspective: If your boat sinks, the contents of your emergency bag will be all that you have. Choose wisely.

Non-Hurricane Heavy Weather

Because a hurricane is the most devastating type of storm, it should be unnecessary to say any more; if you know how to prepare for a hurricane, then surely you know how to prepare for any lesser event. But this is not necessarily true. Ironically, the fact that hurricanes are so dangerous sometimes makes them safer for us because we have adequate warning that a storm is on its way.

When a tropical disturbance begins, no one knows if it will intensify into a monster that will take many lives and cause great property damage, or die out after a few days. Consequently, meteorological agencies carefully monitor a hurricane's progress and continually broadcast its position and expected course by radio and weatherfax. We may know as much as a week in advance that a hurricane is headed our way, and we can take early action to prepare. As soon as they hear the word 'hurricane', most crews will immediately prepare the boat.

However, other weather systems, unrelated to hurricanes, may arrive without much notice but still cause severe damage. The intensity of these storms is often unexpected or unappreciated until it is too late. If it is a sudden event there is seldom time for specific preparation. In that case, survival may largely depend on whatever standard of preparedness you normally maintain on your boat – and on luck.

Levels of Complexity

I consider three levels of difficulty and potential danger for non-hurricane heavy-weather events:

1. *Strong winds* These are winds usually associated with a major weather system such as a front. There is usually some warning that bad weather is on the way if you are monitoring the weather broadcasts or watching the barometer.

2. *Unusual winds* In this case the winds are not necessarily of storm or even gale strength. Rather they are unusual because they come from a direction other than what is expected. This can happen in the tradewind belt when the wind shifts to the south, west, or north. The boat is anchored for normal tradewinds and then, with the passage of a weather system, the winds clock around. Often there is little or no protection from winds that blow outside of the eastern quadrant, and suddenly your boat is on a lee shore that only a short time before served as a convenient wind screen. If this happens at night when anchored in an atoll or other restricted-access anchorage, there will be no choice other than to stay where you are and quickly put out additional anchors.

Problems are often enhanced because there are too many yachts anchored close together. Soon it becomes a scene of mass destruction as boats become caught on each other's moorings or anchor rodes and engines fail because of lines wrapped on props or clogged water filters.

This may be an instance where the disaster could have been avoided by leaving the anchorage when the threat of dangerous weather was first reported. But who is going to be the first to leave? Until someone moves, no one moves. The crew doesn't want to be the first one to go, or else, through lack of experience or timidity, the skipper assumes that he is OK because other boats in the anchorage are staying. It may be that everyone is inexperienced. Finally someone tries to leave, and then everyone tries to leave, but it is too late.

3. *Catastrophic events* Strictly speaking, the dangers in this category are not just heavy weather, although some of them are indirectly related to unusual weather. Catastrophic events are completely unexpected and

there is usually no direct warning of the event. Examples of catastrophic events would be an earthquake-generated tsunami, a landslide into a harbor, or a rogue wave that enters a long, narrow channel.

Cruising sailors who have sailed down the West Coast of the United States and Mexico will know the name Cabo San Lucas which lies at the end of the long Baja Peninsula. The anchorage is an open roadstead exposed to the east and southeast and is a popular gathering place for sailboats. Anchoring here is not easy. There is only a narrow sand shelf in front of the beach, and then the bottom drops off steeply. The usual procedure is to have a bow anchor in about 100 feet of water and a stern anchor in shallow water near the beach.

Cabo San Lucas – A Case Study

In December of 1982 there were 45 cruising boats lying in the San Lucas anchorage. Most had sailed from California and were preparing to set out for the South Pacific in January. They were crowded together and some had their stern anchors less than 30 feet from the beach. So dense was the anchoring that there were three lines of boats and some were less than 50 feet apart. It was a disaster waiting to happen – and it happened.

On the sixth of December the weather broadcast mentioned a stalled cold front about 300 miles west of Cabo San Lucas. The message was repeated on the seventh, and on that day the barometer dropped slightly. The next day a sudden short squall with gusts to 40 knots swept through the anchorage at noon, with a heavy downpour of rain. In that brief encounter three boats dragged their anchors. The blow lasted only about 15 minutes but, in spite of its intensity, it was soon forgotten.

The afternoon weatherfax map showed an approaching gale with southwest winds. Normally, the Cabo San Lucas anchorage would be protected from southwest winds, but it can be argued that the approach of a gale should have put everyone on their guard. In fact only one boat got underway and left the anchorage. It was one that did not have an operating engine.

Late in the day the wind began to pick up, but instead of coming from the southwest, as expected, it was from the southeast and blew directly into the anchorage. By 2200 there were 10-foot waves breaking on the decks of the anchored boats and at midnight they reportedly reached 18 feet with wind gusts in excess of 50 knots.

By dawn the storm had passed and the beach was strewn with wreckage. Of the 45 boats from the day before, 12 were damaged beyond repair. Six were so broken up that their hulls could not be recognized and only pieces were seen lying about. Another six yachts had completely disappeared; apparently swept offshore. Five of the boats on the beach were in good enough condition to be pulled off and salvaged. Remarkably the only serious injury was a man who broke his leg. He was on a boat that got underway and sailed out of the anchorage during the storm. The injury occurred at sea.

It is frightening to imagine what it was like on board the boats in

Cabo San Lucas that night. But there are lessons to be learned by hearing the stories of the men and women who endured the ordeal. Writers Lin and Larry Pardey travelled to Cabo San Lucas a few days after the storm to interview the survivors. Their report appeared in the book, *The Capable Cruiser*, and the following information is from their writing.

Action Taken

Five boats were able to get underway after the storm struck the coast. Four of them survived. One, which was going out under power, was put in peril when its engine quit working. It was not prepared to sail, and in fact it still had its sail covers on. Before the crew could rig and raise the sails the yacht was swept ashore and destroyed.

Other boats tried to get away under power, but were unable to do so. The strong wave action stirred up the sea floor and put a lot of sand and silt in suspension. When this was drawn into cooling water systems, the engines overheated and stopped.

Several boats that tried to use their engines caught anchor lines on their propellers – sometimes their own stern anchor lines, sometimes the abandoned rodes of boats that had been cut loose to get underway. The boats that were able to put to sea successfully had to abandon their anchor rodes and start out under power. But they all had reefed sails ready to hoist immediately.

As with any in-harbor disaster, some damage and the eventual loss of boats resulted from collisions. One was the typical situation in which one boat drags down on another. Boats that were hit may have been properly and securely anchored, but were damaged or ultimately destroyed by dragging boats. Collisions also occurred because boats were anchored too close together. When stern lines parted or were released, there was not enough room for them to swing.

Equipment that Failed

The sudden, energetic waves that struck the coast of Cabo San Lucas put unusual strains on the boats. It is interesting to see what equipment failed, and why. Especially noticeable was the failure of bow rollers. They were damaged on nearly every boat. The loads imposed by wildly plunging bows in the high waves, and the enormous side loads as the boats yawed back and forth, were too much for most bow rollers, and they twisted like pretzels. Some rollers had no retaining pins or bolts across the top of the roller and the chain or line escaped. Once that happened the line was easily chafed.

Commonly the bow roller itself chafed the line. Most bow rollers have fairly sharp edges on the forward edge of the trough. Normally this does not cause a problem. However, if the boat is yawing back and forth or lying to two anchors, nylon line may chafe away in a matter of minutes. Twenty boats at Cabo San Lucas had anchor lines part due to chafe.

There were also problems with chain imposing extreme loading on deck fittings. This caused damage to bow rollers and anchor windlasses on boats that did not have nylon snubber lines installed.

Boats that successfully held through the heavy going at Cabo San Lucas had either CQR or Bruce anchors and chain. In every case they were using anchors that were the next size up (larger) from what the manufacturer recommended for their boat size.

Anchor windlasses were ripped out of the deck on some boats. Probably there were two reasons for this: Owners may have allowed the windlasses to act as cleats or chain stoppers without the chain load taken up with snubber lines as described earlier. Also, some windlasses may have had inadequate backing plates installed.

Lessons Learned

Monitor weather forecasts whenever you are in an anchorage that could, under any circumstances, become a lee shore. Listen to the voice radio forecasts at least once a day, pick up weatherfax reports.

Take a look at your bow roller and anchor windlass before you go cruising. If they need some improvements – and they probably do – make the changes now.

Choose anchoring locations with care, and be sure to have a lot of room between you and the next boat. Anchoring close to friends may be sociable and fun, but it can lead to the loss of your boat, as well as the loss of your friends, in a storm.

When you decide it is necessary to get underway in deteriorating conditions and you must use your engine, have your sails ready to hoist as quickly as possible – the appropriate headsail hanked on, and the main reefed. Both sails can be put in stops so that they can go up in a matter of seconds.

If it is necessary to abandon your anchor, plan how you will cut or release the rode to prevent a delay to your getaway.

Take *timely action* when you suspect that *any action* is necessary. Waiting for things to get better is probably the biggest cause of accidents to sailboats.

Make your own decisions. If you suspect something needs to be done, then it probably needs to be done right now. If it seems like the best thing to do is to leave port, then leave port, and don't wait until someone else decides to do it.

No matter how much you are pressed for time, take a few moments to explain your plan of action to your crew. Be sure they know exactly what they will be expected to do, and how to do it.

32 MAINTENANCE AND REPAIRS

I had done my homework fairly well by the time I began sailing full time, and I didn't encounter too many surprises. I had read and reread numerous books and completed a couple of extensive shakedown cruises. But the one aspect of the cruising life that really surprised me was the large amount of time needed for maintenance.

I have never heard anyone say how much time is needed each year to maintain a typical 30- to 40-foot fiberglass cruising yacht. I would guess it averages more than 400 hours each year. Whenever I make that suggestion, even among cruisers, they sometimes look at me as if I am crazy. 'Why, that's nearly two months for a person working eight hours a day!'

True. But think about how much time you spend during an annual haul-out. Supposedly all you need to do is clean the bottom and apply one or two coats of antifouling paint. But if you have been cruising for several months there will invariably be a long list of 'little jobs' to be done, and it is not at all uncommon for the haul-out to stretch to two weeks or even two months. A husband and wife team will commonly put in over 200 hours of hard work in a two-week haul-out.

A lot of the maintenance that we do escapes our notice, because it is just part of the daily life aboard, but the tasks add up. Repairing sails, changing engine oil, lubricating winches, fixing a leak in the inflatable, putting an eye splice in a halyard, or scraping some barnacles off the bottom, all take time. After five or six years of full-time cruising, a skipper will usually want to stop and spend several months on a fairly major refit. If you are unfortunate enough to experience the 'heartbreak of osmosis' as many of us do, you can easily chalk up months of maintenance time for drying out and repairs. For those who enjoy the beauty of brightwork and having a yacht 'shipshape and Bristol-fashion,' maintenance can be an end in itself.

A crew with a shiny new boat or someone who is only a year or so into a cruise may take exception to my estimate of time needed for maintenance. But these folks are still in a period of grace, benefiting from what Webster's New Collegiate Dictionary refers to as 'unmerited divine assistance given man for his regeneration or sanctification.' Their day will come.

There is *always* some repair to do on a boat. The quotation attributed to Titus Maccius Plautus is as true today as it was 2200 years ago, 'The man who would be fully employed should procure a ship ...'. (Actually the quote is 'The man who would be fully employed should procure a ship or a woman, for no two things produce more trouble,' but it is only the first part of the quote that concerns us here.)

Figure 32.1
*Annual haul-out periods
mean long hours each
day for the crew.*

Doing it Yourself

Those sailors who have become accustomed to having their maintenance work and repairs done by a boatyard will face a heavy reality check when they begin cruising. Repairs and maintenance are not simply financial considerations, they are responsibilities. Even if you have lots of money there will be times when there is no one but you and your crew to make needed repairs. Those who ignore the necessity of routine maintenance do so at their peril.

For many of us, keeping our boats in a seaworthy condition is something we do ourselves so we can afford to go to sea. Knowing what to do, when to do it, and how to do it becomes a way of life, an acquired and hard-won skill built on making a lot of mistakes. There are times when I spend a day or more on a task that an accomplished repair person could easily do in an hour or less. At that, my workmanship is often rather shoddy. But every time I do complete a new job in a satisfactory way, I feel good about it and have the pleasure of knowing that next time it will be easier ... probably.

Don't despair at your ignorance or the mistakes you make. It is part of the game. If you have to do something over and over again to get it right, be happy that it only took you six tries instead of seven. Some people are more adept at working with their hands than others. If you are one of those who has little skill, keep in mind that you are not alone.

There are many of us in the same situation and yet we persevere. I felt better after reading Robert Pirsig's *Zen and the Art of Motorcycle Maintenance* because it explained my place in the world of mechanical things. According to Pirsig I am one of the romantics, creative and inspirational. The other group, the classicists, are bound by reason and logic. You don't take your car to a romanticist for repair more than once.

While there are few jobs that are truly beyond your capabilities, it is sometimes worthwhile to hire someone to work with you or teach you how. Either of those two options is better than just turning over the job to experts and walking away while they do it. Most qualified repair people are expensive to hire, so make the most of your money and work with them if possible or at least watch how they do things. Whenever I have to hire people to work on my boat I stay with them the whole time and make them earn their money by explaining the how and why of what they are doing. Often I take notes so the next time I can do it myself. If the repair person doesn't like that approach I find someone else for the job.

Maintenance and Inspection Schedule

There are certain jobs that should be done on a periodic basis. These include cleaning and lubricating winches and windlasses, changing the engine oil, replacing filters for air, fuel, and water on your engine, renewing zincs on the hull and in the raw water cooling system, and inspecting and cleaning the water and fuel tanks. Instruction books that came with mechanical equipment will give recommended intervals for maintenance. For other items on the boat you will have to set up your own schedule.

Engine maintenance is usually based on operating hours, and I highly recommend having an engine hour meter installed along with other gauges and instruments. Trying to keep track using the logbook can be a hit or miss affair. Cruising boats often accumulate more engine hours in a year than the average weekend cruiser will total in five or six years.

You should make many inspections on a routine basis. You are on your own here. In my opinion, the standing rigging should be examined from top to bottom every time the boat goes offshore. When cruising in tropical waters, I look at the underwater hull about once a week and clean it when necessary. In cold weather this is not so easy, but fouling also occurs at a slower rate. Common sense and experience will help you determine the best procedure for your boat, but a checklist of periodic inspections and maintenance will help you remember when to do it.

Some inspections can be combined with operation. For example, before starting the engine, it is easy to get in the habit of checking the engine oil level, alternator belt tension, the appearance of the fuel filter, and to look for water or oil in the bilge. Once the engine is operating look at the instrument gauges and check the overboard flow of cooling water. Soon all of this will become second nature.

The adage that 'an ounce of prevention is worth a pound of cure' has direct application to yacht maintenance. I once paid this price by spending almost a week freeing up a couple of sheet winches I had let go too long without servicing. I now follow a maintenance program. The more time spent keeping equipment in good condition, the less time and money will be needed to make repairs.

One way to make up an inspection checklist is to go through the boat from bow to stern on deck and below and note everything that needs periodic maintenance. Then set aside a certain time, weekly, monthly, or annually for the appropriate tasks. It might not always be possible to follow this routine exactly, but at least the schedule will serve as a reminder to do the jobs as soon as possible after the prescribed time.

Manuals and Instruction Books

Nearly every piece of new equipment comes with information that gives suggestions on maintenance, cleaning, inspections, and repairs. Keep this information on board. If the equipment becomes mutinous when underway these guides often give you troubleshooting procedures and instructions on how to perform simple repairs. Some have wiring diagrams that a professional repair person will need. If all else fails the instructions should tell how and where to send the item for repairs.

Lists of parts are especially important to have on board. It will save time and money if you have precise information at hand when ordering. Trying to describe some small part in a letter, fax message, or over the telephone to someone who only writes down orders is seldom successful.

Spares

In preparing for a long cruise, consider how you will repair equipment on your boat. This will help you decide what spares and materials to carry. Broadly speaking there are seven categories of 'spare parts' for a boat:
1) Consumables that require replacement on a routine basis such as engine filters for fuel, air, and water.
2) Items which need infrequent and unpredictable replacement such as fuses and light bulbs.
3) Repair kits for overhauling specific equipment such as water and fuel pumps or a marine toilet; usually the manufacturer recommends that when repairs are made a complete set of parts and gaskets be replaced.
4) Specific replacement parts that are often carried as backup items such as a spare engine shaft or a spare blade for the wind steering vane.
5) Unit replacements which are usually self-contained components – a spare electric bilge pump, a spare engine fuel pump or water pump.
6) Various fasteners including screws, bolts, nuts, split pins, and washers.
7) Regularly used materials such as lubricants, adhesives, tape, electric connectors, epoxy, and fiberglass resin.
   Deciding what and how much of any of these items to haul around

as spares may be difficult. Some manufacturers' instruction books include lists of suggested spares. These recommendations merit your attention. If there are no spares recommended with new equipment you might want to write directly to the manufacturers for their opinion on what to take with you. Perhaps the manufacturers only want repairs made by their technicians; you have the option to go along with their recommendation or buy from a different company. Other manufacturers, even though they are supposedly selling equipment for offshore use, don't seem to understand that yachts really do go offshore and are often far from any service facility, or even convenient communications, for advice or ordering parts. If you can explain things to them in that light they may be more helpful.

No matter where you plan to go on your cruise it will probably be easier to buy as many spares and maintenance materials as you can before you leave home. In your own country you have the ease of locating dealers and the advantage of communicating in your own language. Furthermore, when you are still at home you have access to a telephone and transportation. As soon as you are in another country, no matter how friendly or helpful the people may be, finding repair and maintenance parts will be much more difficult and sometimes impossible. In North America and Western Europe, there is a large yachting market, and prices for equipment, spares, repair parts, and consumables are lower due to competition. In other places, even if the parts are available, the costs will be higher. Import duties and the increasingly popular 'goods and services' taxes will drive the prices even higher. In some countries importers often have exclusive arrangements with foreign manufacturers or distributors which eliminate competition. It is not unusual to see name-brand boating items from the U.S. selling in Japan at three times the manufacturers' recommended retail price.

Many of the most enjoyable yacht anchorages are away from large metropolitan areas. Spending hours searching for some insignificant but very necessary part soon becomes tiring and detracts from the enjoyment of sailing.

Of course, there is a limit to how many spares you can carry on board. This is one of the problems with small boats. In general an ideal list of maintenance and repair items for a 30-foot yacht and a 40-foot yacht would not be greatly different in weight and volume, but the larger boat would have much more room for stowage.

After a few years of cruising you will probably come to realize that some of the things you have been carrying around are unnecessary. But before you start throwing things overboard, see if you can find some other boat or local person who can use them, or perhaps you can swap an item for something you need.

Cruising books written 15 or more years ago often recommended carrying an incredible inventory of maintenance materials on board. Certainly it pays to be as self-sufficient as possible, but there are far more boats out cruising today than a few years ago and services are much more readily available. For example, it is hardly necessary to haul around bottom paint or excessive supplies of engine oil these days, unless you are going far off the beaten track. On the other hand don't expect to walk into a chandlery and find a repair kit for your toilet or galley pump at a remote Pacific atoll. As a matter of fact, there won't even be a chandlery.

Tools

While waiting to go through the Panama Canal I helped out as line-handler on a home-built French trimaran crewed by Marc and Felice. In Lake Gatun their outboard engine packed up. Although it is against Panama Canal rules to sail during the passage, our pilot advisor said it would be OK for a while, but that we would have to have the engine operating before we reached the first down-lock. Since no one seemed to know any more about outboards than me, I volunteered to see if I could make it go. I asked Marc for some tools and after rummaging around in the cabin for a few minutes he appeared with a rusty screw-driver and a pair of ancient slip-joint pliers. I asked him why he didn't have more tools and he looked surprised. 'Why I need more tools? Zees was all I use to build zee boat!' I did manage to get the outboard going and although I could appreciate his logic, I did not agree with his philosophy.

As with spares, the time to buy tools is before you leave home. Hand tools are expensive, heavy, and necessary. Trying to complete even a minor repair without the proper tools is frustrating at best and can be somewhere between difficult and dangerous at worst. There will be times when it is imperative to have the right tool. The combination of a badly leaking shaft packing gland and no wrench on board large enough to tighten the nut can give you grey hair in the middle of the ocean.

I recommend having a set of commonly needed hand tools where they are easy to get at on short notice. Include several sizes of phillips and slotted screwdrivers, regular and long-nose pliers, locking pliers (eg. Vise Grips or Molewrench), diagonal cutting pliers, a carpenter's hammer and a plastic-tip hammer, and one or two adjustable wrenches (spanners). Also at hand should be a hacksaw and spare blades, and a small wood saw. I also keep handy a small box of electrical gear including a wire cutter, voltmeter, terminals, and a gas-powered soldering torch.

A set of emergency tools should be located in their own easily accessible locker. On my boat the emergency locker is right at the foot of the companionway ladder, and it contains a three pound sledge hammer, hatchet, wrecking bar, a saw, a very large pair of slip joint pliers, and perhaps most important, rigging wire cutters. These are commonly called rod and bolt cutters in some catalogs. They should be capable of cutting the largest size rigging wire on the boat. The only way to be sure you are getting the proper size is to take a piece of rigging wire with you when shopping for the cutters and make a test. Be sure they cut quickly and easily. In a dismasting you might have to cut loose the stays to a broken spar while leaning over the side of the boat in rough seas.

Appendix 7 is a list of recommended tools for an offshore cruiser.

Bottom Paint

Every cruising boat will need to have the bottom cleaned and painted about once a year. The interval can usually be stretched a bit more if you are willing to put on a mask and snorkel and scrub the bottom now and then. Local conditions, where the boat is moored, how much sailing you do, and type of bottom paint, will also have an influence on fouling. All bottom paints are not the same, and the most expensive are not necessarily the best. A paint that will do an excellent antifouling job in California may not work well in the Mediterranean or New Zealand. Water temperature, salinity, and the type of marine organisms will determine how well a paint works for your boat. If you are in a new area it is often best to use the paint the fishermen use. It will be the least expensive and best for local conditions.

Selecting a Yard for Haul-Out

When you are in a new harbor ask around about the situation of the boatyard, their costs, and the quality of their work. If you plan to have some repairs done by yard personnel, ask local yachtsmen about the ability of the individual workers for various jobs. Sometimes a yard will have an excellent engine repairman and a terrible carpenter or welder. Often a yard will specialize in certain kinds of repairs such as rigging or engine work. It will be to your advantage to find out in advance what their specialty is.

Every yard has an hourly labor charge. Usually it is a flat rate, but the competence of the individual worker may vary considerably. For example the man who is fixing your engine or spray-painting the hull may have many years of experience but someone else may be less qualified than you. It is to your advantage to be around while work is being done on your boat. Some yards will let you help, which may save labor costs and give you an opportunity to learn how a job is done.

Before you commit to a yard inquire about standard services and procedures. For example there is usually a charge to bring the boat out and another to put it back in. High-pressure water cleaning may be an additional charge. If your bottom is already clean, you don't need this service. There is usually a per-day charge for the time you are out and sometimes a flat-rate additional cost for the use of water and electricity. If the yard has showers, they may add a charge for that. In Whangarei, New Zealand, the hauling and launching was done by crane operated by an outside contractor. Because the crane had a minimum charge, it was much cheaper to schedule a haul-out at the same time other boats were being moved in the yard.

Find out the yard's policy for work that is done on the boat and purchase of materials. A few yards require that you buy bottom paint and other supplies from them or else pay an extra fee. This is not legal, but it is done. Most yards will permit you to do your own maintenance, but some require that you hire their workers even for bottom painting. Some yards permit you to hire outside workers to do repairs on your boat and some do not. Ask if there is any restriction on when you can work on the boat – for example at night and on weekends. Are you permitted to live aboard your boat while it is in the yard? Are there toilet and shower facilities available? Does the yard furnish ladders and staging or is that an extra charge? Inquire about extension cords and of course, in a foreign country consider if your power tools will work on the local electric current.

Don't be reluctant to look around the facilities and especially at the haul-out equipment to see that it is well maintained. If possible observe the equipment and yard workers when they are bringing another boat out of the water. If either the equipment or the way things are done make you uneasy, you may want to find another yard or wait until your next port.

There should be a definite understanding prior to haul-out concerning liability in the event of damage to your yacht. Quite possibly the yard, if it is in a remote place, does not have insurance. You will then need to decide if it is worth the risk. If you are like most cruisers you will not have insurance on your boat, so if something happens and no one has insurance you will obviously be the loser. Yards that do have insurance should be willing to give you a signed statement indicating their responsibility for damage during lifting and while the boat is hauled out.

One time in Savannah, Georgia, I was hauled out in a yard that used a Travelift. The morning I was scheduled to be set back in the water the yard boss told me I would have to wait because another boat was coming out. I was unhappy about this because it would mean waiting another day for the proper tide. I protested but to no avail. While I was stewing about my predicament they went ahead with the haul-out of the other yacht. A few minutes later I heard a loud tearing sound and then a resounding crash. In the process of lifting the boat, the stitching in the aft strap of the Travelift had ripped apart. The stern of the boat fell back in the water, and when that happened the 50-foot, keel-stepped mast, whose forestay had been taken off to accommodate the Travelift, fell over and smashed into the stern pulpit. The mast and pulpit were totaled. Had I gone in as scheduled that would have been my boat and my mast. Another time in the Marshall Islands I watched as a strap broke when a crane was lifting out a wooden yacht. The boat dropped on its rudder and the fall did extensive damage to the stern section of the boat. The owner received no compensation for the accident, had to import all of the repair materials, and spent five months ashore before the boat was back in the water.

If you follow the main cruising routes, there will be ample opportunity to hear about the good yards and the bad yards from other sailors. Of course some people are perpetual complainers and nothing makes them happy, but if you frequently hear good or bad opinions expressed about a particular place, pay attention. This is another good reason to belong to the SSCA or some other cruising organization – to read about the experiences of other sailors.

Repair Charges

Be especially leery of cost estimates for repairs. An unscrupulous yard owner can take advantage of you in various ways. Sometimes the yard will be so hungry for work that they will not be realistic in pricing a job, or the man making the estimate may be inexperienced. As the work progresses you will be in deeper and deeper, and the over-run on the job may run to two, three, or more times the original estimate. Some yards will only work on a cost-plus basis or materials plus labor costs. Shop around and shop defensively if you have major jobs to do.

Laws that apply to payment for repairs to ships and boats are different from those for repairs to houses, buildings, or cars. This is to protect the shipyard whose customer can easily run away without paying. These same laws give a dishonest yard owner an opportunity to rip off the unwary customer. Furthermore, the cruising market is an easy target for an unethical repair facility because cruisers are a 'renewable resource' with each year seeing a new crop arriving. Unless you are very well acquainted with the yard, don't rely on an estimate for work to be done. Get a written and signed quote in advance.

If you sail long enough, far enough, and hard enough the day will eventually come when you need to stop for several months and catch up on major repairs and modifications. Usually you have the opportunity to plan for this far enough in advance to select a good stopping place. In making this decision take into consideration the climate, the local cost of living, the availability of maintenance materials and fasteners, sources for spare parts, and the cost and quality of any labor you may need to hire. Don't be too conservative about your estimates of how long a repair period will take. I have never heard of one being completed on schedule. Give yourself at least 50 percent leeway on when you expect to finish. This is especially important if your departure date is weather-dependent.

Haul-Outs

If you are accustomed to hauling out with modern, efficient equipment, you may find some new ways to do it when you are out cruising. In some places the tide is high enough that sailors careen their boats at low tide. With the crew working fast it is possible to clean and paint half of the bottom on one low tide and the other half on a subsequent low tide. Elsewhere a grid is used, in which the yacht is brought between a double row of pilings at high tide; as the tide recedes the boat is kept vertical with fenders and lines tied to the pilings. A somewhat similar procedure is to stand the yacht alongside a bulkhead or pier as the tide goes out. These methods will all benefit from using local knowledge to prevent damage to the boat.

Keel shape will affect how the yacht will sit on the ground. Be sure the keel is positioned correctly to support the boat on a grid or pier. This should not be a problem with a full-keel boat, but may be for a semi-full keel or fin keel. If possible watch or help another yacht do it before you do your own boat.

Not so many years ago experienced cruisers stressed the importance of having a boat that could sit on its own keel to facilitate haul-outs. Today this is less important because there are far more haul-out facilities available than in the past. Also for that reason I would recommend waiting until you are at a yard with good equipment unless you have an emergency.

If you go to a boatyard for a haul-out you will find a wide variety of methods used, including different types of marine railways, Travelifts, and cranes. Any kind of haul-out should be preceded by a conference with the yard manager. The yard should want to see a drawing or photograph of your boat out of the water, so that they will know the best way to block the cradle on a railway or position the lifting straps for a crane or Travelift. If you have added any hull fittings such as a transducer for a depthsounder, through-hull speed sensor, ground plate etc., they should be indicated on the drawing. If you plan to repair or replace any through-hull fittings while hauled out, be sure and tell the yard personnel about that in advance so that blocks or supports are not in the way.

A marine railway, Travelift, or crane are all acceptable methods to haul your boat out of the water if the equipment is in good condition and the operators are experienced and care about what they are doing.

There are different types of marine railways. The most basic is a cradle built on a ways-car with wheels that fit the railway. The yacht is positioned in the cradle and the car is pulled up the track. This is the least expensive set-up for a yard to install, and it takes up little space. In the past it has been the most common haul-out method and is still found throughout the world. The disadvantages are that usually only one boat can be hauled at a time, and if in the process of haul-out some additional work is found necessary, any boats waiting to be hauled will be delayed. There are some railways that can haul more than one boat at a time if they have multiple tracks and switching facilities.

Another kind of railway is one in which the ways-car is a platform, and a wheeled cradle can be moved on and off the car. This has the advantage that the cradle can be moved anywhere in the yard. It also offers a safe and efficient way of positioning the boat in the cradle during haul-out.

The disadvantage of all railways is the possibility for the ways-car to go off the track, or for the boat to slide off the cradle. I have seen cars go off the tracks because of some underwater obstruction, and I have seen a boat nearly slip off a car due to sloppy operation by the cable operator. Whenever a boat is on a car, two or more safety lines should be used to attach the boat to the car. Yards will sometimes fail to do this properly. The workers become complacent and are willing to trust that the wedges, blocks, and staging will hold it in place. All of the blocks and wedges should be clamped or nailed in place. You cannot trust pressure alone to hold them correctly, no matter how carefully they were driven in place.

Although I have seen the straps of a Travelift fail and have heard of other disasters, this is still my favorite way of having the boat lifted in and out, provided the equipment is well-maintained and the operator is experienced. A disadvantage is that the boat's headstay often has to be released before the Travelift can be maneuvered into position. This leaves the mast only partially supported – problem only if the stern should be lowered accidentally. With a Travelift it is important that the straps be properly positioned.

As an added safety precaution, and one that many yards will forego unless you insist on it, the lifting straps of the Travelift or crane should be tied off with safety lines led to cleats or winches on your boat to prevent them from slipping along the bottom of the hull. If possible the lifting straps should also be tied together below the waterline. Even if this cannot be done before liftout it is not so difficult to tie on a preventer line as soon as the boat comes out of the water and it is easy enough to do before lifting back in. With a modern fin-keel hull this is less important than with a full- or partially full-keel, but it is a good safety practice nonetheless with any boat.

Special care is needed to see that the lifting straps don't damage the topsides, and that they don't ruin a new bottom paint job when the boat is being returned to the water. Some yards are careless with their straps and let them accumulate sand and gravel. Considerate yards will have special pads to cover the straps when putting a newly painted boat in the water. They should at least use cardboard or plastic sheeting to protect the hull from scratches by the straps.

Most people consider a crane to be the least desirable way to haul a yacht out of the water. I too was leery of cranes until I saw how it is done in New Zealand, where the crane operators have the finesse and touch of brain surgeons. Elsewhere in the world they are not always so competent. You certainly want nothing less than the best when you see your boat, perhaps the sum total of your material worth, dangling high, sometimes very high, overhead on one slender cable. What if the operator suddenly gets the hiccups, or a wasp flies up his pants leg or, God forbid, he should have a heart attack? Not all of a captain's tests of courage are faced at sea!

All of the precautions accorded the use of a Travelift apply equally to the use of a crane, such as being sure the straps are correctly positioned and that they are tied off to prevent slipping. With a crane, additional care must be taken to fend off the straps from the toerail or bulwark. This is best done using padded spacers between the straps and the hull just below the bulwarks.

In any kind of haul-out operation there should be one person in charge, and all instructions to the equipment operator should come from that individual. The supervisor should be free to move about and check all lines, cables, straps, and blocks. In my opinion no haul-out procedure, even with a Travelift, should be a one-person operation. Trying as it may be, the owner or captain should always be present when his boat is hauled.

On the Hard

Visits to a variety of repair yards around the world will illustrate some of the most innovative and terrifying methods of supporting a yacht while it is hauled out for repair. Before I knew any better I once saw my own boat supported by 55-gallon drums filled with rocks, with supports made from tree trunks, discarded railroad ties, and four-by-four timbers. I wouldn't let that happen again except in an emergency. Yards that rely on such jury-rig methods do so to cut costs and will be unlikely to take any responsibility if an accident occurs.

The only proper way to support a boat that is hauled out for repair is with a strong cradle with adjustable uprights and large adjustable support pads, or else poppets such as pipe stands or screw jacks made specifically for this purpose. There should always be supports beneath the bow and stern.

Watch for how and where the pads on the end of cradle uprights and jack stands are placed on the hull of a fiberglass boat. If the pads are too small or if they are set in the wrong place for an extended period of time, indentations in the hull may result. Perhaps this should not happen to a properly constructed hull, but it can happen, and as hulls become increasingly thinner with high-tech building materials, the chance for this will increase.

A boat's weight when sitting on the hard is mainly supported by the keel, and the uprights and poppets keep it centered and stable. For that reason the uprights on a cradle should be supported with fixed braces or with chains or cables. Likewise poppets should be chained or cabled together to keep them from slipping apart. Any movement of a stand or upright must be done by or under the supervision of yard personnel. In that regard I recommend always going directly to the yard supervisor when you want anything changed on the boat supports. That way if any accident occurs there is no question of responsibility.

Security

It would be nice to think that the danger of heavy weather is over once a boat is in the yard, but it may not be. Even after your yacht is sitting securely in a cradle or on jack stands your responsibility continues regardless of who is paying for insurance. Properly supported, a sailboat should stand tall in any normal wind conditions, but a hurricane is an abnormal event and if one should come your way, added precautions will be necessary. In this case extra tie-downs should be installed to secure the boat to the cradle and to the ground. Be especially wary if the spars are still rigged. Mainsails and roller-furling jibs should be removed. Even under fair weather conditions this is a good idea during a haul-out. If a furled sail should somehow get loose it could lead to a disaster even in a moderate gale.

One last thing to think about when your boat is in the yard is the possibility of theft. You can be sure that the yard where you are hauled out will not have insurance against theft of your property. Anything on the boat including electronics and personal property is completely your responsibility. In some places this is a serious consideration, especially if you are leaving your boat in storage for some time. In that case, you should remove valuables from the boat and store them elsewhere.

33 MAINTAINING GOOD HEALTH

While preparing to go cruising I read every magazine article and book I could find on routine and emergency medical advice for the offshore sailor. Some of it was pretty scary stuff. I pictured myself in each of the medical situations described – all except childbirth.

I began to wonder what I was getting into. Several books recommended long lists of medical supplies to have on hand when sailing. They included pain killers, stimulants, depressants, antibiotic ointment, antibiotic medicine, cures for various illnesses, tools for minor surgical procedures, lots of bandages, tape, and miscellaneous first-aid equipment. Most of the necessary drugs could be obtained only with a prescription, so I took the list to a drugstore and inquired about availability.

The pharmacist scanned the list and looked at me in dismay. 'Do you realize how much this will cost?', he asked. He answered his own question. 'Hundreds of dollars.'

I had not factored this into my cruising budget, so I decided to get a second opinion, and took the list to my doctor, who is also a sailor. John looked over the list of items the books had recommended. 'Are you going sailing or on a medical mission?', he inquired.

'Well, this is what the books said was necessary,' I replied.

'Look,' John said, 'you're healthy now, right? You've never needed any of this stuff before. Why should you suddenly start needing it when you go to sea?'

He prescribed a couple of antibiotics and recommended that I buy some bandages and let it go at that. He was right, too. I suspect that those who follow the recommendations to the letter end up throwing away a lot of expensive outdated medicine after a couple of years.

Of course, each person and each crew have to look at the question of medical supplies in terms of their individual situation. I suspect that the people who write the articles and books have to envision worst-case scenarios, but their shotgun approach to illness often does not take cost or likelihood into account.

In my sailing the only things I have needed so far are bandages, Bacitracin or Neosporin to help heal infected cuts, and once or twice some aspirin for headaches when I have had to deal with uncooperative customs agents or immigration officials. The times I have been sick, once with food poisoning, once with a skin rash from working with fiberglass, and once with an infected cut, have all happened in port. There is almost no way you can get an infectious disease or even catch a cold when offshore. Only when you come to land and get around other people are you liable to become ill.

A few months before leaving on a cruise, all crewmembers should have a complete physical examination and catch up on any needed dental work. I once read that anyone under age 45 who plans to make a long ocean passage should consider having their appendix removed. Seems rather extreme to me. Someone in the crew, and preferably all crewmembers, should take a course in first aid. In most communities short courses are given by the Red Cross.

Take along a general 'what to do and how to do it' first aid book. *The Ship's Medicine Chest and Medical Aid at Sea* is often recommended, but I have found it to be a bit short on realistic information. Much more helpful has been *Where There Is No Doctor – A Village Health Care Handbook*, by David Werner. *Dr. Cohen's Healthy Sailor Book*, by Michael Martin Cohen, M.D., is not a first aid book *per se*, but deals more with preventive maintenance for the crew. It should be read well in advance of leaving on a cruise. Finally, a book that, by its name, would be easily overlooked, is *The Floating Harpsichord*, by Peter H. Strykers, M.D. If I had read this book before sailing, I would have put it aside as too simplistic but after nearly ten years of cruising I can see that it is absolutely spot on! Dr. Strykers' understanding and appreciation of the realities of shorthanded sailing and the likely medical problems of sailors are excellent. His advice on medical supplies and immunization is not equaled in any other book I have read.

Medical Help

Those concerned about the possible need for medical help at sea should consider having a ham or singlesideband (SSB) radio on board. In port, you may be able to find a doctor with the help of the International Association for Medical Assistance to Travelers (I.A.M.A.T.). This service gives a listing of affiliated physicians in 450 cities in 120 countries throughout the world who are prepared to help travelers with medical problems. I.A.M.A.T. also provides current updates and advice on recommended immunizations and information of high-risk malaria areas. I.A.M.A.T. is a non-profit organization and only requests that you make a donation when you become a member.

Medical Costs and Insurance

The cost of medical services vary tremendously throughout the world but they are all less expensive than in the U.S. In quite a few places the only medical facilities are dispensaries that take care of minor problems. They seldom have anything more than the most basic medications, and even those may be exhausted or in short supply. The next step up are clinics, which usually charge little or nothing. Even in cities where good medical advice is available, the charges for services are much lower than in America.

Don't underestimate the talents of the staff in the government dispensaries and clinics. Most of them know their stuff, or at least how to treat the local illnesses, which will probably be the reason why you are seeking their help.

If you plan to continue health insurance when sailing, find out if your insurance covers you when traveling. If not, you may want to consider buying travel insurance. There are some companies that specialize in worldwide insurance, and charge different premiums depending on what countries you visit.

Seasickness

Only in recent years have we come to understand the cause of seasickness, or motion sickness, but there are still many misconceptions about its cause and cure. Everyone is a potential candidate for seasickness, although some people are more susceptible. Those who claim they are never seasick are advised to amend that by saying they have not been seasick yet.

The cause of seasickness is now known to be related primarily to our natural balance (vestibular) system, which is part of our inner ear. The system evolved for life on land, and when we go sailing we significantly disrupt it. Other inputs to our sense of balance are vision and position sensors located in the neck. Our inner ears, position sensors, and eyes continually supply information to the brain, but on a rolling, pitching boat the data can become confused and conflicting. The brain tries to process, understand, and respond to these data. One response to these confusing signals is seasickness although no one seems to understand why this happens.

Anyone who has been seasick will probably remember it as feeling wretched and throwing up. That is the end effect. Usually it is preceded by the face becoming pale and a cold sweat developing. This can be followed by headache, sometimes dizziness, and lethargy or sleepiness. Often your mouth becomes dry. All of these symptoms may be gradual and precede queasiness and nausea. There is usually a loss of appetite and a subtle feeling that all is not well with your stomach. The final stage is vomiting. Not all sailors will make the above step-by-step progression; some will become nauseous almost immediately. Likewise, if the cause of the illness, for example rough seas, abates, or if you are able to adapt to the motion, the progression of symptoms may stop at any point.

In my experience, seasickness slowly creeps up with a general malaise and lethargy. It is well if you can recognize this for what it is. Perhaps you can do something about it, such as moving to the cockpit, where you have a horizon for reference. Changing course slightly may improve the boat's motion significantly, or you may simply be pushing too hard and a sail reduction will improve the situation. However, if you fail to take any action your ill feeling may only increase and, because you feel progressively worse, you will be more reluctant to take any action.

Just as becoming seasick varies from person to person, so does adaptation. Some sailors adapt very quickly, and some take two or three days to get back to normal. A very few are constantly seasick.

One important point that has come with a better understanding of the cause of seasickness is a recognition of what does not cause seasickness. It has nothing to do with how strong or rugged someone is, nor does it have to do with anxiety. Likewise, certain foods or the temperature cannot be considered as causes or factors. However, foods, beverages, or drugs that themselves cause nausea or disequilibrium should be avoided if there is a risk of seasickness. This includes alcohol.

So how, other than staying home, can we avoid or at least reduce the risk of seasickness? One of the most effective ways to ameliorate the problem is to keep active as long as possible. A second is to remain topside, with the horizon as a reference point. During heavy seas the cabin is often buttoned up and the ventilation is poor, so that an already existing feeling of discomfort may be increased. Sometimes in rough going it is necessary to hand steer, and if this task is shared by different crewmembers it may help everyone feel less nauseous. Even if hand-steering is not necessary it may be a good idea to do so as a kind of therapy.

If it is necessary to stay below, it is best to lie down and close your eyes. A yacht's motion is the least violent in a low, central place, and keeping your eyes closed reduces the mixed signals being sent to the brain.

Various drugs are available, but all of them must be taken before the first signs of seasickness appear. In recent years many people have had success with the drug scopolamine, which is administered through a 'transderm' patch. For others it is unsuccessful or produces unpleasant side effects of blurred vision and drowsiness. Other old standbys are Dramamine, Marezine, Bonine, and Antivert. All of these need some lead time to start working; at least two hours, but the recommendation is that they be taken the night before getting underway.

Although some doctors disclaim the scientific validity of wearing wristbands to prevent seasickness, many people have told me they work. Similarly, no one seems to know why, but eating raw ginger or swallowing a capsule of powdered ginger, or even eating gingersnap cookies, will prevent seasickness in many people. Even doctors agree that ginger is successful.

Effects of the Sun

A majority of the cruising destinations are in the tropics, with unrelenting sunshine. Each year we learn more and more about the sun's threat to our bodies – skin cancer, eye damage, dehydration, heat exhaustion, and heat stroke.

Skin Damage

Sunburn is the most immediate and obvious skin danger, but those who spend time at sea must also guard against long-term effects of the sun leading to skin cancer. Ultraviolet radiation (UV) is the cause of sunburn and longer term effects as well. Different people, depending on their skin type, are variously affected by UV, but everyone is subject to its damaging influence.

Sailors may fail to realize how much of the time they are receiving UV rays. We normally associate the danger of overexposure with sunny days and being hot. However, UV rays can penetrate cloud cover, and

Figure 33.1
The sun is the cruiser's friend and enemy. Long sleeve shirts, long pants, adequate foot covering, a broad brimmed hat, sunglasses, and sun block lotion should be standard equipment for the mid-day cockpit crew.

even when we are sailing briskly along and feel comfortable, UV radiation is continuing its relentless attack on exposed parts of our bodies. 'Swim call' is a pleasant way to cool off on a hot day, but it offers no escape from UV radiation, which is absorbed by water. Tropical areas are the most severe areas for receiving UV rays because the sun is closer to the zenith at mid-day, and because the atmosphere's ozone layer, which acts as a UV filter, is thinner at the Equator.

Developing a tan is one way to help reduce the short- and long-term damaging effects of the sun. Exposure to the sun causes the skin to produce melanin, a dark brown pigment, as a defense against UV. But it must be done gradually – the rate depends on each person's skin type. For someone sailing for a long period of time, the slower and more controlled the tanning process is, the better. Start out giving your body maximum protection by wearing a hat, a long-sleeve shirt, and long pants. Use a sunscreen with a Sun Protection Factor (SPF) of 15. Use a total block, such as zinc oxide, on very sensitive areas for initial exposure. If you are cruising for a while you have plenty of time to work up to the natural protection of a tan.

Fair-skinned, blue-eyed sailors from higher latitudes who head toward the Equator in the summer are obviously in the highest UV damage risk group, but these days, with the recognition of a thinning ozone layer, everyone needs to be on the defensive.

Before setting off on a cruise an abundant supply of sunscreen creams or lotions should be on board. In a lot of places they are not available.

When I have guests coming to sail with me I always urge them to bring twice as much sunscreen as they think they will need. Invariably, it turns out that they need it. Certain brands of sunscreen and suntan lotion can stain clothing, and some will permanently stain fiberglass gelcoat and deck cushions.

If someone does get sunburned, use one of the commercially sold sunburn pain relievers such as Solarcaine. Cool-water compresses will give some relief, and aspirin may help to reduce the pain and discomfort. For severe local burns, hydrocortisone cream will help relieve pain and inflammation.

Dehydration, Heat Exhaustion, and Heat Stroke

Heat exhaustion may stem from dehydration when sailing in hot weather. The victim becomes very lethargic and may become dizzy or even faint. It can be treated by increasing water and salt intake. More severe and sometimes fatal is heat stroke. In this case sweating ceases and the skin become very hot and dry. The person affected may become delirious, suffer convulsions, and eventually becomes comatose. Treatment is to reduce body temperature by immersing the body in cool or even cold water.

Eye Damage

Ultraviolet rays are now recognized as the cause of significant eye damage. Particular attention has been focused on pterygium, damage to the cornea, as a concern for those who spend a lot of time at sea. Pterygium results from continuous exposure of the eyes to sun, wind, dust, and especially abrasion from salt. It can occur within as little as three or four years unless prevented by the use of adequate sunglasses. Dark glasses that are polarized are recognized as the best protection. Additional benefit is gained by wearing glasses with side flaps, which help reduce the abrasion by salt.

Sunglasses have become largely a fashion item, and consequently you often pay much more for a designer's name than for quality. In buying sunglasses it is sometimes difficult to decide what is best for you. Recently the U.S. Food and Drug Administration (FDA) has come up with a grading system to quantify the amount of UV protection as well as determining the percentage of visible light offered by sunglasses.

Generally, sailors prefer polaroid lenses because they do a great job of cutting down glare and give better vision for navigating through shoal waters. Further reduction in glare is obtained with mirrored lenses.

Choose frames for their ruggedness and comfort rather than style.

Heavy plastic frames will usually take a lot of abuse. Don't worry about fashion. Very few people will see you on the boat, and if you want designer frames to wear ashore, buy a separate pair of tourist sunglasses.

Keep more than one pair of quality sunglasses on board. They may not survive too many times of being dropped on deck and Neptune is always ready to receive offerings of sunglasses, along with winch handles and tools. Homemade or commercial neck straps will help cut down on losses.

Effects of Seawater

Cuts and abrasions are often slow to heal when sailing. In the tropics especially, cuts are frequently infected by bacteria which thrive on the moist conditions. To speed up the healing process, antibiotic ointments such as Bacitracin or Neosporin should be applied and covered with a bandage. It will probably be necessary to change the dressing frequently. If healing is slow it may be necessary to take some antibiotic medicine. Ask your doctor for a prescription before you leave.

So-called 'swimmer's ear' is not an uncommon problem. To help prevent this infection, make it standard practice to rinse out your ears with hydrogen peroxide after you swim. If you don't have that you can use a ten-percent solution of cooking vinegar.

Inoculations and Illness

Deciding which inoculations are worth getting depends on where you are going. You can get advice from your doctor, from the I.A.M.A.T., from the public health service, and, in the U.S., from the Center for Disease Control in Atlanta, Georgia. In the U.K. the Department of Health publishes advice in *Immunisation Against Infectious Diseases*. Some inoculation series take several weeks to complete.

I have made an effort to keep up with inoculations for yellow fever, tetanus, and typhoid fever. When going into areas known for cholera I have had that inoculation as well. However, the cholera vaccine is only good for about six months. Avoiding cholera is also a matter of being very careful about food in places of poor sanitation.

Hepatitis A is similarly a threat in places where sanitation standards are low, although it can be contracted anywhere. Prevention is the best way to avoid hepatitis as well. This means being careful about water and hand-prepared foods. Even peeled foods can be dangerous if the person handling the food has hepatitis. Raw clams and oysters are notorious for transmitting hepatitis. There are methods of immunization for hepatitis A, but all of them last only a short time. Therefore if you will be in an area of high hepatitis risk the preventive medicine should be taken just before or soon after arriving there. There is also a hepatitis B vaccine, but it takes six months to complete the series.

Malaria is an especially serious illness that still exists in many parts of the world. Although there is no risk in North America, Europe, New Zealand, Australia, or Japan, almost all tropical countries should be considered risk areas. The problem with avoiding malaria is complicated by different strains of the disease that are resistant to certain anti-malarial drugs, and by the fact that you should begin taking medicine before you arrive in a malaria area and continue for four to six weeks afterward. Hence, it is necessary to do some research in advance to determine what specific medicine you need when sailing to certain areas. The I.A.M.A.T. publishes information on malaria prevention and a chart of risk areas.

When sailing in malaria-risk areas, try to keep mosquitos off the boat. Being at anchor and keeping a good breeze moving through the boat helps. Mosquito netting over the hatches is often suggested, but sometimes this so severely cuts down on ventilation that it is intolerable. I have found that burning mosquito coils is the easiest way to keep the critters off the boat at night. When going ashore, repellent is your best bet. This is another item that should be bought before you leave home.

Dengue fever is a mosquito-borne virus common in tropical areas and it affects more than 100 million people annually. It causes high fever, severe headaches, and pain in the muscles and joints. I have met cruising sailors who have suffered dengue fever, and by their accounts it is to be avoided. There is no vaccine or preventive other than to avoid mosquitos in dengue fever areas. Again, mosquito coils and repellent.

Diarrhea is a common affliction of travelers, and sailors are not immune. It can be attributed to a variety of causes, and it is a rare person who will avoid it completely. In most cases it results from the introduction of different bacteria into our gastrointestinal (GI) tract when we come to a new country; especially those with poor sanitation practices. Most often we pick these bugs up from the water. Hence, in a new port special caution should be taken with regard to drinking water. After you have been in a new place for a few days your GI tract will usually adopt the new bacteria and the local water will cease to be a problem. But for the first several days caution is the best policy.

In the past the medication known as Lomotil has been the standard treatment for diarrhea. Now, many doctors advise that no treatment should be given, and that the diarrhea should be allowed to continue until it has eliminated the toxins. Diarrhea can bring on dehydration, so it is important while waiting for it to end to take in extra fluids. This can be done by drinking more fluids, but they must contain glucose to be absorbed by the body. *Dr. Cohen's Healthy Sailor Book* gives recipes for several drinks that will help replace the needed fluids and salts for people suffering acute diarrhea.

Pests

In addition to mosquitos, the cruiser has to now and then put up with a few other pests that take some of the fun out of sailing.

Flying Insects

Sandflies, no-see-ums, and gnats have the ability to drive a normal person right up the wall. In gnat country, the swarms often show up in the late afternoon when the wind drops. Sometimes they come in droves so thick that they get in your eyes, nose, and mouth. But most obnoxious are the bites they give and the welts those bites raise, which may last several days.

Gnats used to give us fits on the Wilmington River estuary in Savannah, Georgia. There is nothing more miserable than a crew of sunburned, beer-filled racing sailors on the fourth-place boat, bucking a foul current in a dying wind, when the gnats descend. Only two things would keep the gnats at bay. One was to light up the most horrible smelling cigar that could be found. It would lay down a smokescreen that no gnat and few people could tolerate. The second, and more effective answer was to slather any exposed areas of skin with an Avon product called Skin-So-Soft. Its designed purpose is to do something wonderful for your skin when you put a tiny bit in a bathtub full of water. As a gnat-buster you use it full strength. It smells only slightly worse than the cigar, but it manages to discourage biting insects.

Cockroaches

Cockroaches are the curse of the liveaboard sailor. Keeping them off the boat is a full-time job when you are in port. But keeping them off is far easier than getting them off once they are aboard. Roaches become crewmembers in several ways. They come aboard as juvenile or adult animals concealed in packages or luggage, or by crawling along mooring lines and fenders when you are tied to a dock or pier. Some species arrive as eggs hidden away in cardboard cartons used for carrying groceries or other supplies on to the boat, and then hatch out in a few days. Less commonly they may fly aboard, but this is restricted to the large American roaches in semitropical and tropical regions. Regardless of how the pioneers arrive, they immediately begin to produce young at prodigious rates.

Every box or bag that you bring from shore to your boat should be inspected carefully for insects and insect eggs before they are brought on the boat. Better yet, don't even bring cardboard boxes on board. When moored alongside empty the box on the dock and hand individual items onto the boat. This same procedure should be followed when at anchor and you arrive by tender. Leave the boxes and bags in the dinghy and hand or set the contents aboard.

In the tropics when I buy a stalk of bananas I tie a rope to it and submerge it in salt water for about 30 minutes before bringing it into the cockpit. The amount of wildlife that can be hidden away in a large bunch of bananas, including lizards, spiders, and cockroaches, is amazing.

Once roaches are aboard you are faced with a battle to remove them. There are various insecticides on the market that are worth trying, but sometimes the roaches seem immune to them. The safest and most popular roach killer is boric acid powder. Whereas cockroaches seem to adapt to other pesticides, boric acid has continued to be successful for many years. The powder is mixed with sugar and sprinkled where the roaches walk. It will be eaten by the roach as food, and it is also ingested when the animal cleans its feet and antennae after walking through the powder. Boric acid is cheap and can be injected into cracks and crevices that roaches inhabit. Silica gel dust can be used in a similar way, but is not as safe as boric acid.

In situations where there is a heavy infestation it may be possible to use a fumigation bomb. This requires that you open all lockers, drawers, etc., then close up the boat and leave it for the day. A second treatment must be done in about two weeks to kill newly hatched roaches. If you use any type of insecticide be careful about the ingredients. Usually if a spray or bomb is used all dishes and cooking and eating utensils should be washed before using. In some countries very strong and dangerous insect poisons are offered for sale with little indication of their effect on humans.

Those who prefer not to use insecticides can bring aboard a spider as a roach killer. For example in Florida there is a spider known as a Housekeeper that kills and eats roaches and other pesky insects. Those who use this technique report that they never see the spider, but it does the job.

Small, commercially available roach baits offer a neat and clean way to control the pests. These are small plastic boxes that contain some food mixed with poison. The cockroach enters the bait box, eats the poison, and then goes off to die in a few days. This method is more expensive than boric acid but is reportedly very effective. It is an especially safe method to use on boats with pets and small children because the poison is beyond their reach.

Rats

Rats exist in every commercial harbor in the world. Do everything possible to avoid tying up in commercial areas. If it cannot be avoided, you might opt for putting rat guards on your mooring lines, just as ships do. It may also be possible to moor your boat with a stern or bow anchor and only one or two lines to the land. Any time you leave the boat in a rat-infested area, be sure and close all hatches and ventilators.

If a rat does get inside the boat, don't waste time trying to get rid of it with a baited rat trap. Start a methodical reconnaissance in the forepeak and work aft, searching out every nook and cranny. Arm yourself with a weapon to stun or kill the beast when it appears, as it eventually will. Otherwise you will be harboring a potential health hazard that will cause no end of petty damage.

I have only had a rat aboard one time. Fortunately, we met on deck, and with a whoop and a holler I drove it into the water and it swam ashore. When you run a rat overboard, watch to see where it goes. It is just as likely to climb back up the anchor line.

Dangerous Organisms

Landlubbers like to think that sailors are constantly battling sharks, giant squid, killer whales, and various other sea monsters. It is not known exactly where this notion comes from although some sailors are not reluctant to spin a good yarn now and then.

Certainly anyone who swims, snorkels or scuba dives in the tropics will occasionally encounter one of the biters, stingers, or rash makers that are a part of that environment. Best, I have found, is to pay attention to the advice of local people and to use common sense. Any islander or atoll dweller who has lived a subsistence existence and is still walking around at age 70 is a good source of information on which marine organisms to avoid.

Dangers associated with marine organisms have been the subject of several books. It is a good idea to have one of them on your boat as a reference. Most of them identify a variety of dangerous organisms, describe why they are dangerous, and offer advice on the preferred cures. I can recommend *Dangerous Marine Animals* by B.W. Halstead.

More dangerous than live organisms are some of the dead ones we eat. Those who sail in the tropics soon learn about ciguatera, a type of food poisoning in fish caused by a toxic dinoflagellate phytoplankton. All of the fish capable of carrying ciguatera are tropical or subtropical and restricted to those feeding in coral reef areas. Various ways to avoid ciguatera, or recognize it, have been proposed but, as yet, there is no sure way. Local knowledge is to be respected, but even this is wrong at times, as coastal and atoll dwellers are frequently victims of the illness.

The severity of ciguatera varies from a mild reaction to extreme illness and even death. The symptoms are stomach pains, nausea, vomiting, and diarrhea. There may be numbness and tingling around the mouth and throat and eventually throughout the body. Following this may be itching or rash as well as dizziness and a feeling of confusion. Generally, however, the symptoms begin to diminish after 24 hours.

Until you are well-acquainted with a local area it is best to avoid eating fish that normally live in reef areas. Most common species carrying ciguatera are sea bass (grouper), snapper, jack, barracuda, and moray eel. Less commonly it is found in parrotfish, surgeonfish, triggerfish, filefish, and porgie. Any fish, however, which feeds on these species can be a carrier. Fish caught on the open ocean can be considered safe.

Taking Routine Medications

Some of the medicines and preventatives for seasickness are not compatible with other drugs. Before taking any of these nostrums, find out if they are incompatible with any medications you take on a routine basis.

A second point: cruisers always have some sort of time schedule in mind, but they seldom achieve it. Whenever you put to sea in a small yacht you stand the chance of being delayed for a variety of reasons. This may be a matter of days but it can be a matter of weeks, and on occasion, months. Anyone who is life-dependent on some medication should have a large supply when they put to sea. Furthermore a certain portion of that medication should be located where it will be sure to be taken with you in the event it is necessary to abandon ship.

SECURITY FOR YOU AND YOUR YACHT

Many stories circulate about pirates. Some of them are true, but there are far more stories than there are pirates. Most of the dangerous sailing places in the world are well known and are reported in cruising association newsletters. Even at that, situations change and often the legends and tales far outlive the dangers. A few years ago when I was sailing along the north coast of South America, Colombia was considered a very dangerous place and yachts were warned not to enter port due to the high crime rate. Recently, boats have gone into these harbors, and the sailors report good things about them. Not so long ago several places in the Bahamas were considered dangerous due to drug smugglers, but now things seem peaceful. Certain parts of the Philippines and Southeast Asia are frequently mentioned as pirate venues, and I am sure that there are indeed a few spots to be avoided. But it is ridiculous to assume that everything west of Hawaii is dangerous. There are several nice island groups out that way, and Hong Kong, Singapore, Thailand, and places in the Philippines are popular with cruisers. Whenever someone starts filling me with stories about dangerous cruising areas my first question is, 'Have you been there?'

Sure, listen to the experiences of other sailors you meet along the way, but ask if their reports are based on experience or hearsay. Try to learn about places from those who have recently been there.

Attitude

How you approach people has a lot to do with the success of your visit in a different country or culture. In spite of the supposedly relaxed lifestyle of cruising, I still see a lot of uptight people out there who are perpetually prepared for the 'natives' to rip them off.

Anse des Pitons, St. Lucia, is one of the most scenic anchorages in the Caribbean. The well-protected tiny bay has a very narrow sand shelf along the beach. You anchor with a bow anchor in about 120 feet (36 m) of depth and a stern line to a palm tree on shore. *Denali* was besieged by 'boat boys' who swam out to meet us or came alongside in small boats as soon as we headed in toward shore. They were all vying to help me anchor and to swim a stern line ashore. I selected a couple of them to help and after the boat was secure they came on board to collect their reward. There was of course a bargaining session and finally we agreed on a fair price that was perhaps a dollar for each helper. They stayed aboard for an hour or so and related stories and information about the local area.

Later that afternoon one of my guests and his wife went ashore in the tender to walk the beach and go swimming. They returned in a couple of hours. Shortly after, we saw one of our 'boat boys' swimming out to our boat carefully holding a pair of shoes clear of the water. As he came alongside the boat he yelled, 'Hey, mon, you left your money on da beach!' My friend John had absentmindedly left his billfold and watch in his shoes when he went swimming and had forgotten to bring them back with him. His billfold contained several hundred dollars in cash and various credit cards. John thanked him sincerely and gave him a generous tip.

A few months later when I was back in the U.S. I read in a boating magazine about a yacht that visited the same anchorage and claimed that they had to fight off the vicious vandals and use a gun to shoot their way out of the harbor. They described how the 'dangerous local natives' had violently tried to board their boat and force them to pay for anchoring when they entered the harbor. They complained that they had been harassed the whole time they stayed there, and that someone had cut their shore line in the night. I find it hard to believe that the local people had suddenly turned savage after I was there.

Theft

By far most of the local people you encounter while sailing are trustworthy. In many of the remote island groups religion plays a major role in the community, and there are strong social and moral codes that put industrial societies to shame. Unfortunately, in recent years the impact of tourism, and that includes folks on yachts, has heightened the desire for 'things' that can only be obtained by money ... or theft. The apparent wealth represented by a yacht may present a great temptation to someone who is poor, and there are a lot of poor people in 'paradise.'

It is impossible to make your boat totally theft-proof, but you can make things difficult for the would-be thief. On *Denali* I have locks for all of my cabinets both in the cockpit and inside the main cabin. While they would not stop someone who really wanted to break in, it does make the job a little harder and will discourage most amateurs or those who just happen to be passing by.

In some places radios and other electronics are especially tempting targets. Your antennas will give away the fact that you have radios on board, but if the receivers are kept in cabinets, the number or quality of radios will not be obvious. Likewise, when in port, binoculars, hand-held VHF radios, and other portable gear are best put out of sight so that a casual visitor, or even the occasional dishonest government official coming on your yacht, will not notice them.

Tenders and outboard motors are especially tempting to thieves. As inconvenient as it may be, the only way to avoid theft in some places is to bring the dinghy aboard at night or to secure it with a steel cable instead of a rope. If the tender has an outboard motor it should be locked to the boat. The screw clamps that attach the motor to the transom have eyes which will hold a lock so they cannot be turned. Another deterrent to theft is to have the yacht name painted in large letters on the transom of a rigid dinghy or on the pontoons of an inflatable.

Petty theft is always a potential problem, and in some places an amateur thief might take something that is of relatively little value but could cause you some inconvenience because it cannot be replaced locally. Such things as diving masks, a snorkel, or a pair of swim fins are examples. When you leave your boat unattended, remove anything from the deck that might be tempting to a casual thief.

Visitors

Inviting strangers on board your boat is a matter of judgment and intuition. If you are alongside a pier or pontoon there may be a steady stream of curious people passing by and often they are anxious to talk to a foreigner. Some of the most valued friends I have made in my travels have been folks who just happened by.

Usually you have the option to discourage people from coming on your yacht. When at anchor visitors may come alongside in small boats but will seldom try to board unless encouraged to do so. Likewise when alongside a pontoon or pier they will usually stand around and strike up a conversation but will not step aboard until invited. If someone is obviously anxious to come on your boat and you don't want them to, they will usually go away if you tell them you are busy just now. If they persist, then you can persist as well, and eventually they get the picture and leave you alone.

In some parts of the world, and especially in places where yachts are seldom seen, local customs may be such that people have no reservations about coming on your boat out of curiosity. These are the most difficult situations because you don't want to be rude, but at the same time you need to maintain your privacy and security. Often in Korea uninvited visitors would step aboard and then stick their head in the main cabin to see what was going on. I did not like it but tried to maintain a degree of politeness. The only time I blew my cool was in a small harbor on the south coast about 80 miles west of Pusan. One morning when I woke up there was a well-dressed man in a suit and tie seated next to my bed and staring intently into my sleepy eyes. I don't know who he was, but if you ever meet him I am sure he will tell you that American sailors are rather rude and inhospitable in the morning.

I always discourage anyone who tries to board without being asked. Sometimes it is necessary to be firm and unyielding to the occasional overly aggressive visitor. Anyone invited into the cockpit is not automatically invited into the main cabin. Few people are so assertive, but the ones who are will almost always back down quickly if you are firm in telling them not to go inside your boat. You should not be reluctant to politely ask someone to leave if he hangs around too long or is obnoxious.

Local people may want to come to your boat to sell or trade. Sometimes they will pester you to the point where you have little privacy. Again a firm but polite refusal will usually suffice. In those cases where you are interested in trading or buying, fresh fruit and vegetables, for example, it is sometimes best to set a certain time each day or to arrange to fly a flag from the spreaders when people may come. Even then it is often necessary to limit the number of visitors or you may find someone busily going through your cabin lockers while his friend keeps you occupied in the cockpit.

Unknown Crew

Some boats take on temporary crewmembers. At any popular harbor throughout the world there are often far more people looking for opportunities to crew than there are places available. In most instances they are folks who are 'hitchhiking' around the world. Often they make good crewmembers and can be expected to chip in for food and to help out with maintenance. Some skippers look for such crew to provide income to offset sailing expenses. I have never taken aboard an unknown crew, but those who do usually have good results. Unfortunately, there have been a few instances where unknown temporary crew have hijacked boats or even killed the owners.

If you do take on temporary crew follow a cautious approach to help prevent difficulties later. This begins with a very detailed interview. Both you and the potential crewmember should be very open and honest about everything. Find out his or her level of sailing experience and be sure to explain what duties you expect the crew to perform. The fact that someone does not have much or any experience may not be very important; everyone has to begin someplace. But if you are embarking on an ocean passage of two or more weeks duration it is important that the neophyte is not too starry-eyed about the romance of the sea. Even if a volunteer is experienced, personality may be much more important than skill. Talk extensively to the potential crewmembers and ask yourself if you want to spend several days or weeks at sea with them.

Determine if there are any medical problems, allergies, or aversion to certain types of food. Ask about the individual's use and tolerance of alcohol. A person who is a heavy drinker or is alcohol-dependent, the so-called functional alcoholic, may become a huge problem at sea. Be absolutely sure it is understood that 'recreational drugs' cannot be brought aboard. In most countries your boat will be confiscated if authorities find illegal drugs – regardless of quantity or ownership. Potential drug and alcohol problems keep a lot of people from taking on unknown crew.

Be sure your temporary crewmember has a passport, and if necessary a visa for the next port of call. As captain you are legally and financially responsible for anyone on your yacht in a foreign port. Check that he or she has an airplane ticket, or the financial resources to buy one, from the next port to their home country. This means asking for proof of these things and not just a verbal assurance. Otherwise you could end up having to pay for a ticket.

If you do decide to take someone on as crew, don't over obligate yourself for the extent of the individual's time on board. Agree on a passage only to the next port but not beyond. If it turns out you and your crew are compatible you can always extend the arrangements. Ask for references and follow them up. Before departing, photocopy the crew's passport or write the name and passport number and leave this information with the immigration officer or some friend. Let your new crew know you are doing this.

All of this may sound harsh or impersonal but it isn't. A responsible crewmember will not object to your thorough investigation. Never take on a an unknown crewmember at the last minute, just before departure. It is better to delay your departure to be sure about the person. It is also generally not a good idea to take more than one unfamiliar person on board.

Some of what has been said about temporary crew can apply to hiring short term craftspeople or laborers to work on your boat when in port. Unless you know the person, it isn't a good idea to give him free run of your boat. It is best for a crewmember to remain on board whenever outside laborers are working.

The subject of carrying firearms on yachts is provocative. Most people have strong views on this issue. On one boat the crew will be absolutely against firearms. The next yacht may be a floating arsenal. I would estimate that more than fifty percent of U.S. sailboats have handguns, shotguns, or rifles, and many Europeans sailors also carry weapons. **Guns on Board**

Almost every year there is another incident of someone shot on a sailboat by accident. More often than not, if a gun had not been on the boat the injury or death could have been avoided. Many people feel a gun gives them added security and safety, but it is good advice that says, 'Never draw a gun or even display a firearm unless you fully intend to use it.' Once you threaten someone with a gun you must be prepared to kill him. Often people do not fully take this into consideration when they decide to have weapons on board.

Why do people consider it necessary to carry firearms on their boat? The usual reasons given are the danger of pirates on the high seas, the possibility of a thief trying to steal money or possessions from the boat, someone wishing to hijack the yacht and crew, or even the chance of terrorist activity. What are the realities of these possibilities?

As already mentioned there are places in the world where piracy has occurred. Most of these places are known and yachts are well advised to stay clear of them. But many pirate stories are like fishing stories and they improve with the telling. Furthermore, if you ever encounter genuine pirates they will likely be better armed and more skilled than you are in the use of guns. Unless you can out-maneuver or out-run them with your boat, it would probably be better to let them have their way. The same is probably true of hijackers. Pirates are more interested in taking money and property than human lives.

Becoming a victim of terrorist activity is remote but not beyond possibility in some parts of the world. Again, high risk areas can be avoided, but if this does happen you will most likely be dealing with professionals or fanatics so dedicated to their cause that violent resistance on your part will do more harm than good.

The most common reason given for having a gun on board is to discourage or repel someone coming aboard to steal. But the problem is seldom as straightforward as it seems. Usually a theft occurs when the owner is away from the yacht. If the thief is a professional, he will watch the boat for some time and plan a visit when you are not on board. In that situation a gun will be of no use and will probably be stolen along with other things.

Sometimes, however, the theft is at night when the burglar may think you are gone or that he is skillful enough to sneak on board and steal without waking you up. Crimes of this type become very complicated.

It is extremely frightening to wake up in the middle of the night and realize a stranger is on the boat, even in the cabin. You lie there trying to act as if you are asleep while you figure out what to do. Your heart is pounding, and you are sure the unwanted visitor will hear it! You have no way of knowing who this is, what they want, if they have a gun or not, if they are alone or part of a group of two or more. What should you do?

Many people have a quick and easy answer to this question. They suggest grabbing your gun and shooting the unknown person. They argue that this person has trespassed on your property without permission and you have the right to assume they may harm you. Someone else will say you should yell a warning with a threat to shoot in hopes that it will scare the unidentified person off your yacht. Another idea is to fire a warning shot. What are the realities of these various scenarios? Let us look at the 'technical' and 'human' aspects of the problem.

Even if you plan to have a gun on your boat, will it be there when you think you need it? In many countries customs officers require that you leave guns in their custody for the duration of your stay in port. This is such a common occurrence that it largely defeats the purpose of having a weapon on board for in-port protection. Some yachtsmen pretend they do not have a gun to avoid this possibility. However, if the customs officers decide to inspect your boat and find a weapon, you will be subject to severe penalties. Even if you are not caught it will be necessary to keep the weapon concealed, and trying to quickly lay your hands on your hidden gun in an emergency will be difficult.

If you have permission from customs to keep a weapon on your yacht, it is seldom a good idea to leave it out where it is handy. A loaded gun is dangerous if there are children on board and it is an invitation to theft if someone should come on your boat when you are not there.

There is also the reality of trying to maintain a gun in proper condition on a yacht. Firearms don't like damp salty conditions. Unless the gun is kept well oiled and out of the open air the metal will quickly rust and pit, making it unreliable as a weapon. Thus if the firearm is kept handy it will probably be unreliable, and if it is kept in proper storage it may be difficult to get to quickly. Consider the complications of getting a gun and loading it without the knowledge of the 'uninvited' visitor in the middle of the night.

If you can overcome the various technical problems, there are the moral and practical aspects of shooting another human. Taking someone's life is something that may not seem difficult as an abstraction, but it is in reality. There is so much violence and murder on TV, in movies, and in popular literature, that killing, even in self-defense, may seem an easy decision. Ask yourself, however, if you can without hesitation end the life of another person, because any time you take up a gun that possibility exists.

Then there are the legal aspects, and finally the potential danger that such an act may create for you and your crew. Suppose for example that you are anchored in an area in which theft and other crimes are known to occur. You have a handgun, rifle, or shotgun where you can get to it quickly. In the middle of the night you wake up and hear someone moving about on or in the boat. You reach for your gun – and then what?

If you shout a warning with a threat to shoot, it may frighten off the visitors, but if they also have a gun they may feel sufficiently threatened to shoot at you. If on the other hand you fire a 'scare' shot of warning, a petty thief may suddenly become someone fighting for his life. A struggle for control of the weapon can easily end up with you or your crew being shot by mistake. People have been killed with their own weapons in this kind of situation. Fighting over a gun, especially a rifle or shotgun in the limited space of a yacht, is likely to result in uncontrolled shots being fired. Furthermore if the intruder is successful in taking control of the firearm, he may be in such a frantic state of excitement that a simple thief becomes an enraged killer.

Now suppose that you do shoot or kill someone who has come on your boat, because you assumed that he planned to rob or harm you. Regardless of how terrified you were at the time the event occurred, or how right it may have seemed then to take the action you did, you may still be found guilty of murder or attempted murder and will have to face the legal responsibilities of your action. If the person you killed or wounded was not carrying a weapon you will probably be in very serious problems with the law. Shooting an unarmed person in self-defense will raise doubts even in a fair, legal court. I know it doesn't work that way on TV, but it does in real life. Add to this that you may be a foreigner in a country where the language, laws, and customs are unfamiliar to you.

Finally consider a situation where a midnight intruder is shot by a nervous yacht owner, and it turns out the shooting victim was only some confused drunk who got on the wrong boat by mistake. In such situations the person firing the gun will surely be found guilty of some crime and will have to carry the burden of his action for the rest of his life.

Again, those who do choose to have guns should fully understand the implications of their use. Just having a gun is no assurance of security. You must know how to use it with precision and be willing to do so without hesitation. Once a gun is shown, the scene becomes one of life and death. If you point a gun at someone for whatever reason you must be prepared to kill.

Perhaps by now I have painted a discouraging picture of the potential dangers of cruising. Actually the possibilities of being the victim of serious theft or assault are quite remote. Many folks have sailed for years

Taking Precautions

without any unpleasant incidents. But when serious problems do occur they receive a lot of attention and publicity; news rapidly spreads through the yachting community and makes headlines in newspapers and sailing publications.

Still it is foolish to ignore the possibility of petty or violent crimes when cruising. So what are some of the options other than relying on violent weapons as self-defense?

First, you must choose your cruising area with discretion. If some country or some part of a country has a clearly established reputation for crime, avoid it. On the other hand be realistic about the source of your information. If there is a place you want to visit but you have heard it is dangerous, be sure of the authenticity of the report. Try to decide if the events described were unusual or incidental. If the victims were sailors, ask yourself if the crime or violence was related to sailing.

In some situations it is impossible to avoid visiting dangerous areas. For example most yachts on a circumnavigation will pass through the Panama Canal. Although sailing in that area is not dangerous, there is a high incidence of theft and muggings in the cities of Colón and Balboa. However, by exercising care when ashore and following the advice of other yachtsmen you meet, it isn't difficult to get around the cities without running into danger.

Always be conservative in appearance and conduct. Wearing expensive jewelry, showing large sums of money, or exhibiting fancy cameras is an invitation to a thief. After all, there are a lot of places in the world where the cost of your camera represents more money than some people will earn in a lifetime. Considering that, perhaps it is remarkable that there isn't more crime.

When you arrive in a new port it doesn't hurt to ask politely about safety and security. Usually customs and immigration officials you meet can advise you if and where any dangers exist or of any special precautions you should take.

Where you moor your boat frequently determines its vulnerability to theft. Anchoring is usually safer than being dockside. A thief has to put forth some effort to visit an anchored yacht. Alongside a dock or pier, your boat presents the possibility of theft to anyone walking by.

The question still remains: How should you defend yourself when someone comes uninvited on your boat at night? Various alarm devices are available to discourage theft and to alert the owner of an intruder. In theory they seem reasonable, but they have some drawbacks. Most of them are electronic devices that are difficult to maintain. Too often they malfunction and set off alarms when you are away from your boat, creating a noise nuisance to other yachts in the vicinity. Try sleeping in a marina when the alarm on the boat of an absent owner accidentally goes off at 2 a.m.

One man I know had stainless steel lifelines connected to a device to give a mild but frightening electric shock to anyone who grasped them to come on board uninvited. The problem was that now and then he forgot to disconnect the system and he or his friends became victims. He eventually abandoned the technique.

Most sailors know the story of Joshua Slocum, the first man to sail solo around the world, and his famous simple burglar detector. He once put small tacks all over his deck at night to discourage some unfriendly local people from boarding his boat while he slept at anchor in South America. According to his account, a cry of pain and the sound of someone jumping in the water in the middle of the night proved the worth of the method. Few of us would want to go to the inconvenience of this procedure. Furthermore, some enlightened thieves wear shoes.

Probably no one will attempt to rob a yacht that has a barking dog on board, especially if it is a large dog. But unless you especially like pets this is not a practical burglar alarm to maintain. Furthermore dogs tend to bark at friend and foe alike.

A very effective device to discourage theft when you are on board is a set of bright spreader lights. If you can surprise and temporarily blind someone trying to sneak on board with exposure to a brightly lit deck, all but the most dedicated robber will beat a hasty retreat; especially if the lighting of the deck is accompanied with a loud yell. Most boat thieves are not very professional operators and can be easily scared away.

The situation of waking up to find someone in your cabin presents a more complicated challenge. I have already pointed out the difficulties and dangers of relying on a gun. But there are a few self-defense techniques that can be highly effective if properly used.

Mace will render someone helpless without permanent injury. Aerosol canisters of this chemical can be as small as a fountain pen. If properly aimed mace should overpower the biggest person and give you control.

There is an alternative to mace that may be even better and safer to use. This is an aerosol spray that is made with pepper. It is reported to put attackers completely out of commission by blinding them for up to 30 minutes. The small aerosol spray canister can be used from five or six feet away and if the victim breathes the pepper spray or gets it in his eyes, he will be instantly disabled.

The advantage of mace or pepper spray is that no one will be accidentally wounded or killed; if the intruder happens to be the confused drunk or even a friend who thinks he is playing a practical joke, it will result in nothing worse than some temporary discomfort.

If you choose this option consider a defensive procedure in advance and be sure your crew understands your plan. The idea is to debilitate the intruder but not yourself or your crew.

FORMALITIES

Entering a foreign country by yacht is sometimes incredibly easy and efficient, with procedures completed in minutes. Other times it can take hours and even days to do all of the required paperwork. The comparative ease or complexity of the maneuver is in no way related to the size, wealth, or sophistication of the nation being visited. Even in one country, entrance formalities may vary significantly depending on the particular port.

If your impression of customs and immigration procedures is based on experiences when arriving by jet at an international airport, brace yourself for a big surprise when you come on a small cruising yacht. Those who arrive by '747' will be sitting next to the hotel pool sipping some exotic cocktail within an hour of arrival, while the poor sailor after several hours at anchor may be just beginning to wait for the customs and immigration agents. When the officials do show up there is often a mountain of forms to fill out. Then the rest of that day and maybe the next will be spent trudging along waterfront alleys trying to find the harbormaster's office or the director of port security.

Be Prepared

Getting ready to enter foreign ports really begins before you leave home. Every crewmember must have a current passport if the boat is on an extended cruise although some neighboring countries may waive the requirements on a reciprocal basis. Some countries require a visa prior to arrival, and others will issue a visa or visitor's permit when the boat clears in. Most countries now allow visitors an initial stay, which can range from a few weeks to two or three months. Rules may vary for citizens of different countries – a problem for crews of mixed nationality. There may be opportunities along the way to obtain visas at embassies or consular offices for countries you plan to visit. The problem is that a visa application usually asks for an arrival date, and yachts rarely meet schedules. This happened to me in Kiribati in the Central Pacific. I had gone to a lot of trouble to get a visa in advance, but by the time I arrived it had expired, and I had to purchase a new one.

Some places that were formerly very relaxed about foreign visitors have now enacted more stringent rules. It may be difficult to obtain information about these requirements but a good cruising guidebook will offer some information. The newsletters of the Seven Seas Cruising Association (SSCA) often report on the latest entry procedures for out-of-the-way places.

Getting a passport, gathering information on entry requirements, and then applying for visas or cruising permits takes time. Passports are easy enough to obtain but may take several days to process. To obtain a visa it is sometimes necessary to send your passport to the embassy or consulate of the country you want to visit. Processing each visa may take a week or more.

Along with the crew's personal documents, the ship's papers must be in order. This includes the yacht's registration papers or documentation. In most countries the customs officer will want to see it. The exact form will vary depending on how and in which state or country your boat is registered. If the boat belongs to someone who is not on board there should be some type of official letter or document to indicate that the captain has permission to operate it. The yacht's registration should list its name, country of registry, its size, and displacement. Commonly you will be asked to enter all of this information on a customs form along with a variety of additional data including size, make and type of engine, capacity of fuel and water tanks and radio call sign. In some countries a brief description of the boat and a list of navigation equipment will be requested.

Quarantine

Upon arriving at a port-of-entry, a boat should follow the standard procedure of flying the yellow 'Q' flag from the starboard spreader below the courtesy flag of the country you are visiting (if you have one). By tradition the 'Q' flag means you wish to be visited and inspected by the quarantine officer and to be granted permission to enter or 'pratique.'

Entry Procedures

Figure 35.1
Frequent encounters with quarantine, customs, and immigration officials are a way of life for the cruising crew.

In some places the quarantine officer will arrive within minutes. But a small yacht can be easily overlooked. If you have a VHF radio try to contact the harbormaster's office or some harbor authorities to let them know you are in the harbor and that you want to contact the quarantine, customs, and immigration officials.

If you are unable to contact anyone by radio, one crewmember may go ashore and try to locate the proper authorities. This is not the time to go sightseeing or shopping, because you are not yet officially cleared into the country.

The boarding or quarantine officer's visit is usually brief. He or she will have a form or two to fill out and will probably ask to see your outward clearance from the last port. Perhaps there will be a few questions about certain foods, plants, or animals on board. Unless there is some irregularity or problem you will receive a Certificate of Pratique which means it is safe for the boat and crew to enter the country.

Occasionally you run into a hard-nosed inspector who will try to force ship regulations on a yacht. Once in Japan, a stubborn quarantine officer forced me to pay for a deratting certificate. It took him five minutes to inspect my boat, and I had to pay about $50 for this service. Usually you can talk your way out of these bureaucratic scams, but other times there is no choice.

Once the boat is given pratique the 'Q' flag can be lowered, and you await the visit of customs and immigration. Unless you already know they are coming to the boat, it may be worthwhile to ask the quarantine office to call them, which he may or may not do.

Customs

Traditionally the role of customs has had to do with the control and taxation of imports and exports. A private cruising yacht is not carrying cargo or engaged in commerce. Thus the main concern of the customs agent is to be sure you are not bringing in any prohibited or restricted goods. In recent years this mainly means 'recreational' drugs, but in some places even prescription drugs, especially pain killers containing any narcotics, are included. Honesty is the best policy.

In some countries customs also looks out for illegal import of products derived from animals which are internationally recognized to be endangered species. For instance, yachtsmen coming to New Zealand are required to surrender shells of giant clams, sperm whale teeth, or products made from turtle shell.

Customs officers will first ask to see the clearance from your last port and then there will be one, or more, or many more, forms to complete. Sometimes they are lengthy questionnaires designed for commercial ships and dealing with cargo and ships stores. Customs officers are seldom very particular about details that obviously don't apply to a cruising yacht. You may, however, be required to list in detail how much tobacco and alcohol is on board. Close estimates are usually adequate, but knowingly putting down false information can bring serious trouble. For example if you put down that you have three bottles of whiskey on board, and an inspection reveals a case or two, you can expect some problems and probably a very thorough search of the boat. This can take hours to complete and even more hours to restow the boat.

Customs officers will almost always ask if there are firearms on board, and in many places they will require that guns be taken off the boat and deposited with customs or police until you depart. If you have them on board you had best admit it. If you lie about it and get found out, you can meet with huge fees or strong penalties. I do not carry guns on my boat, but I do have a flare pistol. I don't mention it unless the inspectors ask specifically.

On very rare occasions customs may ask for a list and serial numbers of all cameras, radios, and electronic equipment on your boat. It is a good idea to prepare such a list in advance.

Now and then customs will want to make some sort of inspection, especially if they are skeptical of some of your answers to their questions. When cruising in an area where smuggling is a common problem, you may have to submit to a very thorough search.

In remote places the customs and immigration officials really have very little to do, and they enjoy the rare chance of visiting a small yacht. If they are in no hurry offer them a cup of coffee and take advantage of the opportunity to find out about the area and especially the location of shops and any points of interest.

Immigration

Immigration is the other major agency to deal with. Immigration officers are interested in the crew and will ask to see passports and collect one or two copies of a 'crew list.' This is a list of everyone on board which includes age, date of birth, place of birth, nationality, and passport number. Each person should be listed with their supposed crew position or assignment. For example, Captain, First Mate, Navigator, Cook, etc. You can be mildly creative in the assignment of job descriptions but don't get carried away. Not everyone may share or understand your humor. But every person on board should have a crew assignment because people on boats are either crew or passengers, and unless you are a registered passenger ship it is better not to list anyone as a passenger. It immediately suggests that you are a business, and this could change your status in the country where you are visiting. Crew lists are often asked for by both customs and quarantine so boats sailing with the same crew for a long period of time can photocopy a quantity of crew lists in advance.

Agriculture

Some countries or areas are very rigid about intentional or accidental importation of food, plants, seeds, and animals. They find this necessary to protect their agricultural industry from possible infestation by harmful and destructive insects and diseases. It may seem a nuisance to go along with some of these regulations, but many countries rely on agriculture for much of their national income. Accidental introduction of harmful pests or plant diseases can cost the country millions of dollars in lost crops and jobs.

The severity of the problem is exemplified by Hawaii, where thousands of new species have been introduced in the past two hundred years. Even today approximately 20 new insect species are accidentally brought to the islands each year. A yacht arriving in New Zealand must dispose of nearly all fresh fruits and vegetables, honey, and popcorn. Some grains, seeds, and milk products, depending on their country of origin, may also be destroyed. In addition the agricultural inspector may want to look at wood or other plant products such as souvenirs from the islands to see if they accidentally contain any harmful insects, insect eggs, or spores.

The thoroughness of the New Zealand agricultural inspectors includes taking off and burning any garbage on the newly arrived boat and even emptying the bag of a vacuum cleaner if you have one. They may also check bicycle tires and tent stakes for dirt that might contain dangerous critters. New Zealand, Australia, and Hawaii are especially tough on pets arriving on cruising yachts, and anyone who comes to those places with dogs and cats can expect a lot of inconvenience and expense. The purpose is the control of rabies, and the animals must either be kept on board or put in a special quarantine kennel for an extended period of time at the expense of the owner.

In New Zealand pets are not allowed off the boat. To assure that the rule is enforced, inspectors will visit your yacht two or three times a week. The cost of the inspector's travel is paid by the pet's owner. Similar rules apply in Australia. In Hawaii all incoming animals are put in quarantine for 120 days (or until you leave if your stay is less than four months) at your expense.

Other Officials

There may still be forms to be completed and fees to be paid depending on where you are. In Fiji a major part of the entry process in recent years has been the inspection by Port Security, which seems to be a branch of the army. They also had a form to fill out and a fee to pay. Some ports require a visit to the harbormaster's office to get permission for anchoring or dock space, and in some cases there will be a fee to pay. In places that see few yachts the fees may be based on tonnage, and therefore very inexpensive for a yacht. In Onomichi on Japan's Inland Sea, I stayed at the very convenient ferry dock for nearly two months at a rate of about 25 cents per day because dockage was based on commercial ships at a rate equivalent to approximately three cents per ton.

Some countries have harbor fees or 'light fees' which supposedly help pay for various navigation buoys and lights. Often in such places the aids to navigation are notoriously unreliable.

Finally all of the hurdles have been jumped, and it is now possible to take it easy, be a tourist, relax on board, do some repairs, or whatever is on the plan du jour, with the knowledge that the paperwork is over – for now. When you leave you have to work back through some of the same procedures to obtain a departure clearance. It is not necessary to contact the quarantine office when leaving, but you will have to obtain an outward clearance from customs, get a departure stamp from immigration, and sometimes check out with the harbormaster.

Usually it is more convenient to complete departure formalities the day before leaving, and most officials will be cooperative when you request to do so. If a departure is set for a Saturday, Sunday, or very early on a Monday morning, it may be possible to check out on a Friday.

Agents

You may arrive in a port and be told you have to have an agent to take care of entry procedures. It is almost never necessary.

A ship's agent is a company or individual who handles all the various clearances for a commercial ship, and arranges docking, berthing, and resupplying of the ship, repairs, and any miscellaneous needs. Agents provide a lot of services, but they are expensive. An unscrupulous official may try and talk you into hiring an agent who happens to be a friend or relative, but this rarely happens. I have, however, had agents show up on board with the government officials.

In places that rarely see visiting yachts an agent may volunteer to help you out of kindness and generosity. Be cautious and make sure there are no strings attached before accepting any help. The few times this happened to me in Japan and Korea I appreciated the help, but it would have been easier to do things on my own.

One exception to the 'no agents' rule is the Suez Canal. There it is inevitable, and there are good and not-so-good agents. Prior to reaching the canal, it is worthwhile to talk to other sailors who have recently passed that way to find out what agents are recommended.

Pilots

It is necessary to have a pilot on board to pass through the Panama and Suez canals. Arrangements in Panama can be time-consuming but at least it is a routine and set operation that is run in an honest way. The procedure includes having your boat 'measured,' paying the fees, being assigned a time to make the trip, and taking a pilot (now called an advisor) to guide you through the canal. Going through the Suez Canal can be easy or difficult depending on how good a job your agent does for you in advance.

Dealing With Officials

Going through entry procedures with quarantine, customs, immigration, and other officials can be trying. Usually we have been at sea for several days or weeks and we may have just come through some difficult sailing before making a landfall followed by a complicated harbor entrance and anchoring.

Suddenly we are faced with several officials who have many questions to ask and a lot of forms to complete. Often they are speaking a language or dialect we do not understand. Perhaps we have been forewarned that officials in this new country are dishonest or are looking for a 'gift' or bribe.

At least 99.9 per cent of the time officials that come to your boat are just people who are doing their jobs. For the most part they are extremely patient and friendly. In fact, the way some cruising sailors treat them makes me wonder how and why they are able to maintain their aplomb and politeness.

There are some ways to make your entry to a new country less traumatic and easier for you and for the local officials. First, try to have the boat neat and clean when quarantine and other personnel arrive. If they have to stumble over sheets and sails on deck, it makes their job that much more difficult. They will need a place to sit and fill out the various forms, and usually they will want to do this in the main cabin. A neat boat will give them a better impression. Likewise the personal appearance of the crew often has some bearing on how you are treated. Maybe you enjoy looking 'salty' at sea, but when you come into port it is a good idea to clean up your act.

It is quite all right to offer the government officials coffee or tea. A cold beer or soft drink is in order if you have it on board and want to be hospitable.

It will save confusion if only one crewmember fills out the forms and answers questions. Perhaps the person who is most fluent in the local language should do this. Be honest and answer questions directly. If you don't understand the question or do not know the answer to a question, just say so. But don't volunteer information that is not asked for. This only confuses the issue. In some countries filling out the forms is an end in itself, and probably no one will ever read them. What is most important is that every line and every box is filled in. One time I was not sure how long I would be staying in a port and wrote, 'unknown at this time' in the box that asked for date of departure. This caused total consternation for the polite customs officers. And after about 45 minutes of diplomatic maneuvering by the customs officer, it dawned on me what they wanted, and I wrote down a specific calendar date. It did not matter what the date was as long as it was somewhere in the future.

As a general rule it is better to overestimate than to underestimate your intended length of stay. Extending a visa or visitor's permit is far more difficult and time-consuming than deciding to leave sooner than expected.

Someone in the crew should stay with the inspectors if they look through the boat. Don't be obnoxious and give them the impression that you do not trust them – even if you don't. Just stay nearby and offer to help them open any cabinets, drawers, and other storage spaces.

While talking to the customs and immigration personnel find out what the departure requirements are. This will save time and problems later. Customs and immigration officers are usually a good source of local information to help you get oriented in a new port.

Eventually nearly everyone runs into a dishonest official. Often they are looking for a 'gift' and will try various ploys to get it. You should resist this to the best of your ability. Often playing dumb is the best approach, as even the most dishonest people will be reluctant to ask outright for a bribe for fear of it being reported. Being forced to give 'gifts' to government officials is inconvenient and expensive to you, and it also makes it that much tougher for the next yacht that comes along.

Usually the places where officials try to solicit gifts are well known, and you can be prepared for this before you arrive. Anytime you are required to pay any fees or charges, insist on a receipt. If the person requesting the money says he forgot his receipt book, tell him you will make the payment at his office.

Sometimes it is tempting to offer a bribe to circumvent a lot of paperwork or to bypass some sticky rule. This can be a risky business; offering a bribe can get you into serious trouble in some places.

If there is one rule about entering and leaving a country, it is to be prepared for just about anything. Procedures may be very formal and serious or incredibly casual. Sometimes the official who comes to your boat may be wearing two or three hats, and will take care of all the paperwork for quarantine, customs, and immigration. That same person may also be the local police constable. In some places customs and immigration will want to come to the boat when you leave to see you cast off your lines and head out to sea. Elsewhere I have been told I could stick around for a couple of days, even weeks after checking out while waiting for good weather. One place I was told that all I had to do when leaving was to write 'I go' in chalk on a blackboard on the front door of the police station.

Most importantly, think of the next guy. If you play the game according to local rules and leave a good impression, the next sailboat that arrives will have it easier. Likewise when you enter a new country remember to be a polite guest. Even if you run head first into a disagreeable or difficult government official keep your cool. It may well be that the curmudgeon you are dealing with has just finished clearing in some condescending and pompous rude sailor and has had two of the last three yachts leave without paying harbor fees. It happens.

Finally don't search for uniformity in these procedures. Last year in Tonga the agriculture officer came on board and required that I throw away all of the fruit and vegetables I had brought from New Zealand. The next day another yacht entered from Auckland but a different inspector boarded it and it was not required to get rid of anything. Try to be philosophical about such experiences. No one ever said paradise would be consistent, and if it does become predictable, it won't be paradise anymore.

36

GETTING ALONG IN OTHER CULTURES

The major reason most of us cruise is to visit other countries and cultures. Unlike most tourists our speed and style of travel often offer us the opportunity to temporarily become a part of the communities we visit. But at the same time we are continually on display and the object of a lot of scrutiny, no matter how obscure we may think we are.

Language

Language difficulties are occasionally frustrating and sometimes humorous. Often our first encounter with a new culture is underscored by differences in language when we meet various officials on arrival. It is impossible to learn all the different languages and dialects where we travel, but it is both possible and important to learn some few basic words and phrases. In most places, knowing how to say hello, good-bye, please, thank you, and good-morning, will put you and those you meet more at ease. Second to that, knowing how to count to 10 will come in handy. Usually, a good tourist guidebook will include these fundamentals. Beyond that, you can pick up useful expressions and phrases quickly if you try. It is remarkable how far you can go with a very few words, some sign language, a smile, and a lot of patience. Carrying a bilingual dictionary will get you through the more complicated situations, but in some countries you will encounter a pidgin that may defy description or book translation.

Along with some rudiments of the language it is important early on to learn the various coins and bills of the local currency. It will save you embarrassment and may also keep you from being overcharged.

Local Customs

You are usually forgiven linguistic mistakes, but going against local customs, even when there is no intention of doing so, is sometimes taken as extreme rudeness. Once you have made a faux pas there is usually nothing you can do except apologize. But with a little effort it is usually possible to avoid major pitfalls. Here again your guidebook will fill you in on the unique or different folkways and mores that you can expect to encounter, and you really should take the trouble to find out this information if you want to have a good visit.

Social standards and local laws often cover a wide range of rules of conduct. Some will be very obvious, such as not consuming alcoholic beverages or not swimming on Sunday, or women not wearing shorts or sleeveless blouses in public. In some countries such rules of conduct are basic courtesies to observe, and if you willfully ignore or resist them, be prepared for the contempt and disrespect you will garner. Mistakes made regarding more subtle patterns of behavior, such as how you sit or stand or bow or shake hands, will usually be overlooked, although they often make the local person feel uncomfortable. The more of these you can learn the easier and more relaxed your visit will be.

Some of the customs you see will seem weird, rude, strange, or even repulsive to you. But don't be too hasty in passing judgement, and especially avoid criticism. Every culture has its share of customs and characteristics that are a bit strange to others. Oriental people are just as shocked that anyone would wear shoes inside a house as westerners are surprised that everyone else doesn't.

Be especially alert to customs, rules, and taboos that pertain to religion. Often this is difficult to do without special information. For example, in some places certain buildings or places have special religious significance even though they are not marked or fenced off. Photographing religious ceremonies may be offensive to the participants. Specific dress standards are often required before entering religious buildings.

The Unique Sailor

Even in countries that have a well-developed tourist trade, cruising sailors are in a special category. Typical tourists are often herded around and live in an artificial world constructed just for them. We who arrive by sailboat see a different and more realistic aspect of the culture and have a better opportunity to meet the people who are characteristic of the country.

In spite of this you will want to be a 'tourist' part of the time in order to visit some of the places of scenic or historic interest. Sometimes it isn't so easy to do. If you wait until after you arrive to find out about a country, you may miss out on some of the most fascinating parts of the culture. In many remote places there will be no information about the area other than what you bring with you, and it is remarkable how often local residents fail to tell you about the things that might be most interesting to you. For example, native crafts will rarely even be mentioned by the residents because they don't consider them to be anything other than part of their daily life.

Whereas the jet-traveling tourist is bombarded with brochures, maps, and pamphlets about the local area, the boater may have to search around for information. In most places there is some sort of tourist office or information center, but it may not be easy to find. To become oriented with a new place, try to obtain information before you arrive. Write to the tourist bureaus in advance. Read your guidebooks as you sail to your destination.

Knowing something about a country before you arrive will significantly add to the enjoyment and meaning of your visit.

Sightseeing

There are numerous ways to go sightseeing. Taking part in a tourist bus trip is usually possible, but it is often either boring or so rushed that there is little depth or enjoyment. It is more pleasant to go at your own pace. Whereas the hotel-staying tourist has only a few days you may have several weeks at your disposal.

Sightseeing is much more than just going to famous places. It can also be just wandering around and following no particular plan. One time when traveling in the Greek islands a friend and I found a great way to go sightseeing. Most of the islands are fairly small, so in the mornings we would catch a bus that went to the far end of the island, get out there and spend the day walking back to the harbor. Usually we would not follow the main highway but rather amble along the farmers' roads. All along the way we were greeted warmly by the people out working in their orchards and fields, and frequently we were invited into their homes for coffee or meals.

In the Caribbean I have often spent pleasant days wandering around looking at the vegetation, talking to farmers, and following my instinct with no plan in mind. When it was time to head back to the boat I would hitchhike or catch a bus.

Photos

Most of us like to take a camera along and capture a few memories. Usually people don't mind being photographed, but sometimes they do. Ask first. In a few places people expect or demand to be paid to be photographed. Usually the requested amount is slight and it is rude to refuse. Often these people are so poor that what is insignificant to you is very meaningful to them. If you don't want to pay, then don't take a picture.

Fishing and Diving

Along the tropical cruising routes there are many places noted for their scuba diving, snorkeling, line or spear fishing, or windsurfing. The cruiser has enough time to take full advantage of these activities. Sometimes local residents will take you to the best fishing spots. Before you go fishing or spearfishing on your own, be sure it is permitted. Local fishermen may resent your fishing and consider it a threat to their livelihood. The best rule is to always ask first. If the answer is no, honor that decision. In some places certain kinds of fishing are prohibited, or there is a charge for the privilege to fish. Don't go against the local rules. If you do, it just makes things that much more difficult for the boats that come after you, and it doesn't do much for the reputation of sailing in general.

Other People's Property

Be very careful about picking fruit or flowers just because they appear to be wild or unclaimed. As sure as you gather some coconuts to take back to your boat, it will turn out the trees belong to someone.

Most sailors are outraged at the increase in crime, especially theft, in some harbors, and decry the fact that often it is impossible to leave their boat unattended. Yet some of these same sailors will go ashore and pick coconuts, gather other fruit, or collect clams and lobsters without asking or offering to pay. In nearly all parts of the world where people live a subsistence agrarian existence, every bush, every tree, and even under-water areas belong to a person, a family, or a group. You may not realize this because there are no fences or signs. For those people there is no need of fences because everyone knows what belongs to whom. It does not occur to them that you don't know, or that you come from a society of fences, locked doors, and printed signs. It causes them great consternation to see someone who appears to be very wealthy, such as a cruising sailor, come and steal their food.

Nightlife

You will probably find the nightlife somewhat limited in many of the places you visit. Away from the large cities and tourist gathering places the lifestyle is rural and often quiet and conservative. On the other hand, if you are in a popular yacht anchorage there may be a lot going on among the various boats. If you like to spend time in bars and discos there is ample opportunity in the larger cities and around the main tourist watering places.

Local Workers

Often local people, especially teenagers, will offer to run errands for you, help you with your shopping, or take you sightseeing. There are dozens of moneymaking schemes they may come up with.

In the Caribbean I have hired local teenagers to wash and wax the hull, or to clean the bottom, and they have done an excellent job at a fair price. These are tasks I would normally do myself, but the kids were anxious to work and only wanted an opportunity to make some spending money. I have also hired teenagers as guides. These turned out to be wonderful experiences because we visited nearby plantations and I learned a lot about the local plants and animals. In Panama, a man saw me varnishing and wanted to help me for a reasonable wage. He ended up doing a much better job than I did, and, in addition, helped me buy local fruit and vegetables at very good prices. If someone has a reasonable service to offer and is anxious to work, it seems to me worthwhile to give him an opportunity to do so. Usually you will also gain an enjoyable introduction to the local culture.

Of course, there may be times when someone attempts to cheat you or take advantage of you in some way. I have had a few bad experiences too, but they are minor in comparison with the good times. Don't become too outraged or self-righteous at someone slightly overcharging you because you are a foreigner. Just take your time in contracting for any services. Talk to other boat crews about the local situation, and try to get a cross-section of opinion. Some sailors are mistrustful and discontented no matter what happens.

Returning Favors

Cruising sailors often receive help and favors from people living in the ports they visit. Naturally, you will want to express your appreciation of their kindness by giving them some sort of gift. Sometime the most treasured gift you can give is an inexpensive souvenir from one of the other places you have visited. If you keep this in mind you can purchase various things along the way that will make nice gifts elsewhere.

In other places a memento of your boat is appropriate. For example I have some small pennants with a picture of my boat and its name printed on it. These are often highly valued by those who receive them.

Often the most appropriate gift is an invitation to visit your boat or to go sailing for a few hours. Many people have never been on a cruising boat, and a short sail may be one of the most memorable events of their life.

As simple as it is to do, a letter or postcard of thanks sent from your next port is often a treasured gift. It only takes a few minutes to write a note of appreciation and the pleasure it brings is beyond measure. If possible have some inexpensive stationery printed before you leave home with a drawing or photo of your boat. In the same vein it is worthwhile to have some name cards printed with your name, the boat's name, and your permanent address.

In underdeveloped countries practical gifts are most appreciated. These include T-shirts, fish hooks, vegetable and plant seeds, perfume, and even pencils and paper. Elsewhere, gifts may be determined by tradition, as in Fiji where you are expected to present a gift of yaqona, the root used to make the drink kava, to the chief of any village near which you want to anchor. Such traditions should not be taken lightly.

Treading Softly

In new places, especially those you may consider 'primitive,' take your time, be observant, and see what you can learn. Often people who are poor by western standards lead lives that are enviably rich and fulfilling. Yes, all societies have their injustices and quirks but many have far less divorce, suicide, alcoholism, and other cultural problems than we do. Talk simply and directly to people you meet. Chances are they know a lot more about what is going on in the world than you think. Likewise, just because some speak your language doesn't necessarily mean they are smarter than those who don't. At the same time don't make assumptions about whom you are speaking to based on their appearance. The humblest person in the village sometimes turns out to be the chief.

Westerners in general, and Americans in particular, tend to be a bit preachy. We often think we have a better way to do just about everything. I don't think this necessarily comes from a feeling that we are better than others, so much as it is a desire to share our knowledge, ideas, and especially our technology. But try not to assume you necessarily have a better way of doing things. A lot of practices in other societies have evolved over thousands of years and may have far more practical significance than we can grasp. Often, even the local people no longer understand the 'why' of certain taboos and customs because it has been lost in antiquity. However, as numerous Peace Corps workers learned to their chagrin, there is often a good reason for a seemingly inefficient technique, and to tamper with it or replace it can unleash a whole new set of problems that no one anticipated.

Share your life and culture with new friends through photographs and stories. If you feel like it and the opportunity arises, share your talents and labor rather than your wealth. Spend a few hours helping out with a community project or with garden work. Attending a church service can be one of the most rewarding experiences you will have in a different culture, and will gain you respect and new friends.

Don't make promises you cannot or will not keep. If someone asks you for a favor, don't say you will do it unless you really plan to do so. This includes promises to send photographs and then not doing it. This happens far too often.

The Seven Seas Cruising Association (SSCA) motto seems a good one to foster. It encourages members to 'leave a clean wake.'

37 COMMUNICATIONS, MAIL, AND MONEY MANAGEMENT

An oft-stated reason for cruising is to 'get away from it all,' to eliminate the 'static and noise' of the conventional way of life, and to get free of the mundane and the routine.

'Ah,' says the fast-track executive who has escaped to go sailing, 'no more phones, no more fax messages, just a slow and easy pace where time is not a priority.' Yet this same Type A personality will be seen pacing back and forth in front of an empty telephone office on an atoll in the Pacific fuming because it is Saturday afternoon and the station operator has gone fishing.

Now and then however even the most laid back cruiser finds it necessary to reestablish contact with the real world. Family and friends want to reach us, we have left business matters behind that require attention, we need to have some money or equipment sent, or we just want to stay in touch.

Communication can take up a lot of time and create as much frustration as some of the most confounding sailing problems. Every cruiser has a few 'war stories' to tell about mail that did not get forwarded or the difficulties of getting a bank draft processed. In almost every port there is some poor sailor waiting weeks for a seemingly insignificant but absolutely essential small part that prevents completion of an important repair.

Phone and Fax

Telephone and fax service is just about everywhere these days, and satellite transmission makes for highly reliable and clear communication. Even remote areas of most countries now have instant communications with the rest of the world.

Often, however, you will pay dearly for these services, and don't expect the convenience you have elsewhere. It may be possible to make a phone call 24 hours a day and seven days a week, but you might have to travel to a phone company office some miles away from your anchorage. Fax machines have come on strong in the most remote places, but often the charges to send and receive are much higher than back home and fax service is sometimes restricted to regular business working hours.

In some countries it is possible to use a telephone credit card. Otherwise it is strictly cash, often in advance, and frequently there is what I call an 'attempt charge,' ie. a service charge to make the call even if no one answers.

Before leaving home explain to family and friends that it is often complicated to call due to time differences and the difficulty of traveling to the local phone exchange. These difficulties can be especially vexing and expensive when trying to contact someone who is coming to go sailing with you. Carefully laid plans made far in advance by mail can save a lot of inconvenient phone calls.

Mail Forwarding

When on an extended cruise it is essential to maintain an address in your own country and have mail sent on to the boat from time to time. Some cruisers find that someone in their family is willing to take on this task, but it is a much bigger job than most people realize, especially if you are leaving behind any business or important financial matters that require special care. Asking a friend to do this is usually not a good idea. At first they may enjoy doing it, but eventually it becomes a burden. It may even wear thin for someone in your family.

The alternative is to contract with a professional mail forwarding service, and pay a monthly or yearly fee for their services, plus mailing costs. With this type of service you can have all of your mail, including packages, sent to you in care of their address. They hold it for you until you give them a forwarding address, at which time they put it in one package and send it on to you.

Most of these agencies are efficient and reliable, but occasionally I hear of one that has turned up its toes. Sailors report that suddenly they

Figure 37.1
Communication with family, friends, and business associates back home is often a now and then event when cruising.

stop receiving mail and eventually learn that the service they subscribed to has shut down without notice. Select a forwarding agent by getting opinions from cruisers who have been using one company for a long time.

If you are absolutely sure where you are going and reasonably certain about your arrival date, you can have your mail sent in advance. After a long time at sea it is nice to come into port and have a bundle of letters waiting. But if you are delayed for any reason or if circumstances make it necessary to change your destination, you may have a problem getting the mail sent on to a new location. A more reliable method is to wait until you arrive to inform your forwarding agent. This can be done by letter, by phone call, or by fax. It usually means you will have to wait in your new port for two or three weeks for the mail, but most port stops are at least this long anyway.

There are various places to have mail sent to you in a foreign port. Sometimes you may have friends where you are going. If so, be sure they will be there when you arrive, and also tell them in advance that mail is being sent to you in care of them. American Express allows its card-holders to have their mail sent in care of their offices in foreign countries. The problem with this is that some offices are far from where you are anchored. Often it is convenient to have mail sent in care of a yacht club that you expect to visit. In either of those two examples be sure that their address is current. If it has changed, the mail will be sent back or may languish in a post office for some time. Also with this system there is often little or no security for your mail.

The most reliable way of receiving mail is to have it sent to a post office in care of 'General Delivery' or 'Poste Restante' with your name and the yacht name. For example:

Mr. John Smith
Yacht Golden Girl
Poste Restante
Vila
VENUATO

Regulations of the U.S. Postal Service require that general delivery mail be held for 10 days, although the post office will often hang on to it for a few days longer before returning it to the sender. The only way it will officially save mail beyond the 10-day limit is if there is a message on the envelope that says to hold until a certain date, for example, 'Hold until July 20.' 'Hold for arrival' does not get any extension beyond 10 days. Other countries have a similar official holding policy but in many places it is not rigidly followed. I have seen mail in some of the Pacific Islands that dated back for more than a year. I have also been impressed with the reliability of seemingly relaxed post office personnel in out of the way places.

Some experienced cruisers recommend sending a postcard or letter to the post office well in advance of arrival to inform them you are expecting mail, and to give a liberal estimate of the arrival date. At the same time you can request that they hold your mail if you are delayed. This may help, but there are no guarantees.

When picking up Poste Restante mail you will usually be asked for identification. If the office is especially strict they may require that you present the passport or a letter of permission from anyone else on the boat whose mail you are collecting.

Before sailing to a large metropolitan area try to find out where you expect to be anchored in relationship to the city center. Some yacht harbors are many miles from the main post office, and it may be more convenient to have mail sent to a branch post office.

Receiving Yacht Equipment

In most countries, but certainly not all, a 'yacht-in-transit' does not have to pay duty on items that are received from the outside by mail or freight, and usually the items will be excluded from other goods and services taxes. Just be sure the imported items are on board when you clear out with customs on departure. I have had customs officers show up unexpectedly just prior to my leaving and ask to see items received weeks before. One time overseas I imported a radar. When it arrived the customs officers were seemingly disinterested and passed it through without comment. But then they began to casually drop by the boat each week for a cup of coffee and a chat until it was mounted on the boat. Another time three customs officers and a driver came by several weeks after I had received two pairs of prescription sunglasses in the mail to be sure they were still on the boat. Each of the uniformed customs men and the driver carefully peered through the glasses to confirm that they were indeed the ones that had been sent from America.

Rules and regulations vary widely from country to country and also depend on the specific items. For example, some countries that have no duty for imported yacht equipment may levy a duty on foul-weather gear, because the customs office considers it clothing rather than boat supplies. Receiving yacht equipment such as engine parts can be extremely complicated and expensive, yet nearly every cruiser will have to do this someday. Often the complications arise from the method of shipping chosen. Because most North American suppliers are only acquainted with domestic shipping, they prefer to use commercial delivery services such as Federal Express or United Parcel Service. This is easier for the shipper, because the delivery services come right to their door. Supposedly it is also better for you too, because deliveries are made to a final destination, such as a yacht club or boatyard, which means you don't have to go looking for the shipment. But often it doesn't work that way.

When overseas parcels are sent from one developed nation to another, delivery services usually maintain their efficient reputation. But be prepared for some significant differences in service. For example, to speed things on to the addressee's doorstep Federal Express in Japan automatically pays the duty and the 3% consumption tax on all the packages it receives. Naturally it then passes that on to the recipient. There is no category for, nor any interest in, a 'yacht-in-transit.' In New Zealand parcel delivery systems understand the meaning of 'yacht-in-transit,' but it still may take several long-distance phone calls to get items cleared through customs and shipped to locations outside of Auckland.

So-called courier services designed especially for sending important letters and documents, such as DHL and TNT, don't work very well in remote places, no matter what they promise. Yes, they have agents and they have routing systems that look good on paper, but sometimes weeks, not hours or days, can elapse before shipments reach you. Even if a packet arrives at its destination country in a reasonable time, it may lie around in some dusty office for weeks, because the agent doesn't know (or sometimes care) where to look for you. If anything, the agent usually expects that you will come asking for the item.

So what is the best way for shipping parcels quickly and efficiently? Surprisingly, I think it is the good old reliable air mail system for anything that will conform to the size and weight constraints put on packages. I have never had a problem with anything sent by air mail if it was labeled with my name, the boat's name and 'yacht-in-transit' in big, bold letters on the package. Invariably it arrives fast and somehow always goes right through customs without a hitch. Some shippers don't like using air mail, however. Companies often refuse to send by the postal system, because it means someone has to take the package to the post office. Thus, if you have a choice of sources for something you need shipped to an out-of-country address, select one willing to send by air mail, and you will be time and money ahead.

Air freight can be the most frustrating and difficult way of all to receive shipments when you are sailing. However, for large bulky items it may be the only choice. When I was in Panama I had a sail sent from England. Even though Panama permits duty-free imports for transiting yachts, it still took me almost two days and cost over $100 in various fees and taxi fares to obtain my sail.

Air freight agents will not come looking for you, so it is important to have some information from the shipper. This means an 'air bill' or 'way bill' number including the flight numbers and time of departure. If possible have the shipper send this to you by fax. With this information in hand it will be much easier to talk to the local air freight agent. Once the shipment has arrived, it is often necessary for you to go to the airport and collect the paperwork from the freight agent and then get clearance from customs. This exercise will be of varying complexity depending on the local situation. There can be all sorts of unexpected glitches introduced, and each of them will usually require some form or stamp, and each one will cost something.

Local people and even government officials may try and coerce you into hiring a shipping or customs agent to handle incoming freight. Usually this is not necessary, and you can do all the paperwork yourself if you are willing to spend the time and can arrange the transportation. The problem is that you may have to visit several widely scattered offices and make one or more trips to the airport. Imagine the difficulties this can entail if you are in a strange place without a car and you don't speak the language. Often the airport is far away from where you are anchored, and public transportation is your only choice short of hiring a taxi or renting a car. In some places a savvy taxi driver can be well worth the investment.

There are a few places where the customs agents or other officials are dishonest and will try to extract some illegal fees and charges. Talk to other cruisers about what they have experienced before you have anything shipped to you. It may be better to wait until your next port.

Money and Banking

Unless you are supporting yourself by working as you cruise, it will sometimes be necessary to have money sent to you from your bank or from someone who is handling your finances. There are various ways to receive money, but all of them have their limitations. Plan ahead so that you arrange to receive money well in advance of needing it. It is incredible how slow the process can be, especially when you are broke.

Having sufficient funds on board is not just a convenience. Sometimes it is a legal requirement. In a few countries you must have onward airplane tickets for all crewmembers or post a refundable bond for the yacht. In addition there are places where evidence of enough money to support yourself and each crewmember for the duration of your visit is required. If you are planning to stay in a country for several months, this can be a sizeable amount of money.

Cash

You should not carry excessive amounts of cash onboard, and what you do have should be carefully hidden in various places on the boat. United States currency is the most widely accepted cash and is recognized everywhere. As part of your cash supply, consider carrying bills of small denomination. Small bills may permit you to hire emergency help in remote places. If you arrive in a new country on a weekend or holiday, and it is impossible to purchase the local currency, you can often get by with US dollars.

Traveler's Checks

Traveler's checks are second only to cash for their convenience, and they are much safer. Although traveler's checks carry a service charge, they often receive a better rate of exchange than cash when converted to another currency. If they are lost or stolen the issuing agency will replace them.

When you first arrive in a new country try to be realistic about how much money you need to convert to local currency. Going to a bank may be inconvenient and time-consuming. When you leave, however, you don't want to have an excessive amount of local currency on hand. Every time you exchange money the bank or exchange agent gets a small percentage, and some currencies are worthless outside of their country of origin.

Credit Cards

In the past credit cards were of little use except in developed countries, or areas with a large tourist business. Now they are becoming increasingly popular even in remote areas. However, not all cards are accepted, and even when cards are used they may not be useful for all services. For example, in the Pacific Island groups of Kiribati and Tuvalu, it is now possible to use Mastercard, but only for cash advances at the bank.

Throughout the world, American Express, Visa and Mastercard are the most popular credit cards. If you have to leave your yacht and fly home unexpectedly, you can buy an airplane ticket anywhere in the world with a major credit card. Credit cards are especially convenient when ordering parts or supplies.

With most major credit cards it is possible to obtain cash advances on your credit card account, or to use the card as a backup when writing a check for cash. Usually this must be done at the regional office of the credit card company or at a cooperating bank. Before you use these services be sure you understand what the handling charges are for this convenience. You may find that one type of credit card is better suited to your needs than another.

If you plan on having a credit card when you are sailing, be sure to get it while you are still employed. Once you are sailing and unemployed, the credit card company will be much less interested in having you as a customer.

Bank Account

The image of cruisers being always on the go is not really correct. Often the boat ends up staying in one country for an extended period of time while you enjoy the country, while waiting out a hurricane season, or during an extended haul-out and repair period. When staying in a country for several months an efficient, convenient, and economical way to take care of money needs is to open a local bank account. It was only after several years of cruising that I realized the convenience of this.

The account can be opened by writing a personal check on your account back home for the initial deposit. There may not even be any service charge for this. It will take perhaps two to three weeks for the check to clear and then you can use the local account. In most places if you maintain a balance of a certain amount there will be no bank charges, and in some places your checks will be free.

Asset-Management Accounts

All of the major brokerage firms now offer some kind of asset-management accounts. There are more than a dozen of these plans available. To open an AMA requires a deposit of anywhere from $1000 to $20,000 depending on the company. Your money is put into a money market fund, but unlike traditional money market accounts you have more convenient services at your disposal. Most AMAs have unlimited, no-minimum, no-fee checking and most important in my opinion is that they all include a Visa, Mastercard or American Express debit (*not credit*) card. That means any charges you make with your plastic card are paid directly from your account and you thereby avoid any interest charges for late payment – a problem that often plagues cruisers whose credit card bills come to them at irregular intervals.

The May 1992 issue of *Kiplinger's Personal Finance Magazine* and the February 3, 1992 issue of *Business Week* both have detailed comparisons of the various AMAs offered in the U.S. At the present time AMAs appear to be one of the most convenient methods of banking for the cruising sailor.

Bank Transfers

Sometimes a bank transfer is the only alternative if you run short of money or if an unexpected major repair job comes up. You will have to send a letter or fax message to your home bank to have the money sent to you. In anticipation of this possibility, talk to your bank before you set out on a cruise to learn exactly how they handle this type of service, how much they charge for making a transfer, and what the exact procedures are for doing it. It might also be worthwhile to check with other banks to see if they are more efficient and convenient. International banks are usually best for this type of service.

When you are cruising and want to make a bank transfer try to find a major, preferably international, bank and ask what you need to do to have money wired from your home bank. Also find out in advance what the service charges are and how long it will take. These days with rapid electronic communications, it should be a simple matter, taking only a few hours at the most. Yet, this process can be very slow, taking as long as two weeks or more.

Sometimes banks will only pay you in the local currency. Here is an example of what can happen: You are somewhere out on the cruising trail and about ready to leave your current anchorage to head for another country. You decide you need to replenish your cruising funds. Because bank transfers usually have flat rate charges, you decide to have a large amount of money sent to you at one time. Perhaps enough for several months. Everything goes according to schedule, and you go to the local bank to pick up your money. You then find to your surprise that the bank will only give you local currency, and it is one of those that is not honored outside of that country. Before it is all over, you end up paying for a service charge and wire charges for your home bank, the service charge for the local bank, the fee for converting dollars to the local currency, and then the fee to convert local currency to dollars or some currency that is acceptable in the region. All in all this can easily come to more than 10 percent of the original value of the money.

Before leaving home determine what your options are for receiving funds from your bank when you are out of the country. Find out what kind of service you can expect from your home bank, give serious consideration to having one or more credit cards, and take along traveler's checks to keep you going for several months, as well as a realistic amount of cash, preferably in U.S. dollars.

38

WHAT IS THE COST OF CRUISING?

The classic answer to this question is, 'As much money as you have!' For many long-time cruising families this facile response is, in fact, correct. They say that when money becomes scarce they continue cruising, but at a more economical level. When the 'cruising kitty' is well-supplied they live more lavishly.

All kinds of boats and all kinds of people go cruising. You can sail around the world in a very simple boat, without an engine, without refrigeration, without electronics, without fancy clothes. You can anchor where it is free, do all you own maintenance, and eat simple but healthy foods, and get by on very little money. On the other hand, if you are able to do so and prefer it, you can have a luxurious yacht with all sort of electronics, air conditioning, a washing machine, freezer and refrigerator, watermaker, and powerful engines and generators. You can stay in marinas, hire others to do your maintenance and upkeep, and spend large sums for your enjoyment in the most expensive ports. You can even hire a captain, crew and cook. There are people who do it that way.

The fact that either choice, or something in between, is possible is one of the nice aspects of sailing. I have met people who were out of money but undaunted, sailing on to the next port, sure that they could find work there.

Twenty years ago many couples reported cruising comfortably for three or four thousand dollars a year. Ten years ago the figures were more like five to eight thousand dollars a year, and now it is perhaps twelve to fourteen thousand. Those are averages and certainly there are people doing it for more or less. It is really tough to come up with specific numbers because people's lifestyles vary so greatly.

Costs that are Reduced

Some expenses disappear or are greatly reduced when cruising. For most people living on land the cost of maintaining a car and paying for other types of transportation consumes a significant part of their expenses. The cruiser has the expense of the boat engine, but that is usually rather small in comparison. For example, *Denali* averages less than 150 gallons of fuel per year when cruising, and now that I have solar panels that will probably become even less.

Sometimes cruising families who stay in one place for several months, for example New Zealand during the austral summer, buy a used car to tour around in, then sell it when they leave for about the price they paid for it. However, it is often possible and really quite pleasant to get around with bicycles that you can carry on board. A lot of places in the world have excellent public transportation, which is also a good way to get to know local people. In many remote areas the local buses are quite cheap. In general, the sailors's need for land transportation becomes less important. The pace of life is slower, and whether you go to town today or tomorrow is seldom very important.

Clothing costs are greatly reduced. There is no need to be fashionably dressed, and few boats can spare the room for clothing that isn't needed. The most expensive clothing on most boats is the foul-weather gear, which will last for years if properly cared for. Popular cruising areas are mainly in tropical waters where shorts and T-shirts are typical apparel at sea and much of the time on land.

Almost all cruising families report that they spend much less on medical expenses when sailing. Cruising is mainly a healthy way of life. Perhaps because there are often no doctors around we manage to get by without their services or their expense.

Entertainment costs are minimal. There are exceptions to this of course, but in the most enjoyable cruising areas there is little need, and often not much opportunity, for these expenses. A lot of entertaining takes place on board, with several yachts getting together for a dinner where everyone brings part of the meal. Alcohol is usually on a BYOB basis. When visitors drop by for a casual visit on board, tea or coffee is typical fare and maybe some cookies or bread if something recently came out of the oven. No one expects lavish food or drink.

If you have been paying for yacht insurance you can probably forget about this expense when you go cruising. Even if you want insurance there are few companies that will write a policy for offshore sailing. Those that do charge high rates. The best insurance most of us have is to buy more and better equipment for anchoring. Being without insurance is not as difficult as it might seem. It puts increased responsibility on the crew, but on the other hand the boat is seldom left unattended for long periods of time. Furthermore, on cruising boats, seaworthiness is maintained at a high standard.

Food costs will surely be less than they were at home if you do your own cooking and learn to enjoy the local foods. Fresh seasonal foods are always the least expensive.

Provisioning wisely, as discussed elsewhere, plays a big role in budget survival. If you shop carefully and buy in quantity you will realize substantial savings.

Costs that Increase

The fact that a cruising boat is continually in use results in more frequent maintenance and repair and, again, the maintenance costs go up with the size of the boat and amount of ancillary equipment on board.

Maintenance costs are mitigated significantly by the amount of upkeep work you are willing to do yourself. Most cruisers do as much of their own repair work as possible. For haul-outs they find yards where the crew is permitted to take care of their own boat and hire outside assistance only for unusually complicated jobs or work that requires special tools or experience. Obviously, staying ahead of maintenance jobs will reduce expensive repairs later on, and having adequate spares on board will make repairs easier.

I have heard some sailors issue the edict that they refuse to have any equipment on the boat that they are unable to repair themselves. While this may seem extreme, especially when it comes to electronic equipment that few of us are capable of repairing it has merit as a general policy. Perhaps a more realistic dictum would be to not have anything aboard that you are not willing to live without if (read: when) it breaks down.

EMPLOYMENT WHILE CRUISING

Some people plan their cruising as an extended vacation. It is a clearly defined event with a specific beginning and end, and well-marked objectives along the way. For others cruising is a much more open-ended adventure. Perhaps a circumnavigation is in mind but there is no set time limit. The philosophy is, 'to see how it goes.' Maybe along the way they will find places they particularly like and may linger there for months or even years. Others start out on the assumption they will be gone for only a few months, and then find they are enjoying themselves so much that the adventure extends indefinitely.

Except for those who are wealthy or have significant savings, most sailors must find work at some point during an extended cruise. No one planning a trip should be misled into thinking that there are jobs everywhere for the asking. Sometimes they are hard to find, and wages may be well below those paid in North America or Europe.

Employment opportunities will occasionally present themselves but more often, you must go out and look for them. Sailors with specific professional or technical skills will be the first to find work. For the rest of us who are in the categories of over- and under-qualified, there is usually work if we are not too fussy about the kind of job.

Legal Aspects

Most countries do not permit foreigners to work unless they have a work permit, special visa, or government permission. That is the rule, but often it is meaningless. Sometimes obtaining permission is easy, and often it depends on the type of work and the length of time you plan to work. For example, if you are a professional in some field, and the country you are visiting needs people with those qualifications, the necessary permits are usually easy to obtain. On the other hand if your employment will, in theory or in fact, replace a local worker, it will be more difficult. A lot of this depends on being in the right place at the right time. Remote, underdeveloped countries often have a need for teachers, doctors, nurses, or engineers.

Even in countries where rules on foreign workers are strict sometimes the enforcement is not and no one pays attention to visiting sailors working. See what other sailors are doing and ask them about the local situation. However, if you are working illegally, you may be forced to leave on very short notice – sometimes within 24 hours.

It may be possible to swap jobs or swap time. For example, a cruising sailmaker might repair a sail for you and you might paint or help paint the bottom of his boat. This type of work is never questioned by the authorities.

U.S. citizens have several opportunities for working in the Pacific. Hawaii, American Samoa, and Guam are all parts of the U.S., and there are no special problems in working. The Marshall Islands and the Commonwealth of the Northern Mariana Islands are independent of the U.S., but they continue to have close ties, including using U.S. currency and the U.S. postal system. In recent years I have visited Guam, American Samoa and the Marshalls, and there were Americans, Canadians, and Aussies working in sailmaking, construction, day care, newspaper reporting, house painting, canvas work, aquaculture, and as nurses and doctors. Many of them were living aboard their boats.

For British sailors there are work possibilities among some of the former commonwealth countries and British dependencies. However, the requirements vary widely and sometimes depend on an individual's age as well as his or her skills. The best advice is to inquire from a consulate of the countries you plan to visit and to do so far in advance of expected arrival time. British Information Services offices can provide you with a list of the names and addresses of information offices of the various countries.

Boat Work

Sailors with boat maintenance skills can almost always find work. If you are a sailmaker, rigger, carpenter, welder, or engine repairman, or you are skilled in woodwork or fiberglass repairs, you will find work if you have the necessary tools and equipment with you. Jobs done on a private basis seldom catch the attention of immigration authorities unless you stay for an unusually long period of time in one place or start to advertise or open a shop.

Even if you are not skilled at boat building or yacht maintenance, there are often related jobs available. The fact that you are a sailor and have experience gained from working on your own boat qualifies you for many jobs. Simple things such as cleaning boat bottoms by snorkeling or scuba is something almost anyone can do. Cleaning and painting hulls during haul-out is not a highly skilled task but one some owners don't want to do themselves. A lot of owners like the look of varnished woodwork and will hire someone to do the work for them.

Occasionally there are jobs teaching sailing to children or adults. To a cruising sailor who is only looking for part-time employment, this can be easy and enjoyable income. Sometimes sailing schools are looking for instructors, and the fact that you are an experienced ocean cruising sailor makes you an 'expert.'

Chartering

Those who set out on a cruise with plans to charter their boat are often disappointed. There is a lot more to chartering than many people realize. Some countries, the United States for example, have very rigid rules and regulations for chartering which are actively enforced. Attempts to circumvent chartering laws are not advised as the penalties are severe. In some places the rules for chartering do permit 'bareboat' charters. In this case you charter only the boat (no crew) with the customer

Figure 39.1
Jobs for cruisers. Regardless of their employment before sailing many sailors find new and often unexpected ways to support themselves as they travel along.

assuming responsibility for the vessel. Cruisers who may have their whole fortune wrapped up in their boat will not be anxious to let someone take their home and sail away. Furthermore, where would you live while the boat is gone? The way around this is for the customer to also hire the yacht's crew. Obviously this is the same as chartering, but it is sometimes done this way to stay within the law.

Chartering also includes liability for your passengers. If someone is injured on your boat when it is in charter, you may become involved in expensive and complicated legal procedures. Chartering is beset with other complications too. If the people you take on a charter vacation are not used to boat life, they may be difficult to get along with, demanding, and careless about the equipment on your yacht. On the other hand a pleasant charter party can develop into a lifelong friendship.

The easiest and most financially worthwhile chartering is to take people on one-day or half-day sailing trips. Usually the amount of money you earn for short trips is good and you still have your 'home' to yourself most of the time. In places where there is an active charter business already established, you will find they do not welcome outsiders offering competition.

Yacht Deliveries

Perhaps you have never considered yacht deliveries as an occupation, but these jobs do come up now and then. Once you have become an experienced offshore sailor, you may be offered delivery jobs. Such work does not usually pay very well if you consider how much per hour you are making. However, if you enjoy sailing, it is a logical way to resupply your cruising budget. Before you take on this responsibility, consider liability, condition of the yacht to be delivered, where to leave your boat while you are gone, and the honesty and integrity of the customer. Whenever you meet another cruising sailor who has done some delivery work, take advantage of the opportunity to learn from his experience and advice.

Writing and Photography

Sailing lends itself to writing. Other than a typewriter or word processor, you need little equipment, and writing is something you can do in your spare time. Your travels will always include interesting adventures, and often the places you visit can only be reached by boat. Reading the popular sailing magazines or looking over a list of sailing books gives the impression that many sailors are writers. It is true that some people are able to supplement their cruising funds by selling articles or even writing books. However, far more manuscripts are submitted than are ever printed, and editors of sailing magazines are deluged with stories.

If you are successful in selling your writing to a major publication, the money you earn will just about help with the groceries, but that's it. There are very few cruisers prolific and successful enough in this endeavor to fully support themselves. Probably the personal satisfaction and enjoyment of seeing their writing or photographs in print now and then is the major reward for many people.

Cruising adventures make good stories, but these are not the only kind of sailing articles to consider writing. New techniques, a different style of rigging, maintenance tips, and 'how to' stories are valuable to readers and less commonly submitted, making them more likely to be picked up by sailing magazines. If you have a new way, a better way, or a unique way of doing something on your boat, consider using it for a story. Have you ever seen a good 'how to' story in a sailing magazine about fishing? I would love to read that story as I am a lousy fisherman.

Sailing magazines, however, represent a very small part of the magazine market. Look around for other magazines that emphasize human interest stories and personal experiences. A few minutes spent looking at *Writer's Market* or *Writers' and Artists' Yearbook* in your public library will introduce you to a large number of potential markets. There are all sorts of associations and professional publications that print stories on a wide range of interests. Once you score with one of these publications, you have a chance to write additional stories because you are a known quantity. The small special interest journals may not pay very much but if you are able to establish a continuing market, the steady flow will be a nice supplement to cruising funds. In addition you can sometimes sell the same story to more than one magazine if the magazines have different markets. The other advantage of writing, even for a low-paying publication, is that it keeps you in the game, and as you continue to write your skills will improve. That in turn may eventually lead to success with one of the more up-market publications.

All sailing magazines look for good photographs that will attract readers' attention. Good photos are especially important when you are trying to sell an article. Editors prefer high-quality 35mm color slides, because they reproduce much better than prints. When taking photographs intended to be sold to a magazine, don't be afraid to take a lot of pictures. Most people will be lucky to get one or two really good photographs suitable for publication from one roll of 36 exposures.

Miscellaneous

Almost anywhere in the world you can find some sort of work if you really want it, and if you are flexible. Jobs you never considered doing at home may be available when sailing. Many – like house painting, construction, or acting as a night watchman – are not complicated nor do they require special skills. Work that might be unpleasant on a continuing basis is not so bad for short periods of time. You may be surprised at how many opportunities come your way if you casually mention that you would like to find some part-time work. Sometimes just noticing something that needs to be done and offering to do it will produce good results.

In Japan some cruising sailors from North America, England, New Zealand, and Australia have managed to make good money teaching conversational English. Although this may sound difficult, it isn't. Mostly it consists of just talking with the students to help build up their confidence in speaking English. Most of the students are adults who are planning to visit abroad for business or for vacations. If you are fluent in other languages, there are opportunities for informal teaching throughout the world. I have met sailors who were teaching dance to children, working in day care centers, even teaching various kinds of ethnic cooking.

Sailors with handicraft skills sometimes sell at craft shows or from their boats. These skills include jewelry making, weaving, scrimshaw, painting, and leather work. It is not unusual to see someone picking up some cruising money by cutting hair on board their boat in a popular anchorage.

40 WRAP UP

After reading this book the most pressing questions you began with may still remain: 'Is cruising what I really want to do? Is the large commitment of time and money for preparation worthwhile for something I'm not sure about?'

As obvious as those questions are it is sad that some people fail to consider them before they rush headlong into cruising. There are far too many examples of folks who simply assumed they would enjoy this way of life and then found out too late that they did not. Some people spend years building a yacht only to learn that it is the planning and the project, not the sailing, that they enjoy most. Others have sold their homes, given up the security of their jobs, and sailed away, only to find within a few months that it was a wrong decision. Sometimes it takes years before they are willing to admit to the mistake. In ports around the world there are boats for sale that represent broken dreams. For a very wealthy person the mistake might be insignificant, but for most of us it can be a blunder that will take years to overcome.

Such a mistake takes an emotional as well as a financial toll on a family. If the crew isn't adequately prepared before setting offshore, the cruise can be sheer hell and eventually even result in the break-up of a family. If the transition from living in a house with a lot of space and modern conveniences to the close quarters and more basic style of a small boat is not made gradually the results are often unfortunate. For those who thrive on having a lot of friends around and an extensive list of activities to occupy their time, the cruising life may be disappointing and lonely. It is easy to say, but it also happens to be true, that no one *really* knows how they feel about cruising until they have spent some time doing it.

If you already have a yacht, no matter what type or what size, it is possible to try some cruising even if it only means occasional gunkholing on weekends and holidays. There are probably far more places nearby to go 'cruising' than you realize. Break away from the common practice of overloading the boat with people and rafting up with a bunch of other boats. Instead take only yourself and your family, if that is who you expect to go cruising with, and sail to an isolated anchorage. Experience being on your own and having to rely on yourself. Being a cruiser does not mean becoming a hermit, but there are still long periods of time at sea and sometimes in port when you are on your own.

If initial attempts prove to be enjoyable, increase the time and distance of your cruising while staying within the capabilities of your present boat. It isn't necessary to sail to Hawaii or Puerto Rico to find out if you like cruising. Even with limited time it is possible to cruise for a few days and then leave the boat in some safe harbor or marina and come back later and continue the trip. Every cruising trip you make, no matter how short or long, will provide new experiences and new challenges. Each time you complete one of these journeys you will come home with some new ideas on how to do it better the next time. Try to anchor as much as possible. This is a skill that can never be overlearned.

Chartering

Another way to test your dream is by chartering. Charter vacations are offered in many parts of the world, and will give a certain flavor of cruising. However, on most charters, even bareboat charters, everything has been done for the customer and the sailing is often highly programed. It is a nice way to introduce inexperienced family members to the concept of 'cruising,' but it will not provide an introduction to independence and the responsibility that only comes by being on your own.

Building Skills

If the dream for offshore voyaging is strong but the reality lies several years ahead, there are numerous skills you can develop in the meantime. Celestial navigation, ropework, sail maintenance, canvas work, fiberglass techniques, and diesel engine repair are a few of the skills to be acquired. There is nothing magic about any of these that makes them beyond your ability to learn if you have the time and desire, and they are all useful whether you eventually go cruising or not. There is probably an evening vocational program nearby that offers courses in some of these subjects. Finally, you can do a lot of reading; there are dozens of books on various aspects of sailing and yacht maintenance.

YACHT SURVEYS

Finding a qualified yacht surveyor is an important part of purchasing the right boat. Ideally the surveyor will be someone with extensive experience in building boats similar to the one you wish to buy, and if you are planning a long-distance cruise your surveyor should have sailed offshore. Good surveyors with the proper qualifications are often hard to find, and in many places anyone can call himself a surveyor, regardless of experience.

In most cases the agreement between the seller and the buyer at the time a deposit is made stipulates that a *satisfactory survey* report must be made within so many days, and that following a successful survey, the buyer must pay the balance or forfeit his deposit. In the meantime the seller cannot sell the boat to another person.

Deciding what is a satisfactory survey report has its grey areas. A survey of *any* used boat will expose many problems. There are no perfect boats, and if the surveyor does the job correctly there may be several pages of problems and recommendations. Most of the faults the surveyor finds will be minor ones, and these will not make the survey 'unsatisfactory.' Faults in the boat which affect its seaworthiness or major problems with equipment, however, are factors that may lead to a negative report. Some of these factors could be: an inoperative engine or one in poor condition, evidence of extensive leaks at the deck-hull seam, cracks around the keel, or other evidence of hull damage, delamination, or significant indications of osmosis.

If the report does prove negative, but you are still interested in buying the boat, you can try and get the seller to either make necessary repairs or to lower the price accordingly. In preparing for this meeting, the buyer should have in mind what the necessary repairs will cost in the event the owner offers to lower the price. Your surveyor may be willing to indicate an estimate in the survey report. This is another reason why the surveyor should be experienced in boatbuilding.

A survey should be made with the boat out of the water. Normally the buyer will have to pay for the haul-out, as well as for the survey. So before you take on the cost of a survey, be sure that this is the boat you want. It is best to do your own survey before you call in the expert.

The following headings are from a survey form I made up when I was shopping for a boat. Even with a boat that is afloat, most of the questions can be answered. It takes several hours to do this job properly, but by the time you have completed it you will have a solid knowledge of the boat.

**Headings for a
Do-it-Yourself
Survey Form**

General Information

Yacht name. Yacht Registration number. Owner's name and address. Yacht type. General description of yacht. Yacht designer's name and address. Builder's name and address. Model name. Hull number.

Value

Original cost. Estimated market value. Estimated insurable value. Estimated replacement cost.

Hull

Gross/net tonnage. Beam. Draft. Displacement. Length overall. Waterline length.

Material and type of construction. Thickness of hull. General condition of hull. Condition and appearance of gelcoat. Evidence of delamination. Evidence of osmosis. External condition of through-hull fittings.

Description and condition of shaft, bearing, and strut. Propeller diameter, pitch, rotation: L/R, number of blades. Propeller composition, condition. Evidence of electrolysis. Are zincs fitted? Condition. Description and condition of rudder and rudder shaft.

Condition of ballast keel/centerboard. Evidence of stress cracks at keel/hull joint. Evidence of damage due to grounding.

Deck

General description of deck layout. Condition of deck surface, non-skid. Condition and appearance of gelcoat. Condition and appearance of woodwork.

Number, size, location, condition of hatches. Condition of hatch gaskets and latches. Type and condition of companionway hatch, OK for offshore sailing?

Evidence of separation or leakage at deck/hull seam.

Condition of lifelines and stanchions. Safety line. Handholds on deck. Condition of bow and stern pulpits.

Anchor windlass: power or manual, chain/rope. Windlass mfg. and model, condition. Condition of bow roller. Condition of mooring cleats and chocks.

Condition of windows. Ventilators installed?

Liferaft size, date last inspected. Location and type stowage for liferaft.

Cockpit

General description of cockpit layout. Number, size and condition of winches. Mainsheet and traveler condition.

Type of steering: wheel, tiller. Autopilot: electric or hydraulic. Wind-steering vane manufacturer, condition.

Condition of engine controls, mfg. Condition of cockpit instrument readouts. Are cockpit lockers waterproof? Type of cockpit locker closures. OK for offshore? Size, number and location of cockpit drains. Are drains of adequate size for cockpit? Cockpit bilge pump type, operable? Bilge pump operates with lockers closed. Man-overboard equipment installed. Cockpit dodger (awning) size, material, condition. Boom gallows type and condition. Cockpit cushions.

Spars

Mast(s) composition, condition. Deck or keel stepped, condition of deck step. Condition of collar. Boom(s) composition, condition. Condition of tracks and hardware on spars. Number, size, location, condition of winches on spars. Mast steps. Spinnaker pole and other spars. Preventer. Type reefing gear, condition. Lazyjacks, condition.

Standing Rigging

Number, position, size and type of shrouds and stays. Proper tensioning of shrouds and stays. Type and condition of all terminals. Turnbuckles and toggles proper size, condition. Chainplate condition. Condition of tangs and spreaders.

Running Rigging

Halyards – internal/external, condition. Condition of sheet tracks and cars. Condition of sheets, downhauls, etc.

Tender

Inflatable or rigid. Storage location. Size. Construction material. Condition. Accessory equipment. Outboard engine for tender, mfg., size, condition.

Yacht Interior

General description and layout. Condition of woodwork, bulkheads and overhead.

Galley

Galley description. Size and type stove, oven. Stove gimbals. Fuel type. Shut-off valve. Condition of stove fuel lines and fittings. Location of stove fuel tank. Galley sink and drains. Fresh-water system manual or pressure. Salt-water supply to galley sink. Icebox or refrigerator, box size and type insulation, location. Refrigeration mfg. and model, freezer. Are compressors correctly mounted? Handholds in galley.

Main Cabin

Non-skid on companionway ladder. Handholds in main cabin. Number of berths and location. Berth or settee cushions' composition and condition. Table installed. Chart desk. Number and location of cabin lights. Cabin sole composition. Type of bilge, capacity, condition. Bilge pump(s) type, operating condition. Emergency bilge pump type and condition. Storage bins and cabinets. Interior condition of windows. Cabin heating system type, mfg., fuel. Type and condition of heater vent system. Heater and pipes clear of woodwork?

Head

Toilet installed. Anti-siphon valve. Wash basin. Shower. Hot-water system. Type heater.

Forward Cabin

Description and condition.

Other Cabins

Description and condition.

Storage Cabinets and Lockers

Description and condition.

Hull Interior

Deck/hull seam condition. Evidence of leakage. Condition of chainplates. Backing plates on through-hull fastenings. Backing plates on stanchions and cleats. Longitudinal stringers installed. Other hull strengtheners. Condition of mast step. Evidence of electrolysis. Number of structural bulkheads and location. How are bulkheads connected to hull, adequate? Number and condition of keel bolts.

Tanks and Plumbing

Fuel tank(s) size, material, location, shut-off valve. Fuel tank(s) fill from deck? Vented to deck? Water tank(s) size, material, location, shut-off valve. Water tank(s) fill from deck? Vented to deck? Number, size, material and type of through-hull valves. Are through-hull valves all operable? Through-hull valves connected to ground system? Double hose clamps on all flexible hose connections?

Electrical System

Number, voltage, location and condition of batteries. Battery tie-downs installed. Battery box condition, adequately vented? Vapor-proof master switch type and location. Electrical wiring all marine grade. Switch panel correctly labeled. Circuit breaker/manual fuse. Shore power connection/converter. Ground system throughout yacht? Ground plate installed? Lightning arrester installed? Navigation lights: type, location.

Electronic Equipment

Radio, condition. Loran, condition. Radar, condition. Satnav, condition. GPS, condition. RDF, condition. Depthsounder, condition. EPIRB(406). Windspeed and direction, condition. Knotmeter/log, condition. Other, condition.

Fire Fighting Equipment

Installed CO_2 system? Area covered, last inspection. Portable fire extinguishers – number, location. Extinguishers last inspection date.

Engine

Engine mfg., size, model, HP. Engine age, total hours, Serial number. Type of cooling. Type exhaust/muffler. Drip pan under engine. Fuel filter. Water filter. General condition of engine. Was engine operated during inspection? Alternator – amps, mfg., model, condition. Condition of engine mounts and bed. Reduction gear ratio. Engine overhaul date. Type carburetor (if gasoline). Flame arrestor. Engine compartment exhaust ventilation. Engine compartment free of fire hazards. Engine-to-shaft coupling type/condition. Type stuffing box and condition.

Ground Tackle and Mooring Gear

Anchors: type, size, condition. Anchor lines: type, size, length, condition. Anchor chain: size, length, condition. Dock lines: number, size, lengths, condition. Fenders: number and condition.

Sails

Sails: type, material, age, condition.

Miscellaneous Equipment

Watermaker type and condition. Awnings for cockpit and deck.
Portable generator. Solar panels: number and amps. Wind/water generator.
Storm windows location and condition.

Inventory

An inventory would include a listing of everything on the boat such as charts, binoculars, sextant, dishes, foul-weather gear, books, manuals, etc. that will be included in the purchase.

DETERMINING ELECTRIC CABLE SIZE FOR VARIOUS RUNS

The following information is furnished through the courtesy of Ancor Marine Grade Products, makers of high-quality electric wire for boats. This type of information often appears in books and magazine articles but it is often poorly understood – especially in regard to the proper way to measure the length of wire needed. So please read the instructions given.

Sailors in the United States and Canada are used to wire that is sized by AWG numbers. However, once you are away from North America all wire size will be in square millimeters and no one will have any idea what the correlation is between the two systems. Therefore the following table is important to keep aboard your boat.

Table 1. Conductor Sizes

AWG	Sq mm	Cm area
18	0.8	1600
16	1	2600
14	2	4100
12	3	6500
10	5	10,530
8	8	16,800
6	13	25,900
4	19	42,300
2	32	66,500
1	40	81,700
1/0	50	104,500
2/0	67	133,000
3/0	81	166,100
4/0	103	210,400

Determining Length

Length (feet) is determined by measuring the length of the conductor *from* the positive (+) power source connection *to* the electrical device *and back* to the negative (−) power source connection. Note that the power source connection may be the battery, a panelboard, or switchboard.

Determining Amps

Current flow (amps) is determined by adding the total amps on a circuit.

Calculations

Conductor sizes not covered in Table 2 and Table 3 can be calculated by using the following formula. After calculating the Circular Mil Area (CM), use Table 1 to determine the proper conductor size. When calculated CM falls between two values use the higher value.

$$CM = \frac{K \times l \times L}{E}$$

CM = Circular Mil (CM) area of conductors
K   = 10.75 (Constant representing the mil-foot resistance of copper)
l   = current (amps)
L   = length in feet
E   = voltage drop at load (in volts)

Example: Suppose an electric winch which draws 50 amps at full load is installed 30 feet from a 12-volt battery. If the installer needs a 3% voltage drop to the winch, what size wire should be used?

$$CM = \frac{10.75 \times 50 \text{ (amps)} \times 60 \text{ (total length of conductor)}}{0.36 \text{ (3\% of 12 volts)}} = 89{,}583$$

Table 1 shows that the next conductor with a CM larger than 89,583 is 1/0 AWG or 50 square millimeters.

Table 2. Conductor Sizes (AWG) for 3% Voltage Drop at 12 Volts

Current (amps)	\ Length (feet) 10	15	20	25	30	40	50	60	70	80	90	100	110	120	130	140	150	160	170
5	18	16	14	12	12	10	10	10	8	8	8	8	6	6	6	6	6	6	6
10	14	12	10	10	10	8	6	6	6	6	4	4	4	4	2	2	2	2	2
15	12	10	10	8	8	6	6	6	4	4	4	2	2	2	2	1	1	1	1
20	10	10	8	6	6	4	4	4	2	2	2	2	1	1	1	1	1/0	1/0	1/0
25	10	8	6	6	6	4	4	2	2	2	1	1	1	1	1/0	1/0	2/0	2/0	2/0
30	10	8	6	6	4	2	2	1	1	1	1/0	1/0	2/0	2/0	3/0	3/0	3/0	3/0	3/0
40	8	6	6	4	4	2	2	1	1/0	1/0	2/0	2/0	3/0	3/0	4/0	4/0	4/0	4/0	4/0
50	6	6	4	4	2	2	1	1/0	2/0	2/0	3/0	3/0	4/0	4/0	4/0				
60	6	4	4	2	2	1	1/0	2/0	3/0	3/0	4/0	4/0	4/0	4/0					
70	6	4	2	2	1	1	2/0	3/0	3/0	4/0	4/0	4/0	4/0						
80	6	4	2	2	1	1	2/0	3/0	4/0	4/0	4/0	4/0							
90	4	2	2	1	1/0	1/0	2/0	3/0	4/0	4/0	4/0								
100	4	2	2	1	1/0	2/0	3/0	4/0	4/0	4/0									

Table 3. Conductor Sizes (AWG) for 10% Voltage Drop at 12 Volts

Current (amps)									Length (feet)									
	10	15	20	25	30	40	50	60	70	80	90	100	110	120	130	140	150	160	170
5	18	18	18	18	18	16	16	14	14	14	12	12	12	12	12	10	10	10	10
10	18	18	16	16	14	14	12	12	10	10	10	10	8	8	8	8	8	8	6
15	18	16	14	14	12	12	10	10	8	8	8	8	8	6	6	6	6	6	6
20	16	14	14	12	12	10	10	8	8	8	6	6	6	6	6	6	4	4	4
25	16	14	12	12	12	10	8	8	6	6	6	6	6	4	4	4	4	4	2
30	14	12	12	10	10	10	8	6	6	6	6	6	4	4	4	4	2	2	2
40	14	12	10	10	8	8	6	4	4	4	4	4	4	2	2	2	2	2	2
50	12	10	10	8	8	6	6	4	2	2	2	2	2	2	2	1	1	1	1
60	12	10	8	8	6	6	4	4	2	2	2	2	1	1	1	1	1/0	1/0	1/0
70	10	8	8	6	6	6	4	2	2	2	2	1	1	1/0	1/0	1/0	1/0	2/0	2/0
80	10	8	8	6	6	4	4	2	2	2	1	1	1	1/0	1/0	2/0	2/0	2/0	2/0
90	10	8	8	6	6	4	2	2	2	1	1	1/0	1/0	1/0	2/0	2/0	2/0	3/0	3/0
100	10	8	6	6	4	4	2	2	1	1	1/0	1/0	1/0	2/0	2/0	2/0	3/0	3/0	3/0

HAM RADIO MARITIME MOBILE NETS FOR CRUISING SAILORS

The following worldwide list of ham radio nets was provided by W6SOT by way of the Gordon West Amateur Radio School and originally published by ICOM America, Inc.

Abbreviations for areas

PAC = Pacific, CAR = Caribbean, No/Car = North Carolina, G.C. = Gulf Coast (Gulf of Mexico), W/C = West Coast of U.S.A., IND OC = Indian Ocean, B/C = British Colombia, E/C = East Coast of U.S.A., G/L = Great Lakes, S/PAC = South Pacific, AUST = Australia, ATL = Atlantic Ocean, MED = Mediterranean, C/PAC = Central Pacific, W/PAC = Western Pacific, N/S/C America = North, South and Central America, PR/VI = Puerto Rico and Virgin Islands, SEA = Southeast Asia, NATL = North Atlantic, NZ = New Zealand.

Abbreviations for Information

WX = weather information; TFC = traffic; EMER TFC = emergency traffic; CW OPER = Morse Code; REC VEH = recreational vehicles; R/C = roll call for reporting in by those on an ocean passage; W/U = warm up session – check ins; M/M = maritime mobile; + = information checked from several sources; ** = no current information – probably outdated; > = From/To times of net; Dual times are listed; / = Standard to daylight, or winter to summer time changes.

TIME (UTC)	FREQ (MHz)	NET NAME/DESIGNATOR	DAYS	AREAS	INFO:	CONTACT
0000>0200+	14.300/313	MAR MOBILE SERV NET	DAILY	PAC/CAR	(ALSO 1600)	KA8O
0030	3.923	Tar Heel Emerg Net	DAILY	No/Car WX	TFC	W4YBQ
0100+	3.952	West Pub Serv Net	DAILY	W/C-BAJA WX	TFC	K6BMW
0100	3.935	Gulf Coast Hurr Net	DAILY	G.C. USA WX,	TFC	WD5CRR
0100**	21.407	Pac-Ind Ocean Net	DAILY	PAC/IND OC	TFC	W6BYS
0130	3.758	B/C Pub Serv Net	DAILY	B/C CANADA	TFC	VE7DDF
0145	3.908	Beaver State Net	DAILY	OREGON	TFC	N7BGW
0200+	21.402	GARRY'S NET (M/M)	M-F	PACIFIC/BAJA		K7YDO
0330/0230+	7.294	SANDIA M/M NET	DAILY	BAJA-W/C	MM SOCIAL NET	KA6HFG
0200	14.334	Brazil/E US Tfc Net	DAILY	E/C-ATL	WX, TFC	K3UWJ
0200	3.932	Great Lakes Emerg/Tfc	DAILY	G/L	TFC	WD8ROK
0200/0100	7.290	Hawaii PM Net	DAILY	HAWAII	WX, TFC	KH6B
0220+	14.300	JOHN'S WEATHER NET	MTThF	S/PAC-NORFOLK ISL	(M/M)	VK9JA
0230	3.905	Calif Tfc Net	DAILY	CALIF	WX, TFC	W7FQ
0300/0200	3.980	Oregon Emerg Net	DAILY	OREGON	TFC	W7VIF
0330/0230+	3.992	Ariz Traffic Net		ARIZ/BAJA	M/M TFC OK	KA7HEV
0200>0400+	14.300/314	SEAFARERS NET (M/M)	DAILY	PAC/W COAST	M/M	WH6J
0300+	14.106	TRAVELER'S NET	DAILY	AUST/IND OC	(M/M)	VK6ART
0300**	7.090	Mexican Emerg Net	DAILY	SONORA	EMER TFC	XE2RME
0300	3.960	Columbia basin Net	DAILY	WASHINGTON	TFC	WB7RUB
0330**	14.040	E/C M/M CW NET		E/COAST	CW OPER	
0400	3.917	Cal/Pac Oper Net t-s		WEST COAST	TFC	W6QLJ
0400+	14.115	CANADIAN DDD NET (M/M)	DAILY	PACIFIC	ALSO 1730	VE7DB
0400+	14.318	ARNOLDS NET	DAILY	SO PAC	M/M	ZKIDB
0400/0300**	14.075	Pac CW Traffic Net	MWF/TTh	PACIFIC	CW OPER.	KH6HIJ
0500/0400+	14.314	PAC MAR NET-WARM UP	DAILY	PACIFIC	W/U, M/M	KH6UY
0500	21.200	VK/NZ/African Net	DAILY	PAC/IND OC	TFC	CK3PA
0500	14.280	USA/Australian Tfc Net		PAC	TFC	
0530/0430+	14.314	PACIFIC MARITIME NET	DAILY	PACIFIC	ROLL CALL	KH6UY
0620	3.944	Traffic Handlers Net	DAILY	OREGON	TFC	KR7L
0630	14.180	Pitcairn Net	MON	SO PAC	TFC	VR6TC
0630	14.320/105	SO AFRICAN M/M NET	DAILY	ATL/IND OC	(&1130)	ZS5GC
0630	14.313	INTERNATIONAL M/M NET		ATL/MED/CAR	ALSO 1700	DKOMC
0700	14.265	Pacific Island Net		C/PAC-W/PAC	TFC	
0700	14.310	Guam Area Net	DAILY	WEST PAC	TFC	
0715+	3.820	BAY OF ISLANDS NET	DAILY	AUS/NZ/S PAC	(M/M)	ZL1BKD

427

TIME (UTC)	FREQ (MHz)	NET NAME/DESIGNATOR	DAYS	AREAS	INFO:	CONTACT
0800	7.287	Australia Traffic Net		AUS/S PAC	TFC	P29CC?P29JM/KX6QU
0800>0830+	14.315	Pac Inter-Island Net	DAILY	S PAC/SEA		G8OS
0800+	14.303	UK MARITIME NET		PAC/MED	(ALSO 1800)	5B4MM
0900	14.313	MEDITERRANEAN MM NET	DAILY	MED	(M/M)	
0900	7.080	Canary Island Net		ATL		
1000	14.313	GERMAN M/M NET	DAILY	ATL/MED	(M/M)	DKOMC
1030	3.815	Caribbean WX Net	DAILY	CAR	WX ALSO 2230Z	VP2AYL
1100/1000+	3.770	Maritime Prov WX Net	M-Sa	NE CANADA SHORE	WX	VE1AAC
1100+	7.237	CARIBBEAN M/M NET	DAILY	CAR		KV4JC
1100+	14.300/313	INTERCON NET	DAILY	N/S/C/ AMER	(ALSO 2200)	K4PT
1100+	14.283	Carribus Tfc Net	DAILY	E/C-CAR	TFC	KA2CPA
1110	3.930	Puerto Rico WX Net	DAILY	PR/VI	WX (ALSO 2310)	KP4AET
1130	14.316	SO AFRICAN M/M NET	DAILY	S ATL/IND OC	(0630)	ZS5MU
1130	21.325	So Atl Roundtable	DAILY	SO ATL/IND OC	ALSO 2330	PY1ZAK
1145	14.121	MISSISSAUGA M/M NET	DAILY	E CAN/ATL/CAR		VE3NBL
1200**	14.040	M/M CW NET		E/C USA	CW OPER	
1200+	14.332	YLEmergency Net	DAILY?	USA	TFC	WB8JDR
1200+	14.320	SO EAST ASIA NET	DAILY	SEA/INDONESIA/AUS		KA4HWN
1200	7.233	RV Service Net	DAILY	East US	REC VEH TFC	8P6DH
1230	7.185	BARBADOS ONFO NET	DAILY	CARR	M/M TFC	8P6DH
1245/1145+	7.268	E/C WATERWAY NET	DAILY	E COAST/CAR	M/M TFC	NU4P
1300>1330+	21.400	TRANS-ATL M/M NET	DAILY	N ATL/MED/CAR	M/M TFC	VE1ZL/VP5SL
1345	3.968	E/C WATERWAY NET	DAILY	E/C, CAR	TFC	
1400	7.292	Florida Coast Net		FLORIDA	R/C, M/M	
1400+	3.968	SONRISA NET	DAILY	BAJA/CAL	TFC	WA6VZH
1500**	7.193	Alaska Net		ALASKA		
1445+	7.294	CHBASCO NET	DAILY	BAJA/CAL	M/M TFC	XE2VJD
1600/1500+	7.238.5	BAJA CAL MAR NET	DAILY	BAJA/CAL	(EX KATES NAVY)	N6ADJ
1600>2200+	14.300/313	MAR MOBILE SERV NET	DAILY	ATL/CAR	(ALSO 2400)	KA8O
1630	14.303	SWEDISH MAR NET	DAILY	IND OC	ALSO 0530/2030	
1630	21.350	Pitcairn Net	FRI	SO PAC	TFC	VR6TC
1630+	7.263	RV Service Net	M-F	W/COAST	REC VEH TFC	K6BYP
1700+	14.340	Cal-Hawaii NET	DAILY	CAL/HAW	TFC	K6VDV
1700+	7.240	BEJUKA M/M NET	M-F	C/AMER/PANAMA	M/M	HP3XWB
1700	14.313	INTERNATIONAL M/M NET	DAILY	ATL/MED/CAR	(ALSO 0630)	DK0SS?

TIME (UTC)	FREQ (MHz)	NET NAME/DESIGNATOR	DAYS	AREAS	INFO:	CONTACT
1730+	14.292	Alaska-Pacific Net	M-F	ALASKA/PAC	(SOURDOUGH)	KL7IJT?
1730+	14.115	CANADIAN DDD M/M NET	M-F	PAC	(SUMMER, ALSO 0400)	VE7CEM
1800>1900+	14.285	KAFFEE KLATCH UN-NET	MWSa	HAW/TAHITI	"NEWS" M/M	KH6S
1800+	14.303	UK MARITIME NET		ATL/MED	(ALSO 0800)	G4ETO
1800	28.303	GORDON ON THE AIR		M/M Info	WB6NOA	
1800	7.076	SO PAC CRUISING NET	DAILY	SO PAC	WX/HARBOR-INFORMAL	
1830+	14.342	MANAMA M/M NET-W/UP	M-Sa	W/C-E/PAC	W/U	KB5HA
1900/1800+	14.305	CONFUSION NET	M-F	PAC/ALASKA	M/M	W7GYR
1900+	14.342	MANANA M/M NET	M-Sa	W/C-E/PACBAJA	WX M/M	KB5HA
1900	7.255	WEST PAFIFIC NET		WPAC		
1900**	7.285	HAWAII M/M NET	DAILY	HAWAII	WX	KH6BF
1900	21.390	Halo Net		N/S AMER	TFC	
1700>1900+	14.280	Int Mission RA Net	M-Sa	C/S AMER/CARR	TFC	WA2KUX
1900+	14.329	BAY OF ISLE NET	DAILY	NZ-S/PAC	(COLIN'S) M/M	ZL1BKD
1900**	3.855	FRIENDLY NET		HAWAII		KH6BF?
1900	3.990	NORTHWEST MAR NET		PAC NW		
2000	3.970	Noontime net	DAILY	WASHINGTON	TFC	W7UU
2000+	7.095	HARRYS NET	DAILY	WEST/SO PAC	M/M	KL7MZ
2000>2200+	21.390	Inter Amer Tfc Net		N/S/C AMER	TFC	
2030	14.303	SWEDISH MAR NET	DAILY	ATL OC	ALSO 0530/1630	
2100+	14.315	TONY'S NET		NZ/SO PAC	WX, MM	ZL1ATE
2130	14.290	E/C WATERWAY NET		E/C USA	M/M	
2200	3.930	West Indies SSB Net	DAILY	P/R-V/I	TFC	WP4BCV
2200	21.350	Pitcairn Net	TUES	SO PAC	TFC	VR6TC
2200+	21.402	PACMAR M/M NET WARM UP	M-F	PAC-BAJA	ALSO 0200	KB7DHQ
2200+	21.412	PAC MAR NET-15 MTR	M-F	PAC	(ALL) M/M	KA6GWZ
2200	3.940	Sea Gull Net	M-S	Maine	TFC	K1GUP
2230	3.815	Caribbean WX Net	DAILY	CAR	WX (ALSO 1030)	VP2AYL?
2230	3.958	Mass/Rhode Isl Net	DAILY	MASS-R/I	TFC	N1BGW
2200>2400+	14.300/313	INTERCON NET	DAILY	N/S/C AMER	(ALSO 1100)	K4PT
2310	3.930	Puerto Rico WX Net	DAILY	P/R-V/I	WX (ALSO 1110)	KP4AET?
2330	21.325	So Atl Roundtable		SO ATL	(ALSO 1130)	
2400>0200+	14.300/313	MAR MOBILE SERV NET	DAILY	CAR/BAJA/PAC	ALSO 1600	KA8O
2400	14.320	SEA M/M NET	DAILY	S&W PAC/SEA	(ROWDY'S)	VS6BE
AS NEEDED+	14.325	HURRICANE NET		A/R ATL/CAR/PAC	EMER WX	

429

VOICE RADIO PROCEDURES

Routine Procedures

VHF radios have a selector switch for low and high power. Low power is usually 1 to 1.5 watts and high power may be between 4.5 and 25 watts depending on type and model. When talking to a nearby station call on low power. This will avoid disturbing more distant vessels or shore stations. The initial call should be on Channel 16. After initial contact is made you and the other vessel should immediately agree to shift to another channel.

At sea, when you are not sure the other vessel has seen you, your initial call on Channel 16 should indicate your relative position. For example:

'Freighter on my starboard bow, this is the sailing vessel *Sunshine* on your port bow, over.' Or, 'Tanker four miles on my port beam, this is the sailing yacht *Moonglow* on your starboard beam, over.'

Speak slowly and distinctly. You never know what the native language of the bridge watch will be. The captains and mates on most merchant ships can speak some English. If they have not seen you, or if their radio is not tuned precisely, it may take them a moment to grasp the message. Usually it is a good idea to repeat the initial contact message. Legally you should also give your radio call sign, but in fact this is seldom done at sea.

After you have established initial contact and switched to a working channel you can convey your message. Typical VHF working channels at sea are 09, 12, 14, 68, 69, and 71. Always remember that Channel 16 is only for making initial contact and for emergency messages. Communicating routine traffic on Channel 16 is illegal and irresponsible because it could block out someone's emergency message.

Emergency Messages

There are three classes of urgent messages and specific ways of sending them.

MAYDAY

A MAYDAY message is *only* to be used in situations where the ship or human lives are in peril and there is a need for immediate assistance. It is a call to anyone, and need not be addressed to any particular station. This is the highest priority call and takes precedence over all others. A MAYDAY can be broadcast on any channel, but it is logical to broadcast on 16 because it is monitored by most stations.

If you hear a MAYDAY call you should listen to see if it is answered and carefully write down the message. If it is answered you should continue listening and keeping a record of the calls. Determine if it is possible for you to assist in aiding the distressed vessel or personnel. If the call is not answered you should answer. Be sure you have understood the message exactly. You should then attempt to give all aid and assistance within your ability. It may be that the actual rendering of help is beyond your capability. However, you may be able to relay the call and continue to broadcast the MAYDAY message for the vessel in distress.

Being able to send a proper and complete MAYDAY message under stressful conditions may be difficult. You should have the following procedure posted near your VHF radio.

1. Turn on the radio.
2. Tune to Channel 16.
3. Set for high-power transmission.
4. Depress transmit button.
5. Send the message slowly and distinctly.
   — 'MAYDAY MAYDAY MAYDAY, this is the vessel _____, _____, _____'. (Give boat name three times).
   — 'My position is _____ '(Position should also be repeated three times slowly. It can be latitude and longitude, or distance and bearing *to* or *from* some specific point or place. Give the best information you can to help others find you).
   — 'My yacht is _____ '
     (Indicate difficulty such as sinking, on fire, etc.).
   — 'There are _____ persons on board'
   — 'Condition of crew is _____'.
     (This is to inform the rescue party if there are injured persons).
   — 'My boat is: _____ length)
                  _____ (type rig)
                  _____ (hull and trim color)
                  _____ (distinguishing marks)
   — 'I am standing by on Channel 16'
   — 'This is vessel _____ '
     (Give boat name and radio call sign).
   — 'Over'.
6. Release the transmit button and wait for an answer.
7. Check to see that your volume control is turned up and squelch control is adjusted.
8. Repeat the message at frequent intervals.

PAN

PAN (pronounced 'Pahn') is a message of urgency – for example if the boat is in jeopardy, if there is a severely injured person on board, or for man overboard.

The message can be sent to a specific name such as the Coast Guard, or you can simply say 'All ships' or 'Any station.'

The message is:
   'PAN PAN PAN. This is the vessel _____ , _____ , _____ ,(boat name and call sign given three times).

Wait for an answer and give your message, or, if possible, shift to another channel and give the message.

Another type of PAN message is PAN PAN MEDICO if a medical emergency exists and assistance or advice is needed. With this type of message the two stations should agree to switch to a working channel as soon as contact is made.

SECURITY

SECURITY (pronounced, say-cure-it-tay) are messages relating to safety, navigational hazard or difficulty, or urgent weather conditions. This might be sent to a nearby Coast Guard station or even sent to 'all ships' or 'all stations'.

The message is:

— 'SECURITY SECURITY SECURITY. This is the vessel _____ (name and call sign).

— Give message or say 'Over' and wait for reply.

The need to broadcast a SECURITY message depends on the situation and conditions. In thick fog you might want to give your position, course, and speed, and end the transmission with 'Out.' If it is a message about some type of hazard to navigation and you are addressing it to a local Coast Guard station you would wait for them to respond before giving the message.

METHODS FOR CORRECTING COMPASS DEVIATION

Deviation is the difference between the compass reading and the correct magnetic reading. This difference or 'error' results from the presence of certain metal objects (or, less commonly, electrical currents) on the boat which are close enough to the compass to deflect it from magnetic north. Some of the deviation can be eliminated, some can be compensated for by adjusting the compass, and some can be corrected by steering.

To eliminate or reduce deviation, look for potential causes when installing the compass. It is better to relocate deviation-producing items than to have the compass in an inconvenient location. Such things as radio speakers or tools can be possible sources of deviation.

Try to keep any metals that could affect your compass at least three feet away. Check any electrical wires in the vicinity of the compass (including the wire to light the compass) to see if there is any difference in the compass reading with the power on and off. It should be possible to eliminate the electrical influence by twisting the wires.

An ever-present problem is the possibility of creating new sources of deviation after the compass has been installed and compensated. This often happens when a small portable radio, flashlight, or winch handle is set down too close to a steering compass. A compass error of only three degrees means an error of one mile over a distance of just 20 miles. Normally this would not be a problem during daylight sailing, but at night or when sailing in haze or fog it could result in a serious accident.

Most deviation can be compensated for by adjusting the compass as described below. Any residual deviation can be accommodated by making steering corrections using a deviation table or card. One of the best discussions of techniques for compass corrections in small yachts is that included in the owner's handbook for Aqua Meter compasses. I have drawn on that source for much of the following discussion.

Compensating or Correcting the Compass

Your compass should have small compensator magnets built into it, and the manufacturer's guide that came with the compass will tell you how to adjust them. If the adjusting is done with a screwdriver or special tool, it will need to be non-magnetic; usually one is provided with a new compass. In every case it is necessary to have flat sea conditions and no significant current. If your sailing area is strongly affected by tidal currents, wait until slack water to make corrections. It is also important to find a place free of boat traffic.

The major effort in correcting goes into eliminating the north-south and east-west deviation. Begin by compensating for east-west deviation, which is likely to be greater because of the magnetic influence from the engine.

Basic Method

Select a fixed (not floating) navigation aid such as a day marker or beacon which you can approach and depart on a north-south and east-west magnetic heading. Begin as close to the navigation aid as is safe, sighting it across the center of the transom, and run out on an east (090) or west (270) compass heading. The objective here is to try and maintain a steady *compass* course. Boatspeed should be adequate to give good steering control. Run the course for at least half a mile, or as much as a mile if possible. Next, slow down, make a tight turn, and steer back to the navigation aid at the same speed as before.

Now you are no longer steering by the compass. Rather you want to steer exactly toward the navigation aid. While doing this a crewmember should observe the compass reading. The difference between this reading and the reciprocal of your course out represents your east-west compass deviation error. The crewmember should then eliminate *one-half* of the error by adjusting the compensating magnets following the manufacturer's recommended procedure. For example, if after running out on a compass heading of 090 you find on the run back that the compass reads 276, your error due to deviation is six degrees. The compass would be adjusted to 273 degrees.

The next procedure is to run out from the navigation aid on a north or south heading and repeat the procedure described above, again eliminating one-half of the difference between the magnetic course and the compass course. Repeat the east-west and north-south runs once or twice again to 'fine tune' your corrections, each time reducing the error by one half.

Range Method

This is the most commonly used method for the do-it-yourself adjuster. In this case you select an east-west and a north-south range to use for compass correction. A range consists of two objects in line on a bearing; you maintain your course along the bearing by keeping both objects in sight and in alignment. Often you can use ranges set up to aid ships approaching a harbor or restricted bodies of water; otherwise you can make up your own ranges by plotting prominent in-line objects that are shown on a chart. However, they should be specific, obvious features such as towers, smokestacks, or fixed beacons or day marks. Less specific features such as hilltops or mountain peaks are not usually suitable.

Try to select ranges close to north-south or east-west bearings; preferably within 10 or 15 degrees. Do not use floating navigation aids, as they may move depending on currents.

To correct your compass carefully steer along the preselected east-west range while a crewmember notes the difference between the course

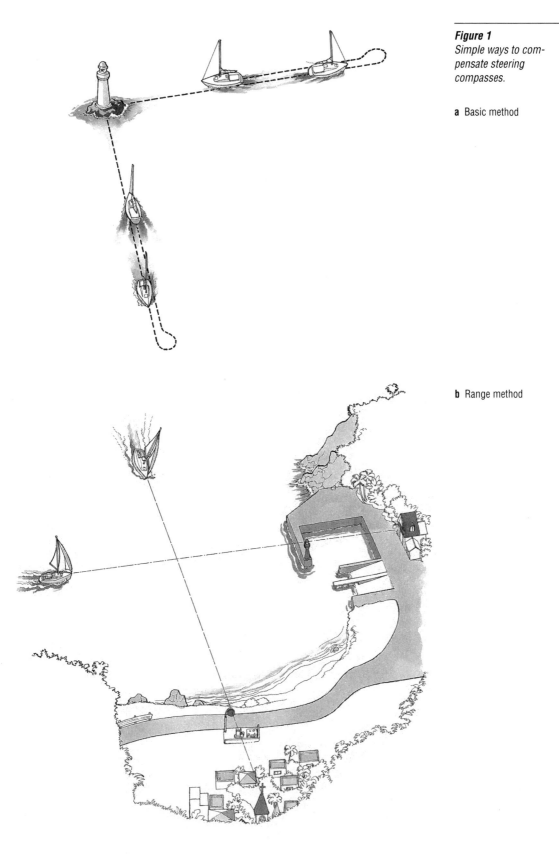

Figure 1
Simple ways to compensate steering compasses.

a Basic method

b Range method

indicated on the compass and the magnetic course you previously determined from the chart. Once this difference is established, the crewmember reduces the error by half using the compass compensator magnets in the same way as described above. You then run the north-south range and make necessary corrections. Repeat the procedures once or twice more on each set of ranges and continue to reduce the error.

Copy Method

This technique is more subject to errors, but if done very carefully, is effective. It should be regarded with some skepticism, and other methods should be used to recheck when convenient.

In this case you find a friend whose compass has recently been compensated and who has a deviation card if necessary. Together, run magnetic courses of east, west, north, and south. The operation will be much more efficient if you are in radio contact. Follow directly in the other boat's wake and adjust the compass as you go. This should be repeated two or three times. Next compare headings at 20-degree intervals around the compass. Record the differences on the intermediate headings but do not attempt to compensate the compass for each one. These readings will be used to construct a deviation chart or card.

Two-Compass Method

If you have two compasses on the boat one should be carefully and completely corrected. The second one can be corrected by using the first one as a guide. Each compass will need its own deviation card.

Professional Corrections

Most yachtsmen can do their own compass compensation. However, for those who choose not to, or for particularly complicated boats, a steel yacht, for instance, it is possible to hire a professional. An amateur can also use the professional methods if the necessary equipment is available.

Pelorus or transit bearings

With the boat in quiet water, bearings by transit or pelorus are taken on a prominent object six miles or more away. This is sufficient distance so that the turning of the boat through 360 degrees will not significantly affect the accuracy of the bearing.

As the helmsman holds a steady 090 or 270 compass heading, the transit or pelorus is sighted on the distant target. The sighting device is then rotated 180 degrees and leveled. Now the helmsman slowly turns the boat, and when the target is sighted again the helmsman is asked to read the compass. If the reading is not 180 degrees from the original heading the discrepancy represents the east-west error, and half of that difference will be corrected. The same procedure is repeated using a 000 or 180 compass heading. Both courses should be repeated once or twice again. After that, smaller incremental readings will be made to develop a deviation card.

Sun compass

A sun compass corrector is a gimballed compass rose. It has a thin, straight pin that sticks up from the center of the compass rose. The boat turns to a compass heading of 090 or 270. When the boat is exactly on course, a crewmember rotates the sun compass rose so that the pin casts a shadow on the same heading. The helmsman then turns the boat slowly through 180 degrees, and a new sun compass reading is taken. Any difference between the boat compass reading and the sun compass reading represents the compass error. As before, one half of the error will be corrected and then a 180 or 000 course will be used and corrections made.

Azimuths of celestial bodies

This is a technique that few yachtsmen will take the trouble to use for correcting deviation, but it can be used to check for compass error when offshore. Usually the sun is used.

It is necessary to know the exact time and the boat's position, and to have a current copy of the *Nautical Almanac*. Most celestial navigation textbooks describe the exact procedure in detail.

Constructing a Compass Deviation Table or Card

Even after you have corrected your compass with the compensator magnets on the cardinal points, there will usually be some additional deviation at the inter-cardinal positions. For this reason it is necessary to make a compass deviation table or card. If you have your compass corrected by a professional, he or she will give you a compass deviation table as part of the labor. Otherwise you can construct your own by running a number of ranges between the cardinal points.

Normally deviation corrections are made into a table with corrections for every 15 degrees. Then, each time you select a magnetic course to steer, you refer to the table and determine the appropriate compass course. This system is fine for a large boat or ship in which there is a navigator to figure out courses. For the cruising sailor it is much easier to make a deviation card by using a compass rose which can be read directly by the helmsman.

This can be made by placing a small compass rose inside of a larger one. Deviation cards can be made from photocopies of the compass card on a nautical chart. The inner rose represents the magnetic course you want to make good and the outer rose represents the course you need to steer for your specific compass. Obviously you will not have a corrected steering course for each compass degree, but you can interpolate between measured corrections. A separate deviation card of this type will need to be made up for each of your steering compasses.

ADHESIVE SEALANTS

There are so many different brands and types of adhesive/sealants offered to boatowners that it is confusing trying to decide which is best for a particular job and which is the best product to have on board for a wide variety of applications. This appendix looks at the three main types of marine sealants – silicones, polysulfides, and polyurethanes.

Silicones

Silicones characteristically have low adhesion and high cohesion. Consequently silicone is not recommended as a binder or adhesive but is excellent as a seal or gasket – especially if it is used in a situation where it is held under compression; for example, where a winch is attached to a fiberglass deck, or for bedding in windows if fasteners are used to hold the ports in place.

Silicones have a rapid set-up time, cure within 24 hours, and retain their elasticity for years and over a wide range of temperatures. Silicone-coated surfaces cannot be painted, and even surfaces that have at one time had a silicone coating will reject paint. In the same way, silicone does not adhere to silicone, so when rebedding a fitting or fixture you must completely remove old silicone sealant and thoroughly clean and sand the surfaces before applying new silicone.

Conventional wisdom says that silicone should not be used below the waterline. This caveat refers to silicone's poor adhesive quality. However, if marine-grade silicone is being used only as a sealant, for example with a plastic through-hull fitting on a fiberglass hull where the fitting is under compression, it is quite appropriate.

On deck silicone is often superior to polysulfides and polyurethanes, for example when bedding a winch or other gear items that will likely have to be removed in the future. With silicone it will be easy to remove the item, but with other high-adhesion products, especially polyurethane, removal may be a major task.

Buy a marine-grade silicone sealant even though it will be higher in price than what you see in a hardware store or builder's supply house. It will usually be a higher quality product and will contain a UV inhibitor.

Polysulfides

Polysulfide is best known for its application as an adhesive sealant when laying down a teak deck and for seam filling in laid decks. It is often referred to as Thiokol from the name of its developer. It is characterized by its bond strength and by its elasticity.

Polysulfides are slow curing but are not affected by the presence of water, high humidity, or high ambient temperature. The curing process will even continue underwater – for example if a boat is launched soon after through-hull fittings have been bedded in.

For bedding between metal, wood, and fiberglass, polysulfide is excellent, but it should not be used with many plastics, like those used in ports and windows, because it can cause them to become brittle. Plastic fittings such as Delrin, nylon, and Marelon, however, are not a problem. It is excellent for bedding metal fittings below the waterline.

Whereas polysulfides can be considered sealant-adhesives, polyurethanes are adhesive-sealants. This emphasis on adhesive may come as a bitter surprise to someone who decides to remove a fitting bedded in polyurethane on a fiberglass boat a few years down the line. It is not at all unusual to see chunks of gelcoat and even the fiberglass itself ripped away when some polyurethane-bedded items are removed. But for strong and waterproof adhesive seals such as deck-hull seams and keel to hull contacts polyurethane is highly recommended. In other ways polyurethanes and polysulfides have some similarities. They can both be sanded and painted when fully cured and they both retain some degree of flexibility.

Polyurethanes

No matter which sealant/adhesive you select, take the time to read the manufacturer's instructions carefully. This applies to surface preparation, recommended application, set-up time, how it will react to sanding and painting, and how it will clean up just after application and once it has set up.

GUIDE TO USES FOR SILICONE, POLYSULFIDE, AND POLYURETHANE COMPOUNDS
(Adapted from *Practical Sailor*)

	Silicone	Polysulfide	Polyurethane
Removability	★ (1)	★ (1)	X (1)
Sandability	X	★★★	★
Paintability	X	★★★	★★★
Flexibility	★★★	★★	★
Chemical resistance	★	★★★ (2)	★
High temp. resistance	★★★	★	★
Adhesion	★	★★	★★★
Cure speed	★★★	★	★★
Suitability for:			
electrical insulation	★★★	★★	★
below waterline	★ (3)	★★★	★★★
Bedding:			
metal/fiberglass	★	★★★	★★
wood trim/fiberglass	★	★★★	★★
wood deck seams	X	★★★ (4)	X
wood hull seams	X	★★★	★
Plastic fittings/fiberglass:			
ABS, Lexan, PVC, acrylic	★	X	X
Nylon, Marelon, Delrin	★	★★★	★★
glass	★	★★★	★★
Gasketing/Sealing:			
fuel and refrigeration	X	★★★	X
exhaust systems	★★★	X	X

Explanation of symbols and notes:

X   not recommended

★   acceptable

★★   better

★★★   best

Notes:

(1) Silicone and polysulfide are removable with some difficulty; polyurethane is virtually non-removable.

(2) Polysulfides are preferred in areas subject to fuel spills, teak cleaners, etc.

(3) Use silicone only for well-secured plastic parts, not for working seams.

(4) Polysulfide preferred for bedding teak, as two-part teak cleaners will permanently soften polyurethane.

ONBOARD TOOLS

I carry the following tools on my boat. I do not suggest that this is the ideal kit for every boat. Rather this list can be used as a reference.

Hammers

- nail or claw hammer.
- plastic-tip hammer.
- 3-pound sledge.
- hatchet.

Wrenches

- 4" adjustable wrench (handy for use on deck for shackles).
- 8" adjustable wrench.
- 12" adjustable wrench.
- set of combination (open and box end) standard wrenches ($1/4$"–$1^1/_{16}$") and/or set of combination metric wrenches.
- set of standard or metric socket wrenches.
- pipe wrench (aluminum).
- set each of standard and metric Allen (hex key) wrenches.

Pliers

- 6" slip-joint pliers.
- 8" slip-joint pliers.
- long nose or needle-nose pliers.
- diagonal cutting pliers.
- straight-jaw locking pliers (Vice-Grips).
- double curve-jaw locking pliers (Vice-Grips).
- long-nose locking pliers (Vice-Grips).
- large plumbers pliers (channel locks), large enough to fit nuts on stern packing gland.

Screwdrivers

- complete set of slotted screwdrivers.
- complete set of Phillips screwdrivers.
- set of very small slotted and Phillips screwdrivers.
- one each large mechanics slotted and Phillips screwdrivers.

Saws

- hand saw (Japanese style are easy to store).
- hacksaw with 10 spare blades (buy the best quality blades and wrap in oiled paper or cloth).

Files

- set of miscellaneous coarse and fine files (wrap in oiled paper or cloth).

Electrical Repair

- inexpensive multi-meter.
- combined crimping tool and wire stripper.
- soldering gun.

Miscellaneous

- two or three sizes of cold chisels.
- two or three sizes of wood chisels.
- center punch.
- hand drill and set of bits.
- wrecking bar.
- small vice (if you have a place to attach it).
- measuring tape (combined standard and metric).
- slide calipers (combined standard and metric or one each).
- Nicropress tools for wire sizes $1/8$" to $1/4$".
- wire cutters (also called rod and bolt cutters) capable of easily cutting largest rigging wire on board – try them out to be sure they do the job.
- wood or rubber sanding blocks.
- variety of paint brushes for bottom painting, varnishing, and interior.
- trimming and cutting knives.
- small T-square.
- small magnet.
- magnifying glass.
- set of standard and/or metric taps and dies.
- hand rivet gun and rivets.
- scissors.

Power tools (for in-port maintenance)

- $3/8$" chuck, reversible drill and set of quality drill bits.
- angle drill head adapter (convenient option).
- small electric (palm) sander.
- high-speed grinder (optional).
- sabre saw (optional).

SPARES AND SPARE PARTS

Before setting off on an extended cruise it is important to collect a supply of spare parts, including consumables such as fuses and bulbs and individual components such as fuel or water pumps. For some equipment it is necessary to use your imagination and try to figure out what you would do if . . . . For example, if you lost the anchor windlass handle overboard, what could you use as an emergency substitute? Perhaps a large screwdriver or another pump or winch handle will get you by. But if nothing else will work, you might want to buy a spare.

Determining needed spares is an ongoing task. Every time a new piece of equipment comes aboard, think about what spares will be needed, record them in your stores notebook, and purchase what you need.

The following list is one that I use. Each boat will have somewhat different requirements. If you are in doubt as to what spares to carry for various items on your boat, read the manufacturers' operating manuals to see what spare parts are recommended. It is also worthwhile to write to the manufacturers and ask what additional spares they recommend for a boat that will be away from its home port for several years.

Engine

- oil (enough for 4 oil changes).
- oil filters (minimum of 4).
- fuel filters (minimum of 4 for each filter – most cruising boats have two filters).
- injectors (minimum of 2).
- copper washers for fuel line connections.
- engine gasket set.
- fuel pump rebuild kit.
- complete fuel pump (optional).
- water pump repair kit.
- complete water pump (optional).
- hoses for fuel line, exhaust, and supply water.
- two sets of engine zincs.
- thermostat.
- cutlass bearing.
- engine electrical system fuses.

Pumps

- overhaul kits for manual bilge pumps (minimum of 2 kits for each pump).
- overhaul kit for toilet.

- overhaul kits or spare parts for all sink pumps.

Hose Clamps
- large selection of all sizes used on board.

Fuses
- selection of all sizes used on board.

Light Bulbs
- selection of all sizes used on board.

Small Batteries
- selection for all sizes on board (don't forget hand-bearing compasses and calculators).

Fasteners
- A wide variety of stainless steel nuts, bolts, washers, lockwashers, split pins, locknuts and screws.

Glues and Sealants
- small quantity of quick setting epoxy and glue.
- underwater-setting, two-part epoxy (minimum 1 quart).
- polyurethane sealant.
- silicone sealant.
- engine gasket cement.
- rubber cement.

Lubricants
- WD-40.
- CRC.
- silicone grease.
- silicone spray.
- anti-seize compound.
- teflon tape (for pipe threads).
- winch and windlass lubricant.
- anhydrous lanolin.

Hatch Gaskets
- manufacturer's replacement or gasket stock.

Rigging
- cable clamps (bulldog clips) for main rigging wire (minimum of 6).
- spare wire as long as longest stay with terminal installed on one end.
- several Norseman or Sta-Lok cones to permit reusing terminals.
- two spare Norseman or Sta-Lok terminals.
- spare rigging turnbuckle (minimum one).

Galley Stove and Heaters

- spare parts or overhaul kit depending on type of unit; check owner's manual. If Primus or similar kerosene burners buy lots of spare parts and one or two spare burners.

Winches and Windlasses

- retaining rings (two or three for each size/brand winch).
- pawls and pawl sprigs (several for each size/brand winch).
- spare winch handle.

Steering

- wind-steering vane spares and replacements as recommended by manufacturer.
- for autopilots spare components (optional).
- spare or emergency tiller.
- for pedestal steering, spares as recommended by manufacturer.

Outboard Engine

- spare spark plug.
- spare starter rope.
- oil for mixing with gasoline.
- lower unit lubricating oil.
- shear pins if required.
- spare prop (optional).

Sails

- sail repair tape.
- sail cloth (minimum of 2 yards).
- selection of straight and curved sail needles.
- waxed sail twine (or twine and wax).
- sailmakers palm.
- leather scraps for chafing patches.
- 6 or more spare hanks.
- 6 or more spare mainsail cars, slugs, and shackles.

LIFERAFT AND EMERGENCY BAG SUPPLIES

The following list includes the supplies carried in my liferaft and abandon-ship bag. It is given here only as a guide. Each crew will want to determine what is needed for their boat.

This list is given in order of priority. As much as possible is packaged together and placed inside the liferaft. What is left is put in the emergency bag.

- reverse osmosis water maker • solar still
- 4 500-ml containers of water
- Class B EPIRB (this is in addition to 406 EPIRB in main cabin)
- 2 500-ml food packets • 3 parachute flares • 3 hand flares
- fishing equipment • flashlight and two sets of batteries
- rigging knife • surgical knife • 2 liferaft inflation pumps
- liferaft repair kit • liferaft repair clamps • survival manual
- first-aid kit • scissors • whistle
- regular and needle-nose pliers • regular and Phillips screwdriver
- sharpening stone • surgical and sail repair needles
- roll of sail twine • magnifying glass • 10' stainless steel wire
- 100 meters 20-lb test fishing line • 100 assorted fishing hooks
- 150 feet 8-mm nylon braid • notebook and 4 wood pencils
- 4 large sponges • 2 large and 10 small plastic bags
- 4 rolls of electrician's tape • drinking cup • spare bailer
- signal mirror • 250 ml of sunscreen • dive mask and snorkel
- strobe • 1 can CRC lubricant • large steel gaff and PVC handle
- 10 hose clamps • 10' of ¼" stretch cord • compass
- plankton net • Very pistol and 6 expired parachute flares
- 3 red and 3 orange expired hand-held flares
  (Expired flares are in addition to new stock listed above. Even though out of date these extra flares are still usable).

PROCEDURES FOR CONTACT WITH SEARCH AND RESCUE (SAR) HELICOPTERS

If it is ever necessary to evacuate a crewmember by helicopter, or to bring aboard a paramedic, or even to receive emergency equipment, it is important to have some advance knowledge of what to expect and how to make the exercise as safe and efficient as possible. It is a given that the crew will be under stress in such an emergency situation. What is often overlooked is the difficulty of communication when working with a helicopter.

The best way to communicate is by VHF radio with initial contact made on Channel 16. Initial information should be discussed before the helicopter is in position over the boat, because once it is hovering the noise level is so great that it is impossible to talk by radio from the cockpit. And with only a crew of two, one of whom may be disabled, it is quite unlikely that the person on the helm will be able to use the radio at all.

So there is tension and noise and finally there is the additional complication of strong downdrafts of air from the rotor blades, which will make it difficult to steer your boat. It is necessary therefore to have enough way on under power to give the boat steerage and directional control. Yes, *under power*. The thought of trying to make any transfer between a helicopter and a small boat under sail boggles the mind. When I brought up this topic with two Coast Guard SAR helicopter pilots they both looked at me and smiled and shook their heads. 'No way.' Both of them lived aboard sailboats.

Before the helicopter arrives, have an orange smoke flare ready to use. This is especially important if there are any other sailboats in the area. Even if yours is the only boat around the pilot may want the smoke to help him determine wind conditions and sea state. When you deploy the orange smoke flare be sure to do it on the lee side of the boat.

Quite often you will see the helicopter before it sees you. You can help the pilot find you by giving him an approximate range and bearing. But keep communications to a minimum as the pilot may have to carry on several radio conversations as well as fly.

In preparation for arrival, clear the cockpit and decks of all loose gear. Any unneeded crew should stay below. If someone is to be evacuated he should be wearing a lifejacket and should have a note well attached to him indicating his medical problem and any medications that have been given.

Any awnings, booms, antennas, or other projecting gear should be lowered. If the boat is under sail it should be put under power and the sails lowered and well secured on deck.

When the helicopter arrives you want to be on a course that puts the wind 30 degrees off your port bow. The helicopter pilot may give you a specific course to steer. Having the wind off the port bow allows the helicopter to make its approach. The pilot is sitting on the left side of the aircraft and can best maneuver into position by approaching your starboard quarter.

Once the helicopter is in position it is critical that the person on the helm remains right on course and does not let himself be distracted or look up at the helicopter. The reason for this is that any deployment of equipment or personnel is done from the starboard side of the helicopter, but because the pilot is on the port side he cannot see your boat. He has to maintain the helicopter's position relative to the boat based on non-stop advice from his co-pilot or from a crewmember.

In some cases the helicopter will drop a line to the boat in preparation to send a crewmember down, to lower a stretcher or sling, or to provide some needed food, medicine, or equipment. Before anyone on the boat grabs the line it should first touch the water or touch some part of the boat to discharge static electricity and prevent a sudden and unpleasant jolt that could knock you over.

Once the line is aboard the boat it must be tended by one or two crewmembers, *but under no circumstances should it be tied or in any way secured to the boat*. If it is, the pilot will immediately order it to be severed at the helicopter.

It is the practice of the British Coast Guard to lower a helicopter crewman to the deck of a small boat with the boat's crew tending the line. The U.S. Coast Guard on the other hand are more likely to drop their crewmember in the water near a boat needing assistance and let him swim to the boat. In that case you will need to help him in boarding. Either way, the rescuer on your boat will supervise the evacuation of a wounded crewmember or whatever is to be done. Whenever you are ready for the helicopter to begin retrieving the line, give a thumbs-up signal.

Obviously Coast Guard helicopter assistance is a tricky and potentially dangerous task for all concerned. However, if everyone knows what to do, it can be performed relatively easily. If it ever happens with your boat, brief your crew on what to expect and assign them specific tasks in advance. Point out that it will be very noisy and gusty when the helicopter is hovering and emphasize the danger of static electricity and the prohibition of tying the helicopter's line to the boat.

SAMPLE CHECKLISTS FOR DEPARTURES AND ARRIVALS

These two checklists are the ones I use on *Denali* and are given here as examples only. You will want to make up your own to suit your priorities and procedures and to match the equipment on your boat. Obviously there is a good bit of redundancy in order to cover most typical situations.

Preparation for getting underway

Day before departure

____ Fuel supply
____ Water supply
____ LP gas supply
____ Food purchases
____ Checkout clearance with customs, immigration and harbormaster
____ Lay out course on navigation charts
____ Enter waypoints on Loran and/or Sat Nav and/or GPS
____ Obtain long-range weather forecast
____ Climb mast and inspect rigging, antennas, etc.
____ Examine standing rigging at deck level
____ Check liferaft tie-downs
____ Check emergency bag
____ Operate anchor windlass

Night before departure

Test all lights:
____ running lights
____ anchor lights
____ strobe
____ compass lights
____ cabin lights
____ flashlights
____ personal strobes
____ Check depthsounder readout, lights and alarms
____ 'Test' EPIRB

Morning of departure

____ Take garbage ashore
____ Obtain weather report
____ Check and record barometer reading
Sails:
____ Jib hanked on, sheets run and ready to hoist
____ Main hanked on, reefed if necessary and ready to hoist

_____ Boom vang installed

Engine:

    _____ Inspect engine compartment and bilge

    _____ Check engine oil level

    _____ Inspect fuel filter

    _____ Inspect water filter

Boat interior:

    _____ All loose gear stowed

    _____ Cabinet doors closed and locked

    _____ Bookcase secure

    _____ Lock gimbals on cooking stove and oven

    _____ Vents and hatches closed and secured

    _____ Check main bilge

    _____ Close through-hull valves to toilet

    _____ Install speed-o transducer through-hull

    _____ Inspect chain locker

    _____ Wind clock

Safety equipment:

    _____ Foul-weather gear ready

    _____ Safety harness ready

    _____ Life vests available

    _____ Man-overboard equipment in place

Deck inspection:

    _____ Spare fuel and water bottles securely tied down

    _____ Tender securely tied down

    _____ Install autopilot

    _____ Install wind-steering vane

    _____ Put winch handles at mast and in cockpit

    _____ Spinnaker pole tied down

    _____ Boat horn in cockpit

_____ Determine departure strategy

Final preparations

_____ Check that stern is clear of lines

_____ Position battery selector switch

_____ Adjust alternator bypass switch

_____ Start engine

_____ Check engine instruments

_____ Check for proper engine exhaust flow

_____ Test engine in forward and reverse

Turn on electronics:

    _____ Loran

    _____ Sat Nav/GPS

    _____ VHF radio on Channel 16

    _____ Radar on standby

    _____ Radar warning indicator

    _____ Autopilot

    _____ Depthsounder

    _____ RDF

____ Review departure strategy
____ Remove mooring lines or bring in anchor

After departure
____ Raise sails
____ Turn off unneeded electronics
____ Stop engine
____ Connect wind-steering vane
____ Disconnect autopilot
____ Check battery selector switch
____ Adjust alternator bypass
____ Inspect engine compartment
____ Remove and stow anchor(s) below
____ Plug hawsepipe
____ Remove and stow fenders and mooring lines
____ Record departure time in log book
____ Haul down courtesy flag

Preparations for entering port

Before arrival
____ ARE YOU TIRED? Would it be better to heave to or anchor?
____ Check and record barometer reading
____ Pump bilges
____ Study harbor and entrance charts
____ Attach anchor to chain and make ready to let go
____ Check operation of anchor windlass
____ Install stern (emergency) anchor and make ready to let go
____ Rig fenders (keep clear of sheets if still sailing)
____ Attach mooring lines (keep clear of sheets if still sailing)
____ Have boat hook available
____ VHF radio on Channel 16
____ Hoist 'Q' flag if appropriate
____ Turn on depthsounder
____ Radar on standby
____ Inspect engine compartment
____ Check engine oil
____ Set battery selector switch
____ Set alternator bypass
____ Check stern for lines in water
____ Start engine
____ Check engine instruments
____ Check engine exhaust
____ Test engine in forward and reverse
____ Connect autopilot
____ Disconnect wind-steering vane
____ Lower and furl sails
____ Remove wind-steering vane

After arrival

Contact officials as necessary (harbor control, quarantine, customs, and immigration)

____ Turn off unneeded electronics

____ Set battery selector switch

____ Take bearings and depth reading if at anchor

____ Add extra fenders as necessary

____ Install spring line on anchor chain

____ Install chafing gear on mooring lines

____ Have emergency anchor ready

____ Fold and stow sails

____ Install cover on mainsail

____ Stow sheets, vangs, etc.

____ Rig anchor light

____ Determine strategy for day or night emergency departure

____ Put tender in water

____ Take garbage ashore

TABLES AND CONVERSIONS

CONVERSION FACTORS

I

Approximate Conversions To and From Metric

known	multiply by	to determine
LENGTH		
millimeters (mm)	0.04	inches (in)
centimeters (cm)	0.4	inches (in)
meters (m)	3.3	feet (ft)
meters (m)	1.1	yards (yd)
kilometers (km)	0.6	miles (mi)
inches (in)	2.5	centimeters (cm)
feet (ft)	30	centimeters (cm)
yards (yd)	0.9	meters (m)
miles (mi)	1.6	kilometers (km)
AREA		
square centimeters (cm^2)	0.16	square inches (in^2)
square meters (m^2)	1.2	square yards (yd^2)
square kilometers (km^2)	0.4	square miles (mi^2)
hectares (10 000 m^2) (ha)	2.5	acres
square inches (in^2)	6.5	square centimeters (cm^2)
square feet (ft^2)	0.09	square meters (m^2)
square yards (yd^2)	0.8	square meters (m^2)
square miles (mi^2)	2.6	square kilometers (km^2)
acres	0.4	hectares (ha)
MASS (Weight)		
grams (g)	0.035	ounces (oz)
kilograms (kg)	2.2	pounds (lb)
tonnes (1000 kg) (t)	1.1	short tons
ounces (oz)	28	grams (g)
pounds (lb)	0.45	kilograms (kg)
metric tons (1000 kg)	1.1	short tons
short tons (2000 lbs)	0.9	tonnes (t)

VOLUME

milliliters (ml)	0.03	fluid ounces (fl oz)
liters (l)	2.1	pints (pt)
liters (l)	1.06	quarts (qt)
liters (l)	0.26	gallons (gal)
cubic meters (m³)	35	cubic feet (ft³)
cubic meters (m³)	1.3	cubic yards (yd³)
teaspoons (teaspoons)	5	milliliters (ml)
tablespoons (tbsp)	15	milliliters (ml)
fluid ounces (fl oz)	30	milliliters (ml)
cups (c)	0.24	liters (l)
pints (pt)	0.47	liters (l)
quarts (qt)	0.95	liters (l)
gallons (gal)	3.8	liters (l)
gallons (gal)	0.13	cubic feet (ft³)
cubic feet (ft³)	0.03	cubic meters (m³)
cubic yards (yd³)	0.76	cubic meters (m³)

II
Miscellaneous Conversions

knots (kts)	1.15	miles per hour (mph)
miles per hour (mph)	0.86	knots (kts)
nautical miles (nm)	1.15	statute miles (m)
nautical miles (nm)	1.8	kilometers (km)
statute miles (m)	1.6	kilometers (km)
statute miles (m)	0.86	nautical miles (nm)
kilometers (km)	0.54	nautical miles (nm)
kilometers (km)	0.6	statute miles (m)
fathoms (fth)	6.0	feet (ft)
fathoms (fth)	1.8	meters (m)
meters (m)	0.55	fathoms (fth)
feet (ft)	0.17	fathoms (fth)
horsepower (hp)	0.75	kilowatts (kw)
long tons	2240	pounds (lbs)
short tons	2000	pounds (lbs)

III
Temperature

Celsius × 9/5 + 32 = Fahrenheit

Fahrenheit −32 × 5/9 = Celsius

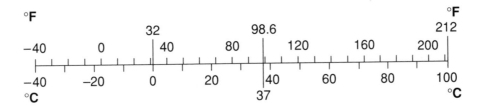

IV
Miscellaneous Equivalents

1 rod	16.5 feet
1 acre	43560 square feet
1 hectare	2471 acres
1 chain (ch)	66 feet
1 statute mile (mi)	5280 feet
1 nautical mile (nm)	2025 yards
1 league	3 statute miles
1 league	4.8 kilometers
1 cable's length	120 fathoms
1 cable's length	219 meters
1 shot (chain lengths)	15 fathoms (90 feet)

V
Fractions of an inch to Decimals of an inch to Millimeters

Inches	Inches	Millimeters	Inches	Inches	Millimeters
$1/64$	.015625	0.39687	$33/64$	.515625	13.09671
$1/32$	.03125	0.79374	$17/32$	.53125	13.49362
$3/64$	.046875	1.19061	$35/64$	.546875	13.89045
$1/16$	.0625	1.58748	$9/16$	.5625	14.28737
$5/64$	.078125	1.98435	$37/64$	.578125	14.68419
$3/32$	.09375	2.38123	$19/32$	.59375	15.08111
$7/64$	.109375	2.77809	$39/64$	.609375	15.47793
$1/8$	.125	3.17497	$5/8$	.625	15.87485
$9/64$	.140625	3.57183	$41/64$	.640625	16.27167
$5/32$	.15625	3.96871	$21/32$	.65625	16.66859
$11/64$	.171875	4.36557	$43/64$	.671875	17.06541
$3/16$	.1875	4.76245	$11/16$	.6875	17.46234
$13/64$	.203125	5.15931	$45/64$	.703125	17.85915
$7/32$	.21875	5.55620	$23/32$	.71875	18.25608
$15/64$	.234375	5.95305	$47/64$	.734375	18.65289
$1/4$	.25	6.34994	$3/4$	.75	19.04982
$17/64$	.265625	6.74679	$49/64$	.765625	19.44662
$9/32$	.28125	7.14368	$25/32$	.78125	19.84356
$19/64$	.296875	7.54053	$51/64$	.796875	20.24037
$5/16$	.3125	7.93743	$13/16$	.8125	20.63731
$21/64$	.328125	8.33427	$53/64$	.828125	21.03411
$11/32$	.34375	8.73117	$27/32$	.84375	21.43105
$23/64$	.359375	9.12801	$55/64$	.859375	21.82785
$3/8$	.375	9.52491	$7/8$	.875	22.22479
$25/64$	.390625	9.92175	$57/64$	.890625	22.62159
$13/32$	.40625	10.31865	$29/32$	.90625	23.01853
$27/64$	.421875	10.71549	$59/64$	.921875	23.41533
$7/16$	.4375	11.11240	$15/16$	.9375	23.81228
$29/64$	.453125	11.50923	$61/64$	.953125	24.20907
$15/32$	.46875	11.90614	$31/32$	.96875	24.60602
$31/64$	.484375	12.30297	$63/64$	.984375	25.00281
$1/2$	.5	12.69988	1.	1.	25.39977

Information in this appendix was compiled from United States National Bureau of Standards Miscellaneous Publication 286 and Special Publication 389. The decimal/inch/millimeter table is courtesy of Broderick & Bascom Rope Company of Sedalia, Missouri.

USEFUL ADDRESSES

It is not practical to list the multitude of sources for products; addresses and suppliers change and much information can be found in sailing magazines or at local suppliers. A good source for virtually all marine products in the U.S. is the annual publication *Sailboat Buyers Guide: The Complete Guide to Boats and Gear*, published by SAIL magazine, 275 Washington St., Newton, MA 02158. A similar buyers guide is published by Practical Sailor magazine, P.O. Box 819, Newport, RI 02840. In the U.K. the source is Sell's Marine Market (Benn Business Information Services, Riverbank House, Angel Lane, Tonbridge, Kent TN9 1SE). Chandlers and specialized bookshops and chart suppliers are also a useful source of information as well as products.

The following associations will provide a cruising sailor with information and assistance in various countries:

Canadian Yachting Association, 1600 James Naismith Drive, Gloucester, Ontario, CANADA K1B 5N4 Phone (613) 748-5687 Fax (613) 748-5688

Cruising Association, Ivory House, St. Katharine Dock, London E1 9AT, UNITED KINGDOM Phone (071) 481-0881

International Association for Medical Assistance to Travelers (IAMAT), 40 Regal Road, Guelph, Ontario, CANADA N1K 1B5

Ocean Cruising Club, P.O. Box 996, Tiptree, Colchester CO5 9XZ, UNITED KINGDOM

Royal Yachting Association, RYA House, Romsey Road, Eastleigh, Hants SO5 4YA, UNITED KINGDOM

Seven Seas Cruising Association (SSCA), 521 South Andrews Avenue, Suite 8, Fort Lauderdale, FL 33301 Phone (305) 463-2431 Fax (305) 463-7183

U.S. Sailing (formerly United States Yacht Racing Union), P.O. Box 209 Newport, RI 02840 Phone (401) 849-5200 Fax (401) 849-5208

14 SAILING AID PUBLICATIONS

The following publications are published by the U.S. Government. They can usually be purchased from chart supply companies or ordered directly from the government.

Those subjects with the notation GPO can be ordered from:
Superintendent of Documents
U.S. Government Printing Office
Washington, DC 20402-9325
Phone (202) 783-3238

Those subjects with the notation DMA can be ordered from:
Defense Mapping Agency – CSC
Attn: PMSR
Washington, DC 20315
Phone toll free 1-800 826-0342

Those subjects with the notation NOS can be ordered from:
Distribution Branch (N/CG33)
National Ocean Service
Riverdale, MD 20737-1199
Phone (301) 436-6990

Pilot Charts (DMA)

Atlas of Pilot Charts – South Atlantic Ocean
Atlas of Pilot Charts – Central American Waters
Atlas of Pilot Charts – South Pacific Ocean
Atlas of Pilot Charts – Northern North Atlantic
Atlas of Pilot Charts – Indian Ocean
Pilot Chart of the North Atlantic Ocean (issued quarterly)
Pilot Chart of the North Pacific Ocean (issued quarterly)

Sailing Directions

Available from Defense Mapping Agency (DMA)

South Atlantic Ocean
    South Atlantic Ocean (Planning Guide)
    Southwest Coast of Africa (Enroute)
    East Coast of South America (Enroute)
South Pacific Ocean
    South Pacific Ocean (Planning Guide)
    West Coast of South America (Enroute)
    Pacific Islands (Enroute)
    East Coast of Australia and New Zealand (Enroute)

Mediterranean
  The Mediterranean (Planning Guide)
  Western Mediterranean (Enroute)
  Eastern Mediterranean (Enroute)
North Atlantic Ocean
  North Atlantic Ocean (Planning Guide)
  Scotland (Enroute)
  Ireland and the West Coast of England (Enroute)
  West Coast of Europe and Northwest Africa (Enroute)
  Nova Scotia and the St. Lawrence (Enroute)
  Newfoundland, Labrador, Hudson Bay (Enroute)
  Caribbean Sea, Vol. 1 (Enroute), Bermuda, Bahamas, and Islands of
    the Caribbean Sea
  Caribbean Sea, Vol. 2 (Enroute), Venezuela, North Coast of
    Colombia and East Coast of Central America and Mexico
North Pacific Ocean
  North Pacific Ocean (Planning Guide)
  West Coasts of Mexico and Central America (Enroute)
  British Columbia (Enroute)
  East Coast of the Soviet Union (Enroute)
  Coasts of Korea and China (Enroute)
  Japan, Vol. 1 – East Coasts of Hokkaido, Honshu, and Kyushu,
    including Nampo Shoto and Ryukyu Islands (Enroute)
  Japan, Vol. 2 – (Enroute), West Coasts of Hokkaido, Honshu, and
    Kyushu, including the Inland Sea
Southeast Asia
  Southeast Asia (Planning Guide)
  South China Sea and Gulf of Thailand (Enroute)
  The Philippine Islands (Enroute)
  Borneo, Jawa, Sulawesi, and Nusa Tenggara (Enroute)
  New Guinea (Enroute)
Indian Ocean
  Indian Ocean (Planning Guide)
  East Africa and the South Indian Ocean (Enroute)
  Red Sea and the Persian Gulf (Enroute)
  India and the Bay of Bengal (Enroute)
  Strait of Malacca and Sumatera (Enroute)
  West Coast of Australia (Enroute)
Arctic Ocean
  The Arctic Ocean (Planning Guide)
  Greenland and Iceland (Enroute)
  North and West Coasts of Norway (Enroute)
  Northern Coast of Soviet Union (Enroute)
North Sea and Baltic Sea
  North Sea and Baltic Sea (Planning Guide)
  English Channel (Enroute)
  North Sea (Enroute)
  Skagerrak and Kattegat (Enroute)
  Baltic Sea (Southern part) (Enroute)

Gulf of Finland and Gulf of Bothnia (Enroute)
Antarctica
Antarctica includes islands south of latitude 60 degrees (Planning guide)

Coast Pilots (U.S. Coastline)

Available from National Ocean Survey (NOS)

No. 1   Eastport to Cape Cod
No. 2   Cape Cod to Sandy Hook
No. 3   Sandy Hook to Cape Henry
No. 4   Cape Henry to Key West
No. 5   Gulf of Mexico, Puerto Rico, and Virgin Islands
No. 6   Great Lakes and St. Lawrence River
No. 7   California, Oregon, Washington, and Hawaii
No. 8   Alaska: Dixon Entrance to Cape Spencer
No. 9   Alaska: Cape Spencer to Beaufort Sea

Lists of lights, including radio aids and fog signals

Available from Defense Mapping Agency (DMA)

Greenland, the East Coasts of North and South America (excluding the continental U.S.A., except for the east coast of Florida), and the West Indies.
The West Coast of North and South America (excluding continental U.S.A. and Hawaii) Australia, Tasmania, New Zealand, and the islands of the North and South Pacific Ocean

U.S. Coast Guard Light Lists

Available from the Government Printing Office (GPO)

Light List (Vol. I) Atlantic Coast (St. Croix, ME to Toms River, NJ).
Light List (Vol. II) Atlantic Coast (Toms River, NJ to Little River, SC)
Light List (Vol. III) Atlantic and Gulf Coasts (Little River, SC to Econfina River, FL)
Light List (Vol. IV) Gulf of Mexico (Econfina River, FL to Rio Grande, TX)
Light List (Vol. V) Mississippi River System
Light List (Vol. VI) Pacific Coast and Pacific Islands
Light List (Vol. VII) Great Lakes (U.S. and Canada)

Radio Navigation Aids

Available from the Defense Mapping Agency (DMA)

Direction-finder and radar stations, time signals, navigational warnings, distress emergency and safety traffic, medical advice, long-range navigational aids, automated mutual-assistance vessel rescue system, emergency communications procedures for U.S. Merchant ships

Available through the Government Printing Office (GPO)
Selected Worldwide Marine Weather Broadcasts (NOAA publication)

Weather Broadcasts

Available through National Ocean Survey (NOS)

Tidal Current Tables

Atlantic Coast of North America
Pacific Coast of North America

Available Through National Ocean Surveys (NOS)

Tide Tables

Europe and West Coast of Africa, including the Mediterranean Sea.
East Coast of North and South America, including Greenland.
West Coast of North and South America, including Hawaii.
Central and Western Pacific Ocean and the Indian Ocean.

REFERENCES AND RECOMMENDED READING

American Boat and Yacht Council, Inc. *Standards and Recommended Practices for Small Craft.* ABYC, Amityville, NY.

Baader, Juan. *The Sailing Yacht.* W.W. Norton & Company, New York, NY. 1979.

Beilan, Michael H. *Your Offshore Doctor.* Putnam, New York, NY. 1985.

Beyn, Edgar J. *The 12-Volt Doctor's Practical Handbook.* Spa Creek Instruments Company, Annapolis, MD. 1989.

Bingham, Bruce. *The Sailor's Sketchbook.* Seven Seas, Camden, ME. 1987.

Brewer, Ted. *Ted Brewer Explains Sailboat Design.* International Marine, Camden, ME. 1987.

Brown, Jim. *The Case for the Cruising Trimaran.* International Marine, Camden, ME. 1983.

Brotherton, Miner. *The Twelve-Volt Bible.* International Marine, Camden, ME. 1987.

Burke, Katy. *The Complete Live-Aboard Book.* Seven Seas, Camden, ME. 1987.

Calder, Nigel. *Boatowner's Mechanical and Electrical Manual.* Adlard Coles Nautical, London, and International Marine, Camden, ME. 1990.

Callahan, Steven. *Adrift.* Ballantine Books, New York, NY. 1986.

Cargal, Michael. *The Captain's Guide to Liferaft Survival.* Sheridan House, Dobbs Ferry, NY, and Seafarer Books, London. 1990.

Cohen, Michael M. *Dr. Cohen's Healthy Sailor Book.* International Marine, Camden, ME. 1983.

Coles, K. Adlard. *Heavy Weather Sailing.* Adlard Coles Nautical, London, and International Marine, Camden, ME. 1992.

Collins, Mike. *Fitting Out a Fiberglass Hull.* Adlard Coles Nautical, London, and Sheridan House, Dobbs Ferry, NY. 1990.

Cooper, Bill and Laurel. *Sell Up and Sail.* Adlard Coles Nautical, London, and Sheridan House, Dobbs Ferry, NY. 1994.

Coote, Jack. *Total Loss.* Adlard Coles Nautical, London, and Sheridan House, Dobbs Ferry, NY. 1985.

Cornell, Gwenda. *Cruising with Children.* Adlard Coles Nautical, London, and Sheridan House, Dobbs Ferry, NY. 1992.

Cornell, Jimmy. *World Cruising Routes.* Adlard Coles Nautical, London, and International Marine, Camden, ME. 1987.

Cornell, Jimmy. *World Cruising Handbook.* Adlard Coles Nautical, London, and International Marine, Camden, ME. 1991.

Cruising Club of America Technical Committee et al., ed. John Rousmaniere. *Desirable and Undesirable Characteristics of Offshore Yachts*. W.W. Norton & Company, New York, NY. 1987.

Dashew, Steve and Linda. *The Circumnavigator's Handbook*. W.W. Norton & Company, New York, NY. 1983.

Dashew, Stephen and Linda. *The Bluewater Handbook*. Beowulf Publishing Group, Ojai, CA. 1984.

Goring, Loris. *Marine Inboard Engines – Petrol and Diesel*. Adlard Coles Nautical, London, and Sheridan House, Dobbs Ferry, NY. 1990.

Gougeon Brothers. *Fiberglass Boat Repair and Maintenance*. Gougeon Brothers, Inc., Bay City, MI. 1987.

Griffith, Bob. *Blue Water*. Sail Books, Inc., Boston, MA. 1979.

Halstead, Bruce W. *Dangerous Marine Animals that Bite, Sting, Shock, Are Non-Edible*. Cornell Maritime Press, Centreville, MD. 1980.

Hammick, Anne. *Ocean Cruising on a Budget*. Adlard Coles Nautical, London, and International Marine, Camden, ME. 1990.

Harris, Mike. *A Guide to Small Boat Radio*. Adlard Coles Nautical, London. 1991.

Henderson, Richard. *East to the Azores*. International Marine, Camden, ME. 1978.

Henderson, Richard. *Singlehanded Sailing, 2nd Edition*. Adlard Coles Nautical, London, and International Marine, Camden, ME. 1992.

Henderson, Richard. *Understanding Rigs and Rigging*. Adlard Coles Nautical, London, and International Marine, Camden, ME. 1990.

Herreshoff, Halsey C. (Ed.). *The Sailor's Handbook*. Little, Brown and Company, Boston, MA. 1983.

Hinz, Earl R. *Landfalls of Paradise*. University of Hawaii Press, Honolulu, HI. 1993.

Hinz, Earl R. *Understanding Sea Anchors and Drogues*. Cornell Maritime Press, Centerville, MD. 1987.

Hinz, Earl R. *The Complete Book of Anchoring and Mooring*. Cornell Maritime Press, Centerville, MD. 1986.

Hiscock, Eric C. *Cruising Under Sail*. Adlard Coles Nautical, London, and International Marine, Camden, ME. 1985.

Hiscock, Eric C. *Voyaging Under Sail*. Oxford University Press, London. 1970.

Howard-Williams, Jeremy. *Care and Repair of Sails*. Adlard Coles Nautical, London, and Sail Books, Inc. Boston, MA. 1976.

Jeffrey, Nan and Kevin. *Free Energy Afloat*. International Marine, Camden, ME. 1985.

Kinney, Francis S. *Skene's Elements of Yacht Design*. G.P. Putnam's Sons, New York, NY. 1978.

Lucas, Alan. *Cruising in Tropical Waters and Coral*. Adlard Coles Nautical, London, and International Marine, Camden, ME. 1987.

Marchaj, C.A. *Seaworthiness: The Forgotten Factor*. Adlard Coles Nautical, London, and International Marine, Camden, ME. 1986.

Maté, Ferenc. *The Finely Fitted Yacht*. W.W. Norton & Co. New York, NY. 1979.

Nicolson, Ian. *Surveying Small Craft, 3rd Edition.* Adlard Coles Nautical, London, and Sheridan House, Dobbs Ferry, NY. 1994.

Norgrove, Ross. *Cruising Rigs and Rigging.* International Marine, Camden, ME. 1982.

Hydrographer of the Navy. *Ocean Passages for the World.* British Admiralty, Hydrographic Office, Somerset, England.

Pardey, Lin and Larry. *Cruising in* Seraffyn. Sheridan House, Dobbs Ferry, NY. 1992.

Pardey, Lin and Larry. *The Capable Cruiser.* W.W. Norton & Company, New York, NY. 1987.

Pike, Dag. *Boat Electrical Systems.* Adlard Coles Nautical, London, and Sheridan House, Dobbs Ferry, NY. 1992.

Proctor, Rick. *The Bullet Proof Electrical System.* Cruising Equipment Co., Seattle, WA. 1992.

Robertson, Dougal. *Sea Survival.* Praeger Publishers, New York, NY.

Robertson, Dougal. *Survive the Savage Sea.* Sheridan House, Dobbs Ferry, NY. 1984.

Roth, Hal. *After 50,000 Miles.* W.W. Norton & Company, New York, NY. 1993.

Schult, Joachim, revised by Jeremy Howard-Williams. *The Sailing Dictionary, 2nd Edition.* Adlard Coles Nautical, London, and Sheridan House, Dobbs Ferry, NY. 1992.

Shane, Victor. *Drag Device Data Base.* Para-Anchors International, Summerland, CA.

Sheahan, Matthew. *Sailing Rigs and Spars – Installation-Maintenance-Tuning.* Haynes Publishing Group, Somerset, England. 1990.

Smeeton, Miles. *Once is Enough.* Sheridan House, Dobbs Ferry, NY. 1984.

Spurr, Daniel. *Upgrading the Cruising Sailboat.* Seven Seas, Camden, ME. 1990.

Street, Donald M., Jr., *The Ocean Cruising Yacht, Volume I and II.* W.W. Norton & Company, New York, NY. 1978.

Strykers, Peter H. *The Floating Harpsichord.* Ten Speed Press, Berkeley, CA. 1987.

Van Doren, W.G. *Oceanography and Seamanship.* Cornell Maritime Press, Centreville, MD. 1992.

Verney, Michael. *The Complete Book of Yacht Care, 2nd Edition.* Adlard Coles Nautical, London, and Sheridan House, Dobbs Ferry, NY. 1993.

Webb, Barbara. *Yachtsman's Eight Language Dictionary, 3rd Edition.* Adlard Coles Nautical, London. 1983.

Werner, David. *Where There Is No Doctor.* The Hesperian Foundation, P.O. Box 1692, Palo Alto, CA 94302.

White, Chris. *Cruising Multihull.* International Marine, Camden, ME, and Waterline Books, London. 1990.

INDEX

INDEX

INDEX

468